NEW GERMAN FILMMAKERS

UNGAR FILM LIBRARY
SELECTED LISTING

Academy Awards: An Ungar Reference Index, Second Edition, updated
    Edited by Richard Shale
American History/American Film: Interpreting the Hollywood Image
    Edited by John E. O'Connor and Martin E. Jackson
American History/American Television: Interpreting the Video Past
    Edited by John E. O'Connor
*America's Favorite Movies: Behind the Scenes/*Rudy Behlmer
The Classic American Novel and the Movies
    Edited by Gerald Peary and Roger Shatzkin
The English Novel and the Movies
    Edited by Michael Klein and Gillian Parker
Film Study Collections: A Guide to Their Development and Use
    Nancy Allen
*From Quasimodo to Scarlett O'Hara: A National Board of Review Anthology
    (1920-1940)/*Edited by Stanley Hochman
*Hollywood's Image of the Jew/*Lester D. Friedman
*Italian Cinema: From Neorealism to the Present/*Peter Bondanella
*Loser Take All: The Comic Art of Woody Allen/*Maurice Yacowar
The Modern American Novel and the Movies
    Edited by Gerald Peary and Roger Shatzkin
Modern European Filmmakers and the Art of Adaptation
    Edited by Andrew Horton and Joan Magretta
*Movies for Kids: A Guide for Parents and Teachers on the Entertainment Film
    for Children/*Ruth M. Goldstein and Edith Zornow
On the Verge of Revolt: Women in American Films of the Fifties
    Brandon French

Other Ungar titles of interest:

*Great Film Epics: The Stories Behind the Scenes/*Michael Munn
Lorrimer Classic Screenplays (Over 50 titles including such classics as *Jules
    and Jim, Bonnie and Clyde,* and *Wild Strawberries*)
A Pictorial History of Television. Second, enlarged edition
    Irving Settel

Complete list of film titles available on request

NEW
GERMAN
FILMMAKERS
From Oberhausen
Through the 1970s

Edited by Klaus Phillips

Frederick Ungar Publishing Co.
New York

To Debbie and Nicole Dawn, for much patience and love

Copyright © 1984 by Frederick Ungar Publishing Co., Inc.
Printed in the United States of America
Designed by
Nancy Sugihara

Library of Congress Cataloging in Publication Data
Main entry under title:

New German filmmakers.

Bibliography: p.
Includes index.
1. Moving-pictures—Germany (West)—History—Addresses,
essays, lectures. 2. Moving-picture plays—History and
criticism—Addresses, essays, lectures. I. Phillips,
Klaus.
PN1993.5.G3N48   1984   791.43'0943   84-2606
ISBN 0-8044-2688-0
ISBN 0-8044-6648-3 (pbk.)

Contents

Introduction

"'THE GERMANS ARE COMING! THE GER-
mans are coming!" one American film critic announced in
1975.¹ Before long, others joined in, heralding a "German film
renaissance"² and concluding that the "new German cinema is the liveliest in Europe,"³ even that "the Germans are
now producing the most original films outside America." Remarkable as this flood of pronouncements was, regarding a national cinema that during the first two decades following World
War II had either been ignored or been summarily dismissed as
probably the worst Europe had to offer, more remarkable still
may be the skepticism, hesitancy, and outright hostility this "new
cinema" encountered on its native soil from critics and the general public alike. Those making such films found themselves
tagged "egocentrics," "subversives," and often worse by indig-
nant tabloid tattlers. Far from the madding crowd of the
metropolis, in the provinces of the Federal Republic, a survey
was unable to detect any specific awareness of a "new" German
cinema as late as 1975. American interest in German films was
all too often discounted as a meaningless love affair of predicta-
bly brief duration by German critics and members of the established film sector. "What other country would take note of its
artists only after they had been crowned with laurels on the
international scene?" one of the relatively few sympathetic voices
lamented.⁴ "New German Cinema: that means a multifaceted
spectrum full of intellectual unrest and nervous dynamism, exciting, contradictory, and systematically radical—one can understand the admiration abroad and is puzzled by the curious ignorance here at home."

The admiration abroad was not unanimous,⁵ and American
attention perforce remained restricted to a small sampling of
films screened at the New York Film Festival or booked by art-
house programmers and campus film societies. For much of the
mid-seventies a triumvirate composed of incongruous figures
from the German film landscape appeared to determine Ameri-

can perception and understanding of the new cinema.[6] From coast to coast, *cinéastes* traded tales of Rainer Werner Fassbinder, the Bavarian "Hell's Angel," a leather-clad *Wunderkind* capable of making a feature film in less time than it took others to say "*Katzelmacher*";[7] of Werner Herzog, a romantic visionary who, on a dare, would fling himself into cacti or eat his shoe, a mad-man who commonly jeopardized his own life and the lives of those around him while working on a film; of Wim Wenders, a shy, bespectacled, gum-chewing fan of jukeboxes and pinball machines, a devotee of Yasujiro Ozu and Alfred Hitchcock. Only a handful of other filmmakers received notice, among them Jean-Marie Straub/Danièle Huillet, Volker Schlöndorff, Margarethe von Trotta, Reinhard Hauff, and—another contro-versial figure—Hans Jürgen Syberberg, alternately regarded as the pariah of the New German Cinema[8] and "a self-advertiser par excellence and romantic martyr eager to disclose his suffer-ings."[9]

America's love affair with the German cinema appears to be continuing into the eighties, and we can hope that some of the reasons behind our initial infatuation may become clearer with the passage of time. Available films are being used and discussed increasingly in German classes and cinema courses;[10] the fea-ture-film lending service at the embassy of the Federal Republic of Germany in Washington, an important (and inexpensive) source of recent German productions for American colleges and universities, experienced a jump in demand from some two thousand lendings in 1979 to more than five thousand two years later; the number of scholarly inquiries into unexplored and underexplored realms of the New German Cinema is rising rapidly;[11] and filmgoers who cultivate screenings of the works in distribution here have begun to grow accustomed to the faces— if not yet all the names—surfacing recurrently in German pro-ductions: Hanna Schygulla, Jürgen Prochnow, Bruno Ganz, Angela Winkler, Klaus Kinski, and many others. Six German films, a greater number than at any time before, ran in com-mercial theaters in New York City simultaneously during one week in February 1982: Helmut Herbst's *John Heartfield, Fotomonteur* (*John Heartfield,* 1977*),* Peter Lilienthal's *David* (1979), Wolfgang Petersen's *Das Boot* (1981), Frank Ripploh's *Taxi zum Klo* (1981), Volker Schlöndorff's *Die Fälschung* (*Circle of*

Deceit, 1981), and Margarethe von Trotta's *Schwestern oder die Balance des Glücks* (*Sisters or The Balance of Happiness*, 1979).

Clearly, much had occurred during the twenty years since February 28, 1962, the date commonly regarded as marking the moment of the New German Cinema's conception, when a group of twenty-six young filmmakers, frustrated by the sorry state of feature film production in the Federal Republic, issued the by now almost legendary proclamation that has become known as the "Oberhausen Manifesto":

> The collapse of the conventional German cinema is finally removing the economic basis from a mentality that we reject. Thereby the new cinema has a chance to come to life.
>
> German short films by young authors, directors, and producers in recent years have received a large number of prizes at international festivals and have met with international critical approval. These works and their success show that the future of the German cinema lies with those who have demonstrated that they speak a new film language.
>
> In Germany as in other countries the short film has become training ground and experimental arena for the feature film.
>
> We declare our objective to be the creation of the new German feature film.
>
> This new film needs new freedoms: freedom from the conventions customary to the industry; freedom from intervention by commercial partners; freedom from domination by special-interest groups.
>
> We have concrete ideas regarding the intellectual, formal, and economic realization of the new German cinema. We are collectively prepared to take economic risks.
>
> The old cinema is dead. We believe in the new.

Without doubt the document's signatories, participants in the eighth Oberhausen Short Film Festival, some of whom had won prizes at international festivals for their short films, were justified in articulating their determination. The previous year the organizers of the Venice Film Festival had turned down all the nominations from the Federal Republic; the German Ministry of the Interior (which had been subsidizing many an Oberhausener's short film and had been giving annual prizes for features as well) declined to present awards for best feature film, best direction, and best screenplay, arguing that nothing of sufficient quality had been produced. From an artistic standpoint the situation could hardly have been worse, leading one German observer to arrive at the following verdict: "The degeneration of realism in the cinema is universal, but in no country has it been accompanied by such a crass desolation of formal means and of the communicative potential of the film as is the case in the Federal Republic."[12]

In the period between the end of World War II and 1949, the year in which the Federal Republic (West Germany) and the Democratic Republic (East Germany) came into being, a couple of promising films were made: Wolfgang Staudte's *Die Mörder sind unter uns* (*The Murderers Are Among Us*) for the Soviet-controlled DEFA company in 1946 and Helmut Käutner's *In jenen Tagen* (*In Former Years*) the following year in the Federal Republic; the former film tells the grim tale of a war criminal now posing as an innocent citizen, the latter takes a look at the immediate past and present in seven vignettes from the vantage point of an automobile whose owners change with the times. If there were any hopes for the emergence of a resolute German cinema, perhaps one with a neorealist bent, the creation of two separate German states quickly shattered them. The centralized film industry in the German Democratic Republic devoted itself to the faithful representation of party ideology; in the western zones roughly forty motion-picture production firms had already sprung up between 1946 and 1948, most of which were actively engaged not in the production of new features but in the marketing of existing French, British, and—especially—American films, or Nazi entertainment films deemed innocuous by the censors. Old Hollywood movies, many of which had been banned in the Third Reich, were now being dubbed into German; bombarding the newborn Federal Republic with relentless intensity, they quickly became the standard fare of many movie houses. By 1950, of the eighty-five motion-picture distribution firms operating in the Federal Republic, most had ties with American companies. The effected American monopoly over the West German film market was not rooted in economic strategy alone, but extended to ideological aims as well. "It was an axiom of the American 're-education' programme that if Germany were flooded with the products of American culture, the Germans would, by some mysterious process of osmosis, be transformed into shining exemplars of Truth, Justice, and the American Way," a British colleague observed.[13]

But what of the films actually produced in the Federal Republic during the next several years against such an unsettling backdrop? At least four prominent categories can be readily discerned (1) *Trümmerfilme* ("rubble" films); (2) *Kriegsfilme* (war films); (3) "exotic" extravaganzas that transferred their audiences to distant shores or offered romanticized portraits of royalty both foreign and domestic; (4) *Heimatfilme* ("homeland" films, depicting the unproblematic activities of simple country folk in settings of natural magnificence and pastoral bliss). Of these four categories the last was by far the most popular—to a degree, ostensibly, because the *Heimatfilme* managed to evoke a mellow sense of nationalistic satisfaction in viewers who, caught up in the infant struggles of what was to become known as the *Wirtschaftswunder* (economic miracle), were interested in forgetting the present temporarily and the recent past permanently. Ilse Kubaschewski, founder of Gloria-Film (initially a distributor of low-budget American "Republic" features, later a prolific source of *Heimatfilme*), was reputed to have set the following guidelines: the main characters must be appealing; no flashbacks, since they tend to confuse an audience; a happy ending at all costs, even if the film has a tragic theme; lots of nature shots; lots of music; always something humorous and entertaining.[14] It would seem that her formula worked. While the German cinema gained few new friends abroad and plummeted from international ridicule to worldwide obscurity, domestic audiences flocked into the theaters in record numbers. During the third quarter of 1952 the ten commercially most successful motion pictures were:

1. *Grün ist die Heide* (*Green Is the Heath*)
2. *Der Wüstenfuchs* (*The Desert Fox*, U.S.A.)
3. *Die Försterchristl* (*Christl, the Forester Maid*)
4. *Hanna Amon*
5. *Heidelberger Romanze* (*Heidelberg Romance*)
6. *Herz der Welt* (*Heart of the World*)
7. *Rebecca* (USA)
8. *Toxi*
9. *Wenn die Abendglocken läuten* (*When the Evening Bells Toll*)
10. *Der große Caruso* (*The Great Caruso*, U.S.A.)[15]

All but three of the films listed are German productions, of which more than half fall into the *Heimatfilme* category. Significantly, films from other European countries are missing completely.

At a time that would later be lamented as the greatest catastrophe, artistically speaking, in the history of a national cinema that once had given the world *Caligari, Metropolis, The Last Laugh*, and *Variety*, business was brisk at the box office. The more than seven thousand movie houses in the Federal Republic sold over 818 million tickets in 1956, the peak year (compared to fewer than half as many movie houses and only some 144 million tickets in 1980).[16] In a nation experiencing rapid economic revitalization and simultaneously trying to shed a lingering losers' complex, many found in the fare made in Germany—however dreary—a welcome source of added self-esteem and pride not totally unlike a soccer victory over another country. For them the films of the fifties, in contrast to the auteur-oriented New German Cinema, showcased German stars whose larger-than-life images adorned enormous iridescent transparencies on many a big-city marquee and whose public and private lives provided steady fodder for West German tabloids.

The selling of the cinema in surburban *Kinos* at times included special morning matinee showings of German entertainment films, sponsored by some detergent or cosmetics manufacturer who had seen to it that every *Hausfrau* in the neighborhood received a complimentary ticket—along with a sales pitch and the prospect of additional intensive product demonstrations right before the film showing. Especially in larger cities, going to the movies frequently involved more than merely the advertised feature film. It was not uncommon, for example, to experience the following chain of events: soft music plays while the theater fills; a gong announces the imminent dimming of lights; as the curtain opens, louder music accompanies slide ads for products or future attractions; a series of short movie commercials; a newsreel; a cartoon or entertaining short film; previews of coming attractions; as the curtain closes and the house lights are raised again, low-noise snacks (chocolates, frozen pralines) are offered for purchase; a gong announces the imminent dimming of lights; the feature film begins. Some metropolitan first-run houses held even greater treasures: Munich's Gloria Palace, for example, offered "tanzende Wasserspiele vor jeder Vorstellung" (a multimedia show incorporating moveable water fountains, colorful spotlights, and stereophonic sounds, which afforded a quasi–ballet experience prior to each performance).

In spite of—or perhaps precisely because of—the star syndrome, pomp and circumstance, and a fair dose of Yankee-inspired know-how, the box-office boom did not last. A meeting of thirty German motion-picture producers in February 1960 in Munich, supported by the nine leading distributors, to compose a ranking of stars who could command from 30,000 to 100,000 marks per film (then roughly $7,500 to $25,000), with 100,000 marks the absolute maximum, brought about an exodus of prominent actors and actresses: Curd Jürgens, Romy Schneider, Gert Fröbe, Maria and Maximilian Schell, Mario Adorf, Horst Buchholz, Klaus Kinski, and many others sought their fortunes abroad, at least for the moment. In addition, the proliferation of television sets in the Federal Republic was beginning to take its toll on box-office profits. Hollywood, faced with the television threat years earlier, had decided to keep Americans going to the movies by offering something they could not get on the home screen: sophisticated technology, ranging from multichannel sterophonic sound to 3-D and anamorphic or other wide-screen photography. Although most existing German *Kinos*, particularly big-city first-run houses, underwent renovation to accomodate wide-screen projection, the changes did little, if anything, to aid German film production. By the end of the fifties the Germans had made only seven anamorphic films, mostly large-scale inter-European coproductions, while Hollywood had cranked out some seventy-five CinemaScope features in 1954 alone. In a desperate attempt to imitate American strategy, the German film industry concluded that it had to keep Germans going to the movies by offering something they could not get on the home screen: a mindless mélange of sex and gore, increasingly aimed at the Federal Republic's sizable *Gastarbeiter* (foreign worker) population.[17]

Some films made in Germany during the fifties and early sixties transcended the prevailing mediocrity, and a handful of productions may be considered forerunners of the New German Cinema, stylistically, thematically, or both: Ottomar Domnick's *Jonas* (1957); Bernhard Wicki's *Die Brücke* (*The Bridge*, 1959); Herbert Vesely's *Nicht mehr fliehen* (*Flee No More*, 1955) and *Das Brot der frühen Jahre* (*The Bread of the Early Years*, 1961);

Wolfgang Staudte's *Rosen für den Staatsanwalt* (*Roses for the Prosecutor*, 1959) and *Kirmes* (*Fairground*, 1960). The potential of such efforts, coupled with the creative intelligence evident in so many of the shorter experimental films that had been screened every year since 1954 at Oberhausen, gradually and increasingly resulted in the emergence of voices that chided the German film industry for its failure to create a meaningful product.[18] Some did more than talk; Doc 59, an organization formed by Haro Senft and Ferdinand Khittl, gave concrete expression to two central goals contained in the Oberhausen Manifesto three years later: raising the overall quality of films and obtaining state subsidies for film projects. The handwriting was on the wall by the time the twenty-six young filmmakers articulated their sentiments in Oberhausen. More than anything, the manifesto was a symbolic gesture, a show of solidarity by a diverse assortment of artists, a protestation couched in rhetoric so self-assertive and defiant that its tenor invites comparison with the rebellious Sturm und Drang effusions nearly two hundred years earlier. The perceived refusal of the *Jungfilmer* (as they came to be called) to be guided by an older, more established director (*Altfilmer*), who might have been in a position to help bridge the gap between the films of the early postwar years and this "new" feature film, led more than one bystander to conclude that the new breed of German filmmaker displayed an ivory-tower mentality.[19] Skepticism burgeoned when a joint session of the Oberhausen group and Gruppe 47, a now defunct German writers' organization, ended in an ungainly split between filmmakers and writers as well as a clash of ideologies within the filmmakers' own ranks.

The year 1962 witnessed the creation of the Institut für Filmgestaltung in Ulm, a training facility for fledgling filmmakers set up by Alexander Kluge (a master theoretician and still one of the New German Cinema's most vocal proponents) and Detten Schleiermacher; one year later the Deutsche Kinemathek opened in Berlin. Although these were encouraging developments, various setbacks tended to obscure any gains: the 1963 Oberhausen festival presented no tangible evidence that German productions were improving; meanwhile the established film sector had released the first in a string of huge commercial successes, Teutonic westerns adapted from the novels of Karl

May. The first concrete result of the manifesto with a substantial and lasting impact on the development of the new cinema was the establishment of the Kuratorium junger deutscher Film in 1965, an institution that made available government funds (at first largely federal money, since 1968 funds provided by the various German *Länder*) for the realization of projects by nonestablished filmmakers. A jury composed mainly of film critics and journalists selected twenty proposals for full or partial subsidization, averaging 300,000 marks per film, between 1965 and 1968.

In January 1966 a prominent Munich film journalist offered this assessment of the postwar German cinema on the occasion of its twentieth birthday.

> There would be no cause for celebrating the event, were it not for the fact that we have been witnessing something virtually incredible during these weeks and months: in this same German cinema where the emergence of a *single* new filmmaker used to create quite a sensation, the first works of no fewer than six filmmakers have made their debut since October 1965. In the upcoming months there will be at least six more. If that continues, we'll see more films by new filmmakers than by the old in 1966.[20]

There was ample reason for euphoria: suddenly German films were being made that found critical acclaim at home and abroad. Celebrated and awarded in Venice, Cannes, and Berlin, films by Jean-Marie Straub and Danièle Huillet, Alexander Kluge, Volker Schlöndorff, and others were being showcased in major European cities as model representatives of this exciting phenomenon initially called *junger deutscher Film*.[21] In December 1967 the German news magazine *Der Spiegel* acknowledged the success of the new German films in a cover story. Prospective talent was able to obtain training in the newly founded Hochschule für Film und Fernsehen in Munich (among its first graduates: Wim Wenders) and the Deutsche Film- und Fernsehakademie Berlin (among its rejects: Rainer Werner Fassbinder). Audiences bored by dull *Altfilmer* offerings and seeking an alternative to dubbed Hollywood imports slowly began to develop a taste for the coarse textures dictated by the new films' restricted budgets and for the thematic concerns informing, in the words of a colleague, "a cinema of disenchantment, reflecting a world not devoid of hopes, but not exactly abounding in clearcut alternatives."[22] Invariably frustrated by inevitable collisions with an unfeeling, uncaring institutionalized bureaucracy, yet impelled by a strong sense of self-assertion, the protagonists in these films embody the mood of German youth during the second half of the sixties.

The passage of a bill mistakenly perceived by some to guarantee easy additional financing for the *Jungfilmer* turned out to be the established motion picture industry's retaliation for the Kuratorium subsidies. When the Filmförderungsgesetz (film subsidy law) took effect in early 1968, the *Altfilmer* were the big winners: the revenues collected through a tax on ticket sales (the *Filmgroschen*), initially estimated at around 15 million marks per year, were to be dispersed by the Filmförderungsanstalt (Film Subsidy Board) in strict observance of guidelines that were clearly designed to discriminate against inexperienced newcomers in need of funding for their first feature film. In order to qualify for a grant, a filmmaker had to have produced a film (the so-called *Referenzfilm*) that during its first two years in distribution had grossed at least 500,000 marks, a figure lowered to "only" 300,000 marks in the case of an award-winning film; obviously such criteria did little to raise the quality of films. To obtain an interest-free loan covering 50 percent of the production costs, up to 250,000 marks, enterprising producers simply devised a formula for a film that was a guaranteed audience pleaser; once that film's box-office receipts were sufficient to meet the criteria established by the subsidy board, the producers collected their grant and used the money for their next project, invariably a sequel or spin-off based on the successful premise of the *Referenzfilm*. New filmmakers, especially those without any feature films to their credit, had good reason to feel shut out. With the Kuratorium's budget severely reduced as a consequence of the new law, many saw bleak prospects—or none at all. Only a minute fraction of the films that had received production grants from the subsidy board by the end of 1971 could be termed "new cinema"; the bulk were commercial creations of unparalleled mediocrity, a singularly unimpressive array of little films with titles like *Bleib sauber Liebling (Keep It Clean, Honey)*, *Tante Trude aus Buxtehude (Aunt Trude from Buxtehude)*, or *Wenn mein Schätzchen auf die Pauke haut (When My Darling Does Her Thing)*.[23] By the middle of the decade annual per capita movie-house visits in the Federal Republic had dropped to a record low of only two, the poorest showing in all Europe.

Amendments to the Film Subsidy Law gradually improved the lot of the struggling filmmaker over the years: the "quality clause," added in 1971, stipulated that films depicting sex and violence in a gratuitous and exploitative fashion were to be ineligible; further revisions of the law in 1974 and 1979 made it easier for newcomers to obtain grant money for project development and screenplay realization. Ultimately the German cinema found a friend in a former rival: television. The *Film/ Fernseh-Abkommen* (Film/Television Agreement), signed by the Film Subsidy Board and the Federal Republic's television networks in 1974, set aside 34 million marks to be used during the next five years for coproductions between filmmakers and the noncommercial, semipublic broadcasting corporations. Under the terms of the agreement such coproductions could be shown in theaters for an initial period of two years before they were cleared for broadcast; the networks were also free to purchase the broadcast rights to a feature film in advance, with the understanding that the film could be shown on television only after five years; the networks could still cooperate with filmmakers on projects intended for initial or exclusive television broadcast. Today some filmmakers charge that the relationship with the networks compromises their political and aesthetic sensibilities; but many more, particularly those whose apprentice work was in television, could not imagine making films without some form of network participation. Compared to young independent filmmakers in other parts of the world, they find themselves in the enviable position of being able to turn to at least four potential funding sources (Kuratorium, Ministry of the Interior, Film Subsidy Board, networks) to supplement any personal resources and money from other channels toward the realization of their projects. But in a country that funnels huge sums of public money into the performing arts every year, a number of filmmakers still feel shortchanged. In 1976 the Federal Republic spent 1.2 billion marks on subsidies for the stage, music, ballet, and opera, with an additional 250 million marks going to the nation's art galleries and museums.[24]

Financing their films has not been the filmmakers' sole concern. After the initial box-office successes of the late sixties, films by new German directors, no longer able to compete within the American-dominated distribution and exhibition mechanisms, were gradually relegated to the art-house circuit. Alternative methods had to be devised. In 1971 a collective of thirteen filmmakers, including Hark Bohm, Hans W. Geissendörfer, Peter Lilienthal, and Wim Wenders, founded the Filmverlag der Autoren. Originally intended as a production organ for its members' films, the Filmverlag began to move into the area of distribution as well.[25] Within the span of a few years, which witnessed a series of in-house feuds, a change of leadership and a rescue from certain bankruptcy by the publisher of *Der Spiegel* in 1977, the Filmverlag became a hallmark for much of the New German Cinema and, as a result of vigorous export strategies, helped create an international audience for German films.

While audiences in selected German cities were given alternatives to the commercial theaters through a growing number of municipal movie houses *(kommunale Kinos)*, the first of which opened in 1971 in Frankfurt, the overall foreign presence grew stronger than ever: in 1975 only 55 German films were produced, compared to 112 four years before; in 1976, the year after foreign critics and audiences had "discovered" the New German Cinema, German films accounted for a scant 12 percent share of the home market. One German critic tried to illustrate the schizophrenic state of the New German Cinema within its peculiar context by means of eight theses and contradictions.

> The German cinema is doing better than ever. The German cinema is finished. The German cinema commands world esteem. The German cinema is provincial. Without government subsidies there would be no German cinema. The German cinema is being subsidized to death. Television is helping the German cinema. Television is killing the German cinema. Every one of these sentences is correct; every one in itself is false.[26]

The ominous ramifications of a repressive political climate, characterized by a near-fanatical terrorism paranoia, appeared to augur an awesome resurgence of German authoritarianism, with ramifications that affected film economics within a system of subsidies from the public sector. Some filmmakers preferred to avoid a showdown and turned toward literature as the basis for a "safe," noncontroversial cinematic venture; during the socalled *Literaturverfilmungskrise* (literature adaptation crisis) of 1976–77 a film addressing the nation's topical concerns head-on, as did the independently funded collective effort *Deutschland im Herbst (Germany in Autumn)* in 1978, was a rarity.[27] Some of the most visible and vocal filmmakers, refusing to serve their audiences bland entertainment in place of an earnest confrontation with important issues merely to appease the policymakers in the network and subsidy board offices, contemplated emigration; but no mass exodus followed. The difficulties one encountered while attempting to make films in the Federal Republic had to be dealt with.

During each of the last three years of the decade, more than half the German films made fell into the category New German Cinema. Annual attendance figures began to climb along with profits, and the number of theaters was on the rise as well, albeit largely resulting from the metamorphosis of older picture palaces into clusters of smaller, more efficient *Kinos*. The familiar logos of American distribution companies prefacing *Nosferatu, The Marriage of Maria Braun,* and *The Tin Drum,* enormous successes both critically and fiscally, were evidence of increasing internationalization of the New German Cinema. With financing and distribution no longer a major problem for the more circumspect filmmakers, much of what the Oberhausen signatories had espoused was now a reality, but just as much, perhaps even more, had been lost.

On September 22, 1979, in an action reminiscent of the 1962 manifesto, filmmakers participating in another film festival issued a statement under the heading "Our Strength Is Diversity" in which they voiced concerns, demonstrated self-confidence, and, above all, proclaimed their solidarity.

> We German filmmakers have come together on the occasion of the Hamburg Film Festival. Seventeen years after Oberhausen we have tried to draw up a balance sheet:
>
> The strength of the German cinema is its diversity. The eighties start in three months.
>
> Imagination cannot be administered. Bureaucrats cannot decree what a productive cinema should accomplish. The German cinema of the eighties can no longer be diverted by commissions, institutions, and special-interest groups as it has been so far.
>
> Above all: we will not let ourselves be divided.
>
> —not feature films from documentaries,
>
> —not filmmakers who have already made films from the newcomers,
>
> —not films that reflect the medium (and do that practically through experimenting) from the narrative film and the commercial film.

We have demonstrated our professionalism. We can therefore not consider ourselves apprentices. We have learned that only the audience can be our ally: they are the people who work, who have wishes, dreams, and interests; they are people who go to the movies, even people capable of envisioning a totally different kind of cinema.

We have to get our act together.

Despite the sense of accomplishment reflected in these words, a cautionary air prevails, evidence that the filmmakers recognized the uncertainties the eighties would hold for a cinema whose evolution had been characterized by alternating waves of triumphs and tribulations. The process of formulating the "new film language" as announced in Oberhausen turned out to be a task with which more than one generation of filmmakers has had to grapple. Of the original group, some are still making films today, others have faded into obscurity, and still others have become part of the establishment they so vehemently denounced in 1962. A second, post-Oberhausen generation of German filmmakers, among whose members the most colorful and controversial figures had given the German cinema such a high profile by the mid-seventies, already could build upon some of the manifesto's realizations and, in turn, was able to provide a heritage of sorts for the hundreds of talented men and women comprising the *Nachwuchsfilmer,* the New German Cinema's newest generations.

The vicissitudes of the sixties and seventies appear to have carried into the early eighties. As the decade began, there was ample reason for excitement: *The Tin Drum,* Schlöndorff's adaptation of the novel by Günter Grass, received the Academy Award for best foreign film in 1980. During the same year the Film/Television Agreement was renewed for an additional five years, its treasury nearly doubled. In line with its enormous budget, Fassbinder's *Lili Marleen,* coscripted and coproduced with representatives of the "established" sector of the German film industry, was premiered in one hundred German *Kinos* simultaneously—a release pattern utterly at odds with convention. In the United States dubbed prints of yet another very expensive German film, *The Boat* ("formerly entitled *Das Boot,*" according to the fine print on the poster), turned up in small-town theaters and drive-ins where no foreign film—let alone one from Germany—had ever been shown before. Wolfgang Petersen, the director of that film (who was nominated for an

Academy Award), began work in early 1983 on a spectacular adaptation of Michael Ende's fantastic best-seller, *The Neverending Story*, at a cost of some 52 million marks—projected to be the most expensive German film ever made.

Such developments, applauded by some, have given others pause to charge that more and more of the new German filmmakers are placing commercial promise and international appeal above artistic values, that their films lack the personal signature so characteristic of earlier works, and that the continuing maturation of the New German Cinema may well be its undoing. Danger signs continually loom over the gains of two decades: During a meeting in Brussels in 1982, commissioners of the European Economic Community advocated the abolition of present German film subsidy schemes in favor of a uniform European pattern based on the British model—a move destined to restrict or even eliminate cinema's national identity. The following year, in an action recalling the events of 1961, the Ministry of the Interior withheld the top German Film Prize. Instead, Interior Minister Friedrich Zimmermann noted that German films accounted for only 10 percent of ticket sales in 1982 and proposed guidelines for the promotion of films with a broad popular appeal both inland and abroad. To what extent the powerful interplay of cultural, economic, and political factors will continue to shape the German cinema remains to be seen.

Against the background sketched in these prefatory remarks, *New German Filmmakers: From Oberhausen Through the* 1970s explores the directions of the New German Cinema by concentrating on twenty-one filmmakers whose films, individually and collectively, convey a sense of the forces and concerns that gave form to the new cinema and helped propel it to worldwide prominence. Names familiar to American students of the cinema (Rainer Werner Fassbinder, Werner Herzog, Volker Schlöndorff, Hans-Jürgen Syberberg, Wim Wenders), some not so well known (Reinhard Hauff, Alexander Kluge, Peter Lilienthal), and some largely unknown here (Herbert Achternbusch, Hark Bohm, Edgar Reitz) have been included.

The chapters, all original contributions written expressly for this volume, focus on specific filmmakers and their major work up to 1980.

—KLAUS PHILLIPS

NOTES

[1] Andrew Sarris, "The Germans Are Coming! The Germans Are Coming!" *Village Voice*, 27 October 1975.

[2] Vincent Canby, "The German Renaissance—No Room for Laughter or Love," *New York Times*, 11 December 1977.

[3] Gerald Clark, "Seeking Planets That Do Not Exist: The New German Cinema Is the Liveliest in Europe," *Time*, 20 March 1978.

[4] Wolf Donner, "Die Deutschen kommen: Warum der neue bundesrepublikanische Film im Ausland schafft, was ihm zu Hause nur mühsam gelingt," *Die Zeit*, 28 November 1975.

[5] Notable among American adversaries of the New German Cinema are Pauline Kael and John Simon. See in particular Simon's "German Measliness," *New York*, 5 September 1977.

[6] Although more subdued, the trend is still present in the early eighties, as shown by David Ansen, "Deutschland Uber Alles" and "Old Gun for Hire," *Newsweek*, 18 October 1982.

[7] The average shooting time for each of Fassbinder's first dozen films is thirteen days. *Katzelmacher*, completed in only three days, holds the speed record.

[8] Steve Wasserman, "Filmmaker as Pariah," *Village Voice*, 14 January 1980.

[9] Eric Rentschler, "American Friends and New German Cinema: A Study in Reception," *New German Critique* 24–25 (Fall/Winter 1981–82): 33.

[10] See also "German Film Courses and Resources: A Special Survey," *Monatshefte* 64 (1977): 305–19. For specific suggestions regarding approaches to the teaching of the German cinema see the following: Richard C. Figge, "The Use of Film in Teaching German Culture," *Die Unterrichtspraxis* 10, 2 (1977): 88–93; Klaus Phillips, "Teaching a Course in the German Cinema," *Modern Language Journal* 62 (1978): 414–19; Eric Rentschler, "Reopening the Cabinet of Dr. Kracauer: Teaching German Film as Film," *Modern Language Journal* 64, 3 (Autumn 1980): 218–28.

[11] The following scholarly journals have devoted special issues to the New German Cinema: "Special Issue: New German Cinema," *Literature/Film Quarterly*, vol. 7, no. 3 (1979); "New German Cinema," *Wide Angle*, vol. 3, no. 4 (1980); "West German Film in the 1970s," *Quarterly Review of Film Studies*, vol. 5, no. 2 (Spring 1980); and "Special Double Issue on New German Cinema," *New German Critique*, nos. 24–25 (Fall/Winter 1981–82).

[12] Klaus Kreimeier, *Kino und Filmindustrie in der BRD: Ideologieproduktion und Klassenwirklichkeit nach 1945* (Kronberg/Ts.: Scriptor, 1973), pp. 175–76.

[13] John Sandford, *The New German Cinema* (London: Oswald Wolff, 1980), p. 9.

[14] See also Curt Riess, *Das gab's nur einmal: Der deutsche Film nach 1945*, vol. 4 (Vienna/Munich: Molden, 1977), p. 221.

[15] Statistics given in *Das sechste Jahrzehnt des XX. Jahrhunderts*, vol. 2, edited by Franz Burda (Offenbach/Baden: Burda, 1961), p. 55.

[16] Figures furnished by Export-Union des Deutschen Films.

[17] Among these are some of the most commercially successful German film exports of recent years, with titles like *Siegfried und das sagenhafte Liebesleben der Nibelungen (The Long, Swift Sword of Siegfried,* 1971), *Insel der tausend Freuden (Island of a Thousand Delights,* 1978), *Graf Dracula (beißt jetzt in Oberbayern (Dracula sucks,* 1979), and the biggest West German box-office hit abroad, *Hexen bis aufs Blut gequält (Mark of the Devil,* 1970), which has grossed more than $8 million in the United States alone. For further documentation see Rolf Thissen, "German Film Industry Goes into a Boom Period," *The German Tribune,* no. 953 (17 August 1980), originally published in German in *Kölner Stadt-Anzeiger,* 1 August 1980.

[18] One of the louder voices was that of Joe Hembus, journalist, film critic, and sometime actor, whose pamphlet *Der deutsche Film kann gar nicht besser sein* (Bremen: Schuenemann, 1961) has achieved the status of a classic. In it he explains, "This book is dedicated to the self-orientation of the German cinema. It wants to point out sources of what is wrong, so that the causes of the ailment become clearly visible. Only when there are no longer any doubts about the causes can a remedy for the ailment be attempted" (p. 3). The original pamphlet has been reproduced in the author's *Der deutsche Film kann gar nicht besser sein: Ein Pamphlet von gestern, eine Abrechnung von heute* (Munich: Rogner & Bernhard, 1981).

[19] Ronald Holloway, "A German Breakthrough?" *Kino: German Film,* no. 1 (October 1979), p. 6.

[20] Joe Hembus, quoted in Robert Fischer and Joe Hembus, *Der Neue Deutsche Film,* 1960–1980 (Munich: Goldmann, 1981), p. 274.

[21] The term "Young German Cinema" eventually gave way to "New German Cinema," a designation coined by American and British critics.

[22] Eric Rentschler, "Critical Junctures Since Oberhausen: West German Film in the Course of Time," *Quarterly Review of Film Studies* 5, 2 (Spring 1980): 146.

[23] One of the first books on New German Cinema, a collection of interviews with filmmakers by Barbara Bronnen and Corinna Brocher, *Die Filmemacher: Der neue deutsche Film nach Oberhausen* (Munich: Bertelsmann, 1973), lists titles of projects and films for which production grants were awarded; see "Statt eines Vorworts," pp. 9–10.

[24] For additional background on film financing in the Federal Republic see Hans-Bernhard Moeller, "New German Cinema and Its Precarious Subsidy and Finance System," *Quarterly Review of Film Studies* 5, 2 (Spring 1980): 157–68.

[25] The Filmverlag distributes a few American films like *The Night of the Living Dead* (George A. Romero, 1968), *The Most Dangerous Game* (Ernest B. Schoedsack, 1932), and a number of Marx Brothers comedies. Filmwelt, a distribution company cofounded by former Filmverlag manager Laurens Straub in 1979, also handles several American films, including Roger Corman's series of Poe adaptations.

[26] For a discussion of the *Literaturverfilmungskrise* see an article by the "Fassbinder" among American scholars of the New German Cinema, Eric Rentschler: "Deutschland im Vorherbst: Literature Adaptation in West German Film," *Kino: German Film,* no. 3 (Summer 1980), pp. 11–19.

[27] Hans C. Blumenberg, "Acht Thesen, acht Widersprüche," *Die Zeit,* 26 August 1977.

HERBERT ACHTERNBUSCH

Celebrating the Power of Creation

by Eric Rentschler

NEW GERMAN CINEMA (NGC) ABOUNDS
with personal visions, but none is as personal as Herbert
Achternbusch's. Numerous West German directors have can-
didly and often painfully disclosed their inner selves before their
audiences, but no one more consistently and poignantly than
Herbert Achternbusch. More direct than all his peers (male and
female), Achternbusch is NGC's most radical individualist. Since
1966, the year the Oberhausen signatories gave the first concrete signs of life, young German directors have surveyed the
real, criticized the given, and conjugated the present tense. In
these endeavors they have continually sought the possible and
plotted the utopian.

Herbert Achternbusch assumes an extreme position in his native cinema—at once a pessimist more virulent than the fatalistic
Werner Herzog and nevertheless an indefatigable activist, a zany
anarchist running amok. Rarely does he get sidetracked in
metaphysical dead ends, in the inexorable circles that enclose
and fetter his colleague's heroes; his despair stems from the
tangible facts of empirical existence, not from the whims of a
cosmos where whirl is king. "This place has wrecked me," the
poet in *Servus Bayern (Bye Bye Bavaria,* 1977) tells an importunate
TV journalist, "and I'm going to stick around until people start

noticing it." How? "I fight back." Nowhere does the NGC rage as vehemently, but these tantrums, provocations, and laments are more than simple self-indulgence or misanthropy. Achtern-busch's is a cinema of disenchantment fashioned by someone enchanted with cinema, simultaneously earnest about the op-pressive quality of the everyday and yet irreverent enough not to succumb to its numbing lack of humor. It celebrates the power of creation despite all odds—which, for someone in the Federal Republic making willfully independent films, can be consider-able. "You don't have a single chance," shouts the hero of *Die Atlantikschwimmer (The Atlantic Swimmers,* 1975*)*, "but go ahead and try anyway."

Achternbusch grew up in Bavaria, a region that has left indel-ible marks on a number of contemporary West German writers and filmmakers. In recent representations, Bavaria has come to connote Germany as dangerous ground: it amounts to a false idyll, a deceptive terrain that looks tranquil at first glance, but whose abounding open spaces and calm forests betray upon closer scrutiny a frightening narrowness. Its inhabitants, hardly the simple folk of postcards and village tales, disdain the foreign, fear the deviant, and torment the singular.

Jagdszenen aus Niederbayern (Hunting Scenes from Lower Bavaria), part of Martin Sperr's *Bavarian Trilogy,* filmed in 1968 by Peter Fleischmann, was one of the most influential declarations of this revisionist view of Bavaria. An outsider enters a village and soon becomes the butt of discussions. Rumors about his past (a jail-bird? a homosexual? a child molester?) swiftly make the rounds. When he tries to flee, a mob tracks him down like an animal. Early Fassbinder works such as *Katzelmacher* (1969) and *Pioniere in Ingolstadt (Pioneers in Ingolstadt,* 1971) also focused on the Bavarian countryside and exploded the myths behind the *Heimatfilme* of the 1950s. These mountaintop dramas set in a pastoral landscape untouched by bombs and Allied occupation forces appealed to a regressively escapist—and chauvinistic—strain in their postwar public. Reinhard Hauff's *Mathias Kneissl* (1971, based on a script by Sperr) and Uwe Brandner's *Ich liebe dich, ich töte dich (I Love You, I Kill You,* 1971) provided a less amicable view of life in the provinces—and a critical view of Germany as a whole. Rural Bavaria: a place where outsiders receive hostile stares and close police surveillance. In the rigid

Herbert Achternbusch
(Courtesy of Export-Union des
Deutschen Films)

structures of these small burgs—political bodies that reflect the latent disquiet in larger Germany—there remains no room for eccentricity or invention.

"I grew up without electricity," reports the autobiographical narrator of Achternbusch's novel *Die Stunde des Todes* (*The Hour of Death*, 1975, p. 7). Born in Munich on November 23, 1938, the filmmaker spent his youth in Mietrachting, a small dot on the Bavarian landscape that was to shape him so crucially. "A man is where he is," says critic Donald Richie in describing the work of Yasujiro Ozu (a filmmaker Achternbusch—like Wim Wenders and Peter Handke—greatly admires); "his environment moulds his character, or induces those choices that taken together become his character."[1] After traumatic treatment at the hands of school officials, Achternbusch studied at the Art Academy in Nuremburg. Supporting himself with odd jobs, he continued to paint for ten years. A return to the city of his birth only increased his feelings of insignificance. Its structures, banks, churches, shopping streets, and fashion-conscious denizens weighed heavily on him. Finding reality so massive, so inhospitable, Achternbusch sought solace and nurture in writing and the cinema. Rather than let daily humiliations beat him into submission, he began transforming them into the substance of his work, producing in time a considerable corpus that includes novels, short stories, film reviews, sketches, radio plays, dramas, scripts, and—as of 1979—six films.

Achternbusch sees no split in his identity as filmmaker and writer. He envisions his entire artistic output in all its variety as one larger work in progress. A complex set of cross-references, recurring situations, and persistent locales and personages lend to these efforts the credibility of a microcosm, at whose center stands the mythos-maker Herbert Achternbusch. "In writing, I become," he says in *Land in Sicht* (*Land in Sight*, p. 63). Writing quite inevitably led to filmmaking; the motivation behind the two activities is the same: "I write and make films to grasp an erotic urge" (p. 69). Literature and film issue from his unique experience; they reflect impotence at the hands of authority as well as visions of possibility, both harrowing nightmare and liberating dream. Film feeds the soul—in a number of ways.

Film is a ubiquitous presence in Achternbusch's prose, especially in *Der Tag wird kommen* (*That'll Be the Day*, 1973),[2] *The Hour of Death* (1975), and *Land in Sight* (1977), three works that bear the designation "novel."[3] Happy, the protagonist of *That'll Be the Day*, talks about his visits to movie theaters. He relates the exact date on which he first saw *Gone with the Wind* and describes subsequent viewings and his reactions on each occasion. "I've gone to the movies alone damned often," he confesses (p. 43). His suffering mother in the same book likewise seeks succor in the dark.

> All my life I was beat up, pushed around, punched out, made fun of, mocked, and things like that. In fact in my whole life I haven't enjoyed a single good hour. Yes, cinema was nice. Cinema was nice. Why? Because it was something different from my constant prayers. Why should I pray? The Almighty doesn't help me anyway. It was a totally different world for me. (p. 89)

Moviegoing as sustenance and salvation: "After I had watched the long steps of the wily Groucho Marx," the narrator confides in *The Hour of Death*, "I once again felt a sense of purpose in my own life" (p. 11). Cinema is more than simple escapism here. If anything, films strengthen Achternbusch's regard for reality, making him aware of another and larger world beyond the one that constrains his every move. Cinema heightens one's sense of the Other. It persists in the mind's eye as one's life unreels.

> On my death bed or lying under some car, as long as my brain hasn't been totally squashed, I will see images from Mankiewicz's *The*

Barefoot Contessa. And when the last waves slip out of my head, I hope they will oscillate somehow images from John Huston's *The African Queen*. And I hope Katharine Hepburn might once again say to Humphrey Bogart, "Charly" (*The Hour of Death*, pp. 11–12).

In the celluloid images unwinding before him, Achternbusch glimpses a liberating alternative: cinema provides compensation for one's frustrating present and the hope of a possible—and better—future one. In his earliest prose, Achternbusch talks of crafting his own images, of becoming the hero in his own film. *The Hour of Death* traces an obsession with cinema from promiscuous moviegoing to critical appreciations of other directors, to scripts taking form in the writer's head, to his performance as an actor in someone else's film.[4] The "novel" ends with the angry Kuschwarda City (one of Achternbusch's amok-running projections) waking up from his punitive fantasies to announce: "Your soul has suffered enough, now it's time to conquer the world" (p. 154). The Kuratorium Junger Deutscher Film has just sent word that his *Das Andechser Gefühl* (*The Andechs Feeling*, 1974) will receive an 80,000-mark subsidy. Weary of acting out film-derived dreams in an unreceptive world, Achternbusch eagerly readies himself to make the first film of his life.

Reading Herbert Achternbusch, as one critic points out, is like watching a brain at work—not in the process of sober reflection, but in the midst of vital necessities, of sweating and dreaming.[5] The author's experience flows before us, not in a continuous manner but in leaps and bounds, jumping from present to past, switching from one perspective to another, shifting at times from diegesis to exegesis. The cinematic consciousness—the profound sense that reality is one never-ending film—inherent in Achternbusch's writing has much in common with Peter Handke's work, but the differences between the two men are even more revealing. A novel like Handke's *Die linkshändige Frau* (*The Left-Handed Woman*, 1976) contains numerous discrete and careful compositions; the narrative moves from one neatly framed moment to another. One finds little of Handke's still lifes in Achternbusch, those precious seconds where one focuses on inanimate objects such as in Keuschnig's "hour of true sensibility."[6] Achternbusch's protagonists continually gaze into the distance, but not in the aimless and detached way we find Handke staring out of his Paris apartment windows in *Das*

Gewicht der Welt (*The Weight of the World*, 1977).[7] Image after
image drifts by Handke's characters, but they remain for the
most part unmoved, outside the reality that surrounds them.
Achternbusch's characters never escape the concrete factors that
circumscribe their lives: even their wildest fantasies recapitulate
the unavoidably given. Dream heightens reality, it does not
elude it. Handke's characters seek self-sufficiency; Achternbusch's figures must always recognize how dependent they are,
no matter where they go.

The apocalyptic images of Achternbusch's prose, the violent
confrontations and outrageous histrionics, have much in common with features in the work of "cinematic" writers such as
Hubert Selby (*Last Exit to Brooklyn*, 1964) and William Burroughs *(Naked Lunch*, 1959*)*.[8] The very garish colors of his
book jackets announce a world of melodramatic tonalities and
vibrant hopes.[9] Achternbusch's tales evidence all the jerkiness of
his films. One passage typically leaps to the next without any
preparation or with only the vaguest binding links. Wisecracks
interrupt long monologues, nonsensical turns of phrase ("Anyone who sings and isn't silly is a scoundrel"[10] or "As long as there
are tall mountains, I refuse to believe in justice"[11]) irreverently
detract from story logic. Visuals coexist with printed pages in
The Hour of Death: a number of grainy black-and-white photographs accentuate Achternbusch's story of a filmmaker's evolution. For example, we see the hero in a long shot taken from
behind him as he strolls over a field into a vast mountain
panorama. A caption reads: "In order to survive one must go
cross-country" (p. 40). It is above all the radical commingling of
elements that lends Achternbusch's prose its singular freshness
and novelty, a blend of disparate textures, moods, and tonalities
that imparts its own convincing integrity to his work. "I always
start with a simple story," Achternbusch says in *Land in Sight*,
"but I tell it so fantastically and wildly and tenderly and abusively
and passionately and urgently that one finds a slice of life in
front of them" (p. 154). This variety of possibilities obtains every
bit as much in the filmic extensions of Achternbusch's writing.

A search for seminal influences on Achternbusch's films repeatedly turns up certain names: Karl Valentin, Charlie Chaplin, Jerry Lewis. Valentin, the grand master of Bavarian stoic
humor, provokes Achternbusch's deepest admiration: "I grew

up on the same dung heap as Karl Valentin," he was quoted as saying in the *Süddeutsche Zeitung* (12 November 1977). "Comedy is when you find laughter and death side by side." Much of Achternbusch's nonsensical sententiousness derives directly from the deadpan wit of Valentin. Achternbusch extols Chaplin as someone who combines social criticism and incisive humor, subversion and laughter. He scorns those who would make a legend out of the Tramp by praising him as an immortal—hence harmless—comic classic.

> Away with your feuilleton tears! Chaplin is finally dead! A throne is vacant. Everyone should scrape under his fingernails as much of him as he can. Chaplin is a moralist. He beats policemen on the head. He kicks directors in the belly. He cannot be tied down, while we allow ourselves to be nailed down. If we see in him only the chance to relax, then the joke is on us.[12]

Much of Jerry Lewis's puerile behavior, his fits of aggression, and his helplessness around women is to be found in Achternbusch's films. And the director—who knows Lewis's *The Total Film-Maker* well—even went so far as to make a pilgrimage to 20th Century-Fox, where he dusted the dirt from Lewis's parking space—a symbolic gesture, indeed one of homage, one of deference: "If Jerry Lewis hadn't appeared to me in a dream, I'd still be a streetcleaner today" (*That'll Be the Day*, p. 236).

Like so many of his NGC colleagues, Achternbusch is an eclectic. His work has humorous and zany tonalities, but it also has many contemplative and quiet moments. To the abiding influence of the low-key Valentin and the high-strung Jerry Lewis must be added the crucial influence that Japanese cinema has had on Achternbusch's development as a filmmaker. He has studied the work of Kenji Mizoguchi and Ozu carefully and learned much from the latter. He prefers the frontality and flatness of image one finds in Ozu. His characters have much in common with those of the Japanese master: they "constantly behave as though they were being observed by others," "their behavior is at times 'public', we might say 'presentational.'"[13] Both directors fashion characters whose psychology is superficial, yet in whose stark directness we find great reserves and depths. The essay "Heart of a Mummy" (in *Land in Sight*) is an appreciation of Akira Kurosawa's *Ikiru*. Achternbusch carefully

recounts the film's line of action, lingering over certain vivid
moments, such as the scene in which Watanabe sits in a swing
during a nocturnal snowfall and sings an old tune: "Quite often
in Kurosawa's films broken people find themselves again in a
lonely song that makes them beautiful" (p. 71). After a retrospective of Kurosawa's films, Achternbusch feels cleansed of the
cerebral bile that quotidian reality usually implants in his mind.
The central thought behind Kurosawa's films could stand very
well as a motto for those of Achternbusch: "We have to scream
out, otherwise we'll find ourselves dead and buried" (p. 82).

To a great extent early Fassbinder films borrow secondhand
experience from the American *film noir*, and Achternbusch similarly borrows from American westerns of the forties and fifties.
Walking down the street in search of a beer, the not-so-self-as-
sured protagonist of *That'll Be the Day* remembers

> that Gary Cooper turned down the lead role in the John Ford west-
> ern *Stagecoach*, the one John Wayne accepted. And in *High Noon*
> Gary Cooper plays the lead role because Gregory Peck had turned it
> down with the explanation that it was too much like his role in Henry
> King's *The Gunfighter*. (p. 127)

More important than all other films, John Ford's *The Searchers*,
"the tragedy of a loner" (p. 242), represents a vision that persists
in Achternbusch's work. The film's closing scene sends chills
through the viewer.

> He [Ethan Edwards] is satisfied. Wayne immediately goes outdoors
> and continues searching, thinking: I just sell sincerity. And I've been
> selling the hell out of it ever since I got going. It doesn't matter what
> that means. But maybe he can someday forget everything. Every-
> thing. If I had made this film, I would have nothing else to say.
> (p. 244)

Achternbusch's subsequent work, quite frank in its debts but in
the end more than the sum of its various influences, provides
clear proof that he has plenty to say—and show.

In Achternbusch's first film, *The Andechs Feeling*, long
panorama shots of the Bavarian countryside alternate with
claustrophobic close-ups of an anxious teacher (as in all his films,
the lead role is played by the director) in his small world. Sitting
at a table on which flies drown in a mug, he confronts a life of

failure: he ignores his wife, neglects his child, shirks his teaching duties, and has little chance of winning tenure from school officials. Only a dream out of the past, the memory of a former liaison with a film star with whom he shared "the Andechs feeling, a feeling that we are not alone" provides sustenance. Suddenly dreams impinge upon reality. His former love arrives and invites him to Italy. Quite unexpectedly he gains tenure in the school. Now he sees himself as being "possible again." But with no *telos* to fuel him, he loses the urge to go on. Tempting fate, in his wife's presence he declares his passion for the actress. The long-suffering spouse delivers a stirring monologue (the first of many by abused wives in Achternbusch's films) about his past misdeeds. She then kills him—"Here's your Andechs feeling!"—and afterward herself. As an ambulance screams, police sirens wail, and a child moans, the actress (played by Margarethe von Trotta) gets into her yellow car and drives away into the distance.

The Atlantic Swimmers, like its predecessor, is a film in a raw state, a work whose primitive frontality, static camera, and lack of transitions paradoxically represent its formal charms. Smooth shot-counter-shot would destroy the kaput world of Achternbusch's weltschmerz-ridden heroes, Heinz and Herbert, perverse variations on Wenders' Robert and Bruno *(Kings of the Road.)*[14] Their dime-store dreams are in the forefront here. They do not have a chance in life, but they decide to try anyway. Responding to Kaufhaus Mixmix's offer to award 100,000 marks to anyone who can swim the Atlantic, they seek to escape their woes. As usual, the familiar Bavariana dominates: the Thalbrückner bridge in Munich, the rundown Gasthof zum Würmbad in Gauting, a garden in the village Herrsching. Herbert, a lifeguard, begins training his friend. Dream reveries flash through the drunken malcontent's mind at one point. Later he meets a pool attendant who looks like his deceased mother. Told he will never find his mother's long-lost second shoe, he goes haywire, dons her dress, and chants poems that recall the more idyllic days of his youth. Soon he believes himself immortal. Alois, an enterprising soul, takes a liking to the verse and plans to print it on toilet paper: "If tomorrow people learn to read with their rears, I'll be the first on the market with something for them." Herbert ultimately parts from Heinz and Alois, who first put Herbert's presumed immortality to the test by pushing him out of a moving car, and then pursue him to Tenerife, where Herbert decides to commence his solo Atlantic swim. As he enters the water, Alois screams, "Get the hell out of here, you stupid pig!" A final long shot reveals Herbert's minuscule head bobbing up and down in the vast ocean.

In 1977 Achternbusch completed two features coproduced with German TV: *Bierkampf (Beer Battle)* and *Bye-Bye Bavaria*. The latter looks decidedly more polished. True, the characteristic flighty ellipses and narrative leaps still abound; nonetheless, the camera work (done by Jörg Schmidt-Reitwein, Achternbusch's—as well as Herzog's—constant collaborator) displays much grace and formal purpose. The film opens with a fluidity not to be found in the relatively static first two works: the camera glides over a frozen scape in Greenland, the manifest destiny of the protagonist as well as an objective correlative to the frigid Bavaria to which we cut. The inner world of the outer world of the inner world: *Bye Bye Bavaria* objectifies and comments on Achternbusch's deepest fears and his most virulent discontents. We first glimpse the poet dressed in papal white sitting before the Bierbichler Inn in Ambach, a *Weissbier* and typewriter in front of him, a dog at his feet. The carefully framed image opens up to reveal the world that has driven him to type the words, "I don't even want to have died in Bavaria." He feels himself pursuid, besieged, and deceived from all sides: by his lovers, his wife, his best friends, and a pushy TV crew. Again and again, both visually (through a series of blue-and-white compositions that link the Bavarian national colors with the snow and water of Greenland) and verbally ("On Greenland there's much more ice," the writer says, "but not as much as we have here"), Achternbusch equates his Bavarian surroundings with an arctic wasteland. Erotic relations have frozen into commodity exchange: Herbert supports his mistress by poaching; she in turn sells the meat to Herbert's wife, who runs an inn. Herbert's friend, the game warden, overlooks this in return for the sexual favors of the poet's lovers. In the end the unruly writer strikes a retreat, but not before his wife has chided him with being a poacher of hearts, a vampire of souls. In a painful and moving single take (with only one momentary cut away to

Josef Bierbichler, Gerda Achternbusch, and
Herbert Achternbusch in *Bye Bye Bavaria*
(COURTESY OF FILMVERLAG DER AUTOREN)

Herbert's burning eyes), the wife (played memorably by Annamirl Bierbichler) confronts her husband before a static camera.

> For you I'm only surroundings. Because the surroundings here ruin
> you, I'm the only thing left for you to take it out on. You can't
> channel your emotions into emotions, but just into aggressions. . . .
> An energy comes from you that destroys me. I'd be better off if I
> were one of your ideas. . . . You, the big outsider, have no insight.
> You write at my cost.

A later image captures the fugitive poet against an icy backdrop,
frozen in the position the painter Johann Heinrich Wilhelm
Tischbein once caught Goethe in after his flight to the Cam-
pagna from Weimar. Various individuals pursuing Herbert—
including the spectacle-greedy TV team—perish in the ice. The
frustrated writer later drinks himself to death. The film ends

with an eerie sequence redolent of Herzog: with polar wolves howling on the sound track, the camera travels over the frosty terrain we saw in the opening sequence.

An equally impressive camera movement opens Achternbusch's next film, *Der junge Mönch* (*The Young Monk,* 1978). The apocalypse has taken its toll: a long pan—shot on Iceland—sweeps over the simmering arid aftermath of a nuclear catastrophe brought about by irresponsible rulers. In the ruins only a few survive. Achternbusch fashions a religion around the new god, a chocolate Easter bunny he finds in a cemetery. Forgetting the old prayers (for they only brought doom), he preaches a hopeful gospel to the elderly housekeeper with whom he dwells in Buchendorf, one of the undevastated areas (Munich exists now as a geyser). Glimpsing a baby carriage rolling down the stairs—ironic shades of *Potemkin*—in a nearby graveyard, Herbert makes the stroller into a mobile church. Sustaining himself on a diet of flies, the new prophet puts himself into a trance and contemplates "the State," the institution that brought so much destruction. A few others also live on: Sepp, who slowly digests himself to death; Branko and Heinz, who form their own group, the Party for *Freiwillige Selbstmordkontrolle* (Voluntary Suicide Control).[15] Herbert, awake from his extended dream reverie, wins Heinz as a disciple, and they travel to Munich, which now houses the Vatican. Herbert becomes Pope with the chocolate deity at his side, but he soon grows weary of his congregation's alcoholic excess. With Luisa, his new secular hope who teaches him a new language, the ex-Pope sets off for Italy. The Alps, the traditional symbol of German yearning, no longer exist. However, Herbert and Luisa never reach the Mediterranean Sea. The pan closing the film reveals the rocky crags on which all human hopes have been shipwrecked.

Unruly elephants wander through a slumbering invalid's mind. Herbert Achternbusch is *Der Komantsche* (*The Comanche,* 1979) who refuses to wake up to a loveless world, preferring his own dreams to life's sad realities. An exotic landscape reflects an existential malaise: characteristically, the images of trumpeting pachyderms give way to long tracking shots through a near-empty hospital where we find the Comanche in an incubator. His fantasies are carefully monitored on a video recorder; in fact, his wife sells them to TV. A devoted staff attends him. A nurse and doctor dedicate their life to him, but with only one patient left it is feared that public funds will be cut off. The dreamer mumbles his visions. As a Comanche he can fly on the wings of his imagination. The doctor explains: "A Comanche says he's going in this direction. Then he goes in that one. And you find him nowhere. He's like the wind." The majority of the film consists of the Comanche's mindscreens: a dialogue with a towering Buddha about his quest for love, reflections on the inexorable God who refuses to be consoled (neither with six million Jews, tourism, nor terrorism), chats with elephants whom he addresses as his wife and child, wanderings in Sri Lanka (which he claims is only forty kilometers from paradise). One later sequence runs like a TV series: "The Comanche: Coyote Crap and Frog Eye in the *Wienerwald.*" Two blood brothers, with live chickens strapped to their heads, seek happiness in a chain restaurant, looking for fellow tribesmen at a beer table.[16] Finally, the slumberer rises and takes flight—the script reads "like Zatopek like John Wayne like Jerry Lewis"—past buses parked outside the Munich Olympic Stadium. Surveying the roaring soccer-match crowd, the camera captures rows of spectators before it stops in front of the massive police contingent. We hear the Comanche's distraught voice: "When I was still dreaming, I had an idea how I could live with people. But now that I'm awake and see people, I don't know anymore. Don't know anymore." He repeats the phrase three more times as the camera closes in on his sorry eyes, the eyes of someone whose dreams have vanished.

Beer Battle (1977), more uncompromisingly than any other Achternbusch film, interweaves private obsession and public experience. As we have seen, the director's films entail both self-aggrandizement and self-destruction; visions of grandeur invariably end in suicide or murder. They dramatize the creator's inner life, but they never cease to stress the imposing reality that has shaped these anxieties, insecurities, and shortcomings. An inexorable social context frames each and every act: narrow Bavarian inns, authoritarian institutions that stifle authentic existence (police, TV, church, schools), organizational structures that define interaction in marriage, love, and friendship. *Beer Battle* is the almost definitive expression of Achternbusch's love-hatred toward Bavaria. During the raucous annual Munich *Oktoberfest*—a reveling mass of thousands, sideshows, beer tents, and sundry other diversions— Achternbusch records the scene with a camera team on what he later described as "a kamikaze mission." Onlookers are included not merely as local color, but rather as part of the staged event. As a result, virtually every shot contains an openness, a fluid sense that reality surrounds the frame and often determines the content of the image. At more than one point the director loses control of his film and takes flight from angry onlookers. For all the seeming *gemütlichkeit* in the crowded beer halls, we sense an undeniable hostility and aggression; especially toward any behavior that interrupts the drunken oblivion. *Beer Battle* blends a documentary account of the 1976 Oktoberfest and Achternbusch's self-stylized passion play. Simultaneously cinema verité, happening, and psychodrama, the film merges fiction and reality in a quintessential embodiment of Achternbusch's film aesthetic, that singular confrontation of the real and the reel.

A would-be policeman (played by Achternbusch, who relishes playing the roles of his oppressors and obsessions, be they school-teachers under whom he suffered or the dead mother for whom he grieves) wanders through the Oktoberfest throng, causing confusion and fomenting anger wherever he goes. In a series of flashbacks we learn that the imposter, chagrined by a life that commands no respect (not even from his wife), has stolen the uniform he proudly flaunts. Two policemen onto his ruse disguise themselves in blackface and pursue him through the beer tents. Meanwhile, the unconvincing peace officer runs from one woman to another, seeking the succor denied him at home. Dogging his steps is another pursuer, his wife. Finally, aware that even in uniform his life is meaningless, he leaves, retreating off-frame; several moments later his corpse is discovered by his friends, lovers, and pursuers. "That's what happens when power gets into the wrong hands," moralizes one of the policemen. "A nobody wanted to be somebody," chimes in his sidekick. "Together we added up to nothing," laments his weeping wife. The film closes with balloons wafting past the commanding statue of Bavaria and disappearing into the dark of night.

Structurally, *Beer Battle* seems at first a series of loosely connected tableaux, shot for the most part from the front, highly gesticulatory in nature; long takes abound, cuts contain abrupt changes of angle. The double pursuit by the police and the wife impart the semblance of plot logic to otherwise coincidentally ordered confrontations. Often the camera lingers as somebody recounts a tale of woe or cracks a joke. Despite these clear signs of arbitrariness, the film contains distinct tightening devices within a narrative frame. It begins and ends with low-angle shots of the towering Bavaria statue on the Theresienwiese. Against the background of a hopeful blue sky, at the foot of the monument, a young girl plays with her dog. In the conclusion, as a song of homesickness is heard, we watch balloons drifting past the matriarch into the distant night sky. A title reinforces the narrative cul-de-sac: "And so it ends." Three flashbacks interspersed throughout the film counterpoint the hero's desperate search for affirmation, providing three commentaries on the same dementia. The first contains the wife's description of the altercation with her husband that triggered his running amok. The second proves to be a lie: Herbert relates how hard it is to be a policeman and fabricates a story in which he steps as powerfully as a sheriff out of a Hollywood western. The final and most complex flashback starts with a policeman recalling the theft of his uniform. Herbert reappears in his filched new identity, and running along an open road halts a truck to check the driver for possible drunkenness.[17] (The scene reenacts Achternbusch's own treatment at the hands of local constables as related in *Land in Sight.*) The imposter eventually drives off with a woman in a sports car, and the camera latches onto his various pursuers.

A dialectic between the discovered and the staged, between the arbitrary and the intentional, the discursive and the precise, governs the form of *Beer Battle.* Nearly every shot has an authentic background (e.g., the Spatenbrabäu and Bräuroß tents),[18] yet for all its found qualities, the film remains highly composed. Unavoidable signifiers of the Bavarian ambience (brass bands, lederhosen, liter mugs, pretzels, wind-up toys, Hackerbräu, dirndls) coexist with aspects of that cultural heritage underlined by the director (quotes from Wagner's *Lohengrin*, hymns of praise to the Virgin Mary, folksongs, naive art). Amateur actors from Achternbusch's stock company intermingle with a cast of thousands. Curious bystanders gape straight into the lens as they pass Jörg-Schmidt-Reitwein; Achternbusch emphatically gesticulates and shouts into the camera at numerous points. *Beer Battle* shows how an environment shapes an individual who in turn is trying to shape his own images of the same space. At one point we see Achternbusch framed with a map of Lake Starnberg behind him while he despairs and suffers his wife's curses. Later on, we glimpse him sketching the contours of that same lake in a beer puddle on a tabletop.

Making reality into one's own film—shaping empirical existence into one's dream of it—Achternbusch readily realizes how limited his manipulative powers are. He must by and large deal with the surrounding world on its own terms, accepting its risks. An extended hand-held take of the beer-drinking crowd provides the film's high point, and is a tour de force. In his script, Achternbusch talks of the eight-minute shot as "this daring leap into the thick of things, into the mass, the attempts to deal with it from one table to the next, its anger and my ability as a policeman." Never, he claims, was he so alive, so physically present, so at one with his own body.[19] The director found that his Groucho- and Harpo-like ploys (skulking down the lanes, insulting people, jumping onto their laps, drinking from unoffered glasses of beer, absconding with food or items of clothing) may cause laughter in the cinema, but in life such shenanigans provoke ire and even violence. Angry bystanders jump into the film and run after the director in unstaged sequences. Fists fly in Achternbusch's face; the punches are real, and he is knocked to the ground. Chased from a hall, Herbert cowers behind a door and then hides under a bench. Like Werner Herzog (who once went to film an angry volcano in *La Soufrière*), Achternbusch journeys into an inferno. Unlike his colleague, however, Achternbusch did experience an explosion—and he did not have to leave the city of his birth to find it.

Herbert Achternbusch's films demonstrate *Autorenkino* in its purest and most radical sense, for they present a world fashioned by an individual who writes his own scripts, plays the lead role, uses his friends and familiar landscapes, directs, produces, and (in some cases) distributes the films. The entire work as a body forms a cyclical and coherent myth in which the creator begets himself on the screen, where he will eventually die or face ultimate perdition only to be reborn in the next film.

Unlike many of his more approachable colleagues, he has never had a particularly comfortable relation with film subsidy boards and television networks. He refuses to pay lip service to current notions of realism, or to conform to what committee heads consider viable cinema. The most difficult thing about everyday experience, he argues, is to emerge from it unravaged. He criticizes other German directors for their pretentiousness and their overdependence on accepted literary properties such as the fiction of Heinrich Böll and Günther Grass and for drawing too little from life, to say nothing of their own imaginations and dreams.

Almost twenty years after the Oberhausen Manifesto, Achternbusch still makes gritty low-budget films that share the willful outrageousness of early Young German productions such as Franz Josef Spieker's *Wilder Reiter GmbH (Wild Rider, Inc.,* 1966) and the anarchistic idiosyncrasy of Vlado Kristl's *Der Brief (The Letter,* 1966) and *Film oder Macht (Film or Power,* 1970). Among all the directors working in the Federal Republic today, Achternbusch most emphatically aligns himself with Sohrab Shahid Saless, an Iranian exile who lives in West Berlin and makes sensitive films about what it is like to be a stranger in a hostile land. Alexander Kluge enjoys Achternbusch's deepest admiration; a film like *Die Patriotin (The Patriot,* 1979), he notes, demonstrates that "dreams need not be an ersatz for an unfinished reality. Reuniting these realms is a task of the individual."[20] Clearly, this impetus stands behind Achternbusch's cinema. Refusing to take seriously the thought-garbage *(Denkschütt)* that clutters the air he breathes, fighting against images that sand off reality's rough edges, denigrate minds, and ruin lives, Achternbusch refuses to be co-opted as yet another middle-class intellectual who sings tales of woe and alienation. Consciously outlandish, he will not settle down: "And I'm not on the ground. Still moving. And I'm afraid to land."[21] Despite contemporary culture's relentlessly assimilative ploys, its way of making pleasing entertainments out of the most avant-garde challenges, Achternbusch stands firm.[22] "In me you find someone you cannot count on," Bertolt Brecht once said. Resisting easy admiration and facile cubbyholing, Achternbusch remains

NGC's most difficult and most direct filmmaker, an anarchist whose raw surrealism stems from a profound regard for the inextricable bonds between the public and the private.

NOTES

[1]Donald Richie, *Ozu* (Berkeley/Los Angeles/London: University of California Press, 1974), p. 165. In *Land in Sight*, Achternbusch expressly mentions that he owns and loves this book (p. 70).

[2]The title stems from an exclamation Ethan Edwards (played by John Wayne) makes at various crucial junctures in *The Searchers*. The rather unidiomatic German rendering is "Der Tag wird kommen;"Achternbusch uses the phrase as his title. The German translation of *The Searchers* (*Der schwarze Falke* or The Black Falcon) likewise leaves much to be desired.

[3]For all their multiplicity of voices, the works do cohere as aesthetic wholes, even if they hardly constitute traditional linear narratives.

[4]He played a schoolteacher in Volker Schlöndorff's *Übernachtung in Tirol* (*Overnight Stay in Tirol*, 1973), a film made for TV. His script *Herz aus Glas* (*Heart of Glass*) was adapted by Werner Herzog in 1976. Achternbusch discusses his collaboration with Herzog (*Land in Sight*, esp. pp. 154–59) in bitter words. He complains that Herzog hypnotized the actors, and he wonders with some trepidation whether his colleague plans to nail his players to trees in future films. An even harsher declaration of Achternbusch's reservations about Herzog is found in his letter to German filmmakers in his *Es ist ein leichtes, beim Gehen den Boden zu berühren* (*It's Easy When Walking to Touch the Ground*) (Frankfurt: Suhrkamp, 1980), p. 119.

[5]Benjamin Heinrichs, "Der Kopf ist ein Abgrund. *Der Tag wird kommen*: Herbert Achternbuschs sechstes Buch," *Die Zeit*, 12 October 1973.

[6]Achternbusch is decidedly more anthropomorphic in his use of objects. They invariably index a character's surroundings and state of mind. In Handke's film version of *The Left-Handed Woman* (1977), we often gaze on images in an unpeopled environment.

[7]This predilection is consistently confessed to by the author in *The Weight of the World;* it is shared by the protagonist of *The Left-Handed Woman*.

[8]Frieda Grafe dubs Achternbusch "the Bavarian bard of beer, the Burroughs of the blue-and-white drug," in "Da fielen Kirchweih und Fasching auf einen Tag: *Bierkampf*, der Oktoberfestfilm von Herbert Achternbusch," *Süddeutsche Zeitung*, 11 March 1977.

[9]The jackets of the reissued complete works of 1978 contain pictures of the poet dressed in white with binoculars around his neck, strolling over the wastes of Greenland, gazing into the distance.

[10]*Land in Sight*, p. 70.

[11]*The Hour of Death*, p. 14.

[12]"Achternbusch on Chaplin: The Throne Is Vacant," translated by Ronald Holloway, *Kino: German Film* (West Berlin), October 1979, p. 23.

[13]A paraphrase of Sato Tadao found in Noël Burch, *To the Distant Observer: Form and Meaning in the Japanese Cinema,* revised and edited by Annette Michelson (Berkeley/Los Angeles: University of California Press, 1979), p. 183.

[14]Benjamin Heinrichs makes this appropriate comparison in "Das Kino in meinem Kopf: Neues von Achternbusch: Der Film *Bierkampf,* der Roman *Land in Sicht,*" Die Zeit, 11 March 1977.

[15]The name is a bastardization of *Freiwillige Selbstkomtrolle,* the West German film censorship board that makes judgments on the appropriateness of films for various audiences. Achternbusch, whose relationship to public institutions is at best strained, also has some choice words to say about the *Filmförderungsanstalt* (Film Subsidy Board), which he dubs the *Filmfötusanstalt* (Film Fetus Board), arguing that is has more to do with aborting films than making them (*It's Easy When Walking to Touch the Ground,* p. 146).

[16]The play on the words *Stammesbrüder* and *Stammtisch* unfortunately has no ready English equivalent.

[17]Jörg Schmidt-Reitwein's composition of the country lane that gently curves into the distance with grass on both sides and trees in the background bears a strong resemblance to the opening shot of another film he worked on, namely Herzog's *Land des Schweigens und der Dunkelheit* (*Land of Silence and Darkness,* 1971).

[18]Although there are moments during which people are absent from the image, these shots never suspend the narrative. We always have a sense that this is an inhabited world and that these structures represent extensions of its denizens.

[19]*Land in Sight,* p. 145.

[20]*It's Easy When Walking to Touch the Ground,* p. 152.

[21]Ibid., p. 138.

[22]Cf. Irving Howe, *Literary Modernism* (Greenwich, Conn.: Fawcett, 1967), p. 24.

HARK BOHM

Films Addressing Questions

by Christian-Albrecht Gollub and Dagmar Stern

BEGINNING HIS CAREER AS A DIRECTOR in 1970, Hark Bohm became involved in an area of filmmaking that was gradually to expand the horizons of the New German Cinema. In a 1978 interview given during the twenty-eighth annual Berlin Film Festival, he explained, "I try to show how the world, and adults, look to an adolescent. But my first film gave me a reputation as a director who is able to work with children."[1] As a direct result of this first feature-length film—*Tschetan, der Indianerjunge* (*Tschetan, the Indian Boy*, 1972 — a new genre evolved in the following decade: *der engagierte Jugendfilm*—the socially relevant film about young people.[2] Viewing his films as "mere" entertainment, however, critics initially labeled them *Kinderfilme* (children's films), *Jugendfilme* (youth films), or *Familienfilme* (family films).[3] Only recently has Bohm been recognized as a pioneer whose films focus on the problematic process of maturation.

In the previous decade, few films dealt with or were made specifically for young people.[4] During the sixties the financial and artistic success of Berhnard Wicki's *Die Brücke* (*The Bridge*, 1969), in which teenage soldiers are left without guidance at a crucial point in their lives, was equaled only by Volker Schlöndorff's *Der junge TörleB* (*Young Torless*, 1965–66), which depicted

Hark Bohm (COURTESY OF F. KILLMEYER)

the sadomasochistic experience of boys in a military boarding school. A cinematic anomaly, it starred, like *The Bridge,* youthful protagonists confronted by the pressures and expectations of the adult world.

While the NGC struggled to establish its identity with films such as *Young Torless,* directors not immediately involved with the movement focused on Germany's youth from a different perspective. Alfred Vohrer and Harald Reinl, established and less innovative figures, continued the unimaginative style of the fifties, directing a commercially successful series of westerns based on the popular novels of the nineteenth-century German author Karl May.[5] It is within this historical framework that Bohm made *Tschetan, the Indian Boy,* in which he combined elements from *The Bridge, Young Torless,* and the May series by offering a youthful protagonist in a western setting.

While Schlöndorff, Vohrer, and Reinl were already seriously involved in filmmaking, Bohm had not yet become actively interested in the art of film. The oldest of four children, he was born on May 18, 1939, to a Hamburg-Othmarschen middle-class academic family in which the father was a dreamer and the mother the fuiding force that held the family together.[6] His childhood was spent on Amrum, the small North Sea island where his ancestors had lived for generations. "They used to say," he recalled, "that there are more Amrum people living in New York than on Amrum because the island is too small to nourish all its inhabitants."[7] Many emigrants from Amrum returned in their old age, and as a child Bohm listened to their recollections. As a result, New York became "the closest metropolis"[8] and America seemed like "something gigantic, like a dream."[9] A grandfather who had managed a Melxican hacienda until 1908 told him stories about the Indios and related family tales about the sea. In addition, boats, violent storms, the raging sea, animals, and seagulls were an integral part of Amrum life. After graduation from the Gymnasium in 1959, he joined the German marine corps. Not surprisingly, he later transferred certain elements of his early years to the screen: Bohm family dynamics, exotic foreigners, and the New World, as well as animals, water, and boats are leitmotifs in his films.

Although as a teenager he had lived close to the legendary art cinema Liliencron, it was not until he studied law at the University of Hamburg that he "discovered cinema."[10] He was particularly interested in the French *nouvelle vague*, westerns, and American gangster films. The American films, especially those of John Ford and Howard Hawks, evoked memories of his childhood and the emigrants' stories.[11]

While at the university Bohm reported on cultural events to the Allgemeine-Studenten Ausschuß, a student board concerned with the political disruption and dissent that were beginning to rock the West German educational system. After further study at universities in Berlin and Lausanne, in 1966 Bohm completed his first Staatsexamen in Hamburg. A year later, he worked as an assistant in a Munich gallery that specialized in expressionist art.

Bohm continued his legal training in the office of Norbert Kückelmann, a lawyer who had worked as a film critic during his own time as a junior barrister. Together with Hans Rolf Strobel and budding filmmaker and fellow lawyer Alexander Kluge, Kückelmann had been instrumental in the founding of the Kuratorium junger deutscher Film in 1965. As a result of his association with Kückelmann, and because his younger brother, Marquard, was an actor, Bohm became involved in the Munich film scene. He contributed to the script of the short feature *Na und (So What)*, a film codirected by his brother Marquard and Helmut Herbst, and in the fall of 1968 met filmmakers Roland Klick and Volker Schlöndorff. The latter, who by that time had made two feature-length films — *Young Torless* and *Mord und Totschlag (A Degree of Murder*, 1966–67) — and was editing his third, *Michael Kohlhaas*, asked him to collaborate on a script about the student movement at West German universities.

"In 1967/68 the radical nature of the student movement enabled me to free myself from petrified traditions," Bohm has written. "Volker's offer revealed a new perspective to me."[12] Because he and his lifelong companion, Natalia Bowakow, a young German-born Kalmuck woman, were short on funds, they moved in with Schlöndorff.[13] While Bowakow did occasional work as a model, the two men worked on the script, which anticipated specific elments that can be found in Bohm's own feature films, particularly *Moritz, lieber Moritz (Moritz, Dear Moritz*, 1977)*. The film was never made, since Schlondorff could not secure funds for the project. However, the script collaboration served its purpose. Encouraged by Bowakow, Bohm reevaluated his own professional plans and began to concentrate exclusively on film.

In 1969 Bohm received a monetary subsidy for his first script and also acted in his first films: Alexander Kluge's *Der große Verhau (The Big Mess)* and Reinhard Hauff's *Die Revolte (The Revolt)*, a West German TV production in which he played a militant in the student movement. When his brother Marquard got the leading role in Rudolf Thome's film *Rote Sonne (Red Sun)*, Bohm took on a small supporting role and also became Thome's main sound man. At the suggestion of Kluge, then head of the film division at Hochschule für Gestaltung in Ulm, Bohm and Bowakow moved to the Bavarian city, where he continued his informal film education. Unlike other filmmakers of the NGC who had studied acting (Fassbinder), theater arts (Herzog) or film (Schlöndorff and Wenders), Bohm was untrained. He was gradually drawn into the film world and learned through personal experience, experience he describes as "hesitating but unceasing."[14]

After acting in Fassbinder's *Der amerikanische Soldat (The American Soldier*, 1970), Bohm began filming *Wie starb Roland S.? (How*

Did Roland S. Die?), his first attempt at directing. Made in March 1970, the short was based on a true incident in which a corpse was found in a hotel near a railway station. Newspaper accounts of the event differed according to their political orientation: some claimed it was suicide, whereas others accused the police of shooting the man. Bohm's film realized thevarious conflicting versions regarding Roland S.'s demise.

The question of murder or suicide also appears in *Einer wird verletzt, träumt, stirbt und wird vergessen (Someone Is Injured, Dreams, Dies, and Is Forgotten)*, Bohm's second short. Made in 1971, it was based on Bohm's impressions of stories by Dashiell Hammett. The film opens with a shot of a severely injured man staggering in the street. While a police commissioner investigates the situation, the dying man hallucinates. In a snowy landscape of the American West, he urges his horse toward a snowbound ranch where a middle-aged woman greets and cares for him. It is uncertain whether she is his mother or his paramour. An older man appears, and a gun battle takes place. At this point the hallucinatory episode ends, and the scene shifts to the commissioner. His investigation of the deceased's room indicates the presence of narcotics. It is possible that while under the influence of drugs the man jumped from the window—or was pushed. The question of murder or suicide remains unresolved. In these first two shorts Bhom establishes the major theme of the feature films that were to follow: a beleaguered individual in conflict with society withdraws into or creates his own reality.[15]   In 1971 Bohm became one of the thirteen cofounders of the Filmverlag der Autoren and has since remained its sustaining force. When six of the original partners withdrew in 1974, Bohm invested some of hisown capital, and in 1977, when the Filmverlag was once again on the verge of bankruptcy, he encouraged Rudolf Augstein, publisher of the German news weekly *Der Spiegel,* to invest in the company. Augstein became a shareholder with 55 percent, while Bohm with 19 percent had the second-largest share. He has directed some of the company's most lucrative films. In 1976 his *Nordsee ist Mordsee (North Sea Is Death Sea)* earned more than 800,000 marks (about $350,000), and the following year his *Moritz, Dear Moritz* was West Germany's top-grossing domestic film.[16]

Throughout his career, Bohm has combined the various aspects of filmmaking. Although he views his acting as only "a job," he has appeared in more than fifteen films in a ten-year period.[17] In addition, he writes film articles for popular and scholarly publications, manages his own production company (the Hamburger Kino Kompanie, founded in 1974), continues to support the Filmverlag, and takes an active part in film festivals throughout the world.[18] Furthermore, he both scripts and directs his films. It is this last element of his involvement in the film industry that he views as most important. For him "life is filmmaking."[19]

Hark Bohm's most significant creative contribution to the NGC is his depiction of the world from the perspective of the male child or teenager, something that has often been misunderstood and incorrectly categorized. As the only German filmmaker in the seventies whose films concentrated exclusively on young people, he was seen as a maker of children's films and not, more accurately, as a maker of films dealing with the adventurous tragicomedy of youth in an essentially adult-oriented world. This very misconception of his work points up one of its essential themes—the proverbial generation gap.

Bohm's films focus on the lack of communication between adults and children. With humanity, affection, and a command of the language and logic of his young protagonists, he captures the subtle differences in their perception of reality and shows them dealing with life's daily conflicts. Although he sometimes tends toward topical subjects, his basic concentration is on the universal and timeless problems of maturation: societal role-playing, society failing its children, physical and mental cruelty, the awakening of sexuality, and the communication gap that is at the heart of the generation gap. Adult-oriented society is seen as doing little, if anything, to aid the prepubescent and teenage youngster; instead it provides additional stumbling blocks in the form of decidedly adult problems: social and economic prejudices, troubled marital relationships, the inability to deal with aging and death. By using their naive wit, spontaneous resourcefulness, and unbridled imagination, Bohm's young people triumph over the adults and their environment.

Bohm's cinematic oeuvre makes it clear that a youngster can

scale life's stumbling blocks and utilize them as constructive elements with which to build a viable, life-supporting existence. Since the child's imagination is not yet fully subject to the order of the adult society, the existence that he fashions for himself proceeds from youthful fantasy and naive idealism, two elements often absent from the adult world. Bohm's cinematically open-ended fantasies provide no definitive solution. The viewer is left to decide whether the idyllic world created by the maturing young can support their dreams or will only lead to ultimate destruction; however, the positive ride-off-into-the-sunset endings suggest an optimism about the future of his protagonists.

The realization of the youthful protagonists' ideal vision finds its structure in simple, loosely woven plots, the complexity of which is determined by the emotional and intellectual capacity of the respective child. Essentially one long cinematic family saga, Bohm's features complement and build on one another as the children mature. The young child is play-oriented, has a relatively short attention span, and reveals discontinuities in his though processes. As his mind develops, he becomes increasingly more conscious of and able to deal with his environment. Bohm makes this maturation process more realistic by filming action from the eye level of the child, thus bringing his audience back to the youngster's level both mentally and physically. As the child grows, so does the camera. Both "heighten" in levels of perception. It becomes clear that the degree of the imprint determines the quality of the print.

A further structuring element is Bohm's use of conflicts and opposites. This is most apparent in his use of the same child actors to portray identical character trypes from film to film. Bohm starred his Oriental "foster son" Dschingis Bowakow, the brother of Natalia Bowakow, in *Tschetan*.[20] In this film and both *North Sea Is Death Sea* and *Moritz, Dear Moritz,* Dschingis, never losing the traits of Rousseau's noble savage, is the pensive and quiet intellectual who first observes and then acts. In contrast, Uwe Enkelmann, also Bohm's foster child, appears in *Ich kann auch 'ne Arche bauen (I Can Also Build an Ark,* 1973*),* *North Sea Is Death Sea,* and *Moritz, Dear Moritz* as the working-class ruffian who acts before he thinks. Antithetical outsiders, they deal with life in their own unique way, eventually finding, particularly in *North Sea Is Death Sea,* that a concerted effort produces the best

Dschingis Bowakow as
Tschetan, the Indian Boy
(COURTESY OF
FILMVERLAG DER
AUTOREN)

Uwe Enkelmann in *North Sea is Death Sea* (COURTESY OF FILMVERLAG DER
AUTOREN)

results. Bordering on the sterotypical, Dschingis and Uwe (as well as all other characters) are the skeleton that Bohm fleshes out with further diametrically opposed elements. The tension of the conflict between young and old, brains and brawn, East and West, silence and sound, nature and civilization, and fantasy and reality, is investigated and brought into a more harmonious balance. Bohm's careful orchestration of plot and mood and the interplay of characters strip these seemingly irreconcilable dualities of their potential banality.

American viewers may approach *Tschetan, the Indian Boy* with a dubiousness about the ability of a German filmmaker to handle the western genre. Bohm, however, appropriates the requisite cliches without allowing them to become leaden. He also gives the plot a unique twist. Around 1880, Jacob "Alaska" Kraft (Marquard Bohm) plans to establish a winter shelter for his flock of sheep on Montana land claimed by the cattle rancher Ben Jackson. Despite threats and harassment, Alaska stands his ground, knowing the law to be in his favor. During one of his encounters with Jackson, the rancher has in tow a 10 year-old Indian whom he accuses of cattle stealing. Alaska tries to make an ally of the boy by freeing him from imprisonment on Jackson's ranch, but Tschetan, recognizing that he has exchanged one form of captivity for another, does not offer Alaska the expected loyalty and assistance. In an effort to escape, the Indian knifes the white man in the hand, and the now incapacitated Alaska forces the Indian boy to carry on the construction of the compound. Tschetan reluctantly agrees, and although he occasionally rebels—at one point he leads the flock to a poisoned watering hole — he even resourcefully implements work-saving methods. His uncertainty about his relationship with the white man is further expressed by numerous unsuccessful attempts to escape. During one of these breaks for freedom, Tschetan finds his family brutally murdered. Faced with the adult task of carrying out Indian funeral rites, he must call upon Alaska, who has followed him, for help in placing the bodies on the ritual bier. In doing so, Alaska demonstrates not only his respect for Indian tradition, but his profound sympathy for Tschetan's loss. Having confronted death together, Alaska and Tschetan next witness the equally moving birth of a lamb. A deep bond forms between the erstwhile loners. Tschetan, who until this point has not spoken with his authoritarian captor, breaks his long silence and admits that he can speak the white man's language.

The growing harmony between the two is disrupted when Jackson and his sons, having discovered that Alaska is harboring the Indian, demand his return. Although the rancher promises Alaska that he will be unharmed if he surrenders Tschetan, the sheep herder affirms his loyalty to the Indian by replying with gunfire. Tschetan wounds one of Jackson's sons and the rancher withdraws. Realizing that he will soon return with reinforcements, Alaska and Tschetan abandon the sheep and head for safety. En route they encounter two of Tschetan's tribesmen. The Indian boy decides to join them and invites Alaska to come along. The latter refuses, but in searching for a cooking utensil that he thinks the boy may have stolen, he discovers instead that Tschetan has generously left him some freshly caught fish. Recognizing the strength of the bond between them, Alaska rides off with his Indian friends in optimistic anticipation of a new and better life in Canada.

By having the group ride off into the sunset, Bohm suggests a quest for a utopian existence in which barriers of race, age, and emotional and intellectual capacity are eliminated. In this ideal world, a human being intuitively comprehends the needs of others without words, which are neither adequate nor necessary. Alaska, the civilized man, discovers the humanity of Tschetan, the noble savage, enters into a friendship with him, and subscribes to his life-style. Two stereotypically antithetical people accept their status as outsiders, realize that their differences can indeed complement each other, and unite to seek an existence more in harmony with humankind and nature. The desire for a utopia stems from their recognition of and disgust with their fellow man's inhumanity.

In *Tschetan* Bohm succeeded in overcoming the often heavy-handed obfuscation of his cinematic contemporaries. His work proved more accessible to audiences of all ages than such NGC milestones as *Strohfeuer (A Free Woman)*, *Die bitteren Tränen der Petra von Kant (The Bitter Tears of Petra von Kant)*, *Aguirre, der Zorn Gottes (Aguirre, the Wrath of God)*, and *Der scharlachrote Buchstabe (The Scarlet Letter)*—all of which, like *Tschetan*, were made in 1972. Although successful in their own right, filmmakers

Schlöndorff, Fassbinder, Herzog, and Wenders failed to take into consideration a new generation of youthful filmgoers, but focused on "message" films for adults. *Tschetan* clothed Bohm's humanitarian message in the popular form of a western, a genre with which the cowboys-and-Indians-oriented youngsters as well as adults could easily identify. Initially, however, German film distributors failed to recognize the film's potential and were hesitant to market Bohm's first full-length feature. Named Film of the Month by the Luteran Film Guild, *Tschetan* was entered in competition at the Moscow Film Festival, given extensive photo-coverage in the popular German periodicals *Bravo* and *Stern,* and enthusiastically discussed on television. As a result of this media exposure, the Filmverlag der Autoren took the film into its program, where it found an appreciative audience of all ages. In the decade that followed, *Tschetan* proved to be a critical if not a financial success and one of Bohm's most enduring films. At the 1980 American Indian Film Festival in San Francisco, it was presented with a recognition award as the first European film to depict Indians in a suitable historical and social framework.

While *Tschetan* was garnering accolades, Bohm began work on the 16mm short *I Can Also Build an Ark.* Unlike the filmmaker's stylized and decidedly commercial German western, *Ark* projects the ambience of a home movie by depicting the adult world exclusively from the perspective of the children, played by non-professional child actors who are outstanding in their portray-als. Their innocence is captured by a naive camera that follows their every move. Its hand-held awkwardness is clearly intentional and complements the content with its very loose form. As the lens records the world through the child's eye, it selectively per-ceives what catches the young mind's attention. The adult level of perception is entirely eliminated.

In *Ark* Bohm has distilled his themes into a seemingly haphazard sequence of scenes that capture the child's world. Three boys (Christoph, Thomas, and Uwe) and two girls (Kirsten and Michaela) between the ages of eight and eleven play innocently and thought-lessly in the congested streets of Hamburg-Bergedorf. After an establishing pan, both the cam-era and the children focus on a van in front of an apartment building in which only two ground-floor stores remain occupied. Over the cacophony of the mechanized city environment—a passing train, a sports car—in carefully orchestrated counter-point, the children's high-pitched jabbering calls the viewer's attention to the human and emotional level. In contrast to the light, playful nature of the youngsters, the adults appear robot-like and callous. An unfeeling pedestrian bent on getting to her destination practically knocks down Thomas, the youngest of the group. The children leave the heavily trafficked thoroughfare and run to the garden behind the nearly empty house, where an unsympathetic man chases them away from an abandoned car, which they fantasize driving. Naturally inquisitive and adventurous, they now investigate the partially vacant building. Uwe, the oldest and ringleader of the group, suggests that Christoph andKirsten somehow gain entry into the locked house to let the others in. When Michaela, Thomas, and Uwe enter shortly thereafter, their companions in advanture have disappeared. The stairs creak. Doors open by themselves. The wind whistles through the empty rooms and corridors. Suddenly two ghosts appear. Christoph and Kirsten are playing a trick on their friends.

Once reunited, the children aim to put the experience of the empty building into perspective. Framed in doorways and windows, wandering through spacious, well-lit rooms, they pick up and examine objects left behind by the former tenants. In one scene Michaela finds a dead goldfish floating in a bowl, momentarily studies it with mild disgust, and blithely tosses it out the window—thereby housecleaning in her own juvenile fashion. Among the many treasures in the attic of the house the children find a Bible. After they read the story of Noah, Uwe claims that he can also build an ark. The group goes to the basement to recreate the biblical episode. While building the boat, the children squabble because Uwe gives orders and does not work. In order to float the craft, the children have to open a water valve. Uwe goes to get a wrench from his father, who barely acknowledges his son's presence; the boy finds the tool himself.

Meanwhile, Christoph, Kirsten, and Michaela continue to build the ark, and Thomas finds mice, lizards, and young doves to put in it. When Uwe returns, he wants to open the water valve immediately, but the others protest that the ark is incomplete. Uwe loses this miniature struggle for power and storms out with Michaela, bolting the cellar door behind him. The others eventually open the water value and the ark floats. As the water rises ever higher, the three discover their entrapment. A window located high above them is the only means of escape. Kirsten, a sassy, streetwise mulatto girl, helps the two youngest by boosting them up to it. Because she is too heavy for them to pull to safety, Christoph and Thomas go to unbolt the door. Meanwhile, Uwe and Michaela return to retrieve the wrench. Their united effort frees Kirsten. Back on the street, they telephone the police to report what happened, then run off in search of further adventures.

After the symmetrical portrayal of an adult-child relationship in *Tschetan*, Bohm presents an extremely one-sided view of the adult world in *Ark*, a world from which the camera all but eliminates grown-ups and in which children seem more mature than their elders. Although typical in their adventurous, haphazard, and naive behavior, unlike the adults the youngsters display a sense of responsibility, maturity, and sincere concern for the well-being of others. Unburdened by society's expectations, schedules, duties, and limitations, they are more humane and mature than the harried, apathetic, and aggressive adults. The interaction of the children stems from instinct and a sense of wonder and discovery. They are what adults should and could be. In the biblical Noah's ark episode, they leave harsh reality behind and create a utopia by escaping into an idyllic fantasy world that represents the quintessence of Bohm's films. The world as we know it, however, cannot support such a utopia, as the nearly fatal final events suggest. Despite the aborted fantasy, the film ends on a positive note.

In 1974 Bohm agreed to make a TV film based on a children's book by Christine Nöstlinger. He recalls the making of this film, *Wir pfeifen auf den Gurkenkönig (We Can Do Without the Cucumber King)*, as a negative experience. Since neither he nor Natalia Bowakow produced the film, he was subject to the restrictions of the three television stations financing the venture. When the producers rejected the "surrealistic madness" of his intentions, Bohm lost interest in the project, which was eventually broadcast in 1976. He now views the experience as little more than *Brot-Arbeit*—work taken on for monetary gain.[21] Having founded his own production company, the Hamburger Kino Kompanie, he exercised complete control over his work, beginning with his next film, *North Sea Is Death Sea.*

North Sea, Bohm's second full-length feature, opens with an establishing long shot of Hamburg that captures its harbor, bridges, and industrialized modernity. As the credits roll by, the mood for the following 86 minutes is set by the raspy, ragged, and apathetically plaintive voice of West Germany's popular rock star Udo Lindenberg.[22] An aural correlative, his song signals the film's theme: disoriented and searching youth.

The lyrics Lindenberg and Bohm coauthored expressly for the film tell of a boy's dissatisfaction with his home life and his dream of stealing a sailboat and letting the wind take him to "a place for a real sharp life." The camera focuses on the antiseptic apartment complex in which 14-year-old Uwe Schiedrowsky lives with his parents. His father, an ill-tempered, drunken tugboat captain, portrayed by Marquard Bohm, terrorizes and brutalizes his wife and son sadomasochistically, projecting his own feelings of inadequacy on his offspring. Dispatched to buy cigarettes, Uwe runs into his young friends. He is the ringleader of the group, and his tight, faded jeans, appliqued jacket, and studded leather wristbands create the image of a young tough. Spotting Dachingis Ulanov waiting for his mother in front of a supermarket, the group makes fun of his oriental features; Dschingis does not respond. Inside the market, his mother encounters more subtle prejudice when the butcher unsuccessfully tries to sell her an inferior cut of steak. Her firmness in resisting is motivated by her conviction that steak and orange juice are necesary for Dschingis's growth and well-being. Once outside, the overprotective mother rids her passive son of his hecklers. The relationships that will dominate the film have been established: Uwe is at odds with his father, whereas Dschingis is the focal point of his mother's existence. However, there is an obvious lack of communication in both family relationships.

Unlike Uwe, Dschingis does not relate to his contemporaries. Withdrawing into a private world in which nature ad animals play an important role, on an inlet of the Elbe River he constructs from debris a raft that he names *Xanadu.* This literary allusion to his Oriental heritage conjurs up visions of Kubla Khan and intimates the teenager's acquaintance with Coleridge's drug-induced poem.[23] A concrete expression of Dschingis's escapist quest, the raft anticipates the realization of a utopia and the escape from daily racial and parental discord.

In a sequence following Uwe's encounter with Dschingis, we see the young tough break into a vending machine and afterward buy a switchblade—a symbol of status and power. He unexpectedly runs into his mother, and together they return to the apartment where the father has been angrily waiting for his cigarettes and now proceeds to beat both his wife and son. In the lengthy, static twilight shot that follows, as the 12-year-old Uwe, framed in a window overlooking bustling Hamburg, sits smoking and drinking beer in an attitude of complete immobility, he confronts his lot and realizes that his life must change.

However, the impetus for this change is not yet strong enough. When, after school, Dschingis goes to work on his raft, he finds it wrecked, and he is again harassed by Uwe and his friends. In the ensuing fight between Dschingis and Uwe, the contemplative Oriental demonstrates physical aggression for the first time, and thanks to his mastery of karate emerges triumphant. Stung by his defeat and his humiliation before his faithful followers, Uwe agrees to rebuild the *Xanadu*. On his way home, he is picked up by the elder Schiedrowsky, who in a moment of surprising affection—or in an attempt at reconciliation—encourages Uwe to take the wheel of his car. Uwe, however, soon misuses this newly acquired skill, and to save face with his friends he steals a car. Informed by the police, the father savagely beats his offspring. Embarrassed to appear at school with a bandaged face, Uwe asks Dschingis to bring him the homework assignments, and when Dschingis complies the two boys fall to talking. "I've thought of running away for a couple of days," Uwe notes, "just to scare them. Sometimes you see in the paper, dear Christoph, please come home. We can work it out. But I don't know where to go."[24] A bond begins to develop between them as they recognize a mutual inability to communicate with and integrate themselves into a society indifferent to their adolescent needs. For both, life has been not a give *and* take but a give *or* take situation: the quietly overbearing Mrs. Ulanov only gives, the elder Schiedrowsky usually takes. Since Mrs. Ulanov has been so generous, Dschingis and Uwe search her out at her assembly-line job, in the hope that she will take the battered boy in; however, she fears legal repercussions and refuses. Disillusioned, Dschingis suggests a solution to the irresolute Uwe:

Dschingis:	We'll run away. You and me.
Uwe:	Don't be silly.
Dschingis:	We'll run away.
Uwe:	It won't work.
Dschingis:	Yes, it will. We'll show her. If you're afraid, you don't have to.
Uwe:	You crazy? I'm not afraid.

Crossing a bridge over the Elbe, they yearn for the freedom beyond the horizon. Xanadu having proved unseaworthy, the boys rationalize the theft of a small sailboat, break into a kiosk for food, escape from the police, and eventually stumble on an intimidating prison. Although they persevere, they begin to reevaluate their utopian ideal and consider returning home:

Uwe:	Dschingis, you sleeping?
Dschingis:	Man, I don't know.
Uwe:	Cold, isn't it?
Dschingis:	Sometimes I wonder, I don't even know how it is going to end, and then I think why don't we go to the police.
Uwe:	I really don't want to go to the police, since I saw that prison on the island yesterday.
Dschingis:	But maybe they don't imprison first offenders.
Uwe:	Why don't you call up and see . . .

But Dschingis speculates that his mother will refuse to take him back, and Uwe fears that his father will kill him. They therefore make a crucial decision: they will keep on sailing toward the North Sea. In a final moment of hesitation, Uwe laconically states, "North Sea is Death Sea. I still got some livin' to do." As the rising sun pierces the mist and the sails catch the first rays of light, their boat begins to move. Resolutely united, the two friends sail westward into a pastel haze. What lies beyond the horizon is left unresolved by the film's open ending.

Although Bohm provides no happy solution to their problems, by having the two dissimilar boys join forces, he suggests the possibility of a better life for both. Uwe and Dschingis are not runaways in the true sense of the word, but rather youths who reject the stifling routine of their parents' world. They have awakened from a social slumber and established a dialogue with each other. By gradually shifting his focus from a mechanized and sterile reality painted in primary colors to a pastel-hued idyll of the sun and the sea, Bohm implies that a realization of the boys' vision is somewhat idealistic but not impossible. They have taken the first meaningful step toward salvation.

The Freiwillige Selbstkontrolle (FSK), a commission that evaluates films released in West Germany, decided that because it set a negative example, *North Sea* was unsuitable for audiences under the age of sixteen. Supported by the press and his public, Bohm countered by citing other NGC films that had not had a detrimental effect on youthful audiences. Six weeks after the film's premier, the FSK lowered the age limit to twelve. Bohm had won his case—and the audience for which his film was made.

The following year, Bohm coscripted and codirected a documentary with his friend and associate Dr. Eric Zimen. *Wölfe (Wolves)* was the result of Zimen's decade-long research on how wolves interact in a pack. Bohm states:

> It deals with the social patterns in the pack, and what different packs do to protect their territory. What we were especially interested in is that the wolf as an animal of prey has a certain function in the whole environment; and also, the wolf is one of the few highly organized mammals who exist in a social group not only to defend themselves but to work together for the common good.[25]

As a naturalist and humanist, Bohm's involvement in the project is not surprising. His films deal with the problems of individual interaction within a social framework, and he feels that the instinctual behavior of human beings is not unlike that of animals; humankind is therefore equally threatened by the destruction of the natural environment. Only highly organized cooperation for the common good can secure the future.[26]

After *Wolves*, Bohm changed direction somewhat by focusing on a single protagonist in his 1977–78 "tender shocker" *Moritz, Dear Moritz.*[27] The rhythmic and lilting tenor music of West Germany's most successful jazz musician, Klaus Doldinger, sets the rambling mood for an opening montage. After a very long establishing shot of a luxury Hamburg villa located on the Elbe,

Dr. Eric Zimen in *Wolves* (COURTESY OF THE FILMMAKER)

the camera zooms in on the Stuckmanns, whose inherited financial security has been undermined by the father's business in-
competence. A recent bankrupt, he has spinelessly withdrawn
into his own world, taking interest in little but his garden. His
wife becomes the family's sole breadwinner, coping as best she
can with the family's financial worries and the demands of her
own job. Testy and high-strung, she is plagued by headaches;
sleeping pills have become an integral part of her life. The recent death of her father and the sickness of her aged mother—
unceremoniously consigned to a nursing home—aggravate her
emotional state.

Within this troubled family milieu, 15-year-old Moritz, an only
child, confronts adolescence with little guidance or sympathy
from his parents. The father can offer only vague platitudes; the
mother guiltily reproaches him for not visiting her hospitalized
mother more often. Sensing an affinity with the old woman—
both are outcasts living on the fringes of the family unit—Moritz
begins to visit her more regularly, sneaks a bottle of schnapps
past the doctors—much to the woman's delight and the nurses'
consternation—and generally comes to enjoy a warm rapport

with his reserved yet loving grandmother. However, he is disturbed by her request for a lethal dose of sleeping pills that would end her suffering and isolation.

Moritz's family models for love relationships are the vapid union of his parents and the nymphomaniacal behavior of his mother's sister. Youthful, attractive, and promiscuous, the latter flaunts her sexuality, teasing her nephew by wandering about the house seductively disheveled, and allowing him to watch through the keyhole as she bathes. At one point, her lover, Christian, emerges nude from the bedroom at an inopportune moment; in juvenile protest, Moritz sabotages his trouser zipper. On the threshold of manhood, Moritz expresses ambivalent attitudes toward sex.

Early in the film, ignoring his mother's calls, he awkwardly jumps onto his bicycle and leaves his stressful and unhappy environment behind. Spotting a beautiful blond teenager, he pursues her until, in the first of many mishaps, he is amost run over. Moritz is to become increasingly involved with Barbara, his first love. He follows her into the subway, to choir practice, and to an art museum. Each encounter is marked by his clumsy adolescent attempts to win the affections of the coquettishly aloof yet obviously interested girl. Time and again the object of his budding sexual interests eludes him, but Moritz perseveres. In his quest for an ideal relationship, he seeks a person not unlike his grandmother, a person who identifies with his problems, comforts him in a moment of need, and loves him for what he is. He anticipates a stable give-and-take relationship with the elusive Barbara and seeks to avoid the give-*or*-take stress situation so typical of the Bohm cinematic family structure.

Moritz's home problems affect his relationship with his classmates, who ridicule him because of his father's bankruptcy. Like Tschetan, Uwe, and Dschingis, he is the outsider. Verbal exchanges lead to physical encounters. Moritz also alienates his teacher by questioning the latter's competency. Only in sadistic visions can the boy compensate for his defeats in life. In his closed inner world, conflicts are resolved solely through bizarre and violent daydreams: young boys gun each other down; he clinically dissects his teacher on a geometric cross; a neighbor's cat gnaws on Mrs. Stuckmann's breast.

Music offers Moritz another means of coping with his problems. His solo accompaniment to jazz records functions as a release for his frustrations. While he plays the saxophone, a domesticated rat and a warty toad, his only true friends, keep him company.

Having sought out Barbara at choir practice, Moritz offers to accompany the group on his beloved saxophone. The choir director finds the idea absurd, but Barbara and the others react enthusiastically. On his way home Moritz falls off his bicycle once again and is helped to his feet by some teenage rock musicians (Dschingis Bowakow and Uwe Enkelmann in cameo roles) who need a saxophonist for an upcoming concert. They invite him to join their band. This episode marks a significant turning point in Moritz's life. His problems begin to resolve themselves through realistic interaction and communication with members of his own age group in the universal language of music.

From this point on, Moritz acts with positive results. He invites Barbara to the upcoming concert, and although she does not immediately accept his invitation, he is hopeful. Buoyed by his success, he finds the courage to deal with his grandmother's problems as well. Realizing that in her case death would be a welcome release, he supplies the lethal dose of pills she initially requested, and he stays with the dying woman until they take effect. Instead of mourning at her funeral, he plays the life-affirming jazz concert, expressing his joy for his grandmother's—and his own—release. During the concert episode that concludes the film, some of Moritz's classmates appear intent on disrupting the performance. In the ensuing battle, Dschingis, the pianist of the group, puts an end to the trouble in a lively and well-filmed karate sequence. The film ends with a freeze-frame close-up of Barbara—who has appeared in the crowd—and Moritz sealing their relationship with a kiss. A unique and respected member of the band, Moritz can now realize his fantasy union with the girl and respond to adult society as a secure individual.

Moritz, Dear Moritz obviously treats the same themes as Bohm's previous films. Although more loosely structured than any of his other works—with the possible exception of *Ark*—the film achieves its unity through the more serious and sophisticated use of Klaus Doldinger's music. Sometimes it sets the mood, at other times it provides leitmotifs. Dark strings accompany scenes with the grandmother and underscore the gravity of her situation. Saxophone music, in contrast, reflects Moritz's own fate. Initially, as the youth starts seeking independence, he briefly and primitively plays the instrument to accompany a recording. His mother often interrupts his simple efforts by crying out his name in a staccato manner. As the young man asserts himself and gains self-assurance, the amount of saxophone playing increases and becomes more accomplished. The acceptance of his saxophone, an instrument associated with jazz and nightclubs, in a church choir signals that the outsider can successfully enter into a social unit. The sphere of social acceptance increases as Moritz plays the instrument with the rock band's guitarist in the family basement. When Moritz finally joins the rock group for the concert and performs his own solo, the integration of the youth and the instrument becomes complete. Much more so than in *North Sea,* in which Udo Lindenberg's sung message anticipates and runs parallel to the action of the film, Moritz's saxophone embellishes and embodies Bohm's highly thematic film structure.

The exotic foreigner, an element in Bohm's previous features, appears here in a more symbolic form. Although Dschingis Bowakow appears briefly, his part is nowhere as important as his roles in *Tschetan* or *North Sea.* To relate the young boy's situation to his previous films, Bohm uses an Indian motif throughout the film in a variety of ways. When, early on, Moritz is injured by a passing car, he draws his fingers across his face—as if feeling for blood—and leaves two very distinct dark stripes, obviously the result of dirty hands smeared with oil. In a parallel scene at the end of the film, when Moritz is scratched after his mother throws the family cat at him, he draws the blood from his temple across his face in deep red stripes. Clearly a fighter, Moritz puts on his war paint, a signal that he will not surrender or go under. The scenes with his grandmother also contain elements of the exotic foreigner. To justify her request for an overdose of sleeping pills, she cites the Indians, for whom, she claims, death was a cause for celebration. Unsure of his responsibilities, Moritz seeks out his father and asks him about the Indians. He is told to consult the encyclopedia, and when he does finds the old woman's claim confirmed. Bohm adds dimension to the Indian leitmotif by treating a topic of current interest—euthanasia.

Like the audiences who saw them in *Tschetan, North Sea, Ark,* or *Moritz,* Dschingis Bowakow and Uwe Enkelmann have, through Bohm's cinematic adventures, matured into adults and are now in their early twenties. In a sense they have become the Jean-Pierre Léauds of the NGC. Similar to Truffaut's Antoine Doinel, they have grown up on the screen. Although Bohm has yet to gain the international following and artistic recognition of his French colleague, he is highly respected by both his German contemporaries and the film public. Fassbinder, a director with whom he had worked on numerous occasions, claimed that *Moritz* was the first West German film to "deeply move" him and said that Bohm was the only NGC director "who understands a little about audience reactions."[28]

How does Bohm see himself in relation to other German filmmakers? "I would say I am more realistic and concrete. I try to take my audience seriously. I think they're not that different from myself."[29]

Other filmmakers of the NGC have followed Bohm's lead. Since the early 1970s, the number of films about young people dealing with the problem of maturation has increased dramatically. One need only mention such filmmakers as Rüdiger Nüchtern, Haro Senft, Gustav Ehmck, Uwe Frießner, Reinhard Hauff, Max Willutzki, and Bohm's former mentor Norbert Kükkelmann to see the ripple effect the adventures of Dschingis Bowakow and Uwe Enkelmann have had.[30] After his most recent film *Im Herzen des Hurrican (In the Eye of the Hurricane),* a film once again starring Dschingis and Uwe, Bohm intends to move away from the cinematic genre that he pioneered.[31] Like his youthful protagonists, he will mature and develop the realistic fantasies of filmmaking.

NOTES

[1] Interview with Hark Bohm, in "Boys' Own Filmmaker," *berlinale-tip. Offizielles Bulletin Internationale Filmfestspiele Berlin,* 28 February 1978, p. 13.

[2] Letter from Hark Bohm to Klaus Phillips, 16 December 1980.

[3] See Hans Günther Pflaum, "Ein neuer Familienfilm," review of *Tschetan, der Indianerjunge, Film und Ton Magazin,* 19 (August 1973): 43–44.

[4] Jürgen Barthelmes and Hans Strobel, "Kinderfilme in der Bundesrepublik:

Situation und Perspektiven," in *Jahrbuch Film* 78/79, edited by Hans Günther Pflaum (Munich: Carl Hanser, 1978), p. 202.

[5] Regarded by literary critics as entertainment and not as serious literature, the Western novels of Karl May (1842–1912) are practically "required reading" for every German youngster. Similar in content to James Fenimore Cooper's Leatherstocking tales, they have been perennial bestsellers. Five adaptations of them are among the more than sixty films Harald Reinl has made since 1949. Alfred Vohrer based three of his forty-five cinema features on the novels. Although the last adaptation was made in 1968, the *Winnetou* series is still a regular part of children's programming on West German television. Critics were quick to compare Bhom's *Tschetan, the Indian Boy* with the series. Throughout his career as a filmmaker, Bohm has had to combat such grade-B stereotyping.

[6] Letter from Hark Bohm to Christian-Albrecht Gollub, 21 April 1981.

[7] Quoted in Judy Stone, "Exciting New German Directors—Peter Lilienthal and Hark Bohm," *San Francisco Examiner and Chronicle, Datebook,* 21 October 1979, p. 20.

[8] Quoted in Thomas Timm and Christoph Meier-Siem, "Mit bewegten Bildern das Bewßtsein des Zuschauers bewegen," *Kino: Magazin für den engagierten Film,* 15 February 1980, p. 31.

[9] Ruth McCormick and Bill Thompson, unpublished interview with Hark Bohm.

[10] Timm and Meier-Siem, "Bewußtsein des Zuschauers," p. 31.

[11] Compare Hark Bohm, "Arbeit, Männergruppen und Frauen: Zu den Filmen von Howard Hawks," *Jahrbuch Film* 79/80, edited by Hans Günther Pflaum (Munich: Carl Hanser, 1979), pp. 27–37. In other interviews and publications Bohm has expressed an admiration for the films of Luis Buñuel, John Cassavetes, Francis Ford Coppola, Robert Flaherty, Vsevold Pudovkin, and Martin Scorsese as well.

[12] Letter from Hark Bohm to Christian-Albrecht Gollub, 24 July 1981.

[13] Stone, "New German Directors," p. 20.

[14] Letter from Hark Bohm, 21 April 1981.

[15] The information on the two short features was provided by Mr. Bohm.

[16] Pflaum, *Jahrbuch Film* 79/80, p. 174.

[17] Letter to Klaus Phillips, 16 December 1980. American audiences will remember Bohm for his portrayal of the pharmacist Gieshübler in *Effi Briest,* the bookkeeper Senkenberg in *The Marriage of Maria Braun,* the police chief Gast in *The Third Generation,* and the pianist Taschner in *Lili Marleen*—all Fassbinder films.

[18] Bohm also assisted in the relocation of the aborted 1978 Munich film festival. With fellow filmmakers Reinhard Hauff and Hans W. Geissendörfer and others, he helped organize a new festival a year later in Hamburg, the city to which he and his family had moved in 1978.

[19] Letter to Klaus Phillips, 16 December 1980.

[20]Although Bohm has not officially adopted Dschingis Bowakow, he considers him and Uwe Enkelmann his sons.

[21]Letter from Hark Bohm, 21 April 1981.

[22]As the "grandfather" of New Wave, Lindenberg began to bridge the gap in 1972 between the eclectic connoisseur's rock underground and the formulaic and trite West German hit parade. He appealed to the young people affected by the 1960s student revolt, which also affected Bohm's life to a great degree.

[23]See John Livingston Lowes, *The Road to Xanadu: A Study in the Ways of the Imagination* (Boston: Houghton Mifflin, 1927), pp. 356–61.

[24]All quotations from the script of *North Sea* are taken from the selections published in *Scala: Zeitschrift aus der Bundesrepublik Deutschland,* January 1977, pp. 17–19.

[25]McCormick and Thompson, interview with Hark Bohm.

[26]Letter from Hark Bohm, 21 April 1981.

[27]Quotation taken from the Filmverlag der Autoren poster used in advertising *Moritz.*

[28]Quoted in Stone, "New German Directors," p. 20.

[29]"Boys' Own Filmmaker," p. 13.

[30]Their films are, respectively, *Schluchtenflitzer (Whizzer), Ein Tag mit dem Wind (A Day with the Wind), Feuer um Mitternacht (Red Midnight), Das Ende des Regenbogens (The End of the Rainbow), Der Hauptdarsteller (The Main Actor), Die Faust in der Tasche (Your Fist in Your Pocket),* and *Die letzten Jahre der Kindheit (The Last Years of Childhood).*

[31]Letter to Klaus Phillips, 16 December 1980.

ALF BRUSTELLIN and BERNHARD SINKEL

A Uniquely Utopian Aura

by Ruth McCormick

ALF BRUSTELLIN AND BERNHARD SIN-kel have worked together harmoniously since the 1960s. "They wish to devote themselves to a new popular cinema, but they go about their work intelligently," writes Friedrich Luft, the distinguished critic, in *Die Welt* (7 September 1977). "They maintain a high standard; but they want to entertain a mass audience, not frighten them away." Although their popularity is well established in Germany, their films have not found a commercial distributor in the United States.

Alf Brustellin was born on July 27, 1940, in Vienna and grew up in the Tyrol. After high school he went to Munich, where he studied German philology and theater and, while still a student, joined the Studiobühne München, a student troupe. Here he met Peter Stein, Roland Gall, and Bernhard Sinkel. From 1964 to 1966 he was director, writer, and actor with the Rationaltheater, a Munich cabaret group, again working with Sinkel. From 1967 to 1971 he served as film and drama critic for the *Süddeutsche Zeitung* and was also a contributor to *Filmkritik, Der Spiegel*, and the *Stuttgarter Zeitung*, gaining a reputation as one of the most interesting young critics in Europe.

It was also during this time that Brustellin began experimenting with super-8 equipment and made the acquaintance of filmmakers Alexander Kluge, Nicos Perakis, Edgar Reitz, and

Bernhard Sinkel and Alf Brustellin (COURTESY OF NEUE CONSTANTIN)

Ula Stöckl, all of whom were affiliated with the Institut für Film-gestaltung Ulm (Ulm Institute for Film Design), a major force in the shaping of the new cinema. In 1968 he made his first film, a forty-minute documentary on Alexander Kluge, *Kluge, Leni und der Löwe (Kluge, Leni and the Lion)* for WDR television.

Remaining closely allied with the Ulm group for the next few years, in 1970 he joined Stöckl, Reitz, and Perakis to found the ULM(Unabhängige Lichtspiel-Manufaktur, independent film handicrafts) production company. He also collaborated with ULM associates and Sinkel on the development of the Kleine Fernsehspiel (little TV show), which, in association with the ZDF television network, produced the films *Geschichten aus meinem Alter (Stories from My Old Age)*, *Sonntagsmalerei (Sunday Paintings)*, *Das goldene Ding (The Golden Stuff)*, *Kino Zwei (Cinema Two)*, and *Die Stadt der Hunde (City of Dogs)*.

In 1970, Brustellin showed his thespian and comedic talents in Stöckl and Reitz's *Geschichten vom Kübelkind (Tales of the Trashcan*

Kid) and in 1970 assumed acting roles in Stöckl's *Sunday Paint-ings* and Reitz's *Cinema Two.* In 1970 he also directed his second film, *Stories from My Old Age,* a 45-minute color film shot in super-8, about two women who imagine what their old age might be like while they reminisce about their childhood; they eventually decide that in the long run only the present matters, "because we always only imagine *what is.*"

In 1971 he and the other ULM founders codirected *The Gold-en Stuff,* a retelling of the myth of Jason and the Argonauts from a modern sociopolitical perspective; the cast was composed primarily of young people between eleven and sixteen years old. In 1972, Brustellin directed his fourth film, *City of Dogs,* a 55-minute 16mm color narrative about a young man attempting to confront his past, his subconscious desire for revenge, and his feelings for a woman. He described the film as "an experiment on the forms and possibilities for telling a story . . . about the impossibility of remembering in a meaningful way."

During 1970–72 Brustellin and Sinkel worked together on fifteen segments of the German version of the *Sesame Street* tele-vision series for children. They were involved in every aspect of the production, from writing and cinematography to editing and animation. Finally in 1973, the two worked together on a feature film, *Clinch,* which was produced by ULM, written and directed by Sinkel, and photographed by Brustellin for the WDR network. The film tells the story of a man and woman whose relationship has deteriorated to the point where language as a form of communication breaks down and leaves the pair in total silence.

Sinkel, who was also born in 1940, in Frankfurt am Main, began his professional life as a lawyer, working from 1970 to 1972 as head of the Archives and Documentation Department for the magazine *Der Spiegel.* Professional legal activities paid the rent, but Sinkel was as determined as Brustellin to make films. The work of Brustellin and Sinkel came to national prominence in 1974 with *Lina Braake oder Die Interessen der Bank können nicht die Interessen sein, die Lina Braake hat (Lina Braake, or The Interests of the Bank Cannot Be the Interests of Lina Braake),* which won the 1975 Bundesfilmpreis for best film. The two coscripted the film, Sinkel directed, and Brustellin again served as cameraman.

Of all Sinkel/Brustellin efforts, *Lina Braake* remains the most

Lina Carstens as Lina Braake (Courtesy of Filmerverlag der Autoren)

popular—and to many critics the best—of their films. In fact, it is one of the best German films of the postwar period. Simple, uncomplicated, and shot on a small budget, it boasts the talents of two of Germany's most celebrated veteran players, the beloved stage actress Lina Carstens (who won the Bundesfilmpreis as best actress for her role), and Fritz Rasp, who will be remembered by film audiences for his usually villainous portrayals in such classics as Fritz Lang's *Metropolis* and *Spies* and G.W. Pabst's *The Loves of Jeanne Ney.*

The clever story not only has a universal appeal, but packs a powerful political message. When her landlord dies and his relatives sell the building to the German Land and Credit Bank, Lina Braake, an eighty-one-year-old widow, is forced out of the small apartment in which she had hoped to spend her last days. The building is scheduled to be torn down to make way for a high-priced luxury project, and since skyrocketing rents make it impossible for Lina to afford another apartment on her pension, the bank offers to resettle her in an old people's home. She refuses, and sues, but she loses the case and must go to the home. It is run by a sanctimonious bureaucrat and an insensitive staff who treat the old folks — many of whom have become passive and now simply wait to die — like children. Deeply depressed and convinced that she has been swindled, Lina takes to her bed until Gustav Härtlein, a feisty eighty-four-year-old ex-embezzler, convinces her that life is worth living—if only to get revenge. Lina livens up, and she and Härtlein begin to plot.

Lina makes friends: Herr Dürr, who jogs to keep himself in shape for his escape from the home; Lawlonski, the handyman who sympathizes with the old folks and detests his bosses; Frau Schöner, the local hairdresser, and her partner Ettore, a Sardinian *Gastarbeiter* who dreams of buying a small farm back home, which, he tells Lina, would cost about 20,000 marks. All are more than happy to help Lina and Härtlein with their scheme.

Härtlein, a financial expert, gets things in motion by teaching Lina to play Monopoly. He tells her that the first step is to establish credit with the German Land and Credit Bank. She establishes a mailing address at a large home in the neighborhood where Lawlonski does yardwork, and, in order to raise a little initial working capital, sells a valuable chest to a ghoulish antique dealer who profits by buying the old people's heirlooms. Frau Schöner and Ettore dress and coif Lina to look the perfect bourgeois lady, and she takes her money to deposit in the bank, where the unsuspecting officials are only too willing to do business with her. Little by little, the stage is set for Lina's big move. She takes out a small loan and repays it. Härtlein, who has in his possesion all kinds of official stationery, makes sure that the bank receives all the necessary "recommendations" regarding Frau Braake's solvency. Eventually Lina requests and receives a 20,000-mark loan. She makes her escape from the home in Lawlonski's truck during a fracas the oldsters cause after Herr Dürr — who had been confined to his room after an unsuccessful escape — shows up at a "social gathering" despite the administration's threats to stop the party. With her 20,000 marks and her precious bicycle, Lina heads for Sardinia, where she is greeted by Ettore's family. During her idyllic stay, she hits on a bright idea: she will use her money to buy a small farm and sign it over to her Sardinian friends, on condition that she can stay there for the rest of her life.

Eventually, of course, the authorities catch up with our heroine, and she is returned to Germany. However, the house she bought is now the property of Ettore's family, and cannot by law be taken from them. Since Lina is eighty–one, a first offender, and penniless, further legal measures against her are pointless and she is simply remanded to the home, happy in the knowledge that she has taken the bank for a bundle—and that she and Herr Härtlein will have a lovely place in Italy to spend their annual vacations.

Lina Braake is a delightful comedy that manages to deal with several serious social problems with grace and compassion. The triumph of the two charming old rogues over the Establishment brought cheers from audiences throughout Germany. The anti-authoritarianism that was to become a hallmark of all Sinkel/ Brustellin efforts manifests itself here in a manner that is both winning and subversive. There is, of course, a fairy-tale quality about the movie that makes beating the system seem a good deal easier then it really is in a world in which the elderly are often neglected or abused by society, in which financial establishments sometimes deal heartlessly with the poor and powerless, and in which "progress" and "urban development" can exact a terrible human cost.

However, *Lina Braake* is a parable about the importance of solidarity; although the injustice of Lina's situation and that of her friends is made clear, it is suggested that, with a little help from our friends, not only can we fight the forces that oppress us, but we can have fun doing it. A strong utopian element is at work here. Although the film sometimes flirts with cuteness— Lina rescues an old three-wheeled cycle from a scrap heap and rides it like a kid, she hustles an "alien" pup for Ettore's children from the humane society — it never loses sight of its serious concerns. There is an especially moving sequence in which the inmates of the home gather for the double funeral of two ladies who, having sunk into silence after years of friendship, die within hours of each other. Unlike Lina, they lost their sense of purpose.

The sunlit outdoor sequences, especially the Sardinian scenes, are bright and lush, while most of the interiors (the bank, the home) seem cold and washed out. (The only exception is Härt- lein's cozy room, where he hatches his plots and peruses his girlie magazines.) For Sinkel and Brustellin, blue skies and green vegetation signify liberation in the best German Romantic tradition. The same is true of other directors as diverse as Herzog and Straub, Schroeter and Lilienthal, Wim Wenders and Rainer Werner Fassbinder. (Usually imprisoned by four walls, Fassbinder's characters may gaze out a window at a landscape when they contemplate possible happiness or escape.) In *Lina Braake,* the filmmakers have succeeded in making that most rare of cinematic creatures, a serious "entertainment" film. Their orientation is popular, and their touch is light, but they have managed to bring to the attention of a mass audience problems that must be faced by any society that strives toward decency. This ability has remained a strength in their work.

Berlinger, subtitled *A German Adventure* (1975), coauthored and directed by Sinkel and Brustellin, is a more complex and ambitious film, and no doubt for that reason never quite as successful. Palpably intended to be a very broad political statement about present-day Germany (West and East, it seems safe to say), it is an intelligent and often very absorbing study of two men who represent two distinct strains in the German historical personality. Lucas Berlinger, scion of an old upper middle-class family engaged in the chemical industry, is a gifted scientist and aviator, a free spirit who questions everything, a romantic indivualist who embodies elements of Nietzsche, Saint-Exupery, Howard Hughes, and Albrecht Berblinger, an eighteenth-century tailor who attempted to invent a flying machine (and who is the subject of a subsequent film, *The Tailor from Ulm* (1978), by Edgar Reitz). Berlinger's childhood friend, Johannes Roeder, a petty-bourgeois overachiever dedicated to conformity, patriotism, and the work ethic, remains loyal "to Germany" after Hitler comes to power. When under orders Roeder tries to convince Berlinger to work for the Nazis, the scientist mocks the fascist regime and tries to get his friend to see the irrationality of the new order. Roeder remains loyal to the Fatherland, but Berlinger assists political refugees, even using a private plane to fly them out of the country by night.

The basic plot of *Berlinger,* which is told in a series of flashbacks and flash-forwards, centers around the conflict between the two protagonists and what they symbolize, from childhood to the late 1960s. The Gestapo, suspicious of Berlinger's activities, arrests his beloved wife, Marlit, who then commits suicide under mysterious circumstances. In 1942, Berlinger makes a heroic escape from Germany by stealing a Luftwaffe plane after setting a military airstrip afire. He goes on to make a fortune in the chemical business in South America. Roeder remains behind, prospering first under the Third Reich, and then under the Occupation, when his hard work and good sense stand him in good stead. He also becomes the guardian of Berlinger's son, who is never seen but becomes, as Roeder assures his associates, "one of us." In 1968, Berlinger returns to claim his family's deserted chemical factory and the land on which it stands. Setting up housekeeping in one of the old buildings, he hires a small staff of workers and devotes himself to research and the care of his possessions—a laboratory, a small red plane, a blimp, and a loftlike dwelling full of plants and featuring a sort of primitive Jacuzzi.

Berlinger is considered an eccentric figure in the neighborhood — admired by some, feared by others — until he again comes into conflict with his old opponent Roeder, now a wealthy land developer and politician whose firm wishes to build a "leisure city" in the vicinity and needs Berlinger's land in order to complete the project. Of course, Berlinger has no intention of selling. Roeder shakes his head: "This isn't the first time he's given me trouble," he sighs. Among Berlinger's supporters is Laski, a young engineer in his employ, and Maria, a schoolteacher and environmental activist with an uncanny resemblance to Marlit. The scientist is immediately attracted to Maria because of her appearance, her dedication to opposing the land developers, and her name (when she tells him her father was a Catholic farmer, he smiles, "Good—otherwise, born when you were, you'd have some name like Brünhilde or Siegtraute!"). They fall in love.

In the end, neither Berlinger nor Roeder wins. Roeder's deal falls through when Berlinger refuses to sell his land, and Berlinger is killed when his plane crashes into a tree. Maria and Laski move into Berlinger's home together, and plan their next move. Though inspired by Berlinger's courage, love of freedom, and respect for the earth, they realize that they must move beyond their mentor's idealism in order to deal with the real world —in which the Roeders and Berlingers are both obsolete.

Berlinger is a confusing film. The numerous flashbacks to different periods make the narrative difficult to follow, and small details are easily overlooked at an initial viewing. Sinkel and Brustellin have attempted to construct a fascinating puzzle, but some of the pieces never fall into place, and certain contradictions are never resolved. The irony implicit in the love/hate relationship between Berlinger and Roeder, opposite sides of the same bourgeois coin, is never fully developed. There is some justification to Roeder's accusation that Berlinger cares only for himself. In one of the flashbacks, Berlinger tells his wife that he is not really interested in having children: "You are my center," he says. When he escapes, he leaves his son and never tries to see him again. His lack of interest can be read as a rejection of the idea of family, but just as correctly as a rejection of responsibility.

This irresponsibility is seen several times: in his childhood, it results in the destruction of his father's laboratory, and later in that of his own airplane and hangar. While this can be read as contempt for property, his contempt for the fascists as lesser beings ultimately results in the destruction of his own wife. Similarly, his contempt for gravity leads to his own death. Berlinger is a golden boy; his gifts are his by nature and by inheritance. The sedulous Roeder, with his dogged insistence on doing the "correct" thing, is the self-made man, and his strivings become pathetic (and almost sympathetic) when compared with the ease with which his *Übermensch* opponent moves through life. The idealistic individualism of Berlinger may be as responsible as the pragmatic materialism of Roeder for the political and psychological problems Germans, and all of us, face today. There are hints of this in the film, as well as the suggestion that intelligent but "ordinary" people like Maria and Laski must remake the world; but that point, which could have been addressed with greater insight—perhaps in a witty confrontation between the two protagonists—is lost amid the plot complications.

Berlinger is a handsome film. As in *Lina Braake,* natural splendor becomes a metaphor for transcendence, and the aerial photography is breathtaking. From here on, Sinkel/Brustellin's cameraman is Dietrich Lohmann, one of the world's finest cinematographers, best known in this country for his work with Fassbinder. Berlinger uses his airplane to escape the repressions of everyday life, and in one stunning sequence, as he passes over the luxuriant Bavarian countryside, the fairy-tale castle of mad King Ludwig comes into view, establishing a relationship between the monarch who worshiped Wagner and the scientist who worships freedom—two aristocratic dreamers whose aspirations can only end in fantasy. Soon after, Berlinger crashes.

The acting cannot be faulted: Martin Benrath, as the libertarian with a talent for dominating others, the skeptical intellectual who is also a sensualist and charming trickster, makes a perfect foil to Peter Ehrlich as the opportunist who can defend the Nazi Party and the American Way with equal righteousness when it suits his interests. The directors have an eye for choosing just the right human types, so the smaller roles are equally well cast. The humor that made *Lina Braake* so engaging appears here in flashes. Like Härtlein, Berlinger has a lot of fun confounding his enemies, and the audience is in on it. There is an especially funny sequence set in a luxury hotel, where Roeder has called a press conference to announce plans for his Alpenarium: hordes of press people, "beautiful people," and just plain freeloaders throng the grand ballroom, chattering, stuffing themselves from groaning buffet tables, swilling expensive booze, and ignoring the long-winded speeches concerning the glories of Scientific Leisure Planning.

Berlinger ambitiously attempts to render the complexity of modern German history in allegorical terms, and at the same time to tell a whopping adventure story with mass appeal. It is possible that the film is actually no more complicated (and at times prolix) than the reality it seeks to illuminate, but in its best moments it is a great deal more amusing.

Der Mädchenkrieg (The Three Sisters; literally, The Girls' War), completed in 1977, was in many ways an even more ambitious undertaking than *Berlinger.* It remains, with *Lina Braake,* one of the directors' two most popular films, and garnered three Bundesfilmpreise—a silver ribbon for the film itself and gold ribbons for actress Katherine Hunter (Katharina) and set designers Hans Gailling and Karel Vacek. It represents several departures for Sinkel and Brustellin: it was shot almost entirely in a studio, with very few of the directors' by now characteristic "nature" sequences; it cannot in any way be described as a comedy or a satire, and it is the first of their films not based on an original story idea, but on a well-known *Bildungsroman* by Manfred Bieler about three German sisters living in Prague during the years 1936–46, the time of the Nazi occupation and defeat. The directors admitted at the time that they wanted "to make a big film in a big way," and they have succeeded. *The Three Sisters* is two and one-half hours long, and would have been longer if it had been completely faithful to the novel.

In 1936, Dr. Sellman, a widower with four children, is appointed branch manager of a large German bank in Prague. His sponsor is Dr. Lustig, an affable Jewish financier with whom he becomes friends. The apple of Sellman's eye is his youngest child and only son, Victor, a gentle child who has been blinded by a severe case of measles. The three daughters, in their middle to late teens, are excited about their new life. Christine, the eldest, is a cool Nordic beauty who dreams of glamour and romance: Sophie, the second, is a warm, sensitive young woman who is studying to become a singer; petite, vivacious Katharina, the youngest, is the family "intellectual" and adventurer. When Germany invades Czechoslovakia, Dr. Sellman's loyalties are torn: he is a good, loyal German, with a good job and children to raise, but he feels it is his duty to help his friend Lustig escape from the Nazis. The three sisters, oblivious to politics, concentrate on their love lives.

Christine falls in love with Jan Amery, a thirtyish porcelain manufacturer whose professed nationalist feelings do not prevent him from doing business with the Germans. Sophie is fond of Pavel Sixta, a fellow music student who aspires to be a composer, but she feels a powerful attraction to Jan, who is something of a womanizer. Katharina's animated friendship with Karol Djudko, a dedicated young Communist scholar, soon turns to passionate love. Eventually, Jan and Christine marry, but her cool narcissism soon turns him toward the vulnerable Sophie, and the two meet secretly. After an attempted elopement, Katharina and Karol are tracked down by their disapproving fathers, and Katharina is sent to a convent in Vienna. The Sellman home becomes a salon for the Nazi elite in Prague, with the elegant Christine holding court, oblivious to her family's apprehensions. Katharina, home on vacation, runs away with Karol to struggle in the anti-German underground. Sophie' "bohemian" singing teacher is arrested by the Nazis and dis appears. After Jan and Sophie are injured in an automobile accident during one of their trysts, her guilt about the relationship prompts her to break with her lover and enter a convent.

The Germans are finally defeated. Dr. Sellman is killed by a stray bullet during the street fighting that ensues as the Russians enter Prague. Christine, who has suffered a nervous breakdown, leaves Jan. Sophie quits the convent and resumes her relationship with Pavel, only to desert him on the night of the premiere of his symphony to return to Jan. Pavel, immediately aware of the situation, makes his way to the hotel where Jan awaits Sophie and bashes his head in with the bottle of champagne that had been intended to celebrate the lovers' reunion and escape to the West. Karol tells Katharina that her nationality and family background are a political liability to him, and breaks with her. The three sisters are cast adrift: their only alternative is to return to Germany, lucky to have escaped with their lives. In the last scene, they stand outside the house to which they had come ten years before with such high hopes, and wonder if perhaps they have deserved to lose everything.

The first third of *The Three Sisters* is Sinkel and Brustellin at their best. Their evocation of a bygone era and a certain middle-European bourgeois environment is completely effective; this is a cozy little world that will soon be shattered by the forces of cataclysmic social change. However, the narrative tends to come apart at the same time that this world begins to disintegrate.

As in all the directors' films, the staging and camerawork are excellent, although one might wish that there had been more location shooting in Prague or a similar city, and less in the studio. Despite the film's length, there is simply too much narrative material to be contained within its perimeters. Elements in the plot are never resolved (what happens to little Victor, who undergoes an operation that restores his sight, and then disappears completely?), and others are fuzzy (at one point late in the film, Christine blurts out that she hates her sisters because they have never understood her and always banded against her —the point is never taken up again, and in the end, despite her politics, Katharina still relates to her, and despite the fact that Sophie was her husband's mistress, Christine still accepts her). The slow pace of the final two-thirds of the film—crammed with plot details and stunning images, but with almost no dramatic confrontation between the characters—makes *The Three Sisters* seem even longer than it is.

In a statement for the film's press book, Sinkel and Brustellin write:

> We wanted to tell a story about young girls who are capable of something more interesting than participation in the collective insanity of that historical period. They take their own very private interests more seriously than any historically important event in the men's world. They are so radically self-involved that they have no time to become involved with mass hysteria or to concern themselves with the fear and terror around them. We like these girls so much that we refuse to criticize them. . . . We don't want to judge them; our public can do that.

Of course, the title "Girls' War," the novel itself, and the directors' statement all imply that women see war differently than men do. While it is true that women are not combatants and seldom have much to do with starting wars, the implication that they are creatures of domesticity and romantic love, caring little for social reality outside their narrow existences, is less true, especially once a war starts. Unfortunately, what the filmmakers find so charming in these "girls" becomes the major flaw of the film.

Never very sympathetic, Christine becomes rather repulsive when she takes up with the Nazis. It is only after her diatribe against her sisters that we get any clue as to her cold, almost dissociated personality. Eventually, she emerges as more stupid than anything else. Sophie's attraction to the arrogant, rather slimy Jan is never quite believable, and her treatment of poor Pavel is at best an indication that she too is weak rather than passionate. Only Katharina comes fully to life and seems capable of personal commitment—if not to a cause, then at least to a man. Of the three women, only she seems more a victim of historical circumstances than of weakmindedness. By the end of the film, the three sisters appear bound together only because they have no one else (read: men) to whom they can turn. A woman's potentially greater proclivity for devoting herself to love and family—and therefore to peace—is reduced in Christine and Sophie to little more than an indulgence in silly romantic daydreams. If these limited creatures have been touched by

Hans Christian Blech and Katherine Hunter in *The Three Sisters* (COURTESY OF FILMVERLAG DER AUTOREN)

Jacques Breuer is the *Good-For-Nothing* (COURTESY OF FILMVERLAG DER AUTOREN)

any war at all, it has been the war of the sexes, and even that seems not to have had much impact on them. As a result, *The Three Sisters* remains a colorful but strangely unmoving spectacle.

Taugenichts (Good-for-Nothing) was directed by Sinkel in 1978 from a script coauthored with Brustellin and adapted from a picaresque nineteenth-century novel by the iconoclastic poet-nobleman Joseph von Eichendorff. With this film the directors returned to the cheerful antiauthoritarianism of their earlier films and indulged to the fullest in their penchant for romantic imagery. *Good-for-Nothing* deals with ideas which, in their fullest development, are embodied in modern characters like Lina Braake and Berlinger. The "good-for-nothing," a miller's son, leaves home to see the world. His adventures take him through every class of society—the now impoverished nobility, *lumpen* world of thieves and artists, and finally his own world, in which he can marry and enjoy petty bourgeois respectability. During his travels, he discusses life and love with a dotty countess, a philosophical porter, and various dislocated poets and painters who have lost the security they enjoyed under the Church and aristocracy with the rise of the "free" bourgeois society. In their press book for the film, the directors wrote:

> Naturally, we have attempted to give the subject matter a modern interpretation. . . . The film takes the necessary and useful literary lessons from Eichendorff, but reinterprets them in terms of modern experience. We do not wish to use these alterations and elucidations against Eichendorff, but, on the contrary, to alert the audience to the "good-for-nothing" principle, which becomes more relevant than ever today, when the "performance principle" is the guiding principle from childhood on.

The most visually beautiful and formally stylized of all the Sinkel/Brustellin films, it seeks to transform a nineteenth-century spoof of the traditional German Romantic "wanderer" tales wherein a youth seeks for the meaning of life in the course of his travels—especially in sunny southern climes—into a parable about the modern hippie dropout who, like his earlier counterparts, is co-opted back into the system after a brief period of rebellion. The attempt is now totally successful, because the film often seems little more than a lighthearted costume "road" picture offering little political or psychological insight into the problems of contemporary alienated, and often jobless, young people. A weakness in Sinkel/Brustellin's approach to their art is most evident in this film: in their desire to reach large audiences, they tend to avoid deep analysis or confrontation with unpleasant realities. Nevertheless, *Good-for-Nothing* is not without charm. The nineteenth-century atmosphere is brought vividly to life, and the directors' affinity for utopian visions has never been put to better use.

In late 1977, in the wake of the assassination of Hanns-Martin Schleyer, the Mogadishu hijacking, and the alleged suicides of Baader, Ensslin and Raspe at Stammheim prison, an ugly mood of reaction set in in the FRG: terrorism and state repression were on everyone's minds, and a group of filmmakers, including Kluge, Schlöndorff, Reitz, Fassbinder, Sinkel, and Brustellin, joined forces with writers Heinrich Böll, Peter Steinbach, and Wolf Biermann, and many of the most gifted editors and camerapeople in West Germany to make an omnibus film, *Deutschland im Herbst (Germany in Autumn)*, in response to the frightening events. Brustellin, Sinkel, and cameraman Lohmann arranged to cover an interview by actor Helmut Griem with Horst Mahler, one-time attorney for the Baader-Meinhof group, who had for seven years been incarcerated in Moabit prison. Mahler discusses his clients and his own case, and expresses doubts about any immediate prospects for constructive social change in West Germany. The filmmakers then turn their camera to Wolf Biermann, a prominent poet already in exile from East Germany. In a moving poem, "The Girl from Stuttgart," Biermann voices his dismay at "the hardening of feelings" in both East and West and wonders whatever became of the postwar dreams for a better society. In a brief sequence about "everyday violence," a man beats a woman. When she escapes, he begins yelling "Kidnap!" and the police soon come running.

In *Germany in Autumn*, Sinkel and Brustellin, who had been accused by some purists of making "Hollywood" films, demonstrated their continued commitment to freedom and social justice. Well received by the German public, the film brought together a number of the founders of the New German Cinema and conveyed a renewed feeling of solidarity.

Difficult social conditions are not avoided in *Der Sturz (The*

Fall, 1978), directed by Brustellin on the basis of a script
coauthored with Sinkel and based on a novel by another emigré
from the East, Martin Walser. We are once more dealing with
the world of *Lina Braake,* a world in which those without money,
or power are constantly threatened with destruction.

Anselm Kristlein, an affable small businessman with a wife
and three children, loses his life's savings when his pinball-ma-
chine franchise falls through. Afraid to go home, he goes on a
drunken bat and falls in with two old friends: Gabriel, an alcoholic swindler, and Glatthaar, a hopeless dropout. Eventually
Anselm's wife, Alissa, convinces him to come home, but is not
happy when he brings his two unconventional friends with him.
Other strange people show up at the Kristlein home, and Alissa
wonders how they will survive. But Anselm remains calm and
philosophical, and there are tender moments even in the midst
of despair. Things soon go from bad to worse: Gabriel stages an
elaborate suicide, and Anselm is arrested for murder. When he
is finally released, he seeks solace from nature, and participates
in an idyllic outing in the woods with some nudists. The Kristlein
children are unhappy because they do not have the money to be
part of the affluent society around them. Anselm and Alissa are
loving and caring, but without money life is impossible. During a
raging storm, Anselm loads his family into a small sailboat and
sails out into Lake Constance.

In an interview quoted in the bulletin describing the film for
the twenty-ninth Berlin Film Festival in 1979, Brustellin stated:

> What interested me was how a man and his wife could, despite all
> these catastrophes, retain a belief in personal happiness and the
> power of love. . . . In contrast to the novel, where this apotheosis of
> true love is a sort of concluding Faustian hymn, it is the main theme
> of the film. That means it has become a quite extraordinary love
> story—extraordinary because it is that of a couple who have been
> married fifteen years, have three children, and are actually always
> fighting. . . . A story like this happens every day; it's horribly true
> and realistic. But I don't want to show only what is realistic; I also
> want to show how something positive can come out of all this, to
> show what could or must be. I am trying to celebrate the victories
> that man can achieve despite his defeats.

A bittersweet film about the clash between imaginative idealism
and the harsh realities of contemporary society, in its best mo-

ments *The Fall* recaptures the fairy tale whimsy of Lina Braake, but in its weakest, it is too unbelievably bleak. It is as if two films —one romantic and visionary, the other naturalistic and harsh— were intercut, without either being fully realized. Brustellin is strongest when he celebrates the power of love and beauty to transform human existence, but weakest when he attempts to chronicle a middle-class family's descent into pauperism. However, because this marriage of two aesthetic approaches has seldom been attempted (and perhaps only achieved successfully by Herzog in *Stroszek*), *The Fall* is one of the most interesting curiosities in contemporary German cinema.

The Fall was Alf Brustellin's last feature film. On November 11, 1981, he was killed in a traffic accident in Munich. He was 41 years old. In 1980, he had coscripted *Kaltgestellt (Out Cold)*, a political thriller, with Sinkel, who directed. In 1981, he also collaborated on the script for the 5-part television version of Thomas Mann's *Adventures of Felix Krull, Confidence Man*, also directed by Sinkel, and that same year wrote for ZDF a script based on John Knittel's novel *Via Mala*. At the time of his death, he had been planning another feature, again to be coauthored and directed with his longtime associate.

For a decade, Alf Brustellin and Bernhard Sinkel worked together so closely and harmoniously that they have come to be thought of as a single entity. It is almost impossible to say which writer-director contributed what to any given script. There is a temptation to speculate that Brustellin — a filmmaker and cameraman from the beginning of his career—was the "visual" one, while Sinkel—a former lawyer and businessman—was the "idea man"; however, this would be misleadingly simplistic. They were collaborators in the truest sense, and *Good-for-Nothing* (directed by Sinkel) is certainly as "visual" as *The Fall* (directed by Brustellin). It is safest to say that theirs has been one of the most successful symbiotic relationships in the history of film.

Though Sinkel and Brustellin's concerns are social, their approach has generally been commercial and characterized by a genial good humor that is rare in contemporary German cinema. For this reason, their films have often been more popular with mass audiences than those by directors more honored at international festivals. Adhering to fairly conventional narrative structures, these films are rich and often witty in characterization, well acted and beautifully photographed. If they lack the innovative, idiosyncratic, or iconoclastic élan that characterizes the films of some of the better known German directors, they have a uniquely utopian aura and generosity of spirit that is all their own.

HELLMUTH COSTARD

The Undisturbed Course of Events

by Russell A. Berman

HELLMUTH COSTARD, BORN IN HOLZ-
hausen near Leipzig on November 1, 1940, studied psychology
at the University of Hamburg, where he participated in the university's Film and Television Work Group. His first film was
commissioned by the university's student union for use in a student government election campaign. "We tried to make it comic
and irreverent, tried even harder to find the correct exposure,"
he recalls.[1]

Costard's next project—an attempt to document Iran's Kur-
dish secessionist movement—was never completed, but its focus
on Third World revolutionaries suggests a growing antiestablishment radicalism in the young director. The Kurds, after all,
were opponents of the Shah, and for the nascent German student movement the close relations between Bonn and Teheran
took on the same symbolic significance as the Washington-
Saigon connection did for the American left.

Previous to 1968 Costard directed several 35mm shorts; the
first three, in black and white, have been compared by Jan Dawson to the early shorts of the French New Wave "with which they
share not only a fragmentary narrative technique applied to the
observation of some volatile and ephemeral human relationships, but also the same feeling of exuberance in the act of

film-making."[2] (Costard, however, claims that he was more profoundly influenced by contemporary Czech and Polish films.) The first of these films, *Tom ist doof* (*Tom Is Tiresome*, 1965) —like the next it was produced by the university work group— depicts how a young man's misbehavior at a carnival ruins the day for his girl friend. *Klammer auf, Klammer zu* (*Open Parenthesis, Close Parenthesis,* 1966) similarly presents an apparently harmless treatment of amorous ties. The film begins with Ole Blaum's decision to leave his job and his girl friend, Carla, to whom, in an unambiguous gesture of finality, he gives his record collection, as he sets out on a journey abroad, hoping to remain away from Hamburg for two years. Full of determination, he begins hitch-hiking and is picked up by a woman in a white Jaguar. She very soon proposes to him, the car is sold to a shepherd, and the pair return to Hamburg.

The structure of the narrative—an attempt to break out of established social patterns followed by the reassertion of those same patterns—explains the title; the "escape" remains a mere interlude within a social structure able to reintegrate all deviant patterns. The implicit social criticism is underscored by a variety of devices. Not only does Ole suggest a relationship between his decision to leave Germany and the recent parliamentary elections, but the voice-over narrator later bluntly says of the film's lightheartedness: "Maybe our stories can be so harmless only because somewhere in the world, people are being shot. Specifically in Vietnam." A newsreel shot of fights between police and demonstrators follows. Finally, a series of disturbing images indicates a present but unclear danger: as Ole walks through the Hamburg suburbs, a man seems to be hanging from a tree, and when tanks drive down the road, Ole feels compelled to jump into a ditch. The tone of the film, according to Dawson, "alternates between unspecified menace and lighthearted love."[3]

In *After Action* (1967), Costard alludes to the tense atmosphere of American crime films and the modernist ambiguity of the French New Wave. The crime remains unclear, as does the fate of the fugitive. Instead there is a brief sketch of a dramatic situation, or better, a brief series of familiar cinematic images. After a tip-off in an Italian restaurant, a man and a woman drive to a railroad station, where she unsuccessfully attempts to obtain something from a locker. As the police arrive, the man assures

Hellmuth Costard at work on *Soccer as Never Before* (COURTESY OF COSTARD)

her of his love and departs hastily. The camera follows him to the apartment of another woman, for whom he seems to care deeply. He asks if she has enough money to survive for two years, urges her to go to the mysterious locker at the train station, and then rushes off, but only after having grabbed the large color television set, the companionship of which he apparently cannot do without.

The 1967 three-minute color short *Warum hast Du mich wachgeküßt?* *(Why Did You Wake Me with Kisses?)* refers to a different but equally familiar aspect of the Hollywood tradition: a monumental opening credit sequence. The dramatic musical score and the sound of thundering surf prepare the spectator for an emotion-packed melodrama. Suddenly the credits are over and the second part of the film begins with shots of a woman— we only see parts of her, never her full body—rising from the bed she has been sharing with a lover and beginning to search through her dresser. The woman has herself been holding the camera and—in the third section of the film—she places it in a drawer, which she then shuts. The screen goes black, while a voice-over narrator describes the magnificent film that would have been shown, had not this mishap occurred.

Despite its humor and extreme brevity, *Why Did You Wake Me with Kisses?* anticipates some of the central concerns that were to relied on cinematic allusions, but here Costard thematizes the camera itself in a very direct manner. Instead of examining the literary and iconographic traditions of film, Costard turns his attention to the medium and its technology. Simultaneously he casts light on the role of the public in the traditional film and how it is manipulated by the language of the established cinema. Like Hans-Jürgen Syberberg, another outsider on the fringes of the New German Cinema, Costard links formal innovation in his films both to reflections on the nature of cinema and to a critical analysis of film's social function.

The year 1968 was the watershed in Costard's career. Having broken off his studies during the previous year, he founded the first Hamburger Filmschau outside the university context. More importantly, he stopped working with 35mm, the medium of the established film industry, and shifted to 16mm, and then to super-8; this issue would later become a central aspect of his overall cinematic project. In 1968 a film by Costard set off a scandal that soon earned him the reputation of the enfant terrible of the West German film scene. In *Besonders wertvoll (Of Special Merit)*, he responded angrily to the new Film Subsidy Law of December 1967, which included a clause designed to deny funding to films judged immoral or politically partisan. Objecting to these restrictions, Costard put together a highly provocative short film (ten minutes) that attacked the new law and its legislative author and easily managed to evoke the ire of the authorities, who banned the film on grounds of obscenity. As a result, an invitation to show the film at the 1968 Oberhausen Festival was withdrawn, which in turn led to the decision of sixteen of the thirty-two invited German directors to withhold their own works. Only after a two-year court battle was the injunction against Costard's film lifted.[4]

The film begins with a close-up of what eventually turns out to be the tip of an erect penis. A narrator recites the morality clause, but the liplike motion of the urethral opening creates the illusion that the penis is pronouncing the law. A series of slide projections of erotic but socially acceptable images follows, and eventually a woman's hand appears, busily stroking the penis. Costard then introduces archival footage from 1956 of Dr. H.C. Toussaint, the former mayor of Essen, who later became the author of the new film law. These black-and-white sequences are spliced with color shots of Costard himself; Costard at times seems to be speaking with Toussaint, but the fanciful nature of the encounter is underscored by the two types of footage. The film returns to the masturbation scene and its climax, and then closes with a candle, blown out by a discreet but audible fart.

Although *Of Special Merit* is primarily an attack on the censorship implied by the new legislation, it makes evident other issues that were to preoccupy Costard. The director's presence as an actor in the film foreshadows subsequent works and thematizes the general problem of the filmmaker. In addition, the slide projections consist largely of soft-core pornographic images, and a contrast develops between the officially tolerated erotic kitsch and the real act of masturbation. The film points out the hypocrisy implicit in society's sexual codes and its antagonism toward politically serious films.

The implicit cinematic issues of *Der warme Punkt (The Hot Dot, 1968)* illuminate Costard's later concerns, although it was not directed by Costard himself but by his friend Thomas Struck (who worked with him on the first student-union film). Costard collaborated on the script and also appears as an actor. Struck focuses attention on the problem of time in film by means of a double-exposure procedure. In the first exposure a white dot is projected onto the film at set intervals; it continually appears and disappears, moves from one corner of the frame to another, and assumes new shapes, eventually turning into a star and finally into an angel. The second exposure is of Costard and Struck wandering through Hamburg, speaking with passersby and engaging in various activities. The final version shows both the curious dot and the street scenes. With the help of a stopwatch and a record of the first exposure, Struck and Costard as actors pretend to examine the dot, discuss its appearance, and even capture it in a cocktail glass. *The Hot Dot* becomes an attempt to maintain rigorous control over the chronology of filming, but the limits of this control soon become clear, since the actors often fail to realize when and where the dot is appearing. This problem would eventually inspire Costard to experiment with a new technology designed to assert chronological order in film.

The structure of *Die Unterdrückung der Frau ist vor allem an dem Verhalten der Frauen selber zu erkennen (The Oppression of Woman Is Primarily Evident in the Behavior of Women Themselves,* 1969) is based on an ironic reference to a socially accepted category of time: the workday of a husband who leaves home at the start of the film and returns at its end. Instead of following this husband on his way through the outside world, the film closely observes the housewife engaged in a daily routine of washing the dishes, making the beds, chatting on the telephone, and pausing for snacks. The documentary camera does not wander from these apparently normal activities, but this normality as well as the pretense of cinematic realism are called into question by the film's most remarkable feature: the housewife is played by a man. As Dawson has observed, the actor provides "a brilliantly accurate female impersonation without ever actually looking like a woman . . . which makes the everyday chores and mannerisms of the 'average housewife' appear at once surreal and crushingly familiar."[5] The socially determined logic of everyday housework seems as inescapable as the conventions thematized in *Open Parenthesis, Close Parenthesis,* while at the same time the actor's gender and the husband's absence highlight the absurd structure of the division of labor. In addition, both the lack of any normal plot development and the presentation of an apparently authentic reality irritate the spectator accustomed to films in which directors thoroughly structure more or less complicated narrative sequences. *The Oppression of Woman* is as much a critique of assumptions regarding sex roles as it is a comment on popular expectations regarding cinema.

The title of *Und Niemand in Hollywood der versteht, daß schon viel zu viele Gehirne umgedreht wurden (And No One in Hollywood Understands That Far Too Many Brains Have Been Turned Already, 1970)* was taken from an article in the German magazine *Stern,* which examined the world of dropouts in California. The implied vision of an alternative subculture opposed to established society corresponds to the intent of the film. Costard had been funded by Bavarian Television to make a film that would explain his concept of an alternative cinema. In the course of preliminary discussions, many notes were prepared and then pinned to a wall. The bulk of the film merely documents these notes; the camera moves across the wall, creating a comic-strip effect, while the sound of crashing waves is heard in the backgound. In the final sequence a super-8 camera moves on electric-train tracks in a circle around the collaborators on the film (and some live pigs as well), while the sound track carries sitar music. The film suggests the difficult situation of the proponents of an alternative cinema. With their inadequate funding they could not turn out a film, but only, in a very literal sense, film the script. More importantly, the image of the circular railroad tracks implies the limits placed on film by the social environment; cinematic change and social change must go hand in hand.

Fußball wie noch nie (Soccer As Never Before, 1970*)* was filmed during a soccer match between the teams Manchester United and Coventry City. It focuses on the well-known player George Best; the camera never loses sight of him but rigorously documents his activities without ever providing an overview of the game. Thus we see the ball, for example, only when it approaches Best. The film depicts a routine activity with the same extreme realism that characterized *The Oppression of Woman.* While the earlier film compressed the housewife's day into a little over an hour, *Soccer As Never Before* establishes a one-to-one correspondence between real time and film time. The viewer watches Best for the full twice forty-five minutes of the match: at irregular intervals Costard even superimposes a digital clock's time record of the game.

The film shows that the star player spends much of his time waiting in isolation. The intention, however, is less a critique of the game and its absurd rules than a demonstration of the power of visual manipulation. *Soccer As Never Before* functions as the diametrical opposite of conventional sports films, which, through editing, montage, and commentary, create a very different picture of a game. Costard's film reveals the degree to which subjective concerns of an ideological nature can enter into the production of images. As Dawson has noted, "Through its own obsessive dialetical process, it shows us that there's nothing anodine or neutral about Germany's favorite leisure activity:

watching sports on television. Conventional sports coverage offers meanings and interpretations which Costard's film persist-
ently challenges."[6]

Der Elefantenfilm (The Elephant Film, 1971) shows an elephant
lifting a tree trunk from a rice field in Sri Lanka, placing it on
the back of a truck, and then, on command, returning the trunk
to the ground. Costard used the film to experiment with a variety of shots and angles. The symmetrical narrative structure,
reminiscent of *Open Parenthesis, Close Parenthesis,* again reflects
Costard's preoccupation with the all-embracing character of the
social system.

In *Teilweise von mir—Ein Volksstück (Partly Mine—a Folk Film,*
1972), the viewer sees 606 passersby sequentially reading fragments of a text prepared by Costard and Thomas Wittenburg.
The implication of the title is clear: each individual has contributed a tiny part to the finished product, which in the end appears as a collective achievement—of the folk. The generic category *Volksstück* also implies a colloquial language and, often, a
simple humor, two features which here result from the wide
variety of participants. For Costard, however, the experiment of
Partly Mine cannot be separated from his vision of contemporary
society in which individuality disappears and rigid forms prevail.
Thus he comments:

> Extreme division of labor appears to eliminate the influence of indi-
> viduals and to emphasize instead the production process as governed
> by the interests of capital or other "foreign powers": a source of
> discomfort for almost everything produced today. The solution of
> this conflict is, however, not only a question of power but also of
> knowledge. The suspicion hardens that even the powerful are essen-
> tially only functioning.[7]

Yet Costard does not merely document the world of taylorist
division of labor. The specific nature of the aesthetic medium
enables him to suggest an alternative to an oppressive age of
mechanical reproduction. He considers film to constitute a dimension of experiment in which alternatives to oppressive social
structures are developed. At the same time, his films examine
the hidden conventions of the established cinema. By underscor-
ing the division of labor in *Partly Mine,* Costard implicitly
criticizes not only the Hollywood tradition but also his own col-

leagues in the NGC, whose films often hide their own collective-industrial origin. Given the nature of the medium, every film is only "partly" the director's, who should therefore not pretend to produce works of art imbued with the same unquestionable originality characteristic of traditional artistic creations.

Ein Nachmittag mit Onkel Robert (An Afternoon with Uncle Robert, 1975*)* is a children's film produced by the Norddeutsche Rundfunk (NDR) for use in its series *Maxi und Mini.* Its apparent message is concerned with how to light a fire in a safe manner. Yet this is not typical educational television for children, since the adult, Uncle Robert, is the opposite of the ideal teacher; he is lazy and untidy, while the child is the actual motivating force in the film.

In the introduction to the screenplay of *Der kleine Godard an das Kuratorium junger deutscher Film (A Little Godard to the Production Board for Young German Cinema,* 1978*),* his most important work to date, Costard writes that "the camera itself is the theme."[8] This is a highly theoretical film about film. Long essayistic discussions of cinematic theory and film technology alternate with narrative sequences, which themselves describe the situation of the filmmaker. The term "a little Godard" was coined by the film critic Thomas Petz in a review of a Costard retrospective in 1976; yet both Godard himself and the members of the production board appear in the film, as do Costard and his less experimental colleagues Rainer Werner Fassbinder and Hark Bohm.

The two central plot lines involve attempts to find public funds for film projects. In the first Costard himself approaches the Film Production Board with a novel idea: instead of first developing a literary structure—the screenplay—that will later be filmed, he hopes to develop a new type of film, which, relying on technological innovations, would document reality in a new manner. We watch Costard apply to the board and see it come to its negative decision; it will fund only fully worked-out projects, not mere ideas or sketches.

In this general context, Costard develops his thoughts regarding the predominance of literary schema in traditional film. Furthermore he complains that most films separate sound and image, only to reunite them artifically in the final product, which hides the seams of its own montage. In contrast, Costard hopes to modify the super-8 equipment in order to be able to film real events with the original sound; by synchronizing several cameras, he can apply the montage techniques of feature films without disturbing the integrity of the sound-image relationship.

> A traditional film consists of a network of exposure moments that the viewer can no longer recognize. . . . Such a film is comparable to an almost completely destroyed wall painting after careful restoration. . . . No one can say to what degree the restorer has inserted his own ideas. Yet films are conceivable that treat the image-tone event as a unit during exposure, i.e., that do not tamper with the synchroneity or at least point out divergences from this principle.[9]

The second funding project—which also fails—involves Costard's efforts, as a member of a Culture Commission, to invite Jean-Luc Godard to Hamburg as an artist-in-residence to work on a project with NDR. Godard indeed arrives to discuss his proposal: a film entitled "Is It Possible to Make a Film in Germany?" Of course, Costard knows very well that German films are being made; he shows us Bohm and Fassbinder on location, while he himself appears carrying a copy of *Newsweek* with a cover story on the New German Cinema. Godard's question, however, refers back to the problem of the relationship between literature and film. Is it possible to make a film that is not simply rehashed literature but a fully independent image? Can film escape the strictures placed on it by a cultural establishment oriented toward literature and itself trapped by bureaucratic regulations? Thus Godard asks, "Is it possible to have imagination? . . . image in the sense of imagination . . . in general, is it possible to make an image in Germany?"[10] Like Costard himself, Godard discovers that the cultural bureaucracy is reluctant to support innovative projects.

These two failed attempts of the avant-garde cinema are set in opposition to footage of the two established young German filmmakers. The distance between Bohm and Fassbinder on one hand and, on the other, the reality of Costard's work, which the viewers have before their eyes, is astronomical. Costard makes no attempt to create a typical illusion; we constantly see the cameras with which he is working and hear him discussing cinematic problems. Meanwhile, his colleagues, each in his own way, busy themselves with the production of a closed fiction.

Jean-Luc Godard and Costard in *A Little Godard* (COURTESY OF FILMWELT)

Bohm anxiously tries to stage a battle scene among children; the behind-the-scenes perspective provided by Costard highlights the artificiality of the event. One suspects, moreover, that a comparison is intended between this staged world of juveniles and the spontaneous play of children at the opening of *A Little Godard*. Costard's lighter, more malleable technology permits him to film authentic events and, by using several synchronized cameras, to use cutting techniques without destroying the original chronology. Bohm, however, is compelled to work with a heavy, inflexible technical infrastructure.

Costard makes the same point with even more intensity regarding Fassbinder's work. We watch Costard with his modified super-8 camera scamper around Fassbinder as the latter, clad in leather and chains, trudges ominously from his luxurious BMW toward the massive 35mm camera. Costard's critique is directed both at Fassbinder's relatively established style of filming as well as at his general behavior, his entrepreneurial demeanor as he

lords over his crew. Thus a close relationship is implied between the formal character of a film and the artistic self-
understanding of the filmmaker.

A Little Godard certainly proves Costard's main thesis: that a
literary screenplay is not a prerequisite for a successful film. The
absence of a rigorously developed narrative does not necessarily
mean that a work will end in chaos. For Costard, literature is
replaced by the authenticity of a moment in time, in which both
sound and image are rooted.

> I found that the very moments of shooting are the significant ele-
> ments of film language. It has been said that the stills or the images
> of the objects, the sounds they produce, and the reflected light are
> the significant elements of motion picture; that they are the equiva-
> lents of written words. But there is only the original moment of
> shooting, that is the instant inseparable from its history (from its
> past), that is all there is.[11]

Perhaps the avant-garde concerns of Costard, specifically his
insistence on the integrity of time, arise in part from the interests
of the young West German generation in uncovering a consciousness of history repressed during the first postwar years.
Costard does not participate in the general "confrontation with
the past," but his protest against the social conventions of time
perception may well represent a parallel issue.

As important as the cinematic theory expressed in *A Little
Godard* may be, Costard has come to recognize that its specific
project has grown outdated. While he struggled to develop
highly synchronized super-8 machinery, the industry came up
with the so-called time-code process for "picture-synchronous
sound recording"[12] in 16-mm. The main goal of this technology
consists of a production speed-up in television in order to eliminate jobs and compete with the video industry, yet Costard
hopes to make use of this innovation in his own future attempts
to use film in a new way: not as the visual reproduction of literature but as the cinematic record of real time and unstaged
events.

NOTES

[1]Quoted in Jan Dawson, *The Films of Hellmuth Costard* (London: Riverside
Studios, 1979), p. 30. The late Dawson's work is the only comprehensive analysis
of Costard's films thus far.

[2]Dawson, *Costard,* p. 31.

[3]Ibid., p. 32.

[4]Peter Handke came to Costard's defense and chronicled the Oberhausen affair in *Ich bin ein Bewohner des Elfenbeinturms* (Frankfurt: Suhrkamp, 1972).

[5]Dawson, *Costard,* pp. 12ff.

[6]Ibid., p. 14.

[7]Quoted in ibid., p. 38.

[8]Hellmuth Costard, introduction to screenplay for *Der kleine Godard* (1978).

[9]Costard, *Godard,* pp. 138A-139.

[10]Ibid., p. 66.

[11]Hellmuth Costard, "Die unschuldige Frau," *Der Spiegel,* 7 November 1977, p. 236.

[12]Herbert Grosskopf and Manfred Stübbe, "Zeitcodierung — ein modernes Hilfsmittel bei der Bearbeitung von Filmen," *Rundfunktechnische Mitteilungen* 20, 5 (1976):183.

RAINER WERNER FASSBINDER

The Alienated Vision

by Anna K. Kuhn

RAINER WERNER FASSBINDER, PRO-
digious *Wunderkind* of the New German Cinema, was born on
May 31, 1946, in the small Bavarian spa town of Bad Wöris-
hofen. His father, a physician, and his mother, a translator, were
divorced in 1951. Fassbinder recalls the household as being
"rather chaotic, devoid of normal bourgeois rules and regulations." Left to his own devices, he grew up "like a little flower."[1]

The Fassbinder household, however, reflected the cultural
aspirations of the German middle classes, and among the director's earliest memories were a volume of Dürer, a gift to the
five-year-old, and a tape of Gounod's *Faust,* presented to him by
his father on one of his infrequent visits. Surrounded by art and
literature, Fassbinder absorbed traditional bourgeois aesthetics,
and this knowledge was to serve him well in his subsequent attacks on conventional literary taste. An unusual component of
Fassbinder's education was introduced by his mother after her
divorce. In order to gain the needed time for her own work,
once he was seven she frequently sent her son off to the movies,
where he often stayed through several showings. This legacy of a
childhood spent watching Hollywood movies is readily apparent
in his own films.

Fassbinder's formal education also had both traditional and

Rainer Werner Fassbinder (Courtesy of
Filmverlag der Autoren)

nontraditional components. Upon completing the Rudolf
Steiner theosophic elementary school, he attended conventional
Gymnasien in Augsburg and Munich until 1964, when, after
jobbing around for a while, he enrolled in a Munich acting
school. There he met Hanna Schygulla, who was to become his
favorite leading actress. Together with Schygulla, Fassbinder
joined the Action-Theater, a cellar-theater outside Schwabing,
whose provocative antiestablishment productions created a
furor. Fassbinder acted, directed, adapted, and ultimately wrote
his own plays; the first, *Katzelmacher,* premiered there in April
1968. Several weeks later the theater was closed by the
authorities, and the group dissolved. Ten members of the
group, including Fassbinder, Schygulla, Peer Raben, Kurt Raab,
and Rudolf Waldemar Brem, founded the *"antiteater."*

An underground, post-Brechtian political theater, it was described as *"antiteater*=ensemble of the Action-Theater, *antiteater*=socialist theater, *antiteater*=information,"[2] and encouraged active audience participation. The *antiteater* was to serve as

the testing ground for Fassbinder's many talents, but it was primarily for his disrespectful adaptation of literary classics that he attained notoriety.[3]

The antagonistically antibourgeois stance of the group's productions is succinctly formulated in the motto Fassbinder affixed to his adaptation of Sophocles' *Ajax*: "The most important thing, it seems to me, is to create discontent regarding the achievements of the bourgeoisie."[4]

The *antiteater* was a short-lived experiment. By late 1969, when the group was given notice to leave by the owner of the Schwabing pub "Witwe Bolte," Fassbinder's cinematic career had been launched and filmmaking took precedence.

Fassbinder had ventured into filmmaking as early as 1965-66 with two shorts, *Der Stadtstreicher* (*The City Tramp*) and *Das kleine Chaos* (*The Little Chaos*), but had been unable to pursue this interest for financial reasons. In April 1969, under his direction the *antiteater* team made a first feature film, with the prophetic title *Liebe ist kälter als der Tod* (*Love Is Colder Than Death*). The film premiered at the Berlin Film Festival in June and received mixed reviews. His second film, *Katzelmacher* (1969), however, won the Film Critics Prize and marked the beginning of one of the most prolific careers in film history. By the time of his death in 1982, Rainer Werner Fassbinder had directed more than twenty full-length feature films (made for movie-theater release) and eleven full-length television productions. For virtually all of these, he wrote the script, and in some played a role. In his last years, he took over the camera work as well.

From his earliest expressionistic self-projections to his later more mimetic works, his films are intensely personal statements. The desperate loneliness of the prototypical Fassbinder hero (quintessentially captured in the title of the 1976 television film *Ich will doch nur, daß ihr mich liebt* (*I Only Want You to Love Me*)) clearly reflects his own lonely childhood. While it is difficult to make any definitive statements concerning the development of such a multifaceted and prolific talent, three phases seem to present themselves. The first of these is delineated by Fassbinder himself, when he concedes that *Warnung vor einer heiligen Nutte* (*Beware of a Holy Whore*, 1970) marks a turning point in his filmmaking, a departure from the onanistic use of autobiographical material.[5] The films that follow *Whore* have a greater social relevance and broader audience appeal: homosexuality (*Petra von Kant*; *Fox and His Friends*), the problem of the immigrant worker, the *Gastarbeiter*, in Germany (*Ali: Fear Eats the Soul*), the bankruptcy of the Left (*Mother Küsters Goes to Heaven* and, to a lesser degree, *Satan's Brew*), and feminist issues (*Martha*; *Effi Briest*) are but some of the themes treated in this period. *Die Ehe der Maria Braun* (*The Marriage of Maria Braun*, 1978) marks a final point of delineation in Fassbinder's development. Both thematically and technically this film breaks new ground: with *Maria Braun* Fassbinder realized his dream of creating the German Hollywood film.

Fassbinder's early films fall into two main categories: the largely derivative Hollywood-style gangster movies (*Love Is Colder Than Death*; *Gods of the Plague*; *The American Soldier*) and the more overt critiques of petty-bourgeois German society (*Katzelmacher*; *Why Does Herr R. Run Amok?*).[6] Common to all, however, are the outsider "hero," the theme of alienation, and (with the exception of *Herr R.*) stylized, static camera work and stylized acting.

In Fassbinder's first film, *Love Is Colder Than Death*, the gangster setting serves largely as a backdrop against which the greater issues of isolation and alienation unfold. A small-time pimp, Franz (Fassbinder), is approached by the syndicate, but refuses to work for them. In retaliation the syndicate sends Bruno (Ulli Lommel), who is to implicate Franz in a crime, thereby making him susceptible to the mob. Franz, however, takes such an intense liking to Bruno that he sets him up with his girl friend Joanna (Hanna Schygulla). Bruno and Franz plan a bank robbery, and Joanna betrays them by going to the police. Bruno's plan to have Joanna killed in the robbery backfires and instead he is killed by the police. Franz and Joanna flee.

Into this darkly pessimistic film, Fassbinder injects moments of comic relief. One of these shows the trio cunningly deceiving a salesperson in order to steal three pairs of sunglasses. In another sequence Bruno and Joanna steal food from a supermarket, their furtive movements, forward lunges, and retreats captured by the tracking camera. Similarly, the death of a motorcyle policeman takes an unexpected turn, when clutching his stomach and doubling over in established Hollywood gangster-movie fashion, he suddenly exclaims in English, "Oh, boy." Fassbinder's sense of irony comes to the fore in this sequence, in which he cites the genre he is emulating only to estrange the viewers by frustrating their expectations. This manipulation of viewer expectations plays an increasingly greater role in his later gangster movies.

Fundamental to an understanding not only of this film but of Fassbinder's entire oeuvre is the conceptualization of the characters as victims of an impersonal, alienated society, who blindly, often violently, lash out, defending themselves as best they can against forces beyond their control. The victims become the oppressors. Fassbinder's characters all seek human contact and warmth but are unable to break out of their innate loneliness and isolation to achieve a real communion with others. Prototypically modern creatures, they lack a means of self-expression. Without a language of their own, they assume the jargon of a preestablished idiom—here that of the gangster movie.

In its focus on the personal interaction of its three main figures, *Love Is Colder Than Death* heralds a favorite Fassbinder theme: the examination of male-female and male-male relationships. While not yet explicit, Franz's inexplicable sympathy for Bruno clearly has homosexual overtones. Fassbinder himself regarded Joanna as the key figure of the film. Conceived as the bourgeois prostitute, interested primarily in protecting her exclusive relationship with Franz, unable to endure Franz's desired ménage à trois, she embodies typical bourgeois values. Perfectly sanguine about selling herself in the hope of cashing in on bourgeois happiness later, she is able to accept prostitution as a means to an end but is unwilling to relinquish her emotionally possessive stance vis-à-vis Franz. Thus the figure of Joanna serves a dual function: as a vehicle for criticizing bourgeois values and as a means of introducing the theme of emotional manipulation, which plays a crucial role in Fassbinder's later work.

Götter der Pest (Gods of the Plague, 1969), Fassbinder's third film, a loose sequel to *Love Is Colder Than Death*, continues the story of Franz and Joanna. The narrative does not directly pick up the events of the earlier film, but the viewer can readily interpolate. The film, which depicts Franz's (portrayed here by Harry Baer instead of Fassbinder) thwarted attempts to find a place in society, opens with Franz's release from prison and traces the reestablishment of his relationship with his former lover Joanna (Hanna Schygulla), now a nightclub singer. Alienated by the proprietary nature of Joanna's affection, Franz rejects her in favor of the less possessive barmaid Margarethe (Margarethe von Trotta). As in the earlier movie, Franz's interaction with women remains unfulfilling. The one moment of genuine human contact is Franz's reunion with his friend Günther (Günther Kaufmann), nicknamed Gorilla. Franz's happiness at being with his friend remains undiminished, even when Günther confesses that he killed Franz's brother, Marian, because he was a police informer. Franz, Günther, and Margarethe drive to the country to visit the aging gangster Joe. There the three men plan a supermarket robbery. Joanna, feeling her love betrayed, betrays them to the police; Margarethe, in turn, betrays them out of genuine concern for Franz. During the robbery, Franz is brutally killed by a gratuitously violent police inspector, who has been having an affair with Joanna. Günther, though mortally wounded, manages to seek out and kill the porno dealer Carla (Carla Aulaulu), who had tipped off Joanna.

By having Margarethe repeat Joanna's betrayal of Franz in *Love Is Colder Than Death,* Fassbinder lays bare one of his main obsessions—the fear of betrayal through and because of love—and emphatically states his belief in the relentless circularity of human behavior. These first two gangster movies demonstrate why Thomas Elsaesser calls Fassbinder's work "a cinema of vicious circles."

> Repetition, reiteration . . . has a particularly important function in his work, on the thematic as well as on the formal level. The films reproduce human relations "as they are", while constantly retracing the contours of a circularity in the utopian hope of finding a way out at the weakest point. Much of the feel and impact of his films—an almost unbearably self-lacerating pessimism shot through with moments of ecstatic (and in the event gratuitous) optimism—seems to come from the need to discover a linearity or dialectic inside a situation emotionally experienced as inescapable, closed, self-perpetuating.[7]

Except for the friendship between Günther and Franz, there is no real human communication in this film; apart from the brief idyll in the country, there is no freedom. These characters are hopelessly doomed to failure and death. The gloomy, dark sets underscore the pessimistic theme of *Gods of the Plague*

by evoking the claustrophobia felt by the characters. Nevertheless, no identification between audience and characters is possible.

In *Gods of the Plague* Fassbinder consciously evokes the Hollywood gangster milieu in order to arouse audience expectations, which he then disappoints. Visually citing American
gangster movies of the forties, both through the garb and demeanor of the actors and the chiaroscuro lighting, Fassbinder
replaces big-time mafiosi with small-time, petty-bourgeois
crooks. His gangsters drive Volkswagens instead of limousines;
they rob supermarkets instead of banks.

In addition to the manipulation of audience expectations,
stylized acting, mannered dialogue, and static camera movement
keep the audience at a distance. Unable to respond emotionally
to the characters and events on the screen, the viewer tends to
analyze the situation and to call into question the society responsible for it. Thus Fassbinder challenges his audience to reevaluate
its conditioned responses both to life and to the art of cinema.

In *Der amerikanische Soldier (The American Soldier,* 1970) Fassbinder bids a fond farewell to the gangster film. No longer content merely to imitate this genre, Fassbinder now parodies it.
Ricky the Killer (Karl Scheydt), a Munich-born American and a
Vietnam veteran, is hired by three Munich policemen (Jan
George, Hark Bohm, Marius Aicher) to liquidate several people
whom they, because of their positions, cannot dispose of themselves. Ricky looks up his old friend Franz Walsch (Fassbinder)
and then gets down to business, first killing a gypsy (Ulli Lommel) and then the porno dealer and informer Magdalena Fuller
(Katrin Schaake). When Ricky demands a woman, Jan, one of
the policemen, sends his lover Rosa von Praunheim (Elga Sorbas). Rosa, who falls in love with Ricky, decides to run away with
the killer. Ricky visits his mother (Eva Ingeborg Scholz) and his
cloyingly dependent brother (Kurt Raab). When Jan learns that
Rosa plans to leave him for Ricky, he gives the killer his final
assignment: to kill Rosa von Praunheim. Ricky, realizing that the
victim is his lover, unhesitatingly fulfills his end of the bargain.
The police, however, renege on their end and lure Ricky into a
trap at the train station, where a showdown takes place. Ricky
is almost saved by his friend Franz, but both succumb when they
are thrown off guard by the unexpected appearance of Ricky's

mother and brother. The film ends with a slow-motion shot of Ricky's hitherto cold and aloof brother clutching the dead Ricky in a desperate, incestuous embrace. Accompanied by the English theme song, "So Much Tenderness," composed by Fassbinder and sung by Günther Kaufmann, the shot is held to the point of audience discomfort.

The parody principle that informs this film allows Fassbinder to unleash his sense of play to the fullest. The operatically hyperbolic death scene is a takeoff on the archetypical Hollywood gangster movie. From the opening scene, the arrival of the Killer, Fassbinder again toys with the audience's expectations. Both in appearance (white suit, black shirt, white tie, felt hat) and in behavior (he throws a woman from his car; he pushes back his hat with his gun), Ricky evokes the familiar idiom, so that the audience, conditioned by this genre, immediately expects a certain behavior from him. Ricky does at times comply with these expectations, (his macho behavior vis-à-vis a chambermaid, for example) but this seeming fulfillment of viewer expectation develops into its direct opposite. Through his ludicrously exaggerated, stylized embraces, Ricky presents us with a deadpan parody of the gangster movie.

The chambermaid (Margarethe von Trotta) is Fassbinder's main vehicle of alienation in *The American Soldier*. Her behavior is consistently inappropriate. Her exaggeratedly rapturous response to Ricky's embraces undermines the seriousness of the situation and thus serves the parody principle. Later, in flagrant disregard of Ricky and Rosa's lovemaking, the chambermaid sits on Ricky's bed and recounts the story of the charwoman Emmi and her *Gastarbeiter* lover, Ali, the basic plot line of Fassbinder's *Angst essen Seele auf (Ali: Fear Eats the Soul*, 1973). This self-contained Emmi-Ali narrative, related so dispassionately, disrupts the narrative flow of *The American Soldier*. As such, it is a particularly obvious use of Brechtian alienation techniques. The stylized suicide of the chambermaid, who stabs herself upon learning that her lover has left her, serves a similar function. Plunging a knife into her stomach, she doubles over and falls onto the banister. Her operatic death stands in sharp contrast to the behavior of Ricky and Rosa, who, having been privy to this entire melodrama, scurry by, feigning obliviousness.

Apart from the content similarities, Fassbinder's gangster

movies attain a coherence through the black-and-white format (to which Fassbinder returned in the 1970 *Gods of the Plague*, after having made several color films) and through the figure of Franz Walsch (Fassbinder's pseudonym as cutter), who appears in all three films. Fassbinder's preference for the name Franz is in no way fortuitous: it clearly reflects an affinity with Alfred Döblin's hero Franz Biberkopf in the novel *Berlin-Alexanderplatz,* which he was to make into a TV serial. In addition to the hotel sequence in *Gods of the Plague,* this connection is made explicit in *Fox and His Friends* (1974), a film in which the hero (Fassbinder) is called Franz Biberkopf. Fassbinder became familiar with Döblin's novel at the age of fourteen, at which point he claims to have "adopted" Franz. Similarly, the porno dealer Magdalena Fuller, whom Ricky kills, is a figure directly out of *Gods of the Plague,* where she is called Carly. Thus *The American Soldier* is not merely a parody of the gangster movie; it is a self-parody of Fassbinder's own mythology as well. Through parody he transcended the derivative genre that had marked the beginning of his career but had ultimately served primarily as a vehicle for presenting his own world view.

Implicit in the gangster movies, the outsider theme becomes the focus of Fassbinder's second, explicitly social-critical film, *Katzelmacher,* which deals with the plight of the *Gastarbeiter* in Germany. The title is a Bavarian colloquialism referring to the presumed uncomplicated sexuality of southern Europeans. Fassbinder's original Action-theater script dealt exclusively with the Greek *Gastarbeiter* Jorgos. The film version sets off his experiences against the relationship of four German couples: Marie (Hanna Schygulla) belongs to Erich (Hans Hirschmüller); Paul (Rudolf Waldemar Brem) sleeps with Helga (Lilith Ungerer); Peter (Peter Moland) is kept by the landlady Elisabeth (Irm Hermann); Franz (Harry Baer) pays to sleep with Rosa (Elga Sorbas).

Katzelmacher is a case study of intolerance and exploitation. The first part introduces the German players and documents the narrow-minded attitudes and the tenuous interaction of these people, trapped in their provincialism; the second part depicts the consequences of such a mentality by showing their victimization of the immigrant worker Jorgos (Fassbinder). From everyone but Marie (who leaves Erich for Jorgos), the

Greek encounters suspicion, intolerance, and antipathy—emotions that ultimately find expression in the totally unprovoked beating of Jorgos. Only Jorgos's landlady, Elizabeth, out of base materialistic motives (she is shamelessly exploiting the *Gastarbeiter)* is willing to endure his presence; the rest are anxious to rid their "community" of this foreign body.

While many of Fassbinder's films employ alienation devices, *Katzelmacher* is perhaps the most extreme in sustaining its level of estrangement. As in a Brechtian *Lehrstück* (didactic play), its characters are one-dimensional figures whose function is to demonstrate certain attitudes and behavior. Although the film is relentless in portraying the *Gastarbeiter* situation, time and again pointing out the prejudiced attitudes of the petty bourgeoisie, it seeks to delve further by pointing out the oppression of the oppressors themselves. It does this primarily through the use of parallelism and repetition. Most of the film is shot against the wall of the *Hinterhof* (back courtyard) of the houses in which these people live, with the characters perched in various positions on railings. The inescapability of their situation is underscored by the choreography of these shots with their placement and displacement of characters. The alternation of interior shots (individual apartments and the pub) with the outdoor *Hinterhof* shots only heightens the monotony by revealing the inherent interchangeability of these peoples' lives. The background of the *Hinterhof* shots, a stark white wall, has the effect of bleaching out the figures. Coupled with the static long takes, this bleaching effect reproduces the boredom, the one-dimensionality of their lives. The claustrophobic circularity of the *Hinterhof* shots is underscored by having alternate pairs (Maria and Helga, Helga and Rosa, Elisabeth and Peter) walk in front of the houses, arm in arm, fantasizing about their "futures." Thier wishful projections (appropriately underlined by the somewhat schmaltzy melody from Schubert's popular *Sehnsuchtswalzer*) stand in sharp contrast to their bleak, mundane existences.

Fassbinder effectively employs the dialogue technique of *Aneinandervorbeireden* (talking past each other) in *Katzelmacher* to demonstrate the alienation of his characters. They rarely face each other when they speak, they usually face the camera instead. Indeed, they rarely address each other, often speaking in the third person. The stylization in *Katzelmacher* is far more disconcerting than in the gangster movies, since the milieu is obviously more immediate to the general public. Perhaps this is why Fassbinder goes to such lengths to prevent viewer-character identification. Confronting his audience with their own prejudices, he seeks to raise their consciousness. The success of his didactic intentions remains questionable. A cold, overly cerebral film, *Katzelmacher* lacks a broad-based appeal. It remains, however, an interesting experiment that reiterates two of Fassbinder's chief concerns: petty-bourgeois narrow-mindedness and exploitation.

Fassbinder's last 1969 film, *Warum lüft Herr R. amok? (Why Does Herr R. Run Amok?)*, is a departure in three respects: it was codirected with Michael Fengler, it is in color, and it is totally devoid of stylization. Indeed, within the context of the NGC, this film is the most naturalistic. By having the actors improvise their dialogue (Fassbinder and Fengler provided merely the outlines of scenes) Fassbinder linguistically fulfills the naturalistic slice-of-life dictum. With disturbing verisimilitude, the film confronts the viewer with the day-to-day life of the technical draftsman, Herr R. By petty-bourgeois standards Herr R. appears a success: he has an attractive wife, a beloved son, a comfortable apartment, a good job, the respect of his boss, the affection of his colleagues, and prospects for promotion. Yet one evening, seemingly unprovoked, Herr R. murders a neighbor, his wife, and his son. The next morning, before the police can question him, he hangs himself in the toilet of his place of work. The answer to the question posed by the title is made explicit through every scene, through endless trivial verbiage, through each meaningless encounter between Herr R. and his fellow human beings to which the viewer is privy. Cracks in the facade of the successful family and career man soon become apparent: tensions surface between Herr R. and his wife and between his wife and his parents; his son is having psychological difficulties in school; Herr R. is overworked, his boss is critical of his work, and it appears he will not be promoted at all. Yet these remain external exigencies and do not explain the murders.

To the viewer privy to Herr R.'s increasing isolation and alienation, confronted with the stultifying boredom of his life, inundated with the endless trivial chatter of his wife and neighbor, Herr R.'s actions are comprehensible. Perhaps the single most disturbing aspect of the film is the fact that in a sense Herr R.

does *not* run amok. There are no passionate outbursts, no signs of frenzy, no epiphanies. Herr R., after listening for some time to the women's babble, quietly picks up a candlestick, lights the candles, and then smashes in his neighbor's, his wife's, and his son's heads. The murders bring no release for Herr R.; their perpetration is the final act of a repressed, oppressed individual, whose only escape is death.

That the protagonist of *Herr R.* is not a shady, semiunderworld character but a commonplace office worker makes his tragedy more immediate to a wide audience, although total identification is still difficult. The overly blue tones of Fassbinder's first color film coupled with conspicuously amateurish camera shots and awkward angles allow the filmmaker to point self-consciously to his medium and make viewers aware that they are watching a film.

Although Fassbinder later disassociated himself from the film, claiming it was actually Fengler's product, *Herr R.* is an important stage in his development because it introduces an element of realism that is to play an important role in his future work. Herr R. is the first of the downtrodden Fassbinder heroes who were to include Hans Epp (*Merchant of Four Seasons*), Franz (*Jail Bait*), Frlank Biberkopf (*Fox and His Friends*), Xaver Bolwieser (*Bolwieser*), and Peter (*I Only Want You to Love Me*), people vainly searching for love; rejected by an indifferent society, they are living proofs that love (or its unstilled need) is indeed colder than death.

The following year, 1970, saw the completion of seven full-length films, including four television productions: *Rio das Mortes, The Coffee House* (based on Goldoni's play), *The Niklashausen Journey,* and *Pioneers in Ingolstadt,* and three commercial film releases: *Whity, The American Soldier,* and *Beware of a Holy Whore.* Like the other films made in what John Sandford calls Fassbinder's "year of experiment,"[8] *Whity* reflects Fassbinder's search for new means of expression. As with other films made that year, such as the comedy *Rio das Mortes* (which deals with the wish fulfillment of two friends who go off to Peru in search of gold) and *The Niklashausen Journey* (a film based on the life of the fifteenth-century revolutionary shepherd Hans Böhm), *Whity* had little long-range formal significance for Fassbinder's development.

Unlike Fassbinder's other early films, *Whity* is a self-contained melodrama devoid of criticism of postwar German society. Set in the West of the United States (the film was shot on the coast of Spain), *Whity* depicts the ultimate decline of the decadent Nicholson family. Ranchowner Ben Nicholson (Ron Randell); his nymphomaniac wife, Katherine (Katrin Schaake); Ben's children by a former marriage, the half-witted Davy (Harry Baer) and the homosexual Frank (Ulli Lommel); and their servant Whity (Günther Kaufmann), Ben's illegitimate son, live together in the family mansion. Whity, who functions as Ben's butler, Katherine's sexual plaything, and Davy's and Frank's attendant, is wrenched out of his submissive stance by the prostitute Hanna (Hanna Schygulla). By making Whity aware of his oppressed situation, Hanna makes him responsive to the demands of members of the Nicholson family to kill other family members. He ultimately shoots the entire family and then flees with Hanna into the desert, where he and Hanna die of thirst. Shortly before their demise, Hanna and Whity carry out a defiant dance of death. *Whity,* the least successful of Fassbinder's films, was unenthusiastically received at its premiere at the Berlin Film Festival in 1971 and was neither distributed commercially nor shown on television. Its significance lies not in its formal or thematic innovations, but in the changes it precipitated in Fassbinder's working relationship with his troupe. The shooting was marred by personal tensions and upheavals and marked the dissolution of the *antiteater* group.

A key film in the development of Fassbinder's oeuvre, *Warnung vor einer heiligen Nutte* (*Beware of a Holy Whore,* 1970), is an actively self-conscious film about filmmaking. The warning (to himself) comes in the form of the film's motto: "Pride comes before a fall." Generally regarded as a breakthrough, marking the end of the obsessively personal style characteristic of Fassbinder's early films and paving the way for a more objective treatment of subject matter, the film records Fassbinder's coming-to-terms with his métier and his assessment of his role within the film crew.

The film is framed by a shot of a young man with blond hair (filmmaker Werner Schroeter) in a field, who recounts a story by Goofy. It then cuts to the lobby of a hotel on the Spanish coast, where members of a film crew await the arrival of their director, Jeff (Lou Castel), and the star, Eddie Constantine (played by himself). The group dynamics of this incestuous troupe constitute the focal point of much of the film. It records the rivalries and jealousies, the various sexual encounters of this dissolute, narcissistic bunch, in an atmosphere vacillating between hysteria and apathy. Into this chaos walks Jeff. Unable to distance himself from the mire of personal relationships, he is immediately involved in a series of sexual encounters. By asserting himself professionally, however, he is able to give the disjointed group a sense of purpose, and he translates his vision of the film about "violence sanctioned by the state" into a workable model.

Beware deals with the filming of *Whity,* and it is hence an intensely personal film; however, it is not merely a projection of Fassbinder's own fears and obsessions; it is more mimetic. The actual figures on which the characters are based are readily identifiable to Fassbinder cognoscenti. Jeff, who wears Fassbinder's emblematic black leather jacket, clearly stands for the director himself. By Fassbinder's own admission, the film documents the breakup of the *antiteater* film collective. Fassbinder's long-cherished vision of filmmaking as a fully democratic collective venture had been revealed as untenable, and the film offers Fassbinder's new understanding of his own function — one in which the director assumes leadership and in which the relationship between him and his film crew is seen as symbiotic. On one hand, the director exploits each member of his crew, living off their various talents in order to realize his idea of the film; for the crew, on the other hand, the director's energy furnishes the galvanizing force and gives the aimless group a sense of purpose. Both director and crew ultimately subjugate themselves, prostitute themselves to the holy whore: the film itself.

While *Beware* successfully captures the whorish aspect of filmmaking (most immediately through the various erotic relationships), the holy component of Fassbinder's definition is less obvious. The Thomas Mann quotation — "I tell you, that I am often tired unto death of presenting the human without partaking of it" — with which Fassbinder concludes the film may offer some insight. Mann's Tonio Kröger, in despair because art is only a substitute for life, underscores the whorish aspect of art. However, he also affirms its sanctity and thereby comes to a new understanding of his own art — which is less esoteric and cerebral and more human. Is this Fassbinder's self-prophecy as well?

Der Händler der vier Jahreszeiten (*The Merchant of Four Seasons*, 1971), Fassbinder's first German popular success, seems to sub- stantiate this reading of the Mann quote. It is regarded by the filmmaker as a turning point in his career, signaling a less onanistic, more objective mode of filmmaking. Its protagonist, Hans Epp (Hans Hirschmüller), is a typical Fassbinder hero: a man who meets betrayal and defeat at every turn. Unable to find happiness, Hans moves from a loveless parental home to a love- less marriage and finally finds release by committing suicide. It is the familiar pessimistic Fassbinder scenario, a variation on the theme of *Gods of the Plague,* and *Herr R.* The novelty of the film lies in the compassionate characterization of its figures. A new humaneness emerges, and with it a new interest in making his characters more emotionally accessible to his audience. No longer viewed merely from the outside, these characters have a new depth. For the first time psychology plays a role in charac- terization; for the first time there is character development. In *Merchant* we are for the first time furnished with information necessary to understand the protagonist's situation. The ubiqui- tous Fassbinder motifs of oppression, repression, and rejection are no longer portrayed for their own sake but are shown to be the causes of Hans's failure.

As a youth, Hans pleads with his mother to be allowed to learn a trade, but she insists that he conform to her bourgeois expecta- tions and complete the traditional academic education. When he returns home from the Foreign Legion (which he had joined in order to escape his mother's tyranny), she greets him with one of the most chilling rejections ever recorded on celluloid: "The best ones don't come back, someone like you has to return." His relatively successful career as a police officer is short-circuited when a prostitute he arrests seduces him in the police station. Dismissed, he becomes a street vendor,[9] and is rejected by the woman he loves (Ingrid Caven) because his new profession ren- ders him socially inferior in the eyes of her family.

A marriage of convenience with Irmgard (Irm Hermann), whose chief ambition is to better their financial position, leads to drunkenness and wife beating. Irmgard leaves him, but returns when he suffers a heart attack. Forced to hire an assistant be- cause of his failing health, Hans employs Anzell (Karl Scheydt), a man with whom his wife had had a one-night stand during her husband's illness. Irritated by Anzell's presence, Irmgard tricks him into dishonesty, and Hans dismisses him but realizes that he has been manipulated. Hans runs into his old friend Harry (Klaus Löwitsch), and takes him into his business, only to have Harry slowly usurp his position, winning the respect of his wife and the affection of his small daughter. Recognizing that he is superfluous, Hans becomes increasingly withdrawn and mute. (Paradoxically, his inarticulateness is eloquent: silence is the linguistic correlative of his loneliness and alienation.) He visits his sister (Hanna Schygulla), the one person with whom he has any real rapport, but his usually astute and sympathetic sibling fails to recognize his despair. Leaving her, he goes to his favorite pub and, in the presence of pub regulars, his wife, and Harry, deliberately drinks himself to death. After his funeral, Irmgard proposes that Harry move in and take over the business. He agrees, thereby formalizing the relationship that had existed before Hans's death.

The fact that Fassbinder makes Hans something of a modern Everyman—his is "a story that almost everyone I know has lived himself. A man wishes that he had made something of his life that he never did. His education, his environment, his circumstances don't admit the fulfillment of his dream"[10]—indicates an important shift in the filmmaker's perspective. No longer preeminently the projection and working through of his own anxieties, the film, with its mimetic orientation, has a broader audience appeal. *Merchant,* Fassbinder's first film after his encounter with the work of Douglas Sirk, is replete with stock melodramatic figures: the prodigal son (Hans), the domineering yet well-meaning mother, the hypocritical brother-in-law, the true love, the long-lost friend, etc. The film makes uses of melodramatic plot development, especially the role of coincidence: the appearance of Irmgard's lover as Hans's business partner, the reappearance of the bosom friend Harry precisely at the moment when Hans needs a savior. Other melodramatic motifs include violent domestic arguments followed by confessions and reconciliations, as well as a romanticized flashback to Hans's Foreign Legion days.

Yet the film never pushes the melodramatic to the point of parody, and it succeeds not despite but in good part because of its melodrama. The melodramatic genre allows Fassbinder to introduce strong emotions into his film, which has an emotional resonance missing in his earlier work. Yet despite Fassbinder's obvious affection for Hans, the viewer never totally identifies with him. Sympathy rather than empathy is the emotional response elicited from the audience.

This is due in part to Fassbinder's deviations from his melodramatic model, primarily in his character depiction. Unlike the typical melodrama, the film avoids simplistic black/white characterizations. Even Hans is not a totally positive figure, as evidenced by the long-drawn-out, albeit stylized, beating of his wife. Even the most unsympathetic characters, Hans's wife and his mother, are presented impartially and nonjudgmentally; Hans's tyrannical mother is also seen as the widowed head of the household, who dearly wants her only son to succeed; Hans's unloving wife is in turn unloved. And Fassbinder, who has embedded the archetypal story of Hans Epp in the specific sociohistorical context of Germany in the fifties, indicates that their materialism merely reflects the postwar *Wirtschaftswunder* (economic miracle) mentality of the society as a whole. Yet Fassbinder's stance must not be confused with a *tout comprendre c'est tout pardonner* attitude. Far from pardoning, Fassbinder challenges the basic precepts of Hans Epp's society. The Brechtian legacy is alive and well in this film, but it is Brecht à la Fassbinder. Less obviously than his earlier films, *Merchant* employs a variety of cinematic distancing techniques that undermine the viewer's identification with people and events on the screen. The characteristic overextended shot is moderated here, but Fassbinder still allows the camera to linger longer than expected, thereby undercutting a realistic mise-en-scène. In another carryover from his early period, he presents us with a preponderance of symmetrical frontal shots, stylized compositions which, together with an abrupt, at times bumpy editing technique, emphasize the filmic medium and also militate against viewer identification. The most overt example of *Verfremdungseffekt* is Hans's beating of his wife. Here the stylized acting is accentuated by the seemingly endless duration of the beating, shifting the emphasis away from an identification with the victim to a condemnation of wife-beating per se. Like Brecht, Fassbinder wishes to appeal to his audience's cognitive rather than its emotional faculties. Hence, neither forgiveness (which implies an emotional identification rejected by Fassbinder) nor rejection is the appropriate response. What Fassbinder strives for is the recognition by the audience of the relevance of these characters' situations for their own lives.

While *Merchant* clearly represents a new phase in Fassbinder's development, the film still betrays several of his ingrained prejudices: his belief in male friendship and his misogynic fear of betrayal. (Hans's downfall, it appears, is directly attributable to five women: his mother, the prostitute, his great love, his wife, and his sister.) However, even these themes receive a more balanced, a more subtle treatment: just before his death, Hans calls Harry's friendship into question; the motivation of the women is more differentiated—they emerge not merely as victimizers, but victims of their petty-bourgeois conditioning. And ultimately it is Hans himself who has internalized the values of this society.

In many ways *Merchant* is a synthesis of Fassbinder's previous oeuvre, combining the alienation-betrayal themes of the pessimistic gangster movies with the *Katzelmacher/Herr R.* indictment of the petty-bourgeois mentality. Yet *Merchant* is to *Katzelmacher* what Brecht's mature plays are to his *Lehrstücke*. Its goal is not only to instruct, but to entertain as well. The characters are at once concrete and abstract, both self-contained and transcendent. It has, in short, achieved a synthesis of *prodesse et delectare*.

Die bitteren Tränen der Petra von Kant (The Bitter Tears of Petra von Kant, 1972), based on Fassbinder's play of the same name, has been called his version of *Death in Venice*. The similarities in plot line are indeed striking: like Mann's Gustav von Aschenbach, the fashion designer Petra von Kant (Margit Carstensen) is at the height of her professional success, when she succumbs to a lesbian passion that leads to her decline.

The beautiful, self-possessed upper-middle-class Petra, once widowed, once divorced, now lives alone with her assistant Marlene (Irm Hermann), whose love she abuses, and whom she utterly subjects to her will. Having, it seems, emotionally coped with the failure of her marriage, she can self-confidently expound to her friend, the Baroness Sidonie von Grasenabb,[11] about nonpossessive love, an ideal she had sought without success in her relationship with her ex-husband. Through Sidonie, Petra meets Karin Thimm (Hanna Schygulla), an indolent young working-class woman, with whom she falls desperately in love. The façade of the self-sufficient, emancipated career woman crumbles as Petra becomes vulnerable to Karin. Karin, whose husband has gone off to Australia, moves in with Petra. Having been exploited by her male lover, Karin now exploits her female lover, allowing Petra to advance her career as a model.

When Karin's husband returns, she unhesitatingly rejoins him. The abandoned Petra at first seems inconsolable, but later maintains that she had never actually loved Karin, had merely wanted to possess her. She offers Marlene, who until then had been a mere object for her, a relationship based on equality and freedom. But Marlene, who does not utter a single word throughout, makes what is the film's most eloquent statement: she packs her bag and leaves in stony silence.

Unlike Mann's novella, the film does not end with the death of the main character. The conclusion is open-ended. It is unclear whether Petra's statement regarding the nature of her relationship with Karin is correct, or whether it is merely a rationalization; we do not know whether Petra will survive the agony of her dependence on Karin, or whether she will be able to reassess her life and attain her ideal of a nonpossessive love. As we see her writhing on the floor in agony, however, one thing becomes indisputably clear: nothing will ever be the same again; Petra's life has been fundamentally changed by her affair with Karin. Marlene's motives remain enigmatic. We do not know whether she is incapable of dealing with a peer relationship based on freedom — whether her departure arises from a masochistic need to be subjugated, or whether, recognizing that Petra is using the identical language and tactics in courting her that she had used in wooing Karin, Marlene's exit is to be seen as a rebellious act of self-esteem and of coming of age.[12] *Petra von Kant* is only superficially about lesbianism. The lesbian relationship serves as a vehicle for probing fundamental questions of dependency and exploitation. The film is as much about Marlene as it is about Petra and Karin. It is Marlene, moreover, who shares many of the attributes of the prototypical (Hans Epp) Fassbinder hero, and who thus helps establish a continuity between *Petra von Kant* and Fassbinder's earlier work.

In *Petra von Kant* Fassbinder has created a totally feminine world. Yet, although no men appear in the film itself, the male sphere of influence is acutely present: Petra's business colleagues are male; Karin's husband exists in the background; and while Petra and Karin both lament exploitation by men, they duplicate this behavior in their dealings with others. Fassbinder visually articulates this implicit male omnipresence by having the interaction between the women occur against the background of an oversize Correggio mural of two male nudes. The action, limited to one room of Petra's apartment, the focal point of which is the bed, recalls a Strindbergian-Expressionist reductionism appropriate to the film's theme. The decor of *Petra von Kant* bears testimony to the fact that Fassbinder has learned to correlate a character and the character's space. The opulent artificiality of Petra's room, with its life-size mannequin and its stylish costumes, reflects her decadent aestheticism. Life for Petra is theater; the artificiality of her life is underscored by a theatrical rather than a cinematic mise-en-scène. Of all of Fassbinder's oeuvre, *Petra von Kant* is the most theatrical. The original five-act division is retained in the film, each act marked by a dissolve into darkness followed by the reappearance of Petra in a different wig, in a different costume. The stylized acting and the exaggeratedly theatrical decor underscore the appearance/reality theme as demonstrated by the revelation of Petra's independence and emancipation as a life lie.

Wildwechsel (*Jail Bait*), based on the play by the same name by the contemporary Austrian playwright Franz Xaver Kroetz, represents Fassbinder's third venture at literary adaptation. The two previous attempts—*The Coffee House,* based on the play by the eighteenth-century Italian writer Carlo Goldoni, and *Pioneers in Ingolstadt,* based on the play by the early twentieth-century Bavarian writer Marie Luise Fleisser, had been (respectively) moderately successful and unsuccessful television productions of 1970.

Jail Bait, Fassbinder's only other commercial theater film of 1972, is thematically and formally the antipode of *Petra von Kant*. In contrast to the upper-middle-class milieu of *Petra von Kant, Jail Bait* depicts lower-middle and working-class milieus.[13] Unlike the highly mannered *Petra von Kant, Jail Bait* employs a realistic mise-en-scène. Together these two films of 1972 paradigmatically embody the stylized and realistic poles of Fassbinder's oeuvre.

Jail Bait deals with the affair of the sexually precocious fourteen-year-old Hanni (Eva Mattes) and the nineteen-year-old worker Franz (Harry Baer). When an envious friend reports them, Franz is sent to prison for seducing a minor. They resume their relationship clandestinely after he is paroled for good behavior. Hanni becomes pregnant and convinces Franz to kill her father (Jörg von Liebenfels), since he is the main obstacle to their love. When the body is found, Franz is arrested for murder. Hanni, who runs into Franz just as he is about to be taken into the courtroom to stand trial, tells him that their baby was born stillborn and deformed. She severs their relationship and denies their love, claiming their relationship had been purely physical.

The chief difference between Kroetz's play and Fassbinder's film lies in their attitudes toward Hanni. While both Hanni and Franz are victims of petty-bourgeois repression, Kroetz's sympathies are with Hanni, whereas Fassbinder's are clearly with Franz. In Fassbinder's hands, Franz becomes another downtrodden hero, vainly in search of love. His commitment to Hanni is greater than hers to him. In the poignant concluding scene, although Franz verbally agrees with Hanni's denial of their love, his gestures (he places his hand on her shoulder, bidding her a final gentle goodbye) and facial expression clearly belie his words. Thus, thematically, *Jail Bait* is a throwback to Fassbinder's earlier films such as *Love Is Colder Than Death* and *Gods of the Plague* in that, once again, a man is betrayed through the love of a woman.

While Kroetz stresses the generational differences, Hanni for Fassbinder is the product of her narrow-minded upbringing. Through numerous close-ups of the many religious pictures and crucifixes in the house, Fassbinder stresses the repressive power of Catholicism in this lower-middle-class Bavarian household. Hanni's internalization of her parents' values becomes clear when she taunts Franz with castration, precisely the punishment her father deems fitting for a "sexual offender." It is Hanni who plans her father's death and who goads Franz into committing the murder. Her triumphant jubilation after the murder parallels her father's "I'd rather gas a million Jews than have him fool around with our child" in its solipsistic disregard for moral considerations.

Kroetz's critical attitude toward the older generation does find resonance in Fassbinder's film. The idyllic opening shot, which rivals the later works of Herzog in the lushness of its colors, is followed by a shot recording the mundane morning ritual of the Drexel family. The juxtaposition of the beauty of the natural landscape and the banal ugliness of their domestic life makes the latter appear all the more repugnant. Herr Drexel articulates sentiments which, of all Fassbinder's expressions, are the most incriminating of bourgeois capitalist society — "no money, no love." Through him, the relationship between capitalist values and fascist ideology is made manifest. Indeed, *Jail Bait* is the first of Fassbinder's films to explicitly evoke the Nazi past. Fassbinder's matter-of-fact, nonaccusatory stance in presenting Herr Drexel's attempt to dismiss the past later became somewhat problematical for the filmmaker.

The film, first shown on television, was severely criticized: the public at large was offended by a close-up of a penis (the shot was subsequently cut); the critics took issue with what they termed Fassbinder's "denunciatory" attitude toward the characters. The most severe criticism, however, came from Kroetz himself, who labeled the film "pornographic" and Fassbinder's attitude toward the characters "obscene." Kroetz sued Fassbinder and won, and Fassbinder was required to cut two scenes he had appended to the original text: a scene in which the father sexually attacks his daughter, and a scene in which Hanni attempts to pick up a *Gastarbeiter* during Franz's stay in prison.

The critics' reception of the film is noteworthy in that Fassbinder goes to what he himself later considered morally questionable extremes to present the characters (particularly the father) in a nonaccusatory fashion. Kroetz's objections seem more justified, since the film, even in its expurgated version, suggests an incestuous attraction between father and daughter— particularly the scene in which Hanni romps around on his lap. Despite its specific sociological context, *Jail Bait,* in its presentation of the repression of youth through the older generation, ultimately deals with archetypal questions.

In his next film, *Angst essen Seele auf (Ali: Fear Eats the Soul,* 1973), Fassbinder again treats a contemporary social issue. *Ali* recounts the improbable May-December romance between a sixty-year-old German charwoman, Emmi Kurowski (Brigitte Mira), and a Moroccan *Gastarbeiter*, El Hedi Ben Salem M'Barek Mohammed Mustaffa (El Hedi Ben Salem), known simply as Ali (because no one can properly pronounce his name), a man some twenty years her junior. Emmi and Ali meet by happenstance when, seeking refuge from the rain, she enters the Asphalt Bar, a pub frequented by immigrant workers. On a dare, he asks the old woman to dance; they chat, he takes her home, she invites him in for a cup of coffee, he makes love to her, stays the night, and moves in with her, and they ultimately marry. Initially their relationship is kept intact by the hostility of their immediate society. Unable to endure the malevolence, Emmi and Ali flee; they go away on vacation. On their return, everything seems magically different: Emmi's children, who had disowned her, are conciliatory—it seems they need a free babysitter; the grocer, who had refused to serve Ali, falsely claiming that the Moroccan's German was incomprehensible, now panders for Emmi's patronage (a new supermarket is giving him competition); the neighbors, who had denounced Emmi to the landlord, now cater to her (they want her to relinquish some of her storage space for their use).

In each case, the motivation for this sudden transformation is materalistic and exploitative. Unhappily, once the external obstacles have been obviated and the couple has attained a semblance of social acceptance, internal problems in the relationship surface. Emmi, who had been the victim, now assumes the role of oppressor. Taking on a proprietary attitude, she commandeers Ali, showing off his muscles to her colleagues, totally objectifying him. Ali quietly resumes his relationship with the pub owner, Barbara (Barbara Valentin). Emmi comes to the pub looking for Ali and the two reconcile by dancing to the same tune as at their first meeting. Vowing to stay with Emmi always, Ali suddenly collapses. The diagnosis, given by the doctor in the hospital to which Ali is taken: perforated ulcer, a common ailment among *Gastarbeiter*, caused by the particular stress to which they are subjected. Prognosis: even should Ali recuperate this time, he will be back in the hospital within six months. Emmi vows that she will prevent a recurrence of Ali's ailment, but the doctor's *"Auf Wiedersehen,"* the final words of the film, assume an ominously prophetic tone.

Ali is the story told by the chambermaid in *The American Soldier,* with the significant difference that the tragic ending of the original version, in which Ali kills Emmi, has been mitigated into

Brigitte Mira and El Hedi Ben Salem in *Ali: Fear Eats the Soul* (COURTESY OF FILMVERLAG DER AUTOREN)

an ambiguous happy ending. What in *The American Soldier* had merely been another of Fassbinder's darkly pessimistic stories takes on distinctly sociocritical ramifications in the later film. Although Fassbinder had not yet come into contact with the work of Douglas Sirk when he conceived the Emmi-Ali story, he had seen virtually all Sirk's films by the time he made *Ali*. Sirk's version of the May-December relationship between a rich widow and her socially inferior gardener in *All That Heaven Allows* (1955) had a great impact on Fassbinder. Melodramatic Sirkian motifs, such as the hero's sudden precarious state of health, which puts everything into perspective and prompts vows of fidelity from the heroine, are incorporated into Fassbinder's *Ali*.

It is, however, precisely at its supremely melodramatic moment, Ali's collapse, that the film transcends melodrama. Ali's illness does not serve as a deus ex machina to unite the couple. Instead, as the doctor's diagnosis and prognosis indicate, Emmi and Ali's happy end is, at best, qualified. The audience is left not with the euphoria of the love-conquers-all Hollywood weepie, but rather with the tragic predicament of the *Gastarbeiter* in West Germany. It is the same situation as in *Katzelmacher*; the difference in the means of presentation is testimony to Fassbinder's artistic growth. Whereas *Katzelmacher* presented a model of petty-bourgeois bigotry, *Ali* imbeds its political message in a melodramatic love story, which presents its characters in a warm, humane, and loving manner.

Fassbinder's next film deals with a more conventional May-December relationship. *Fontane Effi Briest* (*Effi Briest*, 1974) is Fassbinder's masterful interpretation of Theodor Fontane's novel of adultery. Patently the most self-consciously literary of the young German films, its dialogue adheres almost verbatim to Fontane's novel. In addition, Fassbinder retains the third-person narrator off-camera and inserts frames of written tableaus taken directly from the text as intertitles.

Effi Briest is the tragic story of a young woman (Hanna Schygulla), who at the age of seventeen is married off to a stern man of principles, Baron Geert von Innstetten (Wolfgang Schenck), her mother's former suitor, a man twenty years her senior. Neglected and lonely in the provincial town of Kessin, Effi falls into an affair with the garrison commander, Major Crampas (Ulli Lommel). The relationship ends (to Effi's relief) when the Innstettens move to Berlin. There they lead a more interesting and harmonious life, but their happiness is disrupted when Innstetten happens on Crampas's letters to his wife. Despite the fact that the affair is long past (more than six years have elapsed), Innstetten feels compelled to challenge Crampas to a duel. Crampas is killed, and Effi is sent away and denied the right to see her daughter, Annie, whom Innstetten turns against Effi. Effi's parents initially join in the ostracism of their daughter, but they relent when it becomes apparent that she is gravely ill. However, not even the return to her beloved parental home, Hohen-Cremmen, can save Effi, whose will to live has been broken; about a year later, she dies.

Whereas the realist romancier Fontane unfolds the entire panorama of Wilhelmian society, Fassbinder reduces the novel to the microcosm of the Effi– von Innstetten marriage. The thrust of this reduction can be seen in Fassbinder's single deviation from the original—the subtitle he appends to the title: "Or many who have an idea of their possibilities and needs and nevertheless accept the prevailing order in the way they act and thereby strengthen and confirm it absolutely." The subtitle, in its didactic formulation, offers the key to Fassbinder's interpretation of *Effi Briest*: for him the film becomes a study in oppression and repression. It is precisely the juxtaposition of title and subtitle, the tension between source and interpretation that determine the structure of Fassbinder's film. Fassbinder effectively uses narration and stylization to militate against identification with the characters and action on the screen, to jar viewers out of their usual passive stance, to awaken their rational faculties and hence to make them receptive to Fassbinder's engaged interpretation. As with Brecht, the lack of identification is meant to deflect the viewer's focus of attention from the outcome to the process of the action. We are not meant to identify with Effi's fate, but rather to judge it, to see the various junctures at which the seeming inevitability of the events could have been circumvented. This is most obvious in the Wüllersdorf-Innstetten dialogue. After finding the letters, Innstetten sends for his friend Wüllersdorf (Karlheinz Böhm), ostensibly to discuss the options open to him. This discussion, in which Innstetten appears as a man torn by doubt, is the most striking example of the behavior of those alluded to in Fassbinder's subtitle. Innstetten indeed *does* have an idea of his possibilities and needs (he admits that, despite everything, he still loves Effi and that the passage of time *has* made a difference, that he does not personally feel the need to kill his wife's lover). Nevertheless, he accepts the prevailing social tyranny, and by challenging Crampas and sending Effi away, he strengthens and confirms it absolutely. It is Innstetten's special tragedy that he knowingly reaffirms an anachronism and thereby consciously destroys Effi's life and his own. Similarly Effi, who in a moment of lucidity had denounced Innstetten and his misguided concept of honor, before her death forgives him and retracts what she had said. It is her acceptance of Innstetten's oppressive behavior that makes her culpable.

Effi Briest is Fassbinder's masterpiece. It marks the fruition of a long-cherished ambition; Fassbinder had long wanted to film Fontane's novel, but had been prevented from doing so by financial constraints. Clearly the subject matter, with its potential for unveiling manipulative and repressive behavior, appealed to him. He had in fact written and directed a melodramatic version of the same story (*Martha*) for television the previous year. Fassbinder spent a record fifty-eight days filming *Effi Briest* — an undertaking well worth the effort. *Effi Briest* is pure Fassbinder. Without doing violence to the Fontane text, Fassbinder has made explicit what is implicit in the novel. Effi and Innstetten are such perfect products of their society that by focusing in on them Fassbinder presents us with Wilhelmian society *in nuce*.

Faustrecht der Freiheit (*Fox and His Friends*), Fassbinder's other film of 1974, is the mirror image of *Petra von Kant*. It recounts the exploitation and ultimate destruction of the proletarian Franz Biberkopf (Fassbinder) at the hands of his upper-middle-class lover Eugen (Peter Chatel). Franz, an unemployed sideshow actor ("Fox, the Talking Head"), is picked up in a public lavatory by the antique dealer Max (Karlheinz Böhm). Max introduces Franz to refined homosexual circles, where he meets Eugen, the son of a businessman. Eugen quickly abandons his friend Philipp (Harry Baer); he and Franz move into a new apartment. While Eugen contributes his exquisite good taste in decorating matters, Franz (who has just won 500,000 marks in the lottery) contributes the cash. In addition, he saves Eugen's parents' printing business with a 100,000-mark loan. Eugen, embarrassed by Franz's proletarian tastes and manners, tries to refine his lover, to mold him in his own image. The class differences, however, prove to be insurmountable. Eugen leaves Franz and reestablishes his relationship with Philipp. Franz, who has been mercilessly exploited by Eugen (he is cheated out of both his share of the press and the apartment), takes an overdose of Valium. His body is found in an empty subway station by two ten-year-olds, who plunder the corpse. Max and a friend pass by but, fearing involvement, retreat immediately.

Fox, operating with the same constellation of characters as *Petra von Kant*, presents a variation on the theme of the earlier film. Abandoning the stylized acting and artificial decor of the lesbian film, *Fox* is a realistic portrayal of the German gay scene. Fassbinder, by playing the role of Fox himself, publicly admits his own homosexuality. In contrast to his socioeconomic counterpart in *Petra von Kant*, Karin Thimm, Fox is a naive, good-natured fellow. Fassbinder admits that there are many very personal details in *Fox*, but that "I would identify myself much more with the character Eugen than with the character I play, because my relations to people run more that way, but I can't help it, and I try to. That's one of the reasons I made the film—to *change* that kind of relation and become more like Fox." [14] Severely criticized by the gay community for his negative portrayal of homosexuals, Fassbinder maintained that the homosexual theme was secondary. The actual theme of manipulation and exploitation inherently possible within any sexual relationship is merely perpetrated by gays in this instance.

That class, not sex, is primary in *Fox* is best shown in the comedy-of-manners domestic scenes in Eugen's home. His liberal, progressive parents object to their son's lover, not because he is homosexual, but because he lacks the proper social graces: he has bad table manners, he is unable to make the requisite chitchat. It was, however, the final scene that caused the greatest furor in Germany. By having obviously middle-class children pilfer the dead Fox's pockets, Fassbinder violated the child-as-innocent taboo. The closing sequence is, in fact, an emphatic statement about the inevitability of exploitation. Fassbinder was, he maintained, "trying to state in the end that it is a kind of eternal thing that happens. It *is* a circle; it will always happen again. Doing it with children, one sees very clearly that when they grow up they will get into, and they will use, the same mechanism." [15] Thus *Fox* reiterates a theme that goes back to Fassbinder's earliest films: the theme of the eternal recurrence.

If *Petra von Kant* and *Fox* had alienated the gay community, *Mutter Küsters Fahrt zum Himmel* (*Mother Küsters Goes to Heaven*, 1975) incurred the wrath of the German Left. The film is loosely modeled on Piel Jutzi's 1929 prosocialist silent movie *Mutter Krausens Fahrt ins Glück* (*Mother Krausen's Journey to Happiness*), in which the proletarian heroine, old Mother Krausen, unable to repay debts made by her son, fearing debtor's prison, and foreseeing no possible alleviation of her situation, commits suicide by gassing herself in the kitchen. The true measure of her pessimism is borne out by the fact that she attempts to take a young child on her journey to happiness, because she cannot conceive that the child has anything to look forward to in this life. In Jutzi's film the individual tragedy is offset by a collective call to arms. While Mother Krausen succumbs to capitalist exploitation, her daughter, a newly converted socialist, bears promise of a better future. The film ends on an optimistic note, with the masses, marching to the Internationale, leading the way to that more just and equitable future.

In *Mother Küsters* that future hardly seems rosy. The film opens with the news that Hermann Küsters, a worker in a tire factory, has killed a superior and then shot himself. His wife, Mother Küsters (Brigitte Mira), trying to cope with this tragedy, finds herself abandoned by her children. A journalist who has gotten into Mother Küster's good graces writes a sensationalistic, slanderous article. In her time of need, Mother Küsters is befriended by Karl Tillmann (Karlheinz Böhm) and his wife Marianne (Margit Carstensen), members of the German Communist Party, who interpret her husband's deed as an act of desperation on the part of a man who had suffered years of oppression on the job. Mother Küsters initially joins the Party out of loneliness, but gradually becomes politically involved and hopes that the Party will rehabilitate her husband. But the Tillmanns turn out to be armchair Marxists, who use Mother Küsters for their own ends. With elections coming up, the rehabilitation of Hermann Küsters assumes a low priority. Mother Küsters, getting no satisfaction from the Party, turns to an anarchist, who promises to bring the matter to the attention of the public through terrorist action. The terrorist stages a sit-in in the editorial office of the newspaper that had carried the original story. In the original version of the film, the terrorist takes hostages and demands the release of all political prisoners in Germany. Both he and Mother Küsters are shot by the police as they try to flee to their car. In a later version intended for release in America, Fassbinder appended a contrived happy ending, in which the anarchist is too ludicrous to be taken seriously. The editorial staff goes home, the anarchist finally leaves, and only Mother Küsters remains. She goes home with a kindly watchman, a widower who is as lonely as she and who offers her solace in the form of a meal of *Himmel und Erde* (heaven and earth), a concoction of sausage and apples. The new deus-ex-machina ending calls to mind the ending of Murnau's *The Last Laugh*. Utterly unbelievable, it merely underscores the tragedy of Mother Küsters's situation.

Mother Küsters, which caused a furor at its premiere in Berlin, is Fassbinder's least successful film in Germany (American critics reacted much more favorably), where its carte blanche denunciation of the German Left was resented. Yet, despite its unfavorable depiction of antiestablishment revolutionary groups, the film sounds a more optimistic note in that Mother Küsters is the first of Fassbinder's victims who learns, whose consciousness is raised. In this respect she has more in common with the Gorky-Brecht story of the Mother than with Jutzi's *Mother Krausen.*

Satansbraten (*Satan's Brew,* 1975/76) is Fassbinder's most self-indulgent, decadent work. Its cast of characters includes the erstwhile leftist poet Walter Kranz (Kurt Raab), afflicted with writer's block; his long-suffering nag of a wife Luise (Helen Vita); his retarded brother Ernst (Volker Spengler), whose *idée fixe* is having sex with flies; an old-maid admirer, Andrée (Margit Carstensen, deformed with countless facial warts and grotesquely thick glasses); a nymphomaniac, wealthy, aristocratic patroness, Irmgart von Witzleben (Katharina Buchhammer); a prostitute; and an open-marriage couple.

The plot hinges on the elaborately executed practical joke played on Walter by his perpetually horny patroness, Frau von Witzleben: while taking part in one of their sadomasochistic orgies, Walter "kills" his benefactress. The murder serves as a release for Walter, the creative juices flow again, and he produces a poem, "The Albatross," which has the dubious distinction of being identical with Stefan George's Albatross poem (in turn a translation of Charles Baudelaire's poem from *Les Fleurs du Mal*). Unable to admit plagiarism, Kranz convinces himself that he *is* George. He has a George-suit tailored to specifications, hires some handsome young men to function as disciples, dims the lights, lights candles and incense, and celebrates *Georgekreis* poetry readings. The needed cash for his poetic ventures is furnished by Andrée, who willingly subjugates herself to the poetic genius. Walter, considering himself to be in a realm beyond good and evil, cheats his parents and tries to rob a prostitute he had been interviewing. She avenges herself by sending her protectors to beat him up, and Andrée, witnessing the beating and recognizing her own weakness in Walter, abandons him; his wife, whose illness he had ignored, dies. Walter's attempt to pin the von Witzleben murder on his brother backfires. Ernst overhears Walter's conversation with the police and shoots Walter with the murder weapon. The bullets are blank, the blood fake.

Frau von Witzleben and entourage appear, unveiling the "murder" as a hoax. The film ends with an orgy.

Despite some screamingly funny scenes (the poetry readings, Kranz = George's discovery that George was homosexual), the film is devoid of real humor. Cynical, grotesque, and exaggerated beyond credence, it violates good taste in an attempt to *épater les bourgeois.*

In a state of crisis at the time the film was made, Fassbinder was having difficulties adjusting to Frankfurt, where he had gone as director of the Theater am Tor. His play *Die Erde ist unbewohnbar wie der Mond* (*The Earth Is As Uninhabitable As the Moon*) had been rejected. A charge of anti-Semitism had been leveled against his play *Der Müll, die Stadt und der Tod* (*Garbage, the City and Death*). The rejection in Germany of virtually all his films made after *Effi Briest* was aggravated by Fassbinder's acclaim in America.[16] If his response to rejection by German critics was the defiant, spiteful *Satan's Brew,* it proved self-defeating, for it only intensified the alienation of his public.

Fassbinder's next film, *Chinesisches Roulette* (*Chinese Roulette,* 1976), in its extreme formalism is the antithesis of the previous film. Like *Petra von Kant, Chinese Roulette* concerns itself with intense personal interactions and emotional power plays; its abstracted, stylized interactions similarly occur within a spatially confined area. A couple, Ariane (Margit Carstensen) and Gerhard (Alexander Allerson), go off for a weekend with their respective lovers, Kolbe (Ulli Lommel) and Irene (Anna Karina). Through the machinations of their handicapped daughter, Angela (Andrea Schober), the two couples end up in the family's country estate. That evening Angela arrives with her mute nurse Traunitz (Macha Méril). At Angela's instigation, this dual ménage à trois, together with the eccentric housekeeper Kast (Brigitte Mira) and her writer-son Gabriel (Volker Spengler), play Chinese Roulette, a game of truth with consequences. Dividing the group into two smaller groups of four, Angela explains the rules of the game: each member of a group is to pick a person in the other group. The people in the second group must then guess which person has been chosen. Clues as to the identity of the person are given by asking questions such as: "If this person were an animal, what would he be?" or, "If this person were to go off to a desert island forever, what would he take along: a person, a book or thing?" or, "What would this person have been in the Third Reich?"

It becomes clear that Angela, the first player, has chosen her mother for a particularly vindictive retaliation. While the nature of the other relationships remains largely inscrutable, the ties that bind Angela to her parents are based on deep-seated animosity. Imposing in her handicap, Angela is the source of the malevolence that soon permeates the estate. Aware of her parents' paramours, Angela has engineered this encounter in order to force things to a head. It remains unclear whether Angela had anticipated or intended the rapprochement that occurs between her parents, or whether she had hoped to provoke her mother into killing her. Her insolent answers do in fact motivate Ariane into taking a pistol and shooting at the nurse. Traunitz is not killed; she suffers only a flesh wound. After this near catastrophe, Angela goads Gabriel by accusing him of plagiarism. The film closes with an exterior shot, which shows a religious procession passing before the house. A shot rings out and the frame is frozen.

Chinese Roulette is Fassbinder's most enigmatic film. To his open-ended conclusion, Fassbinder adds motifs that are not pursued—for example, an allusion to a recent murder in Paris and the housekeeper's observation, "Now we're the only ones left," conjure up unconfirmed suggestions of clandestine and dangerous criminal or political activity.

The multifaceted nature of the relationships is effectively highlighted by the brilliant camera work of Michael Ballhaus. The most important scenes are shot in the estate dining hall, a room resplendent with mirrors and Plexiglass showcases. Languidly static figures are offset by a perpetually mobile camera that simultaneously captures both the figures and their mirror images—thus involving the viewer in the deception/self-deception of the characters by impairing his ability to differentiate between appearance and reality. *Chinese Roulette* did little to ingratiate Fassbinder with the German public; the critics, while lauding Fassbinder's brilliance as a *metteur-en-scène*, rejected the film on the basis of its cold intellectualism.

Fassbinder's preoccupation with the appearance/reality theme reaches a culmination in *Despair: Eine Reise ins Licht (Despair,* 1977). Based on the story by Vladimir Nabokov (screenplay by

Tom Stoppard), the film takes place in Berlin in the early thirties. The cast of characters includes the Russian emigré Hermann Hermann (Dirk Bogarde), a chocolate-factory owner, his voluptuous and somewhat stupid wife, Lydia (Andréa Ferréol), who is cuckolding him with her cousin, Ardalion (Volker Spengler), an unsuccessful and drunken painter. Hermann, homesick for his motherland, saddled with a floundering business, and concerned about the rise of National Socialism, escapes the horror of his everyday life by disassociating himself from reality. Making love to his wife, Hermann imagines that his role has been taken over by a *doppelgänger,* while he assumes the role of voyeur. On a business trip to Düsseldorf, Hermann meets the itinerant Felix Weber (Klaus Löwitsch), whom he considers to be his double. He offers Felix a thousand marks to change identities with him, at first explaining that it is important that he be seen in two places at the same time, later maintaining that he is making a film. At first reluctant to enter the agreement, Felix later acquiesces, and they exchange clothes. Hermann, who has planned what he considers the perfect crime ("the victim is the murderer"), then shoots Felix, and assuming his double's identity flees to Switzerland, where he plans to start a new life as Felix Weber. Since the two men actually bore little resemblance to each other, the crime is soon discovered and Hermann is arrested.

Despair is unlike other Fassbinder films in several respects: his first elaborate, high-budget production, it is shot in English, and, although set in the Weimar Republic, does not deal with a typically German experience. In this respect it differs from *Bolwieser* (based on the novel by the Bavarian novelist Oskar Maria Graf), which preceded it and influenced its content and form. A two-part television film, *Bolwieser* dealt with the dissolution of a petty-bourgeois marriage. Like *Effi Briest,* it offered insight into the society as a whole; while focusing on the personal sphere, it documented the mentality that fostered the rise of Nazism. In *Despair* Fassbinder again incorporated this theme, and the rise of National Socialism received greater (visual) emphasis than can be found in Nabokov's original. However, like the story, the film essentially documents Hermann Hermann's journey into madness.

In no other film did Fassbinder have less control over the

script, or was he so bound by a text not of his own making.[17] Nonetheless, *Despair* clearly bears the hallmark of a Fassbinder film. Elaborating on the use of glass and mirrors, which had played an increasingly important role since *Chinese Roulette* and *Effi Briest,* Fassbinder has visually rendered Hermann's increasing dissociation by using an elaborate system of mirrors, glass doors, and windows to reflect the distortions and mutations of his mind. The use of reflection in *Despair* is, according to Fassbinder, the cinematic equivalent of Nabokov's linguistic style: "Nabokov is never direct. He handles language as something that reflects, mirrors and rereflects. If I use glass and reflections in the film, it's derived from Nabokov's linguistic structure. . . . The significance of glass in this film is that it's transparent and yet it closes in on the character—and that's Nabokov's style."[18]

The elaborate decor of Hermann's apartment (much of which is a direct carryover from *Bolwieser)* consists of art deco mirrors, glass doors, and windows. This interior stage set serves a dual function: it reflects the entrapment, the claustrophobia he feels and, through the constant reflections, it distorts reality, thus approximating Hermann's mental state. A particularly striking fantasy sequence is shot in the labyrinthine maze of a funhouse. In place of a hall of mirrors, Fassbinder has substituted transparent glass. Hermann and Felix wander around in the glass maze; Felix shoots a gun at Hermann, but after the shot has been fired, wound marks appear on Felix's stomach, he doubles over and falls on the funhouse floor.

The ultimate irony of Nabokov's story, that the resemblance between Felix and Hermann is negligible—i.e., a mere figment of Hermann's imagination—is not revealed to the reader until virtually the end of the novel. Fassbinder had originally planned to duplicate this deception by using Bogarde for the roles of both Hermann and Felix. On the recommendations of Bogarde and Tom Stoppard, however, he agreed to cast another actor in Felix's role. Thus, except for the initial lovemaking scene (in which Bogarde does play Hermann's voyeur-self), the doppelgänger Felix is shown to be the distorted perception of Hermann's distorted mind. The viewer is privy to Hermann's self-deception from the outset. Yet, paradoxically, since the film is shot almost exclusively from Hermann's perspective, this information serves not so much to call Hermann's perceptions into question as our own. Hearing time and again of the incredible physical similarity between the two men, viewers are apt to become confused, question their own perceptions, and search for those resemblances on which Herman so adamantly insists. In the last scenes of *Despair* Fassbinder tantalizes the viewer by manipulating the appearance/reality theme even further. As Hermann gives himself up to the police, he addresses the camera directly: "Good people, we are making a film here. I'm coming out . . . I'm coming out. Don't look at the camera." The brillance of this final shot is that it can at once be interpreted as yet another one of Hermann's distorted perceptions and as an alienation technique designed to shatter verisimilitude.

Fassbinder's contribution to the Young German Filmmakers' collective venture, *Deutschland im Herbst (Germany in Autumn,* 1978), intended as a response to the terrorist kidnapping and murder of the Mercedes Benz executive Martin Schleyer and the resulting conservative backlash in Germany, is by far the film's most personal statement. Like *Beware of a Holy Whore* it is autobiographical, made in the confessional mode. The significant difference is that here the autobiographical component is not disguised as in the earlier film, but presented directly. The sequence portrays the impotence, fear, and rage engendered in a man with leftist leanings in the wake of the Schleyer murder, Mogadishu, and the suspect suicide of the terrorists in Stammheim prison. Fassbinder's segment cuts between scenes shot in his apartment, a garishly lit self-enclosed space that never sees the light of day, and the kitchen of his mother's apartment. The intensity of Fassbinder's reaction is seen most clearly in his affective responses to his lover, Armin Meier, with whom he shares the apartment. Armin, who does not share Fassbinder's concerns, must bear the brunt of his rage. The scenes with his mother (Lilo Pempeit), a stock actress of the Fassbinder troupe, consist of fragments of dialogue in which the two debate questions of law, order, and force in a democratic society. Fassbinder's mother, provoked into articulating extremist views such as advocating killing one terrorist for each hostage taken, and admitting that a benevolent authoritarian leadership is preferable to a democracy, betrays both the proclivity of her generation to

Andrea Ferréol and Dirk Bogarde in *Despair* (Courtesy of Filmverlag der Autoren)

Klaus Löwitsch and Hanna Schygulla in *The Marriage of Maria Braun* (Courtesy of New Yorker Films)

revert to predemocratic solutions in times of crisis, and its inherently authoritarian orientation.

Fassbinder, in contrast, raised in the postwar West German Federal Republic, recognizes the need to adhere to the laws of the democratic state, and adamantly insists on equality before the law for all. While his verbal and political stances coincide, his actions (he sniffs cocaine, is paranoid about being betrayed to the police, forces an itinerant whom Armin had brought home out of the apartment lest he be either a terrorist or a police plant) betray the intensity of his anxiety and fear. The effect of this disparity between word and deed is chilling. Precisely because of its personal relevance, his statement is the most memorable sequence of *Germany in Autumn*.

Die Ehe der Maria Braun (The Marriage of Maria Braun, 1978) presented Fassbinder with his long-awaited box-office breakthrough both in Germany and abroad. Overnight it made Fassbinder a household name and brought Hanna Schygulla the best actress award at the 1979 Berlin Film Festival, making her an international star. It was indeed a German Hollywood film.

The tragicomic opening shots show the wedding of Maria (Hanna Schygulla) and Hermann Braun (Klaus Löwitsch) amid the chaos of a 1943 Allied bomb attack. As the walls come tumbling down, Maria risks life and limb to get the signature of the justice of the peace on the marriage certificate. After half a day and one night of marital bliss, Hermann is sent off to the Russian front. At war's end, Maria keeps vigil at the railway station, hoping for the return of her husband, missing in action. Deciding that life must go on, she eventually takes a job as a barmaid in a club off limits to American GIs. She will, she protests to the family doctor, who must certify her for employment, sell beer, not herself. Her plan to remain loyal to Hermann falters when she hears that he has been killed in action. At the club she seeks out a black GI, Bill (George Byrd), who is in love with her, but with whom she had until then maintained a platonic relationship. Telling him that Hermann is dead, she reveals a vulnerability that she will never again allow herself, and though her affair with Bill brings her happiness, she refuses to marry him, holding fast to her absolute ideal of marriage with Hermann. Nonetheless, she is happy to learn that she is pregnant with Bill's child. Just as she and Bill, rejoicing over the news, are about to make love, Hermann appears, a ghost from a POW camp. Maria, over-joyed, approaches her husband, but the stunned Hermann slaps her. When Bill, trying to protect Maria, restrains Hermann, Maria picks up a bottle and hits Bill over the head, accidentally killing him. She is brought to trial, but Hermann confesses to the slaying and is sent to prison. Maria vows to wait for him, and lives in anticipation of their reunion. Having miscarried Bill's baby, she leaves her home town; on the train she makes the acquaintance of a wealthy industrialist, Oswald (Ivan Desny), and eventually becomes his assistant and his mistress. Her business acumen makes her professionally as well as privately indispensible to Oswald, and working not for herself, but for Hermann and for their future together, she amasses power and wealth. Hermann is completely informed about her relationship with Oswald. When Hermann is finally released, instead of actualizing her happy-forever-after fantasy, he goes off to Australia, leaving behind a letter explaining that he cannot accept the relationship on her terms; in order to be able to live with her, he must regain his identity and self-esteem.

Maria continues to work for Oswald, but their personal relationship has become tormented. Now cynical and hard, she nevertheless clings to the promise of an idealized future with Hermann, who fuels this fantasy by sending her one red rose every month. He does not return, however, until after Oswald's death. The reunion between husband and wife is awkward; both partners have changed, and it is difficult to reconcile their memories and fantasies of each other with the present actuality. Maria and Hermann are the sole benefactors of Oswald's considerable estate. During the reading of the will Maria learns that the love-smitten industrialist, knowing he was dying, had entered into an agreement with Hermann, whereby Hermann would forego Maria until after Oswald's death. Now independently wealthy, they can at long last realize their dream. However, after lighting a cigarette from a gas burner—as is her habit—she absentmindedly blows out the flame without turning off the gas. As a TV announcer excitedly announces the final minutes of the momentous 1954 German-Hungarian soccer game, there is an explosion that sends Maria, Hermann, and their dream into oblivion.

In an epilogue, Fassbinder includes the pictures of four postwar West German politicians: Adenauer, Erhard, Kiesinger, and Schmidt. By so doing, he imposed an allegorical interpretation on the film: Maria is equated with postwar Germany, which in the wake of Americanization has lost its naiveté and high ideals—he does not explain how those survived Hitlerism—and become materialistic and callous. That Willi Brandt is not included in this final array indicates that Fassbinder does not hold this SPD leader responsible for the state of postwar German society.

Like many of Fassbinder's films, *Maria Braun* is rooted in melodrama. The strong-willed, independent heroine, who must fend for herself in a man's world, is a favorite theme of Hollywood "women's films" of the forties. Nevertheless, Maria is in many ways an antifeminist heroine: her desire for power, wealth, and success reflect male values. Advancing herself initially not through merit but through her sexuality, Maria proves herself content to play by male rules in order to achieve her ends. Her success is, however, gained at the price of her own integrity: by internalizing the values of a male society, Maria has become masculine herself.

Maria Braun makes minimal use of the distancing devices common in Fassbinder films. Its heroine is one of the few Fassbinder characters with whom one can identify. Granted, one's sympathy wears thin as the film progresses, but initially the naive, idealistic, loyal Maria is clearly meant as a positive figure. Yet it is clear that her tragedy is one of character as well as circumstance. Maria's inability to relinquish her idea of the perfect love, her romantic yearning for the absolute, prevent her from living fully in the present. By setting up a deferred reality, Maria creates impossible expectations and thereby dooms herself to failure. Interestingly enough, it is precisely those virtues that Hans-Jürgen Syberberg *(Our Hitler)* regards as Germany's greatest virtues: the idealistic striving for the unobtainable, the search for transcendence, which Fassbinder criticizes in the character of Maria Braun.

Fassbinder's changes in the original script show that the Adenauer era was intended as the historical setting. The broadcast of the all-important 1954 world-champion soccer game signifies the end of postwar humiliation for many Germans. Two contradictory speeches by Adenauer are incorporated into the film: the first takes a stand against rearmament, the second advocates it. Initially the script had called for Maria to consciously kill Hermann and herself by driving off a cliff,[19] but Fassbinder chose to make his conclusion ambiguous. While both anticipatory close-ups of Maria at the stove and her reflective pause before lighting the cigarette point to a conscious intent, we cannot be sure. Once again Fassbinder adroitly plays with the audience's expectation.

The commercial success of *Maria Braun* stems in no small part from its affinity with traditional Hollywood rags-to-riches melodrama, replete with the sensationalism of extramarital and interracial sex, murder, and transcendent love. Maria differs from the typical Fassbinder character in that she does achieve upward mobility and at great cost liberates herself from her petty-bourgeois origins. The "political" dimension of the ending seems sufficiently contrived so as not to detract from the film's commercial appeal.

Fassbinder prefaces his next film, *In einem Jahr mit 13 Monden (In a Year of 13 Moons, 1978),* with the following statement:

> Every seventh year is a year of the moon. Those individuals whose existence is primarily influenced by their emotions are especially subject to depressions in these moon years, which also applies, albeit not so pronouncedly, in years with thirteen new moons.
>
> And if a moon year is also a year with thirteen new moons, it often results in personal catastrophes.
>
> There are six years in the twentieth century that are burdened with this dangerous constellation—one of them is the year 1978.
>
> Before that, it was the years 1908, 1929, 1943, and 1957. After 1978, the year 1992 will again endanger the lives of many.

Prompted by the suicide of his lover, Armin Meier (who played in several of Fassbinder's films), *13 Moons* represents Fassbinder's working through of his subsequent guilt and trauma. Set in Frankfurt in 1978, it recounts the last days in the life of the transsexual Elvira Weishaupt (Volker Spengler). The opening shots show Elvira, dressed in male drag, hustling gay Czech *Gastarbeiter,* who in a paradigmatic scene of rejection beat her when they discover she is a woman. Returning home dishevelled and drunk, Elvira is confronted by her lover Christian (Karl Scheydt), who beats and then abandons her. She is consoled by the streetwalker Zora (Ingrid Caven), to whom she confides the story of her life.

The slaughterhouse in which Elvira had worked in her former life as Erwin Weishaupt serves both as the backdrop for Elvira's reminiscences about Erwin's ex-wife, Irene (Elisabeth Trissenaar), and her daughter, Marie-Ann (Eva Mattes), and about earlier, happier days with Christian, a down-and-out actor whom she supported by sleeping with other men. Elvira's sex change had not, it seems, been prompted by deepseated psychosexual desires, but by the offhand retort of concentration-camp survivor Anton Saitz (Gottfried John) to Erwin's confession of love: "Too bad that you're not a girl." Erwin had rushed off to Casablanca for an operation, only to realize, too late, that Saitz had not been serious.

Further light is shed on Elvira's early history through Sister Gudrun (Lilo Pempeit), mother superior of the orphanage in which Erwin was raised. From her Elvira (who has repressed these fourteen years of her life) learns that Erwin was the illegitimate child of a married woman whose husband was at the front. Having once rejected her child, she dealt him a second blow by preventing his adoption by an eager young couple, since this would have meant revealing his existence to her husband. Erwin fell critically ill, and when he recovered became so unpredictable that the nuns, who had doted on him, began to fear and hate him.

Elvira seeks out the now powerful entrepreneur Anton Saitz, getting past his henchmen by using the password: "Bergen-Belsen." Both he and Saitz fail to recognize each other. Saitz accompanies Elvira home, but abandons her in favor of Zora. Elvira cuts her hair, puts on men's clothing, visits her ex-wife and daughter, and vainly tries to effect a reconciliation. Desperately in need of someone to talk to, Elvira visits a journalist she knows, but he initially fails to recognize her despondency. Later, concerned about her, he goes to her apartment where he finds her dead—according to Fassbinder—of a "broken heart."

The transsexual Elvira Weishaupt is Fassbinder's ultimate outsider. Despite its exaggerated circumstances, however, her story is not meant to represent an isolated, improbable phenomenon but to be representative of human relationships in society in which basic human emotions have become atrophied. Elvira's failure to receive help is due not to malice but to the solipsistic inability of the other to reach out to another human being. Fassbinder merely presents the world as he finds it, and Frankfurt, in its characterless uniformity and anonymity, is the logical setting for Elvira's final days.

For this tour de force, Fassbinder not only wrote the script and directed but also did the camera work. The naturalism of the story is offset by brilliant distancing devices, of which the slaughterhouse sequence is the most striking. By having Elvira recount her life against the gory spectacle of animals being herded, slaughtered, and butchered, Fassbinder presents us with his most startling alienation effect. The scene is replete with literary allusions. Elvira's quotation from Goethe's *Tasso* about the redemptive power of art—"But whereas man in his agony becomes mute, a god gave me the power to express my suffering"—clearly applies to Fassbinder himself. The scene is clearly reminiscent of the detailed slaughterhouse sequence that Alfred Döblin introduces into *Berlin Alexanderplatz* with its epigrammatic: "For it happens alike with Man and Beast; as the Beast dies, so Man dies too."

With *In a Year of 13 Moons* Fassbinder completes a prophetic eternal return, hearkening back to the pessimistic world view of *Love Is Colder Than Death*, reiterating in a more sophisticated form the motifs of *Gods of the Plague, Herr R., Merchant of Four Seasons*, and *Fox and His Friends*. It is an extreme articulation of the underlying theme of all Fassbinder's work: inexorable, existential loneliness and alienation.

In it Fassbinder also elaborates on the *Verfremdungseffekt* he had introduced in his previous film: an overload of the sound track. In *Maria Braun* the reunion between Maria and Hermann occurs against the backdrop of the loudly blaring television set, so that the viewer must strain to understand the dialogue. In *In A Year of 13 Moons*, Elvira's narrative is recited against the background of slaughterhouse sounds, and in other scenes the dialogue is juxtaposed against the jarring sounds of a penny arcade. This technique is carried to the extreme in Fassbinder's next film, *Die dritte Generation (The Third Generation*, 1979).

A prologue offers the key to this film interpretation of contemporary terrorism: "A comedy in six parts about social games full of suspense, excitement and logic, horror and insanity."

Fassbinder depicts the contemporary breed of terrorists as mere adventurers devoid of idealism and political commitment, and motivated solely by a desire to escape the emptiness of their affluent lives.

Fassbinder's essential cynicism is underscored by the public-toilet graffiti separating the individual film segments, the first few of which establish the identity of the terrorists: affluent and bored young people who adhere to the Schopenhauerian slogan "World as Will and Representation." By financing the group and manipulating its members into kidnapping him, Peter Lenz (Eddie Constantine), the representative of an American multinational electronics firm, hopes to enhance German sales of computers, which can be used to track down terrorists. Susanne Gast (Hanna Schygulla) his secretary before joining the terrorist group, supplies them with needed information regarding Lenz's habits. After Paul (Raul Gimenez), a killer specially brought in from Africa, is shot by the police, the terrorists go underground and are given new identities—including the name Oskar Matzerath, the hero of Günther Grass's *The Tin Drum*. One by one, the terrorists are betrayed to the police by August Brem (Volker Spengler), a traitor in their midst. In the final scenes the remaining terrorists videotape a statement by the kidnapped Lenz, in which he declares himself a "prisoner of the people." The filming necessitates several retakes, and, like Hermann Hermann's final comment in *Despair*, the sequence at once manipulates the appearance/reality theme and offers an ironic statement not only on the state of terrorism but on the art of filmmaking as well. The videotape shows a complacent Lenz, beaming at the success of his machinations and anticipating the final act of the scenario: the shooting of the terrorists by the police.

The Third Generation—the latest of a group of NGC films on terrorism that includes Alexander Kluge's *Strongman Ferdinand* (1977), Volker Schlöndorff's *The Lost Honor of Katharina Blum* (1975), and the cooperative venture *Germany in Autumn* (1978)—incorporates motifs from the earlier films. Thus Lenz's manipulation of the terrorists for business ends is reminiscent of Ferdinand's stance in Kluge's film, his willingness to go to extremes (staging a terrorist attack) in order to prove the need for his paramilitary security troops. Additionally, Fassbinder has the terrorists kidnap their "victim" on Mardi Gras, thus calling to mind the carnival scenes in *Katharina Blum*. As in *Germany in Autumn,* the film's historical time frame is precisely fixed: a continuously blaring radio informs us (among other things) of the revolution in Iran and of the Vietnamese-Chinese War.

Nonetheless, the film is pure Fassbinder. In typical Fassbinder style it refers back to his own films, elaborates on recently developed distancing techniques, and restates prototypical themes. By having agent provocateur Brem dress in drag, Fassbinder visually cites Volker Spengler's role as Elvira Weishaupt in *In a Year of 13 Moons. The Third Generation* carries to extremes the overloaded sound track, which after *Maria Braun* became Fassbinder's new hallmark. The incessant radio and/or TV is an acoustic affront to viewers' senses—at once an irritant that often prevents them from understanding the dialogue and a challenge that demands their particular attention. Since the dialogue of the terrorists is largely banal, in conjunction with the omnipresent radio and television, it makes viewers acutely aware that his unmotivated third generation is a product of the electronic age.

Ultimately, *The Third Generation* emerges as a variation on the filmmaker's main themes: exploitation and manipulation, betrayal and death. Fassbinder underscores this continuity by including the pseudonymous character Franz Walsch (Günther Kaufmann), who appeared in his first feature film, *Love Is Colder Than Death*. What distinguishes this film from the others is that Fassbinder has transformed an inherently tragic theme into a macabre comedy. In its black humour, in its use of the grotesque, it calls to mind *Satan's Brew*.

The sheer volume of Fassbinder's output, coupled with its breadth and virtuosity, makes any definitive statement on his oeuvre almost immediately invalid. After the release of *The Third Generation,* he completed his monumental thirteen-part television serialization of Döblin's *Berlin Alexanderplatz.* Lauded by the critics, it met with vociferous rejection by the general German public, and is probably the single most controversial production ever to appear on German television. Döblin's novel represents a long-standing interest of Fassbinder's. The figure and fate of Franz Biberkopf remain constant points of reference in his multifaceted work. The downtrodden little man Franz, operating on the periphery of the underworld, is, as we have seen, an important theme in many of Fassbinder's films from

Love Is Colder Than Death to *The Third Generation*. Similarly, Franz's relationship to Reinhold is prototypical of all of Fassbinder's male relationships, and Franz's role as victim-turned-oppressor has relevence for the vast majority of Fassbinder heroes. It therefore seems plausible to view *Berlin Alexanderplatz* as the summation of Fassbinder's previous work.

Much Fassbinder scholarship concerns itself with the question of whether he is a psychological or a political filmmaker. Proponents of the psychological school argue that his work is merely a means for the working through of his own deep-seated personal psychic concerns; it was by his own admission a form of therapy. On the other hand, it is also true that the post-*Merchant* films increasingly incorporated social and political issues—treated in a very personal manner, as in *Fox and His Friends, Germany in Autumn,* and *The Third Generation.* That a filmmaker of Fassbinder's stature dealt with contemporary social and political issues such as homosexuality, terrorism, alienation, and exploitation served to keep these concerns on the forefront of the public's consciousness. Thus the private took on political ramifications.

Editor's note:

On the morning of June 10, 1982, Rainer Werner Fassbinder was found dead in a Munich apartment. The cause of death was heart failure resulting from the interaction of sleeping pills and cocaine.

In addition to the films discussed in this chapter, Fassbinder directed *Lili Marleen* (1980), *Lola* (1981), and *Die Sehnsucht der Veronika Voss (The Longing of Veronika Voss)* and *Querelle* (both 1982). He played the leading role in Wolf Gremm's *Kamikaze 1989* (1982) and acted in numerous films by other directors.

Of the many eulogies and tributes there was perhaps none more moving and perceptive than that by Günter Rohrbach, head of the Bavaria-Atelier. Originally delivered on German television, the text was first published in English in *Kino: Bulletin of the Export-Union des Deutschen Films* (3/82). It is reprinted here:

Even the news of his death sounded like a denunciation. The body was found in his apartment at five in the morning, naked, lying on the mattresses spread out on the floor. "Foul play" could be excluded, said the police record. Yet, what had been avoided discreetly in Romy Schneider's case,* was not spared him, and orders were given for an inquest. Up to his last day he had lived a disorderly life, and even his death was a provocation, for on the day of President Reagan's state visit to Bonn the headlines belonged to the filmmaker Rainer Werner Fassbinder.

He was Germany's most famous director, the only one whose name almost everybody knew although his films were often far from popular. He was called the "Wunderkind" of the German cinema, and yet he was nothing like it. He had started work in the face of the collective prejudice of the film industry and a public more or less devoid of comprehension. Dismissed by many of his older colleagues for what to them were mannerisms and a dilettante approach, he made film after film, with a growing obsession and relentless diligence. And he became a world star before the others had had time to notice.

He, the one they had disdained and despised, had learned to master his cinematic means in virtuoso fashion. However chaotic circumstances might be at home, in the studio he was a precise workman radiating calm and certainty. The man Fassbinder presented to the public, with his posture of rejection and provocation, was a condition of his constantly endangered existence, it was not the man himself.

Admittedly, he was also admired by many, quite early on, the cult figure of a scene which called itself New German Cinema and was determined to achieve world fame. Fassbinder himself never won the Golden Palm of Cannes, nor the Oscar. It was not the fault of his films, but rather, his incapability for correct timing. His way of producing was too impetuous, too quickly was the last film pushed aside by the curiosity engendered by the next one.

The breathtaking speed with which Fassbinder made his films has been much guessed at and also much ridiculed. If you consider that he wrote most of the screenplays for his more than 40 films himself, that he also wrote stage plays in between and was also a theater director, you will get some idea of this man's obsessions. For the psychologist, the case is almost too simple—art as survival training. The only whiff of happiness came to Fassbinder when he stood behind the camera, surrounded by the loyal friends who had for years made up his team and most of whom were almost fanatically devoted to him. As soon as shooting was completed, the fight against depression started, hectic journeys around the world, the flight into drugs, the clinging to new plans and projects. The gulf of loneliness he drew around himself, letting in but a few friends, became more

*An apparent suicide, she died in Paris on May 29, 1982.

and more deep and it was increasingly difficult to return to the life-saving activity of a new film. Too difficult it was in the end.

Fassbinder always had all the preconditions for becoming a legend. The image of his extraordinary existence tickled people's fancy, meeting perfectly the expectations the public has of the artist personality: the artist as part of his own art. The early death, too, fits into the concept. When the body was found, the scenario for his next film, *Rosa Luxemburg,* was lying next to it. He had wanted Romy Schneider for the leading part.

Fassbinder was an important figure also in German television. He never drew a dividing line, as many of his colleagues lay store by doing, between the cinema film and the television film. He wanted to make films and he took the money for them werever he could get it and he looked for his audience wherever he could find it. His two big television series, *Eight Hours Do Not Make a Day* and *Berlin Alexanderplatz,* were television events which nearly broke the television companies.

Directors do not die as long as their films live. Fassbinder remains with us in his melancholic melodramas full of brutality and tenderness. And with us remain the stars he created, above all the women, Hanna Schygulla, Margit Carstensen, Barbara Sukowa, Rosel Zech. The memory remains of a contradictory and vulnerable human being who in his curiously helpless and awkward way shouted in the world: "I just want you to love me."

NOTES

[1]Wilfried Wiegand, "Interview," in *Rainer Werner Fassbinder, Reihe Film* 2, edited by Peter Jansen and Wolfram Schütte (Munich: Hanser, 1979), p. 63.

[2]Yaak Karsunke, "Anti-teatergeschichte: Die Anfange," in Jansen and Schütte, *Fassbinder,* p. 12.

[3]Fassbinder's adaptation of Goethe's *Iphigenia on Tauris,* in which the original text was interspersed with quotes from volatile, contemporary political issues (e.g., trial of a West Berlin commune), comic strips, living theater, Mao, and Paul McCartney, was particularly noteworthy. See Karsunke, "Anti-teatergeschichte," p. 13.

[4]Quoted in Karsunke, "Anti-teatergeschichte," p. 13. My translation.

[5]Wiegand, "Interview,"p. 64.

[6]Since these films constitute two distinct categories, I will not adhere to a strictly chronological discussion of the early films.

[7]Thomas Elsaesser, "A Cinema of Vicious Circles," in *Fassbinder,* edited by Tony Rayns (London: BFI, 1976), p. 25.

[8]John Sandford, *The New German Cinema* (London: Oswald Wolff, 1980), p. 72.

[9]The Film Derives its title from the French *marchands des quatre saisons*, i.e., street vendors who make their rounds with carts of fruits and vegetables.

[10]Quoted in Rayns, *Fassbinder*, p. 55.

[11]The Baroness Sidonie von Grasenabb is a minor character in Fontane's *Effi Briest*. That Fassbinder gives her name to one of his characters in *Petra von Kant* indicates his longstanding interest in this novel.

[12]Fassbinder, who dedicated the film to the person Marlene becomes, was surprised when critics interpreted Marlene's final act as positive. The person Marlene became referred, he maintained, not to the film character, but to the actress Irm Hermann, who took on a more important role in the production end of the Fassbinder troupe.

[13]In its new focus on the working class, *Jail Bait* has a greater affinity with the five-part television series *Eight Hours Don't Make a Day*, made that same year. This series, which revolved around the family life and work place of the working class, is Fassbinder's contribution to the *Arbeiterfilm*.

[14]Norma McLain Stoop, "Rainer Werner Fassbinder and 'Fox,'" *After Dark*, February 1976, p. 43.

[15]Ibid., p. 43.

[16]Cf. Wilhelm Roth, "Kommentierte Filmografie," in Jansen and Schütte, *Fassbinder*, pp. 160–164.

[17]Fassbinder wrote the screenplays for his other literary adaptations: *The Coffee House. Pioneers in Ingolstadt, Jail Bait,* and *Effi Briest*.

[18]Quoted by Dan Yakir in "The Director Explains," *The Boston Phoenix,* 24 October 1978.

[19]Roth, "Filmografie," p. 186.

HANS W. GEISSENDÖRFER

A Precise Craftsman

by Eric Rentschler

''EITHER YOUNG GERMAN FILM IN the Federal Republic will become a political, analytical, reflective film—or one not worth talking about," Wolfram Schütte argued in 1967,[1] the same year Hans W. Geissendörfer made his first feature film. A director hardly prone to topical controversy or sympathetic to ideological endeavor, someone whose films follow manifestly straightforward story lines, an adroit technician who avoids formal experimentation or essayistic discursiveness, Geissendörfer has little in common with more radical advocates of *Autorenkino,* the ardently self-sufficient spirits who drafted the Oberhausen Manifesto in 1962.[2] Not one to man barricades or to insist on absolute creative control, Geissendörfer calls to mind certain Hollywood professionals from the studio heyday, reliable talents like Lewis Milestone and Michael Curtiz.

Contrary to the willful and less tractable talents one commonly associates with the New German Cinema, Geissendörfer insists that film is a popular medium, one whose central purpose is to tell stories in an accessible and direct manner—and in so doing, appeal to a large audience. West German critics have repeatedly claimed that Geissendörfer is at best a skilled craftsman, a plier of tried-and-true genres; his, so they claim, is a cinema of artifice, ciphers, stock situations, and clichés. His directorial vision

Hans W. Geissendörfer (COURTESY OF
THE FILMMAKER)

issues from an adolescent's fascination, from secondhand experience gained in the dark of movie houses. Few would deny his
technical aplomb and visual flair: the prevailing wisdom, however, holds that Geissendörfer's films lack substance, personal
conviction, a unique perspective. No matter how appealingly
packaged, this brand of movie-making remains a synthetic
product, one that would seem—if we listen to the numerous
commentators in West Germany who equate a film's significance
with its sociopolitical content—hardly to warrant closer
scrutiny.[3]

And yet, the work of Hans W. Geissendörfer can do much to
refine accepted notions of what one commonly speaks of as New
German Cinema. His films deserve closer attention—especially
in the United States, where only three titles have been commercially distributed. Perhaps the most accomplished all-around
technician among West German directors, Geissendörfer stands
apart from the *Autorenkino* espoused by his peers. He denies the
widespread—and, until very recently, widely accepted—

assumption that worthwhile films can only arise under conditions that grant a director-producer "absolute financial and artistic control,"[4] preferring instead a more traditional division of labor between the creative and business aspects of the filmmaking enterprise. Unlike so many of his colleagues, who combine the functions of producer, writer, and director in one person, Geissendörfer gladly submits himself to the guidance and organizational powers of another, letting that person take care of fiscal exigencies while the director attends to what he does best, namely filmmaking.[5] No doubt about it, he does not readily fit into the radical framework that observers on this side of the Atlantic commonly ascribe to the NGC. When American critics rhapsodize about West German film, they rarely mention Geissendörfer's name. (Instead, American devotees concentrate on the enfants terribles, the angry young men and women, lauding the perverse flair of their cinema of disenchantment, reveling in their visions of a kaput modernity.)

This state of affairs is unfortunate, for the director has over the years figured as West Germany's most scintillating exponent of genre films, turning out precisely crafted popular movies while others attempted to do so, or merely talked about doing so. One may very well grant that his range of interests does not seem particularly large or diverse when compared with the eclectic likes of Fassbinder, Kluge, Schroeter, and Syberberg. It can likewise be argued that he lacks the subversive energy and offbeat appeal of his eccentric contemporaries, zanies like Achternbusch and Herzog. Nevertheless, for all his dealings with television networks and commercial producers, Geissendörfer has shaped a body of work with an inhering coherence and continuity, both in formal and thematic terms. Neither adhering to the gritty, ambitious, and socially engaged aesthetic of the Oberhausen activists nor comforming to the trendy opportunism of various Schwabing dandies,[6] Geissendörfer has resolutely maintained a middle ground between *Kunst und Kommerz* (art and economics), a territory that until very recently stood all but unexplored by the majority of West German filmmakers.

Geissendörfer's background is one shared by numerous other young German directors. Born in Augsburg on April 6, 1941, the son of a pastor, like so many of his peers he experienced an undefined yet intense fascination for cinema. Attending lectures at four different universities (Marburg, Erlangen, Zürich, Vienna) between 1962 and 1967, he pursued an eclectic set of studies (theater, German literature, and African languages) that did not lead to a degree. He next embarked on extended trips through Europe, Asia, and Africa, and armed with an 8mm camera, he shot his first films. Like Fassbinder and Herzog, he was self-taught and did not learn his future calling at a film academy. His first efforts—documentary and experimental shorts—remain all but unknown. (So much so that Pflaum and Prinzler's otherwise reliable handbook does not list them among Geissendörfer's films;[7] similarly, the nearly definitive work retrospective screened at the 1979 Berlin Film Festival did not include these early films.) Later he served as an assistant director for George Moorse (*Liebe und so weiter* [*Love etc.*], 1968).[8] Finally, Helmut Haffner, a producer at the TV station Bayerischer Rundfunk, impressed by one of the documentaries as well as by Geissendörfer's stint with Moorse, gave the beginner a copy of Lena Christ's *Erinnerungen einer Überflüssigen (Memoirs of a Superfluous Woman)* and asked him to write a screen treatment. Two weeks later Geissendörfer reappeared with a complete shooting script.[9] *Der Fall Lena Christ (The Case of Lena Christ,* 1968) was Geissendörfer's first feature-length film.

The TV-film *The Case of Lena Christ* stands out as an exception to his customary "narrative, epic cinema with suspense and dramatic calculation."[10] Starting with the Bavarian writer's suicide in a Munich churchyard, the inquiry traces a futile quest for happiness: an illegitimate birth, a strained relationship with a mother who torments and exploits her, an attempted flight to a convent, two unsuccessful marriages, an indefatigable desire to express her life's passion in novels and stories. Analytic in its structure, documentary in its design, impressive in its technical precision (especially Robby Müller's solemn and graceful mobile camera), the film painstakingly reconstructs a specific time and place (the rigid Catholic milieu of turn-of-the-century Upper Bavaria). Geissendörfer would later shy away from such incisive observation of social conventions, tending instead toward a close scrutiny of cinematic conventions, and seeking themes and settings of a more universal character. Ever the adapter (this will remain one of the relative constants in his career[11]), the

128   HANS W. GEISSENDÖRFER

filmmaker drew on Christ's memoirs as well as her second husband's chronicle, Peter Bendix's *Der Weg der Lena Christ (The Path of Lena Christ)*.

In contrast to the linear and transparent narratives that were to become his cinematic signature, this debut remains Geissendörfer's most formally adventurous effort, one marked by continual disjunction of image and sound (we frequently listen to Christ talk about an event from the past while we watch its importance in a later experience), constant direct citations (often in voice-over) from the two sources, as well as a story line guided not by chronology but by subjective recollection—in Geissendörfer's words, "memories as a formal possibility."[12] In its thematic approach *The Case of Lena Christ* announces a haunted cinema whose protagonists are plagued by the persistence of past in the present.

In the following apprentice years as a popular filmmaker, Geissendörfer systematically tried out the seminal genres. The vampire film *Jonathan* (1970), his first commercially distributed film, won the coveted Preis der 15 as the best debut *Spielfilm* for that year. A period piece couched in a feudal mid-nineteenth-century setting, *Jonathan* moves among three settings: a staid provincial city troubled by the nocturnal forays of vampires, the baroque castle where the blood-sucking Count and his minions feast on prisoners and hold bizarre rituals, and the ravaged countryside that lies between. Jonathan, a young member of a group dedicated to eradicating the vampires, is sent to the estate on a mission. After an excruciating journey through the devastated landscape, the emissary penetrates into the castle before being taken prisoner. The townspeople follow en masse, opening the castle's filled dungeons, and joining with the liberated prisoners to drive the Count and his followers into the sea. Ostensibly based on Bram Stoker's *Dracula*, Geissendörfer's *Grusical*—musical horror film—owes its clearest debts to several cinematic sources: F. W. Murnau's *Nosferatu* (1921), Carl Dreyer's *Vampyr* (1931), Mario Bava's *La Maschera del Demonio/ Black Sunday* (1960), Roman Polanski's *Dance of the Vampires* (1967), and Ingmar Bergman's *Hour of the Wolf* (1968). Nominally a tale of revolt, the narrative, nonetheless, is not a political parable. Geissendörfer insists that he did not intend an allegory about the student rebellion of the late sixties. Instead, he wanted to play with the genre's possibilities, "to make perfect and beautiful images, to mull over conventions, to quote, to reproduce."[13] For all its eclectic borrowings, *Jonathan* has considerable visual distinctiveness. Bizarre tableaux, elaborate rituals, private ceremonies, ornamental masses—these impeccably choreographed scenes mystify and irritate in equal measure, fascinating and frustrating the viewer with their inexorable strangeness. Robby Müller's moving camera constantly probes previously unseen spaces, teasing the spectator with its gradual and invariably inconclusive disclosures. In the opening sequence, henchmen break down a door and ransack an apartment, their every action followed by a dolly that wends its way through halls and rooms, casting its gaze on furniture and worn walls. One of the intruders asks, "Did you see that painting?" and the camera pans past a painting in another room so quickly that we see it merely for an instant—and only the bottom portion at that. Viewers never really see the "larger picture" in *Jonathan,* nor do they ever gain their bearings: tracking shots lead from one set of horrors to another, images of carnage and plunder. A gliding dolly sweeps us into interiors and forbidden spaces, through shut doors into rooms where inexplicable and unseen events transpire. Geissendörfer's use of music likewise does little to orient the viewer: quite often a tranquil or carefree sound track will blatantly run counter to onscreen violence or foreboding. From its abstract first image of a black-gloved hand with a large ruby ring rapping on a blue-toned door, the film offers a series of encroachments onto terra incognita, so much so that one can readily speak of an "intrusion principle" as the informing structure in *Jonathan.* This propensity will persist as a hallmark of Geissendörfer's personal style.

Geissendörfer's next films increasingly took leave of the rough edges, irritations, ellipsis, and formal spontaneity of *Lena Christ* and *Jonathan,* increasingly moving toward a finely toned and smooth gloss. *Eine Rose für Jane* (*A Rose for Jane,* 1970), a virtual catalogue of quotations from gangster movies compiled by Geissendörfer and Roald Koller, follows a hit man through an entire day. Much in the terse manner of Jean-Pierre Melville's *Le Samourai* (1967), the film amounts to a "meticulous, almost clinical, description of the behavior of a hired killer."[14] In its ninety minutes only 475 words are spoken, and Klaus Doldinger's score

does not fill all the many long passages without dialogue. The
director reduces the action genre to its basic—indeed, ritualistic
—essentials, using characters only as plot elements, staging everything exactly. There is little of the acute exaggeration and
campy contours present in Fassbinder's contemporaneous *Der
amerikanische Soldat (The American Soldier,* 1970). In *A Rose for
Jane* we do not "worry whether the actors themselves can keep
up the pretence."[15] Geissendörfer's highly disciplined cast (especially the expertly understated Heinz Bennent) portray characters that were—in the director's words—"all born on one screen
or another."[16] They exist only in terms of the self-referential
confines of cinematic convention and have little bearing on the
world outside the dark of movie houses.

The next exercise in a popular form, the Bavaro-Western *Carlos* (1971), based very loosely on Schiller's eighteenth-century
play *Don Carlos,* likewise "begins with the first image on the
screen and ends with the last one" (Geissendörfer).[17] Shot in
English with a relatively large budget (2.5 million marks) and an
international cast on location in the Sinai Peninsula, *Carlos* lacks
the historical specificity and high-spirited momentousness of its
classical source. Geissendörfer stripped away the intellectual
framework of Schiller's drama, honing the tragedy down to a
complex of archetypal emotions.

Set in an imaginary Latin American province in the year 1915,
the film portrays a conflict between father and son, between a
tyrannical landowner who ruthlessly oppresses impoverished
farmers and an idealistic youth who bands together with a group
of sympathizers to overthrow the despot. The rebellion comes to
naught; Carlos's shortsighted brashness leads to his violent
death in a showdown with the patriarch. Favorably compared to
the spaghetti westerns of Sergio Leone, *Carlos* demonstrates
Geissendörfer's ever-growing technical skill, evidencing for the
first time his mastery of shot-countershot, the dominant code of
traditional narrative cinema. Increasingly on his way toward becoming a classical exponent of transparent and seamless story
lines, Geissendörfer insisted that despite his film's political background, he had no ideological axe to grind, no message to shove
down the audience's throat.[18] Unlike many other young German
filmmakers who sought to subvert the medium, infusing it with

alternative forms and contents, Geissendörfer staunchly defended popular cinema's usages and appeal—much to the chagrin of numerous West German critics.

In a climate in which style was considered "something slightly suspect, a kind of undemocratic aberration,"[19] film critics in the Federal Republic saw Geissendörfer as an inventive formalist, not without entertaining virtues and creative aplomb, but in the end little more than a showman devoid of substance, a technician more interested in cameras than characters, an aesthete who addressed social problems only in the most general and disinterested way, never really personally involving himself.[20] Geissendörfer's genre films, however, do not merely amount to technical razzle-dazzle, nor do they lack "subjective expression."[21] *Marie* (1972), an atmospheric thriller, reveals much about its creator. "This is my story and I know something about it," Geissendörfer noted in an interview. "I situated it in the time when the Beatles started to become popular, when Bob Dylan's first records came out as well as those of the Rolling Stones and Van Morrison."[22] A title establishes the setting: Stuttgart 1963.

Marie quite adroitly combines Geissendörfer's dominant formal propensity, the intrusion principle, with his major thematic preoccupation: the nemesis of the past. A camera explores the shadowy hallway of a dingy apartment in the film's first shot, starting and stopping in front of half-open doors, hinting at the secrets that lie beyond these thresholds. Marie, a pouty teenager, shares the rundown flat (its walls drip with moisture, the kitchen remains eternally cluttered) with her father, who collapses and dies during a business trip. Numerous indications over the next weeks, both in the apartment where Marie remains until the end of the school year and at her mother's country home, lead the girl to believe that certain long-standing tensions between her parents might have played a role in her father's death. Her suspicions are confirmed: Marie learns that her mother's successful medical practice grew out of a forgery: she assumed the name and title of a doctor who perished in a wartime bomb raid. Fearful that her estranged husband would betray this fraud, the mother submitted to blackmail before she finally murdered him, staging things to suggest a heart attack. After listening impassively to the mother's long confession and ignoring her tearful entreaties, Marie strolls out of the shadowy apartment and its secret-filled closets, no longer a captive of her parents' guilty past.

Marie, more than any other film by Geissendörfer, reconstructs the specifics of a particular time and place. It abounds with artifacts and attitudes from the late Adenauer era: the Elvis Presley poster and Jeanne Moreau records we glimpse in Marie's room, the potted plants and kitschy landscape paintings in the principal's office, the mother's almost erotic experience listening to Rimsky-Korsakov on her new hi-fi. Paralysis and suspicion govern this world in which tranquilizers are ubiquitous. Portraits of John F. Kennedy and Konrad Adenauer stare at pupils from a classroom wall, and everyone nervously keeps close tabs on everybody else: Marie's mother and lover constantly rummage about the father's flat; a French tutor goes through Marie's room when she leaves for a moment; and Marie searches out her parents' secret, rifling through her father's belongings and spying on her mother. Marie will walk out of this past — just as decisively as Garance rides out of Deburau's life in the final scene of Marcel Carné's *Les Enfants du Paradis,* a film from which Geissendörfer quotes at length. The only Geissendörfer character to escape the past, Marie enters a more amicable present. No longer estranged from others and confined to limiting space, dressed in a long white gown, she sits in an outdoor café across the table from a boy her age and enjoys the morning sun, listening to "Them" on a jukebox. The bright refuge is surrounded by greenery (in contrast to the rubber plants in the mother's house or the stormy landscapes Marie encountered elsewhere) and graceful colonnades (unlike the stifling verticality of her father's flat). Framed in a deep focus, Marie now has room to move.

In *Die Eltern (The Parents,* 1973), a WDR production based on an original script, Geissendörfer explores familiar generic territory (the psychological thriller) while surveying new thematic terrain. Shot in just twenty-seven days, this chamber melodrama in the tradition of Alfred Hitchcock's *Rebecca* contains numerous quotations from films by directors such as Luis Buñuel—as well as from Geissendörfer's own work (a scene in the rain recalls a similar moment in *Marie,* as does a reverie in front of a stereo).[23] A movie about the power of fantasy, *The Parents* anticipates the director's more definitive variation on this theme, *Die Wildente*

(*The Wild Duck,* 1976). Anne, the ten-year-old protagonist, refuses to accept her elders' version of reality. "And she remains in
her fantasy world. And this refusal," maintains Geissendörfer,
"is the refusal of a genuine artist before society." [24] Illusions that
clash with an inexorable reality, a conflict in which a child stands
at the center: these elements inform *The Parents* and *The Wild
Duck.*

Ann, played by the fetching Anne Bennent (who would
portray Hedwig in *The Wild Duck*), will not believe that her parents have been killed in the car crash we see at the film's beginning. Taken in by her aunt and uncle, who know—as the parents
did—that the child is sole heir to her grandmother's considerable estate, Ann obstinately insists her parents are still alive. At
several points she claims to see them, but until the film's final
reel, these remain subjective events, visions shared by no one
else: the viewer does not know whether to accept her claims or
not. The foster parents constantly threaten to commit Ann to a
sanitorium, and only another uncle — the black sheep of the
family—takes her seriously. In the end, he discovers that the
parents really are alive. The whole series of mysterious appearances have been staged to drive the child insane so that the
inheritance would then go to the conspirators. The film concludes with a second car accident in which the parents do die.
But Ann remains unmoved. Trusting a fairy tale her father once
told her, she believes that if we lose a loved one, we need only
look hard enough and wish patiently to have them return. This
character creates a fictional world and exists within its self-
referential confines. Ann's resolute trust in her fantasy dupli-
cates Geissendörfer's fascination with the imaginative possibility
of narrative cinema.

Perahim—Die zweite Chance (*Perahim—The Second Chance,* 1974)
—along with *A Rose for Jane* and *The Parents*—belongs to Geissendörfer's most radically hermetic work. An adaptation of Constantin V. Gheroghiu's novel *Gangster Maximilian Perahim* (1952),
the film centers on an ex-gangster who after eleven years in
prison attempts to settle into a normal existence. Returning to
Vienna, he avoids his former cronies, wanting only to work as a
joiner (a trade he learned in jail) and raise his son. Despite his
efforts, he cannot escape his past. A police commissioner and a
prior accomplice distrust him and monitor his every move. Both

his son and an ex-lover perish, and Perahim, feeling responsible, despairs. He takes flight, a fugitive from the law, who — like Eddie in Fritz Lang's *You Only Live Once* (1937)—fights against fate only to discover he cannot win.

Perahim would seem to bear out critical claims that Geissendörfer's dominant theme is the individual at odds with society,[25] but this generalization demands closer scrutiny. It does not apply to works like *Jonathan* and *The Wild Duck,* and in any case, the "society" in the director's films is never more than a vaguely defined entity. The Vienna Perahim moves through, or the metropolis Jones (*A Rose for Jane*) inhabits, could be almost any big city. The spaces possess none of the historical resonance of Ottokar Runze's turn-of-the-century Hamburg (*Der Lord von Barmbek* [*The Lord of Barmbek*], 1973) or the atmospheric density of his present day St. Pauli (*Das Messer im Rücken* [*The Knife in the Back*], 1975); they lack the postwar ugliness and tacky garishness of Schlöndorff's contemporary Frankfurt (*Die Moral der Ruth Halbfass* [*The Morals of Ruth Halbfass*], 1971) or the Munich in Fassbinder's early gangster films. Geissendörfer—except in the cases of *Lena Christ* and *Marie*—presents social conflicts in settings stripped of their social specificity. No sociohistorical context determines his characters' action. Instead, they stand under the sway of rigid genre conventions, of an endemic fatalism that allows at best occasional variations within well-established frameworks. Eschewing the grittiness and realistic endeavors of many NGC films, Geissendörfer continued to stress the fictive character of the worlds (*Scheinrealität*) he creates.

A six-part detective series (*Lobster,* 1975) for WDR followed, a work featuring another insular hero, an offbeat private eye. Geissendörfer then resumed his systematic study of cinematic genres, turning this time to the German *Heimatfilm,* a form as familiar to domestic audiences in the Federal Republic as the western is to Americans. *Sternsteinhof* (*Sternstein Manor,* 1975) contains — thanks to Franz Brühne's consummate outdoor photography—images of windswept meadows and picturesque forests, to be sure; it lacks, however, the false lyricism, nature worship, and emotional excess of traditional *Heimatfilme,* a conservative legacy that stretches back to the teens and continues well into the sixties.[26] Like his peers Reinhard Hauff, Volker Schlöndorff, and Volker Vogeler before him, Geissendörfer infused the popular vein with a radical substance, imparting a sense of the not-so-idyllic conditions ordering life in a countryside still governed by feudal structures. Unlike his colleagues, though, who had drawn on historically documented instances of peasants driven to criminal pursuits, Geissendörfer based his film on a well-known novel, Ludwig Anzengruber's naturalistic classic *Der Sternsteinhof* (1885). Taking considerable liberty with the source's mid-nineteenth-century setting, the director moved the action ahead some fifty years in time. A survey of the rigid class boundaries that separate the peasant girl Sali (who lives in a humble hut at the bottom of a hill) and Toni, the son of a wealthy landowner and the future lord of Sternstein Manor, the film follows the ambitious girl's attempts to escape her station, showing how she manipulates, betrays, even murders, to become the mistress of the estate. Avoiding the documentary verisimilitude of films in which narrators quote from chronicles, supplying actual names, dates, and places, Geissendörfer concentrated instead on shaping impressive tableaux and galvanizing images set against the rural backdrop, hoping that the movie might make up in dramatic effectiveness what it lacked in attention to history and milieu. Seeking to appeal to a large audience both intellectually and emotionally, he stressed that although he wanted to reach "both the head and the heart," he most of all wanted to move the spectator.[27] Entertainingly presenting stories grounded in the cinema of identification, crafted with technical precision, and bound in clearly recognized formulas, Geissendörfer had learned his trade well. He moved now to more ambitious tasks, never forgetting, however, the lessons gained during this period.

The Wild Duck (1976), made during the so-called literature adaptation crisis (*Literaturverfilmungskrise*) in West Germany,[28] follows Henrik Ibsen's drama of 1884 quite carefully, so much so that several commentators chided the film for its bland fealty and lack of perspective. Geissendörfer, like many of his peers who had turned to the classical canon at a time when film subsidy boards and television officials repeatedly rejected critical and incisive projects, came under considerable public attack. He was labeled an opportunist who catered to the governing cultural politics that favored faithful reproductions of bourgeois classics, especially from the nineteenth century. Never particularly enamored of topical concerns or contemporary literature, Geissendörfer vehemently maintained that his *The Wild Duck* had its roots in his intimate relationship to the drama. More than just a technically accomplished and loyal staging, despite its unquestionable deference to Ibsen, the film sums up and brings together the major themes and stylistic traits to be found in the director's systematic study of genre cinema.

Geissendörfer first got the idea for the film after he completed *The Parents*. (He had read the play as a high-school student and had totally identified with Hedwig.) The evolution of the design relates much about the filmmaker's changing attitudes over the years: still somewhat under the influence of his political activist past (he had belonged to a socialist group during the late sixties and had planned several *engagé* films), Geissendörfer had initially wanted to depict Gregers as a positive spokesman for truth, as a sympathetic hero who demasks the false illusions and destroys the *Kleinbürger* smugness of the Ekdal family. As his project took more concrete shape and he lost touch with his progressive aspirations—like a number of disillusioned intellectuals after 1968—he assumed a more critical stance toward the ruthless honesty and the impassioned rhetoric of the student movement. In its enlightenment-at-any-cost thinking, he glimpsed a potential for intransigence, as well as a disregard for personal dreams and private utopias. As a result, in the film as eventually made, Gregers is more sinister and pathetic. A man driven by an unhappy past, Geissendörfer's Gregers seeks to exorcise his private demons vicariously through the Ekdals. Instead of bringing enlightenment, he wreaks havoc. (An early scene foreshadows this: his attempts to light a stove cause smokey havoc in the Ekdal flat.) Doctor Relling, the practical believer in the necessity of illusions, does not pose a convincing alternative to Gregers (as is the case in Ibsen): he indulges in a cynicism that undercuts his persuasiveness. Clearly, Geissendörfer shifted the emphasis to make Hjalmar the dreamer appear as a more sympathetic counter-pole, not just a stick figure representative of empty fantasizing. The family head, for all his indolence and seeming lack of ambition, wanders through the same realm of imagination traversed by Ann in *The Parents* and here inhabited by Hedwig. His pipe dream anticipates an as yet undiscovered possibility: he devotes himself to photography not just to earn a living, but to raise the medium from a mere trade to "an art and a science." In short, his "invention"—which he proudly proclaims will someday stand before "an amazed public"—looks ahead to cinema, the medium in which Geissendörfer has consistently invested his illusion-making hopes. Geissendörfer indeed retains Ibsen's central themes and focuses on the drama of sight and blindness, of brutal truths and life's lies. Nonetheless, the formal vision shaping *The Wild Duck* is that of Geissendörfer, a director who, in perfecting his trade as a genre filmmaker, had raised his craft to an art and a science—while still seeking to reach wide audiences.

Robby Müller's camera moves in a very subdued but elegant manner, always subordinated to the players (and their consummate performances) and the low-lit interiors, never autonomous as an interpreter of events. (This is unlike much of his cinematography for Wim Wenders.) Medium shots and close-ups prevail; dialogues almost invariably occur in alternating one-shots, and not in shot-reverse shot. Geissendörfer isolates characters from each other visually: the initial meeting between Gregers and Hjalmar is framed in the same set of one-shots that we see in Greger's subsequent altercation with his father, a technical effect that only heightens the distance already present in their conversations. (Geissendörfer's characters rarely touch or show physical affection.) The rhythmically spaced intrusions of messengers from the Wehrle family (the servant Pettersen, then Gregers, finally Old Wehrle), a structural device that sustains the play's action, are transformed into cinematic terms, similarly shot scenes that index the growing confusion and ultimate tragedy the Wehrles bring to Hjalmar and his loved ones.[29] Even more compellingly than in *Marie*, Geissendörfer blends the haunting past with the intrusion principle, mingling his most persistent theme with his most striking formal propensity[30]— while nevertheless remaining loyal to the textual basis.

A comparison of *Die gläserne Zelle* (*The Glass Cell*, 1977) and *Perahim*, both of which feature heroes trying to adjust to the outside world after long prison stays, indicates just how impressively Geissendörfer had progressed from a skillful compiler of gangster-movie clichés to an intensely economic stylist with a decisive formal assurance all his own. Although he based *The Glass Cell* on Patricia Highsmith's novel of the same name, Geissendörfer said: "I am making a film *based on* Highsmith, but I am making *my own* film."[31] He left out the entire first half of the novel, reducing Phillip's excruciating five years in prison for someone else's crime to a very short flashback sequence. This past never leaves him, however; it shapes his experiences as he tries to settle back into the Frankfurt everyday, to live with his wife and child in their comfortable *Westend* flat. Images of normalcy surround him, but he rages with disquiet. He views a staid present, but he cannot contain his suspicions and misgiving. Phillip, implicated by the building contractor Lasky for a crime of negligence (a collapsed school killed a number of students), is innocent when he emerges from prison, but he soon becomes a hardened criminal, murderer of his wife's interim lover and his former adversary. Wim Wenders's contemporaneous Highsmith adaptation, *Der amerikanische Freund* (*The American Friend*, 1977), shifted the interest away from Highsmith's amoral and ruthless Ripley, forcing the spectator instead to concentrate on Jonathan Zimmermann and his family, Ripley's victims in his "game." Geissendörfer on the other hand remains completely focused on Highsmith's protagonist, whose perspective governs the narrative. The camera follows his path through Manhattan-on-Main Frankfurt, tracing his frantic steps through a world that amounts to an even larger jail than the one in which he spent five years. The seamless editing reinforces audience identification: when cutting from one scene to another, Geissendörfer repeatedly starts a shot with a zoom or a moving camera, thus "sucking" the viewer into the image, swallowing the spectator up into the narrative flow.[32] *The Glass Cell* was relatively well reviewed and was awarded the 1978 West German State Prize for the best film. A year later, it was nominated for an Oscar as the best foreign film.

A director who has frequently worked for television and who believes in the accepted usages of traditional narrative cinema, a filmmaker more reliant on international models and one less concerned with contemporary issues and present-day West Germany, Hans Wilhelm Geissendörfer represents a curious example of the insider as outsider. An accessible storyteller with a direct appeal, he has never found the wide success he so fervently seeks. Someone who has readily enjoyed financial backing in the past (unlike his colleagues who so often have had to

Katja Rupé and
Peter Kern in
Sternstein Manor
(Courtesy of
Filmverlag der
Autoren)

Helmut Griem and Brigitte Fossey in *The Glass Cell* (Courtesy of Filmverlag der Autoren)

scramble for money to make films, patching together funds from numerous sources), Geissendörfer possesses the confidence of even the most conservative producers in West Germany. Nevertheless, his is a relatively low public profile in the country's film landscape, and few film enthusiasts in the Federal Republic eagerly await "the next Geissendörfer." And among his peers, the filmmakers and critics of his generation, Geissendörfer is suspected of being too accommodating, a man interested in nothing but filmmaking. Although numerous West German directors receive almost cultish devotion from American filmgoers, Geissendörfer is largely ignored. *The Glass Cell*, his most popular film in West Germany, has still not found an American distributor. Meanwhile, Geissendörfer works on, moving from one ambitious project to the next. In 1979 he completed a sweeping eight-part epic for television, a rendering of Bernard von Brentano's 1936 novel *Theodor Chindler*, an account of the fall of Wilheminian Germany shot in 121 days with four thousand extras for nearly 7 million marks. More recently, he was putting the final touches on a painstaking adaptation of Thomas Mann's *Der Zauberberg* (*The Magic Mountain*), one of the most expensive films in German history. Will *The Magic Mountain* prove to be Geissendörfer's *The Tin Drum*? Having completed his journeyman apprenticeship to genre cinema, Geissendörfer is becoming an equally skilled producer of more ambitious films that may win him the recognition in the United States he has thus far been denied.

NOTES

[1] Wolfram Schütte, "Für eine rationale Phantasie im Kino," *Frankfurter Rundschau*, 18 November 1967.

[2] For a discussion of the impetus behind the statement and subsequent historical fact, see Edgar Reitz, "Das Kino der Autoren lebt! Gegen die Verkäufer, Rezeptbäcker und Profiteure," *Medium*, May 1980, pp. 32–34.

[3] The most exhaustive documentation and reiteration of this position is to be found in Klaus Kirschner and Christian Stelzer, *Die Filme von H. W. Geissendörfer —Gespräche, Materialien* (Erlangen: Videogruppe Erlangen, 1979), especially in the closing discussion, pp. 110–25.

[4] Sheila Johnston, "The Author As Public Institution: The New' Cinema in the Federal Republic of Germany," *Screen Education*, nos. 32/33 (Winter 1979/80), p. 70.

[5]Unlike his colleagues who have in many cases formed their own production companies in order to retain total control over their films as well as to hold on to any income resulting from subsidies, recognitions, and prizes, Geissendörfer insists he is a filmmaker, not a businessman, someone who provides ideas and creativity in return for relative economic security. He recognizes that tensions are unavoidable, but sees such a dialectic between director and producer as potentially productive. Indeed one must know how to protect one's own interests; nonetheless, such encounters often enhance the quality of the final result. See his essay, "Abhängiges Arbeiten: Über Regie und Produktion," in *Jahrbuch Film* 79/80, edited by Hans Günther Pflaum (Munich: Hanser, 1979), pp. 108–13.

[6]These advocates of commercial films with flashy people and trendy thematics were particularly active during the late sixties. The most conspicuous representatives include Klaus Lemke (the only one to have enjoyed continuing success over the years), Eckhart Schmidt, Roger Fritz, and Rob Houwer. See Helmut Schmerber, "Kleine Privatrebellion: Junge deutsche Regisseure filmen ihre Generation, Zwischen Widerstand und Anpassung," *Sonntagsblatt*, 9 June 1968.

[7]Hans Günther Pflaum and Hans Helmut Prinzler, *Film in der Bundesrepublik Deutschland* (Münich: Hanser, 1979), pp. 181–83. For a complete listing of the early works, see 10 *Filme von Hans W. Geissendörfer* (Berlin: 29th International Film Festival, 1979), p. 2.

[8]This experience would be a valuable one: the candle-lit scenes in *Die Wildente* (*The Wild Duck*, 1976), Rembrandt-like tonalities within interiors, very much resulted from his work with Moorse, a director who would use this technique most definitively in his 1970 adaptation of Georg Büchner's *Lenz*. See Doris Blum, "Respekt vor Bergman—Bewunderung für den *Weissen Hai*: Vor seiner *Wildente* kam Hans W. Geissendörfer nach Frankfurt/ Ein Gespräch mit dem Filmemacher," *Frankfurt Allgemeine Zeitung*, 4 September 1976.

[9]This anecdote is related by Haffner in "Die Freiheit, Fehler zu machen: Filmarbeit mit Hans Wilhelm Geissendörfer," in Kirschner and Stelzer, *Geissendörfer*, pp. 31–34.

[10]Kirschner and Stelzer, *Geissendörfer*, p. 5.

[11]Exceptions to this are *Eine Rose für Jane* (*A Rose for Jane*, 1970), *Marie* (1972), *Die Eltern* (*The Parents*, 1973), and the *Lobster* series (1975). In all cases, though, Geissendörfer worked with collaborators.

[12]Quoted in Walter Schobert, "*Der Fall Lena Christ*," in Kirschner and Stelzer, *Geissendörfer*, p. 38.

[13]"'Ich liebe Vampire': Hans Geisendörfer [sic] über seinen ersten Kinofilm *Jonathan*," *Münchner Merkur*, 27 March 1970. Elsewhere (Kirschner and Stelzer, *Geissendörfer*, p. 46) Geissendörfer insisted on the "incredible social relevance of the horror genre," especially in reference to its brutality and violence. The director included moments in which production-line murders take place and in which a rat is ruthlessly smashed to death, scenes meant to alienate the audience. These were edited out of the copies that played in West German cinemas, much to Geissendörfer's chagrin. See Geissendörfer's letter to *Die Zeit*, 29 May 1970 (also in Kirschner and Stelzer, pp. 45–47).

¹⁴Rui Nogueira, ed., *Melville on Melville* (New York: Viking, 1971), p. 126.

¹⁵Thomas Elsaesser, "A Cinema of Vicious Circles," in *Fassbinder*, edited by Tony Rayns, 2d rev. ed. (London: BFI, 1979), p. 29.

¹⁶Quoted in W. R., "Geissendörfers TV-Debüt in Amsterdam," *Der Tagesspiegel* (Berlin), 3 August 1970.

¹⁷Quoted in Ingeborg Weber, "Melodramatischer Western," *Der Tagesspiegel* (Berlin), 25 July 1971.

¹⁸See Geissendörfer's comments in Heiko R. Blum, "Western frei nach Schiller," *Frankfurter Rundschau*, 23 November 1971.

¹⁹Jan Dawson, "*Germany in Autumn* and *Eine kleine Godard*," *Take One*, November 1973, p. 14.

²⁰See, e.g., Urs Jenny's review of *Jonathan*, "Vampire in der Tiefkühltruhe," *Süddeutsche Zeitung*, 6 July 1970.

²¹Kirschner and Stelzer, *Geissendörfer*, p. 125.

²²Ibid., p. 13.

²³For a partial catalogue of these references to other films, see Rupert Neudeck, "Krimi oder Pädagogik?" in Kirschner and Stelzer, *Geissendörfer*, pp. 74–75.

²⁴Quoted in Kirschner and Stelzer, *Geissendörfer*, p. 79.

²⁵See ibid., p. 4.

²⁶Cf. Willi Höfig, *Der deutsche Heimatfilm* 1947–1960 (Stuttgart: Enke, 1973).

²⁷Quoted in an interview with Claus Croissant in *Münchner Merkur*, 26 November 1975.

²⁸See my article "*Deutschland im Vorherbst*: Literature Adaptation in West German Film," *Kino: German Film* (West Berlin), no. 3 (Summer 1980), pp. 11–19.

²⁹Cf. H. G. Pflaum, "Mit dem Bildern von Ibsen," in Kirschner and Stelzer, *Geissendörfer*, p. 98.

³⁰Geissendörfer indulges in his intrustion principle even to intruding on the attic space that Ibsen had insisted on leaving unseen.

³¹Quoted in Hans Jürgen Weber, "Suche nach dem Gleichgewicht: Geissendörfer verfilmt einen Roman von Patricia Highsmith," *Tagesspiegel* (Berlin), 8 January 1978.

³²Kirschner and Stelzer, *Geissendörfer*, p. 114.

REINHARD HAUFF

A Cinema of Darwinism

by Klaus Phillips

THE COLORFUL CINEMATIC LANDSCAPE
of the German Federal Republic is inhabited by filmmakers
whose works some critics, rightly or wrongly, have sought to
cubbyhole into neatly surveyable units. Accordingly, one hears
of Achternbusch's zany rampages in a topsy-turvy universe,
Herzog's obsessive quests, Spils's Valentinesque Schwabing
romps, and the early Fassbinder's onanistic self-explorations.
Whatever dangers such attempts at categorization may pose,
they underscore the multifaceted nature of the films produced
in Germany during the past two decades and the vast diversity of
backgrounds, methodologies, and thematic concerns exhibited
by the people making these films. Few would mistake one of
Straub's films for one of Geissendörfer's, one of Syberberg's for
one of Wenders's; similarly, few would fail to discern the progression from the earliest to the more recent works of certain
filmmakers, the professional development that took place between Fassbinder's *Katzelmacher* and *Maria Braun,* Herzog's *Even
Dwarves Started Small,* and *Stroszek,* Wenders's *Summer in the City*
and *The American Friend.*

In the case of Reinhard Hauff the external progression is easy
to summarize. His work is divided into two distinct groups: some
twenty mostly music-oriented variety shows for television be-

tween 1966 and 1968 and, by the end of the seventies, twelve
films, all of which to a greater or lesser extent were made for or
in conjunction with television. Work retrospectives such as the
U.S./Canada tour of 1977–78 and the 1979 *Werkschau* in
Kempten tend to forego the fledgling filmmaker's earliest efforts, but even on the basis of his later work Hauff has not
succeeded totally in removing the stigma of having been
stamped primarily a television director. An intensely serious,
erudite, and personable man in the eyes of his colleagues and
friends, Hauff is best known today as a director of gritty, disturbing films whose intrinsically violent themes frequently surface in their titles: *The Revolt, Open Hatred Toward a Person or
Persons Unknown, The Brutalization of Franz Blum, Knife in the
Head.* In the words of one critic, Hauff favors "contrasts, breaks
and contradictions" and consistently directs his sympathies "towards the socially weak, the underprivileged, the outsiders
neglected by society, the victims."[1] His films are about an often
futile struggle to survive in the face of overwhelming odds. "I'm
fascinated by people who try to survive and keep their human
dignity without having a real chance," he confides, "with more
difficulty than I had in my life."[2]

Nothing in Hauff's biography suggests problems. He was
born in the university town of Marburg on May 23, 1939, into a
Protestant family active in church matters. After studying German literature, theater, and sociology in Vienna, he enrolled in
the Munich Filmhochschule, began acting in a variety of student
theaters (among them the Studiobühne, whose alumni include
Alf Brustellin and Bernhard Sinkel), and took on an assistant's
job with the huge Bavaria-Atelier film studios. What began as a
short-term opportunity for gaining on-the-job experience and
earning pocket money between semesters became a turning
point in Hauff's life. After nearly three years as production
assistant and assistant director, with prolonged on-location filming in France, England, Japan, and the United States as assistant
to the director Michael Pfleghar—including the action-filled but
forgettable *Serenade für zwei Spione* (*Serenade for Two Spies*, 1965),
which was shot with an eight-man team in Las Vegas—Hauff was
offered the chance to direct his own television production. His
work of the next two years was dominated by musical entertainment programs featuring such diverse acts as the singing duo

Reinhard Hauff (Courtesy of
Filmverlag der Autoren)

Esther and Abi Ofarim, the National Ballet of Rumania, and
The Vibrations, as well as personality shows about Ray Anthony,
Wilson Pickett, and Janis Joplin. The encounter with Joplin during her European tour proved to be another turning point in
Hauff's life. To Hauff, Joplin was the starkest representation of
the California drug and rock scene. With cameraman W. P. Hassenstein, who worked on all but one of Hauff's shows and films
from 1966 to *The Brutalization of Franz Blum* in 1974, he
sought to capture her essence as objectively as possible, concentrating on straight documentation and interview rather than the
cinematic fireworks so typical of entertainment programs. "For
me she was the best entertainer and a powerful individual,"
Hauff recalls.[3] "After her, I couldn't go on and work with other
European show business people."[4]

To a certain extent his next project, *Untermann — Obermann*
(roughly: *Man on the Bottom — Man on Top*), shot in a single day
with Volker Koch, who also collaborated on the script, still focuses on show business, but in a broader sense it functions as a
mirror of twentieth-century German history. Produced inde-

pendently for television, the forty-minute documentary illuminates the thirty-year career of acrobats Emil L., Walter W., and their friend Hans B. by recording their revelations to the filmmakers through interviews, conversations, and spontaneous statements. Their confessions add up to a story of men who survived by taking historical developments in stride, performing for the Social Democrats as well as the Nazis and the occupying powers, and ultimately anchoring their trailer in Munich, where they perform odd jobs for a television company while awaiting their pension.

During the same year, 1969, Hauff was able to realize the filming of a screenplay he had written with his friend Peter Glotz. *Die Revolte* (*The Revolt*) afforded the "show director" a chance to break the mold. His first feature film chronicles a desperate and futile flight from the quotidian boredom of a bourgeois existence: Dieter Hartenstein (Hans Brenner), a twenty-five-year-old case worker in an insurance firm, is becoming disenchanted with his job. Instead of showing up for work one morning, he drops in on his bearded buddy, Berger (Raimund Harmstorf), meets a pretty, divorced student (Katrin Schaake), finds a new flat, rents a car, and begins to attend meetings of the APO, a radical political group. Although he and Berger become APO sympathizers, neither has the ideological preparation to comprehend fully what the APO represents. They are caught up by happenstance because they frequent the same bars as these people. Hartenstein is totally unable to analyze his own situation. His new job as sales representative quickly becomes dull, and he finds that he cannot escape social conventions and norms. He steals a car in order to leave the country, but before he can carry out his plan, he shoots his girl friend in a sudden fit of hysteria and then commits suicide.

If this plot is vaguely reminiscent of another film made that year, *Why Does Herr R. Run Amok?* (a film from which Rainer Werner Fassbinder disassociated himself, placing all the credit and blame on his collaborator, Michael Fengler), the similarities in the execution of the two films are even more striking. "There was no rigidly delineated progression of events," Hauff recalls. "The individual scenes resulted spontaneously from contextual logic and from discussions among actors, cameraman Hassenstein, and myself."[5] When the actor portraying Berger first saw the room his character was to occupy, he cleared out its contents, commenting that no room of his would ever by cluttered with such junk, and promptly brought in his own furniture. Not one to consider himself a "conductor" of actors, Hauff likes to be an amplifier who allows his actors to enucleate their natural per-sonalities—an ability he greatly admires in many American ac-tors. None of Hauff's films exemplifies this working relationship more concretely than this, his very first feature.

Both *Herr R.* and *The Revolt* resemble cinéma verité, and both made use of professional as well as nonprofessional actors. The question posed by the title of the Fassbinder/Fengler film is never answered; the series of long, loosely connected tableaux provides no real clue to the ultimate triple murder and suicide. By contrast, the sum of Hauff's scenes adds up to a totality of utter hopelessness that makes the violent eruption at film's end inevitable. Hauff's film does more than ask questions; the tragedy of its hero/victim points up the deficiencies of in-stitutionalized societies. "I wanted to show people who can't find their way," Hauff says. "They spend years sitting in some office without noticing how dreary it all is. Suddenly someone comes and makes them aware of it. They then quickly perk up and quickly do everything completely wrong, because they never learned how to do it right."[6] Hartenstein's crime is the result of an overpowering situation from which there is no way out.

Ausweglos (No Way Out) is the title of another film Hauff com-pleted in 1969, a documentary in which the previous sentence assumes central significance. Collaborating with the noted writer Martin Walser, Hauff based his screenplay on a newspaper re-port about a twenty-four-year-old woman who went into an inn, shot the hostess, and then quietly let herself be arrested. The film scratches away at the circumstances surrounding the appar-ently unprovoked and inexplicable killing by interviewing peo-ple close to the case (the woman's lover, her ex-fiancé, a psychia-trist, several co-workers) without ever showing the woman herself. An outline of her situation emerges, her uncertainties and con-tradictions become graphically obvious—especially in the assessments offered by her lover and the psychiatrist. Having grown up during the war, she later spent part of her youth in the German Democratic Republic before coming to West Germany, where she was confronted with insurmountable problems regarding living and working conditions. Her biography, which so far closely parallels the "fictional" story of Anita G. in Alexander Kluge's *Yesterday Girl,* shows her changing jobs constantly, even working with death-defying stunt drivers at a carnival, before she lands employment as a waitress. Unable to cope, she makes several attempts at ending her life, finally killing her lover's wife.

The actual catalyst for the young woman's senseless act of violence is of far less importance to Hauff than the inescapable environment that he sees as shaping human thought and action. The most disconcerting aspect of Hauff's documentation is that the situation in which the woman finds herself is frighteningly commonplace in modern industrialized society. Hauff characteristically unearths his protagonist's persona without ever attempting a whitewash. Because the woman is not circumscribed in stark monochromes of absolute good or evil, the viewer has difficulty feeling total sympathy or abhorrence. Like a blotter, the woman's biography has soaked up society's defects. Ultimately, *No Way Out* indicts a social system whose authoritarian judicial apparatus emphasizes penalty rather than reform. Hauff attributes his moralist engagement to his Protestant roots: "It so happens that I'm a Protestant, and there's nothing I can do about that."[7]

Having shed the label of "show director," Reinhard Hauff was now perceived as a maker of films dealing with spectacular court cases. With the lessons learned from two documentaries and one feature film, he set out to realize a project that was to become a protest against a penal system under which 65 to 75 percent of all incarcerated juveniles eventually wind up in jail again. "The corrupted youth does not threaten society, society itself threatens youth with corruption," insists an intertitle in *Offener Haß gegen Unbekannt (Open Hatred Against a Person or Persons Unknown,* 1970). The script, written by Philippe Pilliod, Georg Feil, and Hauff, is based on the notes of Heine Schoof, a man jailed in 1967 for attempted manslaughter. Following a violent argument, Schoof had repeatedly stabbed his girl friend, leaving her a quadriplegic. Hauff's film, featuring a cast of nonprofessionals, is a collage of perturbing images gleaned from interviews with juvenile ex-cons, psychologists, and prison wardens, as well as Schoof's own thoughts—a fragmented and fragmentary reconstruction of the circumstances and situations that had a bearing on Schoof's criminal outburst. Through the use of flashbacks and the continual superimposition of Schoof's written statements, relevant passages from Goethe and Wilhelm Reich, statistical formulations, and the screenplay authors' own commentaries on the sound track—occasionally resulting in a near-aestheticized disharmony of picture and sound—*Open Hatred* highlights junctures in Schoof's past that chart the course toward prison: orphanage, mental institution, a home for wayward boys. The blame falls squarely on institutions which, instead of offering therapy and understanding, demand conformity and hypocritical penitence as Hauff presents shots of drudging prisoners, boys graphically recounting instances of subhuman conditions in the reformatories, and nuns callously beating their charges.

Open Hatred, perhaps Hauff's angriest film, was criticized for being unduly biased, overly negativistic and one-sided, and completely ignoring the positive and hopeful impulses emanating from principles of autodidactic behavior and a humanisitic spirit.[8] The film ends on a note of anarchic desperation: a penitentiary is blown to bits.

Halfway through Hauff's next film, angry peasants torch an old mill; near the film's end, police armed with rifles and explosives almost level a farmhouse in their effort to seize the outlaw hiding within. *Mathias Kneissl,* set around the turn of the century, is the first of Hauff's two "historical" films. The year of its completion, 1971, witnessed the release of three other German films that sought to subvert the traditional concept of the *Heimatfilm* (a popular genre in the fifties, typically mixing melodrama, music, and sentimental soap opera set in a pastoral environment untouched by the ravages of war:[9] Volker Vogeler's *Jaider—der einsame Jäger (Jaider—the Lonely Hunter),* Uwe Brandner's *Ich liebe dich, ich töte dich (I Love You, I Kill You),* and Volker Schlöndorff's *Der plötzliche Reichtum der armen Leute von Kombach (The Sudden Wealth of the Poor People of Kombach).* All four films provide a less paradisiacal picture of life and love in the provinces. Although there was no "conspiracy" by the four directors to make these films at this particular time, there are numerous parallels, especially between the two films by Schlöndorff and Hauff. Both are based on factual events from the nineteenth century: Schlöndorff's screenplay, written with Mar-

garethe von Trotta, is derived from an actual chronicle; Hauff
wrote his script with Martin Sperr, a Bavarian playwright (his
Hunting Scenes from Lower Bavaria served as the source for Peter
Fleischmann's 1969 film) who, in turn, drew on documentation
and popular lore. Characters in both films look toward America
as the proverbial land of milk and honey, a country of unlimited
opportunities. Hauff plays one of the poor peasants, a major
role, in Schlöndorff's film; Schlöndorff does a brief cameo as
a railway officer in Hauff's film. The ubiquitous Rainer Werner
Fassbinder, wildly overacting, appears as a sneaky farmer in
both.[10]

Mathias Kneissl, the first of Hauff's films to be shown in theaters and entered at festivals in Cannes and Moscow, begins
harmlessly enough: Hassenstein's camera, in a long take, records
a group of peasants at a rural train station, as they bid farewell to
one of their own, who is heading for America. The overall mood
is lively and cordial, with just a tinge of sadness. The harmonious
scene is marred by the arrival of a coach on the platform, forcing
the camera to track backward and largely obscuring the peasant
farewell while a nobleman emerges from the coach and boards
the train. Soon thereafter, during a protracted portrait shot, the
viewer has time to study the faces of the Kneissl clan: the parents; their children, Alois, Mathias, and Kati; Hans Patsch, a
friend of the family who is interested in Kati; and an elderly man
who does not reappear for the remainder of the film. Their
resolute expressions show a trace of mistrust, except for Kati
(Eva Mattes), who has considerable trouble keeping a straight
face.

The Kneissls, maternally linked to Johann Baptist Pascolini,
a "notorious robber" who was shot to death in the course of a
burglary in 1871, are ostracized as "foreigners." Holed up in a dilapidated country mill somewhere between Augsburg and
Munich, they eke out their miserable existence through occasional carpentry jobs and poaching. One day the mother is jailed
for stealing a monstrance from a shop. The father is hunted
down by a posse and beaten to death in front of his children.
Because of Kati's absence from school, the police often come to
the mill, and in one scene Kati's brothers are arrested when they
try to protect their sister from sexual harassment. The imprisoned Alois dies of consumption. Kati and her mother work as

housekeepers for a sleazy shopowner, who is not above demanding sexual favors from Kati during her mother's absence. When Mathias (Hans Brenner) is released from prison after five years —the sentence, one surmises, was so severe because of earlier offenses, including attendance at a public dance and absence from school—he briefly finds employment as a carpenter, but is fired because his boss fears public retaliation against his business for hiring an ex-con. Homeless after an irate peasant mob sets the mill ablaze and unable to survive within society's suffocative restrictions, Mathias has no recourse but to steal, burgle, and poach. Set up by a farmer to whom he wants to sell mortgage papers stolen during a bungled burglary with Hans Patsch, he shoots down two policemen. Always one step ahead of the authorities, he is alternately harbored by the woman he loves (Hanna Schygulla) and, in exchange for sexual services, by a farmer's wife. Among the many who, like Kneissl, are affected by authoritarian oppression, he soon assumes the dimensions of a popular hero. The warped, romanticized public perception is revealed most strikingly when Kneissl happens upon the shepherd Meier (Martin Sperr) in a field: "I expected you to be better looking," the shepherd confides; "but I hear that women go for you because you always eat celery. Now I've started eating celery too." Despite the growing, well-meant support of many, Kneissl finally is cornered in the attic of a farmhouse. Badly injured, he is rushed to a Munich clinic, where expert doctors restore him to health, so that he can be tried, convicted, sentenced to death, and executed.

Mathias Kneissl is a raw film, a compilation of sixty scenes, in which dialogue (almost entirely Bavarian dialect) is subordinate to visual impact. Kneissl is a parabolic figure whose fate is reminiscent of similar men in other societies—for example, Jesse James—and is not restricted to centuries past, as is illustrated by hostility toward foreign migrant laborers in contemporary Germany. Like Berthold Hoffmann in *Knife in the Head,* Mathias Kneissl is exploited by those around him. For the timid or lethargic oppressed, he becomes an admirable daredevil, a hero. To the authorities he is a rebel, a political tool used to divert attention from other, greater problems. The liberal journalist sees in him an opportunity to expose provincial resentment to his metropolitan readers, but he encounters only mute stares and total inability to communicate among the farmhands he hopes to interview. In the end, *Mathias Kneissl* is a film about an unsuccessful struggle to realize a collective dream, documenting, in the words of Philippe Pilliod, the film's producer, "that heroes and robbers do not grow on trees . . . that they are the products of social conditions, the proletarian rebellion against oppression, a rebellion which, like so many, is turned by the ruling class into the very opposite. A dream of freedom that is perpetuated as a dream and does not become reality."[11]

Pilliod coauthored the screenplay for the next film, *Haus am Meer (House by the Sea* 1972*)*, with Hauff—not a totally successful venture, according to the filmmaker himself, and the only one of Hauff's films to focus on a woman as the central character. "I simply know more interesting men than women," Hauff explains.[12]

At the heart of the story once again is the desire to get away, the dream of starting life anew: the young waitress Hanna (Hanna Schygulla, in her third film with Hauff), having accumulated 15,000 marks from savings and a lottery win, wants to realize her dream of owning a house on some sunny southern island. She makes a careless deal with a realtor and breaks all ties to her homeland. Arriving on the island, she discovers the house, which she had purchased sight unseen, to be a rundown shack, impossible to turn into a small boarding house, as she had planned, without investing substantial capital. But Hanna does not give up. An old friend, a former musician down on his luck, assists her in getting the project started. She falls in love with Antonio, a young Italian, who is eventually shown to have more interest in her money than in her. In a desperate effort to finance the renovation, she becomes the lover of a very wealthy older man, realizing too late that she has sacrificed all her personal values for a vague utopian ideal. The renovation of the property becomes inversely proportionate to her personal degeneration. Hanna has failed to accomplish her primary goal: to become an independent and "free" woman.

House by the Sea, shot in five weeks on a remote Yugoslav island, with two German actors, one Italian, and a cast of some three hundred islanders, reaffirms a central motif from Hauff's earlier work, despite a veneer that makes this film seem totally different: someone seizes an opportunity and does everything

Hans Brenner is *Mathias Kneissl* (COURTESY OF BAVARIA-ATELIER)

completely wrong. Because Hanna dares to take the first step, to break away from her familiar surroundings, Hauff does not see her in a negative light. Her mistake is to think that money could buy happiness. Victimized by colorful ads and commercials that promise true peace of mind in some exotic island paradise, Hanna ultimately no longer acts, but merely reacts.

"Reaction" is a key term in Hauff's last film for the Bavaria-Atelier. Set in a North German metropolis, a Hamburg whose seamier side Hassenstein's camera captures in shots of trashcans, alleys, decrepit tenements, and a menacing maze of tunnels and lights, *Desaster (Disaster,* 1972–73) tells the story of two men whose chance encounter changes their lives forever: Alf Harden, whose efforts to integrate himself into socially acceptable norms have failed, holds up a bank. When a young, very pregnant woman becomes hysterical and faints, he impulsively forgets about bagging his loot and runs to her aid. Responding to the bank's alarm system, Urs Werther, a police officer, arrives and sees a woman in need of attention. He and Harden carry her outside and, before the stunned bank employees have time to react, Harden disappears into the crowd. Faced with a troubled home life and berated by the chief of police, who considers his behavior at the bank unprofessional, Werther finds himself without a wife and a job. When Alf Harden arranges a meeting with the former policeman, Werther, as though compelled to right his earlier "wrong," shoots him. Suddenly comprehending that a common bond unites the two men, Werther takes the badly wounded Harden to a doctor. Together they seek refuge in the country, but their stay is short lived. Disillusioned and penniless, they return to the metropolis, where they kidnap the wife of a bank director. Their scheme ends in tragedy because the bank director does not react to their ransom demand in the expected fashion: he would rather sacrifice his wife than pay the money. Alf Harden is killed. Urs Werther and the forsaken woman head toward an uncertain future, both victims of a misplaced faith in humanity, losers in a world where fundamental values and relationships are betrayed by hypocrisy and corruption.

Despite its intriguing premise and a strong cast, which includes Dieter Laser, Klaus Löwitsch, Eva Mattes, and Margarethe von Trotta, *Disaster* is an oddly unsatisfying film, at times straining credibility. Its disastrous conclusion seems to be that people in a big city can only hope to survive as long as they maintain a mechanized anonymity, and that they are doomed as soon as they fail to "go by the book."

After *Disaster,* Hauff broke his long-standing affiliation with the Bavaria-Atelier, and with Volker Schlöndorff founded Bioskop, a production company headquartered in a smallish Schwabing flat. Since 1974 it has produced or coproduced all their films, those of their spouses, Christel Buschmann and Margarethe von Trotta, and Herbert Achternbusch's first venture. Hauff's first Bioskop production, *Die Verrohung des Franz Blum (The Brutalization of Franz Blum* 1973–74*),* is the last film he did with W. P. Hassenstein behind the camera, the first to enjoy distribution in the United States, and the first in collaboration with Burkhard Driest. A controversial figure, Driest had inexplicably robbed a bank in 1965, only days before he was scheduled to take his law exams, was sentenced to five years in jail, and has received a great deal of bad press since, including a Los Angeles rape charge in 1980, of which he was acquitted. Driest's heavily autobiographical book, which became the basis

Jürgen Prochnow and Burkhard Driest in *The Brutalization of Franz Blum*
(COURTESY OF FILMVERLAG DER AUTOREN)

for the film, was brought to Hauff's attention by film critic
Wolfgang Limmer.

The resulting film is a smoldering study of the atavistic struggle to survive through power: Franz Blum (Jürgen Prochnow,
best known to American audiences for his role as the captain in
Das Boot, 1981), a young insurance-company employee from a
good home, is convicted of bank robbery and sent to prison,
where the warden admonishes him, "You must realize that
you've done wrong; we can't see inside you." He quickly finds
himself in a claustrophobic nightmare world in which ethics and
scruples are tantamount to self-destruction. The intial lessons
are hard: one ear against the lower part of his cell door, curious
about the nature of strange, pigeonlike noises outside, Blum
cries out in pain when Zigzag (Tilo Prückner), the inmate who
made the sounds, gives the door a vehement kick. Another inmate, Bielich, who is a sickly intellectual suffering from a heart
condition, slips Blum some pills to ease his headache. Later in

the prison yard, Bielich, suffering a spell, is knocked to the ground by Kuul (Burkhard Driest), a bully who is the uncontested leader of the prisoners. Having fashioned from a cake of soap a pistol that he covers with shoe polish, Bielich later demands to be taken to the warden, whom he tries to convince of his need for medical attention; he is quickly overpowered.

After Blum files a written report about the attack on Bielich with the prison authorities, who want a pretext for transferring Kuul to another wing, he is lured into a room in which Kuul, celebrating the fifth aniversary of his homosexual relationship with an inmate known as Marie, forces Blum to perform fellatio on him. Blum retaliates with his teeth and is nearly beaten to death. Back in his cell, Blum slashes his wrist.

The film's first half hour delineates Blum's denaturalization, the process of innocence being lost. Hassenstein's customary perspective, his camera cooly observing its subjects at eye level from a distance of a few feet, occasionally is allowed more flexibility: we watch Blum's agonized migraine tantrums through an overhead shot, a vantage point which underscores Blum's caged isolation. When the battered Blum lies in the upper bunk in his cell, the camera closes in on his hand fingering a razor blade from beneath the mattress, stays on the blade as Blum's hand slowly brings it toward his wrist, and comes to rest in a close-up of Blum's clenched jaws as the blade rips through his flesh.

After his attempted suicide Blum is a new person. When an inmate shuts off Blum's water in the shower, he reacts with his fists. Learning that strength attracts followers, Blum gradually muscles his way to the top of the prison hierarchy, a brutal system of slavery and exploitation, in which the powerful provide protection and goods (drugs, coffee, tobacco) to the weak in exchange for services, labor, and loyalty. Where Kuul and others had run the racket instinctively, the cerebral Blum perfects it, blackmailing guards and prompting one of his "business competitors" to remark, "He's even worse than we are." Blum's operation is suddenly jeopardized by Kuul's unexpected return. While the opening sequence of Werner Herzog's *Aguirre* is being televised in the prisoners' recreation room, Blum provokes Kuul, groggy from cottage cheese that Blum had laced with a tranquilizer and beats him in front of the other inmates. Elected head of the prisoners' sports club — an attempt by prison authorities to "let the inmates have a greater say in their own affairs"—Blum institutes a perfidious set of penal rules. Bielich, the embittered intellectual whose support and understanding Blum had sought to cultivate, turns against him, condemning his ruthless authoritarianism. When during a sports session Bielich attempts to convince the others that they are allowing themselves to be used, the angry inmates force him to run with them, pulling and pushing him along the track until his heart fails. Blum is released early because of good conduct. "We can see that you've become a new man," a prison official tells him. "Keep it up!"

The brutalization illuminated in Hauff's film becomes a process of disillusionment for Blum as well as the viewer. The prison life Driest reconstructs is not populated by lookalikes of James Cagney, Edward G. Robinson, or George Raft; it is a place in which people survive by victimizing those weaker than themselves, by trying to adapt to a closed environment where, in the words of one reviewer, "The structure of a society that has initiated this form of punishment manifests itself almost physically."[13] Hauff's film is not an impassioned plea for prison reform. Instead, it exposes how individuals isolated from the corrupt and corrupting rules of a "free" society have no recourse but to embrace those very same rules, corrupting them further and, as a result, being further corrupted by them.

Shot on location at the Fuhlsbüttel penitentiary near Hamburg and the Lührsbockeler Moor, where Driest had served time, *The Brutalization of Franz Blum* is basically a semidocumentary parable of metamorphosis that demands continuous adjustments and readjustments of the viewer's identification with the characters. As Blum sheds his innocence, our sympathy slowly shifts away from him, although (or because) we are aware of his motives. During the last part of the film we may actually begin to feel sorry for "Tiger" Kuul, who, framed by Blum and his followers, has been locked away in solitary confinement. Ultimately we are left with an alienating numbness, a claustrophobic sensation of being imprisoned ourselves. That's exactly how prison is, we conclude numbly.

After *Franz Blum*, a film that reoriented public perception of prison life and that one American reviewer has called "the most tough-minded, compelling, straight look at prison life that I have ever seen,"[14] Hauff again sought to correct popular misconception and misinformation, this time by trying to show that German resistance during the Third Reich was not confined to the isolated actions of a few aristocrats and conservatives, but that there were substantial antifascist sentiments among socialist and communist workers and their families. When the Westdeutsche Rundfunk (WDR) offered Hauff the chance to make a television film based on Franz Josef Degenhardt's semiautobiographical novel, *Zündschnüre (Fuses)*, he studied the material and asked Burkhard Driest to write the screenplay. Shooting on a condemned Westphalian mining estate that was subsequently demolished, Hauff used children from local working-class homes in the leading roles. (The detrimental effects of temporarily tearing them from their accustomed environment[15] was to become the focal point of *Der Hauptdarsteller* [*The Main Actor*] four years later.)

Fuses shows three boys (Fänä, Viehmann, Zünder) and one girl (Sugga), all children from workers' families, constructing their own microcosmic world during the last year of the war. Their activities, a blend of adventuresome game-playing and earnest participation in efforts at organized resistance, are revealed in the episodic fashion of Degenhardt's novel. They assist in the distribution of pamphlets, transmit secret messages from prisoners, slip calls for desertion into packages destined for the front and hide a young Jewish woman and a downed English bomber pilot in their secret headquarters, a den in the woods. The children's world also includes Grandma Niehus, an erudite socialist confined to a wheelchair, for whose wedding feast they appropriate food and wine.

The astonishing verisimilitude of these scenes, filmed in black and white by Frank Brühne's camera and heightened by a conscious and frequent employment of political songs (as in the memorable scene where the tipsy grandfather begins to sing an antifascist tune at the open window), results in a film that uncharacteristically imparts a very real sense of hope and joy as it shows ordinary people successfully preserving their personal dignity through solidarity in a time of oppression. The final minutes of the film qualify the optimism somewhat: after the workers prevent an SS unit from blowing up their factory and the war is over, little Fänä asks, "Is it our factory now?" Her naive question forces the engaged viewer to come to terms with the accomplishments of the years following Germany's capitulation.

Fuses circumvents most of the improbabilities and obscure images in Degenhardt's original text. Fond of quoting Roberto Rossellini's famous line, "One shouldn't separate what reality unites," Hauff is indebted to the Italian neorealist cinema and frequently cites Rossellini's *Roma, Città Aperta (Rome, Open City,* 1945*)*, whose theme closely parallels that of *Fuses,* as one of his favorite films. Unfortunately, because it was the sole producer, the WDR has refused to make the film available for commercial theatrical release.

The cinematic formulation of the struggle against oppression in a near perfect fusion of fictive construction and real situations is achieved in *Paule Pauländer* (1975), a gritty film about a tragic father-son relationship set against the backdrop of atrophying village life in Northern Germany. Working from another script by Driest, which is based on childhood recollections of a fellow prisoner, Hauff cast the leading roles and many smaller parts with laymen, including a boy (Manfred Reiss) and his father (Manfred Gnoth) whose economic and psychological problems corresponded to those delineated in the script.

A long, static establishing shot of a marching band initially suggests a traditional *Heimatfilm* of the fifties: at the village *Schützenfest* (traditional shooting contest) Heinrich, the elder son in the Pauländer household, is crowned champion. The festive images are intercut with scenes of his fifteen-year-old brother Paule and his parents, and the arrival of Elfi, a pretty seventeen-year-old on probation from a city reform school, who finds work at a local service station. When the intoxicated *Schützenfest* participants discover that their newly crowned king cannot pay for the ensuing celebration, as is the custom, they throw him onto a dung heap and shave off half his mustache, whereupon the disgraced Heinrich decides to leave his father's farm.

Paule becomes more emphatically subject to the ruthless tyranny of his father, who is desperately struggling to defend the family farm against the giant industrial concern Zecher. Elfi, resisting the advances of the male villagers, turns to the shy boy for company. For the first time in his life Paule has fun, but his efforts to impress the girl result in repulsively grotesque behavior: in a cemetery, he kills a rabbit by beating its head against a gravestone; while Elfi watches, he defecates on the rectory steps, covers the pile with papers, and sets fire to it. After they steal a tractor engine from the service station, Elfi hides at the Pauländer farm, whose loss old Pauländer has managed to forestall by signing a contract with Zecher for the fattening of two hundred piglets. Sickened by the slaughter of a pig, Elfi quickly realizes that she has to get away. Paule, fearful of losing her, takes her to the fair, where he wins two hundred marks by beating a much stronger opponent in a boxing match. But it is too late; Elfi leaves in a flashy American car with a fellow who promises her work in a city boutique.

Bewildered and disillusioned, Paule joins up with Charly, a dreamer living in a Wild West fantasy world, and spends all his prize money on liquor. Returning home the next morning, Paule finds the farm barricaded and the house locked. In the stalls he comes upon his hysterical mother, his father armed with a shotgun, and heaps of dying pigs. An epidemic has broken out; the farm is lost. Half crazy, the old Pauländer begins to strike his son, but this time Paule hits back and continues hitting until his father collapses on a mound of bleeding, half-dead pigs. The film ends with Paule leaving the farm.

Paule Pauländer's portrayal of adolescence is often compared to Louis Malle's *Lacomb Lucien* and Peter Bogdanovich's *The Last Picture Show,* but the haunting images of Hauff's film defy comparison because of their almost grotesque authenticity: the heaps of bleeding pigs are real; the rabbit, whose head explodes against the gravestone, is real; the chicken Paule decapitates is real; Elfi's vomiting at the sight of the piglet's slaughter is real. Ultimately, the reality of the film was to be eclipsed by the reality of life. Manfred Reiss, the young boy who portrayed Paule, found it difficult to accept his desolate life after the film crew had left: "First they show up and everything's great, and you'd want things to stay that way forever, and then they just simply take off again," he said.[16] Running away from home, Paule showed up outside Hauff's Munich apartment one day in hopes of receiving the support and attention he had come to expect from the man who opened his eyes during the shooting of the film. Hauff found himself unable and unwilling to make such a commitment.

With his wife, Christel Buschmann, Hauff turned this intensely personal experience into the screenplay for his next project, *Der Hauptdarsteller* (*The Main Actor*, 1978), a film which, according to Hauff, "shows how two people, who want to come into contact but cannot, come to terms with each other; an experience shared by many of us: parents and children, teachers and students, the old and the young, the educated and the illiterate, those who never speak up and those who are accustomed to expressing themselves."[17] *The Main Actor* starts on the last day of shooting a film called "Pepe's Life" (the German pronunciation of "Pepe" recalls the initials of "Paule Pauländer"). Temporarily sheltered from the tyrannical aggression of his father (Mario Adorf), fifteen-year-old Pepe (Michael Schweiger), the main actor, begins to idealize Max, the director (Vadim Glowna). When the film people depart, Pepe follows them to an inn, where the filmmakers celebrate the successful completion of their shooting schedule. In his desperate effort to attract the director's attention Pepe starts a fire outside the inn. Max, genuinely concerned about the boy, attempts to intercede with Pepe's father, but the physical and mental abuse becomes more and more insufferable. The pubescent boy's "sex education," for example, is presented in a particularly repugnant scene: the father drags Pepe to a slovenly old prostitute and shoves his head in between her legs. Before long Pepe shows up at the director's home, but Max cannot integrate the boy's demands into his own sphere. Gradually Pepe's admiration for the director turns into hatred and open antagonism, as he realizes that Max is far more committed to the film of Pepe's life than to the reality of that life. He assaults Max, terrorizes him, damages his property, reacts with all the brutality he suffers from his father. During the premiere showing of Max's film, Pepe sets fire to the theater in a final act of senseless violence, a violence directed as much toward himself as toward the filmmaker.

The open ending of *The Main Actor* may suggest various scenarios for Pepe's future: Does he become a full-fledged criminal? Does he return to Max? To his father? Manfred Reiss, the real Paule Pauländer, became a juvenile delinquent and landed in a reform school.

"For many years I have been fascinated by working with young people, since they challenge me on a level that still exists, the level of wishes, hopes, and utopias," Hauff confides; "and again and again I have utilized their experiences. In doing so, I often took on a responsibility which I was unable to assess."[18] Other German filmmakers who work with children and laymen have had to shoulder this responsibility (among them Hark Bohm, Werner Herzog, and Vadim Glowna, whose first directorial effort, *Desperado City,* released in 1981, is about a girl who tries to get away from her surroundings), but none has articulated this responsibility as honestly and convincingly as Reinhard Hauff did in *The Main Actor.*

Asked by an interviewer why he, who has acted in films by Volker Schlöndorff, Peter Lilienthal, Werner Herzog, and Herbert Achternbusch, did not himself portray the director in *The Main Actor,* Hauff responded, "I can't act and direct at the same time."[19] A more compelling reason for Hauff's refusal, one suspects, was the decision to keep a certain emotional distance from the real events on which the film is based. (It was presumably for similar considerations that Burkhard Driest had played the role of "Tiger" Kuul rather than Franz Blum, whose character ostensibly corresponds more closely to his own.) More than a depiction of an isolated personal problem, *The Main Actor* is a metaphorical illumination of the risks and hazards inherent in the making of a film like *Paule Pauländer.*

If *The Main Actor* was the outgrowth of a personal conflict experienced by the filmmaker, Hauff's next film was a response to the ugly climate of terrorist "witch hunts" prevalent in the Federal Republic after the frightening events of autumn 1977, an issue addressed by Rainer Werner Fassbinder, Alexander Kluge, Volker Schlöndorff, and other filmmakers in the collective venture *Germany in Autumn.* Among German films dealing with terrorism, *Messer im Kopf (Knife in the Head,* 1978) is somewhat of an anomaly. *Germany in Autumn* and Schlöndorff's filmic adaptation of Heinrich Böll's novel *The Lost Honor of Katharina Blum* were films rooted in well-known events; Peter Schneider's script was inspired by a friend's near fatal automobile accident that forced him to rebuild his identity from scratch.

The opening sequence of Hauff's film shows us Dr. Berthold Hoffman (a distinguished biogeneticist, we later learn) in his laboratory at the Traut-Institut late at night; he is deeply disturbed by something and on the verge of suicide. "An American in my situation would simply shoot out a window," he mutters to

himself. Hurrying through the neon-lit streets of the anonymous city (Munich), he finds himself in the midst of a police raid
on a radical youth center, where, we discover, his estranged wife
and her lover are working. He rushes into the dilapidated building, a shot rings out, a cryptic freeze-frame brings the action to
an abrupt stop, and the credits begin.

Shot in the head by a young policeman, Hoffmann is taken to
a hospital, where an operation saves his life; but the bullet,
lodged in his brain, has caused partial paralysis, temporary amnesia, and impairment of his motor-speech center. When
Hoffmann comes out of his coma, he has to reassemble his shattered identity and relearn everything from zero: how to eat,
walk, talk, hear, see, feel, think. His wife, Ann, her lover, Volker,
and other radicals try to make Hoffmann a martyr to their
cause, an innocent bystander gunned down by a trigger-happy
policeman. The police and much of the press, on the other
hand, convinced that Hoffmann had brandished a knife and
that the shot was fired in self-defense, paint him as a dangerous
terrorist. Both sides seek to manipulate him for their own purposes, but the scientist, slowly convalescing and under constant
police observation, turns the precept "Truth must be proven"
into an effective weapon against them, as he sets out to recon-
struct that one night. He escapes from the hospital and goes to
the Traut-Institut, but finds no clues there. Ann picks him up
and takes him to the country cottage of Anleitner, his friend and
both his and the radicals' lawyer Persuaded by Anleitner,
Hoffmann decides to return to the hospital voluntarily just before the police surround the home. Soon after, Hoffmann is
released; the police have lost interest in him. Finally free to
"remove the knife from his head," to determine whether he
really held a knife during the raid, he tracks down Schurig, the
young policeman he supposedly stabbed. In Schurig's apartment
Hoffmann forces him to reenact the events of that fateful night,
reversing their respective roles, and learns that he had picked up
one of the tools scattered about on the floor. Schurig has the
faint scar of a superficial scratch on his stomach. The film ends
abruptly as Hoffmann aims the pistol at the policeman's head.

Knife in the Head has become Hauff's most commercially successful film thus far. More than 150,000 people saw it in the first
six weeks in Germany, and it is Hauff's best-known film in the

United States. "Hoffmann—terrorist, harmless citizen, or simply crazy?"[20] the advertising poster's slogan asks provocatively, but the film hardly seems to provide a conclusive answer to the question. Among the largely enthusiastic critical reviews, a few— and it is perhaps significant that they were in the German press —saw the film as a sheep in wolf's clothing, a work guaranteed not to offend anyone. They attacked what they perceived as *Ausgewogenheit* (a currently fashionable term for a calculated attempt to avoid taking sides) and berate the "absurd" open ending.[21]

Hauff does not consider the ending to be open at all: "If the viewers haven't become engaged by then and don't accept a few of the film's premises, they probably won't know what to do with the ending. Whoever followed the premises of the film will be in a position to 'go on filming' for himself after this abrupt ending and to reflect."[22] Hoffmann first has to lose his identity so that he can reestablish his real self. A likable idiot savant after his injury, reminiscent of Herzog's Kaspar Hauser, he instinctively goes after the truth. He is a concrete example of a condition everyone desires, although not under such circumstances. What Hauff demands from his viewers is essentially what is demanded of this film's protagonist: Learn again how to see, hear, speak, and think, before you take a stand!

What most distinguishes *Knife in the Head* from *Katharina Blum, Germany in Autumn,* and other films with a similar theme, is that Hauff consciously avoids a dogmatically didactic treatise on a controversial topic; instead, he spellbinds his audience by emphasizing the traditional cinematic entertainment potential of suspense and humor. Aiming at the intellect as well as the funny bone, Hauff's film contains a number of scenes that are nothing short of hilarious: when the hospital staff ask Hoffmann to identify images on pictures held before him, he immediately points to the one showing a glass of beer and comments excitedly, "A beer!" Seconds later, he dismisses the sight of a hamburger with a spontaneous exclamation of disgust. In what by now may be the film's most famous sequence, the invalid Hoffmann, harassed by the police inspector, exposes his genitals and begins to masturbate, successfully driving the bewildered policeman from his hospital room.

Because such audience-pleasing ingredients surface liberally,

Hauff with Angela Winkler and Bruno Ganz during the filming of *Knife in the Head* (COURTESY OF FILMVERLAG DER AUTOREN)

Hauff's film may be interpreted as a reaction against political films that take themselves too seriously and do little more than bore or alienate their audience. *Knife in the Head* has the desired impact because its cinematic trappings never detract from the substance of its intrinsically sobering theme. Much of the credit goes to Bruno Ganz (*The American Friend, Nosferatu*), who delivers an extraordinary performance as Hoffmann, and to a strong supporting cast that includes Angela Winkler (*Katharina Blum, The Tin Drum*) as Hoffmann's estranged wife, Hans Brenner (*Mathias Kneissl*) as Police Inspector Scholz, and the veteran character actor Hans Christian Blech as attorney Anleitner.

Although *Knife in the Head* grossed more than 2 million marks at the box office, garnered critical accolades, and received numerous awards (including the Prix de la Critique Internationale and the Prix de l'Antenne d'Or at the Paris Film Festival), Hauff had difficulty financing his next film, *Endstation Freiheit* (*Slow Attack*), a quasi-sequel to *Franz Blum* based on a screenplay by Burkhard Driest, who also plays one of the leading roles. After numerous obstacles and delays, *Slow Attack* finally was ready for release in late 1980.

With the exception of *Knife in the Head* and *The Brutalization of Franz Blum* and despite Hauff's tour of major American and Canadian cities in 1977, his films, unfortunately, are not well known here. Intent on comparisons with the "known quantities" in the New German Cinema, American reviewers have offered the conflicting theories that "Hauff is closer perhaps to Schlöndorff than to Fassbinder, Herzog or Wenders"[23] and "Hauff's temperament is clearly closer to [Herzog's and Fassbinder's] than to, say, the more humanistic Schlondörff's."[24]

Compared to many of his better known colleagues, Hauff makes films at a snail's pace—roughly at the rate of one film per year. He emphatically rejects the notion that the director should ultimately be given all the credit for a film's success, views himself as totally dependent on his cameraman, editor, writer, and actors, and considers it his working philosophy to obtain optimum results in close cooperation with cast and crew. An admirer of Francesco Rosi, Roberto Rossellini, John Cassavetes, Martin Scorsese, and the American *films noirs*, Hauff appeals to the exploited, the oppressed, the outsider in all of us. His is a cinema of Darwinism, of individuals struggling to escape from society's labyrinthine dead ends. The films of Reinhard Hauff go on long after they have finished.

NOTES

[1]Klaus Eder in "Reinhard Hauff and His Films: A Program Presented by Goethe Institut, Munich, Films Department," n.p., n.d., p. 12.

[2]Quoted in Judy Stone, "Reinhard Hauff: 'Some Call Me a Moralist,'" *San Francisco Examiner*, 15 January 1978.

[3]Quoted in Lothar Köster and Günter Drechsel, "Interview mit Reinhard Hauff am 15. 12. 1978," in *Reinhard Hauff und seine Filme* (Kempten: Filmklub "e69," 1979), p. 63.

[4]Quoted in Judy Stone, "Hauff."

[5]Quoted in *Reinhard Hauff und seine Filme*, p. 7 (originally quoted in *Abend Zeitung*, 21 October 1969).

[6] Quoted in *Reinhard Hauff und seine Filme*, p. 6.

[7] Quoted in Thomas Timm and Christoph Meier-Siem, "Reinhard Hauff: Ein Protestant in der Unterwelt," *Kino: Magazin für Film und Kultur*, no. 4 (September 1980), p. 33.

[8] *Reinhard Hauff und seine Filme*, p. 9.

[9] To give but two indications of the astonishing popularity of the *Heimatfilm* during the fifties: during the third quarter of 1952, drawing on the summer movie crowds, four of the ten financially most successful films released in Germany were *Heimatfilme*. Two years later the *Illustrierte Film-Bühne*, which between 1945 and 1969 published more than eight thousand different film brochures, experienced higher box-office sales of its program for Alfons Stummer's *Der Förster vom Silberwald* (*The Ranger of the Silver Forest*) than any of its other publications. See also Klaus Phillips, "'Illustrierte Film-Bühne' Resurrected," *Quarterly Review of Film Studies* (Winter 1979): 91–92.

[10] For more information on Schlöndorff's film see Klaus Phillips, "History Reevaluated: Volker Schlöndorff's *The Sudden Wealth of the Poor of Kombach*," *1978 Film Studies Annual* (West Lafayette, Ind.: Purdue Research Foundation, 1979), pp. 33–39.

[11] Quoted in Bavaria-Atelier press kit (reproduced in some—but not all—copies of "Reinhard Hauff and His Films").

[12] Quoted in Timm and Meier-Siem, "Reinhard Hauff," p. 31.

[13] Michael Schwarze in his review of the film, *FAZ*, 26 March 1974 (reprinted in "Reinhard Hauff and His Films").

[14] Judy Stone, "Hauff."

[15] Klaus Eder, "Ein Gespräch mit Reinhard Hauff über seinen Film 'Zündschnüre' nach F. J. Degenharts Roman," *Die Tat—antifaschistische Wochenzeitung, Frankfurt/M.*, no. 36, 7 September 1974.

[16] Quoted in Bioskop-Film press kit ("Reinhard Hauff and His Films" contains a poor English translation).

[17] Quoted in Filmverlag der Autoren press kit.

[18] Quoted in Filmverlag der Autoren press kit.

[19] Quoted in Timm and Meier-Siem, "Reinhard Hauff," p. 35.

[20] The German word *verrückt* is potentially ambiguous in this context: in addition to "crazy" it literally means "shifted," "displaced" (as past participle of the verb *verrücken*).

[21] See Hans C. Blumenberg, "Schere im Kopf: Ein Fall von Ausgewogenheit," *Die Zeit*, 19 January 1979; and the remarks by Helmut W. Banz, also in *Die Zeit*, 1 December 1978.

[22] Quoted in Köster and Drechsel, "Interview," p. 72.

[23] Andrew Sarris, "Starting from Ground Zero," *Village Voice*, 28 April 1980.

[24] Diane Jacobs, "Angst, You're Welcome," *Soho News*, 23–29 April 1980.

WERNER HERZOG

In Quest of the Sublime

by Brigitte Peucker

IN HIS DIFFICULT QUEST FOR THE SUB-
lime in nature and in his films, Werner Herzog often plays the
role of the Byronic hero, shaking his fist at the elements like
Manfred on the brink of the precipice. Herzog literally did just
that in August 1976, when he and his cameraman left Munich in
haste to film the impending eruption of a volcano on the already
evacuated island of Guadalupe. The resulting "documentary,"
called *La Soufrière* after the volcano, includes poignant scenes of
abandonment: empty streets in which traffic lights go on flash-
ing, a television set left on, and packs of hungry dogs ranging
through the city; however, the film's central concern is revealed
as Herzog and his friends—defiant, but hushed with fear and
awe—make their way to the smoldering crater brink.

The gestures of a Manfred or a Faust, resentfully hurled
against what is indomitable in nature, constitute one of the Romantic attitudes to which Herzog frequently returns in his films.
The cloudlike billows of smoke, emerging from the crater and
misting over the abyss, stand as perhaps the central Herzog
image of sublimity enshrouded. The delicacy of these harbin-
gers of death merely reinforces the Romantic context of the
image: whereas the confrontation with death is sublime, the
wraithlike attraction of death itself is the attraction of peace

Werner Herzog (Courtesy of the Filmmaker)

before humanity's fall into knowledge. As if to draw attention away from his ascent, Herzog interviews the few men who would not leave their island, who seem to have found peace already and calmly await death. They, too, are "not afraid," creatures in harmony with the natural order and lacking—perhaps for that reason—the visionary hubris and impatience of the artist.

As is so often the case with Herzog, the film is only superficially a documentary. More tellingly a fable with the filmmaker projected as hero, it has a distinctly mythological cast, to which the resonance of the hushed voice of the narrator, Herzog himself, effectively contributes. Nature has gone awry, and we are reminded of Kleist's *Earthquake in Chili.* The atmosphere of suspense keeps us from taking for granted our knowledge that the volcano will *not* erupt. The feigned embarrassment with which Herzog speaks of "the inevitable catastrophe which did not take place" and the "heroic" Wagnerian chords with which the film closes remind us at once of how fictively the film is composed and of Herzog's capacity for self-mockery—a redeeming strain that is too rarely noticed in his work.

Guadalupe is only one of the exotic landscapes to which Herzog has journeyed in search of the sublime: he has filmed in the Sahara in summertime; he has taken a crew to Skellig Rock off the Irish coast over a violent sea; he has shot in the jungles of the Amazon and the mountains of Peru. His exquisite frames, because of their purity, are like images of Paradise—forbiddingly out of reach. But at the same time, the quests of Herzog and most of his characters are often journeys into the self; the camera searches for visual equivalents of their visionary landscapes. Byronic defiance is counterbalanced by the visionary's spirituality or the pilgrim's reverence. When in 1974 Lotte Eisner was extremely ill, he made a mystical voyage on foot from Munich to Paris so that she might recover. For Herzog the author of *The Haunted Screen* and *Murnau* is a spiritual presence who has given the New German Cinema her sanction and a new legitimacy; it was inconceivable to him that she should be "allowed" to die.[1]

A sense of connection with the great expressionist directors such as Murnau is crucial to Herzog. Although Herzog denies his connection with German Romanticism, his films are populated with figures and moments prominent in this period. Herzog does not deny that *Lebenszeichen (Signs of Life,* 1967*)* is based on a Romantic novella, that *Woyzeck* (1978) focuses on a stunted Romantic visionary who hears voices in the ground, that his Kaspar Hauser quotes from the poet Eichendorff, or that his films contain frames based on the paintings of Caspar David Friedrich. But Herzog's most pervasive affinity with Romanticism appears in the avowal of Lucy, in *Nosferatu* (1978), that "It is of the utmost importance to believe in those things which we know to be untrue." Herzog repeatedly affirms the power of the imagination; its positive side is revealed in Lucy or in Stroszek, while its negative side is perhaps most eloquently expressed in Aguirre. His characters feel humanity's alienation from nature acutely and yearn to revoke the fall from Paradise, to reach out for the Absolute in nature and art.

Herzog grew up in a Bavarian village, a withdrawn child who spent much of its childhood reading the literature of Romanticism and the nineteenth century.[2] He was born Werner Stipetič on September 5, 1942, one of three brothers whose parents were later divorced. The search for extraordinary landscapes began early: by the time he was fifteen, he had hitchhiked to Yugoslavia and Greece, where he was to make his first feature film ten years later. His volatile association with Klaus Kinski started when Herzog's family moved to Munich and shared a house with the actor. In 1961 Herzog received a liberal arts degree and began to make films with a "borrowed" camera while studying literature and history at the University of Munich. On a Fulbright to the United States, he briefly studied film and television in Pittsburgh, then traveled around the country, earning money to produce films (he has generally continued to be his own producer) by working in factories, as a parking-lot attendant, and as a rodeo rider.

By 1964 he had received the Carl Mayer Prize for a screenplay that was to become his first feature, *Signs of Life,* then in 1966 he was awarded 300,000 marks with which to film it. The film received the Silver Bear in Berlin in 1968. With the encouragement of Lotte Eisner he became increasingly less isolated as an artist. In 1972 he was awarded both first prizes at Antwerp for *Auch Zwerge haben klein angefangen* (*Even Dwarfs Started Small,* 1969–70) and *Land des Schweigens und der Dunkelheit* (*Land of Silence and Darkness,* 1970–71), a documentary. In 1975, his *Jeder für sich und Gott gegen alle* (*Every Man for Himself and God Against All, or the Enigma of Kaspar Hauser*) received three international prizes at Cannes. It nevertheless remains true that his reputation is greater in France, England, and the United States than in Germany, where directors with a more overtly political orientation are preferred by the cinematically educated.

Signs of Life (1967) is set in the year of Herzog's birth, 1942, on the island of Cos, where Herzog's grandfather worked on archaeological excavations. The plot is very loosely based on *The Mad Invalid in the Fort Ratonneau,* a novella by the German Romantic writer Achim von Arnim. Stroszek—the name evokes Stipetič—his Greek wife, Nora, and two fellow soldiers—Meinhard and Becker—have been sent to a citadel on Cos, where Stroszek is to recover from war injuries. An island within an island, the citadel exists apart from the war, apart from ordinary life, and seemingly apart from time. Itself lifeless, it nevertheless harbors life signs of various kinds. Stroszek is at loose ends, while Meinhard invents elaborate cockroach traps and contrives plans for making thousands of caterpillars crawl in a circle, avenging himself on nature by inventing a microcosm of which he alone is the sadistic master—or director. In the meantime, Becker, a philologist, attempts to decipher the votive tablets found strewn about as though the explanation for existence were semiotic.

The sun beats down inexorably, and the flickering heat is visible. It always appears to be high noon, the Hour of Pan, when time stops in Greek mythology. The buzzing of the insects nearly drowns out other sounds, and close-ups capture details of grasses, insects, fish, and rocks, while in many wide-angle shots the human beings are lost in the landscape. Stroszek feels panic in the face of the minutiae of nature and evidences of the sublime: the sun and the sea, which threaten him with a diminution of self. Suffering from a serious loss of identity, he and Meinhard are allowed to leave the citadel on a patrol to the center of the island. From a hilltop they survey a panorama of ten thousand windmills—revealed in a pan that lasts a full minute.[3] Madness grips Stroszek, and he fires at the distant whirling windmills in an evocation of Don Quixote's solipsistic quest, a theme that Herzog's later films echo and reecho: madness is the tendency to mistake signs of ordinary life for signs of heroic or transcendent life. Circular movement—windmills, chickens, minnows—is a central Herzog image deriving from the simultaneous absurdity and idealism of Quixote's quest.

Returning in a state of lunacy, Stroszek chases the others from the citadel and threatens to blow up the town in order to "make the earth tremble" and to see "what really lay beneath the surface of things." In so doing, he models himself on the forces of nature, specifically the earthquake responsible for unearthing the tablets and statuary explored by Becker. (In a later film Aguirre will say: "I am the Wrath of God. The earth on which I tread hears me and trembles.") Rebelling against his unresponsive antagonist, Nature, Stroszek fights the sun with fireworks, believing with Lucifer that "one can only counteract light with light." Gradually, indifferently, the sun sets and Stroszek's signs of life blaze across the darkened sky; however, when day breaks, it is not in response to Stroszek but merely as part of the endless cycle—or circling—of day and night. While the narrator mocks Stroszek—"he failed to set the sun on fire"—he nevertheless grants that "there is something titanic in his rebellion against everything." We simultaneously hear the words and see the image of dust thrown up by a truck moving along a lonely wind-ing road and carrying Stroszek away. It is the image with which the film began, another instance of circularity. As we shall see, Herzog's linear plots are repeatedly offset by symmetrically framing elements at other levels of composition, emblems of the way art imposes patterns on particularity.

Fata Morgana (1968–70), Herzog's second feature film, is di-vided into three parts: "The Creation," "Paradise," and "The Golden Age"—each progressively more socialized than the last, yet each a time when humankind and nature were in complete harmony. As elusive and visionary as its title would indicate, the film nevertheless documents discord rather than harmony. It begins with a fixed shot of an airplane landing, like a mytholog-ical bird, in the shimmering heat of a desert under a pink sky. Taken with a telephoto lens, this shot is repeated eight times, and the result is that, one by one, the metallic birds appear to join a flock of real birds startled by the intrusion. The detritus of civilization is repeatedly juxtaposed against the hardiest mar-ginal beings and most impersonal landscapes of nature.

In the first section, the rich voice of the narrator—Lotte Eis-ner—reads from the Popol Vuh, a Guatemalan creation myth.[4] Long traveling shots and 360° pans create a landscape of abstract forms: it is an archetypal scene whose rippled dunes—carefully sculpted by Herzog—visually repeat "the waters" of which the voice speaks. Gradually the scene encompasses a road and then oil tanks and derricks, which at first resemble primitive totems. Desert carrion is replaced by wrecks of trucks. A jarring opposi-tion of image and word serves as a commentary: while we hear of the "coming alive" of beasts, we see their skeletons. The or-ganicity of a peripheral nature merges with the dead mechanics of a peripheral culture.

The sequence called "Paradise" presents portraits of the in-habitants of this region, shot frontally to produce the deliberate awkwardness of a Herzog documentary. This technique in-creases the scorn we feel for the film's displaced human subjects. A goggled scientist reports on the habits of lizards; a German teacher has her African charges repeat "Blitzkrieg is madness." The camera relentlessly denies these subjects an appropriate context; superimposed on the desert landscape, they are dis-placed persons whose only imaginable place is in German cul-

ture. Leonhard Cohen's elegies (which seemed more elegiac in
the sixties than they do today) alternate with texts of a Dadalike
quality, some of them random and some more clearly relating to
the film: "In Paradise, there are landscapes without deeper
meaning"; "In Paradise, plane wrecks have been distributed in
advance." Herzog mocks his subjects, but cinematically admits
that he, too, is an outsider, an ecology-crasher.

Parody is even more evident in "The Golden Age." The central image of this final section has a grotesque, cheaply theatrical
quality: a crooner, wearing goggles, is accompanied by a female
pianist on a primitive stage. Although Herzog presents us with
other images at this point—a diver obsessed with catching turtles
in a decorative pool, for example—he repeatedly cuts to these
cacophonous performers, while a narrator informs us, "In the
Golden Age man and woman live in harmony." Herzog's increasing bitterness subverts the visionary quality of the film, but his
concluding mirage, a fata morgana, implies that if human beings
in general have failed their environment, the visual imagination
remains a viable dwelling place for some.

Fata Morgana was originally planned as a science-fiction film
about a doomed planet; as it stands, the doomed planet is Earth
itself in the Iron Age. Plotless, the film remains essentially an
exercise in the coordination and juxtaposition of images with a
sound track that includes Handel, Mozart, and Blind Faith, as
well as Leonhard Cohen. As a storehouse of ideas, the film
proved crucially important, and Herzog constantly quoted it in
later works: the descent of the birdlike planes recurs in the
documentary *The Flying Doctors*; the image of the temple in the
sand is used for Kaspar Hauser's dream of the Caucasus; there is
a shot of a rock formation that strongly resembles the camel on
its knees in both *Even Dwarfs Started Small* and *Kaspar Hauser*;
the shots of turtles slowly swimming in azure water inspired the
slow-motion treatment of the bats in *Nosferatu*; the chant of the
African Mass is brilliantly repeated in *Even Dwarfs Started Small*;
and the van driving in circles is, of course, a central image in
Dwarfs and *Stroszek* as well.

Even Dwarfs Started Small (1969–70) aroused the German Left
because it was misconstrued as political allegory. Reminiscent of Buñuel—it was shot in Mexico and the Canary Islands—
it is a grotesque tale of the revolt of dwarfs in an institution

whose director is absent, like Pascal's God. After a long pan situating the buildings in a scrub-dotted desert, the film begins at the end, with images showing that the uprising was to fail; a long line of dwarfs sit against the wall, waiting to be questioned, and a dwarf is blinded by the strong lights trained on him during his interrogation. We never see the Big People, but the voice of authority clearly belongs to a man of normal size. In contrast, the final shots of the film include one of a distant city from which the dwarfs are separated by wasteland. Enshrouded in clouds, distant and visionary, the city evokes paintings of the Holy Jerusalem. A key to the film's allegory, it is an image of the state of grace from which the dwarfs are excluded. Their outrage begins as a protest against their deformity, against Mother Nature who has, according to the norms accepted by the dwarfs themselves, created them as freaks and aberrations.

Their hatred for Mother Nature is most graphic in the scene in which they symbolically violate her by pushing a truck into a gaping crater, yelling "Screw Mother Nature." Cursing her repeatedly because they have not understood their deformity as "natural," they misinterpret indifference as cruelty. Their acts of brutality towards animals—the ritualized slaughter of a nursing sow and the hobbling of a camel—are at once retaliatory and imitative acts. By way of commentary, Herzog frequently cuts to scenes of chickens, whose cruelty and stupidity he despises. In one scene they are engaged in killing a lame chicken. Perhaps, as a part of "nature red in tooth and claw," they recognize deformity and destroy it. At any rate, their act is a paradigm for the dwarfs' aggression against animals and humans even more handicapped than themselves.

One dwarf has created a kind of Cornell Box of insects impaled on pins and dressed as members of a wedding. As she proudly displays her work, the others murmur "How beautiful": when the stuff of nature is transformed into art, it is wholly altered (it is dead, for one thing), and only then acquires value. Furthermore, like the world of the chickens and of the institution itself, the Cornell Box is itself a microcosm, but one over which the dwarfs themselves—rather than the head of the institution or the filmmaker—have control. There is yet another of these microcosms: within the institution live two blind, deaf, and dumb dwarfs more diminished than Beckett characters. Their lives are self-contained; we see them at work, at play, and at table. Wearing goggles and leather aviator caps, they resemble insects and, indeed, perceive by means of sticks that they use as insects use feelers. In at least one sense, they are an inversion of the wedding party of insects. Ever intrigued by miniatures, Herzog plays with the idea of the box within a box in defiance of the interpreter who would—with a good deal of justification—read his films as allegories.

The rebel dwarfs have barricaded the dwarf instructor, who is temporarily in charge, in his office, and he, in turn, holds as a hostage the dwarf Pepe, who incarnates the spirit of mockery. Pepe never speaks, but his uncanny laugh echoes throughout the film, and seems to catalyze the pandemonium in the grounds below. By far the most capable looking of the dwarfs, Pepe is the presiding deity of this anarchy, a Lord of Misrule, whereas the other dwarfs express the human spirit in its most pinched, infantile aspects. More than ever unable to enter the celestial city on the horizon, they represent diminished men who have been battling nature since the fall. In another act of violence against humankind and nature alike, the dwarfs symbolically castrate the instructor by burning down his favorite palm tree. When the instructor goes mad, he too challenges nature in an act whose absurdity comments on the revolt itself: he challenges a dead, gnarled tree to hold its "arm" up longer than he. The narrator of *Signs of Life* claimed that there was "something titanic" about Stroszek's rebellion: Herzog's ambivalence about this is revealed here by his miniaturization of rebellion.

Herzog's sympathy probably lies with the most attenuated creatures of *Dwarfs*: the bizarre jousting they do with their sticks—so rarely on the mark, yet their only means of communication with one another—seems an act of quixotic idealism and courage. His documentaries about the handicapped bear this out. The blind, deaf, and dumb protagonists of *Land of Silence and Darkness* (1970–71), for example, have a paradoxical wholeness that the dwarfs lack; they are innocents whose imperviousness to experience guards their unspoiled, naive sensibilities. The symbolically charged final scene of this film centers on one of these innocents who walks into a garden and encounters a tree, which, in a moment of supreme spiritual happiness, he joyously embraces. Such characters rank among those who, like

Kaspar Hauser, remind us of our loss of unity with nature precisely because they themselves in some sense retain it.

Perhaps Herzog's greatest rebel is Aguirre, who like the Satan of the Romantic tradition proclaims, "I am the greatest traitor." The story of *Aguirre, the Wrath of God* (1972) is based on the actual diary of a monk, Gaspar de Carvajal, the film's narrator. A breathtakingly beautiful opening shot simulates a split frame: the left side is all mountain, with a barely perceptible chain of descending figures, while the right side is all sky with swirling fog and Herzog's characteristic, rapidly moving clouds. The movement from the mountains into the flatland is clearly understood as a Descent; as Aguirre says, "From now on it's all downhill." Klaus Kinski portrays the power-crazed lieutenant who eventually makes himself a leader of a group of men split off from Pizarro's expedition in order to seek food and information about El Dorado. Luring his men farther and farther down the river with promises of fabulous wealth, he himself cares only for more lands and greater power. All these factors contribute to make Herzog's film, among other things, a parable of the rebel angels.

Aguirre has a rather conventional beginning: the device of sending explorers to "scout out the territory" is a standard opening for an adventure story. From this point on, the narrowness of obsession closes in, and the film becomes tighter, more focused. Several effects contribute to *Aguirre's* ultimately hermetic quality: its historical and geographical distance as well as the virtual confinement of the action to the mountain-hemmed river and, finally, to the single remaining raft. Although it is claustrophobic, the film nevertheless keeps the viewer at a distance. The voice-over narration has the effect of historicizing the action, reminding us that the film has its origins in an actual diary, the spoken excerpts of which play on our expectations that the speaker will survive to establish a living link between ourselves and what we have seen. What initially seems the story of a quest for riches and self-enrichment becomes instead a meditation on how man's questing spirit gradually impoverishes him. Images of explorers bent on their mission are juxtaposed with images of cannibalism, and the ultimate reduction occurs when monkeys replace the dead men on the raft. Aguirre's announcement that he and his daughter—who is already dead—will together found

a new, pure race is another index of the narrowing of humanity
—and also, of course, a condemnation of Nazism. As befits a
story about megalomania, *Aguirre* juxtaposes questions about
politics and art: Aguirre, who wants "to direct politics as others
direct plays," combines in his person both dictator and
filmmaker. Yet the lust for power is but one dimension of A-
guirre's quest: his search may also be seen as a secularized, per-
verted search for the Holy City, a sublimation of the greed that
motivates his followers. It is in Aguirre that Herzog most successfully exposes the potentially fascistic nature of the indi-
vidualized utopia, and in so doing exposes the negative side of
the artistic imagination.

Not surprisingly, the movement in *Aguirre* (and in several
other films) away from society and toward symbolic abstraction
and the isolation of the self conforms with a Romantic pattern.
Its cinematic narration—what we see on the screen—barely
requires the articulations of a plot but depends on a series of
strong images from which virtually self-sufficient symbols are
generated. The early circular movement of a doomed raft and
the circular movement of the camera itself in the film's final
scene again reinforce the connection between human beings'
darker visionary impulses and art. The river has a life of its own,
and the jungle is a living presence, silent and menacing, the
process world at its most merciless. The jungle is also the home
of the Indians, people at one with nature's rhythms. One of
Herzog's more shocking and compelling images is a close-up of a
drop of scarlet blood on a leaf of vital green. There follows a
point-of-view shot that follows the glance of the soldier who sees
the drop, and the camera reveals an Indian and his Spanish
victim, who seems trapped in the embrace of Indian and tree
alike. Elsewhere, soldiers are snared by nets and ropes that seem
extensions of the perversely luxuriant foliage. Both death and
generation are at home in the jungle: when Inez, mistress of the
executed Ursua, walks silently into the forest, splendidly arrayed
as a bride of Death, the jungle swallows her up and she "van-
ishes without a trace." The Indians, with their poisoned arrows,
emerging between branches and fronds, are agents of this
nature, but it is first the whirling rapids, then the increasingly
becalmed river, and lastly the fever that defeat Aguirre and his
men. But his ravings are not so much the result of fever as the

Klaus Kinski in *Aguirre, the Wrath of God* (COURTESY OF FILMVERLAG DER AUTOREN)

madness of a visionary for whom the imagination has become the sole reality.

The "ski-flyer" Walter Steiner, of *Die große Ekstase des Boldschnitzers Steiner (The Great Ecstasy of the Sculptor Steiner,* (1973–74), also does battle with nature and with death. Made as a documentary for German television, it is thematically consistent with the rest of Herzog's oeuvre. It records Walter Steiner's flights in a ski-flying competition at Plancia, Yugoslavia. Shown in slow motion, he is transformed into a giant bird, an Icarus triumphant, gliding downward to the eerie music of Popol Vuh. When interviewed, Steiner portrays himself as someone constantly struggling with the fear of death, a performer who—like the raven of the story he tells—will be sacrificed by the crowd when he can no longer fly. In all these respects Steiner fulfills ideas that Herzog has of himself (Indeed, Herzog did ski-jumping when he was younger.)

Herzog's presence in the film is pervasive, and although as

narrator he is self-effacing, he clearly suggests an analogy between the ski-flyer and the artist. The film's title points to this
equivalence as well: Steiner is a sculptor in wood as well as in the
air. Herzog's lyrical evocation of Steiner ends with a monologue
spoken by Steiner (based on a text by Robert Walser) from which
the source of Steiner's high seriousness emerges: his desire is to
live isolated on a rock, naked—that is, in a radically reduced
landscape of the soul where he would know no fear.

In *Every Man for Himself and God Against All* (*The Enigma of
Kaspar Hauser*, 1974) Herzog returns to another variant of his
Romantic hero, the "natural man" or true *naïf*, of which Herzog
has found an example in a Berlin street character named Bruno
S. The product of foundling homes and penal institutions, he
was the subject of a documentary that inspired Herzog's determination to have him as an actor.[5] The result was *Kaspar Hauser*.
Bruno S., whose screen presence and canny intelligence are extraordinary, was to represent what was new in the film. At the
same time, however, as Herzog has noted, *Kaspar Hauser* represented a coming to terms with his own work up to that point.[6] To
this end, he brought together actors, images, and themes from
former films: Walter Steiner plays one of the peasants; Lotte
Eisner appears in a crowd scene; an actor plays Hombrecito the
flutist from *Aguirre*; and the dwarf king is played by an actor
from *Even Dwarfs Started Small*. In addition, there is Herzog's
usual menagerie of animal characters: Steiner's raven,
Meinhard's hypnotised chicken, the hobbled camel, and a mon-
key. The film's vision of the Caucasus has its origin in a shot
from *Fata Morgana*, and the vision of the Sahara was shot with
an 8mm camera during the shooting of that same film.

The historical Kaspar Hauser, whose strange mind and
obscure origins caused a sensation in early nineteenth-century
Europe, was a foundling who appeared in the town of Nuremberg in 1828 in a state of semiidiocy and whose life up to that
point had been spent in a "dark prison hole." He first made his
home with a farmer's family, and then was taught by a Professor
Daumer. By 1829, Kaspar had made such progress that he was
able to write his autobiography, which soon made him famous
throughout Europe. In 1832, the Earl of Stanhope, who was
interested in fashionable Romantic ideas (to the literati Kaspar
represented the metamorphosis of Natural Man into Social

Man) continued Kaspar's education together with Anselm von Feuerbach. Kasper quickly proved to be a musical prodigy, and was famous as such by the time of his death from knife wounds in 1833. There were rumors of political assassination and suicide, but Kaspar's death remained as mysterious as his origins.

Herzog fictionalizes Kaspar's biography somewhat. In the film, he is educated by Daumer, who is an amateur humanist, but is not adopted by Stanhope, and does not become a prodigy. Herzog focuses on the complicated mental and emotional history of Kaspar's encounters with "civilization" from his birth into the world of society until his death. Kaspar's inability to understand the world in the terms given to him by others is equaled by their inability to understand him. In Kaspar, Herzog has found a subject that corresponds with his cinematic concerns: Kaspar has the "primordial innocence of vision" that Herzog wishes to recapture for film.

To Herzog, nature is amoral; it is the source of life and death, it is both awe- and fear-inspiring, both fruitful and cruel, and includes both the close-up process world and the distant vistas of the sublime. In *Kaspar Hauser*, Herzog uses landscape in an even more openly allegorical manner than he does in his earlier films, and, in so doing, articulates more clearly the moral ambiguity of the Romantic outlook. When Kaspar is being taken from his dark cellar and escorted to the town by the ominous stranger who has been his keeper, the background landscape is a long sweep of hills and fields, dotted with villages. Significantly enough, this landscape (filmed along the "Romantic Road," a German tourist attraction) and Kaspar's journey lead to Nuremberg, the Romantic town par excellence and the setting of Leni Riefenstahl's *Triumph of the Will*, which documents the infamous Nazi party rally of 1934. Nuremberg thus perfectly illustrates the moral crisis of Romanticism, and Herzog uses an introductory montage of rooftop scenes that echoes Riefenstahl's "awakening of the city" sequence. It is no accident that the film's dedication is to Lotte Eisner—to whom he carried a print on his pilgrimage—and "to all those forced to leave Germany."

The neat gardens with their rows of cabbages, against which Kaspar is so often shown, visually represent the dominating nature-versus-nurture theme. Daumer's garden is a "fallen" but pleasant one in which the apple has become the object of scientific experiment. No longer tempting man with the knowledge of good and evil—man already *has* that—the apple implies man's distant subject-object relation to the inanimate things around him. Using the apple as a prop, Daumer hopes to deprive Kaspar of his primitive animism, but Kaspar refuses to distinguish hierarchically: confirming his view, the apple repeatedly bounces over the outstretched foot that was meant to stop it. For Kaspar, apples too have "Being" and minds of their own, and they seem no different from himself. Similarly, when Kaspar sees his image reflected in a well (the beginning of self-consciousness, an analog of Eve's gazing into a pond in some versions of the fall), he reaches out to "erase" what he sees, rejecting self-consciousness for unity. Kaspar perceives his "appearance in this world" as "a hard fall." He has had to enter a fallen garden, the cultivated garden of "civilization"; ironically, it was precisely in the hermetically sealed condition of his cellar existence that he had experienced unity. Kaspar's at-oneness in his former condition is an index of what he has come to; his symbiotic relationship with the toy horse represents the harmony of the lost paradise, a condition in which physical being and interiority are so much one that dreaming is impossible. Interestingly enough, Kaspar shows genuine cordiality toward most aspects of the socialized world from which he is spiritually and intellectually alienated.

In the fallen world, Kasper begins to have dreams and visions, and to distinguish these from "reality," as he is taught to do. His visions seem to represent nature, but they reveal landscapes Kaspar has never seen, archetypal landscapes of the imagination. Herzog has spoken of his films in terms of their archetypal images, their anthropological nature, and Kaspar's visions, not surprisingly, contain central Herzog images. His vision of the Caucasus consists of hills studded with temples that seem positive counterimages of Stroszek's windmills. In another dream, Kaspar sees many people climbing a mountain to meet Death, as in *La Soufrière* and the later *Stroszek*. A third dream, set perhaps in the Sahara, develops the theme of the blind prophet or seer who relies on intuition to guide a caravan toward the city for which it is searching. Significantly enough, Kasper cannot tell what happens to the caravan after it enters the social arena of

Bruno S. as *Kaspar Hauser* (COURTESY OF CINE
INTERNATIONAL)

the city. Kaspar's imagination cannot reach back toward the
everyday from the Sahara, where reality is a mirage and vision a
reality.

Like filmmaking—especially Herzog's image-oriented filmmaking—dreaming is a matter of creating with natural signs. In
Herzog's view visual signs are preferable to verbal signs, being
more naturalized if not natural; music is also to be preferred
because it, too, is less mediatory than language. Herzog claims
that his films originate from music as well as from landscapes.
Music, an important element in all his films, in *Kasper Hauser*
functions thematically, imagistically, and structurally. Like Herzog, Kaspar thinks of music as a natural occurrence and regrets
to learn that for socialized persons making music is a learned
skill and not simply "like breathing." For Herzog, music carries a
spiritual force akin to the classical doctrines of world harmony;
for example, in the film one of the four "Riddles of the Spheres"
is Hombrecito, an Indian who fears that if he stops playing his
flute the people in the town will die. Another of these riddles,

"the young Mozart," a prodigy who perhaps absorbs that theme from the actual biography of Kaspar, falls into a trance when he is supposed to learn to read and write (words are signs of absence). Instead, he spends his days staring into wells and holes in the ground, "to see"—like Stroszek in *Signs of Life*—" what lay beneath the surface. . . ." A final point: Herzog encloses his film in a musical frame, an aria from *The Magic Flute*, continuing the passage at the end just where he had broken it off at the beginning. It has been pointed out that the score of this film follows the form of a rondo—another circular pattern.[7]

Opposed to the circularity of the music is the linear, episodic structure characteristic of Herzog's narratives: they tend, after all, to be quest romances, for which linear organization is unavoidable. We might call *Kaspar Hauser* a reverse quest, since the hero loses the paradise for which most other characters search. Kaspar's encounters with the pillars of society—the ministers, the professor, the town recorder, the doctor overly concerned with fact—make the same point time and again: Kaspar's intuitions, emphasized by his affinity with animals and children, and sometimes in actual feats of thought, invariably triumph over reason and dogma. His visions present us with a fresh mode of perception, at once imagistic, opaque—and filmic. *Kaspar Hauser* contains an enigma of which Kaspar knows no more than anyone else. It concerns the identity of the unknown figure in black, the man who gives Kaspar life by removing him from his cell and who eventually returns to kill him. The camera seems at first to avoid his face, but when we do see it, its ordinariness provides an identifying clue. When this man strikes Kaspar on the head some time before he returns to kill him, Kaspar has a sublime vision of the primal landscape, the heavens and the waters. Perhaps the title *Every Man for Himself and God Against All* provides a clue to the assailant's identity.

Herz aus Glas (Heart of Glass, 1976) is even less bound to a continuous narrative development than *Kaspar Hauser*; dream sequences and visions expand to such a degree in this film that they nearly constitute the whole. Every day before shooting, Herzog hypnotized his cast because he felt that hypnosis would release their latent power of poetic vision, which self-consciousness has buried. As a result, there is a trancelike heaviness about this film and a flattening out of the characters' powers of response; with the exception of the central character, a visionary prophet—who ironically enough was *not* hypnotized—the film is populated with attenuated half-humans. The screenplay is based on the second chapter of a novel by Herbert Achternbusch (*The Hour of Death*), which was in turn based on a violent and mystical Bavarian folk legend.

The film is set around 1800, and the opening scene reveals Hias, the prophet-shepherd, in a mountain pasture, describing the Apocalypse. Once more an exotic and menacing landscape with scudding clouds and whirling fog is the backdrop for transcendent vision. The film was shot in Wyoming, Alaska, Utah, Bavaria, Switzerland, and the Skellig Islands, and the otherworldly effect of this synthetic landscape is reinforced by Popol Vuh's music. In the valley beneath Hias's pasture, the foreman of a glass factory has died and with him the secret of producing the exquisite ruby glass from which the whole community lives. The factory owner tries repeatedly to find the precious formula, so elusive that he is tempted to think that it is vital, animate. In his madness he hopes to find the secret in the blood of a virgin, and so murders his servant girl. Eventually he sets his factory afire and Hias's apocalyptic prophecy is fulfilled. Madness engulfs the villagers, who imprison not only the factory owner but the prophet who foretold the disaster. At the conclusion of the film, Hias envisions a utopia: on a rocky island live descendants of people who had come to await the Apocalypse; these men are convinced that the world is flat and terminates in an abyss. They nevertheless set out to explore to the edge of the world in a rowboat.

This is perhaps the most extreme formulation of Herzog's disillusioned Romanticism: human vision asserts itself again and again, but its doomed heroic efforts are based on myths as archaic as the flat-earth theory. A self-conscious sense of the insufficiency of vision is conveyed. It is the prophet himself who is spoken of as having the "heart of glass," of caring only for the world of nature and not of humanity. It is the obsessed factory owner who confronts the prophet and recognizes a kindred spirit in him. At the point of visionary intensity, somehow the vitality of art and the mineral coldness of imagination form a destructive synthesis. The cold, glazed starkness of nature in this film is contrasted with hemmed-in, overheated interiors, labyrinthine and arterial, themselves regions of danger because of the mute and seething passions they contain. In a many-chambered tavern, peasants commit silent, drunken acts of violence. The factory is a shell eventually burned away by the seething furnace it houses. *Heart of Glass* takes advantage of the open form of folk and fairy tales to explore the labyrinth of the imagination, with its fatal liability to disguise evil and beauty.

In *Stroszek* (1976–77) the main character, Bruno Stroszek, is a contemporary Kaspar; another one of Herzog's innocents, he is played by Bruno S., whose life, in fact, inspired the story. Herzog's only feature film set in the present, it quickly moves from Berlin to a muted and frozen rural Wisconsin that is simultaneously mythical and precisely detailed. (Herzog has called the United States the "most exotic country in the world.")

The film begins with street-musician Stroszek's release from prison, and his determination to "start a new life." His other-worldliness makes this impossible in the Berlin underworld to which he is confined. Bruno's innocence and gentleness are manifest in his attachments to Beo, his talking bird; to his aged and equally gentle neighbor, Scheitz; and to Eva, a prostitute whom he protects from her pimps. When both Eva and Bruno are beaten, they decide to emigrate with Scheitz to Wisconsin. We witness their excitement as they find Wisconsin on the map—having finally remembered that it is in North America—and we realize that their journey is a quest for a New World and a New Deal.

Like *Aguirre*, *Stroszek* relies increasingly on allegory as the film advances. The opening Berlin sections are full of realistic detail. The interiors and exteriors are reminiscent of Fassbinder, and filmic quotations abound. Then comes a setting that is midway between representation and allegory: in search of transcendence, Bruno climbs a mountain, but the first mountain of this film happens to be the Empire State Building, symbol of the heightened promises of the Land of Opportunity. Later on, the sociology of Railroad Flats, Wisconsin, and the trailer loaded with accurately rendered Americana, but tentatively perched in the vast prairie, is another compromise between reportage and symbolism. Indeed, Herzog manages to make Wisconsin numinous, a land of golden light and perfectly rounded ponds. Nevertheless, signs of attenuated humanity and its faulty technology are everywhere evident in the scattered broken machinery and metal parts that form a concrete metaphor (as in *Fata Morgana*) of an Iron Age that has superseded a more genuine natural Golden Age. As in *Kasper Hauser*, even the Romantic figure of "natural man," the noble Indian, has been reduced to a parodic figure, a sideshow spectacle. Significantly the landscape of this film is at its most Herzoglike, its most visionary, in the final third of the film, when Stroszek again becomes the Romantic Solitary on his metaphysical quest. Like Aguirre, Stroszek becomes increasingly isolated, and his expulsion from what is revealed to be the false paradise of his trailer, preceded by his loss of Eve, sends him on a solitary journey that ends in violence, and perhaps in death. In these scenes various images—a dancing chicken and a frozen turkey—mockingly recall the bird Beo, whom Bruno was not allowed to bring into the country. Stroszek's final meal at an Indian reservation, at which he arrives armed with a shotgun and the turkey—stolen from a supermarket—makes a mockery of the Thanksgiving feast that traditionally celebrates an emigration with a happier outcome. The final mountain of the film is another travesty of the visionary mountain—a ski slope without snow. Stroszek, however, does not climb to the top, but rather sits on a chair lift that repeats the circular movement of the mechanical chickens and of Bruno's truck, whose explosion may or may not stand in for Bruno's own. *Stroszek* ends in intentional obscurity: Bruno may have shot himself; we can only be sure that he has experienced a spiritual death.

Bruno's "primordial innocence," like Kaspar's, is revealed in his feeling for music, Herzog's "language of the soul," and one of the few modes of expression with which Bruno is comfortable. His instruments—a piano, an accordion, a glockenspiel and a bugle—are literally his friends, extensions of himself, and he signals the important moments in his life with his bugle. Bruno's tendency to speak of himself in the third person indicates the degree to which words alienate him from himself. (To explain his emotions to Eva, he builds a "schematic model" of his feelings.) Of course, Bruno's ignorance of English isolates him yet further, particularly during the auctioneer's chant, which Herzog perceives as simultaneously liturgical and profane. On the border between music and language at its most alienating, the chant is a medium of exchange debased in the service of commerce.[8]

Herzog insists repeatedly that his characters "cast no shadows," that they are "creatures of the night," and that his films "come out of the night." Presumably these claims are related to his feeling that films share the reality of dreams or emerge from a "collective unconscious." These ideas are expressed concretely in *Nosferatu—Phantom der Nacht (Nosferatu the Vampyre,* 1978). Count Dracula is just such a creature of the night, and Herzog nearly always surrounds him with dark shadows. (The German subtitle of *Nosferatu* is translated *A Phantom of the Night.*) Herzog's film is a tribute to Murnau's earlier version, which he considers to be the greatest German film ever made. Based on Bram Stoker's *Dracula,* it is the story of Jonathan Harker, a real-estate agent in Wismar, Germany, who is sent to Transylvania to formalize the purchase of a house by Count Dracula. While a guest in the vampire's castle, Harker is bitten by him and sickens. Dracula falls in love with the portrait of Lucy, Harker's young wife, and hurries to Wismar, traveling by sea in a ghostly ship laden with coffins of unconsecrated earth and plague-ridden rats. In the meantime, Harker, weak and ill, travels home overland in an effort to rescue Lucy before it is too late. But Jonathan's own contamination by the forces of evil—his own unconscious—has already begun to take its toll on him by the time he arrives at Wismar, feverish and unable to recognize his surroundings.

Soon Death enters the town in the shape of Dracula's red-sailed vessel, carrying both vampire and plague. The prow of the ship invades the frame and the city's canal, in an echo of the vampire's deadly embrace. Coffins fill the streets as the plague spreads, and finally Lucy, disgusted with the head-in-the-sand Enlightenment rationalism of the Doctor, takes the town's redemption upon herself. Dressed in shroudlike garments, and decked with flowers, Lucy offers herself up as the bride of Death—much like Inez in *Aguirre.* By detaining the vampire at her bedside until the sunrise, she destroys him. Harker's metamorphosis into a vampire is completed upon the death of Dracula, and he leaves Wismar as his successor, riding over a barren desert. Unlike Murnau, Herzog offers no redemption, only his usual circularity. Our last glimpse of Harker, in a landscape with no temporal or geographical determinants, is a reminder that vampirism will be a permanent disease of man unless he "innoculates" himself against its lethal force.

In *Nosferatu* Herzog unequivocally articulates the dangers of the imagination—and hence of art. Jonathan, like Aguirre, is "lost in the land of phantoms" and never emerges. When Jonathan asks an innkeeper to point the way to Dracula's castle, the innkeeper replies, "None such exists except in the imagination of man." That Jonathan's is a descent into an interior, resembling Aguirre's, is clear when he enters underground passageways of rock and at length crosses a bridge to "the other side." In fact, when we first see the castle it is a typical Rhineland ruin, high on a hillside and surrounded by menacing Herzog clouds. This is not what Harker finds when he enters an evidently inhabited castle in excellent repair; when on the following morning he instinctively finds "his" room upstairs, it is as though he were exploring the chambers of his own mind. Harker had expressed the desire to get away from the canals of Wismar "that go nowhere but back on themselves." (Herzog's circle moves from the visual to the verbal and purely thematic dimension in this film.) Harker fails to escape from interiority and solipsism after all.

Nosferatu is constructed by means of doubling and oppositions. Herzog's Dracula is oddly poised between the spiritual and the animal world, and his two heirs, Harker and Renfield, divide these two aspects between them: Renfield becomes the King of the Rats, sovereign over the evils that beset the body; Harker's evil aspect, the sickness of his imagination, is presented in a particularly negative light. We need only contrast his imagination with Lucy's to see that this is so. For Lucy, dreams and the imagination are the agents of faith. "Faith," she says, "is the amazing faculty of man which enables him to believe those things which he knows to be untrue." Her belief in the imagination leads her not into solipsism, into ever-narrowing concentric circles, but outward to the performance of a selfless, social act—which is, however, ineffective. Lucy shares the faith—but also the blindness—of the men who row off to explore the edge of the world in Hias's vision in *Heart of Glass*.

Harker is the Romantic visionary gone mad—not unlike Aguirre, who brings death on all around him as he retreats increasingly into madness. Just as in the earlier film, Herzog points to the connections between solipsism, the artist, and the dictator. Repeatedly he evokes Romantic art in its necrophilic aspect, as with the Caspar David Friedrich-like composition of Lucy viewed from behind among the tombstones, or the motif of the violinist who is also a harbinger of death. His use of Wagner's *Rheingold* overture against the images of ruins like those on the Rhine and scurrying, pestilential rats is a savage reminder of the Third Reich. Taken as a whole—and even Lucy is not exempt from this criticism—*Nosferatu* is a critique of a strain of imaginative spirituality that has gone awry and become dedicated to the worship of death. Thus, as Harker rides into the sublime distance, we hear the strains of "Sanctus, sanctus." Herzog knows how much his own filmmaking is indebted to the Romantic tradition, and he acknowledges its dangers. Like Thomas Mann (many of whose concerns he shares in this film), Herzog derives his creativity from the articulation of those very dangers. Also like Mann, Herzog knows that he is close to the abyss he has revealed.

Nosferatu was Herzog's first big-budget international production, coproduced by Gaumont in Paris and distributed by Twentieth Century-Fox. It starred not only Kinski, whose poignant performance is beyond praise, but also Bruno Ganz and Isabelle Adjani. Five days after finishing *Nosferatu*, eager to begin another film right away, to shoot quickly and on a smaller budget—as though to rid himself of the taint of commercialism—he began to shoot *Woyzeck*, with Kinski and essentially the same crew. Herzog's haste—and the probable exhaustion of all concerned—may account for some of the film's problems.

Based on Georg Büchner's 1836 dramatic fragment, *Woyzeck* (1978) is the story of a soldier who kills his unfaithful mistress, Marie, with whom he has a child. He is led to commit this murder by extraordinary and varied causes: he hears terrifying voices in the ground, he is victimized by his superiors, and he must earn money to support his child by participating in a scientific experiment that forces him to live for months on nothing but peas. Thus psychological, social, and physical factors are equally prominent, and the play sets up a conflict as to which of them is the true source of Woyzeck's madness: is he a visionary

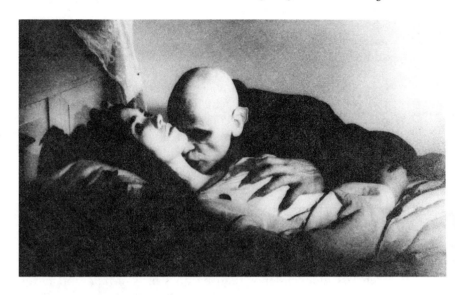

Isabelle Adjani and Klaus Kinski in *Nosferatu* (COURTESY OF 20TH CENTURY-FOX)

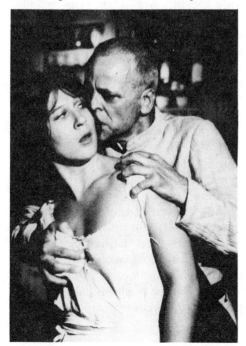

Eva Mattes and Klaus Kinski in *Woyzeck* (COURTESY OF FILMVERLAG DER AUTOREN)

whose visions horrify him because he is too alienated from
nature to derive solace from them, or is he a victim of brutality
and malnutrition? Büchner does not exclude any of these explanations, and neither does Herzog. However, Herzog chooses to
open his film with shots of Woyzeck's mistreatment as a soldier,
rather than the scene in which Woyzeck hears voices from
nature, the scene that is the commonly accepted first scene of the
play. On the other hand, the camera lingers fondly on the bec-
koning but disinspirited landscape, and Woyzeck runs through a
field of strange green pods—the pods, ironically, of opium pop-
pies, the flowers of vision—as the voices in the ground urge him
to kill Marie.

Herzog has a great reverence for Büchner, whose influence is
discernible in a number of his films, and *Woyzeck* is clearly a
cinematic tribute to him, much as *Nosferatu* is a tribute to Murnau. In the filming of *Woyzeck*, however, Herzog allows himself
even less independence than he does in *Nosferatu*, and never
arrives at an independent mode of narrative. Herzog retains
Büchner's text nearly word for word, and tends to do long takes
with a static camera, giving the film a wooden, stagy quality.
Although *Woyzeck* was shot on location in a small Czech town, the
buildings that line the town square seem deliberately framed to
resemble theater backdrops. On one hand, Herzog does not
attempt to make the short, choppy scenes cohere by means of
filmic continuity, and yet, on the other hand, he does not play
upon their choppiness, as Fassbinder would. The result is much
like a series of stills, a preliminary walk-through for a film.
Amazingly enough, Herzog's rendering of *Woyzeck* suffers from
a failure of imagination, for which the choreographed violence
of the climax is no substitute.

As a character, Woyzeck shares qualities with Stroszek and
Kaspar. (Interestingly enough, Herzog originally wanted to
shoot the film with Bruno S.) All three of these characters are
tormented by the disharmony of body and soul, as well as by a
social structure that coarsens their visions. All three are the positive foils of bureaucrats and scientific dogmatists. "We know so
little about people, about life," admits the doctor in *Stroszek*, as he
demonstrates the tenacity with which a newborn baby clings to
life. Science, Herzog implies, cannot begin to comprehend life's

mysteries; the world of the spirit cannot be understood by the accumulation of data or the application of reason.

The same is true of film criticism, Herzog would be quick to remind us. To quote from late Jan Dawson's unfinished book on the New German Cinema:

> In virtually every interview he has given, Herzog has used his considerable linguistic skills to assert his own status as a primitive—and as an incomparable primitive at that. His mysticism serves him as an impregnable fortress, shielding him from analysis. . . . The fact that Herzog denies the value of analysis and criticism does not, of course, detract from the merit of his films. It does, however, leave the best-intentioned critic suspecting himself of an act of bad faith or blasphemy, somewhat akin to tap-dancing in church.[9]

But despite the pose that Herzog has chosen to assume, a primitive is precisely what he is not. He is solidly indebted to a tradition that is *primitivistic,* which looks backward upon an ideal state of nature and also looks forward to a reinstatement of this paradise—if not in life, then in art. It is not too much to say that more than any current writer, and certainly more than any other filmmaker, Werner Herzog is the profoundest and most authentic heir of the Romantic tradition at work today.

NOTES

[1]Of course, Eisner did recover. Later, on the set of *Nosferatu*, she was to say: "I never thought I could be friends with a German again. But here I am. . . . Werner is somehow like Murnau brought back to life." Quoted in Beverly Walker, "Werner Herzog's *Nosferatu*," *Sight and Sound* 47 (Autumn 1978): 205.

[2]Dates and facts are based on Hans Günter Pflaum, ed., *Werner Herzog, Reihe Film* 22 (Munich: Hanser, 1979). Herzog's myth-making is not confined to his films but often extends to his autobiography as well, and statements made during interviews often appear to contradict one another. I have tried always to base my conclusions on the filmmaker's most recent words.

[3]The windmill sequence was filmed in the Lasithi Plain on Crete, where there are 10,000 windmills.

[4]"Popol Vuh" is also the name used by Florian Fricke, who has composed much of the music for Herzog's films.

[5]*Bruno der Schwarze* (1970), directed by Lutz Eisholz.

[6]*I Am My Films (Was ich bin, sind meine Filme,* 1978) is a film about Herzog directed by Christian Weisenborn and Erwin Keusch.

[7] Rudolf Hohlweg, "Musik für Film—Film für Musik," *Herzog/Kluge/Straub, Reihe Film 9*, edited by Peter W. Jansen and Wolfram Schütte (Munich: Hanser, 1976).

[8] Herzog's fascination with the language of auctioneers is documented in *How Much Wood Would a Woodchuck Chuck*, 1975–76.

[9] Quoted in "In Memoriam: Jan Dawson," *BFI Monthly Film Bulletin* (October 1980): 204.

ALEXANDER KLUGE

Mediating History and Consciousness

by *Theodore Fiedler*

ALEXANDER KLUGE — FILMMAKER AND
film educator, attorney and adjunct professor of law at the University of Frankfurt, author of docufiction, theorist and critic of film, the media, contemporary culture and the public sphere, and since 1962 chief spokesman in the arena of cultural politics and policy making for the economic needs and public significance of an indigenous and revitalized German cinema — was born Feburary 14, 1932, in Halberstadt, a provincial city of 50,000 located just northeast of the Harz Mountains in central Germany, now part of the German Democratic Republic.[1] In this city, marked by the socioeconomic and linguistic division of its population and a corresponding separation of its centuries-old public core and its modern industry into an "upper" and a "lower" city, Kluge spent his first fourteen years. He recalls having assimilated not only the sense of order of the "upper" city, where he lived with his upper-middle-class parents (his father was a doctor), but also the historically continuous life-style of the "lower" city, where his father had grown up, with its "sloppiness" and its underlying "profound distrust" of the changing modes of order characteristic of its "upper" counterpart.[2] Otherwise Kluge has had little to say about his direct experience of these years that frame the beginning and end of Nazi rule, although

the Nazi period and its consequences have been a central concern of his adult life.

From this record it would seem that Kluge and his family survived the Nazi period personally unscathed. Yet in the foreword to *New Stories: Notebooks* 1–18, *"Inhospitability of Time"* (1977), his most recent collection of prose pieces, he gives us a personal, if laconic, glimpse of a different order of reality—his first-hand experience of the bombing of the civilian population of Halberstadt on April 8, 1945, when British and American planes destroyed 80 percent of the city, including the Kluge house.[3] Within a year, Kluge's parents divorced and his mother remarried and moved to a western sector of Berlin, where Kluge joined her and continued his education while his sister Alexandra remained with their father. Although Kluge has not commented directly on the impact of this breakup, in a recent interview a reference to the irresponsibility of divorcing parents in disrupting their children's lives suggests that it must have been considerable.[4] The bombing and the divorce may exemplify at its most dramatic a pattern of experience that Kluge, speaking in 1976 about the relationship of his personal life history, his "subjectivity," to his films, identified as the source of his motivation as a filmmaker:

> There's a principle here that I've registered, so to speak, in a series of snapshots throughout my life, namely that in certain moments when I ought to fight, I'm powerless, and the feelings of revenge that then develop, they don't last. On the other hand, this desire for revenge has an elephantine memory, these moments are the entire motivation for my work.[5]

After completing his Gymnasium education in Berlin during 1946-49, years that encompassed the growing rift between the Western Allies and the Soviet Union and the founding of two German states in 1949, Kluge spent the next four years studying law at the universities of Marburg, Frankfurt, and Freiburg, with history and church music as secondary and tertiary disciplines. Passing the first of two state law examinations in 1953, he worked for the next several years as a legal intern in the Frankfurt law practice of Hellmut Becker, a politically engaged attorney who introduced Kluge to the practical politics and possibilities of cultural policy and thus helped prepare him for his later role as chief lobbyist for the interests of the NGC. During

Alexander Kluge (COURTESY OF
FILMVERLAG DER AUTOREN)

these years in Frankfurt Kluge pursued a doctorate in law, which
he received from the University of Marburg at the end of 1956.
These same years brought him into personal contact with
Theodor W. Adorno, the dominant figure of the Frankfurt
School of Critical Theory during the 1950s and 1960s. Adorno's
Marxist-oriented cultural criticism, his critical epistemology, and
his pro-modernist writings in aesthetic theory and criticism
helped shape Kluge's thinking about modern culture as a whole.
In particular, Adorno's *Dialectic of Enlightment* (coauthored with
Max Horkheimer, 1947) had a significant impact on his concep-
tion of the actual production, distribution, reception, and function of established artistic forms and the newer mass-media film
and television in contemporary capitalist society.

Yet it was not Adorno but the literary and cultural critic Walter Benjamin, an associate of the Frankfurt school during the
1930s, who, along with Bertolt Brecht, exerted the decisive influence on Kluge's conception of film and its possibilities. Unlike
Adorno, whose modernist aesthetics and negative analysis of
mass culture led him to an underlying hostility toward film,
Benjamin, like his friend Brecht, was seriously interested in

popular cultural forms and made a case for film as a potentially critical artistic medium specifically suited to the needs and experiences of a mass audience. Kluge's reception of Benjamin's ideas is most evident in his first theoretical discourse on film, "The Utopia Film" (1964); his general conception of film, if not always his filmic practice, has remained consistent over the years with Benjamin's position.[6]

Kluge's initial encounter with filmmaking itself came in late 1958 and early 1959, when thanks to Adorno, who knew Fritz Lang from their days in American exile, Kluge was admitted as an observer (not, as is frequently maintained, an assistant) on the set of Lang's remake of *Der Tiger von Eschnapur* (*The Tiger of Eschnapur*) and *Das indische Grabmal* (*The Indian Headstone*) at the CCC-Studios in Berlin. Kluge's retrospective evaluation of this encounter is contradictory, and his dismissal of it in 1966 as unimpressive is counterbalanced by his recent recollection that his conception of the *Autorenfilm* — the director in the role of producer as well as scriptwriter — had its origins in his observation of Lang's ongoing struggle with the producer of *The Indian Headstone*.[7] In any case, Kluge has consistently identified his determination to make films himself with his viewing of Jean-Luc Godard's 1960 paradigmatic *auteur* film, *A bout de souffle* (*Breathless*).[8] Having already moved to Munich in 1959 where a number of young filmmakers were active, Kluge, working with Peter Schamoni, had by year's end completed his first film, *Brutalität in Stein* (*Brutality in Stone*), a short, innovative documentary on the Nazi period whose simultaneous evocation and deconstruction of the "aura" of Nazi architecture transforms Benjamin's basic concepts into filmic practice.

Constructed on the principle of contrastive montage, a strategy that maximizes the shock effect on perception that Benjamin saw as intrinsic to all film, *Brutality in Stone* opens with shots of the deserted ruins of the Nazi Party meeting grounds on the edge of Nuremburg. A voice-over comments in an understated manner on the archaeological value of architecture in general and then enunciates the film's central concerns: "The deserted structures of the Nationalist Socialist Party reactivate as stone witnesses the memory of that epoch, which ended in the most horrible catastrophe of German history."[9] While the camera, in keeping with Benjamin's assertion of its analytical power, focuses on ideologically significant details of the monumental ruins, their present desolation underscored by music specifically composed for the film, the reactivation of the viewer's memory is advanced by the introduction of a contrapuntal sound — a recording of the enthusiastic screaming of Hitler's supporters at a ritualized rally on the now abandoned site. Hitler's voice itself is then heard above the din: "Only the smallest mind can see the life of a revolution exclusively in its destructiveness. We saw it in the very opposite: a gigantic construction." Following Hitler's pronouncement, an off-camera speaker announces excerpts from the recollection of Auschwitz Commandant Rudolf Hoess, and a second speaker reads Hoess's impersonal, bureaucratic account of his murderous responsibilites in spring 1942 as the systematic destruction of European Jewry began. The opening sequence then closes with a partial reiteration of Hitler's assertion.

The multiple ironies Kluge builds into this sequence are developed and augmented throughout the remainder of the film in a similarly disjunctive manner, as fixed frames of historical photographs, newsreel clips, spoken texts, and titles expressing the ideology of gigantic construction are juxtaposed with others that concretize the immense destruction this ideology helped bring about. The opening archaeological perspective alludes to a widespread tendency among West Germans in the 1950s to "forget" the Nazi period without having come to terms with it, and the remainder of the film is clearly intended to subvert such an attitude, to engage its viewers in a multifaceted, critically mediated reconstruction of their collectively experienced past.

Brutality in Stone anticipates Kluge's rather than Schamoni's later work in film, and it won a first prize on its premiere at the 1961 Oberhausen Short Film Festival. It helped to establish Kluge as a full-fledged member of the emerging generation of young German filmmakers, twenty-six of whom were to sign the so-called Oberhausen Manifesto one year later. Kluge appears to have been one of the prime movers behind this document, which, after proclaiming the collapse of the existing German film industry, claims for its signers the experience, the new film language, and the ideas necessary to create the new German feature film independently of the financial interests and artistic conventions of that industry; it also announces their willingness to share the economic risks involved. Kluge is also one of the few signers to have worked seriously to implement a three-point program—the establishment of educational centers for film-makers, the subsidization of first films, the ongoing subsidization of the short film as a vital form of experimentation—which the Oberhausen group soon formulated but then failed to pursue because of internal dissension. A May 1962 hearing on the state of the German film before the Federal Parliament's Committee on Cultural Policy and Journalism, at which Kluge spoke for the Oberhausen group, failed to produce any results. Shortly after, Kluge and two other members of the group approached Hermann Höcherl, then the Federal Republic's secretary of the interior and a critic of the existing film industry, for federal funds to subsidize first films. Höcherl promised them 5 million marks and in 1964 created the Kuratorium Junger Deutscher Film as the agency charged with the distribution of these funds to fledgling filmmakers. During the years 1965–1968 the Kuratorium was to play a crucial role in the creation of the new German feature film, subsidizing no less than twenty feature films, including Kluge's own breakthrough film, *Abschied von gestern (Anita G), (Yesterday Girl [Anita G]*, 1965–66).[10]

By fall 1962 Kluge and two other members of the Oberhausen group, Detlev Schleiermacher and Edgar Reitz, had advanced another of the group's goals by negotiating with the Hochschule für Gestaltung in Ulm (a self-styled successor of the Bauhaus) the addition of an Abteilung für Filmgestaltung (Division of Filmmaking) to its academic program. Under the direction of Kluge and Reitz the Abteilung, reconstituted as the autonomous Institut für Filmgestaltung in 1965–66, became the first viable training center for filmmakers in the Federal Republic, taking on a small number of students each year for a four-year course of study. In 1970, it ceased its teaching function to concentrate, in Kluge's words, on "research and development."[11] However, it paved the way for the founding in 1965 of the Deutsche Film- und Fernsehakademie Berlin, which still reflects Kluge's concern that film education institutions not train "specialists in the camera, in scriptwriting, production, direction, etc., but rather *Filmautoren*, intellectuals." The Hochschule für Fernsehen und Film established in Munich in 1966, however, had and has as its stated goal the vocational specialization Kluge had cautioned against.[12]

From its inception in 1962—though only intermittently after the end of the decade—the Abteilung and then Institut für Filmgestaltung provided a framework and a center for Kluge's activities as film educator, film theorist, filmmaker, and spokesman for the New German Cinema. The curriculum Kluge helped the Ulm institute develop took as its points of departure the critical theory of the Frankfurt school, the centrality of montage and the camera, and the New Music and modernist literary texts. Kluge himself took a critical look at German education, past and present, in his third short film and first work associated with Ulm, *Lehrer im Wandel (Teachers in Transition,* 1962–63*).*[13] Premiered at the 1963 Oberhausen Short Film Festival, the film opens on the minuet from Luigi Boccherini's *Quintet in E. Major,* while an off-camera speaker relates Socrates' ironic questioning of Callias in Plato's *Apology* about his plans for the education of his sons. The title "Satisfaction with what has been attained" then introduces a sequence documenting a school dedication ceremony in the Federal Republic of the early 1960s, beginning with the school orchestra playing the Boccherini munuet. Thoroughly conventional statements from the various speakers give way to an ironically understated voice-over account, or "minutes," of the proceedings; it captures their ritualized aspect, dwells on the cost and presentability of the new facility, and relegates what ought to be of primary concern—a lively education—to a final sentence. Three-fourths of the way through this account Kluge reintroduces the Boccherini minuet to the sound track, drawing on the symbolic potential of another element of the ceremony to underscore its repetitiveness and ritualized character. The reiteration of Socrates' questioning of Callias at the close of the dedication sequence, clearly an expression of dissatisfaction with what has been attained, introduces a critical, tersely phrased commentary—over historical images punctuated by ironic and factual titles—on the history of German education (and thus of Germany) since the early 1800s. The commentary culminates in the briefly told, exemplary life stories of three committed teachers — their photographs fixed in turn on the screen — who were "choked off" either literally or figuratively during the years 1933-1962.[14] Kluge ends the film where it began, the strains of the Boccherini minuet accompanying a repetition of images from the school dedication ceremony.

Working for the first time with Beate Mainka, the division's instructor of montage, as his editor (she has since edited most of his other films as well) and with three students—Wilfried Reinke, Günther Hörmann and Peter Schubert—as his camera and sound crew, Kluge explored the continuity of German history from another perspective in *Porträt einer Bewährung* (*Portrait of Proven Service*, 1964), a thirteen-minute film that won a first prize on its premiere at the 1965 Oberhausen Short Film Festival.[15] The ostensible life story of one Police Master Sergeant Karl Müller-Seegeberg—a lay actor of that name and occupation indeed appears in the film and narrates as his own story the literary construct that Kluge wrote on the model of his docufictional *Life Stories*—it traces his life from his birth in near-feudal surroundings in 1900 to his forced retirement from the Munich Security Police in 1960. (He had shot at a pair of fleeing lovers surprised in a wooded park.) What emerges from his ingenuous account of having "proven" himself under "more than five regimes" is a schematic overview of German history in the first sixty years of the twentieth century. An exemplary German civil servant, he learned as a youth not to ask "Why?" and spent his adult life striving to serve the existing order, whatever that order might be.

Although Müller-Seegeberg's spoken narrative is the dominant structural element in *Portrait of Proven Service*, it is nonetheless crucially mediated by the film's other elements. For in structuring his first film to be based on a personal story line, Kluge employs various Brechtian strategies to "make the familiar strange," to keep the film's viewers from becoming absorbed either in the narrator or the narrative at the expense of the film's multiple, associatively structured intentions. The film opens, for example, not with the narrative but with the sound of marching music, while a voice-over summarizes Müller-Seegeberg's early-morning activities and the camera follows him walking through several Munich streets. When he begins to tell his story, he does so off camera—a detail shot of a photograph of his face fixed on the screen. Indeed, the entire narration is done as a voice-over. Only a few strategically placed fixed frames of Müller-Seegeberg maintain the link between speaker and story, while the screen is otherwise given over to historical images and film footage that concretize the spoken text. Furthermore, a series of titles interrupts the narrative, momentarily freezing it at crucial junctures, as if to create reflective pauses for the viewer. At one such juncture (title: "The National Socialists come to power: New need to prove oneself") Kluge suspends the narrative for several minutes, allowing a visual and musical montage documenting a Nazi celebration of the seizure of power and a Sturmabteilung (SA) sports meet to speak for itself. At film's end a similarly constructed montage documents a police sports meet in the Federal Republic, suggesting a disturbing continuity in the ceremonial and ornamental nature of various forms of German public life. Thus the film's closing title—"I would clobber anyone who doesn't act democratically. Karl Müller-Seegeberg"—held on the screen for the final fifteen seconds to the sound of marching music, communicates an ominous message within the context of the film's associative structure: the contradictory attitude identified with Müller-Seegeberg in this "signed" assertion is by no means limited to one individual.

Although his short films do not approach the complexity of Kluge's first major *Autorenfilm,* taken together they exhibit most of the structural features characteristic of *Yesterday Girl* as well as of his later films: understated irony as the basic authorial attitude; the use of image, word, and sound as independent structural elements joined in a "constructed" montage rather than a "natural" scene; the interweaving of the documentary and the fictional; the use of commentary and titles; the avoidance of narrative continuity; the use of the camera as an anlytical device; and the reliance on association as a vehicle of meaning. They also establish Kluge's abiding interest in contemporary reality in its relation to the continuum of German history as the subject matter of his films.

These films thus demonstrate Kluge's early determination to employ a new film language appropriate to film's potential as a medium of cognition. This conception of film was initially opposed to film as a medium of mindless illusion in the essay "The Utopia Film" and then elaborated in the companion essay "Word and Film," coauthored with Edgar Reitz and Winifred Reinke.[16] Drawing especially on Benjamin's speculative essay "The Work of Art in the Age of Mechanical Reproduction" and secondarily on Brecht's writings on epic theater, Kluge bases his conception of film on its neglected structural possibilities. He emphasizes the potential similarity of film's movement to the mind's stream of consciousness, the camera's analytical powers, and the capacity of montage both to emancipate image, word, and sound as independent elements of expression and to organize them in a polyphonic manner. Following Benjamin, he posits a movie-going public whose general, historically conditioned apperceptive disposition—critical receptivity in a state of distraction—if not its specific viewing habits and expectations corresponds epistemologically to film's structural possibilities. From this he concludes that a viewer can respond adequately to a new film language based on these possibilities rather than on illusionistic dramaturgical forms:

> There is thus a massing of "snapshots," subjective and objective, literary, acoustic, and visual, that are interrelated in a state of tension. The ruptures between the individual filmic elements that come about in the process of their montage are one of the manifestations of this tension. By availing itself of this layering of its forms of expression, film achieves the effect that its subject matter settles in the areas between these forms of expression. The overall expression does not assume material form in the film itself, but arises in the viewer's head out of the ruptures between the filmic elements of expression.[17]

Writing some three years after the exuberant optimism of the Oberhausen Manifesto, Kluge quickly adds, however, that given the current needs of viewers and filmmakers his conception of the production and reception of film would remain a "program." For film and its realization via a "differentiated" film language clearly depend as much on the "receptivity of a society," on the "filmic imagination of viewers, theater owners, and distributors," as they do on the abilities of individual *Filmautoren*.[18]

Despite this skeptical assessment of his "program's" chances in 1965, Kluge, as the later popular and critical success of *Yesterday Girl* attests, was working hard at making his utopian projections a reality. Indeed, it was his persistent search for funds to make *Yesterday Girl* on his own terms that finally gave him the opportunity to work with film's "epic" possibilities.[19] The film is based on the troubled experiences of Helga Rosenfeld, a young East

German woman of Jewish background who fled to the West in the mid 1950s. Kluge initially recounted her story in "Anita G," one of his *Life Stories of* 1962. As a film *Yesterday Girl* signals its difference at the very start.[20] Instead of opening on a series of shots that create the illusion of a world in which its titular character is to act and exist, Kluge's film confronts its viewers with an aphoristic title: "What separates us from yesterday is not an abyss but the changed situation." In this epigraphic reference to a collective experience — metonymically encoded in the word "yesterday"—the filmmaker, by his use of the pronoun "us," explicitly identifies with his original German viewers. At the same time he argues against one way of making sense of that experience in favor of another. Indeed, given Kluge's reception of Godard—and here one must recall Godard's conceptualization of his early films as essays—the opening title suggests that *Yesterday Girl* is a filmic essay on the relation of Germany's past and present that encourages viewers to think of that relation in situational rather than apocalyptic terms.

The film's second sequence, a parody of a screen test that takes the form of a dramatic reading, draws the viewers' attention to film as a medium of representation and insists on the constructed nature of that representation. Thus it introduces Alexandra Kluge not as Anita G., the central figure of a represented world, but rather as someone involved in the filmic construction of such a world. Laughing spontaneously as the sequence opens abruptly, Alexandra Kluge makes eye contact with someone heard laughing off camera and then looks directly into the camera before resuming her reading. Only after she has read a sentence or so of the text, which consists of a series of ritualized questions addressing the quality of justice meted out by an unnamed authority figure, does her laughter subside and her face assume the serious demeanor appropriate to the text. Yet even as she slips into the dramatic role, the fact that she is seen to be holding food is incongruent with the solemnity of the text and the established conventions of the occasion. It calls additional attention to the role she assumes *as a role* and implicity evokes Brecht's paradoxical theory of gestic acting, according to which an actor should both play a role and make clear that he or she is playing it. Finally, it should be noted that this metafilmic sequence neatly thematizes the quality of spontaneity that Kluge as *Filmautor* values highly.

As abruptly as it begins, the film's second sequence gives way to a series of shots that introduces Alexandra Kluge as Anita G. *in medias res.* The setting is a real upper-middle-class café, whose decor, small orchestra playing dated dance music, and general ambience are distinctly reminiscent of the 1930s. The camera pans from its elevated perspective following Anita as she enters and moves toward a low circular table surrounded by six chairs in the center of the café. A miniature drama unfolds as Anita tries first one and then another chair before finally settling back in a third to survey the café around her in a casual manner, as though she belonged to the world it embodies. That she really does not belong to this world of yesterday—which nevertheless conditions her behavior—is implicit in the drama of the chairs. Her movement from chair to chair, as if to gain the proper position from which to see and be seen, suggests that, however much she may want to identify and be identified with this world, she is playing a social role, playing at being someone rather than *being* that someone. Throughout the film, this particular role and the larger patterns of behavior it entails will trip her.

Kluge emphasizes this crucial aspect of the café sequence in two ways. First, he superimposes the title of his film on precisely those frames that record the drama of the chairs. Second, he holds the diagonal long shot of Anita seated for an extended period, allowing viewers to sense her isolation within her surroundings both visually and aurally. The table and chairs form a circular image that is, both spatially and in terms of form, separated from the linear configuration of the remainder of the scene. Acoustically, the hum of people conversing, added separately to the sound track, vies with the orchestra's playing in volume, suggesting that everyone in the café but Anita is engaged in conversation. Anita's isolation is not broken until a waitress appears on the scene, and although we only *see* the two women speak and gesture and laugh, it is nonetheless one of the few instances of genuine interaction in the film.

This momentary image makes the sudden cut to a courtroom scene seem all the more abrupt. Constituted by a complex sequence of shots that continually shifts and refocuses our attention, this scene provides an ironic view of an instrumentalized judicial system. Its narrow rationality, hierarchial structure, and cultural-historical context limit its agent's ability to comprehend the historically mediated irrationality of Anita's behavior in a "changed situation," be it her flight from East Germany to the West in 1957 or her seemingly unmotivated theft of a cardigan from a fellow nurse in Braunschweig two years later. In questioning Anita about her flight from East Germany—where her parents had rejoined her after the war in 1945 and recovered their confiscated factories—the judge emphatically disputes her tenuous assertion of a connection between her past experiences as a child born to Jewish industrialists in 1937 and the sudden fear that twenty years later led her to come to the West. Significantly, Anita herself appears none too clear about the relation she draws between past and present, merely citing "earlier incidents" as the source of her fear. It is the judge who concretizes these in terms of a rationalistic reconstruction of her *conscious* perception of persecution during 1943–44: "Experience tells us that children suffer no long-term effects from such things." When Anita persists in motivating her departure from East Germany in emotional terms by noting that she "didn't feel safe," the judge counters with a pragmatic motive reflecting the complacent, narrowly materialistic orientation of West German culture of the period: "Wasn't it really the case that you thought your chances would be better here?"

Similarly, in questioning Anita he brushes aside her prehearing statement that she stole the cardigan in a "state of confusion." Half questioning, half lecturing, he asks why pragmatic considerations and/or internalized ethical norms did not keep her from taking the cardigan or make her conceal it once she had taken it. Affirming that she felt cold when she took the cardigan even though it was summertime, she finally responds in keeping with her rudimentary psychological understanding of her behavior: "It was all a matter of feeling." Visibly perplexed, the judge falls back on a legalistic response and then concerns himself with Anita's dossier, as though it held the answer to the enigma before him. In a subsequent shot he reads at length from a convoluted commentary on the West German criminal code that distinguishes between the categories of "possession by a second party" and "ownership as such." While the shot makes clear that the judge is looking for a way out for Anita, it also effectively dramatizes that, in keeping with the institution within which he works and the culture he represents, he can only imagine a legalistic solution to the issue before him. However, Anita's case requires an approach that takes as its point of departure her inarticulate self-understanding rather than current conventional wisdom about human behavior.

Kluge delineates such an approach later in the film in a sequence intersecting Anita's protracted affair with the married cultural functionary Pichota. Interweaving the documentary and the fictional, he structures the sequence around the prominent progressive jurist Dr. Fritz Bauer, who returned from exile in 1949 to a judicial post in Braunschweig and became the attorney general of the West German state of Hessen in 1956, an office he still held when Kluge was filming *Yesterday Girl*. Kluge's voice-over at the start of the sequence informs the viewer that Anita has read about Bauer in a newspaper and is trying to contact him concerning her difficulties with the law. In the final shot of the sequence, as an architect shows him around a traditional courtroom in a new judicial building and points with pride to some technical innovations, Bauer asks his guide whether he can "imagine that some day we'll do a round table, where the prosecuting attorney and the defense attorney and the defendant and the court sit around the table and together struggle for the truth and what we call justice." But in the real world of the Federal Republic, as in the constructed world of *Yesterday Girl*, such thoughts merely outline a utopian counterperspective. Intimidated by the apparatus of secretaries and bright young men that surround the clearly overworked attorney general, Anita never gets through to him. She must thus continue to live with the justice dispensed in the courtroom scene, which ends with a shot that reaffirms the traditional authority of the judge as he returns from chambers. No judgment is spoken. Instead, the camera presents it silently as it cuts first to the gallery of a prison and then to the half-open doorway of Anita's cell.

Having established in the café and courtroom sequences the intersection of past and present in Anita's life, Kluge unfolds Anita's story in a series of discontinuous episodes set in a curiously atemporal West Germany of the early to mid-1960s. No attempt is made to connect individual episodes with major public events of these years such as the building of the Berlin Wall, the *Spiegel* scandal with its instances of police state tactics, or the recession of 1962–63. Instead Kluge marks the passing of time in general cultural terms, alluding to one Christmas season and explicitly setting a scene in another, identifying a day Anita spends with a Gymnasium student at the annual Protestant Day of Repentance, and registering an implicit sequence of winter seasons in scattered exterior shots. Individual episodes have the character of everyday reality, sometimes encompassing large chunks of it in the form of documentary-style footage while still focusing the viewer's attention on Anita's behavior in the here and now of a given situation. At the same time, Kluge establishes the presence of the past in these episodes in various ways: through dramatized attitudes, utterances, and recollections, through the visual and acoustic elements of specific scenes, and — most strikingly — through associative montage, the use of which warrants closer examination.

The first such montage is a polyphonically structured sequence consisting of illustrations from a nineteenth-century children's book that depict two boys frolicking with a mammoth, which one of them has discovered and freed from the ice; Kluge's soft-spoken reading of the accompanying text (his debut as the voice-over speaker of his films) is set against the melody of a children's Christmas carol, "Leise rieselt der Schnee," played on a Hammond organ. It intersects the brief initial prison sequence as though it were Anita's childhood-inspired daydream of freedom, warmth, and community in the middle of her imprisonment. Its utopian aspect also stands in sharp contrast to the oppressive character, in the following sequence, of Anita's forced reintegration into the community at the hands of a domineering, unduly pious, and self-righteous probation officer who only succeeds in driving off her charge before the probationary period is up. The second associative montage joins a series of family photographs from Anita's childhood depicting a solid upper-middle-class existence as lively tango music recalls the dance music of the café sequence. Kluge inserts this montage in a dialogue segment of the lengthy and disjunctively structured episode that follows the probation sequence and is set in Frankfurt. Here Anita works selling language records on commission to passersby, but she becomes her new boss's mistress after he catches her making up a sale. Evoking familial warmth and affluent security, the montage helps explain why Anita is at home in her subsequent role as a kept woman, a role Kluge dramatizes in the framework of documentary footage at a furrier's where Anita purchases a heavy fur coat, a sign of class *and* warmth, with a bundle of 50-mark bills. Anita's not so new existence is cut short, however, by her boss's suspicious wife. To prove his fidelity, Anita's boss, as we learn from Kluge's voiceover comment on shots of Anita packing, decides to press charges against her. The film then cuts to a pan shot of Anita, dressed in her fur coat, walking toward the entrance of the Frankfurt train station with suitcase in hand.

An ironic sequel to the photographic montage in both its formal and thematic structure, the pan shot initiates a recurrent image that becomes emblematic of Anita's transient existence. Indeed, in the flight sequence that marks the end of Anita's affair with Pichota and terminates in her voluntary return to prison, Kluge sets a series of extreme long shots of Anita as a lone figure carrying her suitcase along heavily traveled roadways and across a freeway overpass; tango music alludes to the underlying connection between Anita's consciousness as embodied in the retrospective montage and her present reality. In the Pichota episode itself, on one level an elaborate rerun of Anita's affair with her boss, Kluge draws out the implications of the photographic montage differently: Anita is posed in an evening gown before an ornate map of Bismarck's Imperial Germany hanging on Pichota's wall. This photographlike shot, held for fifteen seconds, recalls the curiously anachronistic photograph of a formal evening party that shows Anita's father standing among his guests, who include a number of officers of the Wehrmacht! In fact, the entire montage is anachronistic, since no German Jewish family lived in the manner it suggests in the early 1940s. However, Kluge's use of the montage to comment on Anita's behavior in the 1960s is invalidated only if we assume that his intention is to reproduce the surface of reality rather than to delineate the structure of reality. Since he has stressed a similarity in the backgrounds of Helga Rosenfeld and his sister Alexandra—whose birthday and year of emigration to the West he lends Anita G. in a more trivial interplay of fact and fiction— it is not surprising that he draws on his family's personalized record of Germany's socioeconomic and political history to explain Anita's disposition to play a self-destructive social role; by doing so he insists on the historical unity of German upper-middle-class existence and points up its continuity in the figure of the *Bildungsbürger* Manfred Pichota.

A final associative montage precedes the Pichota episode and follows a series of scenes at the University of Frankfurt dramatizing Anita's predictable failure to start a new life as a student after being unjustly fired from a job as a maid at a posh hotel. By means of it, Kluge reminds us of another historically mediated motive for Anita's illusory search for warmth, security, and status in her relationship with Pichota. It is fear, embodied in a complex nightmare sequence that integrates elements drawn from Anita's and Germany's past and present as well as from a future totalitarian regime. Anita both flees and confronts her varying pursuers, attacking her probation officer and killing a paratrooper—a representative of the new regime who is about to execute a young boy with his mother's acquiescence—only to have him reappear among a new set of pursuers, including two SA men, a split second later. Again using a montage to convey more than Anita's state of mind, Kluge jolts his viewers in the middle of the chase with the title: "Is yesterday coming tomorrow?"

In the Day of Repentance episode near the middle of the film, Anita self-assuredly tells the student with whom she spends the day that "nobody can learn not to learn." Yet that is precisely what Anita has learned. She is caught between recollections of a plentiful past, a recurring fear whose origins lie in that past, the slogan-simplified reality of the German Democratic Republic, and the complex reality of an affluent Federal Republic that largely ignores Germany's recent past. On her odyssey through the urbanized center of the Federal Republic she encounters no one capable of helping her break through the vicious circle that limits her sense of self and history and restricts her ability to learn from experience. The "teachers" she encounters—the judge, the probation officer, the entrepreneur, two professors, and Pichota—are too caught up in their own all too limited sense of self and the world even to notice Anita's essential dilemma. Their varying attempts to "educate" her only exacerbate her difficulties. When Anita's own muddled sense of her dilemma leads her to seek competent help from Attorney General Bauer, she gives up without reaching him.

Anita's only other solution is to run, although clearly to no avail. In the flight sequence that marks the end of her affair with Pichota, Kluge concretizes her predicament by means of the visual metaphor of a sustained circular tracking shot of Anita sitting on her suitcase in the middle of the grassy interior of a freeway interchange. Not surprisingly, the sequence ends with Anita turning herself in. In the prison sequence that concludes *Yesterday Girl* Kluge leaves open the question whether Anita will learn to make some sense of her life in her ambiguous refuge. It is a physically warm and clean place in which she can give birth to the child conceived during her affair with Pichota, but since she must spend the next four years there she must surrender that child for adoption. The possibility for change is given in the person of a sympathetic social worker who clearly takes Anita seriously as a person in her own right and encourages her to raise questions. Yet their initial dialogue (and the film's last) turns on Anita's formal education and future job possibilities rather than the underlying issues. And the lengthy closing shot of Anita's bewildered face, her eyes peering sadly into the camera, compassionately suggests that the learning process will at best be difficult.

After *Yesterday Girl,* Kluge planned to make a comic film in the tradition of Charles Chaplin and Buster Keaton. "Imagine," he told an interviewer in October 1966, "a person who takes everything very literally walking around in our phrase-ridden environment, for example, a radio station."[21] While this plan sheds some light on his reworking of the Mack Sennett short *Nipp and Tuck* that same year, Kluge's work took a rather different turn under the pressure of subsequent events. At the mid-1967 Berlin Film Festival, he, Edgar Reitz, and film critic Enno Patalas were pelted with eggs by members of the emerging radical student movement. In addition, a new film subsidy law favoring the established film industry was passed in late 1967 despite the year-long opposition Kluge had led against. Both events helped shape Kluge's second feature film, *Die Artisten in der Zirkuskuppel: ratlos (Artists in the Big Top: Perplexed,* 1967–68), a historically situated parable on art, politics, the artist/intellectual, and the public under contemporary capitalism.[22]

From the start *Artists* signals difficulty, dissonance, and contradiction. Inserted among the opening credits, the fixed frame of Hannelore Hoger's as yet anonymous face smiling pleasantly into the camera stands in sharp contrast to the melancholic strains of a hand organ. At the same time an elliptical voice-over commentary—itself a miniature textual montage implying a much longer narrative—leaves the viewer wondering whether it is meant to refer to the woman pictured, represent her thoughts of another woman, or comment by indefinite example on both the difficulty of human relationships and the power of love and sexuality. Similarly constructed montage units joining clear images, opaque texts, and musical fragments recur throughout the film, leaving the viewer groping for connections, looking to make sense of nonsense, questioning what is seen and heard without finding ready answers. In effect, the film forces its viewers to experience perplexity themselves.

Even the general orientation that Kluge provides his viewers as a prefatory gloss on the film's title—"They've worked their way up to here. Now they don't know what next. Just making an effort is absolutely useless"—yields its relevance only gradually. On first viewing neither gloss nor title appear to have any bearing on the following newsreel footage of the 1939 Nazi celebration of the Day of German Art that Kluge edits to ironic effect and identifies in midsequence as "First work of mourning." Hitler and the assembled Nazi elite as perplexed artists? On reflection, that is precisely the association intended. For, as Walter Benjamin observed in his essay on art, politics, and film in the 1930s, fascism, in order to preserve existing property relations, had aestheticized political life. Through the medium of film in the form of newsreels it was made into a cultic, mass-appeal art form that would inevitably lead to war.[23]

"Second work of mourning: Manfred Peickert." Thus Kluge introduces the film's second sequence, which a voice-over commentary ties ironically to the titular gloss: "Genius is the ability to make an unending effort." Peickert, descendant of four generations of apothecaries who valued achievement above all, joins the circus in 1945 in search of a new life. Yet true to his own past he develops unrealizable plans to incorporate elephants into his trapeze act. Frustrated in his efforts to achieve something that "would create a strong feeling," he is, we are told, overcome by melancholy in a routine performance and plunges to his death. Significantly, Peickert's death is by no means the only one linked to performances of ever-increasing difficulty. Kluge hints at a disturbing reality beneath the surface glitter and vitality of the circus: the artists' unreflected efforts to perfect their art and enthrall the public have assumed the form of an unconscious death wish. Moreover, at midfilm Leni Peickert reports, unwittingly to be sure, on the political origins of this existential malady: "First modern circus: Astley in Paris. Time: French Revolution. The achievements of the *artistes*: breathtaking. There is really nothing of which the new revolutionary man is not capable." In retrospect, then, the Manfred Peickert sequence, which carries us into the 1960s, also exhibits an interplay of art and politics in the service of death. Thus it, too, is intended as an instance of mourning or *Trauerarbeit* in an expanded intersubjective sense of Freud's notion.[24] Its function as part of a process of recollection is to make us aware (and here one must keep Kluge's German contemporaries of 1968 in mind as the film's primary intended audience) of our problematical ties to the past, thus enabling us, ideally, to make a new beginning: art and politics in the service of life.

Yet Kluge, whose film as a whole can be viewed as *Trauerarbeit* toward this new beginning, is clearly not very optimistic about its realization. His vehicle for presenting the internal dilemmas and external obstacles confronting the contemporary artist in search of a new art and politics is the story of Leni Peickert's personal act of mourning, her inchoate plan and subsequent efforts to open a reform circus worthy of her father's memory. Not surprisingly, this story recalls the history of the Young German Film from its Oberhausen genesis through 1967 when its subsidization was seriously reduced and restructured. Like the young German filmmakers Leni comes down out of the big top into the world of everyday reality to pursue her plan for a new circus as an entrepreneur. While this move is premised on a miscalculation ("Only as a capitalist can one change what is") and leads to bankruptcy, she and her plan are rescued by an inheritance from a rich friend, an allusion to the funds provided by the Kuratorium during the years 1965–67.

Leni's central, unacknowledged dilemma, a voice-over dialogue implies early in the film, is that she wants to change the circus because she loves it. For this very reason she will not change it, because "love is a conservative impulse." This impulse manifests itself in her unreflected assimilation of the principle of achievement that underlies the existing circus to her evolving political aesthetics. Her rhetoric recalls one of Adorno's most influential postwar dicta: "In view of the inhuman situation the artist has no choice but to intensify the degree of difficulty of his art." Leni attempts to bridge the gap between her intentions and the expectations of her audience by arguing, "Freedom means that the spectator will take what we offer him as entertainment. But what we offer him doesn't need to be that." Her co-workers are unconvinced, and she liquidates the circus in an act of "truthfulness" to her utopian projections.[25] Kluge himself appears prepared to live with the contradictions entailed by Leni's argument. For in making *Artists in the Big Top: Perplexed* he pursues his utopian projections of film and its possibilities to an extreme even as he employs the medium to point up the difficulties—in particular the lack of a disposed public—impeding the realization of a new art and politics.

Kluge's next major film, *Gelegenheitsarbeit einer Sklavin (Occasional Work of a Female Slave)*, had its premiere in Munich in December 1973.[26] Its origins lie in his work with Oscar Negt during 1970–72 on the book *Öffentlichkeit und Erfahrung (The Public Sphere and Experience)*, a formidable analysis of the production, organization, and use value of experience in advanced capitalist society.[27] The book treats the nuclear family as a contradictory organizational form that preserves a matriarchal mode of production. Concerned with real needs and a wholistic experience of time, it nevertheless blocks the transference of this mode of production—in which Kluge and Negt see "woman's true claim to emancipation"—to a public sphere dominated by patriarchal and commodity capitalist forms. In a retrospective defense of his film, Kluge would have us view the film primarily in terms of the implicitly emancipatory "program" of its central character, Roswitha Bronski.[28] Her activities ostensibly "make visible" a radical alternative to the prevailing reality principle. Yet, to borrow a phrase from Kluge's materialist aesthetics of this period, the film itself appears to "organize our experience" differently.

Consider, in particular, the complex opening sequence, which reflects on the film medium as it introduces us to the title figure played by Alexandra Kluge. "Roswitha feels an enormous power within herself. But she knows through movies that this power really does exist," Kluge comments off camera over a shot of Roswitha's face, betraying no irony. Yet the words suggest an ironic stance toward Roswitha that he develops in several ways. First he concretizes Roswitha's movie experience in terms of a brief scene from *Chapayev*, a 1934 Soviet film whose revolutionary romanticism, exemplary hero, and illusionistic mode—all based on the new doctrine of Socialist Realism—conflict categorically with Kluge's own theory and practice as a filmmaker. He then provides an analytical perspective on her reception of film via a title quoting Friedrich Engels: "Everything that gets people moving must pass through their head. But the shape it assumes in their head depends a great deal on their circumstances." At issue here it is not that movies can and do shape our sense of self and thus our actions, but how and why they do so. Given Roswitha's circumstances as shown in the first half of the film, *Chapayev* functions as an external and public means of legitimizing and organizing her private and unacknowledged experience as housewife and mother. Yet the sense of self that Roswitha generates in this manner is illusory and leads at midfilm to a political program that ignores her family as the root cause of her problems and that cannot be achieved by means of her specific mode of production as housewife and mother. It is this interrelated complex of problems that Kluge's decidedly anti-illusionistic film makes visible.

Our first glimpse of Roswitha in the middle of her family takes the form of a harmonious tableau: the Bronskis look out their living-room window onto new-fallen snow. Kluge's voice-over comment—"Inside it's warm, outside it's cold"—takes on metaphorical aspects as the next sequence dramatizes that it also gets "cold" inside. Camera and commentary initially juxtapose two modes of activity in separate spaces: in the kitchen Roswitha and her friend Sylvia looking after their children, in an adjoining room Franz Bronski, a chemist, pursuing studies toward another profession. Roswitha's breaking of a plate signals the sudden interpenetration of these spheres as Bronski, disturbed by the noise, appears in the doorway and berates his wife for disrupting his work, for the general disorder, and for Sylvia's presence. The first of several sequences presenting Bronski as a patriarchal tyrant, this scene also anticipates Roswitha's failure to keep "inside" and "outside" separate while pursuing "occasional

Alexandra Kluge in *Occasional Work
of a Female Slave* (COURTESY OF
FILMVERLAG DER AUTOREN)

work" as an abortionist in order to keep her family together.[29]
Located "in another part of the city," her practice is spatially
insulated from the family, but its illegality draws Bronski's unending opposition even as he lives off its proceeds and eventually brings the police to her door. With Bronski's spontaneous
cooperation she neutralizes this attack from the outside. But
when he afterward makes clear that nothing has changed in
their relationship and takes a job as a chemist, Roswitha resolves
to give up her practice, no longer spend her energy exclusively
on her family, and become socially and politically active.

Kluge, who announces these decisions in a voice-over commentary on a shot of Roswitha and her children in a park, signals his ironic distance by cutting to a shot of ominous storm
clouds—reminiscent of fate montages in German *Heimatfilme*—and setting it and a montage of Roswitha's fantasy of
coming political activities to thunderous piano chords. Significantly, the montage concludes with another clip from *Chapayev*.
Of course Kluge's irony is also directed toward other targets.
Extensive documentary footage of an official study tour of
Frankfurt's social problems, with Roswitha present among a sea
of men, points up the powerlessness of a progressive administration in the face of entrenched interests. A meeting of young
executives and plant security experts unexpectedly thematizes

an underlying problem of advanced capitalist society: the need for a work force that feels secure rather than plants that have been secured. Even Roswitha and Sylvia's naive and disorganized attempt to convince two male newspaper editors of the urgency of their concerns for the nourishment of night-shift workers and the safety of children in traffic suggests it is the editors who need to rethink their ossified categories. Yet in the end Roswitha's personalized approach to political action and her utter blindness to the workings of the existing order, emphasized by Kluge's ironic commentaries and titles, leave viewers shaking their heads.

In 1973, Kluge coauthored a book on the economics, politics, and poetics of postwar filmmaking in the Federal Republic and Europe, and published *Lernprozesse mit tödlichem Ausgang* (*Learning Processes with Lethal Conclusions*).[30] The "first-class individualists in an age of collective struggles" who populate this fiction collection attempt to give their lives meaning by pursuing their work, ideals, or life plans to uncompromising extremes even as the collective bases of meaning continually change. One of the more memorable of these characters, plant security chief Ferdinand Rieche, whom Kluge portrays in the scenario-like narrative "A Bolshevik of Capitalism," became the title character of his next solo feature, *Der starke Ferdinand* (*Strong Man Ferdinand*, 1975–76; 1977).[31]

Played by the diminutive Heinz Schubert, Kluge's Ferdinand is a tragicomic figure decisively at odds with the contradictory and contingent world in which he moves.[32] Frustrated by constitutional constraints on his work as a police detective—the opening scene shows him berating his superior for not seizing a suspect *before* he has had a chance to commit a crime that led to the death of a policeman—Rieche takes a job in the private sector. Yet his initial charge as plant security chief at the German branch of a multinational corporation headquartered in Brussels explicitly subjects him to the same constraints. His predecessor having overstepped legal bounds, he is to return plant security to conformity with constitutional guidelines as quickly as possible. His probationary job status is further threatened because his appointment causes a split within the local board of directors. Board Chairman Ganter has a conception of industrial security that dates back to the sociopolitical upheavals of 1918–

1923, but Wilutzki, a key board member attuned to contemporary reality, opposes a plant security force, arguing that insurance would be only half as expensive and that the savings could be plowed back into production.

Undaunted by Wilutzki, the feisty Ferdinand instructs his charges in the theory and practice of their trade, updates security technology, and, with sledgehammer in hand, reconstitutes his office as a command post in the middle of production. Where his personal needs are concerned, Ferdinand is not above bending the rules. In order to do well on a mandatory physical, he obtains a urine sample from a young clerical worker. Gertie, a plant cafeteria employee, becomes his lover in exchange for his silence after he catches her stealing supplies. Growing restless, he teaches his men how to circumvent the spirit while maintaining the letter of the law in dealing with intruders. Yet Ferdinand's true moment as a radical activist in security matters comes only after a terrorist firebomb damages the plant. Reprimanded for laxity, he is authorized to achieve "total security with all the trimmings." Ferdinand, who thrives on states of emergency, achieves that and more. Besides doubling the security force, adding security hardware, and holding emergency drills that interfere with production, he drills his men as a military unit. Despite his rejection of a former police colleague's politics—"Radical security has nothing to do with radicalism"— he holds joint maneuvers with Kniebeling's neo-Nazi paramilitary troupe, a scene that Kluge structures to comic effect without diminishing its ominousness. As a tour de force he leads a commando unit of his men on a night raid on a competitor's plant, returning the stolen property in broad daylight the next morning. At the same time he finds time to "practice" Christmas in November, with Gertie, determined to leave nothing to chance.

Nevertheless, Ferdinand's professional and personal life begins to unravel even as a threat against the board would seem to make him indispensable. Ganter responds to his request for instructions with an ambivalent message: "You'll have to do more, but you can't do too much." Gertie leaves him while he is embroiled in his illegal handling of a suspected case of industrial espionage. Suspicious of Wilutzki, Ferdinand follows him to Brussels, uncovers secret merger negotiations, and imprisons him in his own house for "treason to the firm." His ignorance of corporate capitalism costs Ferdinand his job when Wilutzki assumes control after the merger. An extreme long shot framing Ferdinand's departure in a plant window captures his essential loneliness and defeat as he trudges off.

Yet an alert and resurgent Ferdinand reappears in the remarkable coda with which Kluge returns the film to its beginning, albeit with a greatly enlarged frame of reference encompassing West German terrorism and the reaction to it by the mid-1970s. To demonstrate both his abilities and the "need" to engage in preemptive detention of "certain groups," he stages an assassination attempt against a cabinet minister. In an interview following his capture, Ferdinand philosophically glosses his intended but bungled near-miss: "Because our lives in general don't have a precise meaning, we can't always shoot precisely."[33] Set against the metaphorical nonsense uttered by the minister in the interview preceding the attempt, his words and his interview as a whole confront viewers with a series of sociopolitical and existential dilemmas characteristic of a pluralistic but badly polarized and hierarchically structured society.

By fall 1977 some of these dilemmas had assumed acute form in the national life of the Federal Republic. On September 9, industrialist Hanns-Martin Schleyer, head of the German Employers Federation, was kidnapped in Cologne and held against the release of eleven German terrorists, including the leaders Andreas Baader, J. K. Raspe, and Gudrun Ensslin, who were imprisoned near Stuttgart. On October 13, a Lufthansa passenger jet was hijacked in Spain to reinforce this demand. On its recapture five days later in Mogadishu, Somalia, by a special unit of the German Border Police, Baader, Raspe, and Ensslin committed suicide with weapons that had been smuggled in to them. Schleyer was found murdered a day later in France. Following six years of intermittent terrorist actions, steadily increasing official countermeasures that frequently violated civil rights, and the constant political demagoguery of Axel Springer's newspapers, this series of events, accompanied by news blackouts and a sustained sense of national emergency, triggered widespread confusion and emotional turmoil.

For Kluge, reminded of the closing months of World War II, the events became an occasion not only to reflect on their relation to German history but also to take a decisive stand against

Heinz Schubert is *Strong Man
Ferdinand* (Courtesy of
Filmverlag der Autoren)

the lethal logic of terrorism and official reprisals in favor of a
"single society" free of civil war.[34] Both concerns inform his contributions to *Deutschland im Herbst* (*Germany in Autumn*, 1978), a
collaborative response of directors, editors, and actors associated
with the NGC to the events of September and October 1977 that
Kluge coordinated and helped give final form. Thus the film, its
final image Kluge's and Volker Schlöndorff's emblematic shot of
a young woman and her daughter walking away from the funeral of the three terrorists, concludes with an unambiguous title.
Uttered thirty-two years earlier by a woman victimized by the
senseless bombing of Kluge's hometown of Halberstadt, it is an
impassioned plea for an end to the violence: "Once atrocity has
reached a certain point, it no longer matters who started it. It
should just stop."[35]

Kluge's most conspicuous contribution to *Germany in Autumn* is
a montage sequence that intersperses diverse images of German
history with dramatized scenes of actress Hannelore Hoger as
history teacher Gabi Teichert, who, in doubt about what to teach
since the events of fall 1977, goes digging in a blue-lit wintry
landscape "in search of the foundations of German history."
Although limited in scope and shaped to fit its context, this
sequence anticipates the radical associative structure and intro-

duces both the title figure and central concern of *Die Patriotin*
(*The Patriot*, 1979), Kluge's idiosyncratic exploration of Germany
from its medieval origins to the present with occasional glimpses
toward an uncertain future.[36] Reshot in a dimly visible nocturnal
setting for *The Patriot*, Gabi Teichert's seemingly random excavations may be absurdly comic on their face, but they are also a
fitting analogue of Kluge's approach to his subject. For in unearthing German history for his viewers, Kluge—also working
in the dark, as it were—appears to draw at random on a disparate array of sources: paintings, landscapes and cityscapes,
comic books, historical and documentary footage, myths, fairy
tales, musical works, photographs, illustrations, interviews,
dramatized scenes, literary texts, proverbs. If, as a consequence,
the film's viewers sometimes experience confusion, they have
paradoxically gained some understanding of what is at issue. As
Kluge comments on a shot of Gabi near the film's end: "Most of
the time Gabi Teichert is more confused than not. That's a matter of the overall context."

The overall context is Germany, and Gabi Teichert's utopian
quest for a "patriotic" version of German history beyond text-
books and centralized curricula is the core fiction around which
Kluge arranges the heterogeneous materials he transmits to his
viewers. Schematically drawn, the figure of Gabi Teichert allows Kluge to move freely between present and past, between
real and symbolic settings. Thus his brief voice-over introduction of her as a history teacher in the West German state of
Hessen and as a "patriot"—someone who "empathizes with all
the dead of the Reich"—both fixes her concrete existence in the
here and now and serves as a prelude to a complex montage
sequence initiated by historical images of death and destruction
on the battlefield. The remainder of the sequence is dominated
by the rambling discourse of a protesting knee, the surviving
remnant of a Corporal Wieland who died in the German debacle
at Stalingrad in early 1943. Introduced via poet Christian
Morgenstern's antiwar "gallows song" "Das Knie," the macabre
fiction of Corporal Wieland's disembodied knee speaking for the
dead of the Reich with a sense of humorous desperation raises
concerns central to the film and Kluge's conception of history:
the physical and emotional reality of individual human beings
both as the victims of history and as its potential subjects, the

contingent nature of historical developments, and the persistence of unfulfilled wishes as well as destructive traditions in a given culture.

The diverse images over which Kluge reads Morgenstern's poem and the knee's discourse serve multiple functions. Including Caspar David Friedrich's painting *Oak in a Thaw*, a nightmarish kneeling figure reaching from an icy slope toward a fortified castle, German landscapes full of spring and summer, and documentary footage of German POWs trudging through the Russian snow, the images freely associate key elements of the spoken texts. Viewed with regard to the film as a whole, they introduce recurrent motifs and selectively embody a richly connotative binary opposition. The polarity between top and bottom informs Kluge's associative presentation of Germany's social, political, military, and ideological history, the hierarchical structure of contemporary institutions and of the human mind and body, and the topography of Frankfurt where Gabi Teichert lives and works. Most easily recognized in the bombing scenes that recur throughout the film (Kluge refers in one instance to the strategies from "above" and "below"), this polarity is also evident in such disparate filmic units as a miniature montage based on a medieval manuscript depicting a peasant being set upon from above by feudal authorities and an entire documentary sequence on the Social Democratic Party's 1977 convention in Hamburg, in the course of which Gabi's seemingly naive efforts to alter the course of German history in a more positive direction help lay bare the hierarchical structure of decision-making in the party.

Although Gabi's quest is represented at the start as all-encompassing—her symbolic excavations are followed by shots of her peering through a telescope at the universe—she is nonetheless aligned through most of the film with its "bottom" pole, the realm of the "folk," of wishes and feelings and experiences rather than that of rationality, rules, and codified knowledge—its "top" pole, which is associated with male authority figures. Thus her teaching of history in terms of the structure of the human body leads to a confrontation with a state educational official who reprimands her for deviating from the standard lesson plan; he finds her inaccessible to reason and lacking a sense of order. In pursuing her interest in folk and fairy tales as a manifestation of eight hundred years of unfulfilled wishes of the German people, she encounters a former high-ranking Hessian school official who has reduced their content to absurd legal issues. Indeed, wherever Gabi Teichert turns, Kluge shows a strident legalism permeating private and public life.

Gabi's implicit response to this state of affairs, as Kluge's own, is "to make an effort," a state of mind and being characteristic of Kluge's utopian protagonists since *Artists in the Big Top: Perplexed*. In *The Patriot* he identifies this condition with a surreal subterranean laboratory: "The interior of a person who makes an effort is comparable to a factory, a workshop, a cellar, or a witch's kitchen." Here, in a thematic setting reminiscent of Goethe's *Faust*, where fairy tales and solid-state physics meet, Gabi Teichert conducts scientific experiments, attacks books with sickle, hammer, saw, and drill, and concocts a witch's brew from orange-juice concentrate and the pages of a book. Back in the real world of her classroom, her efforts leave her sick to her stomach, a sign that her Faustian attempt at unifying the fragmented, at establishing the "inner connections" of German history, fails at a very personal level. In a related scene we see her crying as she drives through Frankfurt. In these scenes Kluge undoubtedly ironizes his own considerable efforts in making *The Patriot*. But his emblematic final shot of Gabi Teichert looking hopefully out into a violent snowstorm on New Year's Eve in anticipation of another 365 days in which to pursue her quest suggests that he, like his cinematic persona, has no intention of giving up.

The specific shape that Kluge's future efforts as a filmmaker will take is anyone's guess. Since *Germany in Autumn* he has repeatedly endorsed the notion of cooperative ventures as a means of overcoming some of the dilemmas inherent in the *Autorenfilm*. His film work in the early 1980s—*Der Kandidat (The Candidate, 1980)*, a sober and sobering portrait of Franz Josef Strauss as a political figure made with Schlöndorff and the newcomers Reinhard Aust and Alexander von Eschwege, and *Krieg und Frieden (War and Peace)*, a film designed to include contributions by Schlöndorff, von Eschwege, and Fassbinder—is in keeping with this position. Even *The Patriot*, the most personal of Kluge's films and the most radical realization of his conception of the *Autorenfilm*, was originally conceived as a group project and contains a scene shot by Margarethe von Trotta. Yet in the end it probably matters little which organizational form Kluge's work as a filmmaker will assume. One way or another the results will reflect the metaphorical summary of his film poetics that concludes his introduction to the screenplay of *The Patriot*:

> Filmmaking is strictly antiacademic, a brash trade; historically grounded, but irregular. At the present time there are enough cultivated entertainment and issue-oriented films, as if cinema were a stroll on walkways in a park. Adhering to the stricture not to leave the walkways has in the past caused the failure of German revolutions. One need not duplicate the cultivated. In fact, children prefer the bushes; they play in the sand or in scrap heaps. Happiness, says Freud, is the fulfillment of childhood wishes. I'm certain that cinema has something to do with wishes. Cinema = Movie = It moves on and on despite all brakemen.

NOTES

[1]Aside from Kluge's scattered autobiographical statements, a major source for the details of his life is Rainer Lewandowski's biographical sketch in *Alexander Kluge* (Munich: C. H. Beck, 1980), pp. 7–14. Kluge gives an indirect account of the ambience of his childhood in a recent portrait of his father entitled "Jahrgang 1892," in *Neue Geschichten, Hefte 1–18, "Unheimlichkeit der Zeit"* (Frankfurt: Suhrkamp, 1977), pp. 313–332.

[2]"Gespräche mit Alexander Kluge," *Filmkritik* 20 (1976): 562.

[3]*Neue Geschichten,* p. 9. In keeping with the primal nature of the experience, Kluge's at once imagined, factual, and analytical reconstruction of the bombing attack on Halberstadt in *Heft* 2 of *Neue Geschichten,* pp. 33–106, contains one of the few instances of overtly autobiographical first-person discourse in his docufictional writing (cf. esp. pp. 50–53).

[4]Rainer Lewandowski, *Die Filme von Alexander Kluge* (Hildesheim & New York: Olms, 1980), p. 38.

[5]"Gespräche," p. 592.

[6]Alexander Kluge, "Die Utopie Film," *Merkur: Zeitschrift für europäisches Denken,* (December 1964): 1134–1146. "The Work of Art in the Age of Mechanical Reproduction," the 1938 version of Walter Benjamin's essay, was first published in 1955 as "Das Kunstwerk im Zeitalter seiner technischen Reproduzierbarkeit" in vol. 1 of the two-volume *Schriften,* edited by Theodor W. and Gretel Adorno (Frankfurt: Suhrkamp), pp. 366–405, after an earlier French version appeared in the then Paris-based *Zeitschrift für Sozialforschung* in 1936. Kluge's source is the later version, which is available in English in Walter Benjamin, *Illuminations,* edited by Hannah Arendt (New York: Schocken, 1969), pp. 217–251.

7For the diverging statements see "Interview," *Filmkritik* 10 (1966): 491, and "Zum Autorenfilm" in Klaus Eder and Alexander Kluge, *Ulmer Dramaturgien: Reibungsverluste* (Munich: Hanser, 1980), p. 103.

8Most recently in Eder and Kluge, *Ulmer Dramaturgien*, p. 103. In another interview published in 1980 (Lewandowski, *Die Filme*, pp. 29–59), Kluge characterized Godard as the "first master teacher whom I fully accepted," as someone whom he "would be proud to have imitated," as someone whose "fundamental assumptions" he would "try to realize in film again and again" (p. 53).

9Lewandowski, *Die Filme*, pp. 288–291, provides a concise summary of and brief commentary on the film, including the two passages cited here.

10A translation of the Oberhausen Manifesto appears in Jan Dawson's critical reconstruction of the politics and economics of the New German Cinema, "A Labyrinth of Subsidies: The Origins of the New German Cinema," *Sight and Sound* 50 (Winter 1980–81): 14–20. Dawson's account substantiates Kluge's crucial role in transforming the rhetoric of the Oberhausen group into reality. For Kluge's account of the meeting with Höcherl see Eder and Kluge, *Ulmer Dramaturgien*, p. 32.

11Quoted in Lewandowski, *Die Filme*, p. 43.

12Kluge, "Die Utopie Film," p. 1140. For official statements of the Berlin and Munich academies, see Hans Günther Pflaum and Hans Helmut Prinzler, *Film in der Bundesrepublik* (Munich: Hanser, 1979), pp. 85–86.

13Kluge and his former students Peter Schubert and Günther Hörmann trace the evolution of the Ulm institute in Eder and Kluge, *Ulmer Dramaturgien*, pp. 31–36. Lewandowski, *Die Filme*, pp. 292–297, provides a brief commentary on and the complete record of *Teachers in Transition*.

14These "life stories" are modeled on Kluge's *Lebensläufe* (Stuttgart: Henry Goverts, 1962). Kluge reinforced this early link between his work in literature and film by including an expanded version of one of the three stories from the film, "Der Pädagoge von Klopau," in the revised edition, *Lebensläufe: Anwesenheitsliste für eine Beerdigung*, published by Suhrkamp in 1974.

15Lewandowski, *Die Filme*, pp. 298–303, provides a brief commentary on and the text of this film. For a precise description and analysis of the four and one-half minutes of the film in which music appears on the sound track, see Rudolf Hohlweg, "Musik für Film—Film für Musik: Annäherung an Herzog, Kluge, Straub," in *Herzog/Kluge/Straub, Reihe Film* 9, edited by Peter W. Jansen and Wolfram Schütte (Munich: Hanser, 1976), pp. 57–61.

16Kluge, "Die Utopie Film," esp. 1144 ff.; "Wort und Film," originally published in *Sprache im technischen Zeitalter*, no. 13 (1965), pp. 1015–1030, has been reprinted in Eder and Kluge, *Ulmer Dramaturgien*, pp. 9–27. A decade later in his wide-ranging interview in *Filmkritik* 20 (1976): 562–93, Kluge disputes the notion that he is/was concerned with "destroying conventional film language" or "discovering a new film language" (pp. 568 f.). But his restatement of his position leaves the substance of his film poetics as spelled out in the mid-1960s intact, although it does emphasize that he has never championed innovation for the sake of innovation.

[17]Kluge, "Wort und Film," p. 15.

[18]Kluge, "Die Utopie Film," p. 1145; "Wort und Film," p. 14.

[19]"Wort und Film," p. 12. In 1963 Kluge founded his own production company, Kairos-Film, and submitted the initial script of *Yesterday Girl* to a federal agency predating the Kuratorium. Several drafts of the script and two years later he had accumulated 620,000 marks, including 100,000 from the Kuratorium. "Das Publikum soll zufrieden sein: Gespräch mit dem Regisseur Alexander Kluge bei den Dreharbeiten zu 'Abschied von gestern,'" *Die Welt,* no. 66 (19 March 1966), gives details of the financing.

[20]Alexander Kluge, *Abschied von gestern: Protokoll,* compiled by Enno Patalas (Frankfurt: Filmkritik, n.d. [1967]), provides a complete record of the final print of *Yesterday Girl.* The story "Anita G." appears in English translation in Alexander Kluge, *Attendance List for a Funeral,* translated by Leila Vennewitz (New York: McGraw-Hill, 1966), pp. 15–34, a volume that contains all but one ("Korti") of the original nine *Life Stories* of 1962.

[21]Quoted in Karsten Peters, "Filme zum Träumen: Gespräch mit Alexandra und Alexander Kluge," *Abendzeitung,* 5 October 1966.

[22]Alexander Kluge, *Die Artisten in der Zirkuskuppel: ratlos. Die Ungläubige. Projekt Z. Sprüche der Leni Peickert* (Munich: Piper, 1968) contains the screenplay of *Artists* as well as the scenarios for two film projects that constitute the initial stages of its genesis. Winner of the Golden Lion award on its premiere at the 1968 Venice Film Festival, *Artists* also received a West German Federal Film Prize in 1968.

[23]Walter Benjamin, "The Work of Art," p. 241. Benjamin singles out the use of elevated long shots in the newsreels to intensify the masses' sense of their own participation in the cultic politics of fascism.

[24]Kluge's use of the concept *Trauerarbeit* is based on Alexander and Margarete Mitscherlich, *Die Unfähigkeit zu trauern: Grundlagen kollektiven Verhaltens,* (Munich: Piper, 1967). A modified psychoanalytic approach to the issue of Germany's unresolved past as an impediment to contemporary politics, it was widely discussed on its appearance and had a second printing in 1968.

[25]At the end of *Artists* Leni and her coworkers make a "new beginning" as technicians in the state-owned TV system, where she is subject to new illusions and obstacles. *Die unbezähmbare Leni Peickert (The Untameable Leni Peickert),* a sixty-minute sequel to *Artists* completed in 1969, shows Leni pursuing her circus plans anew after being fired for secretly broadcasting an erotic film. In the process she discovers she does not really love the circus, and it becomes a mere source of income.

[26]During 1969–71 Kluge and a group of coworkers in Ulm completed two feature-length science-fiction films, *Der große Verhau (The Big Mess,* 1969–70) and *Willi Tobler und der Untergang der 6. Flotte (Willi Tobler and the Demise of the 6th Fleet,* 1971). The former ran briefly in the theaters, the latter premiered on TV and is not in distribution.

[27]Alexander Kluge and Oscar Negt, *Öffentlichkeit und Erfahrung: Zur Organisationsanalyse von bürgerlicher und proletarischer Öffentlichkeit* (Frankfurt:

Suhrkamp, 1972). See pp. 48–50 for a discussion of the family and the status of women.

[28] Kluge's sharpest critics—Marlies Kallweit, Helke Sander, and Mädi Kemper— were associated with the then newly established journal *Frauen und Film*. By his own admission (Jansen and Schütte, *Herzog/Kluge/Straub*, p. 160), Kluge published *Gelegenheitsarbeit einer Sklavin: Zur realistischen Methode* (Frankfurt: Suhrkamp, 1975) largely in response to their criticism. In addition to "Roswithas Programm" the volume contains an account of the genesis of the film; a number of interim scenarios from the years 1970–71, including the version of *Gelegenheitsarbeit einer Sklavin* for which Kluge received an award of 200,000 marks from the Film Subsidy Board in 1971; the final screenplay; and a programmatic restatement of his conception of film with special emphasis on the question of realism. The final screenplay and "Roswitha's Program" are available in English translation in Jan Dawson, *Alexander Kluge and the Occasional Work of a Female Slave* (New York: New York Zoetrope, 1977), pp. 2–24, 42–48. See esp. pp. 47 f. for Kluge's retrospective view of his film.

[29] In one sequence the film insists on an underlying contradiction: "In order to have more children herself, Roswitha runs an abortion practice." There follows a close-up view of a simulated abortion complete with small fetus. Elsewhere Kluge has argued that Roswitha's "helping her children live by killing other people's" is a metaphor expressing "women's competitive relationships" and the "contradiction which exists in any family": "happiness and warmth for one's own family— indifference toward the outside world." (Dawson, *Kluge*, pp. 28, 45). In terms of a formalist dialectic, Kluge's metaphor may work splendidly, but his depiction of Roswitha's personalized care and concern for her patients counteracts its intended thrust.

[30] Alexander Kluge, *Lernprozesse mit tödlichem Ausgang* (Frankfurt: Sukrkamp, 1973). Coauthored by Michael Dost, Florian Hopf, and Kluge, *Filmwirtschaft in der Bundesrepublik und Europa: Gotterdämmerung in Raten* (Munich: Hanser, 1973) was intended as a contribution to the Federal Parliament's reconsideration of West Germany's film subsidy law.

[31] Kluge, "Ein Bolschewist des Kapitals," *Lernprozesse*, pp. 149–178. Skip Acuff has translated key segments of this text as "Excerpts from 'Big Business Bolshevik,'" *QRFS* 5 (1980): 195–203. Kluge began *Ferdinand* as a joint venture with Edgar Reitz, with whom he had collaborated in 1974 on *In Gefahr und größter Not bringt der Mittelweg den Tod,* but he eventually assumed sole responsibility as director.

[32] Kluge's choice of Schubert (a seasoned stage actor widely known to the German public in the mid-1970s from his role as an Archie Bunker character in the TV series *Ein Herz und eine Seele*) for the title role, his use of color, his avoidance of montage sequences and titles, the subordination of voice-over commentary to narrative coherence, and the underplayed seriousness of his comic strategies all suggest that he was trying to reach the broadest possible audience. A failure, especially with critics, on its initial release in 1976, Kluge's film fared far better abroad, winning the International Critics Award in Cannes. In 1977 Kluge reedited the film and placed it with another German distributor in a renewed and modestly successful effort to reach a German audience. The present discussion of the film is based on this version.

[33]The interview is taken nearly verbatim from the first half of another text from *Lernprozesse*, "Wenn man sein Gewissen dressiert, so küßt es uns zugleich, indem es uns beißt," pp. 21–26. Thus the coda as a whole is also based on this text available in Reinhard Mayer's translation as "A Trained Conscience Will Kiss and Bite at the Same Time," *Semiotexte* 4 (no. 2, 1982), pp. 112–23, rather than on "Ein Bolschewist des Kapitals," which concludes with Rieche taking a job with the Bundeskriminalamt, the federal agency charged with the prosecution of terrorists.

[34]Alexander Kluge, "Das Theater der Spezialisten: Gespräch mit Martin Schaub," *Cinéma*, no. 2 (1978), p. 20.

[35]Kluge employs the same quotation to conclude "Der Luftangriff auf Halberstadt am 8. April 1945," in *Neue Geschichten*, p. 106. Kluge's choice of this ending for the film may well have been influenced by the conciliatory gesture of Manfred Rommel, the Christian Democratic Lord Mayor of Stuttgart, who despite public uproar and political opposition from members of his party authorized the burial of the three terrorists in the Stuttgart City Cemetery. Rommel states his reasons in an interview that preludes the burial sequence.

[36]Alexander Kluge, *Die Patriotin: Texte/Bilder* 1–6 (Frankfurt: Zweitausendeins, 1979), contains the screenplay of both *The Patriot* and the Gabi Teichert sequence from *Germany in Autumn*.

PETER LILIENTHAL

Decisions Before Twelve

by Lynne Layton

ONCE THE MASS MEDIA DECIDE WHO IS worthy of attention, the excluded are exiled to a silence and darkness from which escape is nearly impossible. Peter Lilienthal, no stranger to exile, has suffered this fate. Although his first feature film, *Malatesta* (1969), was included in the 1972 Museum of Modern Art program that introduced "Das Neue Kino" to the United States, the press focused on Fassbinder, Herzog, and Wenders; Lilienthal, along with most other New German Cinema directors, was ignored. The self-perpetuating nature of such a blackout was dramatically illustrated by English-language press reports of the 1979 Berlin Film Festival: Fassbinder's *Marriage of Maria Braun* and Herzog's *Nosferatu* were widely discussed, but Lilienthal's *David,* which won first prize, was largely passed over in silence. Nevertheless, in West Germany Lilienthal is considered to be one of the more important new German filmmakers.

At first glance, Lilienthal's films hardly seem personal. His camera is often subjective—we perceive and experience events through the eyes of the characters—and the filmmaker's personal vision is not directly evident. In addition, his recent films deal with political struggles in which groups rather than individuals are the protagonists. Nevertheless, a look at his biog-

Peter Lilienthal (Courtesy of
Christian-Albrecht Gollub)

raphy reveals just how personal even his explicitly political films
are.

Peter Lilienthal was born in Berlin to Jewish parents on
November 27, 1929. At the age of ten, he became an exile when
the family emigrated to Montevideo, Uruguay. He attended a
Jewish high school there and studied art history, while his
mother ran a second-class hotel. Lilienthal's earliest memories
are of talking to German emigrants who had failed to understand what was going on in Germany, had not fought back, and
had later lived by glorifying their less than glorious pasts. He has
remarked of the appearance of such people in his films: "When
they find themselves in an intensified political situation . . . they
must make a decision. The tragedy is that they couldn't make the
decision one minute before twelve, but only one minute after."[1]

In 1954, Lilienthal returned to Berlin for a few months. Two
years later he received a fellowship to the Berlin School of Fine
Arts, where he studied experimental photography and film. Between 1959 and 1964 he worked as assistant producer and director at Südwestfunk (SWF TV) in Baden-Baden, then left to take
a job with Sender Freies Berlin (SFB TV). During the sixties and
early seventies, he directed more than twenty television films
and dramas, most of which reflect markedly different concerns

from the films made after 1968; yet, certain structural and philosophical similarities are noteworthy.

From the beginning, Lilienthal showed a strong interest in literary adaptations and an attraction to authors in political or spiritual exile. Among his earliest films were two adaptations of plays by exiled Spanish playwright Fernando Arrabal, *Picknick im Felde (Picnic in the Field*, 1962) and *Guernica — jede Stunde verletzt und die letzte tötet (Guernica—Every Hour Injures and the Last One Kills*, 1963); later he turned from the absurd to the realistic with two adaptations of stories by Günter Herburger, *Abschied (Farewell*, 1965) and *Der Beginn (The Beginning*, 1966). Lilienthal does not subscribe to the auteur theory of filmmaking; he likes to work collectively and enjoys confrontation with minds active in other media. He has done several films with exiled Chilean author Antonio Skármeta, and the screenplay for *David*, based on an autobiographical work by Joel König, became the collective effort of Lilienthal, Ulla Ziemann, and Jurek Becker, a Jewish East German exile.

Getting his films into the theaters turned out to be a difficult task because of the reputation of his television work. Critics had characterized him as a "beauty-drunk poet of the absurd."[2] The films were denigrated as "asocial and apolitical."[3] "Lilienthal," the filmmaker summed up, "that means esoteric, eccentric, obscure, impenetrable in the most literal sense of the word."[4]

Lilienthal's films are episodic, nonchronological, often as disconnected as the modes of perception and action of his characters. No given event and no individual hero are at the center, but rather a mood of growing menace. Lilienthal is fascinated with the intrusion of the unexpected and inexplicable into everyday life. In the early films, the unexpected took the form of the fantastic or the absurd; in the films of the seventies, it usually takes the form of political repression. In each case, Lilienthal wants to show how people react under such circumstances. In 1964, he noted, "I show the history of people who have no heroic halo, who cannot express themselves, who stand dumb before the horrible and frightening event and really have nothing to say aside from everyday banalities."[5] By 1973 the emphasis had shifted from silence and helplessness to change.

> I prefer people who admit their uncertainties to those who believe they can explain the world. On the other hand, like all uncertain

people, I get tied up in contradictions, for I long for others who can give me certainty. But that's why one makes films: to enter into dialog with people about uncertainties, about what awaits us and what we can change or improve.[6]

In *Farewell* (1965), Lilienthal combined his earlier poetic mode of direction with an uncompromising critical realism. With this production, which ends with a group of youthful observers silently turning their backs on the jaded, boring world of the materialistic bourgeoisie, Lilienthal seems once and for all to have left behind the world of the lifeless and turned to the world of the living.[7]

The placing of hope for change in youth is a motif in nearly all Lilienthal's feature films. Both this and the general change in subject matter are hardly accidental. Occurring in the late sixties, they mark Lilienthal's own evolving reaction to the entry of a new form of the unexpected into everyday life—the new Left in Germany.

Asked to comment on the noticeable change in themes and styles inaugurated by *Malatesta* (1969), Lilienthal replied:

> During the late 1960's, when there were student revolts in Europe and America, I was professor at the Film Academy in Berlin. Everyday life consisted of discussing political events, more from the past than the present, and trying to understand their relationship to oneself and one's hopes. Previously, there was no real internal unrest within Germany, and we were used to discussing the political affairs of others. In 1968–69 that changed: the people were finally affected and went out onto the streets. Going out onto the streets meant getting hit over the head or worse — getting shot like Benno Ohnesorg. These events caused me to test myself and to ask myself where, when, under what conditions, men had fought for their freedom. These questions led me to the story of Italian anarchist Malatesta.[8]

Malatesta, which won the Bundesfilmpreis and was West Germany's entry at Cannes in 1970, must be understood in the context of the political reality of the late sixties, although it is set in 1910–11 London, where exiled Italian anarchist Enrico Malatesta preached nonviolent revolution. The question posed by the film is one of the major political questions of the late sixties and early seventies: Given the violence of the state, must those whose goals are peace and individual freedom resort to violence to institute those goals? Or does resorting to violence destroy the goals?

Malatesta responds to Lilienthal's personal situation as well—that of a forty-year-old professor faced with students ready to commit violence and die for their political ideals. His decision to focus on the relationship between the older, careful Malatesta and the young, naive, spontaneous Latvian refugee, Gardstein, is not accidental but rather entails the moment of "testing oneself" that Lilienthal speaks of above.

In *Malatesta*, two Latvian political refugees rob a London jewelry store so that they can buy weapons for their comrades back home. In the process, they accidentally kill Gardstein, one of their own who had come to warn them that the police were on their way. During the film's climax, which is intercut with documentary footage of the siege of Sidney Street,[9] the anarchists are brutally gunned down by the authorities. This action is subordinate to the relationship that evolves between Malatesta and Gardstein, who, in the course of the film, loses patience with mere words and turns to violence. And even this relationship is subordinate to the film's exploration of modes of oppression and various anarchist responses to oppression.

Intentionally nondramatic and nonpsychological, despite its explosive theme, the film is a confrontation of ideas. Malatesta speaks his lines with no emotion, as though he were reading from his own anarchist writings. This overemphasized Brechtian appeal to the intellect is the weakness of *Malatesta*. In later films Lilienthal is better able to combine the distancing techniques necessary for audience reflection with mood-creating techniques that also involve the viewer viscerally. Many of the distancing techniques, however, remain constant. Three of the most important are the intercutting of documentary material, a dissonance between what is seen and what is heard, and episodic, nonchronological structure.

Malatesta contains many scenes that retard action and function instead to comment on the film's dramatic question: violence or nonviolence? Lilienthal establishes the period mood, its surface stillness, with his use of sepia toned, grainy film; many shots have the look of fragile, beautiful old photos. Repeated shots of a policeman riding a horse down an empty, silent street, pausing to look through the jeweler's window, foreshadow the robbery and contrast the calm with the imminent violence. The tension of the robbery scene is developed through pans and tilts of the empty streets and crowded immigrant tenements, and through parallel editing of the anarchists' break-in and the authorities' search for them; the loud hammering of the anarchist knocking out plaster in the house adjacent to the jewelry store is the only sound heard. The magnified hammering contrasts with the policeman's silent questioning of passersby and neighbors, the unspoken fear of people hastily glancing from windows and standing in doorways.

Critics have argued that Lilienthal maintains an impenetrable distance in this film and does not commit himself to any position. Some even viewed him as an aesthete—a serious matter in the political sixties.[10] While it is true enough that he avoids easy solutions in favor of detailed explorations of an issue, he nonetheless frames *Malatesta* in scenes that question whether revolutionary change is possible without violence. In the end, the young accept Gardstein's view that Malatesta's words alone cannot institute his ideals; however, they recognize the senselessness of his death. Initially, before the film turns to Malatesta, whose first words are "We reject the use of violence," the dramatic question is answered quite differently: documentary footage shows a population in spontaneous revolt, as a voice-over reports in newsreel fashion Graf von Pahlen's reaction to the assassination of his patron, the Czar: "If you want to prepare an omelette, you must first break eggs." Although the film bears Malatesta's name and is sympathetic to the moral purity of his ideal, Gardstein's consciousness and his questioning of Malatesta become central and ultimately appear more rational.

After a documentary about Shirley Chishilm's hopeless campaign for the U.S. presidency, Lilienthal made *La Victoria*, a feature film shot in Chile before and during the March 1973 parliamentary elections that returned the Popular Unity Party to power. Although the film optimistically portrays a change in a young woman's political consciousness and ends with the election of the socialist deputy for whom she campaigned, the hopeful-hopeless dialectic absent from the film itself was reinstated by the circumstances surrounding the film's reception: when Allende's regime was overthrown by the Chilean military, both ZDF and movie houses advanced *La Victoria*'s release to mid-September 1973. Paula Moya, the actress who portrayed and had much in common with the film's heroine, committed suicide shortly after the coup. *La Victoria* allowed Germans concerned about the Rightist victory to view the reality behind the headlines, the true mood of the Chilean people.[11]

La Victoria is the story of Marcela, a provincial Chilean with no political understanding, who comes to Santiago to look for secretarial work. Through her experiences in teaching the poor to read and write, her mistreatment as a part-time office worker, her involvement with the poor women of Nueva Palena, who erected barricades in support of their striking husbands, and her participation in the campaign of socialist deputy Carmen Lazo, Marcela becomes committed to socialism.

In *La Victoria*, which won the Special Prize of the Prague Television Festival as well as the Television Prize of the German Academy of Performing Arts in Frankfurt, Lilienthal dispenses with the intercutting of documentary material and instead works in a genre he later perfects in such films as *Es herrscht Ruhe im Land* (*Calm Prevails over the Country*, 1975) and *Der Aufstand* (*The Uprising*, 1980), which documents the Nicaraguan civil war. Sometimes labeled docufiction, it combines the immediacy of a documentary with a fictional story. It seems well suited to Lilienthal's world view, since he has always portrayed reality and changes in consciousness as the outcome largely of nonreflexive processes, determined as much by the situation in which a character finds himself as by the character's psyche. During the filming an election actually took place, and Carmen Lazo, who plays herself, was indeed elected. The barricades incident occurred shortly before the filming and was recreated by the women of Nueva Palena. All but one of the actors in this film were non-professionals, and much of the film was improvised.

Lilienthal replaces Malatesta's melancholic longing for an unachievable utopia with belief in gradual change. This optimism has much to do with his turn from Europe to Latin America in the period before Allende's fall: "With *La Victoria* I did not want to make a 'socialist film,' nor did I want to show how to build socialism; rather I wanted to show for whom in Chile socialism is made."[12] In choosing to focus on the specific experience of the Chilean people without generalizing, Lilienthal embraces a major principle of Third Cinema, a Latin-American movement of revolutionary filmmaking that burgeoned in the late sixties and early seventies.[13]

La Victoria is the first part of a trilogy which, according to Lilienthal, deals "with political resistance and seduction, the change in possibilities for people during certain specific historical situations."[14] The second part, *Hauptlehrer Hofer* (*Schoolmaster Hofer*, 1974), which won second prize in the 1978 Human Rights Film Festival in Strasbourg, concerns a young teacher's attempt to educate the poor youth of an Alsatian village around 1900. The film is not as programmatically Left as the story on which it is based, especially with regard to the main character's militancy and the ending. Filmed near Strasbourg on a low budget, with six to eight months of preparation and only thirty-five days of shooting, *Schoolmaster Hofer* features only one professional actor, André Watt. The remaining cast consists of villagers and the children of a nearby orphanage.

The film begins on commencement day, as officials loftily announce that the age of darkness is over. While they exhort the teachers "to educate youth to virtue and morality" and "to care for the most precious possession of the people," the camera pans the room of bored listeners. Hofer soon learns that only upper-class children are considered "precious" and that a more appropriate dictum for teaching lower-class children might have been Brecht's "Erst kommt das Fressen; dann kommt die Moral" (till we've had dinner, morality can wait), but the optimism of the "small step forward" pervades the film. *Schoolmaster Hofer* is punctuated by haunting bagpipe music that accompanies the mysterious appearances of a strange figure, Theo, a shepherd. By the film's end it has become clear that the sheep symbolize the peasants' conformity and passivity and that Theo, who disappears with the sheep, is a revolutionary Panlike figure representative of the hope Lilienthal always places in youth. This hope is underscored by Lilienthal's use of light and dark: most scenes emphasize dark colors—blues, blacks, and greens—but the children are always in light.

The children work in the factory, and those who come to school are too exhausted to learn. The powers of society, here the factory management, show no sympathy for the value of education; they are interested in the children only as a source of cheap labor. Although more sympathetically treated, the parents, too, are wary of education, and their children's exhaustion is partly due to their labors in family fields after their factory work is done. The parents need their help to survive. The schoolmaster—a pale, reserved, somewhat awkward figure who does not appear to be a fighter—is forced to hold class in a filthy stable and gradually becomes radicalized in the face of such unbearable conditions. He talks the wary peasants into giving him building materials for a new school, which he and the students build together. Attendance improves; the children love Hofer and enjoy school. After a child dies in a factory accident, Hofer begins a campaign for improved work conditions. When Hofer and the children threaten a strike, the children are clubbed by the police, then fired. When the factory owner makes it clear that he wants Hofer silenced, the peasants, whose language counsels conformity and fatalism, begin to withdraw their children from the school. Theo and the sheep disappear; wool deliveries stop; the factory administrator gets new child labor from an orphanage. Under the direction of a big farm owner, the peasants destroy the school, and the school inspector confronts Hofer in the city hall. The peasants, who like the rich wear black, join with the town powers to have the schoolmaster dismissed; the minister is the only town notable to remain in solidarity with Hofer. Ejected from the village, while the peasants stand silently by like sheep, Hofer stops in a flower field, turns around, and begins to go back. While a boy paints the word SCHULE on a new building constructed by the children, someone mentions that the sheep have not been found. The film ends with an extreme long shot of the joyful Theo and his sheep.

Although critics have discussed *Schoolmaster Hofer* as a film depicting a bygone era, Lilienthal insists on its contemporaneity, noting that in many countries children still work under even worse conditions. Made a year after Allende's fall, the film was in fact intended as a homage to Allende as teacher, in the hope that his "pupils" would follow in his steps.

Calm Prevails over the Country (1975), the final part of the trilogy, won the West German Film Critics' Prize in 1975 and, in 1976, the Golden Bowl, the highest West German film award. Like *La Victoria*, the film takes place in Latin America, and the screenplay once again was the product of Lilienthal's collaboration with Antonio Skármeta. The plot concerns a group of political pris-

Charles Vanel in *Calm Prevails Over the Country* (Courtesy of Filmverlag der Autoren)

oners who arrive in Las Piedras amid rumors that they have been tortured by the military. The citizens begin to form a resistance movement, but the cowardly governor refuses to give permission for a public medical examination. When half the prisoners escape during a break-out attempt, the military declares an emergency and takeover; the remaining prisoners are brutally murdered. During the funeral the people rise up in protest, and the military begins a roundup that leaves the industrialists without a work force. The military, sent to scare one up, finds itself in a face-off with angry women and children.

The film is framed by the story of Grandfather Parra (Charles Vanel), who initially holds a typically petty-bourgeois position: mind your own business, stick to your family, and don't get involved in politics. Eventually, Parra is one of the few citizens not arrested; his entire family, active in the resistance, has been taken away. In a dreamlike sequence at the end of the film, Parra tries to bribe the governor to release his family. When this fails, he decisively packs up a large number of sandwiches, gets a young boy loitering at a deserted taxi stand to drive him to the prison, and walking toward it yells: "Fascists! Criminals!" The viewer, as so often in the course of the film, looks through bars as the gates close on him. The film title flashes, and Parra, another of those who tragically decide at one minute after rather than one minute before twelve, is led off at gunpoint.

The film does not end here. The two prisoners who deplaned first in an opening scene are free and arrive at a strangely shaped white house in the woods, where they are greeted enthusiastically. The resistance goes on. The hopelessness of a jailed citizenry is offset by this ending, silent except for a triumphant blare of the resistance music that runs through the film.[15]

An allegory of oppression and resistance, *Calm Prevails over the Country* recounts the revolt against an imaginary Latin-American dictatorship, but Lilienthal clearly had Chile in mind. Turning once more to docufiction, he intercuts fictional events with documentary material from Argentinian newsreels capturing unrest and military oppression and a coup in Uruguay. More than in any previous film, he shifts attention from the individual to collectives. Some of these collectives are heroic, some are antiheroic, and some (notably the military) are barbaric. A narrative is still distinguishable, but it does not proceed chronologically and is not created by having the viewer identify with any individual fate. A single viewing of the film makes it difficult to sort the characters out. Lilienthal establishes the narrative, which is marked by few events and little dialogue, by alternating between collective and more personal, familial scenes, and by developing moods of anxiety and defiance. The tension between hope and hopelessness becomes the focal point of the drama.

The film's action is the escalating resistance of a people and the corresponding escalation of forces set on crushing that resistance. The sides are drawn in black-and-white terms, but the content of each term remains somewhat ambiguous: the military appears to be an autonomous force propelled by tentative acts of violence to greater acts of brutality, and the resistance is made by a growing but confused group defined only by its conspiratorial everyday existence, its vague rhetoric of "solidarity," "cooperation," and "liberation," and its refusal to capitulate. Yet this vagueness seems to be less a result of political naiveté than of Lilienthal's desire to keep the film allegorical. The point is not to show the relations between politics and economy, but to dramatize the insanity of a situation in which calm can only prevail when an entire citizenry is imprisoned. Here Lilienthal reconciles two of his concerns and shows that there is a fine line between realism and the absurd.

As is often the case in Lilienthal's films, there is irony in his choice of actors. The film was shot in Portugal with Brazilian, Argentinian, and Chilean exiles. The military is played by the Fifth Division of the Portuguese army and soldiers of the Setubal barracks who, one year earlier, had been in the forefront of the Portuguese revolution. In the scene in which a prisoner's coffin is carried through the city, the military brutally breaks up the demonstration and drives off with the coffin. Lilienthal reports that after this scene, the soldiers cried, lifted their countrymen from the ground, hugged them and begged forgiveness. In the tradition of Brecht's *Lehrstücke* theory, Lilienthal seems to want his films to be vehicles for people to reexamine their role in recently experienced social and political events. Here is one place, then, where the level of reflexivity absent in the films is yet reintroduced into Lilienthal's filmmaking.

Lilienthal next turned to another area of personal concern: the plight of Jews during the Third Reich. Although the subject had been on his mind for years, previously it had been too emotionally charged for him to be able to deal with it artistically. Although *Calm Prevails* had won the Golden Bowl, the project committee of the Film Subsidy Board gave him no advance money for *David,* whose screenplay it considered "uncinematographic." The film won first prize at the 1979 Berlin International Film Festival and had its American premiere at the 1979 San Francisco Film Festival.

David must be placed in historical context before it can meaningfully be discussed. In 1978–79, the Holocaust became almost an everyday topic of discussion, a cathartic occasion that touched off a multitude of emotional reactions on the left, center, and right. In the fall of 1978, the Federal Republic officially commemorated the Reichskristallnacht pogrom of November 1938. A few months later, the American television series *Holocaust* was broadcast. The schoolchildren of Germany reacted strongly to this American soap, for many of them had had no clear idea of what had happened to the Jews under the Third Reich. In the days following the series, reactions ranged from horror to new anti-Semitic outbreaks. Syberberg's *Hitler: A Film from Germany* and Lilienthal's *David* premiered in Berlin in late February and early March, when the issue of German-Jewish relations was still very much and very emotionally discussed.

David focuses on the everyday life of an orthodox rabbi and his close-knit family. It begins when David is a small boy in Liegnitz in 1933, the year of Hitler's victory and the first measures taken against the Jews. David is studying Hebrew with his father and learns the prophecy: "Take thee to the mountain, that thou shalt not perish." Shortly thereafter, a Purim celebration is interrupted by the noise of marching Hitler Youth screaming "*Juden 'raus!*" (Jews get out). David's mother, the most astute figure in the film—but too well trained in Jewish patriarchal relations to ever take action alone—expresses her fears. The rabbi, the character most passive and most prone to rationalize and deny what is happening, claims to have heard "*Jugend 'raus!*" (youth come out). Lilienthal places this event during the Jewish holiday celebrating the failure of a Persian plot of genocide; he selects other historical moments of danger as well to suggest that the Jews have not learned from their history.

The story advances to 1938. A grown-up David joins his brother Leo in Berlin, hoping to go to school; Jews are now forbidden to enter school in Liegnitz, and even in Berlin only vocational training is possible. The rabbi visits his sons, and they go to a café. Even Leo's SS uniform, worn with unabashed pride, does not prevent the waiters from recognizing that they are Jewish. When they are refused service, the rabbi shrugs his shoulders, and they leave. The film, which always focuses on the Jews' reactions, gains much of its power from recording the passive way in which they silently accept and adapt to each new violation of their civil and human rights.

With no indication as to how or why he got there, the next scene shows David in Liegnitz during the 1938 pogrom. The rabbi watches his synagogue burn and is arrested. Some time later he returns to his house, disheveled. At dinner, he reports that although the guards had forbidden the prisoners even to think about anything, he had prayed. This pitiful revolt fades behind humiliation when the rabbi removes his hat and reveals a swastika burned in his bald head. He laughs and says, "I'm here and that's what counts." The family is horrorstruck but silent.

Humiliations multiply, scenes shift continuously as David and his family try to survive. The Jewish family, traditionally a com-

Walter Taub and Mario Fischel in *David* (Courtesy of Filmverlag der Autoren)

munity of love and mutual support, is seen in changed historical circumstances to be a dangerous and suicidal illusion.[16] Only after the family is gone is David really able to concentrate on survival and escape. Nightmarish scenes follow—deportations, houses being ransacked, people on the streets pretending to see nothing. After a forbidden ride on the streetcar, a defiant act unfortunately performed at one minute after twelve, the rabbi and his wife are taken. David and his siblings move from place to place. Shots of David hiding in the closet recall shots of imprisonment from *Calm Prevails* as well as the narrow doorway shots in *Malatesta* that foreshadow Gardstein's death. The film's tempo here begins to mime the breathlessness with which David now lives. The nonreflexive nature of the film signifies that the Jews had little time for outbreaks of despair or anxiety; they were fully occupied with such matters as where to get their next meal, where to sleep, where to hide, where to get papers, how to get out.[17]

Berlin is already in flames when David finally escapes in 1943, one of the last Jews to leave. His escape occurs fortuitously through the good will of a German factory owner. His sister's last words are, "Good-bye. This time follow through!" In the final scene, David is on his way to Palestine, and sepia-toned documentary film shows those already there cheering his ship's arrival. The last shot is a black-and-white freeze frame of David's expressive, still somewhat bewildered face.

The film is based on *David: Notebooks of a Survivor* by Joel König (Ezra Ben Gershon). Lilienthal calls it the first German-Jewish film, that is, the first film to focus on the everyday life of the Jews during the Third Reich. It always remains on the level of David's consciousness, never pretending to know more than he. Abrupt scene changes, which tend to confuse the viewer, are meant to reflect the confused response of David and the Jews to rapidly changing historical circumstances. David wanders aimlessly through the thirties and forties—knowing and yet not knowing how urgent it is that he get out as soon as possible, knowing and yet not knowing what is going on around him. The frequent use of shallow focus and of focusing in and out within a shot underscores the haze in which David and the Jews existed. As in *Calm Prevails,* the film builds to a pitch of unbearable anxiety. The psychic horror is so great that there is no need for the scenes of physical violence that viewers have come to expect in films about the Holocaust.

David was written, acted, and directed by survivors of the Nazi Holocaust and their children. During filming on Berlin streets, people turned away from the sight of the Jewish stars on the actors' coats, Jewish youths acting in the film began to ask new questions—of their families who had accepted such treatment and of the Germans who had endorsed it.[18] Clearly, *David* was made for today, to encourage resistance to intolerance of differences wherever it exists. Lilienthal in fact stresses rather than downplays the differences between Jews and Germans.[19] During his Purim sermon, the rabbi quotes Haman, who fostered the plot to kill the Jews: "Their laws are different." For Haman, this is sufficient grounds for genocide. However, Lilienthal's positive emphasis on difference makes for the radicality of his statement against discrimination: the "other" must not be made to assimilate in order to be accepted, but must rather be appreciated as an other.

After *David*, Lilienthal returned to Latin America and made *Der Aufstand* (*The Uprising*, 1980), a docufiction reenactment of the Nicaraguan civil war. The film centers on a young soldier in Somoza's army who gradually decides that he is fighting on the wrong side and ends by joining the Sandinistas; however, the film's stars are the people of Leon, Nicaragua. Lilienthal said that making this film was one of the peak experiences of his life, for he felt that the people's passion and solidarity was unique in the modern world. Many who participated in making the film reported that their reenactments of the traumas so recently experienced were extremely therapeutic. The film ends triumphantly with documentary footage of the people's freedom celebration in July 1979.

One may argue with Peter Lilienthal's phenomenological approach to cinema, which makes his films seem rough and poorly edited. It must be remembered, however, that he is most concerned with capturing the immediacy of experience and thereby creating a mood. If oppression and—more particularly—the circumstances in which people resist and fight for their freedom are to be understood, Lilienthal says, *"das Problem Angst,"*[20] the problem of fear and anxiety, must be kept central. He seems to hope that his films will move audiences to think and act one minute before rather than one minute after twelve.

NOTES

[1]From an interview with Ulla Ziemann in *Dokumentation der 28. Internationalen Filmfestspiele Berlin* (1978).

[2]Werner Nekes, cited in *Dokumentation der Duisberger Filmwoche* (1977), p. 104.

[3]Werner Kliess, "Welche Farbe hat das Grau?" *Film* (Velber) 11 (1968): 22.

[4]Barbara Bronnen and Corinna Brocher, *Die Filmemacher* (Munich, Gütersloh; Vienna: Bertelsmann, 1973), p. 207.

[5]Quoted in Ulrich Gregor, *Geschichte des Films ab* 1960 (Munich: Bertelsmann, 1978), p. 154.

[6]Quoted in Bronnen and Brocher, *Filmemacher,* p. 198.

[7]See Joachim von Mengershausen, "Lilienthal—die Faszination des Abgelebten," *Süddeutsche Zeitung,* 16–17 April 1966.

[8] Lilienthal, interview with Ziemann.

[9] This is based on the Houndsditch jewelry robbery in December 1910, which was mistakenly conceived to have been an anarchist attack. A card with Malatesta's name and address was found near the robbery equipment left in the house adjacent to the jewelry store, and Malatesta was arrested but soon released. "Peter the Painter" died in the home of a woman who had been attending anarchist meetings, and the other two robbers escaped. They shut themselves in a house in Sidney Street in Stepney, and, on the orders of Home Secretary Winston Churchill, they were gunned down by British troops. Lilienthal is wont to interject historical inaccuracies in his films as a distancing or alienation effect. For an account of the siege of Sidney Street and of Malatesta's political career, see James Joll, *The Anarchists,* 2nd ed. (Cambridge, Mass.: Harvard University Press, 1980), pp. 158–64.

[10] See, for example, Alf Brustellin's review, "Schwanengesang auf Idealismus," *Süddeutsche Zeitung,* 26 May 1971.

[11] See Wolfgang Limmer, "Chile im März 73: Ein Pyrrhus-Sieg," *Süddeutsche Zeitung,* 15/16 September 1973.

[12] Quoted in Wolfgang Ruf, "Die Sonne angreifen," *Medium* 3 (1974): 16.

[13] For an explanation, see Fernando Solanas and Octavio Getino, "Toward a Third Cinema," *Cineaste* 4 (Winter 1970–71): 1–10.

[14] Lilienthal, interview with Ziemann.

[15] The music was composed by Angel Parra, a famous Chilean folksinger imprisoned by the military in 1973.

[16] Wolfram Schütte, "Die zerstörte Gemeinschaft der Liebenden," *Frankfurter Rundschau,* 1 March 1979.

[17] Lilienthal, interview with Jeanine Meerapfel, *Dokumentation der 29. Internationalen Filmfestspiele Berlin.*

[18] Lilienthal, interview with Sigrid Schmitt and Heiko R. Blum, "' . . . um Erkenntnis zu zeigen, ist es meistens zu spät,'" *Medium,* no. 3 (1979).

[19] B. Ruby Rich, "David," *The Reader,* 25 April 1980.

[20] Lilienthal, interview with Schmitt and Blum.

EDGAR REITZ

Liberating Humanity and Film

by *Ingrid Scheib-Rothbart and Ruth McCormick*

ONE OF THE SIGNERS OF THE 1962 Oberhausen Manifesto, Edgar Reitz has enjoyed a long and fruitful collaboration with Alexander Kluge, who called him "the most consistent German filmmaker . . . the one who deals in the most relentless fashion with the ambiguity of sense consciousness."[1] In a 1981 interview, Kluge added, "Reitz is a superb craftsman, open to experiment. His talent is far-ranging; it cannot be 'domesticated'; you could ask him to do something totally different, for example, to build a bridge, and he would be able to do it."[2]

Unlike Kluge, an intrinsically political person who came to film through legal studies and philosophical investigations, Reitz began by wanting to make films. Born on November 1, 1932, in the Hunsrück region, he studied literature, theater, and journalism in Munich with a view toward becoming a filmmaker. As a student he often saw two or more films a day, studied acting, started an experimental theater company, wrote essays and poetry, founded and coedited a literary magazine, and took up photography. "My idea of how to become a filmmaker," he says, "is to spend five or six years doing every possible job connected with films."[3]

Reitz worked for a number of film companies as production

assistant, script supervisor, and camerman before beginning to make experimental films and industrial shorts in 1957. By 1962, he had made fifty industrial films, and as chief of the department of experiment and development for Insel-Film GmbH was able to pursue his passion for developing new cinematic forms. His *Kommunikation (Communication, 1961)* and *Kino I—Geschwindigkeit (Cinema I—Speed, 1962)* are considered by Kluge and others to be two of the best experimental postwar German films.

Communication was commissioned by the German Federal Postal Service, which granted the filmmaker complete artistic freedom for its realization. Reitz explains his film as follows:

> Communication, the theme of the interrelation of man and technology, the idea of translating human experiences into technical expressions and codes, can be presented from different perspectives. Therefore, we tried to create images and sequences that would leave a certain calculated latitude to the viewer and his associations.[4]

The eleven-minute film has 259 takes, intertwined with one another in such a way that images dissolve and are superseded by others within the framework of a tightly organized time structure. The sound track, composed by Josef Anton Riedl, consists of spoken language electronically processed into a kind of music.

Cinema I—Speed—first of a projected series of films that were to investigate aspects of cinematic theory—was inspired by Fernand Léger's dictum, "Let the landscape be blurred with the speed of an express train." Reitz developed three new technical processes specifically for the film: a camera capable of taking shots at a changing but precisely determinable frequency, and two processing techniques by which single frames from a chronologically photographed sequence might be selected according to periodic or random patterns and then reassembled. The result is a fascinating study of movement that suggests how a fast-flying insect might see the world. To counterpoint the images, Riedl composed a score for various percussion instruments. Both *Speed* and *Communication* were inspired by principles of the Vienna School of "new music"—Arnold Schoenberg, Alban Berg, and Anton von Webern—which neo-Marxist philosopher Theodor Adorno has called the only truly revolutionary music of our century.

Edgar Reitz (COURTESY OF EDGAR
REITZ FILMPRODUKTIONS GMBH)

When Reitz signed the Oberhausen Manifesto in 1962, he had yet to make a feature film. (In fact, several of the twenty-six "directors" who signed the manifesto had never made a film, while others were actually writers and scholars.) The German film industry—which had never really recovered from the mass exodus of creative talent from Hitler's Reich and the dismemberment of the German studio system by the Allies after the war—was still in a precarious state. Only 69 feature films were made in Germany in 1961—the lowest annual production rate in ten years—and cinema admissions had dropped by 14 million marks in one year. To make matters worse, German feature films had an international reputation for low quality. The Ministry of the Interior reacted by announcing that beginning in April 1962 it would make available grants for feature film projects, scripts, and script outlines. At the Oberhausen Short Film Festival in February of that year, Reitz, Kluge, and a group of other young people working in film protested against the policies by which the grants were to be administered, arguing that the government money already expended to subsidize feature films had gone into the wrong hands and was being used to make the wrong films. In their manifesto, they demanded the right to create a new German cinema. Inspired by the French *nouvelle vague,* they took up the slogan "Le cinema de papa est mort." Within days, little green stickers saying "Papas Kino ist tot" appeared everywhere—walls, trees, sidewalks, cafés, and even lavatory seats. Young filmmakers whose short films had been praised at international festivals were demanding a chance to show what they could do. As Reitz told critic Jan Dawson in 1978:

> It was such a tough time, the film industry was such a closed business. . . . One day we simply made a list of all the prizes we'd won at international festivals, and realized that we'd already attracted more attention abroad than all the German feature films.[5]

Government policy makers were, in essence, challenged to save German cinema. Kluge, a lawyer versed in political struggle, and Reitz, already a sophisticated film theoretician, were Oberhausen's most vocal proponents in those early years. They urged that talented new filmmakers deserved a chance to enter a closed (and at this point, hostile) industry by being eligible for funds with which to make a first feature film. They also called for the founding of a film school in which prospective directors could get formal training in cinematic theory and practice.

Their first goal was reached in 1965, with the establishment of the Kuratorium junger deutscher Film (Board of Curators of the Young German Film), an autonomous nonprofit organization which, although not tied to any political party or group, was funded by the Länder (Federal states) in order to create opportunities for first feature films.

In 1966, Kluge, Reitz, and several of their associates achieved their second aim with the opening of the Institut für Filmgestaltung (Institute for Film Formation) in Ulm. Founded on the principles set forth at Oberhausen, it was dedicated to the development of an overall program for a truly new cinema, as well as to the training of a new generation of filmmakers. For ten years, it was a major factor in a German film world previously devoid of educational opportunities.

Reitz and Kluge established contact with the Ulm School of Advanced Design, a private college dedicated to Bauhaus studies and financed by the Geschwister-Scholl Foundation, and it agreed to allow them and eight other members of the Oberhausen group to set up a film school under its roof. The theoretical principles of the institute were based on the *politique des auteurs,* and contact was established with the Lodz Film

School in Poland and l'Institut des Hautes Etudes Cinématographique (IDHEC) in Paris. Every aspect of film was taught, and from 1963 on, Kluge and Reitz were the theoretical leaders. Reitz taught dramaturgy, directing, and theory of cinematography. Kluge remembers:

> The curriculum was planned by all the people involved, none of whom had ever made a feature, only short films. Ideas came from Edgar Reitz, from Detten Schleiermacher, and from me. Before long, Vlado Kristl appeared, and during the semester break, he made the film *Der Damm* together with the students. The new forms he introduced proved to be so exciting that our classes during the second year were devoted to a discussion of them. . . . We didn't orient ourselves to foreign film schools. It must be understood that our program didn't grow out of just any academic viewpoint: one element was Critical Theory (the neo-Marxist theories of the Frankfurt School, which included thinkers like Max Horkeimer, Theodor Adorno, Walter Benjamin, Herbert Marcuse, Jürgen Habermas, and others). The second component, montage and cinematography, was handled respectively by Beate Mainka-Jellinghaus and Edgar Reitz; film was always approached in terms of editing, and variations in camera perspectives were also very important. Third and finally, we took our models from literary sources and from the new music more than from cinema itself. If professional cinema played a role at all, it was actually only in our studies of the films of the 1920s. Narrative cinema was more or less ignored. As far as we were concerned, a new beginning for German cinema could never come out of the prevailing order.[6]

The institute continued the development of its pedagogical theories through the teaching of filmmaking until 1968; after the founding of the Munich and Berlin film academies, practical training in Ulm was discontinued, and the school now devotes its efforts toward research and theoretical work.

While Reitz was connected with the institute, he served as cameraman for Kluge's first feature, and made four films of his own. He also developed VariaVision, a system of simultaneous projection on sixteen screens, in collaboration with the architect Paolo Nestler and Insel Film under the auspices of the German Federal Railroad. In 1965, the first production using this system, *DB-Vision,* was presented at the International Traffic Exhibition in Munich. The basic concept of VariaVision, to create a synthesis of images, text, and music, was used in *DB-Vision* to emphasize certain aspects of travel like speed, safety, distance, rails, arrival, and departure. On four rows of four screens each, floating in the dark above the heads of the passing spectators, synchronized images relate to one another in a continuous presentation. The same motifs complement one another or join together into images spanning several screens, while in "pools" of sound, dialogue (by Alexander Kluge) and electronic music complement the flow of visual patterns.

Having served as director of photography on Kluge's *Abschied von Gestern* (*Yesterday Girl*), Reitz wrote and directed his own first feature film, *Mahlzeiten* (*Mealtimes*) in 1966. Both in form and content, it was a radical departure from conventional film fare and so engendered excitement and bewilderment. Reitz had established himself as the maker of cool, structured, highly innovative films dealing with concepts and form.

In 1967, the film won the prize for best first feature at the Venice Film Festival. Reitz recalls the glories and difficulties of that early period.

> I was particularly proud to win a prize at Venice for *Mahlzeiten* because I was standing next to Buñuel on the stage: he was awarded a prize for the last film of his life, which was how he'd presented *Belle de Jour,* and I was awarded the prize for the best first film. The feeling was that from now on everything was going to change. And when I got back from the festival, the distributors had pulled out my film. I called to ask why it was no longer showing anywhere, because the Venice prize had attracted press coverage and could have been a big publicity boost, and the dumb answer I got from the head of distribution, in a German slang that is virtually untranslatable, was, roughly, that prizes kill audiences. That wasn't the real reason, but it was a year before we saw what had happened.[7]

At the end of 1967, the Film Development Act was voted into law. It retroactively specified that any film grossing more than half a million marks in its first two years of distribution was eligible for subsidies. Had the films of the "new" directors been widely exhibited and competing at the box office, they would have received a large share of the newly voted subsidies. By pulling these films out and putting their own into the cinemas, industry old-timers were trying to boost their films over the half-million point in order to get the lion's share of the subsidies. This was the underlying reason for the disappearance of New German Cinema films after only a year. The young filmmakers

founded the Arbeitsgemeinschaft neuer deutscher Spiel-
filmproduzenten (Syndicate of the New German Feature Film
Producers) to counteract the commercial lobby. As Reitz notes:
"We could not get back into the cinemas with new films the
following year because, being eligible for hardly any of the new
production money, we produced almost nothing."[8] German
cinema became a fight between two camps, and it continues to be
waged more as a conflict between cultures and generations than
as an economic power struggle. Reitz remembers:

> We became isolated. During the sixties, we developed a kind of an-
> ticinema sentiment. It was not what we originally wanted, but we
> maneuvered ourselves into a corner, into a kind of polarization
> against the film industry, and in so doing, we sought salvation in
> opposition to everything that was called cinema up to then. . . . We
> had grown up with a love for the cinema and we became its enemies
> because hostility dominated the world of cinema.[9]

Mealtimes was almost guaranteed to displease traditionalists. It
tells the story of Elisabeth, a young woman who embraces life,
makes many friends, and loves food, sex, and having babies.
While studying photography, she meets Rolf, a medical student,
whose unhappy childhood makes him want to dedicate his life to
the service of humanity. Interested in everything he does,
she follows him to his classes and absorbs his interests. In
springtime, they begin a motor bike tour, enjoying the cuckoo's
call and making love on top of haystacks and in flowering
meadows; Elisabeth feels engulfed—according to the narrator—in a big, romantic love affair. She comes home pregnant.
   They marry and live in an attic apartment dominated by a
large double bed. Giving up photography, Elisabeth enjoys
domesticity and "long, wonderful talks" about their love and
their happiness. After the birth of a second child, Rolf gives up
his full-time studies to work part time. Elisabeth regales her
friends with tales of her happiness, and expresses disapproval of
Irina, an independent young woman still experimenting with
her life. Since she considers birth control "unhealthy and vul-
gar," she becomes pregnant a third time, and Rolf is forced to
give up his studies completely. Unhappy, he feels the need to be
alone, and takes a job in Rotterdam as an unskilled worker. A
despairing letter from Elisabeth makes him return just before
the third child is born.

Elisabeth decides that living in the country will renew their romantic love. "Man and woman—one body," she says. "But not all the time," replies Rolf. A fourth pregnancy is followed by an abortion and—soon after—a new pregnancy, which Rolf allows her to see through. Elisabeth is tempted to leave Rolf for a former boy friend, but decides that the latter is too involved with professional success. In due time, she has her fifth child.

Here the film shifts its emphasis from Elisabeth to Rolf and his "poor life," as it is described in one of the recurring intertitles. He has become a traveling salesman and sees his wife infrequently. In his lonely hotel room, he mindlessly kills and skewers flies. Meanwhile, Elisabeth, meeting two American Mormons, decides that "God wants us to be happy in this world." Eventually, she and Rolf are baptized Mormons in a riverside ceremony.

"Is Rolf capable of saving himself through the help of his brain?" the narrator asks. Driving his Volkswagen deep into the woods, he seals the windows and starts the engine. This suicide is treated matter-of-factly and is strangely juxtaposed with ensuing scenes. After an angry encounter with Rolf's mother, Elisabeth, veiled in black lace and carrying flowers, performs an almost somnambulistic mourning ritual.

Abruptly the scene changes again. Elisabeth meets a young American, Brian Leak, and a new relationship rapidly unfolds. She puts flowers in her hair, and the pair make love in a meadow. As we watch her children eat spaghetti, the narrator tells us how glad they are that their mother is happy again. Veiled in white and crowned with flowers, she marries Brian while her Mormon friends look on.

Elisabeth emigrates to America with Brian and her five children to start a new life. We see a snapshot of her family in front of a small house, and one of her letters is read: "It is wonderful to start a new life and to be able to experience such great love, especially in a foreign country. . . . Everything is generous, free, and, if one is cut out for it, completely individual. . . . It lets me think of Rolf. Whatever one touches with loving hands must become twice as beautiful." (Reitz had actually seen a similar letter, and it inspired him to make the film.)

In the film's last shot, a black ocean liner moves slowly into the frame.

In films like *Mealtimes,* Reitz and his colleagues made good the promise of the Oberhausen Manifesto. They dealt with present-day realities in German society and swept away old cinematic stereotypes, challenging audiences to give up outmoded habits of identification and to accept new kinds of forms, character development, narrative, and imagery. Although Reitz seems to be telling a fairly realistic love story, he injects an element of ambiguity. The viewer is thrown off course repeatedly by abrupt changes, reversals, and, particularly, by the ending of the film.

Critic Enno Patalas has written,

> The film is not identical with its story and the characters of its protagonists. Neither the children nor Rolf's behavior are responsible for the catastrophe. They drive the story to its extreme, they make it into a "case," a paradigm. The ending, above all, makes it appear as such. Elisabeth's new conjugal bliss reiterates the story of her marriage to Rolf and gives it a degree of generality which, isolated, it does not possess. The ending is really the beginning of the film. . . . It calls for observation, discovery, comparison.[10]

The element of ambiguity is further strengthened by the relationship of language to the imagery. Dialogue is complemented by voice-over narrative/commentary and graphic intertitles. When Elisabeth notes that "the only interesting thing is the human face," we see a close-up of her face. Again and again phrases and images combine to unmask cliches and point to social contradictions. "The actors speak in order to conceal the thoughts of the characters; their bodies deceive deliberately," Reitz explains.

> The relationship between Elisabeth and Rolf is dominated by endless talk of happiness . . . the speaker does not see the unhappiness around him, but the audience can see it better. . . . In literature, language is always equally subject matter and conveyor of thought. In film, there is a possibility, so to speak, to portray language photographically as evidence of the physical reality of people.[11]

"The threat of hunger, the waiting woman, destroy us all." This quotation from James Joyce's *Ulysses,* which appears as the prologue to the film, characterizes the position of Rolf, who is increasingly drawn into total dependence on his wife. He never acts, only reacts, and when he finally does show initiative, it can only be expressed in an act of self-destruction.

Elisabeth, the central character in this potentially misogynistic kaleidoscope of modern middle-class marriage, turns out to be a strikingly artificial character. Reitz described her as "endowed with a certain healthiness, a powerful female aura, that makes her attractive to men without their taking into account that her way of looking at things might be frightening.[12]

The mouthpiece for every bourgeois notion of love and marriage, either directly or through the narrator, Elisabeth voices as her own ideas that seem to come from pop tunes. By contrasting her with her friend Irina, a "liberated" woman with a capacity for critical thinking and a desire to explore her options in life, Reitz exonerates himself from charges of misogyny.

Fußnoten (Footnotes), a 90-minute "commentary" on *Mealtimes*, is made up of outtakes from the latter film. Two films follow, both in collaboration with the Ulm School: *Uxmal*, a science-fiction drama, and *Filmstunde (Film Hour)*, a 16mm experimental documentary.

In 1968–69, Reitz wrote and directed *Cardillac*, a modern adaptation of the novella *Das Fräulein von Scuderi* by E. T. A. Hoffmann. The title character, a renowned goldsmith, commits suicide with a homemade electric chair. His body is found surrounded by hundreds of pieces of jewelry—his entire life's work. Unable to part with any of his creations, Cardillac had reacquired them by robbery and even murder. The respectable goldsmith had led a sinister second life as a criminal.

The film reconstructs Cardillac's life, but the emphasis increasingly shifts to his daughter, Madelon, the product of a short, illusion-filled relationship between the goldsmith and a beautiful black woman from Guadelupe. Dominated by her demanding, authoritarian father, Madelon has become a cold, emotionally unresponsive young woman. The only other important person in Cardillac's life is Olivier, his assistant, who, while attempting to follow in the footsteps of his master, lacks talent and originality. Alongside the fictitious characters, real-life people appear in this film happening, among them the industrialist Gunter Sachs, whose encounter with Cardillac illustrates the relationship between the artist and art business.

In a radio portrait of Reitz in 1980, critic Karsten Witte pointed out:

> What Reitz attempted, through a constant grueling dialogue with his film team, was a reflection on the theme of the social responsibility of the artist to society. . . . Certainly, the film bears the traces of the inner strife rampant in the group who worked on it, who were split by irreconcilable differences. One sees clearly that *Cardillac* is a product of the tumultuous 1968 period. But in contrast to the resultant sectarian films of the period, which increasingly narrowed their trust to fit dogma and were designed for a specific audience, *Cardillac* does not block out any opinion, even the most outrageous. . . . The film is lacking in political perspective, but compensates with its chaotic, overflowing richness. What the actors think about themselves and their roles has the same importance as a role itself.[13]

In 1970, in collaboration with Ula Stöckl, Reitz wrote and directed *Geschichten vom Kübelkind (Tales of the Trashcan Kid)*, and, in the same year, together with Ula Stöckl, Alf Brustellin, and Nicos Perakis, formed a production company called U.L.M. (Unabhängige Lichtspiel-Manufaktur, or Independent Film Handicrafts). The word *Manufaktur* denotes "hand-crafted," referring to films not made through mechanical production. In 1971, the four filmmakers teamed to write, produce, and direct *Das Goldene Ding* (literally, *The Golden Stuff*, actually *The Golden Fleece*).

Reitz's hometown in the remote Hunsrück region west of the Rhine is the locale for *Die Reise nach Wien (The Trip to Vienna)*, 1973). His first film on Germany's recent past (coscripted with Alexander Kluge) avoids heroics and focuses on the everyday life of two young wives whose husbands are serving in the army. It is spring 1943, and after Stalingrad the war takes a turn for the worse. Toni and Marga are bored by the restrictive life of a quiet town untouched by war events. Lonely and frustrated, they long for excitement and dream about a trip to Vienna, where dashing officers and real heroes abound.

An unexpected discovery of a money cache gives them the opportunity to realize their romantic dream. However, once in Vienna, they fall into the hands of a racketeer who cheats them out of their money. As for heroes, they encounter only two elderly officers on sick leave who help them to recoup some of their money and other valuables, which they must partially barter away on the long trip back.

Illusions lost, they arrive home, only to find that Marga is about to be arrested by the Nazi authorities for having failed to report the slaughter of a pig. To save her, they manage to implicate the local Nazi official on rape charges. He is punished and transferred to the Russian front, where he is soon killed. The film ends in 1945, when the first American tank rolls into town—a new era is beginning.

Based on a true story—Reitz's mother and a friend went on an adventurous trip to Vienna in 1943—and Reitz's own childhood memories, the film is both a chronicle of everyday life in Nazi Germany during World War II and a portrait of women in wartime. A star cast (Elke Sommer, Hannelore Elsner, and Mario Adorf) and meticulous period settings made for wide audience appeal. The experiences of Marga and Toni, as Reitz comments, "Build a microstructure on which the superstructure of history unwinds." The film shows the connection between private life and the National Socialist system from the perspective of Toni and Marga. It does not attempt to make a value judgment of National Socialism, but to direct attention to the biographical factors which, in reality, carried the system.

In May 1979, amid heated discussions about the TV production *Holocaust*, Reitz offered an interpretation that serves as a commentary to his own films about the period.

> If we want to come to terms with the period of the Third Reich and its atrocities, we can only approach it in the same way in which we gather information day by day about the world in which we live at present. We suffer from a hopeless lack of worked-out, structured, and aesthetically conveyed experiences. As a consequence, our reflexes have atrophied to the point where we are unable to "smell out" bad events, to spot the neo-Nazi by his small gestures; we are unable to sense physically the anxiety of our fellow citizens: real compassion no longer occurs spontaneously, in simple personal interactions. The atrophy of our reflexes is a very serious matter. We lose the only means we have to change things positively and qualitatively. We need to rid ourselves of the fragmented way of thinking—most precisely with regard to the worst part of our fascist history. We have to clarify our historical consciousness as often as we can. In this way, we will be able to create films, literary works, images that will heal our damaged reflexes.[14]

In 1974, Reitz again collaborated with Alexander Kluge, this time on *In Gefahr und größter Not bringt der Mittelweg den Tod (In Danger and Great Need the Middle Road Leads to Death)*. This curious title is taken from the writings of Friedrich von Logau, a German mystic of the Reformation, another period of great social upheaval. Reitz and Kluge combine fiction and fact in a "collage" of events in Frankfurt during a ten-day period in February 1974. The film is modeled on the *Wochenschau* (weekly newsreel), a cinematic form about which Hans-Magnus Enzensberger wrote in his 1957 essay "Fragmented World: Anatomy of a *Wochenschau*": By giving us a look at the world, [the *Wochenschau*] remains itself invisible; its methods remain invisible; the laws of the world which it presents to us remain incomprehensible. . . . The central theme of the *Wochenschau* is destruction: it is discernible throughout."[15] In their *Wochenschau*, Kluge and Reitz further deconstruct the already fragmented by leaving out the traditional voice-over commentary which in a conventional newsreel attempts to make sense of what is shown on the screen, and by letting images and events "speak for themselves." In this way, the audience is made aware of how mystifying the *Wochenschau* really is; without the reassuring and unifying commentary, the world becomes utter chaos. Two fictional characters, Inge Maier (Dagmar Boddrich), a woman who "sleeps around" and steals from her lovers whenever possible, and Rita Müller-Eisert (Jutta Winkelmann), an East German spy, wander through the urban landscape of the film, witnessing its "real-life" events, which include the annual Fasching (Mardi Gras) celebrations, police actions against squatters in buildings slated for demolition to make way for urban renewal, a political convention, a conference of "junior executives," a beauty contest, a meeting of astrophysicists.

The directors had originally intended to call the film "Eyes from Another Land." These "eyes," it seems, are not only those of Rita the spy, who agrees with Marx (and the directors) that "sense experience is the basis of all knowledge," but also those of Inge, who sometimes gets the feeling, as she puts it, of having fallen into a phony film; they are also our own eyes taking in this crazy-quilt world. Other "characters"—a police official, a politician, the "Prince" of the festival, the boss of the demolition firm, an aging fireman, an up-and-coming businessman, a janitor—speak of their lives in an almost meaningless, dissociated manner. Inge is very unhappy with her hand-to-mouth existence, but sees no way out; Rita, who reports everything she sees, is finally relieved of her duties because her contact cannot make sense of her detailed accounts of the craziness around her.

Images collide: scenes of the police arresting protesters at the demolition site give way to a police choir singing a *Schlager* called "The Magic of Spanish Nights." A pot sits on top of some volumes of Marx, and the title reads "Noodles." People celebrating Fasching seem to be forcing themselves to have a good time. A newscaster announces the latest of Henry Kissinger's "peace missions" to the Middle East. Physicists discuss black holes. The sound track is also a collage, mixing Wagner, Verdi, the march from the film *Bridge on the River Kwai,* Hanns Eisler, songs from old UFA musicals, and a children's chorus from East Germany. The film ends with a children's nonsense rhyme about a room filling up with water.

In Danger was criticized in some quarters for not having made a more concrete political statement, but this was obviously not what Kluge and Reitz had in mind. Viewers are to draw their own conclusions. The film is a series of ironic aphorisms resembling, in visual form, those by Theodor Adorno and Max Horkeimer in the final section of *The Dialectic of Enlightenment,* a radical critique of contempory mass culture that poses questions, not solutions. If the "plot" of the film seems consistent with Kluge's work, the images are clearly the result of Reitz's early experimental efforts. We see a world moving very fast, but going nowhere; the image of the destruction of perfectly useful buildings in the name of "renewal" becomes a metaphor for postindustrial society and its obsession with mindless growth, hurtling through chaos to what may well be total annihilation.

Stunde Null (*Zero Hour*), which won a 1977 Bundesfilmpreis, is often considered Reitz's best film. Based on a script on which he collaborated with Peter Steinbach, it concerns a group of people in a small town near Leipzig in the immediate postwar period. Germany has been divided by the Allies, and the American occupying forces are moving out to make way for the incoming Soviet troops. Fear of the "barbaric" Russians is mixed with a guilty awareness of the sufferings previously inflicted on them.

Joschi, a former member of the Hitler Youth, idolizes the American victors and wears a U.S. flight jacket. On a motorbike stolen from the German army, he heads toward Möckern, where, according to a map he has, the Nazis have buried jewels and other valuables. In exchange for some cigarettes, Nattiske, an old railwayman who now runs a bicycle repair shop, allows Joschi to stay with him. He makes friends with Frau Unterstab, a widow; Paul, a one-legged veteran; and Isa, a somewhat older teenager who, fearing that the Russians will rape her, takes refuge in Frau Unterstab's greenhouse. Joschi tells Isa about the buried treasure and his plans to escape to the American zone. Together, they find the cache and hide it in the greenhouse. When the Russians arrive, Isa hides, and as both she and the treasure are about to be discovered, Joschi threatens the Russians with a pistol. A fight is avoided only after the townspeople convince the Russians that Joschi is merely protecting his girl friend. While the new occupiers drink and amuse themselves with a carousel in the village square, Joschi and Isa head for the American zone. A jeep pulls up alongside them, and laughing American soldiers take Joschi's jacket, his loot, and Isa. Driving off, they leave him stunned and bewildered on the deserted road.

Reitz says of his film:

> The people I have described in my film, and some of them are members of my own family, were capable of being part of the Third Reich. My own memories seem to contradict the judgment that has been passed upon our parents' generation. To me, it still remains a mystery how Hitler's Germany could have come about: all that murderous brutality on a political level, and at the same time, that feeling of warmth and cozy well-being in the privacy of our own homes. As a result of this, I have learned to live with this ambivalent love/hate feeling that is typical of my generation in Germany. The war is still far from over. In this film, my perspective is that of the young cyclist, who will only understand much later what he now watches with such great curiosity.[16]

Zero Hour is a powerful, warm, and moving film. Especially memorable among the characters are Frau Unterstab, a sharp-tongued woman who blames the Nazis for her soldier-son's death, and Matek, a resourceful Pole who had been doing forced labor for the Germans, and who has stolen a carousel, which he now takes from town to town. The characters communicate a thoroughly believable feeling of being caught in a historical "zero hour," a moment between fear and cautious hope for the future.

In late 1977, Reitz joined in the collective production of *Deutschland im Herbst (Germany in Autumn)*, a left-wing response to the assassination of ex-Nazi industrialist Hanns-Martin Schleyer, the Mogadishu hijacking, and the alleged suicides of three members of the Baader-Meinhof gang at Stammheim prison.

Each director involved approached the subject in his or her unique way. Fassbinder presented a carefully staged account of his personal life at the time. Kluge introduced the young history teacher Gabi Teichert, another of his female witnesses. Schlöndorff, in collaboration with novelist Heinrich Böll, gives an account of a television production of *Antigone*—shelved because of its potentially explosive political content—interweaving it with the real-life drama of Christiane Ensslin, sister of the dead activist Gertrud Ensslin, who strives to assure her sister and the other two prisoners a decent burial. Reitz's contribution is based on an actual experience related to him by the writer Peter Steinbach, who had been searched by guards at the Franco-German border. The sequence is short and frightening, an incident of everyday fascism, as a couple run into a Kafkaesque interrogation by officials looking for the Schleyer kidnappers. In one of the most effective moments in the film, the incident ends with a stern salute from a guard as a raised gate comes down and cuts the frame in half.

In 1978, Reitz directed his most ambitious project, *Der Schneider von Ulm (The Tailor from Ulm)*. He had long been fascinated with the character of Albrecht Berblinger, who in the latter part of the eighteenth century had used his knowledge of fabrics and engineering in an attempt to construct flying machines. Reitz wrote the script with Petra Kiener, who also worked as assistant director. Reitz described the film.

> From a filmmaking point of view, the character of Berblinger has one enormous advantage: very little is known about him. Which means that there are virtually no limits to one's imagination. Or rather, the only limits are the few recorded facts. We structured our material in such a way as to ensure allusions to these facts: but in the final analysis the film is a fairy tale, in which the role of history is merely to substantiate the legend. In other words, it's not an authen-

Tilo Prückner in *The
Tailor from Ulm* (COURTESY
OF FILMVERLAG DER
AUTOREN)

tic film, based on historical research, about the life of Albrecht
Berblinger, but rather a work of fiction.[17]

An entertaining film with serious political and philosophical
overtones, *The Tailor from Ulm* was intended for a mass audience.
Reitz spared no expense in his attempt to bring the eighteenth
century to life and to make the flying experiments as realistic as
possible. Berblinger is seen as an amiable idealist who sacrifices
his family and fortune to his obsession. It is the time of the
French Revolution, and Berblinger becomes friendly with a
Jacobin, Caspar Fesslen, whose revolutionary notions add fire to
his own enthusiasm and imagination. He finally succeeds in
creating a machine that gets him up for a fine flight. But when
he attempts to repeat his feat for the benefit of the local aristocracy, he fails. Forced to flee from Ulm, he nevertheless keeps his
creative urge intact.

Berblinger is presented not as a hero but as an ordinary man
with an (almost) impossible dream. There is little dramatic tension, and the political discussions between Berblinger and

Fesslen are rather out of touch with the concerns of the politicized youth of the sixties and early seventies. The visual elegance of the film—especially in the aerial sequences— heightened by Nikos Mamangakis's score, is impressive, but it nevertheless cannot compete with the more poetic and disturbing beauty of the films of directors like Herzog, Wenders, or Hauff.

For the past few years, Reitz has been working on a 10-part television series, *Made in Germany*. Based on a script cowritten with Peter Steinbach, it is simultaneously the chronicle of a rural family and a whole region, an account of sixty years in Reitz's native Hunsrück. Shot entirely on location with a nonprofessional cast drawn from the area, the ten segments will vary in length and use both black and white and color. A documentary about the work in progress was produced by Reitz in 1980, and the entire series itself was scheduled for release in 1983.

There can be no question that Edgar Reitz is one of the most consistent and influential figures in contemporary German cinema. His films deal not only with the liberation of men and women who strive to shake off social oppression, but with the liberation of film itself from outmoded and obsolete forms. His dedication to innovative social and aesthetic theory is surpassed only by his commitment to the real world and its betterment. As long as he continues to make films, it seems certain that we will always be able to expect the unexpected from Edgar Reitz.

NOTES

[1] Karsten Witte, "Edgar Reitz: A Radio Portrait," broadcast by NDR, 8 January 1980.

[2] Alexander Kluge, interview with author (I.S.-R.), 20 January 1981.

[3] Edgar Reitz, interview with author (I.S.-R.), 20 January 1981.

[4] Quoted in *Information über den Film "Kommunikation,"* 1962, p. 3.

[5] Quoted in Jan Dawson, "A Labyrinth of Subsidies," *Sight and Sound,* Winter 1980–81, pp. 15–16.

[6] Klaus Eder and Alexander Kluge, *Ulmer Dramaturgien: Reibungsverluste* (Munich & Vienna: Hanser, 1980), pp. 33–35.

[7] Quoted in Dawson," A Labyrinth of Subsidies," p. 17.

[8] Quoted in ibid., p. 18.

[9] Witte, "Radio Portrait."

[10]Enno Patalas, reviewing the film in *Die Zeit*, 7 April 1967.

[11]Witte, "Radio Portrait."

[12]Quoted in Frieda Grafe and Enno Patalas, "Tribüne des jungen deutschen Films. 6. Edgar Reitz," *Filmkritik*, March 1967, pp. 128–132.

[13]Witte, "Radio Portrait."

[14]Ibid.

[15]Hans-Magnus Enzensberger, "Fragmented World: Anatomy of a *Wochenschau*," 1957; quoted by Wilhelm Roth in *Film/Korrespondenz*, February 1975.

[16]Quoted in *Neue Deutsche Filme* 1976/77, 27th Berlin Film Festival, 1977.

[17]Quoted in the program notes for the 29th Berlin Film Festival, 1979.

VOLKER SCHLÖNDORFF and MARGARETHE VON TROTTA

Transcending the Genres

by Christian-Albrecht Gollub

THE MOST SUCCESSFUL GERMAN FILM-making couple since Thea von Harbou and Fritz Lang in the 1920s, Margarethe von Trotta and Volker Schlöndorff have individually and collaboratively done work that has won international acclaim and garnered prizes at film festivals everywhere. Schlöndorff's first feature, *Der junge Törleß (Young Törless,* 1965–66), based on Robert Musil's novel, not only established his reputation but set a precedent for the films that followed. With few exceptions he continued to work in adaptation, and in 1975, when box-office receipts for domestic films were disastrous, he and von Trotta coscripted and codirected *Die verlorene Ehre der Katharina Blum (The Lost Honor of Katharina Blum),* based on Heinrich Böll's novel, which became one of the year's most successful releases. The couple's final collaboration, *Der Fangschuß (Coup de Grâce,* 1976), was based on Marguerite Yourcenar's novel.

The following year was critical for both filmmakers. Margarethe von Trotta wrote and directed her own first feature, the highly acclaimed *Das zweite Erwachen der Christa Klages (The Second Awakening of Christa Klages).* With a script based not on fiction but on the facts leading to the arrest of Munich teacher Margit Czenki, von Trotta emerged from her husband's cinéliterary

Margarethe von Trotta (Courtesy of the Filmmaker)

shadow. At the same time, although literature was proving box-office poison, Volker Schlöndorff embarked on his most ambitious adaptation—Günter Grass's *Die Blechtrommel* (*The Tin Drum*). The film broke worldwide records in 1979, the same year von Trotta released *Schwestern oder Die Balance des Glücks* (*Sisters or The Balance of Happiness*), a film that established her as a feminist director with access to distribution at home and abroad. Although in many ways atypical, the two filmmakers had become internationally recognized mainstays of the New German Cinema.

Born in Wiesbaden on March 31, 1939, Volker Schlöndorff lost his mother during a bombing raid in World War II. As a youngster he longed to become a circus performer—over thirty years later this fantasy would be partially realized in his filming of *The Tin Drum*'s circus sequence—but in the early 1950's he developed an interest in film. Because German films were not being shown in Wiesbaden, he saw primarily foreign films and cites the work of Jean Cocteau, Alfred Hitchcock, Carol Reed, and Elia Kazan as particularly memorable. Vacations were often spent in France, and young Volker came to view Paris as the "capital of the world": "In order to cure me of my artistic tendencies," he recalls, "my good Protestant father sent me to a Catholic lycée in France. I was a good student but I remained a devoted cinéphile. Fortunately, the priests at the lycée encouraged me to attend the Cinémathèque."[1] Schlöndorff subsequently studied economics and political science.

He had also been attending the Cinémathèque regularly—seeing between six and seven hundred films in a two-year period—and observing the rise of the *nouvelle vague* and the films of Chabrol, Godard, and Truffaut. Moreover, he had spent one year at the Institut des-Hautes Etudes Cinématographiques (IDHEC) and had met Louis Malle, subsequently working as his fourth assistant on *Zazie dans le Métro* (1960), an adaptation of Raymond Queneau's novel. That same year he made his first short, *Wen Kümmert's* (*Who Cares*), his own assistant director being Bertrand Tavernier. Schlöndorff continued to work with Malle and was assistant director for *Vie privée* (*A Very Private Affair*, 1962), *Le feu follet* (*The Fire Within*, 1963), and *Viva Maria* (1965). In addition he assisted Alain Resnais on *L'Année dernière à Marienbad* (*Last Year at Marienbad*, 1961), a film based on nouveau romancier Alain Robbe-Grillet's cinénovel, and Jean-Pierre Melville on *Léon Moron, Prêtre* (1961), based on Béatrice Beck's novel, and *Le Doulos* (*The Fingerman*, 1962).[2]

Upon his return to West Germany in the mid-1960s, Schlöndorff made *Young Törless* (1966), the success of which led to three films in short succession. His *Ein unheimlicher Moment* (*An Uncanny Moment*, 1967), was to be an episode in *Der Paukenspieler* (*The Kettledrum Player*), but the feature was never released. Schlöndorff's own two features *Mord und Totschlag* (*A Degree of Murder*, 1967), and *Michael Kohlhaas—der Rebell* (*Michael Kohlhaas*, 1968–69) were attempts to appeal to a broader audience. Both films having been lambasted by critics and ignored by moviegoers, Schlöndorff gave up the idea of a "Hollywood career" in Germany and made a television adaptation of Brecht's *Baal* (1970), which starred Rainer Werner Fassbinder and members of the *antiteater*. The role of Sophie was played by Margarethe von Trotta, a young actress with whom Schlöndorff would collaborate on his next seven films and whom he would marry in 1971. Born on February 21, 1942, in Berlin, she was the daughter of artist Alfred Roloff, who died while she was still quite young, leaving von Trotta and her aristocratic mother nearly penniless. At her mother's insistence, she attended a trade

Volker Schlöndorff
(Courtesy of the
Filmmaker)

school, but after a brief period as a secretary she left for Paris, where she lived as an *au pair* girl—and began to spend a coniderable amount of time in the Cinémathèque, where she met directors, joined in discussions, and worked for various film collectives. With a group of friends she collaborated on scripts and codirected a number of shorts.

Returning to West Germany in the early 1960s, she briefly pursued university studies before attending a Munich acting school. "I wanted to direct films—and then again not," she subsequently explained. "I didn't have a role model. At that time, in the early 1960s, there weren't any female directors in the Federal Republic. So I became an actress."[3] In 1964 von Trotta temporarily gave up acting for marriage and a child, but, feeling creatively stifled, soon returned to her career. Beginning in 1967 she worked with such directors as H.G. Schier, Gustav Ehmck, Franz-Josef Spieker, Klaus Lemke, Rainer Werner Fassbinder, Reinhard Hauff, Claude Chabrol, Herbert Achternbusch, and Volker Schlöndorff. Three years later, while she and Schlöndorff collaborated on the script for his film *Der plötzliche Reichtum der armen Leute von Kombach* (*The Sudden Wealth of the Poor People of Kombach*), she divorced her husband. The ensuing custody battle for her son was the source for the semiautobiographical *Strohfeuer (A Free Woman,* 1972*),* a film that brought her a number of acting awards.

In 1961, shortly before the Oberhausen Manifesto, Schlöndorff told *Cahiers du Cinéma* that he planned to "return to my country in order to make films, because they have none there."[4] He had already spent five years in France, and despite his assertion that "my main goal, apart from the cinema, was to forget that I was German,"[5] he had begun to subscribe to *Filmkritik,* the Munich journal that would soon publish his reports on the French cinema.[6] As a voice-over translator of German subtitles in films shown at the Cinémathèque, he became acquainted with German film history through the films of such directors as F. W. Murnau and G. W. Pabst. Moreover, he knew Lotte Eisner and Fritz Lang personally and saw the latter's films.[7] As a German expatriate, Schlöndorff was repeatedly questioned about his homeland. "This made me curious to find out what it is to be a German," he recalled. "My films deal with that."[8] Both passively and actively reminded of his German heritage. Schlöndorff felt "in all naiveté"[9] that he could make a contribution to the foundering film industry in his native Germany. In retrospect his decision to return there to make his first feature was a timely one.

Schlöndorff was working as assistant director on a Paris production of Robert Musil's drama *Die Schwärmer (The Visionaries),* when German film critic Enno Patalas informed him that the West German Ministry of the Interior was granting monetary support for screenplays. Knowing his admiration for Musil, Patalas suggested the author's *Young Törless* (1906) as a possible project. In 1962 Schlöndorff contacted Dr. Otto Rosenthal, who held the rights to the Musil work, but Rosenthal feared that the novel would suffer in the transition. While assisting Louis Malle, Schlöndorff wrote a script for the proposed film and submitted it to the West German government, but he failed to receive a grant. However, he soon interested producer Franz Seitz in the project and in the summer of 1965 again approached Rosenthal, who after reading the script agreed. Before a contract could be signed, however, Luchino Visconti contacted Rosenthal and likewise expressed interest in *Young Törless.* After considerable negotiation, three months later Rosenthal sold the rights to Franz Seitz for 20,000 marks. Schlöndorff then returned to

Matthieu Carriere in *Young
Torless* (COURTESY OF
REITER/NORA)

Munich where he discussed the script's possibilities with another
aspiring filmmaker: Werner Herzog. With 200,000 marks that
Seitz had been granted by the West German government and
with additional financial backing from Louis Malle, Schlöndorff
began filming in November 1965. Six months later, after its
premiere in Nantes, France, on May 20, 1966, *Young Törless* won
the Max Ophüls Prize, the first of numerous international
awards.

The film opens with an establishing pan of the bleak and hazy
landscape surrounding the Neudorf train station, where Coun-
cilor Törless and his wife are being seen off by their son Thomas
and a group of his friends—Reiting, Beineberg, and Basini—all
students of a nearby boarding school. The elder Törless anxiously asks Beineberg, a self-confident young man, to keep an eye
on his son. After an emotionally restrained "My child!" Frau
Törless boards the train, which departs as mother and son exchange glances that indicate a strong bond. Returning to the
school, the dark-uniformed boys pass some peasant women who
glance meaningfully at Törless, who silently returns their stares.
When Reiting caustically probes, "Well, is the little boy
homesick?" Törless manages a forced smile. The boys stop at an

inn, where Basini orders a round of wine and loses money playing craps. The boys continue on, and the school looms ominously in the evening shadows. In these opening scenes we are
given a brief character sketch of the four young men: Törless,
withdrawn and observing; Reiting, sarcastic and perceptive;
Beineberg, seemingly mature and reliable; and Basini, the outsider and loser.

In class, at the clock ticks away, close-ups betray the boys'
boredom. Beineberg marks off the days on his desk, and Basini
draws a chalk line to separate his territory from that of the boy
alongside him. The bell finally signals release. The teacher,
overhearing Törless remark on the tedium of it all, assigns him a
pensum from Horace.

As the boys prepare for bed, Basini asks Beineberg for an
extra day in which to repay a loan. Beineberg agrees on the
condition that Basini do whatever he tells him to, no matter how
unpleasant. As the others sleep, Basini breaks into Beineberg's
locker and steals some money. The following Sunday, the boys
are in a café. Törless dreamily observes both a waitress and
Beineberg with an intensity that is captured in sensuous close-
ups that betray his sexual tension. A shattering glass brings him
back to reality, and he and Beineberg discuss their future. Törless confesses to knowing nothing about what he wants or is.
Meanwhile, Reiting accuses Basini of the theft, and in return for
silence makes him agree to do whatever is requested of him.

Beineberg and Törless visit Božena, an unwed mother who
supports herself by entertaining male visitors. Fascinated but
reserved, Törless loses his temper when Božena comments on
his mother's beauty. Božena angrily retorts that having lived in
Vienna, she knows that people are the same everywhere. Törless
is impressed by her unflattering portrait of the people who have
thus far shaped his life. The following day, Reiting tells Törless
of Basini's theft, and Törless histrionically insists that the thief be
punished. He is told, however, that "a variety of pleasures" may
be derived from the situation, and although he fails to understand, the homosexual implications are clear to the viewer. This
sexual element increasingly comes to dominate relations
between the boys.

The next day, as Törless and Beineberg watch, Reiting forces
Basini to submit to a variety of humiliations—including a sug-

gestive hosing—in exchange for silence. The others will hence-forth "control" various aspects of Basini's life. Reiting and Beineberg constantly deflate Basini's various pretensions to mas-culinity, and their relationship with him takes on a decided sadomasochistic tone of which Törless is unaware, as he is oc-cupied with his own problems with the concept of imaginary numbers. An appeal to a teacher brings only an equivocal "It's all feeling, even mathematics," and since Törless is not in touch with his feelings he remains unenlightened.

Beineberg informs Törless of a homosexual scandal at the school some time ago and indicates that Reiting and Basini are engaged in similar activities. Feeling his own masculinity threatened, he resolves to "torment" Basini, and in an attic that evening Reiting and Beineberg physically abuse Basini as Tör-less contemplatively looks into a mirror or into the camera. He records his own alienation in his diary, which Reiting finds and reads. Reiting and Beineberg leave for a vacation, and it is sug-gested to Törless that during their absence he visit Božena. In-stead, Törless spends his time with Basini, who obliquely admits the homosexual acts into which the others have forced him. Törless vainly tries to get him to verbalize his reasons for submit-ting.

On their return, Reiting and Beineberg escalate their abuse of Basini in attic sessions during which Törless ignores the latter's calls for help. Later, Basini complains that previously he had been "so nice" to him, and at this allusion to their sexual in-volvement Törless orders him to be still: "That was not I." As Basini is displaying his bruises, Reiting appears and accuses them of secret meetings. Törless denies the accusations, and, expressing his new awareness that the "clean" and "dirty" as-pects of life are not mutually exclusive, announces that he no longer wants to be involved in Basini's humiliation.

The next day Basini is provoked when a letter from his mother is read to the entire class. The students barricade Basini in the gymnasium and hang him from a set of rings. Schlöndorff films this episode in part with a hand-held camera, both from the students' perspective and from Basini's, so that the film, which has until now been relatively static, is literally turned on its head and attains a feverish pace. Basini finally escapes his tor-mentors and vomits.

As the others rehearse a version of these events suitable for the authorities, Törless seeks solitude in the outdoors. Meeting Božena in a café, he announces his intention of leaving the school, to which he then returns. A lengthy monologue explains his now mature attitude: "What looks so dreadful, so untouchable from a distance, simply occurs, very quietly and obviously. And therefore one has to be wary of it."

With no sign of remorse, Törless accepts the faculty's decision to expel him. As the film ends, he climbs into his mother's carriage, and the camera pans the vast and hazy landscape surrounding the school.

Young Törless was seen as either a commentary on Austria's upper classes at the turn of the century or as a filmic rendering of critic Wilfried Berghahn's interpretation of Musil's novel as a prophecy of the Nazi atrocities.[10] But the filmmaker stated that he considered it "the attempt to represent an 'atmosphere' and behavior patterns 'per se'—not through abstractions but rather with plastic and acoustic means."[11] Schlöndorff's evaluation provides the key to his subsequent films.

However one may interpret the sadomasochistic relationships in *Young Törless,* viewed within the larger context of Schlöndorff's work the behavior patterns to which the filmmaker referred have as their central issue the violence with which both society in general and interpersonal relationships in particular are imbued. Indeed, seen as a unit, the films comprise an iconography of violence that spans the spectrum. Its various manifestations may be the starting point of a film (*A Degree of Murder*), the final desperate act of a frustrated individual (*The Morals of Ruth Halbfass* and *Coup de Grâce*), or the result of injustices to which a previously relatively passive person has been subjected over a period of time (*Michael Kohlhaas, The Lost Honor of Katharina Blum,* and *A Free Woman*). A selfish act may mushroom into an uncontrollable and perverse situation directly related to the political and social tenor of the period (*Young Törless, The Sudden Wealth of the Poor People of Kombach, The Tin Drum, The Lost Honor of Katharina Blum*). That society's laws or expectations do not correspond to an individual's governing principles or motivating factors—however off-center or illogical either may be—is evident throughout Schlöndorff's work. His films are a running commentary on the power struggle between two seemingly irreconcilable sets of values.

The success of *Young Törless* eventually led to negotiations with American film companies, and prior to the release of *A Degree of Murder,* the film's producer, Rob Houwer, sold the international distribution rights to Universal Pictures. Soon after, a contract with Columbia Pictures guaranteed Schlöndorff international distribution and funding of his subsequent pictures. While the filmmaker remained in Germany, he had, in essence, "gone Hollywood," the first director of the NGC to do so. In an effort to give *A Degree of Murder* a broader appeal, Schlöndorff hired internationally recognizable Anita Pallenberg and Brian Jones to work with him. In addition, eschewing literary sources, he collaborated on an original script set in contemporary Germany.

A Degree of Murder is the story of a young waitress, Marie, who murders her former boy friend, Hans, and then tries to dispose of his corpose with the aid of Gunther, a young man she has met in a bar. Together with Gunther's friend, Fritz, they wrap Hans's body in a carpet and transport it to a highway construction site. After disposing of the body, they pay Fritz's aunt a brief visit and return to Marie's apartment building. The young woman's friend Elfi, invites the two men upstairs, but neither one accepts. When Marie enters her apartment, she sees a photograph of Hans on her night table and begins to scream. The camera cuts to the cafe where she works. Once again she is serving coffee, and her customer tries to pick her up. In the final scene of the film, a bulldozer is moving dirt at the construction site, and a crane lifts Hans's body high into the air.

The film met with catastrophe at the West German box offices.[12] Neither Anita Pallenberg's nymphomaniacal portrayal of Marie, the at times sharp dialogue, nor Brian Jones's score were of much help. While sex, crime, and music added certain "entertainment" values, they also caused the film to appear superficial. Schlöndorff himself later described it as a "trivial film."[13] Indeed, audiences were unable to find adequate justification for Marie's initial act of violence or her "serious" conversations with other women in the film. Marie, it seems, is dissatisfied with her life as a waitress, but her errant and occasionally crude behavior makes it difficult to see her as anything other than a troubled and frustrated young woman who lives for the moment. Although awarded a Filmband in Silver and 300,000 marks, neither it nor the director's subsequent feature lived up to the critics' expectations.

In 1968, Schlöndorff once again turned to literature as a source for his next film. Based on the 1810 novella *Michael Kohlhaas* by Heinrich von Kleist, the film attempted to relate the injustices suffered by the horse dealer Kohlhaas in the sixteenth century to the political upheaval and student unrest of the late 1960s. However, the use of contemporary documentary footage at the beginning of the film seems forced and trite. While Schlöndorff considered the film "very beautiful," he admitted that the venture was a failure. The overabundance of brutal—and often poorly filmed and awkwardly staged—action sequences overwhelm the viewer and surely contribute to what Margarethe von Trotta later referred to as Schlöndorff's "Kohlhaas trauma."[14] As the credits roll we see footage of demonstrations in Paris, Tokyo, New York, and Berlin. The camera then cuts to the property of the horse dealer Michael Kohlhaas, and a voice-over commentary informs us that Kohlhaas was a hardworking, peaceable, and orderly man, and that these very virtues led to rebellion, arson, and murder. Elisabeth, Kohlhaas's wife, emerges from their house, hands her husband two saddlebags, and kisses him good-bye. Kohlhaas is taking some of his horses to market.

He reaches a tollgate on the property of the landowner von Tronka; because he does not have the required permit, he must leave two of his best horses as collateral. When he returns two weeks later, he finds his animals thin, unfed, and overworked. Kohlhaas requests retribution, but von Tronka's men chase him and his people away. Soon thereafter, Kohlhaas takes the matter to court, but the officials' sole question seems to be the condition of the dealer's horses when he left them with von Tronka. Learning that the court considers him the instigator of the affair, Kohlhaas is enraged and seeks vengeance. He demands that von Tronka, who has conveniently disappeared, be turned over to him, and he and his men storm Wittenberg, where the landowner is thought to be hiding. While houses are plundered and set on fire, the horse dealer murders the city's mayor and watches as his men rape the local women.

The busy Kurfürst in Dresden feels that some action must be taken, and one of his advisors, a religious named Martin Luther, suggests that Kohlhaas not be treated like a criminal but rather be ordered to Dresden and be freed on parole, if he agrees to disband his followers. The Kurfürst accepts the arrangement, as does Kohlhaas, who comes to Dresden, where he is promised that his case will be reexamined. He sees his children again and finds his horses. While in Dresden, Kohlhaas has been appointed a guard for his "protection," but the horse dealer feels himself to be more of a prisoner; he makes his way to the local prison and, not finding the warden there, waits outside the door the entire night. When the Kurfürst hears of this, he reverses his decision. Kohlhaas is condemned to die, but before he is executed he frees his two horses. As they gallop across the meadows, his legs and arms are broken, and he dies, tied to a large wooden wheel raised high above the crowd. As the film ends, his children are shown playing with Luther. His horses, the cause of his death, gallop freely on a distant field.

Michael Kohlhaas exhibits the psychological turmoil and physical encounters so typical of Schlöndorff's work; however, despite the documentary footage prefacing the tale, the horror of the action sequences cannot be related to the upheavals of the late 1960s and is therefore little more than a cheap thrill geared toward an international market. As becomes evident, the director's forte lies not in action films or contemporary crime dramas but rather in such personal and intimate compositions as *Young Törless*. His camera is at its best when it acts as a quiet and withdrawn observer, rather than as an overly active visual recording device.[15]

Following his new debacle, Schlöndorff took two major steps in his career. In 1969 he severed his Hollywood ties and, with Peter Fleischmann, founded Hallelujah Film, his own production company. He subsequently adapted Brecht's *Baal* for German television. Coproduced by Hallelujah Film, the Hessische Rundfunk (HR), and the Bayerische Rundfunk (BR), it was shown in April 1970, when Schlöndorff had already begun his first script collaboration with Margarethe von Trotta, whom he had directed in the television production. Their film, *The Sudden Wealth of the Poor People of Kombach*, was, like *Baal*, conceived as a television production and coproduced by Hallelujah Film and the Hessische Rundfunk. Unlike *Baal*, however, the film was intended for general theatrical release following its first television airing.

Schlöndorff and von Trotta based their script on a nineteenth-century chronicle by Carl Franz, a court secretary who documented the 1821 robbery of a money transport by a group of peasants. Six men from Kombach plan and, after numerous thwarted attempts, execute the robbery, a crime first suggested to the young worker Jacob Geiz by a Jewish peddler. In the Geiz family kitchen, the spoils are divided among the robbers, and the golden thalers soon appear in the village. When a reward is offered for the capture of the criminals, the villagers report the strange behavior of the Geiz family. The elder Geiz, his son Jacob, and Soldan, one of their accomplices, are subsequently jailed, and although no money is found they remain suspects. Heinrich, Geiz's older son, and Ludwig Acker are also questioned. In the course of the questioning, the latter admits to his guilt and implicates his accomplices. Soldan and Volk, the sixth robber, commit suicide, and the others are condemned to death. Everyone except Heinrich atones for the criminal act, but his wife, Sophie (Margarethe von Trotta), finally convinces him to reveal where the money is hidden. Heinrich can now receive Holy Communion. Of those involved in the crime, only the instigator of the crime escapes death; he flees to America. The film ends as it began, with a voice-over narration describing the events on the screen. One by one, the four men are decapitated.

Schlöndorff's preoccupation with the German past stems from, as he stated, his "non-German" years in France. In the filmic transformation of a literary work, the director has a particular goal in mind.

> Literature helps me to understand those things I cannot deal with if I don't have literature, those things I cannot formulate correctly. I have almost always used literature as a source of information. In literature I look for, above all, information regarding the question What is a German? . . . What is German about me? What actually is the German identity?[16]

While Carl Franz's nineteenth-century court chronicle is only tangentially literary, as a historical document it suited Schlöndorff's purposes. The didactic nature of the film finds expression in the voice-over narration—quoted directly from the chronicle—and other Brechtian alienation effects that remind viewers that they are seeing a film and cause them "to reevaluate one moment of history."[17]

The Sudden Wealth of the Poor People of Kombach, Schlöndorff's most successful film since *Young Törless,* won the German Filmband in Gold for best direction and was seen by a larger audience than any of his previous features—due primarily to the television airing prior to its theatrical release. The reaction to the film was not, however, overwhelmingly positive. Critics now began to label Schlöndorff an "art film" director, both because of his allegiance to historical and literary sources and because of his seemingly apathetic attitude toward current events. His failure as an "entertainer" had been demonstrated by *A Degree of Murder* and *Michael Kohlhaas.* As fate would have it, Schlöndorff set his next film, *Die Moral der Ruth Halbfass* (*The Morals of Ruth Halbfass*), in contemporary Germany. His script—coauthored by writer Peter Hamm—was based on the 1971 trial of Minouche Schubert, wife of a wealthy industrialist who had allegedly been shot by hired killers.

As the film opens, Franz Vogelsang, a high-school art teacher, is reading a passage from Ibsen—Schlöndorff cannot completely avoid the literary—to his lover, Ruth (Senta Berger), wife of wealthy businessman Erich Halbfass. Although Ruth cherishes her relationship with Franz, she refuses to divorce her husband for reasons of prestige. Dissatisfied, Vogelsang plots with Francesco, Ruth's hairstylist, to kill Halbfass. Although himself married, Franz would very willingly leave his wife, Doris, for Ruth. The two women are distinct opposites. While Ruth enjoys her status in society, Doris is a simple woman devoted to her husband.

When Halbfass discovers his wife's illicit relationship, he meets with Doris and asks her to handle the matter. Later, Doris phones to make an appointment, at which she shoots him. As a result, the original murder plot is revealed, and Franz is arrested. Having recovered from his wound, a few months later

Halbfass is on the way to Spain with Ruth. Their teenage daughter, Aglaia, reads a newspaper account of the apparent suicide of the imprisoned Doris, who has steadfastly refused to comment on her motives. As the film ends, Aglaia punctuates her reading with the comment "Simply anachronistic," and takes some snapshots of her departing parents. Franz, meanwhile, has been exonerated.

In the film's most significant scene, Franz's remarks on the relationship between art and society are an appropriate comment on Schlöndorff's own work: "The dominant topic of our era is violence, violence in politics, violence in society, violence in interpersonal relationships. Art cannot and should not ignore this violence."

While not without its moments, for the most part the film is a mass of clichés—the rich wife and her middle-class lover, the homosexual hairstylist, the streetwise teenage daughter, the devoted wife, etc.—and moves alternately among various cinematic genres: social satire, drawing-room comedy, love story, and murder mystery. Lacking focus, it is often confusing, and the director was later to express regret at having made it.[18]

Schlöndorff now began to concentrate almost exclusively on strong female protagonists who, like Božena, Marie, or Ruth were not merely "the second sex." *Strohfeuer* (*A Free Woman*, 1972) is what he had conscientiously sought to avoid previously: a problem film. On the suggestion of von Trotta, with whom he wrote the script, he examined the plight of a young divorcée in a male-oriented world. A docufictionalization of von Trotta's own divorce, the film is the most significant, although by no means the most effective, of their collaborations.

As the credits roll, Elisabeth Junker (von Trotta) braves Munich's morning traffic on her motor scooter, responding to honking with an obscene gesture. At the courthouse, where her divorce from Hans Helmut is to be finalized, she freely admits having deserted both him and their son, Nicolas. She begins her new life by removing her wedding ring and purchasing a black wig. Meeting some publishing friends, she makes an unsuccessful pitch for a job and then asks Oskar Merz for a lift to Frankfurt. At a rest stop, after throwing up, she discusses her divorce with him. Later, while waiting for him to complete some business, she phones her lawyer (a woman) in Munich and is told there are complications about the custody of her child. Returning home immediately, she finds that her mother is taking care of Nicolas during Helmut's absence and is advised to patch up her marriage. She angrily refuses, and when Helmut returns he objects to her presence and refuses to allow her to remove some belongings.

Since custody depends on steady employment, she looks for work, but is offered nothing that does not exploit her attractiveness as a woman. To develop her talents, she takes singing and dancing lessons, but when results are slow in coming accepts work as a saleswoman in a fur store. Preferring to remain independent, she rejects Oskar's offer of financial help. In a black-and-white daydream sequence she sings a song rejecting the various roles into which women are forced.

Weary of the custody struggle, Elisabeth tries to get a friend to swear that he is the boy's true father. Her scheme gets little encouragement from her lawyer, who overwhelms her with criticism and technical jargon. Her attempts to expand her horizons turn up examples of the subordination of women in all aspects of life and art. Only marginally independent and fearful of losing custody of Nicolas, Elisabeth accepts Oskar's suggestion that they marry. The film ends with a series of wedding photos. This ending, seen by some as an abject surrender, is perhaps better interpreted as a joining of forces with a man sympathetic to her struggle to establish herself in a male-dominated world.

After *A Free Woman,* advertised as a "film by Volker Schlöndorff and Margarethe von Trotta," von Trotta began to develop her own themes and expand on them in her remaining collaborations with Schlöndorff. Both in the two television features and in *The Lost Honor of Katharina Blum* and *Coup de Grâce,* a woman's actions and reactions reflect the freedom she seeks from society's expectations and strictures. The women in these films stand up for their rights. Their refusal to be social pawns often has negative results, but their assertive natures show them to be as strong as, if not stronger than, their male counterparts. Not until von Trotta directed her own features, however, would women emerge as the dominant sex. For her, *A Free Woman* marked the beginning of a transition period.

Following the television features *Overnight Stay in Tirol* (1973) and *Georgina's Reasons* (1974)—a contemporary drama and a

Henry James adaptation focusing on marital discord and emancipation—Schlöndorff and von Trotta coscripted and codirected *The Lost Honor of Katharina Blum*. In December 1971 the West German *Bild-Zeitung*, a newspaper not unlike our *National Enquirer*, "reported" a bank robbery by the terrorist Baader-Meinhoff gang, and when novelist Heinrich Böll took issue with the slanted and sensationalist account he was promptly labeled a sympathizer and intellectual accomplice of the group, and his house was subject to a police search. These experiences led to a novel in which Böll described four days in the the life of a young woman victimized by unfair tabloid practices. He sent the galley proofs to Schlöndorff and von Trotta, who were working on an adaptation of his *Group Portrait with Lady*, and they immediately switched to collaborating with him on the screenplay for the still unpublished novel.

Katharina Blum, a quiet and reclusive housekeeper, meets fugitive Ludwig Götten at a party and spends the night with him. When in the morning Commissioner Beizmenne and his men break into her apartment, Ludwig manages to elude them with her help. Katharina is taken in for questioning, and the story is "reported" in the *News* by Werner Tötges, a slick young journalist who also seeks out and interviews members of Katharina's family, including her former husband. Meanwhile another *News* reporter interviews her employers, the lawyer Blorna and his wife, Trude. In the published accounts, information is greatly embellished, insignificant details are blown out of proportion, and individuals are "quoted" as to Katharina's character. As a result, she begins receiving obscene phone calls and letters. To escape harassment, she moves in with her aunt, whose phone is immediately tapped. Katherina's attempt to contact Ludwig leads to his arrest.

Katharina asks Tötges to meet her at her apartment, and when he makes sexual advances toward her, she shoots and kills him. At his funeral, colleagues eulogize him as a victim of "terrorism" and a martyr for a "free press." The film ends with a disclaimer that prefaces Böll's novel: "Should the description of certain journalistic practices result in a resemblance to the practices of the *Bild-Zeitung*, such resemblance is neither intentional nor fortuitous, but unavoidable."

According to von Trotta, she directed the actors and Schlöndorff handled technical matters on *The Lost Honor of Katharina Blum*.[19] Whereas Heinrich Böll narrated the story of Katharina Blum—subtitled "How Violence Develops and Where It Can Lead"—in fifty-eight sections filled with flashbacks and commentary, the film presents it as a very straightforward and chronological sequence of events. The camera acts as a passive recording device and—as in *Young Törless* and *The Sudden Wealth of the Poor People of Kombach*—most of the scenes are studied and static. When scenes depicting violence or injustice do occur, they erupt volcanically and thus jar the viewer from a composed portrait in which the sounds of silence are deafening. Since Schlöndorff is not a particularly daring or innovative director, but rather a solid technician, he uses his technical virtuosity to narrate and not to explain. In contrast, von Trotta's strength lies in the direction of her actors, through whom she creates her story. The film is thus a prime example of the complementary talents of both filmmakers.

Many critics considered the film too slick and described the supporting cast as too stereotyped to be believeable.[20] American critic Molly Haskell, who, like many of her West German counterparts, preferred Böll's mosaic structure to the filmmakers' linear treatment, saw the film as a cinematic sibling of *A Free Woman*.

> In striking out, the struggling divorcée of *A Free Woman*, like the intensely private, even prudish Katharina Blum, forfeits the protections of the law and the solicitude of men, vouchsafed her for as long as she abided by the rules of the game. . . . For a woman to cultivate an area of the self that owes nothing to men, as these heroines do in vastly different ways, is an offense against patria and patriarchy and, as both films show conclusively, doomed to ridicule or failure.[21]

That Katharina Blum turns herself into the police is, however, not an indication that she has failed, nor is Elisabeth Junker's remarriage the surrender of a weak individual. Unwilling to live without Ludwig Götten, she seeks revenge; she will bide her time in prison until she, like Ludwig, is released. Both women make utilitarian use of an institution to their own advantage. For both giving in does not mean giving up.

The Lost Honor of Katharina Blum was the most successful German film of the mid-1970s. It brought the filmmakers a step toward international recognition. Rather than capitalize on their success with a topical subject, for their next and final collaboration they selected Marguerite Yourcenar's 1939 novel *Coup de Grâce*—a work that had interested francophile Schlöndorff since the 1960s—which he directed and she starred in after completing a script with Jutta Brückner and Geneviève Dorman. This newest undertaking was anything but commercially oriented and was, as Hans C. Blumenberg somewhat exasperatedly pointed out, "again a cinematic adaptation of literature, again a story about a woman, again a treatment of emancipation."[22]

In 1919 the soldiers Erich von Lhomand and Konrad von Reval return to the latter's home, the castle Kratovice in the Baltic provinces. A civil war has broken out, and Konrad's sister Sophie (von Trotta) and their elderly Aunt Praskovia are forced to live a relatively withdrawn existence. Sophie falls in love with Erich, but he is more interested in cultivating "friendships" with members of his own sex. Sophie seeks solace in superficial encounters with men socially below her. Moreover, she continues to associate with Grigori Loew, a Jewish communist whose political views she shares. After repeated attempts to seduce Erich, she leaves the castle and joins the radical faction. During a confrontation, her brother Konrad is killed. Later Grigori Loew is shot when he attempts to flee from the brick factory in which he, Sophie, and other sympathizers have been hiding. Erich is in charge of the operation and captures Sophie, who is dressed in a man's partisan uniform. As each of the prisoners is shot, Sophie requests that Erich be her executioner. He delivers the "coup de grâce" as requested and departs with his troops. As his train pulls away, the film ends with a shot of a servant who, shovel in hand, is preparing to bury the dead.

While *A Free Woman* and *The Lost Honor of Katharina Blum* were strong statements regarding a woman's role within a particular political framework, in *Coup de Grâce* the historical events surrounding the 1919 civil war in the Baltic play a subordinate role to the love affair(s) on which the film focuses. Sophie, a headstrong and independent young woman, refuses to accept Erich von Lhomand's repeated rejections, and her numerous tawdry affairs are intended to provoke him. In what may be viewed as a final act of emancipation from an impossible personal situation, she joins the rebel forces. Because she is aware of

Erich's homosexual tendencies—referred to, as in *Young Törless*, in euphemistic terms—Sophie dresses as a man and defies him to execute her. His "coup de grâce" is her bittersweet revenge. Although Erich pulls the trigger, it is Sophie who delivers the final blow. In death she triumphs over him and what she considers his weakness. Their confrontations are not the result of political machinations but evolve from the private rather than the public struggle. Although the script retains a number of elements from Yourcenar's novel (Erich, for example, narrates Sophie's story in continuous voice-overs), despite some exquisite black-and-white compositions the film is little more than a vehicle for von Trotta's considerable talents as an actress.

Following *Coup de Grâce*, the filmmakers parted company professionally. Having already staged Leoš Janáček's opera *Katja Kabanova* in Frankfurt in 1974, Schlöndorff proceeded to stage *Wir erreichen den Fluβ* (*We Reach the River*) by Hans Werner Henze, who wrote the scores for *Young Törless* and *The Lost Honor of Katharina Blum*. In 1977 Schlöndorff made the television documentary *Only for Fun—Only for Play: Kaleidoscope Valeska Gert*, a profile of the iconoclastic seventy-seven-year-old actress/dancer. Gert, best known to modern audiences for her roles in G. W. Pabst's films *The Three Penny Opera* and *The Joyless Street*, had appeared in *Coup de Grâce* as Aunt Praskovia. In addition, Schlöndorff began his adaptation of Günter Grass's *The Tin Drum*, work that he interrupted in order to contribute to the collaborative *Germany in Autumn*. During the time Schlöndorff was involved in these numerous projects, von Trotta, after nearly ten years of collaboration, was preparing her own first feature: *Das zweite Erwachen der Christa Klages* (*The Second Awakening of Christa Klages*). "I prefer the so-called private topics," she explained, "problems of living together. How do women try to get out of restricting situations? Those things don't affect him, can't interest him."[23] By severing her professional ties with Schlöndorff, von Trotta was now free to pursue "women's films," a term that she herself refuses to use in describing her own work.[24]

Collaborating with Luisa Francia, she based her new script on the true story of a Munich kindergarten teacher who robbed a bank to provide funds for her alternative day-care center. The film opens with Christa in a totally bare apartment. As the opening credits end, she comments in voice-over, "I had to create my own prison before I could understand what had happened to me." The film then relates her story in flashback. As Christa and her friends Werner and Wolfgang rob a local bank, Lena Seidlhofer, a hostage, has ample time to study her disguised face. Wolfgang is soon apprehended, but Christa and Werner escape to a small village where Wolfgang's friend, the pastor Hans Grawe, puts them up for the night. When, however, he discovers their crime, he forces them to leave after supplying them with clothes and hair dye for Christa, to whom he is obviously drawn.

Meanwhile, the police question Lena Seidlhofer, who when shown a photo of Christa insists that she can only identify her in person. Returning to her cheerless apartment, Lena compares a snapshot of herself with a newspaper photo of Christa. On her own initiative, she visits Christa's apartment and questions Reingard, a young woman caring for several children.

Christa and Werner seek help from Ingrid, a cosmetician who works out of her home. Unhappily married to a man who is seldom at home, she reluctantly allows them to stay and is soon drawn to the free-spirited Werner. She agrees to take the stolen money to Reingard, who, however, refuses to accept it. Christa vents her frustration by running through the woods and screaming.

The return of Ingrid's husband forces the departure of the fugitives, and soon Werner is stopped and shot down by the police. Christa seeks help from Hans, and although he is unable to be honest about his attraction to her he does arrange for her to work on a cooperative farm in Portugal, where she is soon joined by Ingrid. Sharing both grief and joy, the two women become close friends, but they must soon quit the farm because of rumors of the robbery and of the suspicious nature of their relationship. ("Women think and feel differently here," Christa is told.)

Leaving the stolen money behind, and with it the idea that she might do "something significant," Christa returns to Germany with Ingrid. In a bare apartment she reads poetry and scrawls "Be Able to Wait" on the wall. Her despondency about her powerlessness leads to an abortive suicide attempt that in turn leads to a determination to rebuild her shattered life with the help of Ingrid and Reingard. Meanwhile, Lena, who has been continuing her investigations, notes with disgust that the former day-care center is now a porno shop.

Venturing into the world to buy groceries, Christa is spotted and arrested. At the police station, she is outfitted in her former disguise, and Lena is called in to identify her. Staring directly at Christa, she announces with the ghost of a smile, "No, I'm sure that she's not the one." Lena's false testimony liberates both herself and Christa, who achieves her "second awakening," the emergence from the repressed and contemplative existence shown in the initial moments of the film. Following not the letter but the spirit of the law, both women emerge not as victims but as victors, as does Ingrid, who sheds socially acceptable patterns and emerges from a restrictive marriage into a communal relationship with her own sex.

Unlike Schlöndorff, who begins with a story on which actors are imposed, von Trotta begins with fully conceived characters and asks herself, "What could happen to them? In what relationship do they stand to one another, to their environment? What conflicts do they live?"[25] Since women are the focus of her story, male characters necessarily play a minor or supporting role. While Schlöndorff somewhat fatuously clung to literary sources in his investigation of "Germanhood," she began exploring the relatively new territory of "Womanhood." In their subsequent films they were to continue on their own paths.

Günter Grass's *The Tin Drum* burst on the German literary scene in 1959 with a clash of symbols and cymbals. Sixteen years later Franz Seitz, who had earlier produced *Young Törless,* discovering that a number of proposals for the film rights had fallen through, renewed an earlier proposals of his own.[26] At the time, box-office receipts for domestic films had plummeted, the Filmverlag der Autoren—the largest distributor of West German films—was on the verge of bankruptcy, and directors such as Fassbinder, Wenders, Syberberg, and Herzog had announced their intention of working abroad. The West German film industry was clearly in dire straits.

After reading a fifty-page treatment, Grass assigned the rights to Seitz, who wrote an initial screenplay. After considering Roman Polanski as a possible director, Seitz contacted Schlöndorff, who accepted the "provocation,"[27] as he termed it, and in June 1977 began meeting with Seitz and Grass in the first of many conferences. After preparing a well-honed script, he began assembling his cast. Eschewing the suggestions of United Artists, a financial backer and distributor of the film, that he use Isabelle Adjani, Dustin Hoffman, or Keith Carradine for major roles, he settled on a largely German cast, leavened by such international stars as Andréa Ferréol, Charles Aznavour, and Daniel Olbrychski. In addition, his behind-the-scenes crew included Federico Fellini's makeup artist, Rino Carboni; Jacques Tati's editor, Suzanne Baron; David Lean's composer, Maurice Jarre; and Luis Buñuel's scriptwriter, Jean-Claude Carrière. *The Tin Drum* was not quite the typically "German" film he said he was dedicated to, which may account for the fact that in its first year some 3.5 million Germans paid to see it.

Seitz, Carrière, Schlöndorff, and Grass himself fashioned a final script in which material from the first two parts of the three-part epic was used. In his diary, Schlöndorff noted, "What is important for me is that I made a good film, not that I please the author."[28] Upon viewing the completed film, Grass commented, "I forgot the book and saw a film."[29] Although the plot had been simplified and distilled, the spirit of the author's literary vision had been retained.

In a voice-over, Oskar Mazerath (David Bennent), an omniscient narrator, introduces his ancestors. We watch as young Anna Bronski (Tina Engel), eating potatoes on a desolate Kashubian field, gives shelter under her voluminous skirts to an arsonist pursued by the police. Taking advantage of his privileged position, Joseph Kaljaiczek impregnates her. The sequence has the jerky movement and sad comedy of a silent film. A child, Agnes, is born, but when the police reappear sometime later, Kaljaiczek dives into a river, surfacing, according to rumor, as a Chicago millionaire, Joe Colchic, whom we see contentedly puffing on his cigar. In the Danzig market place, meanwhile, Anna with Agnes nearby sells geese, butter, and eggs. An iris shot ages her. During World War I her wares turn to turnips.

Given to contemplative stares and reticent admiration of men, Agnes (Angela Winkler) comes out of her shell when she meets her future husband, Alfred Mazerath (Mario Adorf), a physically imposing older man whose basic interests are cooking, photography, and politics. Agnes consoles herself with her cousin, Jan Bronski (Daniel Olbrychski), a delicate military reject

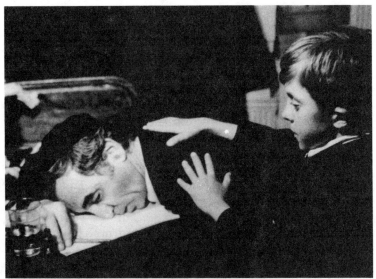

Charles Aznavour and David Bennent
in *The Tin Drum* (COURTESY OF BIOSKOP-FILM)

Tina Engel in *The Tin Drum*
(COURTESY OF BIOSKOP-FILM)

whose strength is limited to the bedroom. Agnes's growing lack of restraint is signaled by the colors of her clothes, which during the course of the film go from muted greens and blues to scarlets and blood reds.

The result of this ménage à trois is Oskar himself, whose birth is intimately rendered in a series of special effects. After a fall down a flight of cellar stairs at the age of three, Oskar decides to stop growing and concentrate on a tin drum given him by Agnes. He also discovers that he has a high-pitched scream that can shatter glass and can therefore be used against all potential enemies and nuisances.

To allow for her weekly tryst with Jan, Agnes deposits Oskar with Sigismund Markus (Charles Aznavour), a Jewish toy dealer. But Oskar slips away, follows his mother to the Pension Flora, and climbs to the top of the nearby Stockturm for a better view as Agnes and Jan tumble into bed. Oskar's screams mingle with Agnes's cries of ecstasy as windows everywhere shatter in a magnificent slow-motion sequence. When Agnes subsequently visits Markus's shop he tells her that given the political situation she should dispense with Bronski and set her sights on a German. He himself has recently been baptized, and he offers to take her and "the little prince" to London. She refuses, and as she returns to the family grocery shop Hitler's voice echoes through the streets.

The Mazeraths visit a circus, and Oskar, fascinated by the dwarf Master Bebra (Fritz Hakl)—his different effect on the entire family is captured in close-ups—steals behind the scenes to meet him. When he demonstrates his own shattering talents, Bebra suggests that he join the troupe, but Oskar prefers to remain a private observer. "People like us must play and determine the course of events," Bebra warns, "otherwise the *others* will do it!"

Bebra's comments are another expression of the simmering political atmosphere threaded through the film. Never the total focus of the action, it takes the form of polite suggestion (Markus's comments and offer to Agnes) or a "minor" variation (Oskar and the neighborhood children parade across the street as an SA troop marches by). Bebra's observations serve to mature Oskar both artistically and mentally. Despite his diminutive size, he must utilize his ability as a true artist, an ability which until now has caused him to be viewed as an oddity. In his brief conversation with Bebra, he dispenses with laconically ungrammatical baby talk and uses complete and eloquent sentences. In the company of adults, however, he will continue to speak like a three-year-old. More so than in the past, he will "determine the course of events," both privately and publicly.

As the Nazi movement grows in intensity, Alfred joins the party, a portrait of Beethoven is replaced by a picture of Hitler, and a newly purchased radio allows the family to listen to political propaganda. Attired in his party uniform, Alfred berates Bronski for his political apathy and states, "We are experiencing days which will go down in history. One just can't stand on the sidelines! One has to be part of it!" After Alfred leaves for a rally, Oskar, who has "the blue eyes of the Bronskis," climbs onto a chair so that he may better hear the early radio coverage of the rally as the lovers—his mother and "uncle"—whisper.

The rally itself begins as a capsule analogy to the 1934 Nuremberg rally in Leni Riefenstahl's *Triumph of the Will*: the enthusiastic crowd, the various groups of Hitler Youth, and the symmetrically aligned swastikas. But as partly official Albert Forster enters to the accompaniment of a military march, Oskar—who has by now snaked under a tribunal—begins to beat a three-quarter rhythm on his drum. In a humorously orchestrated sequence, the Hitler Youth band members gradually take up the beat, and the march is transformed into the *Blue Danube Waltz*. As the marching officials attempt to adjust to the waltzing rhythm, the crowd pairs off and begins to dance. Everything has gone haywire; the symmetrical alignment and strict organization are in shambles. A sudden thunderstorm disperses the crowd. As Bebra had suggested, Oskar has played a role in determining events.

A 1938 Good Friday outing on the North Sea beach is one of the most visually impressive sequences in the film. Agnes, her alizarin crimson garments contrasting with the dark male figures and the washed-out whites, blues, and beiges of the surroundings, removes her stockings with Bronski's "help" as Alfred takes their picture. When a horse's head teeming with live eels is pulled from the water, something within Agnes snaps. The horse's teeth and her husband's dentures are strikingly similar; the squirming eels are phallic representations of Bronski's lively bedroom antics. As Alfred and a fisherman shove the eels into a sack, Oskar beats his commentary on his tin drum; Bronski comforts Agnes, who is vomiting. The beach scenes are at once appealing and disgusting, filled with conflicting emotions and characterized by grotesque and tender sexuality.

At home, Agnes refuses to share in the eels and retires to her bedroom, where she prays as the camera pans to a painting of Mary Magdalene. Bronski enters and slips a hand between her legs, and her weeping gives way to low moans. Parts of the scene — witnessed by Oskar from the armoire—are captured in a Fassbinderlike mirror perspective. A change takes place in Agnes. She emerges from the bedroom, sits down at the table, resolutely takes the platter of eel and, without the slightest trace of emotion, eats in large bites.

An abortive attempt to confess her sins—Agnes in red, the church all white—is interrupted by Oskar's drumming. At home Agnes incessantly devours herrings and sardines from the family grocery. Anna is summoned and immediately realizes that Agnes is pregnant. As Alfred and Oskar pound on the bathroom door, a scream is heard, and the scene cuts to a cemetery. Markus appears to pay his respects to the dead Agnes, but is driven off with anti-Semitic insults. Later the baptized Jew returns in a yarmulke to mumble a Hebrew prayer over her grave. A scene of a funeral repast at which friends eat, drink, and sing ends with Anna and her grandson seated near a bonfire. Anna lifts her voluminous skirts and the boy seeks comfort under them.

In voice-over narration Oskar comments on ensuing private and political events as the camera pans the hazy Danzig skyline:

> Once upon a time there was a guillible folk that believed in Father Christmas. But in reality Father Christmas was the gasman! Once upon a time there was a toy dealer whose name was Sigismund Markus and who sold white-red enameled drums. Once upon a time there was a drummer whose name was Oskar. Once upon a time there was a toy dealer whose name was Markus and who took with him all the toys of the world.

The camera cuts to a burning synagogue and to Markus's ruined shop. His conversion having proved meaningless, the toy dealer has committed suicide. As his enumerating litany comes to a climactic close, Oskar discovers the body. A music-box melody tinkles in the background, the aural correlative of a fantasy world destroyed.

Oskar's narration continues into the invasion of Poland, on which day the boy lures Bronski into the Polish post office, where patriots are holding out against the Nazis. Oskar wants to reclaim his drum, which is being repaired by the caretaker. As the defenders surrender, Bronski and his son are building a house of cards that suddenly collapses. Led away to a firing squad, Bronski holds up the Queen of Hearts, a sensuous reminder of his lost Agnes.

Oskar, Alfred, and some neighbors join an enthusiastic crowd awaiting the Führer. As he is driven past them, Oskar beats his tin drum; the multitudes cheer. The Führer's face is never shown. His outstretched and raised arm is filmed from a backseat perspective, as in *Triumph of the Will.* Unlike the Nuremberg rally parody, rendered from Oskar's subjective point of view under the grandstand, the filming of Hitler is basically objective, and one has the sense of watching a newsreel.

The film takes on a quieter tone with the arrival of Maria Truczinski, the sixteen-year-old who will assist Alfred in the grocery. She enters clutching two large cabbages to her chest, a visual foreshadowing of her impending sexual involvement with both Alfred and Oskar.[30] In a voice-over, Oskar admits that she was his "first love," and later consummates the relationship after placing a candylike fizz powder in her navel. The sequence humorously and poignantly renders Oskar's childlike approach to sexuality.[31] Shortly, Oskar discovers Maria and his father in sexual congress, and by pressing his tin drum into the man's back, forces him to ejaculate. When Kurt is born to the now married couple nine months later, Oskar calculates that only he could have fathered Maria's child. During the baptismal repast—not surprisingly, Maria wears one of Agnes's red dresses—Oskar privately promises the baby a tin drum for his third birthday. Moreover, should Kurt so wish, he will show him how to stop growing. Oskar is now ready to pass on his own experiences to a younger generation.

Oskar continues his sexual education with Lina Greff (Andréa Ferréol), wife of the homophile vegetable salesman and scout leader who prefers his sensuous potatoes and the muscular physiques of his scouts to his wife's callipygian charms and insatiable sexuality. A frozen cactus at her window ledge represents her unsatisfactory marriage. Oskar comes to the rescue with his "third drumstick." Because Lena's scenes in the film are limited, there is neither a contrast nor a conflict between right and wrong as had been the case with Agnes. The schoolgirl innocence which brought about Maria's pregnancy is likewise absent. Lina embodies the union of a seedy seductress and a frustrated wife, a woman who knows no bounds and feels no guilt.

Oskar again meets Master Bebra, now dressed in a military uniform, and the lilliputian mind reader Roswitha Raguna, who urge him to join their troupe of entertainers. The scene cuts to the Eiffel Tower, where a uniformed Oskar holds Roswitha's hand and gives her a kiss. At a theater, Oskar demonstrates his shattering talent. On a Normandy bunker the troupe dines on Hungarian salami, Dutch chocolate, and Russian caviar. During its next performance there is a blackout, and Oskar and Roswitha take shelter under a table. The scene then cuts to their bedroom as Bebra enters and announces that the Americans are coming. They head for their truck, but Roswitha lingers for a cup of coffee and is killed by a grenade. Her death ends Oskar's career as a performer.

Oskar returns to Danzig on Kurt's third birthday, and he presents the indifferent child with a tin drum. As Danzig burns, Alfred replaces Hitler's picture with the Beethoven portrait. ("Beethoven. *He* was a genius!") The family takes shelter in the basement; as Russian soldiers enter, Oskar presses his father's Nazi insignia pin into his hand. Alfred tries to hide the insignia in his mouth and chokes on it as the Russians rape Lina Greff and Maria screams. A soldier empties his machine gun into Mazerath's body.

At the cemetery Oskar, in voice-over contemplation, decides on his future: "Oskar. Should I or shouldn't I? You are now in your twenty-first year, Oskar. Should you or shouldn't you? You are an orphan, Oskar. Should I or shouldn't I?" After Alfred's makeshift casket is lowered, Oskar resolutely throws his tin drum into the grave. ("I should. I must. I want to grow.") At that very moment, young Kurt, who has been tossing pebbles, throws one at his brother/father's head and wounds him. Oskar begins to grow.

There being no possible future in Danzig—the drab, stripped

Mazerath apartment with its Mary Magdalene portrait visually conveys this fact—Oskar leaves for the West with Maria and Kurt. What the future holds for the three Mazeraths—the third and as yet unfilmed section of Grass's novel—is left unanswered in Schlöndorff's work.[32]

The film's final scenes are carefully orchestrated color compositions. Wearing a dark coat that contrasts with his white and grotesque head bandage, Oskar is seated in a baggage-loaded cart, which the somberly dressed Maria pushes toward the train station. Accompanied by Grandmother Anna and Kurt, they join the crowds looking for a place in the freight cars heading westward. As the train pulls out, Oskar suddenly realizes that his grandmother is not going with them and calls out to her in an emotion-laden scene. An extreme close-up of her face reveals her anguish. The film ends as it began, with a shot of a Kashubian potato field. As the train heads toward the horizon, we see an elderly woman working near a smoldering fire. The greens and blues of the landscape are muted by a hazy smoke and give this final and very lengthy shot—nearly five minutes in duration—an artificial and dreamlike ambience.

Before he actually began to film the novel, Schlöndorff theorized in his diary:

> The wealth of characters and episodes are more side by side in the film than one after another as in the novel. A fresco is generated, a narration that proceeds along the horizontal rather than along the perpendicular. Between the major tableaux, as in a variety revue there can be short montages in which Oskar occasionally speaks as a commentator, not to give information, but rather to formulate his thoughts about himself and the events.[33]

Schlöndorff's film brings out the sexual, societal, psychological, religious, and political stagnation or awakening in Grass's novel through a series of *tableaux vivants* joined by Oskar's presence in nearly every episode, parallel scenes rendered in slight or stark counterpoints (such as Markus's toy shop, the family dining room, Oskar's sexual escapades, the cemetery), leitmotifs (the tin drum, the ubiquitous fish, the earsplitting screams), sharp color contrasts, and the young drummer's voice-over narration. What Grass produced was the result of a cascade of language. Schlöndorff achieves a similar effect through a broad stream of images.

The film, like the novel, lives in details, and its message is similarly bleak and humorously unsparing. Both are a montage, a concatenation and a juxtaposition of moral, political, and linguistic passion, but what shocked readers in 1959 does not necessarily overwhelm contemporary film audiences. Schlöndorff lifted and glorified Grass's contrasts between the real world and Oskar's perception of it in a heightened spectrum of visual sensitivity. The viewer must read Schlöndorff's fresco much as 1959 readers had to visualize Grass's text. By accepting the "provocation," Schlöndorff proved that Grass was not unfilmable, as many critics had long thought.[34]

The Tin Drum appeared to mark a turning point in the history of the NGC. Awarded West Germany's most coveted film prize, Die Goldene Schale, and 500,000 marks, it also shared the Palm d'Or with Francis Ford Coppola's *Apocalypse Now* at the Cannes Film Festival.[35] In addition, Schlöndorff, producer Franz Seitz, and Fred Sorg, a representative of United Artists, were given the 100th Goldene Leinwand, an award for which films qualify only if they have recorded more than 3.5 million viewers within an eighteen-month period, a figure that *The Tin Drum* had surpassed six months earlier. In April 1980 Schlöndorff won an Oscar, a milestone in the history of the German cinema, and *The Tin Drum* was named the best foreign-language feature of the year.

Nevertheless, as critic Ulrich Fischer noted: "One tin drum does not a concert make."[36] As Margarethe von Trotta prepared and directed her second feature, *Schwestern oder Die Balance des Glücks (Sisters or The Balance of Happiness, 1979)*, German audiences were still less than enthusiastic about German films. Since the director had been awarded the West German Filmband in Silver and 300,000 marks the previous year for her first film, financing was less difficult than it might have been. She considered working with the same actresses, but because she "could no longer steer the story" in their direction, it "moved away" from her concept of their characters. The relationships between the women in this second film grew in intensity, and von Trotta eventually completed her script as the story of two sisters.[37]

Maria, the older of the two, is a successful, efficient, and emotionless woman, who works as an executive secretary in a large Hamburg firm. Although she assumes the costs of Anna's medical studies, she expects her to apply herself. A dreamy self-

Gudrun Gabriel and Jutta Lampe in *Sisters*
(COURTESY OF FILMVERLAG DER AUTOREN)

doubter, the younger woman questions the validity of her studies and is worried about her approaching exams, but in her role of supervisor and guardian Maria impatiently urges her to press on. When Maria becomes involved with Maurice, her boss's son, the totally dependent Anna becomes despondent and commits suicide.

Feeling that she has been remiss in her sisterly duties, Maria compensates by taking in Miriam, a lively young woman who works for the same firm, and offers to pay for her language studies. Unconsciously replacing Anna as the object of Maria's somewhat askew affections, Miriam fights a similar dependence on her. Although she continues her studies, she is also interested in pursuing a career as a singer and dreams of going to America. When she passes her exams, she realizes what control Maria has over her and leaves the apartment they have shared. Only then does Maria attempt to come to terms with her sister's death. As the film ends she states: "I will learn to dream while I live, Anna. I will try to be Maria *and* Anna." Only by this union can the balance of happiness be achieved.

Sisters is a considerably more internalized and psychological film than von Trotta's first feature, in which the crisis was a result of external pressures. Here we are dealing with a conflict that arises from internal feelings of interdependence and guilt. Anna tries to accept Maria's conception of her, but utterly lacking in outlets she only succeeds in becoming increasingly distraught. Maria, on the other hand, has her work and her affair with Maurice, an affair that appears more practical than personal. Unable to dissolve her ties to her sister, Anna can find escape only in death. Rather than face her emotional response to this suicide, Maria, the level-headed and efficient organizer, finds a replacement for her sister. However, Miriam's departure forces Maria to confront her own emotional inadequacies.

Because of its mind games, von Trotta's second film is not as readily accessible as the more externally oriented *The Second Awakening of Christa Klages*. Critics found that there was insufficient motivation on the part of the three "sisters" to justify their actions. Audiences responded quite differently, however, and saw the film as a more carefully tailored study of dominance and subordination. Again the question of a "women's film" arose. The director took issue with the term.

> What does it mean? Every Hollywood film in which women are playing the lead calls itself a "woman's film." I would like to eliminate this genre description from the face of the earth. It is a film about relationships. Male directors make "relationship films" also. The relationship between the two sisters in my film could just as well be the relationship between a man and a woman. It rests on interdependence. Then again I think that the manner in which this film is made is perhaps tied to a woman. How the characters and their feelings are portrayed—the stress lies not in the story but rather in the emotional flow which runs through this story—is perhaps a specifically feminine manner of expression.[38]

While von Trotta has been repeatedly cited for her oustanding original scripts dealing with women's problems, her husband has been taken to task for his allegiance to history and literature. As early as the mid-1960s young directors and Schlöndorff's contemporaries criticized him because he chose not his own "socially relevant pains" but rather Robert Musil's *Young Törless* as script material.[39] With regard to the relationship between literature and film, he commented:

> The highest form of a script is naturally a work of literature because it is something in which people are described with great precision: where they are, what they do, and what they feel. Usually an author works on a book for years, and if he is not writing, then he constructs it internally. It accumulates internally and is then expressed at some point. . . . For writing a script let's assume you have eight weeks, let's say maybe three months. The end result cannot be the same. I don't want to disqualify the script. I only want to say that I prefer literature to film because I don't know anyone who could sit down to write a script with comparable seriousness, and especially not me.[40]

By choosing to interpret a literary classic filmically, a director inevitably runs the risk of being compared with the work and its author and will automatically be at a disadvantage. Schlöndorff, however, does not consider his literary bent an albatross. By ignoring the negative attitude that critics and audiences alike have toward cinematic adaptations of literary works and by exploiting his interest in the written medium, he has produced several of the NGC's most accessible and enduring films.

Another evaluation of Schlöndorff is that he is a "director without a style."[41] At face value this statement appears to be a criticism, but on closer examination it reveals the filmmaker's adaptability to his material. Unlike his contemporaries, whose films often exhibit easily identifiable idiosyncratic techniques, Schlöndorff is not even vaguely manneristic.

> I have absolutely no film-theoretical concept. I follow a type of moralistic imperative. That is to say, I feel that certain films have to be made. For me this corresponds to a feeling of justice and stems from a very personally perceived pressure.[42]

Like Schlöndorff, von Trotta has no film-theoretical concept of cinema, avoids and resents labeling of any sort, and does not claim to have been influenced by any particular school of thought. As critical and audience response to her work has demonstrated, the fact that she makes films for women does not preclude a male audience. Of the growing number of female filmmakers in West Germany, she is the most visible, most successful, and most accessible.

This accessibility is the key to both von Trotta and Schlön-dorff. While withdrawing to what some may term cinematic ivory towers—women's films and literary adaptations, respectively—the filmmakers have transcended whatever limitations the genres may have and have broadened the critical perspective of the New German Cinema.

NOTES

[1] John Hughes, "*The Tin Drum*: Volker Schlöndorff's 'Dream of Childhood,'" *Film Quarterly*, no. 3 (1981), p. 3.

[2] Regarding his first meeting with Schlöndorff, Melville commented:

> I met Volker one evening at the Ciné-Club du Lycée Montaigne. Bertrand Tavernier had dragged me there to see that monstrosity called *Johnny Guitar*. . . . Beside Tavernier there was a small boy to whom I paid no attention: Volker Schlöndorff. That was in the spring of 1960. In the summer of the same year, this boy telephoned me to ask if he could become my assistant. I had him come to my office in the rue Jenner. We got on at once. Almost immediately I felt that I had met my spiritual son, and I still feel the same way about him today.

Melville on Melville, edited by Rui Nogueira (New York: Viking, 1972), p. 89.

[3] Quoted in Hans Jürgen Weber and Ingeborg Weber, eds., *Die bleierne Zeit: Ein Film von Margarethe von Trotta* (Frankfurt: Fischer, 1981), p. 86.

[4] Quoted in Robert Fischer and Joe Hembus, eds., *Der Neue Deutsche Film: 1960–1980* (Munich: Goldmann, 1981), p. 11.

[5] Hughes, "*The Tin Drum,*" p. 3.

[6] See, for example, Schlöndorff's article "Alain Resnais' neuer Film," *Filmkritik*, no. 5 (1961), pp. 236–38.

[7] Eisner introduced Schlöndorff to Lang and the two corresponded regularly until the German-American director's death in 1976. In 1963 Schlöndorff wrote about Lang's experiences in post-World War II Germany. The article, entitled "L'Etranger" ("The Stranger"), appears in Luc Moullet's book *Fritz Lang* (Paris: Editions Seghers, 1970), pp. 146–47.

[8] Florian Hopf, "Ein offenes Gespräch mit Volker Schlöndorff—dem Mann, der bewiesen hat, daß wir als Filmemacher wieder wer sind," *Playboy Interview* (Munich: Moewig, 1980), p. 77.

[9] Quoted in Corinna Brocher, "Volker Schlöndorff," *Die Filmemacher: Zur Neuen deutschen Produktion nach Oberhausen 1962*, edited by Barbara Bronnen and Corinna Brocher (Munich: C. Bertelsmann, 1973), p. 80.

[10] Wilfried Berghahn, *Robert Musil* (Reinbek: Rowohlt, 1963), pp. 28–29.

[11] "Tribüne des Jungen Deutschen Films. 1. Volker Schlöndorff," *Filmkritik*, no. 6 (1966), p. 309.

[12]Werner Kliess, "Protest," *Jahrbuch der Filmkritik VIII*, edited by Arbeitsgemeinschaft der Filmjournalisten (Emsdetten: Lechte, 1969), p. 57. Schlöndorff himself describes the film as "one extremely big catastrophe." See Jens Wendland, "Was ist deutsch an meinen Filmen? Der Filmemacher Volker Schlöndorff und seine Liebe zur deutschen Literatur," *Deutsche Zeitung*, 28 September 1979.

[13]Brocher, "Volker Schlöndorff," p. 84.

[14]Quoted in Willi Bär and Hans Jürgen Weber, eds., *Schwestern oder Die Balance des Glücks: Ein Film von Margarethe von Trotta* (Frankfurt: Fischer, 1979), p. 133.

[15]In 1979 Wolf Vollmar's *Michael Kohlhaas*, conceived but never aired as a series for West German television, was reedited for theatrical release by its director and, in spite of moderate critical acclaim, experienced a fate similar to Schlöndorff's film.

[16]Wendland, "Was ist deutsch."

[17]Klaus Phillips, "History Reevaluated: Volker Schlöndorff's *The Sudden Wealth of the Poor People of Kombach*," 1978 *Film Studies Annual* (West Lafayette, Ind.: Purdue Research Foundation, 1979), p. 37.

[18]Hopf, "Ein offenes Gespräch, pp. 81–82.

[19]Quoted in *Variety*, 20 January 1982.

[20]See, for example, Siegfried Schober, "Die Heilige Johanna der Schlagzeilen," *Der Spiegel*, no. 41 (1975), pp. 169–70. Schober describes the film as "too slick, closed and perfect."

[21]Molly Haskell, "Katharina Blum Loses Honor and Finds Sainthood," *The Village Voice*, 5 January 1976.

[22]Hans C. Blumenberg, "Trotzköpfchen als Terroristin. Nach *Katharina Blum* wieder eine Literaturverfilmung, wieder eine Frauengeschichte," *Die Zeit*, 22 October 1976.

[23]Quoted in Angelika Wittlich, "Margarethe von Trotta," *Frauen Filmbuch* (Munich: Medien-Arbeitskreis der Demokratischen Fraueninitiative, 1978), pp. 172–77.

[24]Quoted in Christa Maerker, "Was ich sagen möchte, kann ich so billig sagen: Gespräch mit Margarethe von Trotta und Helke Sander," *Jahrbuch Film 78/79: Berichte/Kritiken/Daten*, edited by Hans Günther Pflaum (Munich: Hanser, 1978), p. 78.

[25]Quoted in Willi Bär and Hans Jürgen Weber, eds., *Schwestern oder Die Balance des Glücks: Ein Film von Margarethe von Trotta* (Frankfurt: Fischer, 1979), p. 153.

[26]Volker Schlöndorff, *"Die Blechtrommel": Tagebuch einer Verfilmung* (Darmstadt: Luchterhand, 1979), p. 21.

[27]Quoted in ibid, pp. 37–39.

[28]Schlöndorff, *Tagebuch einer Verfilmung*, p. 91.

[29]Quoted in ibid., p. 121.

[30]See Ernest Borneman, ed., *Sex im Volksmund: Der obszöne Wortschatz der Deutschen* (Reinbek: Rowohlt, 1974), Vol. 2, Section 32.2. The German idiom *seinen eigenen Kohl bauen* means "to engage in incestual relations.

[31] The fizz powder may also be interpreted quite graphically. The German idiom *jemandem Brause füttern* (literally "to feed someone fizz powder") is slang for fellatio. See Borneman, *Sex im Volksmund*, Section 36.4.

[32] After he had decided to limit Grass's novel to the first two sections for his film, Schlöndorff commented in his diary: "The postwar period, Oskar Mazerath in Düsseldorf, that would be a second film with a different actor. Work for later. Why not really make a film about this era which I myself remember, the 1950s, a *Tin Drum, Part Two?*" See ibid., p. 44.

[33] Ibid., p. 38.

[34] Hans Günther Pflaum and Hans Helmut Prinzler, eds., *Film in der Bundesrepublik Deutschland* (Munich: Hanser, 1979), p. 47. Prior to *The Tin Drum*, only one work by Grass had been adapted for the screen. Hansjürgen Pohland's 1967 *Katz und Maus (Cat and Mouse)* was based on the novella by the same title. *The Tin Drum* and *Cat and Mouse* represent the first two parts of Grass's Danzig Trilogy. The novel *Hundejahre*, the third book of the Trilogy, remains unfilmed.

[35] According to French writer Françoise Sagan, the film jury in Cannes had intended to award the Palm d'Or to *The Tin Drum* alone but acquiesced to the demands of festival organizer Robert Favre Le Bret and recognized Coppola's film as well. See Hans Günther Pflaum, ed., *Jahrbuch Film 80/81: Berichte/Kritiken/Daten*, (Munich: Hanser, 1980), p. 202.

[36] Ulrich Fischer, "Eine Blechtrommel macht noch kein Konzert," *Frankfurter Allgemeine Zeitung*, 10 September 1980.

[37] Bär and Weber, *Schwestern*, p. 154.

[38] Ibid., p. 155.

[39] Eckhart Schmidt, "Der Filmemacher Volker Schlöndorff: Professionell, pragmatisch, ambitioniert," *Medium*, no. 6 (1973), p. 15.

[40] Quoted in Christel Buschmann, "Das Kino wird im Keim erstickt: Stoffe, Drehbücher, Drehbuchautoren," *Jahrbuch Film 78/79: Berichte/Kritiken/Daten*, edited by Hans Günther Pflaum (Munich: Hanser, 1978), p. 115.

[41] Hans C. Blumenberg, "Das war der wilde Osten," *Die Zeit*, 4 May 1979.

[42] Hopf, "Ein offenes Gespräch," p. 77.

MAY SPILS and WERNER ENKE

Beyond Pure Entertainment?

by *Christian-Albrecht Gollub*

THE FILMS OF MAY SPILS AND WERNER Enke represent an audience's dream and a critic's nightmare. Should they be treated as superficial fare or serious comedy? In the mid-1960s the first post-Oberhausen Manifesto commercial and critical successes had signaled West Germany's cinematic rebirth. On the coattails of such films as Alexander Kluge's *Yesterday Girl,* Volker Schlöndorff's *Young Törless,* and Ulrich Schamoni's *It* rode aspiring filmmakers who likewise sought to do away with the tedium of Grandpa's Cinema with films that are now—with few exceptions—dismissed as entertaining fluff. Since Kluge's and Schlöndorff's second features were box-office flops, theater owners and distributors became reluctant to include young German filmmakers in their programs. They preferred instead the popular films of Marran Gosov, Eckhart Schmidt, and Michael Verhoeven featuring scantily clad, impatient virgins or pubescent young men. Marran Gosov, a Bulgarian who came to West Germany in 1960, explains how he came to make *Engelchen oder Die Jungfrau von Bamberg* (*Engelchen or The Virgin of Bamberg,* 1966) "[Producer/director Rob] Houwer and I were of the opinion that one should try to resuscitate the comedy genre, precisely because the young German film had until then neglected it."[1] Houwer, whose first full-length production, Schlöndorff's *A Degree of Murder,* had been a commercial failure, decided to explore the untapped genre, and *Engelchen* became a success. Other directors quickly followed suit. Roger Fritz's *Mädchen Mädchen (Girl Girl,* 1966), Will Tremper's *Playgirl* (1966), Franz-Josef Spieker's *Wilder Reiter GmbH (Wild Rider Inc.,* 1967), Eckhart Schmidt's *Jet Generation* (1968), and Michael Verhoeven's *Engelchen macht weiter (Engelchen Keeps On,* 1969), were similar in form and content to Gosov's first film. *Engelchen*'s Gila von Weitershausen, *Playgirl*'s Eva Renzi, and *Girl Girl*'s Helga Anders became cult stars. The directors tried to capitalize on their successes, but the poor quality of their subsequent ventures caused most of them to fade from the filmmaking scene by the early 1970s. Following such sexploitation fare as *Erotik auf der Schulbank (Eroticism in the Classroom,* 1968) and *Männer sind zum Lieben da (Men Are for Loving,* 1969), Schmidt gave up filmmaking and turned to film criticism. Commenting on his *Jet Generation,* he noted:

> In all respects [the film] is the exact opposite of the productions of the Young German Film until now: not an ugly film about ugly people in ugly milieus, but rather an attractive film with attractive people in attractive milieus; not a film about—for me and 200 million others—totally uninteresting little problems of postwar Germany, not a boring analysis of boring West German Philistine psyches, but rather a film about people with people who stamp the face of the world with their ideas: with new looks, new sounds, new images.[2]

When May Spils and Werner Enke's *Zur Sache, Schätzchen (Go to It, Baby,* 1967) burst upon the West Germany film scene, audiences were vacillating between the analytic young German filmmakers and the light-hearted erotic comedies of Gosov, Schmidt, and Verhoeven. Spils felt that the former group represented films that were "too cineastic" and "too artistic" and herself experienced the boredom to which Schmidt had referred in 1968.[3] Moreover, the social and cinematic upheaval of the late 1960s did not preclude what Spils considered a most vital element of filmmaking: unadulterated entertainment. *Go to It, Baby* attempted to bridge the gap between the two seemingly irreconcilable cinematic camps.

May Spils has generally been grouped with the directors of sexploitation comedies. However, while her films feature at-

Werner Enke and May Spils
(COURTESY OF THE FILMMAKERS)

tractive and semi-nude young female stars, their plots do not involve a spring awakening or the loss of virginity. Compared with the erotic comedies of the late 1960s and early 1970s the films are, as Werner Enke stresses, "totally prudish." Because Spils's formulaic film titles are sexually suggestive, her work appears closely related to the sexploitation genre, but on closer examination the films themselves reveal minimal sexual content. Spils herself unconsciously provided a sexual element that led to the false categorization. As the first successful female director of the New German Cinema, she made good copy, and the fact that she often went about her work clad in a bikini promoted the image of the sexploitation comedy.

Maria-Elisabeth "May" Maier-Spils was born in Twistrigen, a small town near Bremen, on July 29, 1941, and originally studied to become a foreign correspondence secretary for English and French, a career that she felt would afford ample free time to pursue her interest in film and theater. In the late 1950s, it was not unusual for her to see three films a day. Especially attracted to the French *nouvelle vague* and American films, she admired such young stars as Brigitte Bardot, Audrey Hepburn,

and James Dean. Soon, in addition to language courses at the
Berlitz School, she began to take acting lessons—an activity she
had to keep a secret, since involvement in the theater was
frowned on within the family. Nevertheless, she and a group of
friends organized a small *Kneipentheater* and produced two plays
in a local pub—a detective comedy and "something half-
religious." Without any organizational training or extensive
theatrical background, Spils directed the plays, was in charge of
costumes and props, and wrote both scripts. As the productions
were "done very unprofessionally," the group disbanded after
its second effort. The venture had proved to be a financial failure.

Undiscouraged, Spils continued to work creatively. While
completing her language training, she wrote a novel, a play, and
a number of short stories—works never intended for publication and subsequently destroyed. While working in Hamburg
for an advertising agency, she enrolled in a modeling school and
soon found occasional work as a fashion model. Six months later, finding the people of Hamburg were "too pig-headed and
north German," she moved to "swinging" Munich, where she
began working as a fashion model and an extra in films—"totally
uninteresting stuff."

Nevertheless, it allowed her to meet Peter Schamoni, signer of
the Oberhausen Manifesto and director of fifteen shorts. Schamoni, who had collaborated with Enno Patalas, Alexander
Kluge, Rob Houwer, and Carl Lamb, was soon to direct his first
full-length feature, *Schonzeit für Füchse* (*Closed Season for Fox
Hunting*). Spils also met Klaus Lemke, an aspiring young
filmmaker who was preparing his first short film, *Kleine Front
(Small Front,* 1965), and Werner Enke, the film's codirector and
star. In one way or another, all three—Schamoni, Lemke, and
Enke—were to play an integral part in her career as director.

In 1965, Klaus Lemke and Spils attended the Oberhausen
Short Film Festival. "I took a look at all the films and said, I can
do that too," she recalled. She began planning her own first
short, *Das Porträt (The Portrait),* using some inherited property as
collateral. Meanwhile, she had obtained practical filmmaking
experience by watching Lemke as he worked on his own projects. *The Portrait,* written by and starring Spils, depicts a young
girl who wants to become a painter and struggles to produce

what she thinks is high art. Eventually she attaches her own photo to the canvas, and, satisfied by what she sees, signs it.

The ten-minute short won a prize at Mannheim's International Filmweek, and, encouraged by this initial success, Spils began work on her second short, *Manöver (Maneuver)*. Spils scripted, produced, edited, and acted in the ten-minute short, which also featured Werner Enke. Like *The Portrait, Maneuver* was semiautobiographical and set in form and content the tone for the films that were to follow it. A young man (Enke) not particularly interested in working prepares for his first full-time job by vacationing with his girlfriend (Spils). During his last days of freedom, the two of them play out various work situations so that he will be ready to face the real world. Farcical effects and sight gags abound. Shown at the Oberhausen Short Film Festival, *Maneuver* was very well received by critics and audiences alike. It was clear to Spils and Enke that they had found their cinematic niche: verbal and physical slapstick with undertones of pseudophilosophical irony. Their off-balance humor needled a society that took itself much too seriously. Spils was convinced that her true vocation lay behind the camera and not in front of it.

In contrast, Werner Enke knew early that he wanted to become an actor. Born in Berlin on April 25, 1941, Enke grew up in Göttingen. As a ten-year-old, Enke drew his own "films" in notepads and soon noticed that he could make his fellow students laugh by the manner in which he related his often bizarre stories. Later, though enrolled at the university in Munich to study theater arts, French, and German, he often cut lectures and wrote plays. Having been rejected by acting schools in Berlin and Munich, he took private acting lessons. Unable to find steady theatrical employment, he began working in television and eventually drifted into Munich's film industry. In 1965,he met May Spils, and teaming up with her and Klaus Lemke attempted a short-lived career making promotional shorts for local merchants. Enke, however, continued to work with Spils. In 1966, he costarred in Volker Schlöndorff's *A Degree of Murder,* and following a starring role in Franz-Josef Spieker's *Mit Eichenlaub und Feigenblatt (With Oak and Fig Leaves, 1967)* he collaborated with Spils on *Go to It, Baby.* She was the first to recognize his true comic flair.

With regard to their collaboration, Spils observes, "No other
director could have made that film. But no other actor either."
Enke became typecast as the work-shy ne'er-do-well with a decidedly off-balance view of and unique attitude toward quotidian reality. It is an image that he and Spils have explored,
cultivated, and refined in their subsequent cinematic efforts.
Like Enke, Spils was also typecast; she became known as a director of comical farces. Both have, however, used this labeling to
their advantage. In their opinion, they complement one another
and function best as a team; and the fact that they work on
opposite sides of the camera seems unimportant. With this truly
collaborative perspective in mind, both have turned down all
offers to work independently.

Spils and Enke approached *Go to It, Baby* from a very personal,
unstructured, and yet determined perspective. Set in a humorous and light-hearted vein, *Maneuver* had depicted a young
couple's attempt to come to terms with established values and
societal routine. Within the framework of the late 1960s, *Go to It,
Baby* both elaborated on the short and narrowed its focus to one
central character. At the time, student unrest at West German
universities dominated the news media, and the film picked up
on this new social tenor. Ambivalent with regard to the first
successes of the NGC, in an article published in *Der Spiegel* in
December 1967, Spils and other neophyte directors—Maran
Gosov, Eckhart Schmidt, and Klaus Lemke among them —
expressed their discontent with the films of such "established"
directors as Alexander Kluge and Volker Schlöndorff.[4] Spils
noted: "They should do away with the boredom in the cinemas,
and that's something the gentlemen of the Young German
Cinema have hardly accomplished yet."[5] In the months following the opening of her film, critics echoed her view. In Munich's
Abendzeitung, for example, Ponkie wrote: "At the beginning of
the glut of young filmmakers May Spils has earned a small note
of distinction for herself: She has delivered the first light entertainment film in the midst of a large supply of self-reflexive
sorrow and satirical generation mustiness."[6] To be sure, weighty
analyses of social conditions and the problems faced by West
Germany's young people were areas Spils and Enke studiously
sought to avoid in the preparation of their script. Although fully

aware of what was going on around them—both in the cinema and in society—they primarily considered film as a medium for entertainment rather than as celluloid social commentary. Their films, however, do make a social statement.

Collaborating with Rüdiger Leberecht, Spils and Enke took several months to write the script for *Go to It, Baby*. Spils was prepared to produce the film herself, but Peter Schamoni read their script and insisted on producing the film. During the actual filming, the young filmmakers chose to ignore the producer's suggestions, and in retrospect Spils comments, "I had a great deal of initiative and courage, quite a bit of courage." Schamoni continued to be skeptical, as he felt that audiences would not tolerate certain scenes as envisioned.

In Schwabing, Munich's Greenwich Village, we watch as Martin prepares for bed, turns out the lights, and slips between the sheets. As the credits appear, the camera cuts to the street—it is broad daylight. And so begins a film which, in recounting a somewhat fantastic day in the life of its offbeat hero, constantly cheats our conventional expectations of behavior.

An admirer of the cartoonist Wilhelm Busch, who gave us the immortal *Max and Moritz* and other comically pessimistic tales of disaster, Martin is convinced that "it'll all come to no good," the "it" remaining unspecified. Laid back and resistant to quotidian reality, Martin can be counted on to respond to it in an outrageous manner. He not so much fights off as sloughs off his marriage-oriented girl friend, Anita. He is equally successful in frustrating the representatives of authority. For example, when his friend Henry convinces him—at pistol point—to report a robbery in his apartment building, he makes a hash of the routine questions asked by the police, claims to be a Nazi of Bedouin descent, and demands to be allowed to ask questions in turn. Quickly tiring of the game, he slips through the police station window while the officers confer in confusion, but returns through the front door arrayed in dark glasses, obviously phony whiskers, and a winter coat. "What's most important now is to act very inconspicuous," he announces to Henry as the two emerge into the summer day.

While they are at a swimming pool, Martin is reminded by Henry that they have promised to deliver song lyrics to Bloch, a wealthy eccentric who runs a store where he buys and sells "ideas." Glancing around him at the buxom young female bathers, Martin rattles off:

> Go to it, baby
> Don't be crazy
> In bed let's be lazy
> Let's smoke till it's hazy

While Henry enthusiastically runs to phone Bloch, Martin meets Barbara, a girl from a middle-class family, whom he immediately sets about impressing with wild tales: "You should have seen me fifty years ago jitterbugging with Selma Lagerlöf." Leaving the pool—Martin is in his bathing trunks, having set fire to his trousers after an argument with the woman who runs the locker room—the trio runs into and escapes from the police, who now suspect Martin of having himself committed the robbery he came to report. They stop at a zoo, where while Henry races off to phone Bloch about a new bit of doggerel tossed off by Martin, the latter continues his idiosyncratic courtship of the somewhat fascinated Barbara, whose staid upbringing has not prepared her for an imaginative approach to existence. Observing a caged lion, Martin notes that its adventures in that small enclosure are greater than they could be in the jungle, since the drama of tracking its prey must necessarily become more vivid. "Fantasy grows with the limitation of space," he assures her in one of his pseudophilosophical yet trenchant observations. The sequence at the zoo ends in a wild chase scene during which Martin and Barbara race around with a goat ensconced in a child's purloined stoller.

In a following sequence, they engage in a lighthearted conversation filled with innuendos.

Martin: They're fiddling up there.
Barbara: Fiddling, what's that?
Martin: Well, when I do like this. (He touches her neck.) This, this isn't fiddling yet. (More intensely) But this, this is fiddling clear and simple. (Less so) This perhaps isn't quite fiddling yet. (More intensely) But this now is quite obviously fiddling. (He pets her neck. It is clear that Barbara does not mind. Martin pulls his hand away.) Darn it, it's clear that I just fiddled!

Barbara: Fiddler!
Martin: Well, yes, who doesn't like to fiddle? The whole world fiddles. (Barbara puts her hand on Martin's knee).
Barbara: Is that fiddling?
Martin: Not quite yet. It could have happened quite by chance, quite unconsciously.
Barbara: And this?
Martin: Getting there.
Barbara: And this?
Martin: Fiddling pretty much. (Barbara strokes Martin's knees. She quickly pulls her hand back.)
Barbara: Darn it, it's clear that I just fiddled!
Martin: Right!

Encouraged by her encounter with the freewheeling Martin, Barbara skips a family ritual—an excruciating after-dinner violin concert by her father—and meets with Martin, but the two are soon picked up by the police. To give Martin a chance to escape, Barbara uncharacteristically performs an impromptu striptease that distracts the police. When she later meets up with Martin again they go to his cluttered apartment, where at his euphemistic suggestion they engage in "a little match." Meanwhile, Anita is furious when Martin fails to keep his promise to show up at a party given by the lecherous Bloch and supplied with females by Henry.

Back at the apartment, Martin is suggesting another "little match" to Barbara, who refuses and departs both from the scene and the picture. Enter the angry Anita, and to placate her Martin suggests "a match" just as the police break in. Martin admits to the burglary—which he may or may not have actually committed—and in a farcical scene with the police is shot. However, just as Anita is lamenting his death, he pops us and "pardons" the cop who shot him. As he is being led away, the camera offers us a static shot of Anita, once more alone and frustrated.

In the late 1960s, strong female characters dominated the West German screen. As Martin, therefore, Werner Enke offers a contrast with the males portrayed in films of the era. Robert Fischer and Joe Hembus have observed:

> In its early years the New German Film bore witness to the male filmmakers' fascination with lively and admirable women who were more bound to their own strong temperament than to convention;

the specific quality of these women fundamentally determined the quality of the film: this extends from Tremper's *Playgirl*-Eva Renzi to Schlöndorff's *A Degree of Murder*-Anita Pallenberg, Kluge's *Yesterday Girl*-Alexandra Kluge, Reitz's *Mealtimes*-Heidi Stroh, from characters portrayed by Helga Anders, Sabine Sinjen, and Hannelore Hoger to Fassbinder's Hanna Schygulla. In comparison the men were uninteresting: The only fascinating and imaginative male character during this period is Werner Enke from *Go to It, Baby*, a film made by a woman. Otherwise one only saw ill-humored heroes of a mumbler syndrome and of a whimpering inner nature, in addition to some marionettes and stoical victims of feminine initiative.[7]

In *Go to It, Baby* the sexual tables are indeed turned. In contrast to the multidimensional and curiously puzzling male lead, the female characters are one-dimensional stereotypes used mainly to further the plot, to act as foils for Martin, and to express the boredom and banality of normalcy. Barbara is a young upperclass woman whose proper upbringing automatically relegates her to a subservient position. Martin easily, almost passively, manipulates her, as she is attracted to elements in his life-style that are totally foreign to her: his spontaneity, his singular sense of humor, and his remarkably ambivalent attitude toward tradition and authority. Only once does Barbara demonstrate initiative—when she disrobes in the police station—and even then she is acting for Martin's sake rather than her own. Although she appears in various states of undress, Barbara's sexuality is downplayed and she remains Martin's foil. In contrast, Anita is depicted as an aggressive and emancipated female, who supports herself and never mentions familial obligations. However, although she seems strong and independent, Anita, a frustrated nag, has only one goal in mind: marriage. Refusing to acknowledge or to make allowances for Martin's idiosyncracies, this eternal Xanthippe fails to explore alternate possibilities or relationships; she has trained her one-dimensional sights on someone beyond her realm of limited comprehension. Her tirades are tediously repetitive, and whenever she appears on the screen, the audience knows what to expect from her. By playing out her role as a marriage-oriented, pseudoliberated stereotype, Anita throws Martin's eccentric and unpredictable behavior into relief. Always in full control, he dominates the women around him by means of sheer passivity.

However minor their roles, Spils's women are portrayed in a less than favorable light. For example, the young women Henry picks up and takes to Bloch's villa are mindless bikini-clad nonentities interested only in having a good time. Like the women at the public swimming pool, they function only as decorative figures—little more than products for masculine consumption. It may be surprising to some that Spils, an emanicipated woman by her own admission and actions, chose to depict female characters with such vapid personalities. A simple role reversal becomes evident when we remember how male filmmakers in the early years of the NGC rendered the male psyche through "ill-humored heroes," "marionettes," and "victims of feminine initiative."

While Barbara and Anita are older but by no means more complex versions of the American Gidgets in Bikini Beach movies, Martin is considerably more cerebral than his American counterparts. The shallowness of his song lyrics, byproducts of his fertile imagination, is clearly intentional. Fully aware of the "business" relationship between Henry and Block, he feeds his friend material to "sell." However, he avoids direct contact with a man who stoops to buying and selling ideas. In addition, he flexes not his muscles—little in evidence--but his mind. For example, when at the police station he turns the tables on his questioners by asking, "Who or what is Schopenhauer?" he is testing the psychological adaptability of his interrogators—they are baffled by this non sequitur. When he tells Barbara that he jitterbugged with the Nobel Prize-winning Swedish author Selma Lagerlöf, we laugh with him both at the anachronism and the ridiculousness of the image. Through language Martin takes advantage of and points to the weaknesses of those around him. He always manages, however, to restrain his (sub)conscious attacks with a comic tether. Werner Enke quotes with approval Karl Valentin, a German Chaplinesque tragicomic cabaret and film personality: "Laughing is like crying; it just comes out backward."

Enke describes *Go to It, Baby* as "one cut above a radio play," i.e. an aural text with optical amplification—but an audience unattuned to Martin's often neologistic Schwabing chatter will be struck by the visually humorous sequences that tie the verbal interchanges together. The verbal is indeed augmented by what

Spils terms "optical texts" in which physical humor is represented in all its facets. While Enke is not above jumping out of a window or dressing like a buffoon to evoke an audience response, at times his humor can be extremely subtle. Although not overtly contemplative, Martin is a sensitive individual whose banter and physicality are tragicomic statements about his perception of society and its restrictions.

Go to It, Baby was premiered on January 4, 1968, and was to be the West German entry at Cannes, but Robert Favre Le Bret, the head of the festival, rejected it as "too light."[8] A month later, at the eighteenth annual film festival in West Berlin, the film was cited for its dialogue, and Werner Enke was awarded the Filmband in Gold as the best young actor of the year. "I haven't yet seen a film in the new German wave in which there is so much freedom,"[9] said one critic, and another described Spils's "talented debut film" as "deftly cheerful" and "uncomplicated."[10] Audiences flocked to the film, one of the few that year to succeed both critically and financially.

In retrospect, Spils views the making of *Go to It, Baby* as cathartic and spontaneous. Her second feature, *Nicht fummeln, Liebling! (Don't Fiddle, Darling!)* utilized a "similar mechanism," but Spils feels that "the naiveté was gone." Production began in 1969 on a script by Peter Schlieper.

Charly, a hypochondriac, spends his day mumbling "The old rhythm is gone," and is eventually turned out by his girl friend. Urged on by his friend Harry, he gets a job as a film extra. Chaos ensues, and although he loses his job he does meet two starlets who team up with Harry and himself. The two couples become involved with some arsonists in a Schwabing commune, and everybody shortly lands in jail. Charly manages to escape disguised as a cop, teams up with an attractive blond driving a convertible, and a number of new escapes and chase scenes bring the film to an end.

In spite of the fact that Spils and Enke had little to do with the writing of the script, *Don't Fiddle, Darling!* appears to be the second installment of a Spils-Enke comedy saga; however, it differs from its predecessor in one major respect. Whereas *Go to It, Baby* achieved a balance between the spoken word and the visual image, there are more optical texts and sight gags in the follow-up. To be sure, Werner Enke explores further aspects of the

Werner Enke and Gila von Weitershausen in *Don't Fiddle, Darling* (COURTESY OF CIC)

Werner Enke and Henry van Lyck in *Give It To Him, Lad* (COURTESY OF CIC)

Martin/Charly image in his language and mannerisms, and there are sequences of comic intensity, but what had seemed refreshingly provocative during a period of student uprisings now came across to some as an exploitative and superficial rehash. *Der Spiegel's* reviewer complained:

> "It'll all come to no good"—the Schwabing ne'er-do-well Werner Enke said it time and again to his baby. And so it happened. What was cheerful protest against conformity and the bourgeoisie in May Spils's first film, *Go to It, Baby,* is a limp joke in the second Spils film, a cramped remake of the intelligent grumbling of yesteryear.... What Charly-Enke says while sitting on the toilet is true: "The old rhythm is gone."[11]

Nevertheless, young audiences who had sought comic relief with Martin were fascinated by his alter ego Charly, and an older public enjoyed established stars Erika Beer and Karl Schönböck in cameo appearances. Only slightly less successful at the box office than *Go to It, Baby,* the film was not a total critical failure. In the year of its release Spils and Enke were awarded the coveted Ernst Lubitsch Prize.

For their third full-length collaboration, *Hau drauf, Kleiner!* (*Give It to Him, Lad!,* 1973), Spils and Enke wrote the script themselves. Charly is now a more mature but still bizarre hippie. Like the Greek Cynic philosopher Diogenes, he makes his home in a barrel, cultivating the easy life in a garden behind an old building in Munich's Altstadt. His passive existence is interrupted when he is called up for reserve duty and must exchange his blue jeans for a uniform. Too much of a pacifist to engage in war games, after his ineptness sabotages his unit's maneuvers he throws this rifle into the Isar River and disappears. Hunted as AWOL, he effortlessly eludes his pursuers and joins up with his friend Henry. What follows are a series of harum-scarum adventures as promoters of a hair restorer and as detectives assigned to shadow a sausage vendor discover whether or not he chews gum! Eventually, Charley retires to his barrel with a young lady named Caroline, but after a night of bliss he is arrested by the army and led off to jail as the film ends.

In preparing their script, Spils and Enke concentrated more on the story line and less on sight gags and visuals. The plot is more tightly woven and elements are combined and refined— the authoritarian figures are now represented by the national military. Nevertheless, the film caters openly to the audience's expectations, and there are few surprises and even less originality. As for Spils, she found it "too intellectual," and not in keeping with the team's original intentions: entertainment. Nevertheless it was one of 1974's most successful comedies.

1979, the year of their fourth feature *Wehe, wenn Schwarzenbeck kommt . . . (Watch Out When Schwarzenbeck Comes)* proved to be a critical test for Spils and Enke. Stories of rampant terrorism coupled with the 1977 kidnapping and murder of politician Hanns-Martin Schleyer had dominated the media in the five years since the light-hearted *Give It to Him, Lad!* Prominent filmmakers treated political themes—both past and present—in their works. Hans Jürgen Syberberg's *Our Hitler,* Margarethe von Trotta's *The Second Awakening of Christa Klages,* Reinhard Hauff's *Knife in the Head,* and the collaborative *Germany in Autumn* were only a few of the controversial films that sought to raise the consciousness of the West-German citizens. How would audiences react to a comedy in the light of such weighty competition?

The script was written by Enke and Jochen Wedegärtner (Spils's input was minimal) and had little if anything to do with West Germany's current unrest. As always, Werner Enke's Charly is the central character in the film. For once he appears to have a job. He is the director of a flea circus that is in dire financial straits. Since he cannot pay his debts, his business and star performers are confiscated by the authorities, and Charly moves in with his friend Ramirez and his obese wife. During one of his nightly wanderings, Charly happens upon a strange sight. The scrap dealer Schwarzenbeck, an elderly, rotund gentleman, has tied himself to railroad tracks in the true fashion of the silent cinema. With a simulated suicide he hopes to avoid having to pay taxes on his business. Charly saves Schwarzenbeck's life, and the latter thanks the young man by giving him a job as a car salesman. Fascinated by Schwarzenbeck's business expertise, Charly comes to view him as a role model and father figure. On one of his many escapades—he is caught shoplifting in a department store—Charly meets a young women named Charlotte and promptly falls in love with her. She is behind in her rent, and he resolves to help her. At a neighboring fair he takes on the Strangler from Metzelberg, a renowned boxer, and wins a hundred marks. Schwarzenbeck, who is once again at the mercy of the revenue board, now talks Charly and his friends into joining him in a plot against the revenue office. A few days later the surprised citizens of Munich find tax rebates, generated by a reprogrammed computer, in their mailboxes. Having taken over as the local mailman, Schwarzenbeck delivers the checks himself.

Of the filmmakers' four features, *Watch Out When Schwarzenbeck Comes* is the most visually oriented film. The "intellectual atmosphere" of *Give It to Him, Lad!* gives way to an abundance of pantomime, a plethora of sight gags, and a carefully selected group of humorously and grotesquely dressed stock figures. Charly's neologisms—"now acceptable in polite company" according to critic Wolfgang Limmer—take a back seat to optical texts. When Charly jumps onto a tandem to escape the store detective after the shoplifting episode, the chase scene is visually condensed, since the detective takes the seat behind him. Try as he might, the aggressive Strangler cannot compete with his puny opponent. The humor in this scene stems not only from the absurd confrontation between the denim-clad young man and the aging boxing star, but also from the oversized gloves, the Victorian boots, and the brightly patterned boxing briefs the portly fighter wears. Regarding the lengthy boxing sequence, a tribute to Werner Enke's idol Charlie Chaplin, Wolfgang Limmer observed, "One rarely sees ten minutes of such concentrated comedy in a German film."[12] Next to the Strangler, Ramirez's room-filling wife and Schwarzenbeck, Charly, and Charlotte appear excessively normal and straight-laced. Enke, the "last knight of the German film comedy,"[13] and his collaborator Wedegärtner have created a series of classic vignettes tied together by a very loose plot. The life of Charly becomes the plot, but, paradoxically, he no longer dominates each scene. As a result, the tedium of following a character whose screen persona is well known before the film even begins is eliminated.

Commercially *Watch Out When Schwarzenbeck Comes* was one of the great screen successes of 1979. At the box office it ranked third behind *The Tin Drum* and *The Marriage of Maria Braun*, proving once again that Spils and Enke have their fingers on the pulse of German film audiences, to whom they gave something that could not necessarily be found in other films of the past twenty years: comedy, humor, and entertainment.

It is not surprising that film scholars more often than not dismiss Spils and Enke as superficial in their approach to filmmaking. Although a number of critics in various film histories acknowledge that *Go to It, Baby* was a milestone in the early years of West Germany's cinematic rebirth, they eschew interpreting it or the subsequent films, and content themselves with platitudes about the first genuinely and repeatedly successful female director of the NGC. What they fail to recognize is that the comedic approach of Spils and Enke goes beyond pure entertainment. In fact, the seemingly superficial antics of their characters can be interpreted as covert social criticism. Comedy and tragedy are not mutually exclusive. In a Spils/Enke collaboration a "devilish seriousness" lies waiting to be discovered under the carefully and cautiously cultivated guise of humor.

NOTES

[1]Quoted in Barbara Bronnen and Corinna Brocher, eds., *Die Filmemacher: Zur neuen deutschen Produktion nach Oberhausen* (Munich: Bertelsmann, 1973), p. 94.

[2]Quoted in Robert Fischer and Joe Hembus, eds., *Der Neue Deutsche Film, 1960–1980* (Munich: Goldmann, 1981), pp. 216–17.

[3]All statements by May Spils and Werner Enke, unless otherwise noted, stem from a personal interview conducted by the author on January 21, 1982.

[4]Kluge and Schlöndorff had actually made only one or two films at this time.

[5]"Bubis Kino: Ach, der Papili," *Der Spiegel*, no. 53 (1967).

[6]Quoted in Fischer and Hembus, *Der Neue Deutsche Film*, p. 42.

[7]Ibid., p. 37.

[8]Quoted in "Dialog mit Taubstummen," *Der Spiegel*, no. 22 (1968).

[9]Peter W. Jansen, "Zur Sache, Schätzchen," *Filmkritik*, no. 2 (1968), p. 129.

[10]"Striche in Schwabing," review of *Zur Sache, Schätzchen*, *Der Spiegel*, no. 2 (1968).

[11]"Männchen im Getreide," review of *Nicht fummeln, Liebling*, *Der Spiegel*, no. 5 (1970).

[12]Wolfgang Limmer, "Böse Bunken: *Wehe, wenn Schwarzenbeck kommt*," *Der Spiegel*, no. 4 (1979).

[13]Franz Manola, "Was arbeitslose Jungendliche fühlen: *Wehe, wenn Schwarzenbeck kommt . . .*" *Die Presse* (Vienna), 17 February 1979.

ULA STÖCKL

How Women See Themselves

by Marc Silberman

ULA STÖCKL IS AMONG THE HANDFUL OF
German women directors who began making films in the sixties.
She shares with other established women directors such as Erika
Runge and Helma Sanders-Brahms a certain distance to the
organized women's movement in West Germany and, as a result,
has been subjected to a mixed reception among feminists. Yet
Stöckl, like the outspoken feminist Helke Sander, is one of the
few women directors who has insisted on focusing her attention
in all her films on women and how women see themselves.

Ula Stöckl's biography suggests little that would lead one to
suspect a budding cinéaste. Born in Ulm on February 5, 1938,
she left school at sixteen and became a secretary. At twenty she
left Germany to study languages in Paris and London, later
working as an executive secretary. Although Stöckl wrote and
published stories and travel reports during this time, it was not
until 1962—when she became an editor in the television department of a music production company—that she turned to
screenplay writing. Stöckl quickly realized that as a woman she
would have to know her métier much better than the male competition.[1]

Returning to Ulm in 1963, she studied with Alexander Kluge
and Edgar Reitz at their newly founded Institute for Filmmak-

Ula Stöckl
(COURTESY OF THE FILMMAKER)

ing in the Ulm School of Design. Although her original intention was to spend only two years learning how to write screenplays, she stayed at the institute for the full five-year program and became its first graduate in 1968. Stöckl was decisively influenced by her experiences at the Ulm Institute. Kluge and Reitz were then in their formative period of adapting French auteur-cinema to the realities of the German production scene. *Autoren-kino*, derived from the concept of the autonomous author, refers to the utopian role of the filmmaker as author of a film insofar as he or she retains control of all production phases. In other words, *Autorenkino*, at least in the mid-sixties, was a means to assert the individuality of the filmmaker, to claim the film as the product of an individual, and to counter the notion of film as a mass commodity. The training in filmmaking organized by Kluge and Reitz was based on the production of miniatures. The Ulm Institute concentrated not on epic forms but on the smallest unit of coherence, fragments from which longer, linear narratives might be constructed. The influence of this episodic element characterizes the structure of Ula Stöckl's films. *Autoren-kino* in the tradition of Kluge and Reitz also meant that Stöckl assumed the triple function of screenwriter, director, and producer in more than two-thirds of her eleven feature-length films.

Ula Stöckl's films revolve thematically around the problems of affective relationships: marriage (what mechanisms of oppression it develops, how it fails as soon as the woman claims her autonomy), role-playing among women, the opportunity for women to engage in unconventional behavior, the impossibility or inability on the part of adults to express adequately their needs, and, finally, the search for forms of communication other than verbal. That is not to imply that Stöckl's films are only about women. Although men appear almost exclusively as peripheral, stereotyped figures, the lives of the women revolve around men implicitly and explicitly. Stöckl shows women who are breaking out of conventional relationships but who cannot find an alternative, women who refuse to be treated as objects of male prerogatives but who nonetheless conceive of their own emancipation in patriarchal terms.

As a student at the Institute for Filmmaking, Stöckl directed three shorts on her own, and she assisted in directing both Alexander Kluge's *Abschied von gestern (Yesterday Girl,* 1966), one of the first and most important contributions to the New German Cinema, and Edgar Reitz's *Mahlzeiten (Mealtimes,* 1967), his first feature-length fiction film. Her own first feature film, *Neun Leben hat die Katze (The Cat Has Nine Lives),* was completed in 1968 with a grant from the Kuratorium junger deutscher Film. First conceived in 1965, the screenplay originally contrasted a girl's dreams about professionalism and independence with the reality of a world that offers few opportunities to women. After three years of research and rewriting, the final script introduces *four* female protagonists. The film seeks to investigate the relationships between these women and their differing self-images in counterpoint to a programmatic statement by the voice-over commentary: "Never have women had so many opportunities to make something of their lives. But now they must simply realize that they are capable of wanting." Instead of presenting a broad social panorama, the film delves into the private lives of the protagonists. Like the French experimental filmmaker Agnes Varda (*Cléo de 5 à 7,* 1962; *Le Bonheur,* 1965), Stöckl shows not the process of development in her women characters but its results. Similarly, her focus on the private sphere is not aimed at escapism but provokes the reality of emptiness that characterizes the lives of her female figures.

The Cat Has Nine Lives (COURTESY OF BASIS-FILM)

The plot of the film resembles that of a soap opera. The four women represent four different role models. Each tries to break the bonds of dependency but, as a product of patriarchal society, finds she cannot succeed. Katharina, a journalist, lives alone, has ambitious plans, and is involved with Stephan, a married man. She lives a life full of compromises, recognizing that even her professional achievements are unsatisfying. Ann, too, is unable to find fulfillment in her everyday life, but in contrast to her friend Katharina, she finds compensation in the realm of play and fantasy. Unsure of her future after a recent divorce, Ann arrives from Paris to visit Katharina in Munich in the naive hope of improving her life by changing its geographical context. Ann soon becomes involved in a relationship with Sascha, whom Katharina "steals" as a narcissistic proof of her own attractiveness. Ann then approaches Stephan, only to discover that his notion of love is no more than mindless consumerism. Magdalene, Stephan's deceived wife, meanwhile sits at home and contemplates suicide. The fourth woman, Gabriele, is a popular singing star whom Katharina interviews for a newspaper report.

She is the opposite of Katharina and Ann: financially independent, basking in the narcissism of her glamorous image, and able to seduce Stephan casually, without hesitation or regret.

The women presented here are sociological clichés. Katharina represents the reality principle: she constantly seeks approval from her environment and those around her. Change is important, no matter what the chance of success, for Katharina sees herself as someone who can and must learn. In one sequence, for example, she pretends to apply for a secretarial opening just to prove to herself that she can compete successfully; in another she assumes her editor's stubborn and ridiculous logic when she defends an article against his criticism. In contrast to Katharina, Ann represents the pleasure principle, and in the division of labor constructed by the film, she lives her imaginative life while Katharina pursues her profession. Ann, too, is verbal: she argues convincingly with Sascha for her freedom and against his possessiveness; and she gives free rein to her spontaneous emotions: she joins an anti-Vietnam demonstration because "some things you just have to do." Yet Ann never tries to change herself. She "exists," and her playfulness becomes autistic and ultimately constrained. Stöckl interrupts the film with intense dream projections that characterize the repressed aspects of Ann's personality: anger when she burns a hole in her nylons with a cigarette and rips them apart, infantile envy when she incessantly gobbles up candy and lollipops, jealousy when she dreams of killing Stephan, and hurt when she projects Katharina as an unloving, elderly mother figure. Ann finally gives herself up to a mythological fantasy; in her mind she turns Katharina into the legendary Circe, the dream image of a woman who freely asserts her female sexuality and exerts her power over men by turning them into swine. Circe, however, remains only in the imagination, an optical cipher that carries the negative inscription of the protagonists' experience in the everyday world.

Magdalene, the deceived housewife, represents the death wish, the traditional agent of women's internalized violence. Briefly introduced as the loyal homemaker and devoted spouse, she finds her only recourse in suicide as a response to the loss of her husband's affection. In a tritely edited sequence she sits on her bed, pistol in hand, as the camera begins to revolve around her. The claustrophobic and dizzying image of despair remains, however, unmediated and ineffectual. Gabriele, the star, in contrast, is the self-projection of male ideology. Flirtatious and sexy, she assumes that she is hated and envied by all women. Her success as a woman is attained at the price of total objectification: her freedom is that of a commodity governed by the laws of the patriarchy. Katharina observes Gabriele at the rehearsals for a recording session of the film's title song ("The Cat Has Nine Lives"). As Gabriele's star image becomes displaced by the reality of the labor of a singer, Katharina begins to perceive how ridiculous this image is. Her admiration for the self-generated glamor of Gabriele parallels Ann's wish projection of Circe. Both use imaginative constructions to shape a utopia deformed by their own inability to satisfy their need for solidarity. Each of the four women fails to perceive that her anxiety has something to do with the society in which they live. They can only express their insight negatively—the realization of their lack of knowledge as to how to behave differently. As one character explains: "I can formulate my notion of happiness only negatively. I imagine the consequences of a decision and then I know what I don't want."

The problem of female self-representation is at the center of the film. How can women say what they want to be when a fundamental lack of language characterizes their existence, when they only learn to re-act? One means of escape from the restraints on independence and freedom imposed by the patriarchy is proposed in a masturbation scene. Self-induced pleasure leaves the tension between the women still on a latent level but removes them from the repressive mechanisms they have been taught. Moreover, the frequent laughter of the women throughout the film suggests a means of escape from the domination of verbal rationalizations identified with the male characters. The film reflects these concerns on the formal level as well in the mixture of narrative elements: action sequences, reflective commentary, metaphoric images, and dream sequences. Stöckl establishes tension in the discrepancy between plot (dramatic high points, confrontations, emotions) and presentation (arrhythmical, fragmentary, uninflected), as if the world of these types were in conflict with what the camera records: faulty communication, muddled meanings, and misperceived signals.

Stöckl intentionally left the film unfinished and fragmentary. She refuses to structure scenes toward narrative closure or to provide sharp, concise dialogue. Even in those sequences distinguished by verbal interplay, the dialogue serves more to reveal behavior patterns than to communicate a specific meaning. For example, in a discussion between Ann and Sascha about her demands on life and her need for freedom, Sascha struggles to speak French—Ann's language—when responding to her views, but when he wants to stress his own sense of possessiveness, he shifts to his native German. The abstract nature of Sascha's "objective" reasoning barely conceals his effort to manipulate the conversation and Ann. In all her films Stöckl focuses on human emotions, on those moments when people are pushed to a breaking point or when life begins to crumble around them. Like John Cassavetes (in *Woman Under the Influence* or *Gloria*), she does not intensify these dramatic moments, but rather she concentrates the camera on dead moments, banalities, and lost dreams. Two bedroom scenes with Katharina and Stephan illustrate the point. Both are short sequences taken from one angle and almost devoid of dialogue. Like painted images, the scenes show no crisis but communicate the chaos of emotions within Katharina, the "emancipated" woman. Similarly, the sequences with Gabriele focus not so much on the rush of events that constitute her exoticism and glamor, but on Katharina's fascination with the fluctuation of Gabriele's character as she deals with her self-image and the work to produce that image.

Stöckl employs two distinct camera techniques in *The Cat Has Nine Lives*. In the cinéma-vérité sections (particularly in the first half of the film, which introduces the characters and their relationships) she uses on-location filming, natural light, and improvised dialogue. Yet even here distance is built into every sequence. The camera frames faces and decors, not events. Particularly striking is the use of opulent color, with the result that many images are melodramatic: Ann playing with white blossoms while sitting in a rowboat on a lake bathed in sunlight, or Ann in a red sweater standing in a field of bright yellow blossoms. Such kitsch, reminiscent of advertisements in teen magazines, is not sentimental but hard and direct; it eschews the romanticism of French filmmaker Claude Lelouch in *Un Homme et une femme* (1966) and *Toute une vie* (1974) in favor of the shock effect of static, statuesque images. The impression is one of nakedness, the brutal effect of unlived wish projections and misdirected desire. Stöckl disrupts this melancholy atmosphere by shifting to another stylistic level for the dream sequences. Contrary to the realism in early films of the NGC, which usually relies on the image to connote event and motivation, Stöckl introduces metaphors, traumatic visions, and fantastic myths to depict the repressed conflicts of the women. Especially remarkable are the sequences that involve an archetypal dimension: Katharina sits as the accused before a group of old women who argue reproachfully that there is no such thing as nonmarriage; a group of children watch a rabbit being skinned—the boys laugh and the girls run away. Such interruptions provide a subjective entry into the psychological motivations of the characters while enabling the viewer to perceive them as members of a more general social constellation.

As a first independent production, *The Cat Has Nine Lives* does reveal weaknesses in direction and editing. It is clear that Stöckl became more comfortable with improvised dialogue as the filming progressed and as she began to trust her group of professional and nonprofessional actors. Also, the filmmaker tends to emphasize the obvious at times by relying on overt symbolism and repetitive editing. However, such weaknesses do not justify the lack of interest and understanding with which the film was met on its release. As the first postwar German film by a woman to take up explicitly women's issues (only ten years later was it recognized as such), it aroused the blatant sexism of the male film critics. Leftists accused the film of being apolitical, others bemoaned the lack of well-rounded male characters, and one critic damned it as a film by ladies for ladies. As a result, it never found a commercial distributor and was confined to isolated showings in some art-film houses and at a few festivals.

Stöckl's next two films were both coproductions with her former mentor Edgar Reitz. *Geschichten vom Kübelkind (Tales of the Trashcan Kid,* 1969–70) was an attempt on their part to transcend the limitations of traditional aesthetic, production, and distribution demands. It consists of twenty-two independent episodes, varying in length from one to twenty-five minutes, about a rebellious young woman who constantly clashes with the expectations of her social environment as she moves from one adventure to another. The name of the title character, the Trashcan Kid, derives from an Austrian expletive referring to a worthless person. In the first episode, Kübelkind is literally born full-grown from a placenta thrown into a trashcan. This marks the beginning of her unjust situation, because—as the voice-over comments—such "monsters" should never be raised in a "normal" society in the first place. Wearing a black pageboy wig, and always attired in the same red dress, stockings, and shoes, she is the visual symbol of the outsider who, do as she will, can never become like those "normal" people around her. Kübelkind is, indeed, the antithesis of respected social structures, a polymorph-perverse, infantile being without a past or a personality. She is introduced to all the education and upbringing demanded by society, yet in each instance she proves too much the human being, too much the child, to surrender to the expectations of the middle-class do-gooders who plan to save her. In fact, Kübelkind seems to become the very deformation of that propriety she is supposed to develop. Equipped with the lessons she is taught, she draws literal conclusions: she, too, murders, whores, steals, is murdered, and, finally, returns for sweet revenge.

As a purely stylized figure, Kübelkind is a vehicle for social criticism, attacking hypocritical attitudes and the behavior they generate. In particular, her aggressive sexuality represents a provocation to male and female role-playing. Besides criticizing dominant social inhibitions, the film also implicates the traditional preferences and expectations of the movie audience. Thus, the directors refuse the deception of depicting reality in the accepted sense. The serial structure, with its titles, quotes, sound collages, repetitions, and anachronisms, defies narrative harmony and continuity as means of resolving conflict and contradiction. As a result, Kübelkind can die in one episode and reappear in the next. Moreover, each episode comprises a parody of traditional film genres such as the western, the musical, slapstick comedy, gangster, horror, sci-fi, or Tarzan movies. For example, several sequences based on Dumas's *Three Musketeers* are presented here in fragmentary sections throughout most of the film as a caricature of traditional narrative logic in the novel.

Tales of the Trashcan Kid has been characterized as one of the most interesting contributions to experimental film in the early seventies.[2] Well aware of the impossibility of distributing such an unusual film in West Germany, the filmmakers created a *Kneipenkino* (movie bar) in Munich where guests could drink and choose episodes from this and other films on the menu. Reprinted in a super-8 cassette format (originally it was planned as a ten-hour sequence with forty-three episodes), the episodes were an attempt to utilize the anthology structure in exhibition as well. The spectators saw whichever episode they chose, but only when enough other spectators were also prepared to watch; in effect, the film was assembled as a group activity.

Stöckl's next four films were all produced for television, including the feature-length, modernized version of the Golden Fleece myth called *Das goldene Ding* (*The Golden Stuff*, 1971). Once again she participated in a collective directorial effort, this time with Reitz, Alf Brustellin, and Nikos Perakis. The production was cast with children, and the traditional myth was slightly altered to demonstrate that the Argonauts were able to escape the dangers of war without the aid of the gods or heroic courage but through the powers of rational thought alone. The other three films are lengthy shorts that examine an individual's attempts to escape social pressures: *Sonntagsmalerei* (*Sunday Painting*, 1971) depicts a woman who, in the form of a diary, tells how she is unable to realize her dreams of happiness; in *Hirnhexen* (*Goblins of the Mind*, 1972), a young man investigating the suicide of his friend is himself driven to suicide as he becomes aware of the emptiness around him; and in *Der kleine Löwe und die Großen* (*The Lion Cub and the Grown-ups*, 1973) a young boy learns to fight the rigid ideas of child-raising held by adults. Each film exposes some aspect of superficiality in the middle-class conception of liberal life-styles.

A similar theme provides the point of departure for Stöckl's next major film, funded by and coproduced with a television network (ZDF, the "cultural" network). *Ein ganz perfektes Ehepaar* (*A Quite Perfect Couple*, 1973) utilizes elements from the sentimental love film and the crime story to create a satirical social critique of trendy life-styles in the manner of France's Claude Chabrol in such films as *Le Beau Serge* (1958), *Les Bonnes femmes* (1960), and *La Femme infidèle* (1968). Angela and Robert swear everlasting fidelity within the framework of an open marriage. Each may enter into other relationships, but should such an arrangement threaten their marriage, the partner may then use any means necessary to win back the other. After ten years, Robert faces the stress of a midlife crisis. When he brings home his new girl friend and begins to dream of starting life again with her, Angela finds an opportunity to kill her without leaving a trace. Having saved her marriage, in revenge she then seeks out a lover and prepares to leave with him, expecting Robert to hold her back. The two men, however, find that they like each other, and Angela, to her dismay, is the loser. That would be a realistic reading of the story, but Stöckl's images are rarely unambiguously realistic. The film also projects a metaphorical level of meaning about the role of fantasy in human relationships and the experience of a woman who comes to realize that her husband lacks the imagination she demands of him.

A Quite Perfect Couple is not really about an emancipated woman but about the different emotional constitutions of men and women and the degree of affirmation they require in a partnership. The film is told largely from Angela's perspective and is meant to provoke in women the need to articulate their desires in spite of their socially underprivileged position. To that extent, Angela represents a negative model: she constructs an antimoralistic arrangement with Robert which, in the end, produces a new morality of possessiveness just as suffocating as the traditional marriage they had previously rejected. Both of them are professionally involved in marriage counseling—Robert as a theorist in a research institute and Angela as a television journalist who interviews women with marriage problems on her show "Partnership: What Does It Mean?" Ironically, their liberal views expressed in a professional framework only serve to expose the hypocrisy of their own marriage.

Although Stöckl had more money for the production of A Quite Perfect Couple than for her previous features, the film definitely suffers from a reduction in imaginative cinematography. This, however, is due less to Stöckl's own artistic limitations than to the increasing inflexibility of the television "censors" and the hostility of her (male) critics. Shot in black and white, the film is less demanding both on the material and on the viewer. The editing shows only minor traces of the experimentation in The Cat Has Nine Lives and Tales of the Trashcan Kid. The music is sparse (three American blues songs) and disappointingly banal as commentary on Angela's attitudes. In only one sequence does well-timed editing and quick camerawork adequately capture the physical presence of Angela's emotions. Angry at being excluded from the easy camaraderie between Robert and her lover, Angela retreats to the greenhouse in the garden and cuts off all her prized rose blossoms. Through the changing camera angle the viewer sees her distorted face from below, then the results of her destruction from above. Other than a double flashback immediately following this scene and the climactic final slow-motion dream sequence in which Angela envisions Robert poisoning her lover, the film does little to reinforce aesthetically or comment on the emotional contradictions. As a result, Stöckl draws an unintentionally ambiguous line between desire to love and desire to possess.

A Quite Perfect Couple was not well received by television critics, but Stöckl continued to obtain money from the networks to produce at least a film a year through 1977. *Hase und Igel (Hare and Hedgehog,* 1974*)* returns to the issue of a woman who tries to find happiness with more than one man. The protagonist organizes a business and house collective with five men, but she quickly realizes that the men develop stronger bonds among themselves than they do with her. Her utopian community becomes reality when each man finds his own "private" girl friend, and she is left alone. *Popp und Mingel (Popp and Mingel,* 1975*)* is Stöckl's only literary adaptation (based on a story by Marie-Luise Kaschnitz), a well-received film about the lively fantasy life of a child whose working parents have no time for him.

Erikas Leidenschaften (Erika's Passions, 1976) continues a thematic preoccupation that Stöckl addressed in her first feature film and in *A Quite Perfect Couple*—the conflict between the need for emotional security and the drive for independence. Also co-produced with television-network funding, the film returns to a friendship constellation like that between Ann and Katharina in *The Cat Has Nine Lives.* In her later film, however, Stöckl conducts an autopsy on the relationship. Franziska and Erika (played by two well-established actresses whose careers began in the fifties) had met as secretaries, the former recently divorced and the latter intensively in love but unhappy. Franziska found herself caught up in a number of activities, never able to decide which one was most meaningful for her, whereas Erika was practical and always ready to sacrifice for others. They decided to live together; Erika earned the money and Franziska became involved in whatever struck her fancy: political organizing, cultural activity, or feminism. Ten years later, in an evening of intense discussion, they begin to articulate some of the reasons for the failure of this relationship, while they repeatedly fall into the same patterns of repressive behavior that had driven them apart four years earlier. The opening sequence introduces each figure separately: Franziska, self-assured, lets herself into their former apartment while Erika is out and then immediately begins to rearrange the furniture and to try on Erika's clothes. Erika, in contrast, enters as a more spontaneous, affectionate type. The first confrontation establishes their well-practiced roles — Franziska is critical and aggressive; Erika awkwardly drops a frying pan and burns herself with hot oil.

The film relies almost exclusively on dialogue for its analytical thrust. Through careful editing, the camera reinforces the subjective view of the women toward each other with its frequent alternation between high and low shots and with close-ups that capture each gesture or change in facial expression. The two women gradually peel off layers of defensiveness as they analyze how they manipulated and admired each other. Both had become dissatisfied—Erika because she felt exploited and Franziska because she could not understand why Erika allowed herself to be used. At the same time Erika is fascinated by her friend's capacity for enthusiasm. Franziska, in turn, envies Erika's capacity to feel strong emotions, to fall in love time and again, even though her affairs never end happily. In the course of the evening, the two women inadvertently lock themselves in the bathroom. Their confinement and forced intimacy becomes a metaphor for the spiraling movement in their self-analysis. Faced with their crumbling self-images, the two women begin to reveal to themselves how and why they are vulnerable to each other. The film ends as both women explode in shared laughter, a leitmotif in Stöckl's films for the moment that prefigures the elusive utopia of free, uninhibited relationships.

Erika's Passions focuses on the functioning and dysfunctioning of a partner relationship. By concentrating on two women, Stöckl avoids the question of sexuality, even though lesbian overtones are expressed in the latent rivalry and are clearly reflected in stereotypical aspects of a "masculine" and a "feminine" woman. Stöckl's own skepticism about friendship seems to govern the dynamics of the film, for she consistently exposes the illusion of equality as an excuse for exploitation. Yet neither the suggested sadomasochism of human relationships nor the implied critique of Franziska's hollow leftist phrases are convincingly balanced by the personality of Erika, with whom the filmmaker's sympathies seem to lie. Erika's "feminine" qualities (willingness to sacrifice for others, emotionalism) glorify clichés without submitting them to the kind of critical scrutiny that the film's format would indicate.

Stöckl's most recent film, *Eine Frau mit Verantwortung (A Woman with Responsibility,* 1977), typifies the dilemma of a filmmaker who has been professionally marginalized within the system of television funding. Utilizing a screenplay written by the director Jutta Brückner, it is a one-hour segment for a television series based on case studies from the files of a psychiatric institute. The film presents a convincing and well-acted portrait of a woman who becomes compulsively neurotic under family and child-raising pressures. As in all her previous films, Stöckl best demonstrates her strengths in showing the effects of male domination in women's lives, but the minimal budget and the constraints of the series format leave little room for the directorial energy and creativity that was so promising in her first films. Since 1977, the filmmaker has tried to reenter the commercial film market, but her identification with television production has been a barrier. In addition, Stöckl has recently gained a belated reputation as one of the first feminist filmmakers in West Germany, and was honored by retrospectives in Berlin and Edinburgh in 1977. This has pushed her further into the ghetto of problem films about women, at least in the eyes of West German funding agencies. Some feminists have criticized Stöckl's films because the protagonists rarely break out of their misery and subjection. In the private and privatized search for self-realization and love, they do not embody positive images of self-confidence and resistance. Yet these films prefigure many of the concerns in the current women's movement, and as such they represent an important contribution to social enlightenment. In a sense, Stöckl's debut as a filmmaker was ten years too early, for only in the past few years have we seen the emergence of a critical audience and distribution network capable of responding to the courageous formal and thematic innovations in her films.

NOTES

[1]Some of the information for this article was obtained in a conversation between Ula Stöckl and the author in June 1979.

[2]Ulrich Gregor, *Geschichte des Films ab* 1960 (Munich: Bertelsmann, 1978), pp. 171–72.

JEAN-MARIE STRAUB and DANIÈLE HUILLET

Oblique Angles on Film as Ideological Intervention

by Maureen Turim

THE FILM PROJECTS OF JEAN-MARIE Straub and Danièle Huillet stand on the margins of governmental and industrial exploitation, on the margins of the New German Cinema. This marginality is marked by a filmic expression that serves meaning obliquely, indirectly, and by a concern with film as ideological intervention.

The films of Straub and Huillet avoid the compromises inherent in much commercial production, and implicitly critique the self-indulgence of other auteurist flourishes. Behind the austerity and rigor, behind the insistence on discourse, is a cultural critique, a theory of art and ideology growing out of modern German critical thought.

Jean-Marie Straub and Danièle Huillet met in Paris when Straub was working as assistant director for Jacques Rivette on *Le Coup du Berger.* Straub had been a student at the universities of Nancy and Strasbourg, at which time he directed the ciné-club of Metz. Straub and Huillet moved to Munich, where they married in 1959. They had already begun work on the script for a film on Bach, but this project, along with another to film Heinrich Böll's *Billiards at Half-past Nine,* was postponed for lack of sufficient funding.

Instead Straub made his first film, a short entitled *Machorka-Muff,* in 1963. Straub and Huillet's collaboration seems to have always been an intimate sharing of ideas and plans, but initially Straub received sole directorial credit. Huillet was credited with collaboration on the screenplay of *Nicht versöhnt* (*Not Reconciled,* 1964–65) and the screenplay and editing of *Chronik der Anna Magdalena Bach* (*The Chronicle of Anna Magdalena Bach,* 1967) and *Geschichtsunterricht* (*History Lessons,* 1972). She shared directorial, writing, and editing credit on *Othon* (1969) and again on *Moses und Aron* (*Moses and Aaron,* 1974) and then on all the films since.

The filmmakers share a commitment to a vision of what cinema should be. Straub has expressed this in an interview as seeking to achieve the same measure of expressive image and original synchronous sound he admires in Jean Renoir's *La Nuit au Carrefour.* He has also likened his form of Brechtian cinema to that of John Ford in *Fort Apache,* since Ford questions the mythology of the hero in the final scene. But despite Straub and Huillet's sense that their cinematic vision has such historical antecedents, their extremely unconventional work on the relation of sound to image and their transformations of narrative form and film acting has meant a long-term struggle to finance, produce, and distribute each film. This struggle has been aided by friendships with and support from critics at *Cahiers du Cinéma, Ça,* and *Filmkritik,* French and German film journals whose theory of film closely parallels their own. This liaison with Paris film circles has been a major factor in the presentation of their films to a broader public; their work, however, is still primarily seen at international film festivals and on the German cultural television channel. Their struggle for distribution and recognition of their work evokes one's respect, especially in the face of the uncomprehending criticism in the popular press.

Straub and Huillet's intellectually demanding cinema requires that the spectator bring substantial prior knowledge to the experience of viewing. The spectator depends on the written texts, the scripts, the critiques, and the interviews as supplements to fill

Jean-Marie Straub and Danièle
Huillet (COURTESY OF GIOVANNI
GIOVANNETTI)

in, to explain. Sometimes the filmmakers themselves offer
explanations, as in Huillet's notes on the making of *Moses and
Aaron*.[1] Often critics and theorists provide elaborate *explications
de texte* in which they attempt to explain the meaning and functions of various shots and montage constructions. Straub and
Huillet are the filmmakers that film theory—in its current
semiotic and ideological pursuits—has desired, for they develop
an ideologically motivated process of signification. They use
shots whose angle, internal construction, duration, movement,
and montage are considered as conceptual parameters. An arcing pan, an oblique track-in, or a quick insert frames information in a unique way that necessitates the use of that technique;
form is literally put to the task of making sense.

History Lessons (1972) provides two different examples of how
such conceptual organization can be used. The narrative inquiry
into the commerce of Ancient Rome, which takes the form of a
series of costumed dialogues, forms one series of segments. The
narrative here is derived from Brecht's novel *The Business Affairs*

of Mr. Julius Caesar. A young man interviews a poet, a jurist, a peasant, and a banker. The interviews select from Brecht those portions most directly involved in political machinations and commercial exchange: the slave trade, the struggle of peasants and craftsmen, the war against the mountain people, the history of the mining industry, the debates in the senate. The system of filming is a series of oblique angles in a montage that produces surprising spatial articulations. Straub and Huillet have carried the techniques used by Robert Bresson to film the series of conversations on benches in *Au Hasard Balthazar* (1967) several steps further.² They extend Bresson's departure from the standards of shot/reverse shot into a more pronounced variation of spatial positions and increase the rupture of spatial continuity between any two shots.³ The resulting complex sequences frame and focus our attention on the dialogue: images serve the exposition of the text in much the same way that they do in *Othon.*

The other type of sequence in *History Lessons* is constituted by three segments of the young man driving into contemporary Rome and then through its streets. In the film comprised of fifty-five shots, the segments are inserted as shots 5, 38, and 45, each having approximately the same duration (8′ 40″, 10′ 20″ and 10′ 39″) for a total of almost exactly thirty minutes of film time. Since the shots are taken from a single position behind the drivers, they form a repeated insertion of another space and time—another conceptual principle in the rendering of Brecht's novel.

The critical response to these driving segments is often to turn them into metaphors, to assign them meanings.⁴ The frames within frames are said to represent the camera and perspectival representation. The journey through the streets ruled by the force of daily circumstance is said to be an analysis of the contemporary context of the city.

The car segments clearly do refer to transportation modes and daily street activity in Rome, to the framing of vision in contemporary existence. But what these images convey is not analytical information; it is a calling forth, through insistent framing, of our knowledge of issues outside the text. For those aware of sociological theories of the city, circulation, and commerce, the filmic trope constituted by this tracking shot resonates with the contemplation of these issues. For many other viewers, these images are empty, puzzling, uninformative, or the time allotted them far exceeds the viewer's desire to continue to speculate on what principles are involved. In either case they serve as punctuation of the rest of the film, time to think about the insistent onslaught of dense dialogue in other segments, time to think about filmmaking and the image.

The demand on the viewer in the driving segments is essentially the same as it is in other avant-garde films that use abstraction. These images ask us to explore reduction, control, bold presences and absences, sound and silence, metonymic framings, and "empty" spaces—to find visual challenge and pleasure, as well as meaning. They ask for our patience, for a free-floating and associative attention. They ask us to work with them, as we allow them to work themselves out in a duration that may exceed our expectations.

As with all imagery that avoids the didacticism of a self-evident or "full" representation, the redundancy of a verbal explanation of all things that are shown, this filmmaking practice tends to displace the didactic function onto the critic. Writing about Straub and Huillet can amount to *writing-in* all that is merely indicated. I prefer to indicate the process of a juxtaposition that remains disjunctive; the two types of segments in *History Lessons* remain in conceptual tension, each problematizing the other. They remind critics that one cannot simply formulate a conjunction of semiotics and ideology in the image and its montage. One must allow for that which evades such formulas.

Here is the real pleasure of Straub and Huillet's films and their real difficulty. One easy way to gain access involves seeing the films again, or remembering them as one thinks, in another context, of the subject matter they address. It is in light of this kind of comparative remembering that I will discuss a number of their films.

The Chronicle of Anna Magdalena Bach, for example, is a bold "recollection" in light of such film biographies as Charles Vidor's *A Song to Remember* (1945, the life of Chopin) and *A Song Without End* (1960, the life of Liszt). In each of the Vidor films, the composers' intertwining biographies are narrated as romantic fictions so "Hollywood" in style that the characters of Sand, Chopin, and Liszt, in relationship to one another, are not even consistent between the two films, and the mythology shifts depending on which composer is the heroic focus. Furthermore, in *A Song to Remember,* the lush Technicolor decors mask the revolution of 1848, although Chopin's Polish nationalism is presented so it can be placed in opposition to the fantasy portrayal of Sand as dominatrix. The music is romantically performed, and its composition is always given narrative motivation.

In contrast, *The Chronicle* is an expanded version of Bach's second wife's diaries. It never presumes to tell us more about the characters' motivations or personal lives than the historical evidence offered in the chronicle, although some additional narration was generated in the same tone, with the same attention to births and deaths, economic and political circumstances, and musical publications and performances. The film enters into the telling of history with a mixture of effects, some of which strive for the "real" of historicity. Other effects remain as markers of the discursive position of the film. Despite the accurate reconstitution of costume and instrumentation, of language and architecture, the film actively denies the possibility of a complete reassemblage of the past. It acknowledges the deception inherent in all historically reinacted documentary films by a few techniqies that do not serve "reconstitution"; for example, the actors do not age with the passing years. Thus as spectators of history, the viewers of *Chronicle* learn their own place as well as how to focus on the textures and conflicts of another century; the film reinforces this tension of placement and perspective. Its own rhythms, its sound-image articulations of space and time are resolutely modernist; temporal extensions are contrasted with abbreviated accentuations, stasis with fluidity, silence with lyric entrances—all with a penchant for emphatic surprise. In this new formal framing, the tensions of the Baroque are released from the constraints of its own splendor. The music is not so much enchanting as it is intriguing, and (despite the flatness of the filmic sound or, perhaps, because of it[5]) something new is heard.

Similarly *Othon* reverberates in memory as one experiences Corneille à la Comédie Française, since the faithful theatrical representation gives us theater as artifact, tradition intact, while *Othon* disengages from this appreciative mode. The film is troubled by three temporalities: that of ancient history; that of seventeenth-century dramatic literature; and that of contempo-

The Chronicle of Anna Magdalena Bach (COURTESY OF THE FILMMAKERS)

rary filmmaking practice. The filmic mise-en-scène (the costumed players on a hill above modern Rome with traffic sounds intervening) emphasizes the embedding of one historical moment in another, the shifting and reframing of the context of reperception. It is useful to compare *Othon* to Ariane Mnouchkine's theatrical and film versions of *Molière*. The play which preceded that film used dual stages to accentuate the split between the play as historical biography and the historical plays embedded within that frame. Since the audience had literally to shift directions of their seats at the Théâtre du Soleil, there was a marked disjunction between the two theatrical instances; in the film version, cinema's capacity to integrate disparate spaces, to embrace alternating sequences as part of its traditional presentation, lessened the disjunctive aspect. *Othon* goes to extremes to enforce a tension between the referenced time periods. Through disruptive sound, mise-en-scène, and montage the contemporary audience holds onto a critical position on historical theatricality.

Theater in film is also one of the issues presented in Straub and Huillet's *Der Bräutigam, die Komödiantin und der Zuhälter (The Bridegroom, the Comedienne and the Pimp,* 1968). This film condenses Ferdinand Bruckner's *Krankheit der Jugend* into a ten-minute segment comprised of a unitary oblique long shot, which is then made the centerpiece of a triptych structure framed by two segments that fill in what becomes incomprehensible in the revised play. The first segment is a long, descriptive tracking shot of a street of prostitution; the third segment is a pared-down narration of a woman's attempting to escape her pimp to get married, and it ends with her shooting the pimp after he has chased the couple to their new home. The triptych mode of collage frames the theatrical expression of alienation with images of entrapped social relations and violent rebellion. This film practice releases a theatricality that exceeds staging. It is, rather, located in the split, the gap, the disjunction within a combinatory practice of montage. The "surrounding" sequences elucidate the play framed between them, giving new grounds for the theoretical debate about the relationship between theater and film.

Not Reconciled (1965) exists in a similar relationship to Heinrich Böll's *Billiards at Half-past Nine,* on which it is based. The moving tableaus of the film do not replace the novel, but reposition its imagery as images of memory and history. However, a knowledge of the novel is essential to a narrative comprehension of the film.[6] The visual is structured as a commentary on the text's implications. The film has a different point to make, one that assumes the novel in its metacritical approach. This strategy can be contrasted to Volker Schlöndorff's in *The Tin Drum,* in which the director sought filmic analogues to Günter Grass's evocations of the novel's subjective imagery through illustrated voice-over narration.

American television's *Holocaust* or *Playing for Time,* and Bernardo Bertolucci's epic *1900* also bring contrasts to mind. In approaching the family or the group in history, these other films create lengthy linear fictions in which we follow the emotional events of individuals presented as a mélange of stereotyping and "rounded" characterization. *Not Reconciled* presents figures who are enigmatic and flat, whose social actions are presented elliptically, in a temporality that continually inserts past in present without demarcations, explanations, or clear motivations. This

Hanna Schygulla and Rainer Werner Fassbinder in *The Bridegroom, the Comedienne and the Pimp* (COURTESY OF THE FILMMAKERS)

troubled relationship between past and present, between subjectivity and history, produces the conceptual impact of the film.

The documentary film or filmic essay is the type of film that one remembers as one watches the filmmakers' *Einleitung zu Arnold Schoenbergs Begleitmusik zu einer Lichtspielszene (Introduction to Arnold Schoenberg's "Accompaniment to a Cinematographic Scene,"* 1972) and *Fortini/Cani* (1976). Both films use images to convey and contextualize uncut texts read in voice-over. In the case of *Introduction,* the texts are letters exchanged between Schoenberg and Kandinsky discussing anti-Semitism in Germany in 1923. In *Fortini/Cani,* the text is Franco Fortini's polemical analysis of the Italian stance on the Israeli-Palestinian conflict written immediately after the Six-Day War. The films treat the texts as documents to be granted a respectful, full reading in the light of film imagery, which counterpoints the arguments of the essays or letters.

Rather than strain at the discursive within the image, the filmmakers have developed a strategy in which the verbal text performs a significant and autonomous discursive task. The visual series comments on that verbal argument, rather than the inverse. The visual in *Fortini/Cani* assists the discourse as a metacritical reframing of the original essay, and one is tempted to replace the image/voice-over paradigm with voice/image-over, as images surround the voice, supplying new spaces and meaning through which it can be heard.

The presence of the text, as graphic trace and as object, marks the verbal/visual tensions in *Fortini/Cani*'s strategy of argumentation. The text appears (or is indicated in the absence of its direct appearance) in the following sites, which create a structure of intervals over the forty-one-shot film:

> Shot 1, a close-up on a worn edition of Franco Fortini's *I Cani del Sinai* precedes the titles of the film. It is framed against the diagonal stripes of floor boards.
>
> Shot 2, a closer shot on the book open to the prefatory note mentioned earlier. The trace of the absent reader is marked by a pair of black glasses reposed at the bottom left-hand corner of the frame.
>
> Shot 12, in close-up as an open book resting on Fortini's knees, held by his hands, as he reads, the rest of his body off frame.
>
> Shots 21, 23, 25, and 31–36, the text is itself an off-frame presence, since Fortini is presented in medium shot, the book itself indicated through his sightline as he looks down to read. The series 21–25 is punctuated by other intervening shots, while 31–36 is punctuated only by black leader.
>
> Shots 24, 26, and 39 as handwritten red ink on white background text, arranged in short lines, like poems.
>
> Shot 41 begins with Fortini reading in long shot, framed on the same terrace of the Villa Contoncello, Isle of Elba, as the camera pans right, past him across the house, the terrace, the sea, and the hill, which is in frame as the film ends.

As these shot descriptions indicate, the act of reading and being read to infuses the entire film. Images of reading include those in which the physical text is either only presence, or the sighted absence just below the screen, in which the glasses left against the frame line serve as a marker of an absent reader as the spectator takes his/her place. All are evidence of the process through which the spectator/reader is called into presence by a spectacle/discourse and asked for assistance in generating its discursive activity. If, as in Straub/Huillet, textual elements are refined to the minimal, reordered with gaps and disjunctions, punctuations of indeterminant grammars (themselves becoming minimal elements), then, as less is made obvious, the greater this calling out to the viewer can be. Elements of a disjunctive visual collage perform anasemically, holding meaning in abeyance, available to be filled in afterward. Viewing, reading is neither linear nor circular; it is striving by memory toward that which it has not yet understood.

As the voice of Fortini reminisces, accompanied by the first image of the villa, we see a shot of the sea from the terrace, which could well be a subjective shot from the vantage point we later (shots 21, 23, 27) see Fortini occupying.

> Thirty years earlier, in July I think, in front of the same sea, in a family hotel, my father's copy of *Corriere della Sere*: something had started to happen there where the sun was setting, in Spain. When was it that they killed those blacks in America? (Last summer, or the summer before?) Memory serves to level everything.
>
> On the asphalt of the streets the fresh blood congeals again where it flowed before in years past.
>
> Nothing can be changed.

This musing on memory, this attempt to be ironic about static or circular views of history, points up that this film cannot simply be content with a modernistic circularity. Its weavings, its imbrications of diverse threads cannot afford to lose perspective on why cynicism is a "gain for the cause of conservatism." Memory, textual activity, discourse are presented as serious operations of resistance.

One function that aids this resistance is the analysis of information, its dispersion and its reception, here represented by four examples of the Italian news media woven into the image. First, Italian television news, as presented by the well-known commentator Arrigo Levi, occupies shot 4, so that its own semiotic conjoining of discourse and image is embedded as counterexample within *Fortini/Cani*'s disruptive context. Levi laments the outbreak of fighting, insinuating that the withdrawal of UN troops brought on the war. This leads Levi to suggest that the UN (U Thant, the Pope, President Johnson) are the forces that should settle the conflict. Fortini interrupts Levi with ironic commentary: "My name must not count. I am information, service to the public; I represent democracy, fair play, civilization, good." The UN looms behind the news commentator's shoulder, an icon that replaces images of the struggle in its own terrain, in its own terms. In order for Fortini to interpret this dream of an impartial, correct bourgeois justice and mediation, he will defer the issue, its return a reference to other cited news texts.

"La Cultura Vince," an article by Arrigo Benedetti in *L'Espresso* (what Fortini calls the "bourgeois-radical press"), occupies shot 8. Fortini juxtaposes this image with an indirect commentary on the racism, self-interest, and ethnocentrism that shapes the Italian perspective. Then, curiously, the film presents portraits of two individuals—Luciana Nassim and Adriano Apra—who state their position almost as if they are embodiments of Fortini's analysis, the appreciative audience of the *L'Espresso* article. To relatives, Jews who cannot understand his criticism of Israel, to those whose poster manifesto celebrated the "values of civilization performed by the Israelis" and who accused him of having sold his soul to the Italian Communist Party (PCI), Fortini responds with another citation of an external text, which he in turn subjects to his own critical view. The response is delayed until shot 25, consisting of an insert of an article by Bernard Levin in the *Daily Mail,* bearing the headline, "This dangerous talk of Jews shirking their duty." Citing both Sartre and Marx, Fortini tries to analyze anti-Semitism in terms of class interests and then apply the same principle of class analysis to the anti-Arab sentiment. Fortini establishes his position in opposition to Levin, even though the two are superficially similar—Jews who have refused to support Israel; Fortini, unlike Levin, expresses no personal indignation at "false accusations," as he acknowledges that he has betrayed the class interests of his accusers.

The understanding of how important this critique of the discourse of the press is to the film is underlined by Fortini's statement at the beginning of shot 40, an extreme close-up of text from *L'Unità,* the PCI daily.

> It has to happen in spite of everything that *L'Unità*, in the midst of its clumsy stupidities, and in spite of its constant defense of a politics of coexistence, of Nasser and his generals, of Paul VI and his encyclicals, nevertheless, after a few days, printed something that was more true, and more just—also because more desperate than all the rest of the Italian press.

This is followed by a lengthy scanning of the entire article, allowing the film's viewer to read the text in full. The slow, downward scanning is interrupted only by a horizontal movement across a graph depicting the relative population of Jews and Arabs in Palestine from 1919 to 1961. Fortini insists, the film insists, this text, this historical analysis, this commentary is to be read, to be comprehended, it is both image and voice, it demands full attention. This strikes me as one of the most extreme examples in the history of cinema of the foregrounding of the written/spoken text. The argument in *L'Unità* closely echoes and expands Fortini's own analysis of the "political and military affairs of Israel and the Arab countries," read in shots 33–35 (the punctuated medium shot of Fortini discussed earlier). One must hold the details of the arguments together across their dispersion in the film; for example, how to assimulate the information on the population chart given in the *L'Unità* argument with Fortini's insistence on a figure of historical memory:

> Until the June war had been fought and won, to outsiders it would remain unclear to just what degree Israeli political leadership was committed to class policies, to loyalty to the imperialist cause. Unclear, that is, to those who had forgotten the war of 1956 and the violence of the reprisals which killed, on average, four Arabs for every Israeli.

If one remembers, then, over the course of the text, the chart indicates more than geographical displacement of Arab peoples, but a statistical account that includes genocide within its shifting configurations.

This experimentation with the complexity of the essayist mode is perhaps the most innovative and profound contribution Straub and Huillet have made to filmmaking. It continues the research and creativity of France's Jean-Luc Godard and Chris Marker. Even the narrative films, such as *Chronicle*, share this essayist quality through the placing of documents such as eighteenth-century maps and published music within the frame of fictional narration.

Straub and Huillet's film essays begin to operate intertextually; critiques of anti-Semitism and Zionism are articulated in relationship to one another, from film to film. Their earlier attention to Schoenberg's letters (the political consciousness of a musician, the need he had to embrace his Jewishness in the face of political persecution) and their subsequent concern with Fortini's analysis of the Israeli state connect and resound in the work they made between these other films, their film of Schoenberg's opera, *Moses and Aaron*. Positioned between the essays, the spectacle of the opera is also a complex articulation of the relationship between belief and power.

As with many of Straub and Huillet's films, *Moses and Aaron* met with considerable ignorance and contempt among mainstream critics. For instance, one reviewer commented after the New York festival showing: "What I find is an almost total lack of visual reward, a style that is obliterating dull and so much reading of subtitles that you might as well be curled up with a book on Moses and monotheism."[7]

Ironically, this sarcastic reference to Sigmund Freud's *Moses and Monotheism* not only illuminates the antiintellectualism of American journalism but unwittingly brings up a conjunction worthy of our attention. The publication of Freud's essays on Moses in *Imago* in 1937 and the withholding of the third part until the 1939 publication in England during his exile from Vienna curiously parallels the history of Schoenberg's writing of *Moses und Aron*. Schoenberg began the opera in Vienna in 1928 and completed it in 1932, leaving the third act unfinished, without a musical score. He then left Vienna for the United States.[8]

This parallel is perhaps more than an uncanny coincidence. Freud and Schoenberg were both intellectuals of Jewish birth who worked in early twentieth-century Viennese culture, having renounced their religious ties to Judaism. In both instances, they were confronted by the anti-Semitism of colleagues and a society that resisted the threatening innovations of their work. (This link is addressed in two recent cultural histories of Vienna: Janik and Toulmin's *Wittgenstein's Vienna* and Carl Schorske's *Fin-de-Siècle Vienna*.[9]) In addition, as the footnotes to *Moses and Monotheism* alone indicate, the preoccupation with Moses, ancient history, religion, and mythology was part of a much larger scholarly debate on the founding patriarch of Judaism in Jewish/Germanic culture at that time.[10]

The letters cited in *Introduction*, discussed earlier, also give us a sense of the social atmosphere. Schoenberg's willingness to identify himself as a Jew was a political act undertaken despite his conversion to Protestantism. It appears from his letters that Judaic religious principles became increasingly important to him. He wrote Alban Berg in 1933:

As you may surely have noticed, my return to the Jewish faith occurred long ago, and is discernible even in the published sections of my work ("Thou shalt not, thou must" as well as in *Moses and Aaron*, of which you have known since 1928, but which goes back for at least another five years; it is particularly noticeable in my drama *The Biblical Way*, which was conceived in 1922 or 1923, but not finished until 1926–27).[11]

Freud's investigations into Judaic heritage remained a critical analysis of psychoanalytical mechanisms operative in the formation and therefore the deciphering of mythologies, but Schoenberg's commitment to Old Testament stories and Jewish liturgy was a statement of his religious conviction. For Straub and Huillet, Schoenberg's religious convictions are problematic, considering their own critical position; the solution was to look upon the film project as a reframing, analyzing religion from a philosophical view that is much closer to Freud's than to Schoenberg's.[12]

Moses und Aaron was never performed in full in Schoenberg's lifetime. It was first staged in Zurich in 1957, then in Berlin in 1959. Both stagings borrowed from German expressionist style, the visual style that marked Schoenberg's own paintings as well as the portraits of him done by Oskar Kokoschka in 1924 and Man Ray in 1927. The Zurich production had elaborate "Caligari" sets, including ramps painted in swirling high-contrast abstractions.[13] The Berlin sets ranged from constructivist platforms of angular geometrics, abstract mobiles, and shaped spotlighting, to the expressionistically shadowed body leotards of the "Dance Around the Golden Calf." These stagings are not only logical choices from an art-historical point of view but emphasize the romantic, expressionistic qualities of Schoenberg's music—its emotive properties, rather than its compositional complexities and theoretical significance.

But Straub and Huillet's decision to make the film of *Moses und Aaron* was a reaction to the Berlin performance of 1959, their first exposure to the opera. Straub has said of the Berlin version, "What I saw was very 'stage' abstract; misunderstood abstraction. What was there immediately was: under open sky, contrary to what I had seen."[14] In reworking the opera in their conceptual filmic mode, the filmmakers attempted to displace the opera's religious, spiritual overtones, its latent expressionism and Romanticism, edging toward a more theoretical and dialectical rendering of Schoenberg's music and its social references.

The first step was to fulfill the desire to move the performance outdoors, to the Alba Fucense amphitheater for the first two acts and to Lake of Matese for the brief third act—sites Straub and Huillet found on a trip made for this purpose through Southern Italy.[15] To concentrate all the action of the first two acts in the abstract space of the amphitheater is not to turn filmed opera into the stylized realism of Joseph Losey's *Don Giovanni*. Losey fell into the trap of having his singers sauntering through landscapes as they sang, fundamentally violating opera's necessity for a still space that allows the voice to perform. Straub and Huillet instead chose to keep their singers stationary within an oval space of ancient theatrics and to introduce the visual kinetics entirely through camera movement.

The mise-en-scène and camera work not only clarify the action and contrasts inherent in the opera but undercut and criticize certain aspects of the Moses myth. As the opera presents the myth, Moses is the strict interpreter of monotheism as a belief in the idea without tangible images as manifestations. The part is entirely *Sprechstimme*, the form of vocalization Schoenberg developed, which consists of intonations rather than designated musical notes. Aaron is the practical interpreter of Moses, translating his ideas into song, constructing metaphors for power and faith. It is a rich tenor part, contrasting and sometimes overlapping with Moses' speech. Moses and Aaron, Rabbi and Cantor, Discourse and Figure, Intellect and Emotion, Logos and Instinct, Spiritual and Sensual, the opposing forces are at first combined in a dual leadership. Aaron serves Moses by being his voice, providing the link to the people who find the ideas of Moses too intangible. This element is derived from the Biblical text, which says that Moses has a "speech impediment," a point that Freud discusses extensively for its symbolic content within the myth.[16]

Inherent in Schoenberg's text is a fascinating debate on the basic question of semiotics: how do ideas get expressed in language and represented in images? How do certain metaphors serve ideas and others misrepresent them? Is metaphorization or imaging always a debased form of the concept?

Straub and Huillet approach Schoenberg's opera with a filmmaking practice that critiques Aaron's method of turning

Shot no:

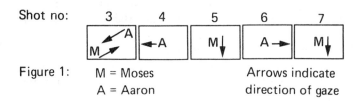

Figure 1:   M = Moses   Arrows indicate
             A = Aaron   direction of gaze

Diagram of Act I, Scene 2

ideas into expressive images. Their strategy is to reduce the expressive to the minimal traits of indication, to treat the filmic image as a conceptual function. The opera's flamboyant images are reduced to sparse representations, in which camera movement and character position in space (spatial and kinetic signifiers) are more important than represented "objects." The space between, the relation, the movement that connects or contrasts, are what signifies within their system—that is, always in relation to the voice, which dominates signification.

In the first scene of Act I, they make a major change in the mise-en-scène of the opera by omitting the burning bush. Moses, alone in the image, has a dialogue with the voice of the chorus, the people, who are never represented on screen in this scene. The entire scene is done in a single shot, with the camera leaving Moses about midway through the scene to begin an extensive pan up to the left at a diagonal, across the empty arena, along the steps, the hillside, craning left across the top of the hill, to the sky. The fluidity of motion through space, an emblem of a quest, a mission, a struggle, is given without the certainty of a god figure in representation, even metaphorically.

The second scene is composed entirely of a dialogue between Moses and Aaron as they meet in the desert. The film portrays this scene in a space of abstraction derived from the arena interior, beginning with a shot that places them on opposite ends of a diagonal with Moses in the lower left, Aaron in the upper right. Like the discussions on the benches in *History Lessons*, this scene is a carefully wrought variation of camera angles. Martin Walsh points out that the first shot of this sequence is the only time in the film that Moses and Aaron are seen facing each other, and that the shots that follow break with continuity editing expectations, given the strong 180° editing line established by that shot.[17] The sequence sets up a pattern of antagonism; Moses is fixed in a frontal view, Aaron can shift, impossibly, to seem to surround him. Moses is the law, Aaron is clever, as Aaron will sing later. This accords with Karl Wörner's analysis of the musical part of Aaron.[18]

> There are many moments in the score—when Aaron weaves into his song the themes and symbols that belong to God, and his mandate to Moses, and are thus part of Moses' world; this happens whenever Aaron, unwittingly rather than deliberately, receives some intimation—grasps the shadow—of this world. But his proper realm is that of the image, of eternal change. And thus, both his song and his musical characterization by the orchestra are subject to perpetual change.

Aaron questions Moses, asking how the people can be politicially united (freed from Pharaoh's harsh bondage) considering Moses' insistence that this unity be formulated on the complex philosophical concept of power that eludes representation. At the end of the act he yields to Moses' concept, but in the scenes that follow it is clear that Aaron can function only within representation, images, metaphors.

The last two scenes of the first act most stringently use the space of the arena as an indicator of the lines of force in the power struggle, the play of ideas and affinities. A diagram in the Woods/Huillet production notes[19] indicates that the chorus is grouped on the far side of an ellipse, with the priest on one side and the man, young man, and maiden (the only solo parts besides Moses and Aaron) on the other. The camera movements take advantage of this semicircular arrangement in scene 3 to sweep the space between the figures in arcing pans that follow the course of the sung dialogue preceding Moses and Aaron's arrival in scene 4. Their arrival is anticipated by the chorus, whose sung lines serve to underscore the value of Straub and Huillet's spatially signifying mise-en-scène.

> See Moses and Aaron!
> Moses's powerful head!
> Moses, his rod in his hand,

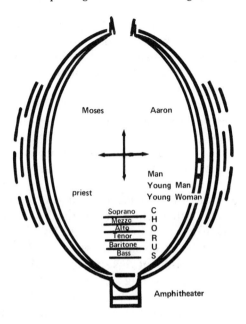

Diagram of Act I, Scenes 3 and 4

moving slowly, reflective,
seems to stand still,
now moves somewhat.

Does he wait? Is he moving?
Moses waits!
No, he's walking slowly!
He waits! No, he moves! . . .

Aaron, a young man no more,
moves along with a light step far before him,
and yet stands close to him!
Is Aaron close to Moses?
no, he goes before!
Is Aaron at Moses' side now?
front or in back of him?
They are moving, but not in space.
Are nearer, are farther, are deeper,
are higher—have vanished wholly!

Scene 4 is a virtual cinematic analogue for the chorus's description. The quizzical attempts at interpreting proxemics and ges-

tures are paralleled by shot compositions that emphatically re-
state the space of confrontation with movements and angles that
turn static positions into shifting views and relations. Moses and
Aaron are separated from the chorus by the full length of the
amphitheater; the chorus is arranged in six rows (a change from
the customary four used on the stage) so that their rectangular
formation either fills the frame, or, when they are seen from a
canted high angle, floats as a parallelogram diagonally within it.
The questions of leadership, communication, and antagonism
are visually rendered. Particularly spectacular in this regard is
shot 13, which frames Moses in the left foreground, with Aaron
on a diagonal in the upper right, then subjects this to a pivoting
camera movement to the right, which turns the shot into a frontal view of the two, only to swing back to the left, returning to the
original framing, before the shot closes with a swish pan to the
chorus. The choreography of this shot marks Moses and Aaron
at their most united, attempting a combined effort at answering
the chorus's persistent questioning of their god. The punctuation at the end of the shot enforces the resistance of the people,
as the men of the chorus sing, "Then we must be forsaken, since
we see him not!"

It becomes necessary for Aaron to provide metaphors to reach
the people. Here Straub and Huillet reduce the flamboyant images to sparse representations, as in the transformation of rod
into snake, which Aaron uses to establish Moses' (and God's)
phallic power:

> Moses is shown on the left of the image, in medium shot, his head
> lowered. He looks up and says, "My idea is impotent as Aaron said."
> As he finishes the line the camera pulls back to show Aaron, who
> reaches over to grab Moses' staff, as the chorus, voice off, asks,
> "Aaron, what are you doing?"
>
> There is a cut to a new angle on Aaron with the staff, composed as
> a diagonal, lower left to upper right, as he throws down the staff.
>
> Cut to a high angle on a small snake, slithering on the ground, as
> the chorus (off) expresses fear, musically, in elaborately repetitive
> phrases. Aaron sings in voice-over of the meaning of the symbolism,
> not as regards the people, but as ironic commentary on the Moses-
> Aaron power struggle: "The rigid staff of Moses is the law, the ser-
> pent of Aaron is cleverness."
>
> Then a final shot shows Moses large, in left foreground; Aaron,
> smaller, more distant to the right, in a diagonal composition, against

the background of the hill beyond the stadium. Aaron hands the staff back to Moses.

These four shots are edited without matches on action, avoiding possible cinematic tricks to present magical transformation. Like primitive American cinema, the action unfolds in its own, straightforward pictographic mode, with a hint of discontinuity due to the absence of any continuity conventions. The snake is also inadequate to the reaction it evokes. Yet this understatement has an elegance, a surprise that emphasizes other elements of the incident. Moses' gesture of lifting his head before making his pronouncement is given as much dramatic focus as Aaron's gestures with the staff, and the simplicity of the snake image allows the voice-over lines of the chorus and Aaron to dominate, rather than having a monstrous snake steal our attention to an iconographic expression.

Similar litotes present the leprous hand of Moses in close-up with the chorus's reaction as voice-over. The third shot in the hand series begins on the chorus confined to its distant grouping on the other side of the arena, until a swish pan arcs across the distance to Moses, on the other side of the arena, whose cured hand is now held up by Aaron. This is immediately followed by a shot that mirrors this camera movement in reverse, by starting on Aaron and moving back to the chorus. Here the double, mirror pans are used as relational indices, allowing the space between the people and the brothers, Moses and Aaron, to speak to the issue of performance and leadership. The combination of concept and expressive image seals the gap; the people will continue to struggle, united under their leaders.

This first act is by far the most successful in the film. The second act, which traces the people's disaffection from the concepts of Moses during his absence and Aaron's compensatory solution of offering the people the Golden Calf, receives far less affective enaction. This may be due to Straub and Huillet's decision to avoid the spectacle of an orgy as a decadent bourgeois cinematic mode.[20] As with the snake and leprous hand, they present the orgy scenes as a series of tableau, indications of sex, drunkenness, and debauchery; unfortunately, with the notable exception of a brilliant shot that shows the sacrifice of the virgins, and one that isolates their blood being poured as a ritual offering, the orgy shots are labored and clumsy. The scene asks for Schoenberg's expressionistic staging, which is precisely what Straub and Huillet need to avoid in order to remain within the conceptual use of cinema.

Does the unevenness here imply an inability to cope with the libidinal, the death instinct, the terrorism of a boundary crossed in which orgy becomes murder? This terrain can only be explored by a kind of voyeuristic cinema of affective participation antithetical to Straub and Huillet's tenets of conceptual reduction and distancing. Their orgy becomes a curious sign of the limitations of their approach to cinema, which is not to condemn the film. It ends tersely, presenting Schoenberg's unfinished act of punishment as a simple coda. A theoretical transformation worthy of note is their decision to end on Aaron's release rather than his death. This encourages an interpretation of the film, which, in Straub's words, is "partly in contradiction to the opera," in that it sides far less with Moses than does Schoenberg. In Straub and Huillet's decentering of the Moses and Aaron mythology, no ultimate truth, no God-given law reigns supreme. If the libretto remains unchanged, if Schoenberg's words are presented in his music just as he intended, the film uses its own modernist imaging system to interfere with the position Schoenberg held, opening history and cultural mythologies to new interpretations.

Straub and Huillet are theoretical, elliptical, innovative, and challenging. They move Brechtian distancing out beyond its interference with popular spectacle, working instead with texts that are not readily accessible to audiences whose attention to and expectation of literature, music, and film is conditioned by limited exposure and experience. Those who are familiar with Bach and Schoenberg and remember college lectures on Corneille are directly addressed by this film. A critique of the intelligentsia in its own terms, Straub and Huillet's approach is also an artistic practice in which structural experimentation and the ideas formed by this reconstruction form an oblique angle on the vitality of cinematic possibility.

NOTES

[1]Danièle Huillet, "Notes on Gregory's Work Journal of the Filming of *Moses and Aaron*," *Enthusiasm*, no. 1 (December 1975).

[2]See Maureen Turim, "The Textual System of *Au Hasard Balthazar*," Master's thesis, University of Wisconsin–Madison, 1975, for a detailed discussion of Bresson's analytical camera work and editing in bench conversation scenes. This is related to the notion of nonsutured filmic discourse presented by Jean-Pierre Oudart in his article "La Suture," *Cahiers du Cinema*, April 1969, pp. 36–39.

[3]Martin Walsh, "Brecht and Straub/Huillet: The Frontiers of Language," *Afterimage*, Summer 1978, pp. 12–32.

[4]See Walsh, "Brecht and Straub/Huillet," p. 19; and Gilberto Perez, "Modernist Cinema: The History Lessons of Straub and Huillet," *Artforum* 17 (October 1978): 46–55.

[5]A more detailed discussion of the function of the directional sound (as well as other aspects of *Chronicle*) can be found in Maureen Turim, *"Ecriture Blanche*: The Ordering of the Filmic Text in *The Chronicle of Anna-Magdalena Bach*," *Purdue Film Studies Annual*, 1976, pp. 177–192. The directional sound recording was linked to the camera movements (mike behind camera, following its diagonal tracks in and out) to emphasize this spatial dimension to the work. Many viewers object to the quality of the sound, especially on the 16mm prints, but it can be argued that the method of Straub and Huillet is an effort to insert the presence of their filmmaking system into the sound track for ideological reasons, which include a departure from stereophonic fidelity (impossible with optical sound in any case).

[6]Melanie Magisos, "Not Reconciled: The Destruction of Narrative Pleasure," *Wide Angle* 3 (1980): 35: "It is nearly impossible to grasp the narrative without knowledge of the plot obtained from the novel on which *Not Reconciled* was based. . . . At times it is even a struggle to identify the main characters."

[7]New York Post, 9 October 1975.

[8]Freud's essays were republished with the addition of a third part as the book *Moses and Monotheism*, translated by Katherine Jones (New York: Knopf, 1939 and 1967). The history of the writing of *Moses und Aaron* is presented in H. H. Stuckenschmidt, *Arnold Schoenberg* (London: John Calder, 1959), pp. 107, 145–152.

[9]Allan Janik and Stephen Toulmin, *Wittgenstein's Vienna* (New York: Touchstone, 1973); Carl E. Schorske, *Fin-de-Siècle Vienna* (New York: Knopf, 1980).

[10]The historical-thematic connection between Freud and Schoenberg is explored in theoretical terms by Jean-François Lyotard in his essay "Plusieurs Silences" in *Des dispositifs pulsionnels* (Paris: 10/18, 1973), pp. 281–303. Lyotard asserts, "Schoenberg was the Luther of new music, serialism its reformed church, as Freud was the Luther of the unconscious, as Deleuze and Guattari have said" (p. 296), meaning that Schoenberg and Freud represented a parallel critical practice within their respective realms of music, science, and therapy.

[11]Ervin Stein, ed., *Arnold Schoenberg's Letters* (New York: St. Martin's Press, 1965), p. 184.

[12]Interview, *Jumpcut*, December 1976, pp. 61–62.

[13]See photos of Zurich staging in Stuckenschmidt, *Schoenberg*, opposite p. 96.

[14]Interview, *Enthusiasm*, December 1975, p. 23.

[15] Interview, *Enthusiasm*; interview, *Jumpcut*.

[16] Freud, *Moses and Monotheism*, pp. 37–38.

[17] Martin Walsh, "Moses and Aaron, Straub and Huillet's Schoenberg," *Jumpcut*, December 1976.

[18] Karl Wörner, *Schoenberg's Moses and Aaron*, translated by Paul Hanesurger (New York: St. Martin's Press, 1963), p. 83.

[19] Huillet, *Enthusiasm*.

[20] Interview, *Enthusiasm*, p. 24. Straub said, "In Vienna [a presentation of the opera] you couldn't understand anything, neither the score nor the libretto, complete confusion. . . . I sat there and suddenly couldn't even hear the notes, besides it looked like Pigalle 1900," to which the interviewer, Andi Engel, added, "There was the production in Hamburg, which turned into an orgy. The bourgeois were delighted."

HANS-JÜRGEN SYBERBERG

Of Fantastic and Magical Worlds

by *Russell A. Berman*

HANS-JÜRGEN SYBERBERG WAS BORN on December 8, 1935, in Nossendorf in Pomerania, a region he would later characterize as the homeland of both the romantic painter Caspar David Friedrich and the iron chancellor of German unification, Otto von Bismarck. This vision of a historically rich landscape in which cultural tradition converges with the politics of German identity provides an important key to Syberberg's cinematic work.

Having spent his boyhood in a classically conservative atmosphere and his adolescence in the East Germany of the Stalinist era, he missed the flood of postwar American influence after 1945 and grew up "without chewing gum and pinball machines." Instead he was introduced to the established canon of great works and to the ideology of the victors from the East.

> My first impressions were really Faust and Brecht, unforgettable, while others [in West Germany] proceded along very different paths. . . . While many [in the West] listened to their ministers playing jazz, we heard Beethoven and Bach, *Carmen* too, and read "Diamat," dialetical-historical materialism. . . . Thus an art education . . . until 1953 with the high cultural heritage and socialist realism of Soviet origin in the East German culture colony, [led] to a spiteful rejection of the new so-called progress that came from Moscow.[1]

This background undoubtedly explains many of the features that distinguish Syberberg from other new German filmmakers: the constant references to a wealthy cultural tradition, particularly of the nineteenth century; his "whole German" (*gesamtdeutsch*) perspective not fixated on specifically West German issues; and finally his immunity, or better, antagonism toward Hollywood and the cinematic traditions that have proved so attractive to several of his colleagues.

Syberberg spent his early years in the countryside, but in 1947 his family moved to Rostock, and his new urban surroundings offered opportunities for regular contacts with theater, music, and film (largely Soviet works). In this period Syberberg began his own work with film, including 8mm versions of Chekhov stories as well as documentaries of demonstrations and sports events. In Rostock he met Benno Besson of the Berliner Ensemble, and this led to an invitation from Bertolt Brecht to come to Berlin. There Syberberg was permitted to film Brecht's rehearsals of *Mother Courage, The Mother, Puntila,* and Goethe's *Urfaust*; this 1953 footage was later worked into his 1971 documentary *Nach meinem letzten Umzug . . . (After My Last Removal. . . .)*

While Brechtian aesthetics profoundly influenced Syberberg, he was equally fascinated by the French films he could now see for the first time in West Berlin, such as *Orphée, Les enfants du paradis*, and *La Belle et la Bête*. In 1953 he left East Germany and, after completing school in Minden, traveled to France, England, Austria, and Italy; finally he settled in Munich in 1956, where he entered the university to study literature and art. He describes the environment as a "hell of artistic inactivity,"[2] and when he completed his studies in 1962 with a thesis on elements of the theater of the absurd in the plays of the Swiss dramatist Friedrich Dürrenmatt, he took work in Bavarian television, since no jobs were then available in the German film industry itself.

During the following three years, he turned out cultural reports on the Munich scene, topical films for holiday seasons, and films of regional interest. The 185 films of this period varied in length from three to thirty minutes. These were years of apprenticeship, and he recalls making every effort to maintain control of all aspects of production—the shooting, the cutting, and the sound—and here one may discern roots of his mature oeuvre: the technical mastery of the medium, the interest in

Hans-Jürgen Syberberg (COURTESY OF THE FILMMAKER)

Young Syberberg (COURTESY OF THE FILMMAKER)

cultural documentation, and above all the familiarity with the established culture industry that would later become the target of his bitterly radical criticism.

In 1965, still working for Bavarian television, Syberberg undertook his first major project, the documentary *Fünfter Akt, siebte Szene: Fritz Kortner probt Kabale und Liebe (Fritz Kortner Rehearses Schiller's Intrigue and Love)*. As in the case of the Brecht film, Syberberg directed his attention to a grand old man of the theater at work in the realization of classical drama: the climactic death scene of Ferdinand and Luise. No outside financing was available, and the crew was reduced to a bare minimum. Its task consisted of following Kortner on stage continuously in order to capture the development of the scene in the course of the rehearsals. Even in this early film, the unique character of Syberberg's documentary work is apparent. Unlike the normal German television documentaries, with their voice-over narrations and the emphasis on behind-the-scenes sensations, the Kortner film rigorously observes the artist at work without extraneous commentary or tendentious montage.

A short sequel to the Kortner film, *Kortner spricht Monologe für eine Schallplatte (Kortner Speaks Monologues for a Record*, 1966), depicts the actor in some of his most impressive roles, including Richard III and Shylock. Meanwhile Syberberg was working on a documentary on the actress Romy Schneider that had been commissioned for German television. Although he initially intended to show her at a critical stage in her career, wavering between Germany and France, he was hindered by the demands of Schneider's manager, who was anxious to present a purely wholesome image to the German public. Legal suits followed, and Syberberg eventually withdrew his name from the film. This conflict represents one step in a series of confrontations with a culture industry motivated, according to Syberberg, only by profits and hostile to any aesthetic sensitivity.

Syberberg continued his documentaries of cultural figures in 1967 with *Die Grafen Pocci (The Counts Pocci)*. The Pocci family joined the Bavarian court in the late eighteenth century, and its most renowned member, Franz Pocci (1807–1876), a master of ceremonies and court jester for Ludwig I, created the famous figure of Kasperl for the Munich puppet stage. Syberberg's film traces the history of the Pocci and their traditions by exploring the family estate, Castle Ammerland, while profiling the sixty-three-year-old Count Konrad. The thematic complexity, the division into a series of chapters, and the use of montage and collage anticipate formal features of Syberberg's later work. Similarly the fundamental motif of the film—the wealth of a heritage in danger of extinction—would soon find an echo in the major projects. In the final sequence, Konrad Pocci, seated at a hunting post in the forest, insists that he would never sell his land, since money could never replace the happiness provided by the nature he so deeply loves. This romantic anticapitalism, a central theme in Syberberg's works, is coupled with a search for the multidimensionality of a mystic vision.

> These sentences of Pocci, taken seriously, would mean a revolution. A revolution of our activity, our thinking and spirit: no longer buying and selling everything . . . no longer modernizing as far as possible, cutting down trees, widening streets, covering kilometers with asphalt . . . for once tolerating secrets in pictures and sound and riddles . . . with respect for ancient myths, wisdom, and warnings.[3]

Syberberg's notion of an alternative to the world of banal modernization—the beach beneath the concrete of the metropolis—was nourished by the countercultural currents that would soon overflow in the uprisings of 1968.

Reminiscent of the closing ideas of *The Counts Pocci*, Syberberg's first feature film, entitled *Scarabea—Wieviel Erde braucht der Mensch?* (*Scarabea—How Much Earth Does a Man Need?* 1968), is based on a story by Tolstoy in which the devil tempts a poor peasant to seek ever greater land holdings. He enters into an agreement with nomads of the Asian steppes: for a set sum he may have title to all the land he can stake out on foot before sunset. Greedy as he is, he overexerts himself, and although he returns to the starting point just before dusk, he dies of exhaustion; a simple grave, six feet deep, is all the earth he then needs. Syberberg sets his film in Sardinia, replacing the Russian nomads with highlands bandits and the land-hungry peasant by a German tourist eager to gain possession of the promising coastal property. In the course of the day, however, the German's value system, based on investment and profit, gives way to a yearning for peace and a new life in the sensual constancy of a primitive South. Syberberg has synthesized Tolstoy's fable with a traditional motif of German literature (the parallels to Thomas Mann's *Death in Venice* are obvious), while updating the material in order to criticize contemporary European culture. Less attention is paid to a coherent plot than to a series of images with mythic associations: noonday sun glistening on the water, mysterious caves, a festival replete with folk dancing and bloodletting. On a formal level, this de-emphasis of a suspense-filled plot represents a rejection of the Hollywood cinema still predominant in Germany. In fact, a parody of the prototypical Hollywood genre—the western—is inserted into *Scarabea*; the film itself becomes the battlefield of the opposing forces of civilization and myth.

Syberberg treats cinema with all the seriousness of an aesthetic revolutionary, viewing it as the art form of the modern age, the new *Gesamtkunstwerk*, the "continuation of life by other means." It has the potential of providing the images of dreams and utopias otherwise banished from a thoroughly rationalized everyday life. Yet, he argues, this cinematic potential has rarely been realized because the market pressures and profit motives, which operate throughout society, corrupt all the activities of the film industry. Art is replaced by lucrative endeavors, such as pornography, a problem that Syberberg investigated in his 1969 documentary *Sex-Business Made in Pasing*. As in his earlier films, he records the process of cultural production by following one figure at work, but Brecht and Kortner are now replaced by Alois Brummer, a director of Bavarian pornography films, as "the symbol of the inhumanly mercenary cinema."[4] Syberberg is not interested in the sensationalism of the topic (Brummer makes a rather trivial impression) but in its significance as a major component of the German film market. Consequently, he punctuates the film with interpolated comments and statistics regarding the current state of the industry.

His increasingly profound criticism of commercial cinema (as well as financial losses incurred by *Scarabea*) led him to join other young directors in an effort to avoid the established channels of distribution by establishing direct contacts with theaters. This strategy was intended to foster an autonomous film culture outside of and hostile to the predominant world of porno and kitsch, and Syberberg's first contribution to this organizational advance in the history of the New German Cinema, *San Domingo*

(1970), reflects similar considerations. Based on a novella by Heinrich von Kleist in which a mulatto woman feigns love for a white officer in order to detain him long enough for the black rebels to arrive, the film was originally to be set in the former German colonies in Africa. However, because of financial difficulties and a desire to attract a German audience, Syberberg transposed the story to Munich. A naive and idealistic middle-class youth anxious to run off to Africa hesitates because of his attraction to the abandoned daughter of a black G.I. Meanwhile, her accomplices, a gang of toughs, attempt to extort money from his parents.

The choice of a nonexotic setting parallels other neorealistic aspects of *San Domingo*: all figures, except for the central youth, are lay actors, and they speak a heavy Bavarian dialect. In general the film emphasizes the overwhelming influence of milieu by focusing on drug parties, motorcycle forays, and the connection between juvenile delinquency and radical politics. Syberberg considers the film an early warning against terrorism, and it ends, in fact, with a dramatic Eldridge Cleaver quotation on the danger of ignoring the alienation of contemporary young people.

With *San Domingo*, the initial phase of Syberberg's career drew to a close. Since the Kortner films he had developed a unique documentary style, a set of central thematic concerns, and, most importantly, an increasingly elaborate critical analysis of postwar German cultural life. In 1972 he commenced a series of five films investigating the roots of contemporary cultural problems in the past century of German politics, art, and myth. The three main films are built around key figures in modern German consciousness: King Ludwig II of Bavaria, the popular author Karl May, and Adolf Hitler. While these major works are often treated as a closed trilogy, their production alternated with two other films; the first was devoted to Theodor Hierneis, a cook at Ludwig's court, and the second to Winifred Wagner. Important in themselves, as monologues they provide contrast with the sovereign epic sweep through a philosophical landscape that characterizes the three central films.

Throughout the whole series, Syberberg's examination of tabooed issues has regularly provoked an often acrimonious public debate; his investigative reporting is directed not at sensational political transgressions but at the unsuspected conspiracy of ideas. This is a decidedly intellectual cinema whose rich imagery never overpowers language; illusion remains subordinate to enlightenment. "If film is to live," writes Syberberg, "and not merely as entertainment for a few pleasant hours, then we must work in that open sphere where politics and the search for truth border on one another."[5]

The title *Ludwig—Requiem für einen jungfräulichen König* (*Ludwig—Requiem for a Virgin King*, 1972) is less intended to suggest an atmosphere of mourning than the rigor and complexity of musical form. Syberberg's animosity toward the simple narrative films of the culture industry explains the formal structure of *Ludwig*: a series of nearly thirty Brechtian episodes tied to one another in terms of content but not linked together within a sequential plot. Each is introduced by a title, often with an ironic undertone. The actors are placed within stylized tableaux, the background consisting often of back-projections of scenes from Ludwig's castles. Narrative continuity is further interrupted by casting the same actor in several roles. This technique both prohibits any facile identification with the figures—another part of Syberberg's Brechtian legacy—and establishes connections by means of visual quotations: when Peter Kern appears as Ludwig's hairdresser Hoppe and later as the SA leader Ernst Rohm, Syberberg's thesis of a continuity between Ludwig's vision and aspects of the National Socialist ideology is underscored.

Quotation is essential to Syberberg's overall use of montage, the careful juxtaposition of heterogeneous elements on the levels of spoken text, image (including the rich inconography of each shot), and sound. Ludwig's complex historical relationship to Wagner, for example, is echoed in the sound track: the film begins with the opening of *Rheingold* and closes with *Götterdämmerung*; the frame of the film is marked by the beginning and end of Wagner's *Ring*. Music and idea correspond similarly when Elisabeth of Austria's warning to Ludwig is accompanied by the music of Brangäne's warnings to Isolde. Consequently, Ludwig's attraction to the myth-maker Wagner takes on an ominous coloration in which erotic tones cannot disguise the shadows of impending doom. Thus music functions as a component in a highly structured associative montage, in which it is as important as other compositional elements: props, gesture, text, and settings.

Ludwig describes a series of incidents associated with the Bavarian king in order to suggest that the problems Ludwig perceived—the evils of industrialism, the ambivalence of German unification under Prussian pressure, the erosion of myth in the modern age, and its rebirth in frightening forms—were central to a cultural malaise that would eventually engender fascism. Yet Syberberg argues neither that Hitler fulfilled Ludwig's legacy nor that Ludwig somehow foresaw and rejected the Hitlerian possibility. Rather, Ludwig appears as a helpless visionary, unable to prevent the rapid industrialization of Germany despite his awareness of the cultural crisis it would precipitate. A romantic anticapitalist, he searches desperately for the security of myth—his affinity to Wagner—but ultimately allows the forces of modernization to gain control. Eventually, in the case of Hitler, myth and modernization combine in a paradoxical catastrophe that releases the worst of both as the culmination of Ludwig's hopes and fears.

Theodor Hierneis oder: Wie man ehem. Hofkoch wird (*Ludwig's Cook*, 1972) is based on the memoirs of Theodor Hierneis, who began his culinary career as a cook's helper at Ludwig's court. The film is a long monologue in which the actor Walter Sedlmayer as Hierneis recalls his past and his vision of Ludwig as seen from the kitchen. Hierneis appears as the subject of a (fictional) documentary, but certain methods of distancing have been employed to prevent any placid identification with this pedestrian hero. For example, while the bulk of his speech is in the first person, it begins and ends in the third person. Furthermore, the castle rooms described are often not shown, and the viewer, required to imagine them, is forced to be both Hierneis's interlocutor and his distanced observer.

The English title of the film suggests the comic element inherent in the servant's view of the master, the fantasy of Ludwig's romanticism next to the down-to-earth experience of the cook. Thus Hierneis recounts how his sleeping quarters were located under one of the artificial lakes in the castle and that a bothersome leak forced him to take an umbrella to bed.

The film's German title, however, captures another aspect: *Theodor Hierneis or How One Becomes a Former Royal Cook*. After leaving Bavaria, Hierneis became a successful restaurateur who capitalized on his illustrious past. Tenaciously loyal to his former servitude, he has thoroughly internalized the authoritarian mechanisms of society. As a study of subjugation, the film captures both the cook's fascination with power and his reproduction of hierarchial attitudes. *Ludwig's Cook*, which Syberberg describes as "chamber music," is certainly not as complex as the requiem *Ludwig*, but the central interests of both films converge in the examination of domination in mass society.

Like Ludwig, Syberberg's Karl May stands at the threshold of the twentieth century. Nostalgic about the vanishing world of romanticism, he is also apprehensive about the age being born. In this modern, rational society that has relentlessly eradicated myth, an attraction to the irrational unexpectedly recurs; hence the title *Karl May—Auf der Suche nach dem verlorenen Paradies (Karl May—In Search of Paradise Lost, 1974)*. May is presented as "the last great German mystic in the age of dying legends,"[6] whose immensely popular novels provided utopian images set against the exotic colonial background of 1900. The novelist anticipates the development of film, which is for Syberberg the specifically modern form of fantasy production. This thematic relationship between the popular author and cinema explains the film's brief homage to the French director Georges Méliès, whose works are considered to be the epitome of cinematic imagination.

Similar considerations of cinematic history motivated Syberberg to select a cast composed of German stars of the thirties: Helmut Käutner, Lil Dagover, Kristina Söderbaum, Mady Rahl, and others. The choice of these actors had nothing to do with the Nazi nostalgia of the 1970s; instead, the presence of these actors constituted a visual quotation implying a hidden affinity between May's fantasies and the aura of the film stars. For Syberberg, the erosion of traditional society initiates a "search for paradise lost" that ranges from May's literary visions to images on a movie screen. Appropriately enough, passages from Gustav Mahler's *Resurrection* Symphony dominate the soundtrack of *Karl May*. The central figure is well aware that the attraction to an irrational alternative to the modern order can easily lead to a catastrophe. "Woe, if the wrong man comes," he warns toward the end of the film, and indeed, invited to speak in

Vienna, May attracts the attention of the young Hitler. While Syberberg does not equate the two figures ideologically, he suggests a proximity within "the spiritual panorama of European people at the onset of the proletarian mass age":[7] utopia and its perverter, aesthetic compensation and the aestheticization of politics.

In *Winifred Wagner und die Geschichte des Hauses Wahnfried von 1914–1975* (*The Confessions of Winifred Wagner*, 1975) Syberberg continues his investigation of the interdependence of the Wagnerian tradition and the growth of National Socialism by returning to the documentary form of his earlier films. In 1915 Winifred Williams married Richard Wagner's son Siegfried, and, when he died in 1930, she gained control of the Bayreuth Festivals and remained in power throughout the Nazi period. Her friendship with Hitler began in 1923 before the Munich putsch and lasted until 1945; her continued unrepentant loyalty to him as recorded by Syberberg resulted in strong public controversy, as well as her family's repudiation of the film. The English title's connotation—a confession of guilt—is therefore inappropriate. The absence of any self-criticism or willingness to examine the past characterizes her account, the superficial objectivity of which is captured in the dry but precise original title: *Winifred Wagner and the History of the House of Wahnfried* 1914–1975.

The film is fundamentally a study of Winifred Wagner recounting her past, particularly her relationship to Hitler. In the West German context, her expression of unshaken loyalty to Hitler is a rare exception; however, her unwillingness to examine closely what she euphemistically calls his "dark" side is paradigmatic. This inability to reconsider Hitler or her own role betrays a rigidity hostile to change and intolerant of contradictions. "Basically I'm an insanely loyal person," she remarks. "Once I develop admiration for a person, it remains through thick and thin. Well, I mean, then I simply stand by him [Hitler], not to his errors, but as I say, they just don't affect my relationship to him. I separate the two completely." Were Hitler to appear today, she adds, she would greet him as warmly as ever. Her repeated assertions of this separation of personal and political dimensions and of her own fully unpolitical character rapidly become grotesque; when Syberberg asks about her reaction to the attacks on Jewish artists and the banning of certain works, such as the music of Gustav Mahler, she merely replies that she had never liked Mahler's music and therefore the matter did not bother her at all.

The motif of loyalty, stability, and steadfastness, which she consciously invokes, is part of the Wagnerian ideological heritage in which the wholesome, the homogeneous, and the pure (including race) constitute the opposite of the mixed, the differentiated, the changing.[8] At the Wagner family's request, Syberberg agreed to an epilogue in which Winifred could allow for errors of memory—but not any critical distancing from the substance of her presentation. Syberberg wrote this disclaimer, which she reads in voice-over narration to a series of still shots. At the end, she rhetorically explains why after thirty years she broke her public silence: "Why not?" Syberberg reports that Winifred was amused by this ultimate gesture and described it as a "Jewish ending";[9] she means that its openness and levity contrast with the remorseless loyalty she upholds.

Winifred represents the opposition to any change on principle, and the film examines the relationship between a frozen vision of the past and the morbid stability of the present. By uncovering this connection, Syberberg attempts to initiate a "work of mourning," the confrontation with the past necessary for a free life in the present. He describes the film as "a matter of breaking a spell with cinematic means."[10] It is a biopsy of a conservative society that still looks askance at former opponents of Hitler and in which Winifred is certainly not alone in her view that Willy Brandt's enlisting in the Norwegian army in order to oppose Nazi aggression was an unforgiveable act of treason.

By means of Winifred's monologue, which contains both fascinating, and trivial information, Syberberg underscores Hannah Arendt's thesis of the "banality of evil," using it as one of the quotations that divide the film into chapterlike sections. Otherwise the film consists only of close-ups and medium shots of Winifred speaking, spurred on occasionally by Syberberg's very broad questions. The slow movement of the camera follows the rhythm of her discourse, betraying a nonpolemical tenderness toward the subject. Syberberg has attempted to let her speak without imposing a tendentious perspective via the usual documentary methods; there is no voice-over narrator who argumentatively explains Winifred's errors, nor has Syberberg introduced extraneous material—footage of Nazi rallies or of concentration camps—as a montage to contradict the text. Only in the final sequence has he included extraneous images, in particular shots of the early years of the National Socialist movement and the Wagner family in 1923. This is no heavy-handed exposé, but a profound analysis, radical because of its sensitivity. The extraordinary length of the original version—five hours—indicates the director's unwillingness to muffle his subject's words. Ultimately Winifred, despite her efforts to de-politicize Hitler's attraction to Bayreuth, confirms Syberberg's thesis: "The Hitler we hate and the Wagner whom we love are linked inextricably to each other, from the beginning and without an end."[11]

After *Ludwig* and *Karl May*, Syberberg's examination of modern German culture and its relationship to political and artistic legacies culminates in the 1977 magnum opus: *Hitler, ein Film aus Deutschland (Our Hitler: A Film from Germany)*. Syberberg again makes no attempt to provide a conventional documentary of historical events with the help of authentic footage and the instructional commentary of a narrator. The film is not concerned with the actual Hitler, the private person, the politician, and the dictator, but with Hitler as a figure of popular fantasy; hence the emphasis on the mass support behind Hitler's legal—and, as Syberberg underscores, democratic—accession to power. Yet even more important is Hitler as a fascinating figure outside Germany and after 1945: Chaplin's Hitler, Hollywood's Hitler, Hitler as the incarnation of evil for the popular mind. This emphasis on Hitler as image, implicit in the title of the work, evokes Syberberg's second theme: film. The many motifs associated specifically with Hitler and National Socialism are intertwined with references to the history of film, including Méliès, Thomas Edison, Sergei Eisenstein, Erich von Stroheim, the expressionists, Leni Riefenstahl, and the Hays Office. These two thematic orientations even converge in the monologues of Fritz Ellerkamp, Hitler's personal projectionist, who describes the latter's addiction to film. Yet the proximity of these two levels is less a matter of Hitler, the film buff, than a consequence of key elements in Syberberg's thought. As suggested in *Karl May*, the rationalized world of modernity suffers from a lack of myth; the fantastic images of cinema might offer a substitute, or the utopian promises of an unscrupulous politician might mobilize the masses. Aesthetics or politics, film or Hitler—Syberberg regards them as twin solutions within the single historical context of the modern industrial world.

Because of its highly political and emotionally charged topic, the film has met with a good deal of opposition from critics who would have preferred a more traditional discussion of the specific background of National Socialism. Instead of describing Hitler as a lackey of heavy industry or a necessary result of German backwardness, the film treats him as a typically modern phenomenon, not unrelated to contemporary developments in Stalin's Soviet Union or in Hollywood's America. (In this Syberberg is surely indebted to the critical theory of Max Horkheimer and Theodor W. Adorno.)

Despite the provocative nature of the film's arguments, one suspects that the fervor of Syberberg's critics stems largely from a hostility toward the film's formal features. Constructed on a scale that dwarfs Riefenstahl and rivals Wagner, the film, more than seven hours long, is divided into four distinctly titled parts, which are themselves in turn divided into a total of twenty-two sequences similar to the chapter units in *Ludwig*; here, however, the chapters are not introduced by titles designed to orient the audience in its reaction to the rich and highly complex material. More importantly, Syberberg's tendency to downplay narrative continuity reaches a climax in *Our Hitler*. The biographical framework inherent in *Ludwig* and *Karl May* has dwindled; historical chronology gives way to the primacy of an intellectual argument carried out in the different layers of cinematic material. The very breadth of that argument, concerning the relationship of Hitler and "the age of the masses," necessitated the development of a form less constraining than a simple story line and closer perhaps to that of the modern novel. Despite humorous as well as profoundly moving passages, *Our Hitler* is a difficult film, not immediately accessible; it demands repeated viewing and reflection.

Syberberg has continued to work with the tableau as a collage of heterogeneous materials suggesting affinities or Brechtian contradictions. Each shot contains five formal positions: the projected background, the foreground (which can contain di-

Heinz Schubert in *Our Hitler* (Courtesy of Export-Union des Deutschen Films)

Syberberg and Amelie Syberberg on the set of *Our Hitler* (Courtesy of Export-Union des Deutschen Films)

verse elements), the music, noise on the sound track, and the spoken text (generally monologues, in keeping with the anti-realist character of the film). For example, at one point an actor portraying the young Goebbels appears in a room of manne-quins, dressed and arranged in order to suggest an elite social gathering of 1923. In the background we see a slide of the Venus grotto from Wagner's *Tannhäuser*; Syberberg intends to refer both to the content of the opera—erotic entrapment in an otherworldly utopia—as well as to his own *Ludwig* film, where the same slide is used during the nightmare sequence. The sound track includes street sounds, machine-gun fire, political songs, a Hitler speech, contemporary popular music, and the spoken text itself, in which the actor recounts the excitement of his initial meeting with Hitler. Syberberg's point here is not that the fundamentally uninteresting person Hitler was irresistibly convincing but that within a specific cultural context the search for leaders who appear charismatic—who can be misperceived as messianic—eclipses traditional values.

As a corollary to this collage structure, Syberberg has relied on a complex system of quotation, ranging from the direct montage of authentic recordings of Nazi speeches or Allied broadcasts to the cinematic parody—as for example when Peter Kern in an SA uniform speaks the final monologue from Fritz Lang's *M*. Similarly, the visual images are often quotations of important paintings, especially those of the German Romantics, and one of the key props is a large black stone modeled after an image in Dürer's *Melancolia I*. Furthermore, the musical sound track is composed of quotations from both popular and serious compo-sitions.

The development of the sound track is fundamental to the structure of the work. On one level, the montage of radio broad-casts generally proceeds chronologically, from the recordings of the early Nazi movement in the first part of the film to the Allied announcements of victory at the end. This provides a weak but consistent time line, homologous to the biographical approaches in the earlier films, around which the central themes can be organized. More significantly, Syberberg uses excerpts from Haydn, Mozart, Beethoven, Wagner, and Mahler in a com-plicated fashion: not as background mood but as a precise cita-tion within the associative complex of each tableau.

A brief description of this musical system can illustrate the key developmental lines of the film. Here, as in *Ludwig,* Syberberg has consciously employed a musical model by creating four semi-independent symphonic movements, each centered on different problems. The first part, with its emphasis on the rise of National Socialism, returns repeatedly to excerpts from *Rienzi,* Wagner's opera of the populist revolutionary. Syberberg underscores his point by juxtaposing *Rienzi* with the Horst Wessel song and, later, with radio braodcasts of the book burnings in Berlin. The second part turns to the problem of utopian elements in the National Socialist vision; the key musical citations include *Parsifal* and, above all, the resurrection passage of Mahler's Second Symphony, suggesting associations familiar from *Karl May.* As the radio reports shift to the military developments of 1944–45, *Götterdämmerung* is quoted in the third part. Finally, in the initial passages of the fourth section, only brief references to *Rienzi* and Haydn's "Kaiserquartett" (with its nationalist connotation) are heard; otherwise, the realm of high culture seems to disappear from the sound track, because, as Syberberg complains, business has replaced art in the modern world. Only at the very end, analogous to his notion of the ultimate goal of authentic art, does the promise of resurrection again resound: Mahler's resurrection, *Parsifal,* Tristan's plea for salvation—"O sink hiernieder, Nacht der Liebe"—and the chorus from Beethoven's Ninth Symphony.

This musical system demonstrates that the thematic centers of the film include resurrection, revolt, and defeat. Syberberg presents a theology of the modern world in which the gods have disappeared but not the yearning for paradise. Banished from the heavens, Lucifer, as in Dürer's engraving, may brood and plot, but he is condemned to stare off in the wrong direction. Syberberg's Hitler similarly takes on the guise of the devil, who is desirous of divine status and promises utopia while in fact fanning the fires of hell. In the context of this basic parable, many elements of the film take on particular significance: the brief, almost parenthetical, reference to Thomas Mann's *Doktor Faustus* (from which Syberberg has borrowed a good deal); the Weberian call for charismatic leadership in the second section of the film; and the biblical allusion to faith moving mountains in a 1943 Goebbels speech heard at the beginning of each of the last three parts. Finally, the interplay between musical system and spoken text suggests the ultimate failure of Hitler's heaven-storming dreams. The cosmic motifs (reminiscent of Stanley Kubrick's 2001) that open the film and reappear at the end of each of the main sections are regularly accompanied by excerpts from Mozart's Piano Concerto in D minor, but within the code system set up by the film Mozart assumes a particular meaning. In one of the most memorable sequences of the film, Hitler, clad in a Roman toga, rises from the grave of Richard Wagner, and reports from the afterworld that Mozart was the one spirit who refused to respect him. Thus Mozart, whose music fills the divine spheres, is set in contrast to Hitler, the fallen angel, who may promise utopia to the godless masses of modernity but for whom paradise remains forever unattainable.

As controversial as the film's examination of Hitler's popularity is the theme of the legacy of National Socialism. One is reminded of the proposition in Jorge Luis Borges's "Deutsches Requiem" that the defeat of Germany constituted, paradoxically enough, a necessary condition for a further spread of National Socialist ideas. Thus, in the important "dialogue which is really a monologue" between Hans Baer and the puppet of Hitler, we hear the latter laud the postwar world: "Praise from Adolf Hitler to the world after me. What is the short span of my human life compared with the eternity of my subsequent victory? Can I not be satisfied with immortality?" He then proceeds to recount those developments of which he approves—the thoroughly changed map of Europe under American hegemony, Stalinist terror and the persecution of dissidents in the East, the anti-Zionist resolution of the United Nations and the success of Idi Amin, torture in South America, the Berlin Wall, and West German terrorists. All this pleases him and compensates for his own posthumous unpopularity. If the list seems cantankerously eccentric, Syberberg has provided in an earlier section two visions of the "Hell around us" in which the cultural life in each of the two German states is attacked in specific terms as a perpetuation of the fascist catastrophe.

In general, Syberberg's understanding of Hitler's legacy focuses on the fundamental discrediting of idealism. By placing his mark on utopia, Hitler rendered it unpalatable. As André Heller complains in one of the final sequences: "You have taken away the sunsets, sunsets of Caspar David Friedrich. You are guilty that we can no longer see wheat fields without thinking of you. You have trivialized Old Germany with your simplistic pictures of workers and peasants." He has destroyed the legitimacy of any dignified life, and left only the pursuit of money as a possibility. Here, as elsewhere, Syberberg denounces the postwar world as the locus of unfettered capitalism: Hitler's most devastating bequest. Interestingly, this interpretation of postwar Germany is not extraneous to the West German Left's thesis about the continuity of class society. However, whereas the Left emphasizes problems such as ownership of capital, Syberberg suggests a broader notion of capitalist culture: its hostility toward an authentic culture.

A high point of the film occurs in the fourth part when the mayor of Berchtesgaden and the director of tourism gleefully calculate the potential success of a German Disneyland at the site of Hitler's alpine home, replete with personal memorabilia, sensational facsimiles, and even stuffed models of Hitler's dogs. With the energy of vaudeville performers and a mercenary spirit worthy of figures from Ibsen, the two put forth their plan: "Business is the freedom of the democrat. And democracy is only possible with economic growth. Hitler is clearly the international top product, with real cash possibilities. . . . Nothing esoteric. Culture is extinguished. We want real popular taste." Despite complaints that the film lacks a critical perspective, in this scene Syberberg has masterfully described an affinity between capitalism and fascism with a keen, satirical hand: commercialized culture as the legacy of Hitler and, perhaps, the condition of his rebirth.

Syberberg's linking of the venal materialism of modern culture to Hitler's unbroken influence echoes an important dissident note in postwar West German culture—for example, Günter Grass's early complaints that his compatriots had abandoned their ideals in exchange for the consumerist pleasures of the *Wirtschaftswunder.* The source of this critique, however, was the controversial book of Alexander and Margarethe Mitscherlich, *The Inability to Mourn,* which argued that postwar consumerism represented a sublimation of the collective trauma of 1945; frenetic economic activity allegedly provided an alternative to a therapeutic confrontation with the past.[12] The Mitscherlichs, key figures in the establishment of West German psychoanalysis, used the term "mourning" in its full Freudian significance as a productive process of overcoming emotional loss. Freud labeled its alternative "melancholy," implying a pathological fixation on the loss and an inability to come to terms with reality.[13]

This background allows one to understand Syberberg's cinematic goal all the better. The "work of mourning," which he invoked at the close of *Winifred Wagner,* still inspires *Our Hitler,* and therefore the emblems of melancolia in the film represent precise symptoms of the postwar ailment. Through film Syberberg hopes to heal; hence his antipathy toward an entertainment industry that destroys cinema's curative powers. Film, he insists, must be serious art in the grand tradition, and it is obligated to examine those traditions that have led to catastrophe. At its best, it can unveil utopian forms in an otherwise melancholy world, where dreams have given way to pedestrian routine: film as the reappropriation of eroded ideals, a tentative projection of paradise regained.

NOTES

[1] Hans-Jürgen Syberberg, *Syberbergs Filmbuch* (Munich: Nymphenburger Verlagsbuchhandlung, 1976), p. 307.

[2] Ibid., p. 111.

[3] Ibid., p. 310.

[4] Ibid., p. 79.

[5] Ibid., p. 109.

[6] Ibid., p. 39.

[7] Ibid., p. 46.

[8] Cf. Richard Wagner, "Was ist deutsch?" in *Gesammelte Schriften und Dichtungen,* vol. 10 (Leipzig: E. W. Fritzsch, 1898), 36–53.

[9] Syberberg, *Filmbuch,* p. 285.

[10] Ibid., p. 293.

[11] Ibid., p. 263.

[12] Alexander and Margarete Mitscherlich, *Die Unfähigkeit zu trauern: Grundlagen kollektiven Verhaltens* (Munich: Piper, 1968). The American edition is *The Inability to Mourn: Principles of Collective Behavior* (New York: Grove Press, 1975).

[13] Sigmund Freud, "Mourning and Melancholia," in *A General Selection from the Works of Sigmund Freud,* edited by John Richman (New York: Liveright, 1957), pp. 36–53. Cf. Susan Sontag, "Eye of the Storm," *New York Review of Books,* 21 February, 1980, p. 40.

WIM WENDERS

Wenders in the Cities

by Kathe Geist

WILHELM ERNST WENDERS WAS BORN IN
Düsseldorf, on August 14, 1945, only days after the Japanese
surrender heralded the end of World War II, the beginning of
the nuclear age, and, with these, the dominance of the United
States in world affairs. Germany had surrendered three months
earlier, and America's presence and influence were to loom large
in Wenders's consciousness and profoundly affect his films.

The son of a doctor, Wenders grew up in the Ruhr town of
Oberhausen and was introduced to films early when his father,
Heinrich Wenders, bought him a handcranked projector, some
prints of old Chaplin and Keaton comedies, and, eventually, an
8mm movie camera. Though the elder Wenders had once
owned a sizable collection of American silent comedies, he
thought of movies as nothing but a hobby and was decidedly
unsympathetic to the westerns and *film noir* adventures with
stars like Alan Ladd and Robert Mitchum that were coming out
of postwar America. Nevertheless, his son saw these regularly—
if discreetly.

In his youth, Wenders initially toyed with the idea of becoming a priest but at sixteen he was lured away from church by the
local pinball parlor. Pinball was symptomatic of Wenders's rebellion against German high culture, which to many in his
generation seemed oppressive and tainted by Nazism. They
turned instead to the popular youth culture, with its casualness
and promise of easy freedom, that issued from the occupation
barracks of American GIs. Wender's deep fascination with the

gadgety of modern youth is evident in the images of Coke machines, jukeboxes, transistor radios, television sets, cassette recorders, record players, and pinball machines so abundant in many of his films.

Wenders began studying medicine in Freiburg in 1965 but was repelled by the authoritarianism he encountered both at the university and in the hospital where he worked as an orderly. After a brief stint at studying philosophy in Düsseldorf, in 1966 he decided to develop his talents as an amateur water-colorist and he went to Paris to study painting at the École des Beaux Arts. Rejected—life drawing seemed an impossible subject to Wenders — he eventually became an apprentice of abstract printmaker Johnny Friedländer. Wenders loved the work in Friedländer's studio, but he loved even more the afternoons spent watching films at the Paris Cinémathèque. He often saw three or four films a day; filmmaking suddenly became a serious option for him. He applied and was accepted into the initial class of Munich's newly formed film school.

In his film school years, 1967–70, Wenders made six short films and found himself at the center of an aesthetic movement known as the New Sensibility. The term was applied particularly to introspective filmmakers associated with the Munich film school; they were primarily interested in recording passing phenomena in very long takes that were not necessarily used to create plot. In fact, these young filmmakers often dispensed with plot altogether. Along with their high regard for "just showing" phenomena, the group had some other rather bizarre notions, such as the theory carried out in *Silver City* (1969), a Wenders short, that called for the periodic insertion of two or more frames of black leader (blank, exposed film) to imitate eye blinking.

Of the six short films, only *Alabama* (1969) was made for the film school. It contained the seeds of much that would characterize Wenders's later feature films: an only vaguely suggested story with a gangsterish plot, little dialogue, a rock score, plentiful "driving sequences"—those shot from a moving car and concentrating on the view out the window—and a distinctive black-and-white photography rich in silhouettes and low-light effects by Robby Müller, who would collaborate with Wenders on all of his German features.

Wim Wenders (Courtesy of
Export-Union des Deutschen
Films)

During his film school years Wenders also wrote film and rock
music criticism for the magazine *Filmkritik* and Munich's *Süddeutsche Zeitung*. Wenders associated film and rock closely: both
were part of the American-born youth culture he adored, both
seemed to embody a hard-traveling, free-living, totem-smashing
life-style that promised release from German stolidity. When
Wenders began writing for *Filmkritik*, its criticism was changing,
following a path laid down by French New Wave critics a decade
earlier. From disdaining popular American films, the *Filmkritik*
critics had come to idolize films by 'directors like Samuel Fuller,
Nicholas Ray, John Ford, Don Siegel, Alfred Htichcock, and
Anthony Mann. Like the French New Wave critics-turned-
directors before him, Wenders was deeply influenced by American films. Following Godard's lead in using Hollywood directors
as actors, Wenders had Sam Fuller and Nicholas Ray act in several of his later films.

Wenders attended film school at the height of the student

movement that climaxed in a series of demonstrations throughout Germany in the spring of 1968, after SDS leader Rudi
Dutschke was shot in the head by an anticommunist fanatic. The
Easter demonstrations of 1968 protested against the yellow
journalism of the Springer press, whose red-baiting practices the
students blamed for the assassination attempt against Dutschke.

Arrested for allegedly hitting a policeman, Wenders denied
the charge in court. His short *Polizeifilm* (1970) was a tongue-in-
cheek documentary explaining the new "tactics of tolerance"
adopted by the Munich police when they realized that police
brutality had created widespread sympathy for the demonstrators. The film, which made liberal use of Donald Duck comics,
was commissioned (though never shown) by Bavarian television.

During part of 1968 and 1969, Wenders lived in a political
commune, but he often had trouble communicating with his
fellows: "I went to see westerns every night, and they were talking about imperialism and fighting this and fighting that. . . .
Anyway I had a hard time with them."[1] As the student movement dissolved into terrorism, many of the commune's members
went underground, and Wenders left.

His own course of self-destruction was more passive and in
keeping with the interiority of the New Sensibility: he went
through a heavy drug period and landed in a hospital. Part of
the problem was his overwhelming shyness, the difficulty he had
in communicating with people. Wenders and his film-school colleagues had worked around this defect by making it a point of
style to exclude people from their films and deal primarily with
objects. But the disposition took its toll.

Wenders's uncommunicativeness was reflected in his first feature, *Summer in the City* (1970), made as his diploma film for the
school. The main character, Hans (Hanns Zischler), wanders
through Munich and Berlin, seeing the sights and visiting old
friends, but speaking little and conversing less. Woodenly alone
in his world, Hans has no idea of how subtly offensive his behavior is, and one wonders if even Wenders realized it at the time.
He calls *Summer* a film about depression, about the way people
felt in the late 1960s—"an enormous disappointment . . . a
feeling of being completely powerless"[2]—because political
activism had failed. Figures like Hans appear in almost all Wenders's subsequent German films, but he learned to see them

more objectively. He would understand them, know what he was creating with them, see their uncommunicativeness as a problem to be overcome. At the time he made *Summer*, Wenders was too much Hans, too depressed himself, to be objective about his character. Therapy and filmmaking would, however, eventually lead Wenders out of the emotional abyss in which he found himself.

In *Summer* Wenders continued techniques used in *Alabama*: a rock score (the film is named for a song by the Lovin' Spoonful), numerous driving sequences, black-and-white photography that played with silhouettes, reflections, and extreme low-light conditions. Like *Alabama* it concerned young people on the edge of society.

In *Summer,* however, the hero is trying to escape his old gang. The escape theme probably reflects Wenders's own preoccupations at the time. No longer part of the commune or the drug scene, he also felt the need to break with the rarefied atmosphere of film school and the New Sensibility, to make it in the hard-hitting world of commercial cinema. Replying to a critic who remarked on the determination of the protagonist of *Falsche Bewegung (Wrong Move,* 1975) to become a writer, Wenders said, "And that's my story too."[3]

In the mid-sixties Wenders met Peter Handke, the Austrian enfant terrible of German letters, whose gift for self-promotion had made him well known while still a very young man. After de-dramatizing German-language drama with plays in which the characters address themselves almost exclusively to the audience, Handke turned to a subjective, highly descriptive prose. Labeled the New Subjectivity, it was a close cousin to the New Sensibility. Wenders and Handke became close friends. Although never the extreme intellectual Handke was, Wenders nevertheless shared most of Handke's passions, including American detective fiction, American films, and rock music. At one time they were even in love with the same woman. In 1969 they collaborated on the short *3 American LP's,* a colorful paean of praise to American music, movies, and the American landscape.

Wenders was frequently the first person who read Handke's manuscripts, often as they came out of the typewriter. He read *Die Angst des Tormanns beim Elfmeter (The Goalie's Anxiety at the Penalty Kick)* in this fashion and joked at the time about making a film from it. The joke became a reality when in 1971 Wenders obtained a grant from the Kuratorium for his first feature. (He did not tell them about *Summer in the City.*) German and Austrian television and the Filmverlag supplied enough additional funds to allow for the use of professional actors and fairly sophisticated equipment. "I thought I was the richest filmmaker in the world. I had twenty meters of tracking, which seemed like a mile."[4] The result was a tight, professional-looking film that perfectly captured the mood and feeling of Handke's book.

The Goalie's Anxiety at the Penalty Kick tells the story of Josef Bloch (Arthur Brauss), an Austrian soccer goalie. The film begins when he misses a goal and is thrown out of the game for arguing with the umpire. He bums around Vienna and eventually picks up a woman (Erika Pluhar) who sells tickets at the movie theater he attends. He spends the night with her and in the morning, annoyed by her mindless chatter and further attempts to flirt with him, he strangles her. In a vague attempt to flee the consequences of his crime, Bloch takes a bus to a Burgenland village that borders on Hungary and Yugoslavia. He stays in the village hotel and each day reads newspaper accounts of the investigation into the murder. Although he does nothing to keep from being caught, the ignorance of the local villagers, who seldom read the papers, ensures against his quick discovery. When a composite drawing of the murderer appears in the paper, a drawing that greatly resembles him, the hotel's chambermaid (Libgard Schwartz) looks straight from the picture to Bloch and comments, "He'll most definitely have grown a mustache by now."

Bloch whiles away his days by visiting a former girl friend— the reason he chose this particular village—and walking through the countryside. The murder-thriller we have been conditioned to expect never materializes. The film constantly works against all expectations. In one scene Bloch discovers the body of a mute boy who has been missing since Bloch came to the village. A shot of Bloch standing on a wooden bridge over a stream is followed by a shot of the stream from his point of view. Barely visible in the background is the boy's body. It is never shown in close-up. Bloch leaves, but does not hurry away from the stream, and he never tells anyone what he has seen. His discovery of the child's body has no bearing on the plot whatsoever; it is simply another event in the subjective world of Josef Bloch.

Audience expectation is frustrated, too, by Jürgen Knieper's eerie music, which punctuates the film, not when Bloch faces real danger, but whenever he is reminded of danger. The music occurs, for example, when he sees the child's body, when he passes a pile of pumpkins after having learned the unlikely fact that a local child was killed when pumpkins were thrown at him, and whenever he sees a local policeman—although they are as ignorant as everyone else of Bloch's identity. Instead of cluing the audience as it would in a normal suspense film, the music reflects Bloch's inner thought—just as the camera, for the most part, captures his perceptions.

Frustration of audience expectations itself contributes to an overall motif in the film: the difficulty of ever knowing what to expect. A customs guard at the border explains to Bloch with absurd exactness how hard it is to determine which way a culprit will run; the film ends with Bloch telling a fellow spectator at a soccer game how hard it is for the goalie to know which corner to guard.

> If he knows the kicker from earlier games, he knows which corner he usually goes for. But maybe the kicker is also counting on the goalie's figuring this out. So the goalie goes on figuring that just once the ball might go into the other corner. But what if the kicker follows the goalie's thinking. . . .

The result is the paralysis Bloch demonstrates in the film's first sequence, when, standing immobile, he lets the ball go by him into the goal. It likewise explains his indifference with regard to the police search. He sees no point in trying to evade or outwit it.

Indecision and paralysis also invade Bloch's relationship with his old flame, Hertha (Kai Fischer), who runs a tavern on the border. Hertha finds him attractive and leads him on, but she also taunts him with the news that she is sleeping with the local estate owner's son. When he eventually makes a pass at her, she rejects him. Unnerved by her conflicting signals and unable to play her game, Bloch wanders off after each encounter with her, the relationship always at a stalemate.

In the same way, conversation in the film never leads anywhere. While the characters in *Summer in the City* rarely conversed, those in *Goalie* converse at cross purposes. For example:

Hertha: Somebody died next door yesterday.
Bloch: Does your waitress wear health shoes?
Hertha: That is definitely the bike.
Bloch: What bike?
Hertha: The mute schoolboy's.
Bloch: If these shoes came in other colors, they might become the fashion. Did the well-digger come back again?
Hertha: He couldn't even call for help.
Bloch: Who?
Hertha: The boy.

The police net closing in on Bloch is the only logical force in the film's absurd world. Its unseen, unheard presence is suggested at one point by the camera when it dollies toward the sink in Bloch's hotel room, toward Bloch in his bed, toward a triple mirror reflecting Bloch; finally it captures him in a bird's-eye shot from directly overhead. The sequence gives an overwhelming impression of Bloch's psychic isolation as well as of the net inevitably closing in on him. Behind the foreground of a bumbling, confused, and paralyzed humanity, the police search is logical and relentless. It has the cosmic overtones of death. It *will* overtake Bloch, but not within the confines of the story.

If metaphorical death lurks in the background of *Goalie*, physical death is also constantly present in the story: a woman is murdered, a schoolboy drowns, a boy has been killed by pumpkins, and a wake goes on next to Hertha's tavern. These elements are all taken from Handke's book, but they serve Wenders's own fascination with death — strong even in the early shorts. For example, after finding his friends massacred, the protagonist of the *Alabama* dies behind the wheel while driving down a country road; his death is indicated by the camera's slowly closing aperture. Later films such as *Wrong Move* and *Im Lauf der Zeit (Kings of the Road,* 1976) contain several suicides, attempted suicides, and an attempted murder, and in *Der amerikanische Freund (The American Friend,* 1977) a dying man is persuaded to commit murder. (Wenders's preoccupation with death is most intense in his American film *Lightning over Water* (1980), both a document of Nicholas Ray's last days and a meditation on death. And in his subsequent *The State of Things* (1982) a main character says, "Death, Friedrich. . . . It's the greatest story in the world.")

In nearly all of Wender's films, America in one form or another is a major motif. In his short films Wenders is unambivalently enthusiastic about America, and friends say this was indeed his attitude in real life. In *Summer in the City,* before he learns about visa restrictions, Hans intends to escape to the United States.

Although in *Goalie* Wenders is as enthusiastic as ever about American music and movies, when a Coca Cola truck passes Bloch in the village, it suggests that there is as little escape from American consumer products as from the Viennese police. Indeed, Wenders connects the two when he enables the police to trail Bloch thanks to the American currency he inadvertently leaves behind him (currency left over from his team's tour in the United States). Significantly, this plot device is not in Handke's book. American "capital" betrays Bloch even as—Wenders felt— it was betraying Germany, particularly the German film industry, largely strangled by American-owned distribution companies. "It (American culture) is something you treasure," he told one interviewer, "but at the same time you see it's taken over like a Moloch: the American cultural debris and the imperialistic dictatorship of the American film distributors."[5]

Wenders also became aware of a need to assert his own identity as a European artist, to free himself somewhat from the tremendous influence American films had had on him: "I realized while I was shooting *The Goalie* that I wasn't an American director; that although I loved the American cinema's way of showing things, I wasn't able to recreate it, because I had a different grammar in mind."[6] A year or so after *Goalie,* Wenders discovered the films of Japanese director Yasujiro Ozu, whose filmmaking career stretched from the 1930s to the early 1960s. Wenders immediately sensed a soulmate, a filmmaker deeply influenced by the American film who nevertheless preserved his own unique style. He later called Ozu his "only master,"[7] yet he had used Ozulike techniques before ever seeing an Ozu film. His debt to Ozu was not a particular style or method; rather it was learning to trust his own vision.

Goalie's critical success opened the way for Wenders's next film, *Der scharlachrote Buchstabe (The Scarlet Letter,* 1972), based on

Nathaniel Hawthorne's novel. A costume drama, the film was a German-Spanish coproduction with name stars and a comfortable budget, and it was intended to reach a much wider audience than the esoteric *Goalie*. In two years Wenders appeared to have successfully infiltrated the ranks of commercial cinema in Germany. However, the complexity of the production took most of the control out of his hands: "I felt as though I were sitting on the wagon without the reins."[8] The name stars—Senta Berger and Lou Castel—did not fit their roles as Hester Prynne and Arthur Dimmesdale, and neither was convincing. Wenders's own choice of actors, Yelena Samarina and Rüdiger Vogler, would undoubtedly have rendered more interesting and complex performances. In addition Wenders lost interest in the project because the requirements of a historical costume drama prevented him from using his camera spontaneously. "You can't improvise with the past," he recalled. "I hadn't realized how hard it would be to leave out . . . every kind of *trouvaille*. If there was a ship on the sea, we had to wait until it had gone."[9]

Lack of control and lack of spontaneity were not the film's only problems. Wenders also weakened the film by rewriting the script prepared by playwright Tankred Dorst. Wenders himself gives no adequate explanation for turning Dorst's script, a fairly faithful interpretation of Hawthorne's story, into a semiwestern in which Hester's husband Chillingworth (Hans Christian Blech) appears as a robust backwoodsman, Dimmesdale is murdered by a vengeful governor, and Hester manages a last-minute escape to her waiting ship. Neither Dorst nor Wenders had been particularly interested in Hawthorne's preoccupation with the effects of sin on the human heart, but Dorst, attracted to the tension between utopian experiments and societal limitations, viewed the Puritan colony as a utopian experiment undermined by human passion and its normal outcome. Like Hawthorne, he saw mortals and society as inherently limited and imperfect. Such a resigned view was not shared by Wenders, still a very young man, who only five years before had been fighting social injustice in the streets. He used *The Scarlet Letter* as a forum to blast social oppression. When the Puritan governor murders Dimmesdale and then moves quickly to try to prevent Hester from leaving the colony, he takes on overtones of the West German police cracking down on student dissent and terrorism. The

mad Hibbins, truly an old witch in Hawthorne's novel, is played
by the beautifully bedraggled Yelena Samarina, and her madness is attributed directly to the oppression of women. When
Dimmesdale reveals his own scarlet "A," Hibbins laughs hysteri-
cally and revengefully. Seeking a more liberal society, Hester
wastes no time wishing she might be united with Dimmesdale in
heaven (as in Hawthorne), but scurries off to the waiting ship.

Although the film proved Wenders as much master of a traditional narrative style as anyone, the critics were quick to detect
his immaturity, both because of the shallow production and because he had revealed his impatience with the production to the
press. (Ten years later, having worked under similarly oppressive and unfruitful conditions making *Hammett* for Francis Ford
Coppola, Wenders gave hardly a hint to the press of the myriad
frustrations that had beseiged him.)

The professionalism of *Goalie* had been largely the result of
Wenders's deep understanding and sympathy for Peter Handke's thought and work, and this because Handke's thought was
so similar to his own. Although his considerable talent had made
it relatively easy for him to break into commercial film-making
in Germany, Wenders was unable to suppress his own individuality sufficiently to submerge himself in other people's endeavors. He was only viable as an auteur-director, an independent.

With the personal, critical, and box-office failure of *The Scarlet
Letter*, Wenders's only thought was to work small again, to write
his own story, to give himself room for spontaneity. His next
film fulfilled these conditions. *Alice in den Städten* (*Alice in the
Cities*, 1974) was made from his original script. The story of a
man and a child traveling together, it was quite similar to *Paper
Moon* (1973) before Wenders saw the Peter Bogdanovich film
and altered his own script. The film stars Yella Rottländer, Wenders's greatest dividend from *The Scarlet Letter*, in which she
played the child, Pearl.

Philip Winter (Rüdiger Vogler), a German journalist, returns
to New York with writer's block and a pack of Polaroid snapshots
after a psychically exhausting trip across the United States. In
trying to book a flight home, he finds that an airline strike has
made Amsterdam the closest possible destination. He meets Lisa
(Lisa Kreuzer) and her little girl Alice (Yella Rottländer), who

are also trying to get back to Germany: Fed up with New York, Lisa is willing to leave the man she lives with to get home, but finds that her boy friend's desperation at the prospect of her departure necessitates a brief return to him. She asks Philip to take Alice ahead to Amsterdam, knowing that with Alice in Europe she will have to return.

Philip complies, but when Lisa does not appear in Amsterdam at the arranged time, both he and Alice panic, he thinking he will be stuck waiting in Amsterdam indefinitely and Alice fearing she will be abandoned. They agree to look for her grandmother, who lives in Wuppertal, according to Alice's best recollection. When a street-by-street search of Wuppertal produces no grandmother, Alice concludes she has made a mistake, and Philip takes her to the police. No longer burdened by Alice, Philip seems, nevertheless, in no particular hurry to return to his home base in Munich. He stays in Wuppertal, attends a Chuck Berry concert, and returns to his hotel to find that Alice has run away from the police and returned to him. He laughs helplessly and agrees to continue what he certainly perceives to be a hopeless search.

Philip is the archetypal Wenders hero, a traveling man just past thirty who has trouble relating to people. While he was still in New York, his former girl friend Angela (Eddie Köchl) told him: "You came here so somebody would listen to you, you and your stories, that you're really just telling to yourself. It's not enough, dear, not after awhile." His writer's block is symbolic of his inability to communicate, for which he tries to compensate with the images he makes with his Polaroid camera. Neither woman in New York is able to help: Angela is tired of his egocentricity, and Lisa is too preoccupied with her own problems to notice his. But Alice, with her child's magic and her relentless insistence on being cared for, breaks through his barriers. No doubt he has missed her during his day alone in Wuppertal. In any case, he takes her back and no longer complains about her tying up his time. As long as his writer's block persists, he really has nothing else to do anyway.

Before she left them, the police told Alice her grandmother's last name and suggested she lived somewhere in the Ruhr district. From this information and a picture Alice has, the two eventually find the grandmother's house, but Grandma doesn't

Rüdiger Vogler and Yella Rottländer in *Alice in the Cities* (Courtesy of Filmverlag der Autoren)

live there anymore. Given over to the idea of wandering around with Alice, no matter where, Philip suggests they go swimming. At the beach they meet a beautiful young woman (Didi Petrikat) who invites them home to supper. Unlike the women in New York, she is concerned about Philip and compassionate. And, unlike the New York women, who decline to have sex with Philip, she welcomes him into her bed. Of course, Alice, not Philip, has provided the liaison both in having brought Philip around to an emotionally receptive state and in having first approached the woman. But Alice is not content to remain only a catalyst to adult romance. She is jealous, and in the morning she drags Philip out of bed and insists that they continue the journey.

Out of money, Philip concludes he must take Alice to his parents, who live on the other side of the Rhine. Crossing in a ferry, they meet a detective from Wuppertal (Hans Hirschmüller), who tells them that Alice's mother and grandmother

have been located in Munich and asks why Philip never reported back to the police. Philip's only reply is another helpless
laugh.

Phillip takes the train with Alice, who at the last minute produces sufficient cash for his ticket. When Alice asks him what he
intends to do in Munich, he replies that he will write the story of
their travels. His writer's block is broken. The film ends with a
helicopter shot of the two of them leaning joyously out the window of their train as it disappears down the Rhine Valley.

Alice is a charming story if one ignores the implications of
a man who relates successfully to a girl child, but not to grown
women. All of Wenders's heroes (with the exception of Hammett, who is not entirely a Wenders creation) have trouble relating to adult women. Wenders sees this difficulty as a reflection of
his times: "Relationships between men and women became more
unsure, and everybody I met and all relations I saw became
more and more confused."[10]

Wenders's heroes find no access to those women who have
their own problems to solve and their own lives to lead. Except
for the Didi Petrikat character, whose only function in *Alice* is to
nurture Philip and Alice by giving them food and shelter, Wenders, to do him credit, always pictures women as independent
individuals. Marianne in *The American Friend* has standards that
come into sharp conflict with her husband's new career as a
criminal (and in a large portion of the original script, all of which
ended up on the cutting-room floor, she has her own career as
an actress); the lone woman in *Kings* is determined to live by
herself and make her own way, and in *Wrong Move*, Therese, an
actress, is rebuffed when she goes to the pretentious writer-hero
for solace in her own career dificulties. The hero admits his
failing—"I was unable to help Therese and just used my work as
an excuse, although I knew very well that it didn't deserve the
name of 'work' if I weren't open to Therese at the same
time"—but he doesn't admit it to her. The inability of Wenders's
heroes to relate to women who are people in their own right is
almost total, and it reflects in the extreme, perhaps, a widespread problem in contemporary Western culture.[11]

In *Alice* the Germans living in America are homesick and
speak negatively about the United States. This has led some
European critics to assume that Wenders shows America in a bad

light. In fact, what Wenders *shows* contrasts markedly with what the characters *say*. Wenders shows precisely those kinds of structures in America that fascinate him wherever he films: gas stations, old houses, and trains (the elevated in Queens). He shows Manhattan's skyscrapers from the bottom looking up and from the Empire State Building looking out. He deliberately compares America and Germany, selecting shots of similar locations from both countries: rows of old houses, hot dog stands, Wuppertal's suspended railway, which compares with Queens' Flushing Line, the Ruhr's water towers standing in for Manhattan's skyscrapers, and virtually the same shot of Philip driving into a modern gas station in each country. If portions of what Wenders shows of America seem delapidated and junky, so does Wuppertal, where the street outside Philip's hotel is being torn up, and the Ruhr, where old workers' houses are being torn down. The problem Wenders's characters have is not America, but what they have come to expect from America. Wenders shows that America and Germany are not so very different. We see Philip attending a Chuck Berry concert in Wuppertal, a bottle of Coke in his hand. America is the land of Philip's myths, as it was Wenders's. For both, the real America was disillusioning— perhaps because it was not different enough and perhaps because the detritus of modern civilization on a scale the size of the United States was too overwhelming.

Like Dorothy in *The Wizard of Oz*—and Alice makes the comparison less far-fetched than it might be—Philip discovers there is no place like home. When America fails him, he is finally able to accept himself and his country for what they are— Americanized, but his own. Going home, accepting one's roots, is an important theme in Wenders's films, an important station for his alienated heroes on their way to wholeness, and one that reflects his own route. *Alice, Kings,* and *Wrong Move* all have sequences in the Rhine/Ruhr area because Wenders grew up there. In the course of making the films, he, like his heroes, felt the need to come to terms with his origins.

For his next film, *Falsche Bewegung* (*Wrong Move*), Wenders again collaborated with Peter Handke. Handke wrote an original script based loosely on Goethe's *Wilhelm Meister's Apprenticeship,* the grandfather of the German *Bildungsroman,* the personal development novel, in which a young man travels to discover his place and purpose in the world. The genre obviously appealed to Handke and Wenders, for Wenders's *Alice* drew on the tradition as did, far more consciously, Handke's novel *Short Letter Long Farewell*.

Unlike the charming *Alice, Wrong Move* concerns characters so rigorously alienated that not one is likeable. The hero, Wilhelm Meister (Rüdiger Vogler), wants above all to become a writer, although he wonders if he can manage it, since he does not like people. Given to inaction, Wilhelm begins his travels only when his mother (Marianne Hoppe) decides that he should leave her and see something of the land and the people he intends to write about. He boards a train for Bonn and is immediately adopted as patron by two vagabonds, an old man (Hans Christian Blech) and a young girl, Mignon (Nastassja Kinski). Wilhelm and a young actress aboard another train are attracted to one another, and she wires him her phone number. After he and his companions check into a hotel in Bonn, Wilhelm calls the actress, Therese Farner (Hanna Schygulla), who agrees to meet him the next day. The four go walking on the outskirts of Bonn, and pick up a fifth companion, a would-be poet, Bernhard Landau (Peter Kern). Bernhard invites them to stay at his uncle's estate, but mistakes the house, and they come upon a rich industrialist (Ivan Desny) who is about to shoot himself. Happily detained from his suicide, the industrialist invites them to spend the night. Therese is eager to sleep with Wilhelm, but in looking for her room that night he goes astray and finds Mignon's. Following, as usual, the course of least resistance, he sleeps with the teenager instead of Therese.

The next day another hike takes the five into the hills above the Rhine. The old man, who has alluded several times to his secret past, admits he was a concentration camp commandant, and Wilhelm privately determines to kill him.

When the hikers return, the industrialist has hanged himself. The group travels south to Therese's home in Frankfurt, losing Bernhard on the way. Once in Frankfurt, Wilhelm finds that his own self-absorption makes him an unsuitable companion for Therese, and he determines to leave. First, he attempts to kill the old man by throwing him off the Main ferry. He relents at the last minute, however, and the old man flees. Leaving Mignon in Therese's care, Wilhelm visits the Zugspitze, Germany's highest mountain. As he stands on the observation deck at the top, we hear an interior monologue in which he ponders his inability to act:

> I stood on the Zugspitze and waited for something to happen like I was waiting for a miracle. But the snowstorm didn't come. Why had I run away? Why was I here instead of with the others? Why had I threatened the old man instead of letting him tell me more? It seemed like I had missed something, and as if I was always missing something with every new move.

Handke's stamp is clearly on *Wrong Move*. The cutting is faster than that of *Kings* or *Alice* and more precise. Far more leisurely, *Kings* and *Alice* tend to spill over with scenes and scenery that are sometimes redundant or superfluous but which contribute to the relaxed pace of those films. *Wrong Move* moves along with more discipline and like *Goalie*—Wenders's other collaboration with Handke—sometimes deliberately frustrates audience expectations. For example, when Wilhelm's train passes a station, an exterior shot shows the platform clock just as the second hand has come to rest on the twelve. The shot is cut just before the minute hand springs forward and thus creates the bizarre impression that the clock has stopped. A stopped clock is thematically relevant to Wilhelm's state of being, but disorienting for the audience. Handke helped with the cutting of *Wrong Move,* and thus the pace of the film and disorienting shots like that described above may well be the result of his direct input.

Like *Goalie, Wrong Move* is peppered by casual violence—or the mention of violence—for which the audience is seldom prepared. In an early scene, Wilhelm looks out his window at the village square and suddenly puts his fist through the plate glass. After an exuberant chase down the mountainside, the group reenters the industrialist's house and finds hanging from a bannister the body of the man they had saved from suicide only the previous night.

A "Wenders hero" like Josef Bloch and Philip Winter, Wilhelm Meister has such a weak sense of identity that he relates poorly to people. More than the goalie, who always seems psychically isolated whether or not he is with people, Wilhelm prefers to be alone. But like the goalie and unlike Philip Winter, Wilhelm is unable to act and unable to change. Wenders found himself disliking Handke's character, primarily because of his inability to change, and commented sourly: "At the end, Wilhelm isn't a hero anymore, not even in his own eyes. He could become a man; but that would be another film."[12] Thus the two films derived from Handke differ from Wenders's others in being less positive, in picturing an immobilized and immobilizing world in which the characters and the audience are frequently disoriented and never at ease. Neither the world nor the characters seem capable of change. There is no way out.

Handke's genius nonetheless helped to give *Wrong Move* a formal precision missing in the mellower *Alice* and *Kings*. Vincent Canby remarked that the cool beauty of *Goalie*, in contrast to *Alice* and *Kings*, made him think that Wenders needed "a collaborator of Mr. Handke's discipline and intellectual enthusiasm."[13] While Wenders aficionados would miss the warmth and exuberance of *Alice* and *Kings*, judges at the Berlin Film Festival in 1975 responded to *Wrong Move*'s perfectionism with prizes for best film, director, screenplay, editing, music, and cinematography. It was a triumph for Wenders and his crew, which still included Knieper as composer, Müller on camera, and Peter Przygodda, who had edited every Wenders film since *Summer in the City*.

For Wenders the ability to change is essential, and his next film, *Im Lauf der Zeit* (*Kings of the Road*, 1976), illustrates how. The film pairs two Wenders heroes, Bruno Winter (Rüdiger Vogler) and Robert Lander (Hanns Zischler), who meet when Robert, recently separated from his wife, tries to commit suicide by driving his Volkswagen into the Elbe. Tiring of the attempt as soon as the car starts to fill with water, he climbs out the top and scrambles to shore while Bruno, an itinerant movie-projector repairman, watches alternately amused and amazed. Bruno lives in a moving van, and he invites Robert to travel with him, at least until his clothes dry out. The two hesitantly overcome mutual distrust and form a bond of friendship that expresses itself more in actions and antics than in words as they travel Bruno's circuit through decaying villages along the East German border.

The absence of women is a fundamental motif in the film. Robert is estranged from his wife; his mother has been dead for eight years, and his father, whom he visits at one point, recalls that his own mother died at his birth. Bruno has apparently had one or two unsuccessful love affairs, which have caused him to swear off women. When he meets Pauline (Lisa Kreuzer), a cashier in a movie theater, he flirts with her, and they spend all night in the theater, but they do not have sex, despite her willingness. Like the western heroes in the movies of his youth, Bruno is an isolate and a celibate. Sex renders him too vulnerable. He complains to Robert later that he feels deeply lonely when he is having sex—probably because he has never been emotionally open enough to touch another person with his heart. After visiting his father, Robert decides they should visit Bruno's childhood home, an island in the Rhine where he had lived alone with his mother. The house is dilapidated, and his mother no longer lives there. He appears to have lost contact with her altogether. Another young man in the film is beside himself because his wife has just committed suicide, thus another absent woman.

Kings explores the black hole left by women in the world of Wenders's men, and one evening Robert—agitator for change throughout the film—insists that they must somehow learn to live with women, rather than like dead men. "If it [living with women] is impossible, you've got to make it possible. You can't go on living the way you are now, if you can't imagine anything else or don't even want to change." In the morning he leaves Bruno, presumably to take up his former life. He tacks a note to the door of the abandoned U.S. Army hut where they have camped: "Everything must change."

Shocked, Bruno determines to change his life as well. In the film's last shot, he tears up his repairman's itinerary.

Kings touches on many of the themes from Wenders's earlier films, often with more deliberation. The salutary effects of examining one's origins are demonstrated when Robert and Bruno visit their childhood homes. The ambivalence regarding Americanization is taken up specifically when the men spend the night in the army hut. They confront the source of their beloved rock and roll, and Robert makes his much-quoted statement: "The Yanks have colonized our subconscious!" The remark is prompted by Bruno's recalling a personal crisis in which he remembered the tune but not the words to a rock and roll song whose words, it turned out, were exactly appropriate to the situation.

In his previous films Wenders had referred to cinema frequently but casually. He becomes more specific in *Kings,* where he examines the plight of provincial movie houses in Germany, which, via block booking practices, are forced to show primarily pornography and related trash. All but one of the major distributors are American-owned, and Wenders reserves his serious anti-Americanism for the film distributors.

Germany's Nazi period is referred to twice in *Kings.* In the film's opening sequence, Bruno talks with an old movie-house owner, who explains that he was not allowed to run his theater for years because he had been a member of the Nazi Party—only he cannot quite remember the party's name. Bruno smirks. He is willing to follow Wilhelm Meister's hindsight and learn from the old man rather than condemn him. Later, when Bruno meets Pauline, she is carrying a candle in the shape of Hitler's head. Wenders included the head at Lisa Kreuzer's insistence. She had found the candles for sale at a gas station near the border and told Wenders she wished to appear with the candle. He had her carry it in the carnival scene: she has apparently won it at a concession. Later Wenders cut the sequence with the Hitler candle between scenes of Robert confronting his father, a newspaperman, with whom he has never had an easy relationship. The Hitler candle thus silently identifies the father as belonging to the Nazi generation and helps account for the difficulty between father and son.

Wenders's generation tended to blame at least some of its confusion on the Nazi period, which, among other things, obliterated modern culture in Germany, leaving the younger generation to start from scratch *and* to work from an American model in trying to catch up. Germany's own great tradition of modernism was virtually unknown to postwar youth in their formative years. A generation gap appeared early, exacerbated by the Nazi generation's reticence about discussing the period with its children. Encouraged by prosperity, a national amnesia took over in the fifties and sixties (typified by the old theater owner in *Kings*) that confused the youngsters, who grew up somewhat a-shamed of being German, although not always sure why. They resented their parents' silence and scorned them for having belonged to that unmentionable past. The attitude is best expressed by Wilhelm in *Wrong Move,* who wants to kill the old

Nazi and suggests the oppression the old man's very existence poses for him when he tells the old man his dream:

> I dreamed that you should die. . . . A child would keep you company until the moment of your death. The child sat next to you and the mausoleum was closed with a huge stone. I dreamed . . . of the absolute darkness in which the child must stand until your death. It was my child.

Wilhelm's reaction is typically immature, for killing the old man will not lessen his own problems. In contrast, the *Kings* characters show a greater willingness to understand the past. They visit their childhood homes, and Robert, although still at odds with his father, tries to communicate with him. Unable to say what he wants aloud, he writes him a treatise instead.

The legacy of Nazism is apparent in the divided Germany, along whose border Robert and Bruno travel. Like the border town in *Goalie,* the East German provinces are totally stagnant. Hitler-head candles are manufactured there. Circulation of the elder Lander's newspaper is so low that he now issues it only three times a week. The village movie houses show only trash, and many have closed. As in *Goalie,* the breakdown in communication between East and West is mirrored by a breakdown in communication within the local populations. Wenders often speaks of the sense of liberation he experiences when he crosses borders, i.e., travels in foreign countries. But the men in *Kings,* like Josef Bloch in *Goalie,* travel along borders that cannot be crossed, an indication that the stagnation in their souls keeps company with the tragedy of contemporary Europe. The parallel gives Robert's charge heightened urgency: Everything must change.

Young people felt themselves directly addressed by *Kings of the Road,* which broke house records in Munich and Berlin. With the success of this very personal film, Wenders turned his attention to the filming of Patricia Highsmith's thriller, *Ripley's Game.* The German press cheered: Wenders was finally going to make a real "movie." The promise was fulfilled: *The American Friend* moved quickly, if sometimes repetitiously, and included numerous murders, narrow escapes, a gun battle, an explosion, and so on. The story was a little confusing, but so, Wenders noted, was *To Have and Have Not.* He had succeeded in making a popular movie. But behind the façade of an action film, Wenders told the same stories he had been telling all along, stories of men who do not get along with women and prefer the companionship of other men, stories of an uneasy love for America, stories about the uniformity, the lack of geographical identity, in the modern world.

Jonathan Zimmermann (Bruno Ganz), a framemaker of slender means, lives in an old apartment block near Hamburg's waterfront with his wife Marianne (Lisa Kreuzer) and their son. Jonathan suffers from a blood disease that could claim his life at any time. An old-world craftsman of pure values, he refuses to shake the hand of Tom Ripley (Dennis Hopper), an expatriated American art dealer of shady reputation. Ripley deals in paintings from an American artist named Pogash (Nicholas Ray), who pretends to be a dead and much collected artist named Derwatt. Ripley, a neurotic, dresses like a cowboy, talks to himself on a cassette recorder, and lives alone in a huge dilapidated mansion filled with "American Pop" artifacts: a jukebox, a Coca Cola machine, a fluorescent Canada Dry sign hanging over a pool table. Like Chaucer's Pardoner, Ripley seems either "a gelding or a mare"—he manifests no interest in women, knows only men, hugs and kisses Pogash by way of greeting him.

Ripley is evidently attracted to Jonathan when they first meet, for Jonathan's snub wounds him deeply. When a gangster friend of his, Raoul Minot (Gérard Blain), asks for a man with a clean record to murder rival gangsters for him, Ripley suggests Jonathan, then regrets his rashness. In an attempt to make amends, he visits Jonathan and offers friendship; this time Jonathan is more fascinated than repelled by Ripley and his gauche Americanisms. But Ripley is too late to head off Jonathan's corruption at the hands of Minot, who woos him with fear (that his disease is getting worse), money, and the promise of a specialist's diagnosis.

Meanwhile Jonathan's marriage, which initially appears warm and supportive if not passionate, begins to disintegrate. His wife, Marianne, grows suspicious of what she senses are his shady dealings; moreover, she feels abandoned and sees Ripley as her competitor, as indeed he is. Wenders at no time suggests a homosexual liaison between Jonathan and Ripley, although the

Dennis Hopper in *The American Friend* (Courtesy of Filmverlag der Autoren)

relationship is clearly homoerotic, based on an attraction of opposites, shared enthusiasms, and a lust for adventure.

Eventually one group of gangsters discovers the Jonathan-Ripley-Minot connection and prepares a nighttime attack on Ripley's mansion. Jonathan helps defend it, and he and Ripley dispatch the entire gangster contents of a commandeered ambulance. Marianne appears and offers Jonathan a reconciliation, but Ripley advises her that he and Jonathan have work to do first. She agrees to drive for her exhausted husband while Ripley drives the ambulance full of bodies. They arrive on a lonely beach, where sand, sea, and sky are pearl-colored in the early morning light. Ripley sets fire to the ambulance, whose orange explosion contrasts expressively with the white background. It climaxes Jonathan's adventure with Ripley. He pushes Marianne back into their car and drives off across the beach without Ripley. He intends to resume his family life. But exhausted and euphoric, he drives off the road, blacks out, and dies as the car heads toward the ocean. Just before it reaches the sea, Marianne pulls on the hand brake. She gets out and looks glumly at Ripley sitting on an old pier post and singing to himself. The sound of waves dominates the sound track and carries into the next scene in which Pogash, sitting atop New York's West Side Highway, decides to stop pretending to be the dead Derwatt and return to life. It is a mystical moment, as though Jonathan's death—present in the sound of the waves—had called Pogash to life. The male bond goes on even in death.

The American Friend has an intense mood that sometimes verges on hysteria. It is heightened by the cutting, the lighting, the music, and the strange ways Ripley is characterized. In one scene he lies on his pool table and photographs himself repeatedly with a Polaroid camera, letting the finished pictures rain down on him. In another he is photographed through a red filter in a bedroom decorated with red curtains and red satin sheets. Elsewhere he is illuminated by a green light. Garish colors embellish the film generally, particularly the evening skies, which are electric orange or purple. Knieper's music—dissonant chords repeated periodically—jangles the nerves as does the disorienting cutting from New York to Hamburg to Paris. In keeping with these devices, Wenders's themes take on a feverishness not present in the earlier films.

Wenders deliberately confuses the cities. Sequences in Hamburg as well as New York take place in waterfront locations. In Paris Wenders chose to use a section called "little Manhattan" where a small replica of the Statue of Liberty stands in the Seine. One interurban sequence is cut as follows:

—pan of the Paris cityscape over "little Manhattan," shot from Jonathan's hotel room.
—shot of the phone ringing in Jonathan's Hamburg apartment.
—the skyline of real Manhattan (from Brooklyn).
—a sequence in Derwatt's loft (Manhattan).
—Jonathan's Paris hotel room, where his telephone rings.
—Minot talking on the telephone from his balcony.
—another pan of the Paris cityscape from Jonathan's hotel (in which Jonathan is able to spot Minot).
—a close-up of an elevator counter (Jonathan's hotel).
—a close-up of a medical report in Jonathan's hands (Minot's apartment); the camera pulls back to a medium long shot of

Jonathan, which now includes the view out the balcony windows; as Jonathan closes the report, the Statue of Liberty in the Seine is visible.

Following the line of thinking Wenders had pioneered in his America-Germany comparison in *Alice,* the sequence gives the impression that all cities are one and hints broadly that their unity follows an American model. It also connects Jonathan's betrayal with America: via camera placement the Statue of Liberty replaces the faked medical report in his hands. The doctor who prepared the report is an American as is Ripley, who set Jonathan up in the first place. But the accusation implied here seems to go beyond the confines of the story and to see Jonathan's corruption by money (not actually American money here) allied to Germany's "economic miracle": moral sloth and economic energy, superintended by Uncle Sam.

Wenders's real anger, however, is still primarily directed against American film interests in Germany. Fassbinder raved against the "economic miracle" in general for its blunting of German moral acuity, but one feels that its principal significance for Wenders is the precipitous downhill slide taken by German cinema as soon as prosperity set in. Jonathan is associated with "good cinema," in particular early cinema, cinema in its age of innocence. He owns, for example, an antique Zoetrope, an early device for making pictures move. The gangsters are associated with "bad cinema," in this case pornography, which they produce and distribute internationally. Significantly the filmmaking gangsters are Americans, and, although they die, innocent cinema (Jonathan) is nevertheless corrupted.[14]

Like all of Wenders's films, *The American Friend* is ambivalent about America. Ripley helps to corrupt Jonathan, but he also offers him adventure, freedom from a deadening domesticity. He and his peculiar world of American Pop lure Jonathan like a siren—just as America lures Wenders.

The internal evidence of ambivalence in *The American Friend* is borne out by Wenders's next career decision. Impressed by the angst-filled thriller, Francis Ford Coppola invited Wenders to come to California to make a film for him. Wenders accepted the offer and moved first to San Francisco, then to Los Angeles, and finally to New York, where he lives at this writing. He has not made a German-language film since *The American Friend.* In

1982 he directed Peter Handke's play *Across the Villages* at the Salzburg Festival. Plans to make a film from this and several other recent works by Handke were widely publicized, but no money for the project was forthcoming in Germany. Potential backers told him they could have done it a few years ago, but not now. There just was not enough interest in that sort of film anymore. So Wenders remains in the United States and continues to make films in English, and an era in German filmmaking closes behind him.

NOTES

[1] Wim Wenders to author, Los Angeles, 1 August 1980.

[2] Quoted in Jan Dawson, *Wim Wenders*, translated by Carla Wartenberg, (New York, 1976), p. 19.

[3] Quoted in Walter Adler, "Das große Geld, die Angst und der Traum vom Geschichten Erzählen," *Filmkritik*, December 1978, p. 683.

[4] Quoted in Dawson, *Wenders*, p. 22.

[5] Fritz Müller-Scherz and Horst Wiedemann, "Wim Wenders über 'Im Lauf der Zeit,'" *Film und Ton Magazin*, May 1976, p. 54.

[6] Quoted in Dawson, *Wenders*, p. 8.

[7] Quoted in ibid.

[8] Wim Wenders to author, Los Angeles, 2 August 1981.

[9] Quoted in Dawson, *Wenders*, p. 22.

[10] Edward Lachman, Peter Lehman, and Robin Wood, "Wim Wenders: An Interview," *Wide Angle*, 2 (1979): 78.

[11] Mas'ud Zavarzadeh writes of Jean-Jacques Beineix's *Diva* (1982) that it represents the black or Third-World woman as soft, feminine — a sex object, with whom white men feel they can relate, in place of the white woman, whose push for equality has apparently rendered her too threatening to today's white male heroes. (*Film Quarterly*, Spring 1983, pp. 54–59.)

[12] Quoted in Hans Günther Pflaum, *Filmkorrespondenz*, 2 (1975):11.

[13] Vincent Canby, "The Goalie's Anxiety," *New York Times*, 14 January 1977.

[14] Eventually Jonathan dies, too, although from a priori causes, not corruption. His inevitable death reflects Wenders's view of "innocent" cinema as no longer possible in our present world where cinema, in its last age, has become too self-conscious. See Claudia Sandner von Dehn, "In der Endzeit des Kinos," *Hessische Allgemeine* (Kassel), 9 July 1977.

Acknowledgments

NUMEROUS INDIVIDUALS AND ORGAN-
izations contributed information and advice. The authors wish to express their special gratitude to the following: Clara Burckner and Ursula Miesch (Basis-Film); Michael Röhrig, Brigitte Huthmacher, Ute Frerichs (Bavaria-Atelier); Irma Rotsch (Bioskop-Film); Hark Bohm and Natalia Bowakow; Barbara D. Steinsch (Neue Constantin Film); Helga Sauré (Embassy of the Federal Republic of Germany, Washington, D.C.); Gabriele Rohrer and Petra Fouque-Bader (Export-Union des Deutschen Films, Munich); Jochen Wilke (Filmförderungsanstalt, Berlin); Karen Cooper (Film Forum, New York); Enno Patalas (Filmmuseum im Stadtmuseum, Munich); Katharina Hembus (Filmverlag der Autoren); Margaret Kellner (Filmwelt); Sidney Finger; Norbert and Inge Fischer; Uta Hoffman (German Information Center, New York); Ramona Curry (Goethe Institute, Chicago); Christoph and Inke Wecker (Goethe House, New York); Tim Grady; Tom Prassis (Gray City Films); Miriam Hansen; Joe Hembus; Werner Herzog; Ulrich Kurowski (Archiv der Hochschule für Fernsehen und Film, Munich); Danièle Huillet; Hilla Jaenicke; Edwin Jahiel; Don Krim (Kino International); Alexander Kluge; Detlef Krumme; Norbert Kückelmann; Richard Leskosky; Peter Lilienthal, Peter Christian Hall (*Medium*, Frankfurt/M.); the staff of the Museum of Modern Art Film Stills Archive and Film Study Center; Debbie Lewis and Mary Lugo (New Yorker Films); Sylvia Noack; Monika Kind (*Playboy* Germany); Detlev and Barbara Schlöndorff; May Spils and Werner Enke; Ula Stöckl; W. Green (Syberberg Filmproduktion); Bill Thompson; Karsten Witte; Stephen Zietz; Tess Haley (Zoetrope). The editor is indebted to the VMI Foundation for travel grants. Finally, the authors would like to thank Stanley Hochman for his untiring support, patience, and faith.

Notes on the Contributors

RUSSELL A. BERMAN received his B.A. from Harvard and then studied German literature in Munich and Berlin and at Washington University in St. Louis, where he received his Ph.D. The author of *Between Fontane and Tucholsky: Literary Criticism and the Public Sphere in Imperial Germany* and various essays on critical theory, modern German literature, and the relationship between film and literature, he is assistant professor of German studies at Stanford University.

THEODORE FIEDLER has written on critical theory, East German poetry, Brecht, Hofmannsthal, Trakl, and Hölderlin. He is associate professor of German and chairman of the Department of Germanic Languages and Literatures at the University of Kentucky.

KATHE GEIST is an art historian with a Ph.D. from the University of Michigan. Her doctoral dissertation is on the films of Wim Wenders, and her subsequent publications include articles on Wenders and on his favorite filmmaker, Yasujiro Ozu. Kathe Geist wrote the subtitles for the 35mm release of *Alice in the Cities*. She currently teaches film at Illinois State University.

CHRISTIAN-ALBRECHT GOLLUB has published articles on modern Austrian poetry and the New German Cinema, interviews with Arthur Miller and Christopher Isherwood, and translations from French and German. His own poetry and prose have appeared in a number of Little Magazines in Europe and the United States.

ANNA K. KUHN received her Ph.D. in German Studies from Stanford University. She is the author of *Der Dialog bei Frank Wedekind* and has published articles on modern German literature and on literary adaptations in the New German Cinema. She has taught at Harvard and is presently assistant professor of German at the University of Pennsylvania.

LYNNE LAYTON received her Ph.D. in comparative literature from Washington University. Her publications include articles on Enlightenment literature and philosophy, nineteenth-century realism, and film. An associate editor of *Telos*, she is assistant professor of humanities at Boston University.

RUTH McCORMICK has worked as a film publicist for Contemporary/McGraw-Hill Films, Avco-Embassy Pictures, and Toho International. A former editorial board member of *Cineaste*, she has written numerous articles on film and women's issues and translated a book on Fassbinder. She has taught film at the Free Association and the School for Marxist Education in New York.

BRIGITTE PEUCKER received her Ph.D. from Yale. A Woodrow Wilson Fellow and a Morse Fellow, she currently holds a Mellon Fellowship at the Whitney Humanities Center at Yale, where she is Charles Murphy Associate Professor. She has written articles on film and lyric poetry as well as a book, *Arcadia to Elysium: Preromantic Modes in Eighteenth Century Germany*.

KLAUS PHILLIPS received his Ph.D. from the University of Texas at Austin. He has written articles on German and Yiddish drama and on film; was cotranslator of *Rainer Maria Rilke: Nine Plays* (Frederick Ungar, 1979); and is host of *The Sounds of Germany*, a weekly radio program he originated in 1977. He has taught at the University of Illinois, the Virginia Military Institute, and is currently associate professor of German studies at Hollins College.

ERIC RENTSCHLER studied in Stuttgart, Bonn, and Prague, before receiving his Ph.D. from the University of Washington. He is the author of *West German Film in the Course of Time* and editor of *West German Film in the* 1970s, a special issue of the *Quarterly Review of Film Studies*. His other published work includes articles on New German Cinema, film and literature, and eighteenth-century German drama. He is associate professor of German literature and film studies at the University of California at Irvine.

INGRID SCHEIB-ROTHBART grew up in Berlin and Cologne, where her first film experiences were a mixture of Hollywood and Third Reich. After training as a translator for English and French and a career as a textile designer, she emigrated to the United States. Since 1962 she has been working in cultural programming at Goethe House New York, where she coordinates and organizes film packages, retrospectives, and appearances by German filmmakers. She maintains a film information and liaison service with special emphasis on the films of the New German Cinema.

MARC SILBERMAN was educated at the University of Minnesota, the Freie Universität Berlin, and Indiana University, where he received his Ph.D. in German. He has published books and articles on literature in the German Democratic Republic and German film as well as translations of the playwright Heiner Müller. He teaches German and humanities at the University of Texas in San Antonio.

DAGMAR STERN received her Ph.D. in German from Indiana University. Her publications include a book, *Hilde Domin: From Exile to Ideal*, and articles on various aspects of cultural life in the German Democratic Republic. She has taught at the University of Illinois, Brown University, the University of Arkansas, and Columbia University.

MAUREEN TURIM has written and lectured on the films of Jean-Marie Straub and Danièle Huillet and is currently finishing a book, *The Flashback in Film: Memory Processes and the Subjectivity of History.* She is associate professor of cinema studies at the State University of New York at Binghamton.

Filmographies

THEATRICAL FEATURE FILMS PRODUCED through 1979 are listed chronologically. The inclusion of shorts, documentaries, and television productions was left to the discretion of the authors. English translations follow original titles in parentheses, where different; unofficial (literal) renderings are given for films not distributed in the United States. Films are black and white unless noted. Filmography information includes length in minutes, producer (P), script (S), camera (C), principal actors (PA), and distributor (D); where applicable, U.S. distributors follow in parentheses; copies available free of charge to educational groups and institutions for nonprofit screenings *exclusively* from the Washington Embassy of the Federal Republic of Germany film library carry the designation "FRG Embassy."

The following abbreviations are used for distributors and television production companies: Filmverlag der Autoren (Filmverlag), Cinema International Corporation (CIC), Bayerischer Rundfunk (BR), Hessischer Rundfunk (HR), Norddeutscher Rundfunk (NDR), Südwestfunk (SWF), Süddeutscher Rundfunk (SDR), Sender Freies Berlin (SFB), Saarländischer Rundfunk (SR), Westdeutscher Rundfunk (WDR), Zweites Deutsches Fernsehen (ZDF), Arbeitsgemeinschaft der öffentlich-rechtlichen Rundfunkanstalten der Bundesrepublik Deutschland (ARD), Österreicher Rundfunk (ORF), Radiotelevisioneitaliana (RAI), Office de radiodiffusion-télévision française (ORTF).

HERBERT ACHTERNBUSCH

Das Kind ist tot (The Child Is Dead); 1970; short.

Das Andechser Gefühl (The Andechs Feeling); 1974; color; 68 min; P: Bioskop; S: HA; C: Jörg Schmidt-Reitwein; PA: HA, Margarethe von Trotta, Walter Sedlmayr, Barbara Gass, Reinhard Hauff, Ingrid Gailhofer, Alois Hitzenbichler; D: Filmwelt.

Die Atlantikschwimmer (The Atlantic Swimmers); 1975; color; 81 min; P and S: HA; C: Jörg Schmidt-Reitwein; PA: HA, Sepp Bierbichler, Heinz Braun, Margarethe von Trotta, Alois Hitzenbichler, Ingrid Gailhofer, Barbara Gass, Gunter Freyse; D: Filmwelt.

Bierkampf (Beer Battle); 1977; color; 85 min; P: HA/ZDF; C: Jörg Schmidt-Reitwein; PA: HA, Sepp and Annamirl Bierbichler, Heinz Braun, Margarethe von Trotta, Barbara Gass, Gerda Achternbusch; D: Filmwelt.

Servus Bayern (Bye Bye Bavaria); 1977; color; 87 min; P: HA/SDR; S: HA; C: Jörg Schmidt-Reitwein and Jörg Jeshel; PA: HA, Sepp and Annamirl Bierbichler, Heinz Braun, Barbara Gass, Karolina Herbig, Gunter Freyse, Gerda Achternbusch; D: Filmverlag.

Der junge Mönch (The Young Monk); 1978; color; 84 min; P and S: HA; C: Jörg Jeshel; PA: HA, Heinz Braun, Karolina Herbig, Barbara Gass, Luisa Francia, Sepp Bierbichler, Gerda Achternbusch; D: HA.

Der Komantsche (The Comanche); 1979; color; 83 min; P: HA/ZDF; S: HA; C: Jörg Schmidt-Reitwein; PA: HA, Annamirl Bierbichler, Barbara Gass, Heinz Braun, Brigitte Kramer, Franz Baumgartner; D: HA.

HARK BOHM

Wie starb Roland S.? (How Did Roland S. Die?); 1970; 25 min; P: HB.

Einer wird verletzt, träumt, stirbt und wird vergessen (Someone is Injured, Dreams, Dies, and Is Forgotten); 1971; 20 min; P: HB.

Tschetan, der Indianerjunge (Tschetan, the Indian Boy); 1972; color; 94 min; P: HB/Filmverlag; S: HB; C: Michael Ballhaus; PA: Marquard Bohm, Dschingis Bowakow; D: Filmverlag (FRG Embassy).

Ich kann auch 'ne Arche bauen (I Can Also Build an Ark); 1973; color; 51 min; P: HB/Filmverlag; S: HB; C: Dietrich Lohmann; PA: Uwe Enkelmann, Kirsten Wardinsky; D: Atlas (FRG Embassy).

Wir pfeifen auf den Gurkenkönig (We Can Do Without the Cucumber King); 1974; 96 min; P: SR/SDR/WDR; D: Atlas.

Nordsee ist Mordsee (North Sea Is Death Sea); 1975; color; 86 min; P: Hamburger Kino Kompanie; S: HB; C: Wolfgang Treu; PA: Uwe Enkelmann, Dschingis Bowakow, Marquard Bohm, Katja Bowakow; D: Filmverlag, Atlas (FRG Embassy).

Wölfe (Wolves); 1976; 48 min; P: Hamburger Kino Kompanie; C: Eric Zimen, Udo Hirsch, Henning Zick.

Moritz, lieber Moritz (Moritz, Dear Moritz); 1977; color; 96 min; P: Hamburger Kino Kompanie; S: HB; C: Wolfgang Treu; PA: Michael Kebschull, Kyra Mladeck, Walter Klosterfelde, Grete Mosheim, Kerstin Wehlmann, Dschingis Bowakow, Uwe Enkelmann; D: Filmverlag.

ALF BRUSTELLIN and BERNHARD SINKEL

Kluge, Leni und der Löwe (Kluge, Leni, and the Lion); Director: AB; 1968; 40 min; P: WDR.

Geschichten aus meinem Alter (Stories from My Old Age); Director: AB; 1970; color; 45 min; P: AB for ZDF; S and C: AB.

Das goldene Ding (The Golden Stuff); Directors: AB, Ula Stöckl, Edgar

Reitz, Nicos Perakis; 1971; color; 90 min; P: Edgar Reitz; S: AB, Ula Stöckl, Edgar Reitz, Nicos Perakis; C: Edgar Reitz; PA: Christian Reitz, Ramin Vahabschadeh, Mario Zöllner, Michael Jeron, Katrin Seybold; D: Basis.

Die Stadt der Hunde (*City of Dogs*); Director: AB; 1972; color; 55 min; P: AB for ZDF; S: AB; C: Christoph Brandt.

Clinch; Director: BS; 1973; color; 65 min; P: BS/U.L.M. for ZDF; S: BS; C: AB; PA: Ursula Kreiss-Fense, Michael Krüger.

Lina Braake oder Die Interessen der Bank können nicht die Interessen sein, die Lina Braake hat (*Lina Braake, or The Interests of the Bank Cannot Be the Interests of Lina Braake*); Director: BS; 1974–75; color; 85 min; P: BS/U.L.M. for WDR; S: BS; C: AB; PA: Lina Carstens, Fritz Rasp, Herbert Bötticher, Erika Schramm, Benno Hoffmann; D: Filmverlag, Atlas.

Berlinger; Directors: AB, BS; 1975; color; 115 min; P: ABS/Independent for ZDF; S: AB, BS; C: Dietrich Lohmann; PA: Martin Benrath, Peter Ehrlich, Hannelore Elsner, Tilo Prückner; D: Neue Constantin (FRG Embassy).

Der Mädchenkrieg (*The Three Sisters*); Directors: AB, BS; 1976–77; color; 143 min; P: ABS/Independent/Maran/Terra/SDR; S: AB, BS, from a novel by Manfred Bieler; C: Dietrich Lohmann; PA: Adelheid Arndt, Katherine Hunter, Antonia Reininghaus, Hans Christian Blech, Matthias Habich, Eva-Maria Meineke; D: Filmverlag (FRG Embassy).

Taugenichts (*Good-for-Nothing*); Director: BS; 1977; color; 90 min; P: ABS/Solaris; S: AB, BS, from a novella by Joseph von Eichendorff; C: Dietrich Lohmann; PA: Jaques Breuer, Eva-Maria Meineke, Sybil Schreiber, Wolfgang Reichmann, Matthias Habich, Mareike Carriere; D: Filmverlag (FRG Embassy).

Deutschland im Herbst (*Germany in Autumn*); Directors: AB, BS, Fassbinder, Schlöndorff, Kluge, et al.; 1977–78; color and b/w; 134 min; P: Pro-jekt Filmproduktion im Filmverlag/Hallelujah-Film/Kairos; D: Filmverlag (New Line Cinema).

Der Sturz (*The Fall*); Director: AB; 1978; color; 103 min; P: ABS/Independent/Maran/von Veitinghoff/SDR; S: AB, BS, from a novel by Martin Walser; C: Dietrich Lohmann; PA: Franz Buchrieser, Hannelore Elsner, Wolfgang Kieling, Eva-Maria Meineke, Kurt Raab; D: Filmverlag.

HELLMUTH COSTARD

Tom ist doof (*Tom Is Tiresome*); 1965; 12 min; P: HC.

Klammer auf, Klammer zu (*Open Parenthesis, Close Parenthesis*); 1966; 22 min; P: Arbeitskreis Film und Fernsehen/Knoop Film.

After Action; 1967; 11 min; P: Studio 1 Filmproduktion.

Warum hast Du mich wachgeküßt? (*Why Did You Wake Me with Kisses?*); 1967; color; 3 min; P: HC.

Besonders wertvoll (*Of Special Merit*); 1968; color; 10 min; P: HC/Petra Nettelbeck.

Die Unterdrückung der Frau ist vor allem an dem Verhalten der Frauen selber zu erkennen (The Oppression of Woman Is Primarily Evident in the Behavior of Women Themselves); 1969; color; 64 min; P: HC/WDR; S and C: HC; PA: Christoph Hemmerling; D: Freunde der deutschen Kinemathek.

Die Postkarte (The Postcard); 1969; color; 8 min; P: HC.

Und Niemand in Hollywood der versteht, daß schon viel zu viele Gehirne umgedreht wurden (And No One in Hollywood Understands That Far Too Many Brains Have Been Turned Already); 1970; color; 95 min; P: HC for BR; Collaborators: Peter Dahl, Christoph Hemmerling, Andy Hertel, Thomas Struck, Klaus Wyborny.

Fußball wie noch nie (Soccer As Never Before); 1970; color; 99 min; P: Studio Filmproduktion for WDR; C: Stanislav Szomolányi, Manfred Treutel, Diethard Matzka, Fritz Schwennicke, Wolfgang Fischer, Jürgen Jürges, Peter Kaiser; PA: George Best.

Der Elefantenfilm (The Elephant Film); 1971; color; 24 min; P: HC.

Teilweise von mir—Ein Volksstück (Partly Mine—A Folk Film); 1972; color; 53 min; P: HC/Radio Bremen; S: HC, Thomas Wittenburg; C: HC; D: Freunde der deutschen Kinemathek.

Ein Nachmittag mit Onkel Robert (An Afternoon with Uncle Robert); 1975; color; 24 min; P: HC for NDR.

Der kleine Godard an das Kuratorium junger deutscher Film (A Little Godard to the Production Board for Young German Cinema); 1978; color; 81 min; P: HC/ZDF; S: HC; C: Bernd Upnmoor, Hans-Otto Walter, Hanno Hart, HC; PA: HC, Ivan Nagel, Hark Bohm, Rainer Werner Fassbinder, Harry Baer, Andréa Ferréol, Uwe Nettelbeck, Jean-Luc Godard; D: Filmwelt.

RAINER WERNER FASSBINDER

Der Stadtstreicher (The City Tramp); 1965; 10 min; P: Roser Film.

Das kleine Chaos (The Little Chaos); 1966; 9 min; P: Roser Film.

Liebe ist kälter als der Tod (Love Is Colder Than Death); 1969; 88 min; P: Antiteater-X-Film; S: RWF;C: Dietrich Lohmann; PA: Ulli Lommel, Hanna Schygulla, RWF; D: Ceres.

Katzelmacher; 1969; 88 min; P: Antiteater-X-Film; S: RWF; C: Dietrich Lohmann; PA: Hanna Schygulla, Lilith Ungerer, Elga Sorbas, Doris Mattes, RWF, Rudolf Waldemar Brem, Hans Hirschmüller, Harry Baer, Peter Moland, Hannes Gromball, Irm Hermann; D: Filmverlag (New Yorker).

Götter der Pest (Gods of the Plague); 1969; 91 min; P: Antiteater; S: RWF; C: Dietrich Lohmann; PA: Harry Baer, Hanna Schygulla, Margarethe von Trotta, Günther Kaufmann, Carla Aulaulu; D: Filmverlag (New Yorker).

Warum läuft Herr R. amok? (Why Does Herr R. Run Amok?); 1969; color; 88 min; P: Antiteater/Maran-Film for SDR; S: Michael Fengler, RWF; C: Dietrich Lohmann; PA: Kurt Raab, Lilith Ungerer, Amadeus Fengler, Franz Maron; D: Filmverlag (New Yorker).

Rio das Mortes; 1970; color; 84 min; P: Janus Film und Fernsehen/Antiteater-X-Film.

Das Kaffeehaus (The Coffee House); 1970; 105 min; P: WDR.

Whity; 1970; color; 95 min; P: Atlantis Film/Antiteater-X-Film; S: RWF; C: Michael Ballhaus; PA: Günther Kaufmann, Hanna Schygulla, Ulli Lommel, Harry Baer, Katrin Schaake, Ron Randell; copy on file with Berliner Synchron.

Die Niklashauser Fart (The Niklashausen Journey); 1970; color; 86 min; P: Janus Film und Fernsehen for WDR.

Der amerikanische Soldat (The American Soldier); 1970; 80 min; P: Antiteater; S: RWF; C: Dietrich Lohmann; PA: Karl Scheydt, Elga Sorbas, Jan George, Margarethe von Trotta, Hark Bohm, Eva Ingeborg Scholz, Kurt Raab, RWF; D: Filmverlag (New Yorker).

Warnung vor einer heiligen Nutte (Beware of a Holy Whore); 1970; color; 103 min; P: Antiteater-X-Film/Nova International; S: RWF; C: Michael Ballhaus; PA: Lou Castel, Eddie Constantine, Hanna Schygulla, Marquard Bohm, RWF, Ulli Lommel; D: Filmverlag (New Yorker).

Pioniere in Ingolstadt (Pioneers in Ingolstadt); 1970; color; 84 min; P: Janus Film und Fernsehen/Antiteater for ZDF.

Der Händler der vier Jahreszeiten (The Merchant of Four Seasons); 1971; color; 89 min; P: Tango Film; S: RWF; C: Dietrich Lohmann; PA: Hans Hirschmüller, Irm Hermann, Hanna Schygulla, Gusti Kreissl, Kurt Raab, Klaus Löwitsch, Karl Scheydt, Ingrid Caven; D: Filmverlag (New Yorker).

Die bitteren Tränen der Petra von Kant (The Bitter Tears of Petra von Kant); 1972; color; 124 min; P: Tango Film; S: RWF, based on his play; C: Michael Ballhaus; PA: Margit Carstensen, Hanna Schygulla, Irm Hermann; D: Filmverlag (New Yorker).

Wildwechsel (Jail Bait); 1972; color; 102 min; P: Intertel for SFB; S: RWF, based on a play by Franz Xaver Kroetz; C: Dietrich Lohmann; PA: Jörg von Liebenfels, Ruth Drexel, Eva Mattes, Harry Baer; D: Atlas (New Yorker).

Acht Stunden sind kein Tag (Eight Hours Don't Make a Day); 1972; color; 5-part TV series; Part 1: 101 min; Part 2: 100 min; Part 3: 92 min; Part 4: 89 min; Part 5: 89 min; P: WDR.

Bremer Freiheit (Bremen Freedom); 1972; color; 87 min; P: Telefilm Saar for SR; D: (FRG Embassy).

Welt am Draht (World on a Wire); 1973; 2-part TV production; color; Part 1: 99 min; Part 2: 106 min; P: WDR.

Nora Helmer; 1973; color; 101 min; P: Telefilm Saar for SR.

Angst essen Seele auf (Ali: Fear Eats the Soul); 1973; color; 93 min; P: Tango Film; S: RWF; C: Jürgen Jürges; PA: Brigitte Mira, El Hedi Ben Salem, Barbara Valentin, Irm Hermann; D: Filmverlag (New Yorker).

Martha; 1973; color; 112 min; P: WDR; D: (Teleculture).

Fontane Effi Briest (Effi Briest); 1974; 141 min; P: Tango Film; S: RWF, based on the novel by Theodor Fontane; C: Dietrich Lohmann, Jürgen Jürges; PA: Hanna Schygulla, Wolfgang Schenck, Karlheinz Böhm, Ulli Lommel, Ursula Strätz, Irm Hermann, Hark Bohm, Lilo Pempeit; D: Filmverlag (New Yorker).

Faustrecht der Freiheit (Fox and His Friends); 1974; color; 123 min; P: Tango Film/City Film; S: RWF; C: Michael Ballhaus; PA: RWF, Peter Chatel, Karlheinz Böhm, Harry Baer; D: Filmverlag (New Yorker).

Wie ein Vogel auf dem Draht (Like a Bird on the Wire); 1974; color; 44 min; P: WDR.

Mutter Küsters' Fahrt zum Himmel (Mother Küsters Goes to Heaven); 1975; color; 120 min; P: Tango Film; S: RWF, Kurt Raab; PA: Brigitte Mira, Ingrid Caven, Karlheinz Böhm, Margit Carstensen, Armin Meier; D: Filmverlag (New Yorker).

Angst vor der Angst (Fear of Fear); 1975; color; 88 min; P: WDR; D: (Teleculture).

Ich will doch nur, daβ ihr mich liebt (I Only Want You to Love Me); 1975–76; color; 104 min; P: Bavaria for WDR; D: (FRG Embassy).

Satansbraten (Satan's Brew); 1975–76; color; 112 min; P: Albatros Productions/Trio Film; S: RWF; C: Jürgen Jürges, Michael Ballhaus; PA: Kurt Raab, Margit Carstensen, Helen Vita, Volker Spengler, Ingrid Caven; D: Filmverlag (New Yorker).

Chinesisches Roulette (Chinese Roulette); 1976; color; 86 min; P: Albatros Productions; S: RWF; C: Michael Ballhaus; PA: Margit Carstensen, Anna Karina, Alexander Allerson, Ulli Lommel, Andrea Schober, Macha Méril, Brigitte Mira; D: Filmverlag (New Yorker).

Bolwieser (Bolwieser; also known as *The Stationmaster's Wife)*; 1976–77; color; 2-part TV production; Part 1: 104 min; Part 2: 92 min; P: Bavaria for ZDF; D: (Teleculture).

Frauen in New York (Women in New York); 1977; color; 111 min; P: NDR.

Despair: Eine Reise ins Licht (Despair); 1977; color; 119 min; P: NF Geria II Film/SFP Paris/Bavaria; S: Tom Stoppard, based on the novel by Vladimir Nabokov; C: Michael Ballhaus; PA: Dirk Bogarde, Andréa Ferréol, Volker Spengler, Klaus Löwitsch; D: Filmverlag (New Line Cinema).

Deutschland im Herbst (Germany in Autumn); 1977–78; color with b/w segments; 134 min; Fassbinder episode 26 min; C: Michael Ballhaus (Fassbinder segment); PA: RWF, Lilo Pempeit; D: Filmverlag (New Line Cinema).

Die Ehe der Maria Braun (The Marriage of Maria Braun); 1978; color; 120 min; P: Albatros Productions; S: Peter Märthesheimer, Pea Fröhlich, based on an idea by RWF; C: Michael Ballhaus; PA: Hanna Schygulla, Klaus Löwitsch, Ivan Desny, Gottfried John, Gisela Uhlen, Günter Lamprecht, George Byrd; D: United Artists (New Yorker).

In einem Jahr mit 13 Monden (In a Year of 13 Moons); 1978; color; 124 min; P: Tango Film/Pro-ject Film Produktion im Filmverlag; S: RWF; C: RWF, assisted by Werner Lüring; PA: Volker Spengler, Ingrid Caven, Gottfried John, Elisabeth Trissenaar; D: Filmverlag (New Yorker).

Die dritte Generation (The Third Generation); 1978–79; color; 110 min; P: Tango Film/Pro-ject Film Produktion im Filmverlag; S and C: RWF; PA: Volker Spengler, Bulle Ogier, Hanna Schygulla, Harry Baer, Vitus Zeplichal, Udo Kier, Margit Carstensen, Günther Kaufmann, Eddie Constantine, Raul Gimenez; D. Filmverlag (New Yorker).

HANS W. GEISSENDÖRFER

Befriedigung (Satisfaction); 1966; documentary.

Dynamitfischerei (Dynamite Fishery); 1967; documentary.

Fastentage in Griechenland (Days of Fasting in Greece); 1967; documentary.

Netzfischfang im Aegäischen Meer (Net Fishing in the Aegean Sea); 1967; documentary.

Eins & Eins (One and One); 1968; short.

Manfred Schoof Quintet; 1968; documentary.

Anna Kahn; 1968; short.

Der Fall Lena Christ (The Case of Lena Christ); 1968; 90 min; P: BR; S: HWG, based on Lena Christ's *Erinnerungen einer Überflüssigen (Memoirs of a Superfluous Woman)* and Peter Bendix's *Der Weg der Lena Christ (The Path of Lena Christ)*; C: Robby Müller; PA: Heidi Stroh, Edith Volkmann, Sophie Strelow, Paul Stieber-Walter, Eberhard Peiker, Wilhelm Meyer, Peter Dornseif, Peter Hallwachs, Luigi Malipiero.

Jonathan; 1969; color; 100 min (German version; American release version 103 min); P: Iduna Film/Telepol; S: HWG, loosely based on Bram Stoker's *Dracula*; C: Robby Müller; PA: Jürgen Jung, Ilse Künkele, Paul Albert Krumm, Hertha von Walter, Oskar von Schab, Ilona Grübel, Hans-Dieter Jendreyko, Henry Liposca, Arthur Brauss; D: Obelisk (New Yorker).

Eine Rose für Jane (A Rose for Jane); 1970; color; 91 min; P: WDR; S: HWG, Roald Koller; C: Robby Müller, Willi Trautner; PA: Heinz Bennent, Martine Brochard, Paul Albert Krumm, Hammi de Beukelaer, Eddie Constantine, Klaus Lemke, Rolf Zacher, Wim Ponica, Ton Lesnsink, Harry Weitner, Barbara Witow, Giovanni Lipolis, Albert von Dorn.

Carlos; 1971; color; 107 min; P: Iduna Film/WDR/BR; S: HWG, based loosely on Schiller's *Don Carlos*; C: Robby Müller; PA: Gottfried John, Anna Karina, Geraldine Chaplin, Horst Frank, Thomas Hunter, Sheike Ophir, Bernhard Wicki, Lorenza Colville, Ruven Steffer, Sabi Dor; D: Beta-Film.

Marie; 1972; color; 95 min; P: Bavaria/WDR; S: HWG, Klaus Bädekerl; C: Robby Müller; PA: Anna Martins, Maria Schell, Heinz Bennent, Lis Verhoeven, Wilfried Klaus, Heidi Stroh, Ilona Grübel; D: (FRG Embassy).

Die Eltern (The Parents); 1973; color; 96 min; P: Bavaria/WDR; S: HWG, Klaus Bädekerl, Bernd Eichinger; C: Robby Müller; PA: Anne Bennent, Heinz Bennent, Henri Serre, Barbara Rütting, Gunter Malzacher, Diane Bennent, Siegfried Kristen, David Bennent, Franz Josef Steffens, Hans Elwenspoek.

Perahim—Die zweite Chance (Perahim—The Second Chance); 1974; color; 104 min; P: Filmverlag/ZDF; S: HWG, Bernd Eichinger, Ulli Edel, based on Constantin V. Gheroghiu's *Gangster Maximilian Perahim*; C: Robby Müller; PA: Heinz Bennent, Anna Martins, Blanche Aubry, Richard Münch, Leon Askin, Michael Janisch, Kurt Jaggberg, Annemarie Düringer.

Lobster; 1975; color; 6-part TV series, each installment 58 min.

Sternsteinhof (Sternstein Manor); 1975; color; 125 min; P: Roxy Film/BR; S: HWG, Hermann Weigel, based on Ludwig Anzengruber's *Sternsteinhof*; C: Frank Brühne; PA: Katja Rupé, Tilo Prückner, Peter Kern, Agnes Fink, Gustl Bayrhammer, Irm Hermann, Ulrike Luderer, Horst Richter, Maria Stadler, Elfriede Kuzmany; D: Filmverlag.

Die Wildente (The Wild Duck); 1976; color; 105 min; P: Solaris-Film/WDR/Sascha-Film; S: HGW, based on Henrik Ibsen's play; C: Robby Müller; PA: Jean Seberg, Peter Kern, Bruno Ganz, Anne Bennent, Martin Flörchinger, Heinz Bennent, Heinz Moog, Sonja Sutter, Robert Werner, Guido Wieland; D: Filmverlag (New Yorker).

Die gläserne Zelle (The Glass Cell); 1977; color; 90 min; P: Roxy Film/Solaris-Film/BR; S: HWG, Klaus Bädekerl, based on Patricia Highsmith's novel; C: Robby Müller; PA: Helmut Griem, Dieter Laser, Bernhard Wicki, Brigitte Fossey, Walter Kohut, Gerlinde Egger, Claudius Kracht, Günther Strack, Klaus Münster, Hans Günther Martens, Christa-Maria Netsch; D: Filmverlag.

Theodor Chindler; 1979; color; 8-part TV series, each installment about 60 min.

REINHARD HAUFF

Untermann—Obermann; 1969; 40 min; P: RH/Bavaria/SDR; S: Volker Koch, RH; C: Dieter von Soden.

Die Revolte (The Revolt); 1969; color; 90 min; P: Bavaria/WDR; S: Peter Glotz, Volker Koch, RH; C: W. P. Hassenstein; PA: Hans Brenner, Raimund Harmstorf, Kathrin Schaake, Hanna Schygulla.

Ausweglos (No Way Out); 1969; 80 min; P: Bavaria/SDR; S: Martin Walser, RH; C: W. P. Hassenstein, Paul Ellmerer, Kurt Brückner.

Offener Haß gegen Unbekannt (Open Hatred Against a Person or Persons Unknown); 1970; color; 88 min; P: Bavaria/ZDF; S: Philippe Pilliod, Georg Feil, RH, based on the notebooks of Heine Schoof; C: W. P. Hassenstein; PA: Akim Ahrens, Jürgen Mathes, Paul Scherbe.

Mathias Kneissl; 1970–71; color; 90 min; P: Bavaria/WDR; S: Martin Sperr, RH; C: W. P. Hassenstein; PA: Hans Brenner, Ruth Drexel, Frank Frey, Eva Mattes, Hanna Schygulla, Kurt Raab, Martin Sperr, Rainer Werner Fassbinder, Volker Schlöndorff; D: (FRG Embassy).

Haus am Meer (House by the Sea); 1972; color; 98 min; P: Bavaria/Triglav Yugoslavia/WDR; S: Philippe Pilliod, RH; C: W. P. Hassenstein; PA: Hanna Schygulla, Rolf Becker, Paolo Bonetti, Branko Plesa, Milan Srdoc.

Desaster (Disaster); 1972–73; color; 95 min; P: Bavaria/WDR; S: Manfred Grunert; C: W. P. Hassenstein; PA: Klaus Löwitsch, Dieter Laser, Ruth Maria Kubitschek, Eva Mattes, Georg Marischka, Margarethe von Trotta.

Die Verrohung des Franz Blum (The Brutalization of Franz Blum); 1973–74; color; 104 min; P: Bioskop/WDR; S: Burkhard Driest; C: W. P. Hassenstein; PA: Jürgen Prochnow, Burkhard Driest, Eike Gallwitz, Tilo Prückner, Karlheinz Merz, Kurt Raab; D: Filmverlag (New Yorker).

Zündschnüre (Fuses); 1974; 101 min; P: WDR; S: Burkhard Driest, based

on the novel by Franz Josef Degenhardt; C: Frank Brühne; PA:
Michael Olbrich, Bettina Porsch, Thomas Visser, Kurt Funk, Tilli
Breidenbach, Hans Beerhenke, Tana Schanzara.

Paule Pauländer; 1975; color; 95 min; P:Bioskop/WDR; S: Burkhard
Driest; C: Jürgen Jürges; PA: Manfred Reiss, Angelika Kulessa, Man-
fred Gnoth, Katharina Tüschen, Achim Sauter, Werner Eichhorn,
Margret Homeyer; D: Atlas (FRG Embassy).

Der Hauptdarsteller (The Main Actor); also known as *The Star* and *The
Protagonist)*; 1977; color; 94 min; P: Bioskop/WDR; S: Christel Buschmann, RH; C: Frank Brühne; PA: Mario Adorf, Vadim Glowna, Michael Schweiger, Rolf Zacher, Hans Brenner, Akim Ahrens, Angelika Kulessa; D: Filmverlag (Teleculture).

Messer im Kopf (Knife in the Head); 1978; color; 108 min; P: Bioskop/
Hallelujah/WDR; S: Peter Schneider; C: Frank Brühne; PA: Bruno
Ganz, Angela Winkler, Hans Christian Blech, Hans Brenner, Heinz
Hönig, Eike Gallwitz; D: Filmverlag (New Yorker).

WERNER HERZOG

Herakles; 1962–65; P: WH; redone 1965: for Cineropa Films.

Spiel im Sand (Game in the Sand); 1964; P: WH; not released.

*Die beispiellose Verteidigung der Festung Deutschkreuz (The Unprecedented
Defense of the Fortress Deutschkreuz)*; 1966; P: Werner Herzog
Filmproduktion/Arpa-Film.

Lebenszeichen (Signs of Life); 1967; 90 min; P: Werner Herzog
Filmproduktion; S: WH; C: Thomas Mauch; PA: Peter Brogle,
Wolfgang Reichmann, Athina Zacharopoulu, Wolfgang von
Ungern-Sternberg, Wolfgang Stumpf; D: Filmverlag (New Yorker).

Letzte Worte (Last Words); 1967–68; P: Werner Herzog Filmproduktion.

Maßnahmen gegen Fanatiker (Precautions Against Fanatics); 1968; P:
Werner Herzog Filmproduktion.

Die fliegenden Ärzte von Ostafrika (The Flying Doctors of East Africa); 1968–
69; P: Werner Herzog Filmproduktion.

Fata Morgana; 1968–70; color; 79 min; P: Werner Herzog Filmproduk-
tion; S: WH; C: Jörg Schmidt-Reitwein; PA: Wolfgang von Ungern-
Sternberg, James William Gledhill, Eugen des Montagnes; Narrators:
Lotte Eisner, Wolfgang Bächler, Manfred Eigendorf; D: Filmverlag
(New Line Cinema).

Auch Zwerge haben klein angefangen (Even Dwarfs Started Small); 1969–70;
96 min; P: Werner Herzog Filmproduktion; S: WH; C: Thomas
Mauch; PA: Helmut Döring, Paul Glauer, Gisela Hertwig, Hertel
Minkner, Gertraud Piccini, Marianne Saar, Brigitte Saar; D: Filmverlag (New Yorker).

Behinderte Zukunft (Handicapped Future); 1970; P: Werner Herzog
Filmproduktion.

Land des Schweigens und der Dunkelheit (Land of Silence and Darkness);
1970–71; 85 min; P: Werner Herzog Filmproduktion; D: (FRG Embassy).

Aguirre, der Zorn Gottes (Aguirre, the Wrath of God); 1972; color; 93 min;

P: Werner Herzog Filmproduktion; S: WH; C: Thomas Mauch; PA: Klaus Kinski, Helena Rojo, Del Negro, Ruy Guerra, Peter Berling, Cecilia Rivera; D: Filmverlag (New Yorker).

Die große Ekstase des Bildschnitzers Steiner (The Great Ecstasy of the Sculptor Steiner); 1973–74; P: Werner Herzog Filmproduktion.

Jeder für sich und Gott gegen alle (Every Man for Himself and God Against All, or The Enigma of Kaspar Hauser); 1974; color; 109 min; P: Werner Herzog Filmproduktion; S: WH; C: Jörg Schmidt-Reitwein, Michael Gast, Klaus Wyborny; PA: Bruno S., Walter Ladengast, Brigitte Mira, Hans Musäus, Willy Semmelrogge, Michael Kroecher, Enno Patalas, Elis Pilgrim, Clemens Scheitz; D: Filmverlag (New Yorker).

How Much Wood Would a Woodchuck Chuck?; 1975–76; P: Werner Herzog Filmproduktion.

Mit mir will keiner spielen (No One Wants to Play with Me); 1976; P: Werner Herzog Filmproduktion.

Herz aus Glas (Heart of Glass); 1976; color; 94 min; P: Werner Herzog Filmproduktion; S: Herbert Achternbusch, WH; C: Jörg Schmidt-Reitwein; PA: Josef Bierbichler, Stefan Güttler, Clemens Scheitz, Volker Brechtl, Sonja Skiba, Brunhilde Klöckner; D: Filmverlag (New Yorker).

La Soufrière; 1976; P: Werner Herzog Filmproduktion.

Stroszek; 1976–77; color; 107 min; P: Werner Herzog Filmproduktion, Gaumont; S: WH; C: Thomas Mauch, Ed Lachmann; PA: Bruno S., Eva Mattes, Clemens Scheitz, Wilhelm von Homburg, Clayton Szlapinski; D: Filmverlag (New Yorker).

Nosferatu—Phantom der Nacht (Nosferatu the Vampyre); 1978; color; 107 min; P: Werner Herzog Filmproduktion, Gaumont; S: WH, based on F. W. Murnau's *Nosferatu* and Bram Stoker's *Dracula*; C: Jörg Schmidt-Reitwein, Michael Gast; PA: Klaus Kinski, Isabelle Adjani, Bruno Ganz, Roland Topor, Walter Ladengast; D: Twentieth Century-Fox (Films Incorporated).

Woyzeck; 1978; color; 81 min; P: Werner Herzog Filmproduktion; S: WH, based on Georg Büchner's *Woyzeck*; C: Jörg Schmidt-Reitwein, Michael Gast; PA: Klaus Kinski, Eva Mattes, Wolfgang Reichmann, Willy Semmelrogge, Josef Bierbichler, Paul Burian; D: Filmverlag (New Yorker).

ALEXANDER KLUGE

Brutalität in Stein (Brutality in Stone); 1960; 12 min; P: AK/Peter Schamoni.

Rennen (Race); 1961; 9 min; P: AK. Rolf A. Klug.

Lehrer im Wandel (Teachers in Transition); 1962–63; 11 min; P: AK.

Porträt einer Bewährung (Portrait of Proven Service); 1964; 13 min; P: Kairos.

Abschied von Gestern (Yesterday Girl); 1965–66; 88 min; P: Kairos/Independent-Film; S: AK; C: Edgar Reitz, Thomas Mauch; PA: Alexandra Kluge, Günter Mack, Hans Korte; D: Filmverlag (Liberty).

Pokerspiel (Poker Game); 1966; P: Kairos

Frau Blackburn, geb. 5. Jan. 1872, *wird gefilmt* (*Mrs. Blackburn, born 1/ 5/1872, is being filmed*); 1967; 14 min; P: Kairos.

Die Artisten in der Zirkuskuppel: Ratlos (*Artists in the Big Top: Perplexed*); 1967–68; b/w and color; 103 min; P: Kairos; S: AK; C: Günter Hörmann, Thomas Mauch; PA: Hannelore Hoger, Alfred Edel, Siegfried Graue; D: Filmverlag (FRG Embassy).

Feuerlöscher E. A. Winterstein (*Firefighter E. A. Winterstein*): 1968; 11 min; P: Kairos.

Die unbezähmbare Leni Peickert (*The Untameable Leni Peickert*); 1967–69; 60 min; P: Kairos for WDR.

Ein Arzt aus Halberstadt (*A Doctor from Halberstadt*); 1969–70; 29 min; P: Kairos.

Der große Verhau (*The Big Mess*); 1969–70; color and b/w; 86 min; P: Kairos; S: AK; C: Thomas Mauch, Alfred Tichawsky; PA: Vinzenz and Maria Sterr, Hannelore Hoger, Siegfried Graue; D: Filmverlag.

Wir verbauen 3 x 27 Milliarden Dollar in einen Angriffsschlachter (*We're Sinking 3 x 27 Billion Dollars into an Attack Cruiser*); 1971; 18 min; P: Kairos.

Willi Tobler und der Untergang der 6. Flotte (*Willi Tobler and the Demise of the 6th Fleet*); 1971; color and b/w; 96 min; P: Kairos; S: AK; C: Dietrich Lohmann, Alfred Tichawsky, Thomas Mauch; D: Alfred Edel, Hark Bohm, Helga Skalla.

Besitzbürgerin, Jahrgang 1908; 1973; 11 min; P: Kairos.

Gelegenheitsarbeit einer Sklavin (*Occasional Work of a Female Slave*); 1973; 91 min; P: Kairos; S: AK; C: Thomas Mauch; PA: Alexandra Kluge, Franz Bronski.

In Gefahr und größter Not bringt der Mittelweg den Tod (*In Danger and Great Need the Middle Road Leads to Death*); Directors: AK, Edgar Reitz; 1974; 90 min; P: Reitz-Film/Kairos; S: AK, Edgar Reitz; C: Edgar Reitz, Alfred Hürmer, Günter Hörmann; PA: Dagmar Bödderich, Jutta Winkelmann; D: Filmverlag.

Der starke Ferdinand (*Strong Man Ferdinand*); 1975–76; 1977; color (new version color and b/w); 90 min (new version, 97 min); P: Kairos/ Reitz-Film; S: AK; C: Thomas Mauch, Martin Schäfer; PA: Heinz Schubert, Verenice Rudolph; D: Filmverlag (Liberty).

Die Menschen, die die Staufer-Ausstellung vorbereiten (*The People Preparing the Staufer Exhibit*); 1977; 42 min; P: Kairos/Institut für Filmgestaltung.

Nachrichten von den Staufern (*News of the Staufers*); 1977; 10 and 12 min (two films); P: Kairos/Institut für Filmgestaltung.

Deutschland im Herbst (*Germany in Autumn*); with Fassbinder, Schlöndorff, et al.; 1978; color; 134 min; P: Pro-ject Film produktion/Hallelujah-Film/Kairos; D: Filmverlag (New Line Cinema).

Die Patriotin (*The Patriot*); 1979; color and b/w; 121 min; P: Kairos; S: AK; C: Jörg Schmidt-Reitwein, Thomas Mauch, Werner Lüring, Günter Hörmann; PA: Hannelore Hoger, Dieter Mainka, Alfred Edel, Marius Müller-Westernhagen; D: Munic Films.

PETER LILIENTHAL

Picknick im Felde (Picnic in the Field); 1962; P: SWF.

Guernica—Jede Stunde verletzt und die letzte tötet (Guernica—Every Hour Injures and the Last One Kills); 1963; P: SWF.

Abschied (Farewell); 1965; P: SFB.

Der Beginn (The Beginning); 1966; P: SDR.

Horror; 1968; P: SDR.

Malatesta; 1969; color; 90 min; P: Manfred Durniok/SFB; S: PL, Heathcote Williams; C: Willy Pankau; PA: Eddie Constantine, Vladimir Pucholdt, Christine Noonan; D: Durniok, Freunde der Deutschen Kinemathek (FRG Embassy).

Die Sonne angreifen (Attacking the Sun); 1970; 83 min; P: Iduna/SFB; S: PL, based on *Verführung* by Witold Gombrowicz; C: Gerd von Bonin; PA: Jess Hahn, Willy Semmelrogge, Ingo Thouret, Peter Hirsche; D: Obelisk.

Jakob von Gunten; 1971; color; 90 min; P: ZDF; S: PL, based on the novel by Robert Walser; C: Dietrich Lohmann; PA: Hanna Schygulla, Alexander May, Sebastian Bleisch, Reinhard Hauff.

Shirley Chisholm for President; 1972; 60 min; P: ZDF.

La Victoria; 1973; color; 84 min; P: Produktion 1 im Filmverlag/ZDF; S: PL, Antonio Skármeta; C: Silvio Caiozzi; PA: Paula Moya, Vincente Santa Maria, Carmen Lazo, the people of Nueva Palena; D: Filmverlag.

Hauptlehrer Hofer (Schoolmaster Hofer); 1974; color; 100 min; P: F.F.A.T.-Film/WDR; S: PL, Herbert Brödl, Günter Herburger, based on the story by Günter Herburger; C: Kurt Weber, Ulrich Heiser; PA: André Watt, Sebastian Bleisch, Kim Parnass, Tilo Prückner; D: Basis (FRG Embassy).

Es herrscht Ruhe im Land (Calm Prevails over the Country); 1975; color; 104 min; P: F.F.A.T.-Film/ZDF/ORF; S: Antonio Skármeta, PL; C: Robby Müller, Abel Aboim; PA: Charles Vanel, Mario Pardo, Eduardo Duran, Zita Duarte, Henriqueta Maya; D: Filmverlag (New Yorker).

David; 1978–79; color; 125 min; P: von Vietinghoff/Pro-ject/ Filmverlag/ZDF/F.F.A.T./Dedra Pictures; S: PL, Jurek Becker, Ulla Ziemann; C: Al Ruban; PA: Walter Taub, Irena Vrkljan, Eva Mattes, Mario Fischel, Dominique Horwitz; D: Filmverlag (Kino International).

EDGAR REITZ

Schicksal einer Oper (Fate of an Opera); 1958; 16 min; P: Filmstudio Leckebusch.

Baumwolle (Cotton); 1959; color; 35 min; P: Studio Linnebach.

Krebsforschung (Cancer Research); 1960; color; 2 films, 30 min each.

Yucatan; 1960; 12 min.

Kommunikation; 1961; color; 11 min.

Post und Technik (Mail and Technology); 1961; color; 45 min; P: Bavaria.

Ärztekongress (Medical Congress); 1961; color; 30 min.

Moltopren 1–4; 1961; color; 4 films, 20–30 min each.

Kino I—Geschwindigkeit (Cinema I—Speed); 1962; 12 min; P: Insel.

Varia Vision; 1964–65; approx. 60 hrs; simultaneous projection of 36 strips of film on 120 movable screens; P: Insel, for 1965 International Traffic Fair in Munich.

Die Kinder (The Children); 1966; 12 min; P: ER.

Mahlzeiten (Mealtimes); 1966–67; 97 min; P and S: ER; C: Thomas Mauch; PA: Heidi Stroh, Georg Hauke, Nina Frank.

Fußnoten (Footnotes); 1967; 90 min; P and S: ER; C: Thomas Mauch; PA: Heidi Stroh, Georg Hauke, Nina Frank.

Uxmal; 1968; color; 75 min; P, S, and C: ER; PA: Petra Schürmann, Peter Berling.

Filmstunde (Film Hour); 1968; 120 min; P and S: ER; C: Dedo Weigert, Thomas Mauch.

Cardillac; 1968–69; color; 95 min; P and S: ER; C: Dietrich Lohmann; PA: Hans Christian Blech, Catana Cayetano, Liane Hielscher, Rolf Becker.

Geschichten vom Kübelkind (Tales of the Trashcan Kid); Directors: Ula Stöckl, ER; 1969–70; color; 210 min; P: ER; S: Ula Stöckl, ER; C: ER; PA: Christine de Loup, Alf Brustellin, Werner Herzog; D: Basis.

Kino Zwei (Cinema Two): 1971; color; 90 min; P, S, and C: ER; PA: Urs Jenny, Vlado Kristl, Werner Egger.

Das goldene Ding (The Golden Stuff); Directors: Ula Stöckl, ER, Nicos Perakis, Alf Brustellin; 1971; color; 90 min; P and C: ER; S: Ula Stöckl, ER, Nicos Perakis, Alf Brustellin; PA: Christian Reitz, Ramin Vahabschadeh, Mario Zöllner; D: Basis.

Die Reise nach Wien (The Trip to Vienna); 1973; color; 102 min; P: ER; S: ER, Alexander Kluge; C: Robby Müller; PA: Elke Sommer, Hannelore Elsner, Mario Adorf.

In Gefahr und größter Not bringt der Mittelweg den Tod (In Danger and Great Need the Middle Road Leads to Death); Directors; Alexander Kluge, ER; 1974; 90 min; P: Reitz-Film/Kairos; S: Alexander Kluge, ER; C: ER, Alfred Hürmer, Günter Hörmann; D: Filmverlag.

Bethanien; 1975; color; 30 min.

Picnic; 1975; color; 28 min.

Wir gehen wohnen (We're Going to Play House); 1975; color; 28 min.

Stunde Null (Zero Hour); 1976; 108 min; P: ER/Solaris/WDR; S: Peter Steinbach, ER, Petra Kiener, Karsten Witte; C: Gernot Roll; PA: Kai Taschner, Klaus Dierig, Herbert Weissbach; D: Prokino, Atlas.

Deutschland im Herbst (Germany in Autumn); Directors: ER, Fassbinder, Schlöndorff, Kluge, et al.; 1978; color; 134 min; D: Filmverlag (New Line Cinema).

Der Schneider von Ulm (The Tailor of Ulm); 1978; color; 115 min; P: ER/Genée; S: ER, Petra Kiener; C: Dietrich Lohmann, Martin Schäfer; PA: Tilo Prückner, Hannelore Elsner, Vadim Glowna; D: Filmverlag.

Susanne tanzt (Susan Dances); 1979; 16 min.

VOLKER SCHLÖNDORFF and MARGARETHE VON TROTTA

(all films directed by Schlöndorff *only*, unless noted)

Wen kümmert's (Who Cares); alternately titled *Wacht am Rhein (Watch on the Rhine)*; 1960; 11 min; never released theatrically.

Der junge Törleß (Young Törless); 1965–66; 87 min; P: Franz Seitz/Louis Malle; S: VS, Herbert Asmodi, based on the book by Robert Musil; C: Franz Rath; PA: Matthieu Carrière, Bernd Tischer, Marian Seidowsky, Herbert Asmodi, Barbara Steele; D: Atlas (New Yorker).

Mord und Totschlag (A Degree of Murder); 1966–67; color; 87 min; P: Rob Houwer-Film; S: VS, Gregor von Rezzori, Arne Boyer, Niklas Frank; C: Franz Rath; PA: Anita Pallenberg, Hans Peter Hallwachs, Manfred Fischbeck, Werner Enke.

Ein unheimlicher Moment (An Uncanny Moment); 1967; 13 min; P: Franz Seitz; made to be included in the episodic film *Der Paukenspieler (The Kettledrum Player)*, which was never released.

Michael Kohlhaas—der Rebell (Michael Kohlhaas); 1968–69; color; 100 min; P: Oceanic Film Produktion/Rob Houwer-Film; S: VS, Edward Bond, Clement Biddle-Wood, based on the story by Heinrich von Kleist; C: Willi Kurant, Herwig Zürkendörfer; PA: David Warner, Anna Karina, Kurt Meisel, Inigo Jackson, Emanuel Schmied, Gregor von Rezzori, Peter Weiss, Anita Pallenberg; D: Warner-Columbia (Corinth).

Baal; 1969; color; 87 min; P: HR/BR/Hallelujah-Film; S: VS, from the play by Bertolt Brecht; C: Dietrich Lohmann; PA: Rainer Werner Fassbinder, MvT, Sigi Graue, Hanna Schygulla.

Der plötzliche Reichtum der armen Leute von Kombach (The Sudden Wealth of the Poor People of Kombach); 1970; 102 min; P: HR/Hallelujah-Film; S: VS, MvT; C: Franz Rath; PA: Georg Lehn, Reinhard Hauff, Karl-Josef Cramer, Wolfgang Bächler, Harry Owen, Harald Müller, MvT, Rainer Werner Fassbinder; D: Atlas (New Yorker).

Die Moral der Ruth Halbfass (The Morals of Ruth Halbfass); 1971; color; 89 min; P: Hallelujah-Film/HR; S: VS, Peter Hamm; C: Klaus Müller-Laue, Konrad Kotowski; PA: Senta Berger, Peter Ehrlich, Susanne Rettig, Helmut Griem, MvT, Marian Seidowsky; D: CIC.

Strohfeuer (A Free Woman); 1972; color; 98 min; P: Hallelujah-Film/HR; S: VS, MvT, C: Sven Nykvist; PA: MvT, Friedhelm Ptok, Martin Lüttge, Walter Sedlmayer, Georg Marischka; D: Filmverlag, Atlas (New Yorker).

Übernachtung in Tirol (Overnight Stay in Tirol); 1973; color; 78 min; P: HR; S: VS, Peter Hamm; C: Franz Rath; PA: MvT, Reinhard Hauff, Herbert Achternbusch.

Georginas Gründe (Georgina's Reasons); 1974; color; 65 min; P: Bavaria for WDR/ORTF; S: Peter Adler, based on the story by Henry James; C: Sven Nykvist; PA: Edith Clever, Joachim Bissmeier, MvT.

Die verlorene Ehre der Katharina Blum (The Lost Honor of Katharina Blum); Directors: VS, MvT; 1975; color; 106 min; P: Paramount/Orion/Bioskop-Film; S: VS, MvT, based on the story by Heinrich

Böll; C: Jost Vacano; PA: Angela Winkler, Mario Adorf, Dieter Laser, Heinz Bennent, Jürgen Prochnow, Hannelore Hoger; D: CIC (Films Inc.).

Der Fangschuß (*Coup de Grâce*); 1976; 95 min; P: Bioskop-Film/Argos-Film/HR; S: Geneviève Dormann, MvT, Jutta Brückner, based on the novel by Marguerite Yourcenar; C: Igor Luther; PA: MvT, Rüdiger Kirschstein, Mathias Habich, Valeska Gert, Matthieu Carrière, Franz Morek; D: Filmverlag (Cinema 5).

Nur zum Spaß—nur zum Spiel: Kaleidoskop Valeska Gert (*Only for Fun–Only for Play: Kaleidoscope Valeska Gert*); 1977; color; 60 min; P: Bioskop-Film; S: VS; C: Michael Ballhaus; PA: Valeska Gert, Pola Kinski; D: Bioskop-Film.

Deutschland im Herbst (*Germany in Autumn*); 1977–78; color; 124 min; P: Project Filmproduktion Hallelujah-Film / Kairos-Film; S: Heinrich Böll; C: Colin Mounier; PA: Angela Winkler, Franziska Walser, Helmut Griem, Heinz Bennent, Mario Adorf, Dieter Laser; D: Filmverlag (New Line Cinema).

Das zweite Erwachen der Christa Klages (*The Second Awakening of Christa Klages*); Director MvT; 1977; color; 88 min; P: Bioskop-Film / WDR; S: MvT, Luisa Francia; C: Franz Rath; PA: Tina Engel, Sylvia Reize, Katharina Thalbach, Marius Müller-Westernhagen, Peter Schneider; D: Filmverlag (New Line Cinema).

Die Blechtrommel (*The Tin Drum*); 1979; color; 144 min; P: Franz Seitz/Bioskop-Film/Artemis-Film/Hallelujah-Film/GGB 14/Argos-Film/Jadran-Film/Film Polski; S: Jean-Claude Carrière, Franz Seitz, VS, Günter Grass, based on the novel by Grass; C: Igor Luther; PA: David Bennent, Mario Adorf, Angela Winkler, Daniel Olbrychski, Katharina Thalbach, Heinz Bennent, Tina Engel, Berta Drews, Andréa Ferréol, Charles Aznavour; D: United Artists (Films Inc.).

Schwestern oder Die Balance des Glücks (*Sisters or The Balance of Happiness*); Director: MvT; 1979; color; 91 min; P: Bioskop-Film / WDR; S: MvT, Luisa Francia, Martje Grohmann (Martje Herzog); C: Franz Rath; PA: Jutta Lampe, Gudrun Gabriel, Jessica Früh, Konstantin Wecker, Rainer Delventhal, Agnes Fink, Heinz Bennent; D: Filmverlag (Cinema 5).

MAY SPILS and WERNER ENKE

Kleine Front (*Small Front*); Directors: WE, Klaus Lemke; 1965; 23 min.

Das Porträt (*The Portrait*); Director: MS; 1966; 10 min; PA: MS.

Manöver (*Maneuver*); Director: MS; 1966; 10 min; PA: MS, WE.

Zur Sache, Schätzchen (*Go to It, Baby*; also known as *To the Point, Darling, Not Now, Darling*, and *Let's Get to the Point, Dearie*); 1967; 80 min; P: Peter Schamoni; S: MS, WE, Rüdiger Leberecht; C: Klaus König; PA: WE, Uschi Glas, Henry van Lyck, Inge Marschall, Helmut Brasch; D: Filmverlag, Meteor (FRG Embassy).

Nicht fummeln, Liebling! (*Don't Fiddle, Darling!*; also known as *Don't Fondle, Darling!* and *Don't Fondle Me, Love!*); 1969; 89 min; P: Cinenova;

S: Peter Schlieper, from an idea by Christian Karich; C: Hubs Hagen, Niklaus Schilling; PA: WE, Gila von Weitershausen, Henry van Lyck, Benno Hoffmann, Elke Hart (Elke Haltaufderheide), Karl Schönböck; D: CIC.

Hauf drauf, Kleiner! (Give It to Him, Lad!; also known as Pound on It, Shorty!); 1973; color; 82 min; P: Cinenova; S: MS, WE: C: Gernot Roll; PA: WE, Henry van Lyck, Mascha Gonska, Franz Mosthav, MS; D: CIC.

Wehe, wenn Schwarzenbeck kommt . . . . (Watch Out When Schwarzenbeck Comes; also known as Beware of Schwarzenbeck); 1978; color; 80 min; P: Cinenova; S: WE, MS, Jochen Wedegärtner; C: Petrus Schloemp; PA: WE, Benno Hoffmann, Sabine von Maydell, Helmuth Stange, Werner Schwier, Elma Karlowa; D: CIC.

ULA STÖCKL

Neun Leben hat die Katze (The Cat Has Nine Lives); 1968; color; 90 min; P: US, Thomas Mauch, S: US; C: Dietrich Lohmann; PA: Liane Hielscher, Christine de Loup, Heidi Stroh, Elke Kummer, Alexander Kaempfe, Jürgen Arnd, Hartmut Kirste; D: Basis (FRG Embassy).

Geschichten vom Kübelkind (Tales of the Trashcan Kid); 1969–70. (See Edgar Reitz.)

Das goldene Ding (The Golden Stuff); 1971. (See Alf Brustellin and Bernhard Sinkel.)

Sonntagsmalerei (Sunday Painting); 1971; color; 45 min; P, S, and C: US; PA: Ursula Fense, Alf Brustellin, Bernhard Sinkel; D: Basis.

Hirnhexen (Goblins of the Mind); 1972; 45 min; P and S: US; C: André Dubreuil; PA: Volker Matzen, Jürgen Rudi, Christian Preuss, Jürgen Alex, Hilda Heimböck, Helga Gross, Jutta Münch; D: Basis.

Der kleine Löwe und die Großen (The Lion Cub and the Grown-ups); 1973; 50 min; P and S: US; C: André Dubreuil; PA: Martin Halm, Hans-Peter Hallwachs, Gaby Gasser, Flory Jacoby, Rolf Zacher; D: Basis.

Ein ganz perfektes Ehepaar (A Quite Perfect Couple); 1973; 90 min; P and S: US; C: André Dubreuil; PA: Doris Kunstmann, Gerd Baltus, Susanne Schaeffer, Hans-Peter Hallwachs; D: Basis.

Hase and Igel (Hare and Hedgehog); 1974; color; 60 min; P and S: US; C: Franz Rath; PA: Claudia Rückert, Hans Lori, Günter Overmann, Helmut Zernickel, Karl Plag, Richard Kirchbichler; D: Basis.

Popp und Mingel (Popp and Mingel); 1975; 50 min; P: Artus-Film; S: US; C: Thomas Mauch; PA: Patrick Kreuzer, Lisa Kreuzer, Paul Neuhaus; D: Basis.

Erikas Leidenschaften (Erika's Passions); 1976; 64 min; P and S: US; C: Thomas Mauch; PA; Karin Baal, Vera Tschechowa; D: Basis (FRG Embassy).

Eine Frau mit Verantwortung (A Woman with Responsibility); 1977; color; 72 min; P: Eikon-Film; S: Jutta Brückner; C: Mario Masini; PA: Christina Scholz, Nikolaus Dutsch, Erwin Keusch, Evi Hörbiger, Francine Brücher, Philippe Naoun, Susanne Reitz; D: Basis.

JEAN-MARIE STRAUB and DANIÈLE HUILLET

Machorka-Muff; 1962; 18 min; P: JMS-DH/Atlas/Cineropa-Film; S: JMS, DH, based on the story "Hauptstädtisches Journal" by Heinrich Böll; C: Wendelin Sachtler; PA: Erich Kuby, Renate Lang, Rolf Thiede, Günther Strupp, Johannes Eckardt, Heiner Braun, Gino Cardella; D: Referat für Filmgeschichte (New Yorker).

Nicht versöhnt oder Es hilft nur Gewalt, wo Gewalt herrscht (*Not Reconciled*); 1964–65; 55 min; P: JMS, DH; S: JMS, DH, based on the novel *Billard um halbzehn* (*Billiards at Half Past Nine*) by Heinrich Böll; C: Wendelin Sachtler, Gerhard Ries, Christian Schwarzwald, JMS; PA: Henning Harmssen, Karlheinz Hargesheimer, Heiner Braun, Heinrich Hargesheimer, Martha Ständer, DH, Wendelin Sachtler; D: Referat für Filmgeschichte (New Yorker).

Chronik der Anna Magdalena Bach (*Chronicle of Anna Magdalena Bach*); 1967; 94 min; P: Franz Seitz Filmproduktion/ RAI/ IDI-Cinematografica/ JMS-DH/ Kuratorium Junger Deutscher Film/ Filmfonds/ HR/ Telepool; S: JMS, DH; C: Ugo Piccone, Saverio Diamanti, Giovanni Canfarelli, Hans Kracht, Uwe Radon, Thomas Hartwig; PA: Gustav Leonhardt, Christine Lang-Drewanz, Joachim Wolf, Rainer Kirchner, Ernst Castelli; D: Referat für Filmgeschichte (New Yorker).

Der Bräutigam, die Komödiantin und der Zuhälter (*The Bridegroom, the Comedienne, and the Pimp*); 1968; 23 min; P: Janus Film und Fernsehen/ JMS-DH; S: JMS, DH; C: Klaus Schilling, Hubs Hagen; PA: Rainer Werner Fassbinder, Lilith Ungerer, James Powell, Peer Raben, Irm Hermann, Hanna Schygulla, Rudolf Waldemar Brem; D: Referat für Filmgeschichte (New Yorker).

(Othon.) Les yeux ne veulent pas en tout temps se fermer ou Peut-être qu'un jour Rome se permettra de choisir à son tour/Die Augen wollen sich nicht zu jeder Zeit schließen oder Vielleicht eines Tages wird Rom sich erlauben seinerseits zu wählen (*Othon*); 1969; color; 82 min; P: Janus Film/JMS-DH; S: JMS, DH, based on *Othon* by Pierre Corneille; C: Ugo Piccone, Renato Berta; PA: Adriano Aprà, Anne Brumagne, Ennio Lauricella, Olimpia Carlisi, Anthony Pensabene, JMS; D: Freunde der Deutschen Kinomathek, Referat für Filmgeschichte (New Yorker).

Geschichtsunterricht (*History Lessons*); 1972; color; 88 min; P: JMS-DH/ Janus Film und Fernsehen; S: JMS, DH, based on the novel fragment *Die Geschäfte des Herrn Julius Caesar* by Bertolt Brecht; C: Renato Berta; PA: Gottfried Bold, Johann Unterpertiger, Henri Ludwig, Carl Vaillant; D: (New Yorker).

Einleitung zu Arnold Schoenbergs Begleitmusik zu einer Lichtspielszene (*Introduction to Arnold Schoenberg's "Accompaniment to a Cinematographic Scene"*); 1972; color and b/w; 16 min; P: JMS-DH for SWF; S: JMS; C: Renato Berta, Horst Bever; PA: Günter Peter Straschek, DH, Peter Nestler, JMS; D: Referat für Filmgeschichte (New Yorker).

Moses und Aron (*Moses and Aaron*); 1974; color; 110 min; P: ORF/ ARD/HR Janus Film und Fernsehen/JMS-DH/RAI/ORTF/Taurus-Film; S: Opera by Arnold Schoenberg; C: Ugo Piccone, Saverio Diamanti, Gianni Canfarelli, Renato Berta; PA: Günter Reich, Louis Devos, Eva

Csapò, Roger Lucas, Richard Salter; D: Prokino (New Yorker).

Fortini Cani/Die Hunde von Sinai (Fortini/Cani); 1976; color; 83 min; D: Referat für Filmgeschichte (New Yorker).

Toute Révolution est un Coup de Dés/Jede Revolution ist ein Würfelwurf (Every Revolution Is a Roll of the Dice); 1977; color; 11 min; D: (New Yorker).

Dalla nube alla resistenza/Von der Wolke zum Widerstand (From the Clouds to the Resistance); 1978–79; color; 103 min; D: (New Yorker).

HANS-JÜRGEN SYBERBERG

Fünfter Akt, siebte Szene: Fritz Kortner probt Kabale und Liebe (Fritz Kortner Rehearses Schiller's Intrigue and Love); 1965; 110 min; P: BR.

Romy: Anatomie eines Gesichts (Romy: Anatomy of a Face). 1965; 90 min, shortened to 60 min; P: Rob-Houwer-Filmproduktion; C: Kurt Lorenz; current version not authorized by Syberberg.

Kortner spricht Monologe für eine Schallplatte (Kortner Speaks Monologues for a Record); 1966; 90 min; P: Syberberg Filmproduktion/Presier-Records; C: Kurt Lorenz, Mac Lloyd, G. Hamory.

Die Grafen Pocci (The Counts Pocci); 1967; color; 92 min; P: HJS.

Scarabea—Wieviel Erde braucht der Mensch? (Scarabea—How Much Earth Does a Man Need?); 1968; color; 90 min; P: TMS Film; S: HJS, based on a story by Leo Tolstoy; C: Petrus Schloemp; PA: Walter Buschhoff, Nicoletta Macciavelli, Franz Graf Treuberg, Karsten Peters; D: HJS.

Sex-Business Made in Pasing; 1969; 100 min; TMS; D: Atlas.

San Domingo; 1970; 138 min; P: TMS; S: HJS, based on a novella by Heinrich von Kleist; C: Christian Blackwood; PA: Alice Ottawa, Michael König, Hans Georg Behr, Carla Aulaulu, Peter Moland; D: HJS, Atlas.

Nach meinem letzten Umzug . . . (After My Last Removal . . .); 1970; 72 min; P:HJS; D: Freunde der deutschen Kinemathek.

Ludwig—Requiem für einen jungfräulichen König (Ludwig—Requiem for a Virgin King); 1972; color; 134 min; P: TMS; S: HJS; C: Dietrich Lohmann; PA: Harry Baer, Peter Kern, Peter Moland, Hanna Köhler, Ingrid Caven, Ursula Strätz; D: Atlas (American Zoetrope).

Theodor Hierneis oder: Wie man ehem. Hofkoch wird (Ludwig's Cook); 1972; color; 90 min; P and S: HJS; PA: Walter Sedlmayer; D: HJS.

Karl May—Auf der Suche nach dem verlorenen Paradies (Karl May—In Search of Paradise Lost); 1974; color; 187 min; P: TMS/ZDF; S: HJS; C: Dietrich Lohmann; PA: Helmut Käutner, Kristina Söderbaum, Käthe Gold, Attila Hörbiger, Willy Trenk-Trebitsch, Mady Rahl, Lil Dagover, Rudolf Prack, Rainer von Artenfels, Leon Askin, André Heller; D: Warner-Columbia.

Winifred Wagner und die Geschichte des Hauses Wahnfried von 1914–1975 (The Confessions of Winifred Wagner); 1975; 303 min; P: HJS; D: Atlas (Liberty has 100-minute version).

Hitler, ein Film aus Deutschland (Our Hitler: A Film from Germany); 1977; color; 440 min; P: TMS/WDR/INA/BBC; S: HJS; C: Dietrich

Lohmann; PA: Heinz Schubert, Peter Kern, Harry Baer, Hellmuth Lange, Peter Lühr, Peter Moland, Martin Sperr, André Heller; D: HJS (American Zoetrope).

WIM WENDERS

Schauplätze (Settings); 1967; 10 min; P, S, and C: WW (lost).

Same Player Shoots Again; 1968; b/w tinted; 12 min; P, S, and C: WW; D: (Gray City).

Silver City; 1969; color; 25 min; P, S, and C: WW; D: (Gray City).

Alabama; 1969; 22 min; P: Hochschule für Fernsehen und Film (HFF); S: WW; C: Robby Müller, WW; D: HFF (Gray City).

3 amerikanische LPs (3 American LPs); 1969; color; 15 min; P: HR; S: Peter Handke; C: WW; D: (Gray City).

Polizeifilm; 1970; 12 min; P: BR; S: Albrecht Göschel; C: WW; PA: Jimmy Vogler, Kasimir Esser; D: (Gray City).

Summer in the City; 1970; 125 min; P: HFF; S: WW; C: Robby Müller; PA: Hanns Zischler, Edda Köchl, Libgart Schwarz, WW; D: HFF (Gray City).

Die Angst des Tormanns beim Elfmeter (The Goalie's Anxiety at the Penalty Kick); 1971; color; 101 min; P: Filmverlag/ORF/WDR; S: WW, Peter Handke, based on Handke's novel; C: Robby Müller; PA: Arthur Brauss, Kai Fischer, Erika Pluhar, Libgart Schwarz, Rüdiger Vogler; D: Filmverlag, Atlas (Gray City).

Der scharlachrote Buchstabe (The Scarlet Letter); 1972; color; 90 min; P: Filmverlag/WDR/Querejeta; S: WW, Bernardo Fernandez, from a script by Tankred Dorst based on the novel by Nathaniel Hawthorne; C: Robby Müller; PA: Senta Berger, Lou Castel, Hans Christian Blech, Yelina Samarina, Yella Rottländer, Rüdiger Vogler; D: Filmverlag (Gray City).

Alice in den Städten (Alice in the Cities); 1974; 110 min; P: Filmverlag/ WDR; S: WW, Veith von Fürstenberg; C: Robby Müller; PA: Rüdiger Vogler, Yella Rottländer, Lisa Kreuzer, Edda Köchl, Didi Petrikat, Hans Hirschmüller; D: Filmverlag, Atlas (Gray City).

Falsche Bewegung (Wrong Move); 1975; color; 103 min; P: Solaris/WDR; S: Peter Handke, freely adapted from Goethe's *Wilhelm Meister*; C: Robby Müller; PA: Rüdiger Vogler, Hanna Schygulla, Hans Christian Blech, Nastassja Nakszynski (Kinski), Peter Kern, Ivan Desny, Marianne Hoppe, Lisa Kreuzer; D: Filmverlag, Atlas (Gray City).

Im Lauf der Zeit (Kings of the Road); 1976; 176 min; P and S: WW; C: Robby Müller; PA: Rüdiger Vogler, Hanns Zischler, Lisa Kreuzer, Rudolf Schündler, Marquard Bohm; D: Filmverlag (Gray City).

Der amerikanische Freund (The American Friend); 1977; color; 123 min; P: WW/Road Movies/Les Films du Losange/WDR; S: WW, based on the novel *Ripley's Game* by Patricia Highsmith; C: Robby Müller; PA: Bruno Ganz, Dennis Hopper, Gérard Blain, Lisa Kreuzer, Nicholas Ray, Samuel Fuller, Peter Lilienthal; D: Filmverlag (New Yorker).

Selected Bibliographies

EDITOR'S PREFACE

This bibliography lists books and articles that offer useful information about general aspects and problems of the New German Cinema. Items about specific filmmakers are to be found in the respective chapter bibliographies.

In English

Baker, Rob. "'New German Cinema': A Fistful of Myths." *Soho News*, 23 March 1978, pp. 21–23.

Bean, Robin. "The New Generation in German Cinema." *Films and Filming*, September 1965, pp. 12–13, 28.

Canby, Vincent. "The German Renaissance—No Room for Laughter or Love." *New York Times*, 11 December 1977.

Clarke, Gerald. "Seeking Planets That Do Not Exist: The New German Cinema Is the Liveliest in Europe." *Time*, 20 March 1978.

Cohen, Jules. "The Chronic Crisis in West German Film." *Film Comment* 3 (Winter 1965): 32–35.

Corrigan, Timothy. *New German Film: The Displaced Image*. Austin: Univ. of Texas Press, 1983.

Dawson, Jan. "The Industry: German Weasels (Filmverlag Follies)." *Film Comment* 13 (May/June 1977): 33–34.

Donner, Wolf. "Films Around the World: The Germans Are Coming." *Atlas* 23 (March 1976): 29–30.

Durgnat, Raymond. "Caligari to 'Hitler.'" *Film Comment* 16 (July/August 1980): 59–71.

Eidsvik, Charles. "Behind the Crest of the Wave: An Overview of the New German Cinema." *Literature/Film Quarterly* 7 (1979): 167–81.

Elsaesser, Thomas. "The Postwar German Cinema." In *Fassbinder*, 2nd rev. ed., edited by Tony Rayns. London: British Film Institute, 1979, pp. 1–16.

Franklin, James. *New German Cinema: From Oberhausen to Hamburg*. Boston: Twayne, 1983.

Gregor, Ulrich. "The German Film in 1964: Stuck at Zero." *Film Quarterly* 18 (Winter 1964): 7–21.

————. *The German Experimental Film of the Seventies*. Munich: Goethe-Institut, 1980.

Grenier, Richard. "Screen Memories from Germany." *Commentary* 69 (June 1980): 65–77.

Holloway, Ronald. "Who's Who in West German Film Industry: A Directory of Directors and Filmmakers over the Period 1957–1977." *Variety*, 2 June 1977.

————. "A German Breakthrough?" *Kino: German Film*, no. 1 (October 1979), pp. 4–17.

————. "The German Cameraman." *Kino: German Film*, no. 6 (Spring 1982), pp. 41–45.

Horne, Jed. "Faces from the Edgy World of German Film." *Life*, May 1981.

Jansen, Peter W. *The New German Film* (exhibition catalog). Munich: Goethe-Institut, 1980.

Johnston, Sheila. "The Author As Public Institution: The 'New' Cinema in the Federal Republic of Germany." *Screen Education* 32/33 (Winter 1979/80): 67–78.

Manvell, Roger, and Fraenkel, Heinrich. "The Nineteen-sixties and the New German Cinema." In *The German Cinema*. New York/Washington: Praeger, 1971, pp. 124–33.

Moeller, Hans-Bernhard. "Brecht and 'Epic' Film Medium: The Cineaste, Playwright, Film Theoretician and His Influence." *Wide Angle* 3 (1980): 4–11.

————. "New German Cinema and Its Precarious Subsidy and Finance System." *Quarterly Review of Film Studies* 5 (Spring 1980): 157–68.

Overbey, David L. "From Murnau to Munich: New German Cinema." *Sight and Sound* 43 (Spring 1974): 101–3, 115.

Phillips, Klaus. "Exotism in the German Cinema of the Fifties." In *1976 Film Studies Annual*. West Lafayette, Ind.: Purdue Research Foundation, 1976, pp. 171–76.

Rentschler, Eric. "*Misère-en-scène*: Young German Filmmakers on Dangerous Ground." *Movietone News*, no. 49 (April 1976), pp. 18–24.

————. "Critical Junctures Since Oberhausen: West German Film in the Course of Time." *Quarterly Review of Film Studies* 5 (Spring 1980): 141–56.

————. "Deutschland im Vorherbst: Literature Adaptation in West German Film." *Kino: German Film*, no. 3 (Summer 1980), pp. 11–19.

————. "American Friends and New German Cinema: Patterns of Reception." *New German Critique*, no. 24/25 (Fall/Winter 1981/82), pp. 7–35.

————. *West German Film in the Course of Time*. Bedford Hills, NY: Redgrave, 1984.

Sandford, John. "The New German Cinema." *German Life and Letters* 32 (April 1979): 206–28.

————. *The New German Cinema*. London: Oswald Wolff, 1980.

Sarris, Andrew. "The Germans Are Coming! The Germans Are Coming!" *Village Voice*, 27 October 1975.

Vogel, Amos. "A Nation Comes Out of Shell-Shock." *Village Voice,* 4 May 1972.

In German

Bronnen, Barbara, and Brocher, Corinna. *Die Filmemacher: Der neue deutsche Film nach Oberhausen.* Munich: Bertelsmann, 1973.

Dörrie, Doris, and Fischer, Robert, eds. *Kino 78: Bundesdeutsche Filme auf der Leinwand.* Munich: Monika Nüchtern, 1978.

Fischer, Robert, ed. *Kino 79/80: Bundesdeutsche Filme auf der Leinwand.* Munich: Monika Nüchtern, 1979.

————, and Hembus, Joe. *Der Neue Deutsche Film: 1960–1980.* Munich: Goldmann, 1981.

Gmür, Leonhard H., ed. *Der junge deutsche Film.* Munich: Constantin, 1967.

Gregor, Ulrich. *Geschichte des Films ab 1960.* Munich: Bertelsmann, 1978, pp. 122–84.

Hembus, Joe. *Der deutsche Film kann gar nicht besser sein: Ein Pamphlet von gestern, eine Abrechnung von heute.* Munich: Rogner & Bernhard, 1981.

Kreimeier, Klaus. *Kino und Filmindustrie in der BRD: Ideologieproduktion und Klassenwirklichkeit nach 1945.* Kronberg/Ts.: Scriptor, 1973.

Möhrmann, Renate. *Die Frau mit der Kamera: Filmemacherinnen in der Bundesrepublik Deutschland — Situation, Perspektiven, 10 exemplarische Lebensläufe.* Munich: Hanser, 1980.

Pflaum, Hans Günther, and Prinzler, Hans Helmut. *Film in der Bundesrepublik Deutschland.* Munich: Hanser, 1979.

Chapter bibliographies are divided into English and German sections; in the case of Volker Schlöndorff some sources in other languages are given as well. In instances where a filmmaker has received substantial critical attention in English-language newspapers, journals, and books, German entries are limited to the most important items. Publications prior to 1981 are listed, but in isolated cases (e.g., Rainer Werner Fassbinder) selected later works are also included. The following abbreviations are used to identify German newspapers: *Süddeutsche Zeitung (SZ), Frankfurter Allgemeine Zeitung (FAZ), Frankfurter Rundschau* (FR).

HERBERT ACHTERNBUSCH

In English

Achternbusch, Herbert, and Greenberg, Alan. *Heart of Glass*. Munich: Skellig, 1976 (contains the script to the film interspersed with Greenberg's notes on Herzog's making of the film).

Besas, Peter. "*Bierkampf* (Beer Chase)." *Variety*, 13 July 1977.

Holloway, Ronald. "*Die Atlantikschwimmer* (The Atlantic Swimmers)." *Variety*, 7 July 1976.

———. "*Der Comanche* (The Comanche)." *Variety*, 19 September 1979.

———, trans. "Achternbusch on Chaplin: The Throne Is Vacant." *Kino: German Film*, October 1979, pp. 21–23.

Kael, Pauline. "Enfant Terrible." *New Yorker*, 13 November 1978, pp. 223–28 *(Bye Bye Bavaria)*.

In German

Achternbusch, Herbert. *Hülle*. Frankfurt: Suhrkamp, 1969 (3 stories).

———. *Das Kamel*. Frankfurt: Suhrkamp, 1970 (4 stories).

———. *Die Macht des Löwengebrülls*. Frankfurt: Suhrkamp, 1970 (story).

———. *Die Alexanderschlacht*. Frankfurt: Suhrkamp, 1971 (prose).

———. *L'Etat c'est moi*. Frankfurt: Suhrkamp, 1972 (story).

———. *Der Tag wird kommen*. Frankfurt: Suhrkamp, 1973 (novel).

———. *Die Stunde des Todes*. Frankfurt: Suhrkamp, 1975 (novel; includes the scripts to *Heart of Glass* and *The Andechs Feeling*).

———. *Land in Sicht*. Frankfurt: Suhrkamp, 1977 (novel; includes as integral parts the scripts to *The Atlantic Swimmers* and *Beer Battle*).

———. *Servus Bayern*. Gauting: Kirchheim, 1977 (filmscript).

———. 1969/*Die Alexanderschlacht/Die Atlantikschwimmer*. Frankfurt: Suhrkamp, 1978 (three-volume reordering of the complete work, including the script to *The Young Monk* and the play *Ella*).

———. *Der Komantsche*. Heidelberg: Das Wunderhorn, 1979 (filmscript).

———. *Es ist ein leichtes, beim Gehen den Boden zu berühren*. Frankfurt: Suhrkamp, 1980 (includes the scripts *The Comanche* and *Black Erwin*, the plays *Susn, Gust*, and *Kuschwarda City*).

———. "'Ich bin der direkteste Filmmacher in Deutschland': Ein Gespräch mit Herbert Achternbusch über sich und die anderen." *FR*, 6 January 1979.

Blum, Doris. "Der Film *Das Andechser Gefühl*: Herbert Achternbusch und das Kino." *FAZ,* 25 March 1973.

Drews, Jörg. "I'm Dunkeln einen nassen Baum ersteigen: Herbert Achternbuschs drittes Buch." *Die Zeit,* 23 February 1971 *(The Mighty Roar of the Lion).*

————. "Ein grantiger Freund." *Der Spiegel,* 2 November 1980 *(The Comanche).*

Fink, Adolf. "Ein Wilderer im Revier des Lebens." *FAZ,* 20 August 1980.

Grafe, Frieda. "Da fielen Kirchweih und Fasching auf einen Tag: *Bierkampf,* der Oktoberfestfilm von Herbert Achternbusch." *SZ,* 11 March 1977.

Grohmann, Martje. "Die Flucht in das Eis: *Servus Bayern.*" *Die Zeit,* 3 February 1978.

Hage, Volker. "Von Selbstmördern und Atlantikschwimmern." *FAZ,* 12 September 1977.

Handke, Peter, and Widmer, Urs. "Der zu Recht geehrte Achternbusch."*Die Zeit,* 24 June 1977 (laudatio for Achternbusch's reception of the Petrarch Prize, which the author turned down in an act of protest).

Heinrichs, Benjamin. "Der Kopf ist ein Abgrund: *Der Tag wird kommen* —Herbert Achternbuschs sechstes Buch." *Die Zeit,* 12 October 1973.

————. "Katastrofen-Prosa: Herbert Achternbusch: *Die Stunde des Todes* — Beschreibung eines unbeschreiblichen Buches." *Die Zeit,* 21 March 1975.

————. "Das Kino in meinem Kopf: Neues von Achternbusch: Der Film *Bierkampf,* der Roman *Land in Sicht.*" *Die Zeit,* 11 March 1977.

Knapp, Gottfried, "Eiszeit am Starnberger See: Herbert Achternbuschs neuer Film *Servus Bayern.*" *SZ,* 27 January 1978.

Limmer, Wolfgang. "Die Plagen der Fantasie." *Der Spiegel,* 2 July 1976 *(The Atlantic Swimmers).*

Maurer, Michael. "Es lebe das Kino meiner Träume: Ein Porträt des Schriftstellers und Filmemachers Herbert Achternbusch." *Film und Ton,* August 1977, pp. 54–56.

————. "Jedes Bild ein neuer Anfang: Der Schriftsteller und Filmemacher Herbert Achternbusch bei den Dreharbeiten zu *Serves Bayern.*" *FR,* 29 August 1977.

Niehoff, Karena. "Ein bayerischer Mensch: Herbert Achternbuschs Film *Bierkampf.*" *Tagesspiegel* (Berlin), 29 April 1977.

Schmidt, Eckhart. "Eine Chance Für zwei Bayern: Herbert Achternbuschs Parabel *Die Atlantikschwimmer.*" *Deutsche Zeitung/Christ und Welt,* 9 July 1976.

Schödel, Helmut. "Die Riesen des Wahnsinns: Notizen aus der Münchner Anarcho-Bohème." *Die Zeit,* 7 September 1979.

Schütte, Wolfram. "Im Packeis treibend: Herbert Achternbuschs neuer Film *Servus Bayern.*" *FR,* 11 March 1978.

Storch, Ulrike. "Die Filmographie—Herbert Achternbusch." *Die Information* (Wiesbaden), July/August/September 1977, pp. 93–96.

Thieringer, Thomas. *Bierkampf/Die Atlantikschwimmer/Das Andechser Gefühl.*" *Medium,* May 1977, pp. 24–26.

Walser, Martin. "Das Unmögliche kann man nur darstellen: Herbert Achternbuschs zweiter Film." *FR*, 9 August 1976 *(The Atlantic Swimmers).*

HARK BOHM

In English

"Boys' Own Filmmaker." *berlinale-tip. Offizielles Bulletin Internationale Filmfestspiele Berlin*, 28 February 1978, pp. 12–13 [interview with Bohm].

Brown, Geoff. Review of *Moritz, lieber Moritz. Monthly Film Bulletin*, January 1980, pp. 9–10.

Filmverlag der Autoren. *Moritz, lieber Moritz.* Munich: Filmverlag der Autoren, 1978 (illustrated pamphlet with plot summary and comments by Bohm).

Holloway, Ronald. Review of *Nordsee ist Mordsee. Variety*, 16 June 1976.

———. Review of *Moritz, lieber Moritz. Variety*, 29 March 1978.

———. "Germany's 'Second Generation' Filmmakers." *International Herald Tribune*, 21–22 June 1980.

Kafka, J. Review of *Tschetan—der Indianerjunge. Variety*, 18 April 1973.

Stone, Judy. "Exciting New German Directors—Peter Lilienthal and Hark Bohm." *San Francisco Examiner & Chronicle, Datebook*, 21 October 1979.

In German

Blaich, Ute. "Stuyvesant in Niggertown." *Der Spiegel*, 3 May 1976 (Review of *Nordsee ist Mordsee*).

Blumenberg, Hans C. "Bockmayers *Flammende Herzen*, Bohms *Moritz, lieber Moritz.*" *Die Zeit*, 24 March 1978.

Bohm, Hark. "Entfernung aus der Sicherheit esoterischer Ästhetik: Perspektiven für das kommende Filmjahr." In *Jahrbuch Film 77/78*, edited by Hans Günther Pflaum. Munich: Carl Hanser, 1977, pp. 54–55.

———. *"Moritz, Dear Moritz." Medium*, 10 (1978): 10–11.

———. "Lauter Erfolge ohne Publikum." *Der Spiegel*, 8 July 1978.

———. "Arbeit, Männergruppen und Frauen: Zu den Filmen von Howard Hawks." In *Jahrbuch Film 79/80*, edited by Hans Günther Pflaum. Munich: Carl Hanser, 1979, pp. 27–37.

Czybulka, U. Review of *Tschetan—der Indianerjunge. Jugend Film Fernsehen* 17 (1973): 159.

Dawson, Jan, and Fründt, Bodo, eds. *Moritz, lieber Moritz.* Berlin: Internationale Filmfestspiele Berlin, 1978 (includes comments by Bohm).

Eder, Klaus. "Young People, Taken Seriously," *medium* 10 (1978): 2–7.

Hobsch, Manfred. Review of *Im Herzen des Hurrican. Filmbeobachter* 5 (March 1980): 5–6.

Karasek, Hellmuth. "Hamburg, Hamburg: *Moritz, lieber Moritz.*" *Der Spiegel*, 13 March 1978.

Knorr, Günter. "Äußere und innere Bewegung: Hark Bohm über seinen neuen Film." *Filmjournal* 20 (February 1980): 11–14, 33–39 (general interview with Bohm upon completion of *Im Herzen des Hurrican*).

Koegel, W. Review of *Ich kann auch 'ne Arche bauen*. *Jugend Film Fernsehen* 18 (1974): 228–29.

Kurowski, U. Review of *Tschetan—der Indianerjunge*. *Filmkritik* 17 (September 1973): 427.

Mohn, E. Review of *Moritz, lieber Moritz*. *Medien + Erziehung*, 22 (1978):110–13.

"*Moritz, lieber Moritz*." In *Kino 78: Bundesdeutsche Filme auf der Leinwand*, edited by Doris Dörrie and Robert Fischer. Munich: Monika Nüchtern, 1978, pp. 132–37.

"*Nordsee ist Mordsee*." *Scala: Zeitschrift aus der Bundesrepublik Deutschland*, January 1977, pp. 17–19 (script excerpts with brief commentary).

Pech, Klaus-Ulrich. "Vom braven Wolf." *FAZ*, 26 October 1978.

Pflaum, Hans Günther, "Ein neuer Familienfilm." *Film und Ton Magazin* 19 (August 1973): 43–44 (Review of *Tschetan—der Indianerjunge*).

————. "Zwei Jungen auf der Suche nach dem Ich: Hark Bohm über *Nordsee ist Mordsee*." *Film und Ton Magazin* 22 (June 1976): 52–53.

Ruf, Wolfgang. "Nicht nur ein toter Indianer ist ein guter Indianer." *Die Zeit*, 29 June 1973 (American edition).

Schatzdorfer, G. Review of *Nordsee ist Mordsee*. *Medien + Erziehung* 21 (1977): 138–40.

Schwarze, Michael. "Hark Bohms Spielfilm *Nordsee ist Mordsee*." *FAZ*, 22 May 1976.

Timm, Thomas, and Meier-Siem, Christoph. "Mit bewegten Bildern das Bewußtsein des Zuschauers bewegen." *Kino: Magazin für den engagierten Film*, 15 February 1980, pp. 27–42 (includes lengthy interview with Bohm).

ALF BRUSTELLIN and BERNHARD SINKEL

In English

Holloway, Ron. "*Berlinger*." *Variety*, 6 July 1976.

————. "*Der Mädchenkrieg*." *Variety*, 14 September 1977.

————. "*Taugenichts*." *Variety*, 29 March 1978.

In German

Blumenberg, Hans C. "Bernhard Sinkels *Taugenichts*, Wolf Gremms *Tod oder Freiheit*." *Die Zeit*, 27 January 1978.

Brustellin, Alf. "Super(acht)-Glossarium." *Filmkritik*, no. 12 (1970), pp. 627–28.

————. "Cannes-Notizen." *Filmkritik*, no. 7 (1971), pp. 339–42.

Buschmann, Christel. "Das Kino wird im Keim erstickt: Stoffe, Drehbücher, Drehbuchautoren." In *Jahrbuch Film 78/79*, edited by Hans Günther Pflaum. Munich: Hanser, 1978, pp. 111–19 (includes extensive commentary by Brustellin and Sinkel).

Fischer, Robert, ed. "*Der Sturz*." In *Kino 79/80: Bundesdeutsche Filme auf der Leinwand*. Munich: Monika Nüchtern, 1979, pp. 134–37.

Karasek, Hellmuth. "Kraut und Rüben: *Der Mädchenkrieg.*" *Der Spiegel,* no. 38 (1977).

————. "Freier Fall: *Der Sturz.*" *Der Spiegel,* no. 7 (1979).

Luft, Friedrich. "Der Film *Mädchenkrieg* von Brustellin und Sinkel angelaufen: Er langweilt mit Niveau." *Die Welt,* 7 September 1977.

Schmidt, Eckhart. "Kristleins doppelte Pleite: Alf Brustellins *Der Sturz* nach dem Roman von Martin Walser." *Deutsche Zeitung,* 25 February 1979.

Schmitz, Helmut, "Lest Walser: *Der Sturz,* verfilmt von Alf Brustellin." *FR,* 28 February 1979.

Schütte, Wolfram, "Neues Terrain gewonnen: Staatsanwaltschaft beschleunigt Frankfurter Premiere von *Berlinger.*" *FR,* 29 November 1975.

Steinborn, Bion. "*Deutschland im Herbst* mit: Alf Brustellin, Alexander Kluge, Edgar Reitz, Volker Schlöndorff, Bernd Sinkel—und Theo Hinz (Filmverlag)." *filmfaust: Zeitschrift für den internationalen Film,* no. 7 (1978) (lengthy interview regarding *Germany in Autumn*).

von Mengershausen, Joachim. "Wir arbeiten ganz anders als der Jungfilm: Gespräch mit Ula Stöckl, Edgar Reitz und Alf Brustellin." *Filmkritik,* no. 10 (1971), pp. 542–47 (interview with Stöckl, Reitz, and Brustellin).

Zimmer, Dieter E. "Kino: Alf Brustellins *Der Sturz* frei nach Martin Walser, Angst der Verkäufer—Der Wahnsinn ist überall." *Die Zeit,* 16 February 1979.

HELLMUTH COSTARD

In English

Dawson, Jan. *The Films of Hellmuth Costard.* London: Riverside Studios, 1979.

————. "Germany in Autumn and Eine Kleine Godard." *Take One* 6 (November 1978).

Holloway, D. "Der kleine Godard (A Little Godard)." *Variety,* 22 November 1978.

In German

Blumenberg, Hans C. "Kino der dritten Art: Hellmuth Costard und sein neuer Film 'Der kleine Godard.'" *Die Zeit,* 30 June 1978. Reprinted in Hans C. Blumenberg, *Kinozeit: Aufsätze und Kritiken zum modernen Film,* 1976–1980. Frankfurt: Fischer, 1980, pp. 133–139.

Bohrer, Karl Heinz. "Vom schwierigen Umgang mit den Bildern: Herzog, Costard und die Amerikaner oder der Experimentalfilm als Kritik des Kulturbetriebs: Bemerkungen zum Internationalen Filmfestival in Edinburgh." *FAZ,* 31 August 1978.

Brunow, Jochen. "Über das Bildermachen." *Tip* (Berlin), no. 21 (1978), p. 22.

Costard, Hellmuth, *Herberts Reise ins Land der Uhren.* Reinbek bei Hamburg: Rowohlt, 1974.

————. "Die unschuldige Frau." *Der Spiegel,* 7 November 1977.

————. "Spielfilme vollkommen phantasielos drehen: Ein Spiel-filmvorhaben" (unpublished ms., 1978; includes *Der kleine Godard*).

Ebert, J. "Kann man in Deutschland Filme machen?" *Filmkritik* 22 (December 1978): 618–53.

Grafe, Frieda. "Aus Bildern Bildung: 'Der kleine Godard'—Ein Film von Hellmuth Costard." *SZ*, 11 November 1978.

Kuhlbrodt, Dietrich. "Costard, immer einen Schritt voraus." *SZ*, 22 September 1968.

————. "Costards Dreh am Rad der Filmgeschichte: 'Der kleine Godard' über Filmemachen in Hamburg." *FR*, 1 July 1978.

Petz, Thomas. "Frühe Filme—später Ruhm." *SZ*, 7 October 1976.

RAINER WERNER FASSBINDER

In English

Aitken, Will. *"Despair."* *Take One* 7 (January 1979): 6–8.

Alvarado, Manuel. *"Eight Hours Are Not a Day."* In *Fassbinder,* edited by Tony Rayns. London: BFI, 1976, pp. 37–41.

Baker, Rob. "Germany Bounces Back." *Soho News,* 1 November 1979.

Berman, Bruce. *"Merchant of the Four Seasons."* *Take One* 4 (November/December 1972): 39–40.

Borchardt, Edith. "Leitmotif and Structure in Fassbinder's *Effie Briest.*" *Literature/Film Quarterly* 7 (1979): 201–7.

Britton, Andrew. *"Fox and His Friends*: Foxed." *Jump Cut,* no. 16 November 1977), pp. 22–23.

Canby, Vincent. "Fassbinder's 'American Soldier' is Bold and Interesting." *New York Times,* 30 January 1976.

————. "Early, Exuberant Fassbinder." *New York Times,* 12 November 1976 (*Beware of a Holy Whore*).

————. "Rainer Fassbinder—the Most Original Talent Since Godard." *New York Times,* 6 March 1977.

————. "Fassbinder Hits the Mark Again in a Pessimistic 'Mother Küsters.'" *New York Times,* 7 March 1977.

————. "Fassbinder, in 'Jail Bait,' Explores Danger of Women Through Girl, 14." *New York Times,* 16 May 1977.

————. "'Katzelmacher' Hypnotizes and Amuses." *New York Times,* 4 June 1977.

————. "'Gods of the Plague,' 1969 Fassbinder Film, Is Quintessential American Gangster Movie." *New York Times,* 11 June 1977.

————. "Fassbinder Sneers at German Affluence." *New York Times,* 8 November 1977 (*Herr R.*).

————. "Fassbinder's 'Year of 13 Moons.'" *New York Times,* 8 October 1979.

————. "'Maria Braun' from Fassbinder." *New York Times,* 14 October 1979.

————. "Why Critics and Audiences are Prone to Disagree." *New York Times,* 14 October 1979 (*Year of 13 Moons*).

————. "At the Film Festival: 'Ali.'" *New York Times,* 21 October 1979 (*Maria Braun*).

Cant, Bob. "Fox and His Friends: Fassbinder's *Fox.*" *Jump Cut,* no. 16 (November 1977): 22.

Clarens, Carlos. "Moon over Mon Ami(e)," *Soho News,* 11 June 1980.

Combs, Richard. "Chinese Roulette and Despair." *Sight and Sound* 47 (Autumn 1978): 258–60.

Dawson, Jan. "Women—Present Tense." *Take One* 7 (July 1979): 10–12 *(Marriage of Maria Braun).*

————. "The Sacred Terror: Shadows of Terrorism in the New German Cinema." *Sight and Sound* 48 (Autumn 1979): 242–45 *(The Third Generation* and other recent films).

————, and Medjuck, Joe. "Misc.: Fassbinder: A Year (or so) in the Life." *Take One* 4 (July/August 1974): 26.

Denby, David. "The Brilliant, Brooding Films of Rainer Fassbinder." *New York Times,* 1 February 1976.

Elsaesser, Thomas. "A Cinema of Vicious Circles." In *Fassbinder,* edited by Tony Rayns. London: BFI, 1976, pp. 24–37.

Farber, Manny, and Patterson, Patricia. "R. W. Fassbinder." *Film Comment* 11 (November/December 1975): 5–7.

Fassbinder, R. W. "Fassbinder on Sirk," translated by Thomas Elsaesser. *Film Comment* 11 (November/December 1975): 22–24.

————. "Insects in a Glass Case: Random Thoughts on Claude Chabrol," translated by Derek Prouse. *Sight and Sound* 45 (Autumn 1976): 205–6, 252.

Fell, John L. *"Despair." Film Quarterly* 33 (Fall 1979): 59–61.

Franklin, James C. *"Beware of a Holy Whore:* A Review." In 1976 *Film Studies Annual.* West Lafayette, Ind.: Purdue Research Foundation, 1976, pp. 132–35.

————. "Method and Message: Forms of Communication in Fassbinder's *Angst Essen Seele Auf." Literature/Film Quarterly* 7 (1979): 182–200.

————. "The Films of Fassbinder: Form and Formula." *Quarterly Review of Film Studies,* Spring 1980, pp. 167–181.

Gilliatt, Penelope. "Fassbinder." *New Yorker,* 14 June 1976, pp. 93–96 *(The Bitter Tears of Petra von Kant).*

————. "No Sadness That Art Cannot Quell." *New Yorker,* 28 March 1977, pp. 118–22 *(Mother Küsters Goes to Heaven).*

————. "Prodigy." *New Yorker,* 30 May 1977, pp. 104–5.

Gow, Fordeon. "Obsession." *Films and Filming,* March 1976, pp. 12–17 (on Fassbinder in general).

Greenspun, Roger. "Film Festival: 'Merchant of Four Seasons.'" *New York Times,* 9 October 1972.

————. "Phantoms of Liberty. Thoughts on Fassbinder's *Fist-Right of Freedom* [*Fox*]." *Film Comment* 11 (November/December 1975): 8–10.

————. "White Heat." *Soho News,* 29 January 1976 *(The American Soldier).*

Greig, Simon. *"Fox." Films and Filming,* February 1976, pp. 34–35.

Haddad-Garcia, George. "A Conversation with Rainer Werner Fassbinder." *Christopher Street,* June 1982, pp. 48–55.

Harrigan, Renny. *"Effi Briest, The Marquise of O . . .* Women Oppressed!" *Jump Cut,* no. 15 (July 1977), pp. 3–5.

Haskell, Molly, "Sisterhoodwinked: Panting for Power." *Village Voice*, 25 October 1973.

Horak, Jan-Christopher. "Fassbinder Faces Life." *Village Voice*, 3 October 1974.

Hughes, John. "Why Herr R. Ran Amok: Fassbinder and Modernism." *Film Comment* 11 (November/December 1975): 11–13.

―――, and Riley, Brooks. "A New Realism: Fassbinder Interviewed." *Film Comment* 11 (November/December 1975): 14–17.

―――, and McCormick, Ruth. "Rainer Werner Fassbinder and the Death of Family Life." *Thousand Eyes*, April 1977, pp. 4–5.

Iden, Peter. "Making an Impact: Fassbinder and the Theatre." In *Fassbinder*, edited by Tony Rayns. London: BFI, 1976, pp. 17–23.

―――. "The Sensation Maker: Rainer Werner Fassbinder and the Theater." *Wide Angle* 2 (1977): 4–13.

Keneas, Alexander. "Marriage of Maria Braun." *Newsday*, 15 October 1979.

Kling, Vincent. "The Dynamics of Defeat: Aspects of Rainer Werner Fassbinder's Art." In 1976 *Film Studies Annual*. West Lafayette, Ind.: Purdue Research Foundation, 1976, pp. 157–66.

Kremling, Helmut J. "Fassbinder's *Beware of a Holy Whore*." In 1976 *Film Studies Annual*. West Lafayette, Ind.: Purdue Research Foundation, 1976, pp. 167–70.

Kroll, Jack. "The Boom Goes Bust." *Newsweek*, 29 October 1979 *(Maria Braun)*.

Leaming, Barbara. "Structures of Alienation: *The Merchant of Four Seasons*." *Jump Cut*, nos. 10/11 (June 1976), pp. 39–40.

―――. "Rainer Werner Fassbinder's Fear of Fear." *Take One* 5 (July/August 1977): 14–15.

Lellis, George. "Retreat from Romanticism: Two Films from the Seventies." *Film Quarterly* 28 (Summer 1975): 16–20 *(Merchant of Four Seasons)*.

Limmer, Wolfgang. *Fassbinder*. Munich: Goethe Institut/Filmverlag der Autoren, 1973.

Mayne, Judith. "Fassbinder and Spectatorship." *New German Critique*, no. 12 (Fall 1977), pp. 61–74.

McCormick, Ruth. "*Fox and His Friends*." *Cineaste* 7 (1976): 43–44.

―――. "Fassbinder and the Politics of Everyday Life: A Survey of His Films." *Cineaste* 8 (1977): 22–30.

―――. "*The Marriage of Maria Braun*." *Cineaste*, (Spring 1980), pp. 34–36.

―――, ed. and trans. *Fassbinder*. New York: Tanam, 1981.

McGuinnes, Richard. "The Eyes Have It." *Soho News*, 2 October 1975 *(Fox and His Friends)*.

Nooman, Tom. "Maria Braun." *Film Quarterly*, (Spring 1980), pp. 40–45.

Rayns, Tony. "Fear Eats the Soul." *Sight and Sound* 43 (Autumn 1974): 245.

―――. "Forms of Address: Tony Rayns Interviews Three German Film Makers." *Sight and Sound* 44 (Winter 1974/75): 2–7 (Fassbinder/Wenders/Syberberg).

————. "Notes on Form and Syntax." In *Fassbinder*. London: BFI, 1976, pp. 42–44.

————, ed. *Fassbinder*, 2nd rev. ed. London: BFI, 1980.

Roud, Richard. "Journals: Berlin." *Film Comment* 12 (September/October 1976): 4f. (*Satan's Brew*).

Sandford, John. "Rainer Werner Fassbinder." In *The New German Cinema*. London: Oswald Wolff, 1980, pp. 63–102.

Sarris, Andrew. "Can Fassbinder Break the Box-Office Barrier?" *Village Voice*, 22 November 1976.

————. "Further Thoughts on Fassbinder." *Village Voice*, 11 July 1977.

————. "The Heart of the Masterpiece." *Village Voice*, 15 October 1979 (*The Marriage of Maria Braun*).

————. "Fassbinder's Gayness Without Gaiety." *Village Voice*, 16 June 1980.

————. "Fassbinder and Sirk: The Ties That Unbind." *Village Voice*, 3 September 1980.

Sparrow, Norbert. "'I Let the Audience Feel *and* Think'—An Interview with Rainer Werner Fassbinder." *Cineaste* 8 (1977): 20–21.

Stern, Michael. "The Inspired Melodrama and the Melodrama It Inspired." *Thousand Eyes*, January 1976, pp. 3–4ff.

Stoop, Norma McLain. "Rainer Werner Fassbinder and 'Fox.'" *After Dark*, February 1976, pp. 43–45.

Thomas, Paul. "Fassbinder: The Poetry of the Inarticulate." *Film Quarterly* 30 (Winter 1976/77): 2–17.

Thompson, Bill. "Germany, Fassbinder and Those Waves." *Cinegram*, no. 3 (1976/77), pp. 38–42.

Thomsen, Christian Braad. "Fassbinder's Holy Whores." *Take One* 4 (July/August 1973): 12–16.

————. "Interview with Fassbinder (Berlin, 1974)." In *Fassbinder*, edited by Tony Rayns. London: BFI, 1976, pp. 45–49.

Tyler, Ralph. "The Savage World of Rainer Werner Fassbinder." *New York Times*, 27 March 1977.

Whitney, Craig R. "Fassbinder: A New Director Movie Buffs Dote On." *New York Times*, 16 February 1977.

Wilson, David. "Anti-Cinema: Rainer Werner Fassbinder." *Sight and Sound* 41 (Spring 1972): 99–100.

In German

Baer, Harry. *Schlafen kann ich, wenn ich tot bin: Das atemlose Leben des Rainer Werner Fassbinder*. Cologne: Kiepenheuer & Witsch, 1982.

Eckardt, Bernd. *Rainer Werner Fassbinder*. Munich: Heyne, 1982.

Karsunke, Yaak, et al. *Rainer Werner Fassbinder*, 3rd rev. ed. Munich: Hanser, 1979.

Limmer, Wolfgang. *Rainer Werner Fassbinder, Filmemacher*. Reinbek bei Hamburg: Rowohlt, 1981.

Pflaum, Hans Günther, and Fassbinder, Rainer Werner. *Das bißchen Realität, das ich brauche: Wie Filme entstehen*. Munich: Hanser, 1976.

Raab, Kurt, and Peters, Karsten. *Die Sehnsucht des Rainer Werner Fassbinder.* Munich: Bertelsmann, 1982.

Zwerenz, Gerhard. *Der langsame Tod des Rainer Werner Fassbinder.* Munich: Schneekluth, 1982.

HANS W. GEISSENDÖRFER

In English

Baker, Rob. "The Wild Duck." *Soho Weekly News,* 28 April 1977.

Canby, Vincent. "Screen: A German *Wild Duck.*" *New York Times,* 29 April 1977.

Crist, Judith. "Middle-Aged Adolescence and the Seven-Year Itch." *Saturday Review,* 11 June 1977, pp. 44–45 *(The Wild Duck).*

Gilliatt, Penelope. "The Current Cinema: Humbug." *New Yorker,* 9 May 1977 *(The Wild Duck).*

Hoberman, J. "Excuse the Expressionism." *Village Voice,* 5 February 1979, p. 42 *(The Glass Cell).*

Holloway, Ronald. "*Sternsteinhof* (Sternstein Manor)." *Variety,* 14 July 1976.

_____. "*Die Wildente* (The Wild Duck)." *Variety,* 8 September 1976.

Simon, John. "Well-Intentioned, Ill-Conceived." *New York,* 9 May 1977, pp. 70ff. *(The Wild Duck).*

Steene, Birgitta. "Film As Theater: Geissendörfer's *The Wild Duck* (1976)." In *Modern European Filmmakers and the Art of Adaptation,* edited by Andrew S. Horton and Joan Magretta. New York: Ungar, 1981, pp. 295–312.

In German

Donner, Wolf. "Dracula im Bayerischen Wald." *Die Zeit,* 14 May 1970 *(Jonathan).*

_____. "Schöne Rituale: Der Filmmacher Hans W. Geissendörfer." *Die Zeit,* 30 October 1970.

_____. "Der Mörder in uns." *Die Zeit,* 7 April 1978 *(The Glass Cell).*

Geissendörfer, Hans W. "Abhängiges Arbeiten: Über Regie und Produktion." In *Jahrbuch Film 79/80,* edited by Hans Günther Pflaum. Munich: Hanser, 1979, pp. 108–13.

Günther, Wilfred. "*Die Wildente.*" *Medium,* October 1976, p. 34.

Internationale Festspiele Berlin. 10 *Filme von Hans W. Geissendörfer.* Program, 29th International Film Festival Berlin, 20 February–3 March 1979.

Jenny, Urs. "Vampir in der Tiefkühltruhe." *SZ,* 7 June 1970 *(Jonathan).*

Kirschner, Klaus, and Stelzer, Christian, eds. *Die Filme von H. W. Geissendörfer—Gespräche, Materialien.* Erlangen: Videogruppe Erlangen, 1979.

Kroetz, Franz Xaver. "'Mein Heimatfilm war das nicht.'" *Der Spiegel,* 5 April 1976 *(Sternstein Manor).*

Pflaum, Hans Günther. "Erfahrungen beim Verfilmen von Ibsen, Anzengruber und anderen: Gespräch mit Hans W. Geissendörfer aus

Anlass seines Films *Die Wildente.*" *Film-Korrespondenz,* 5 October 1976, pp. 3–5.

Schiller, Jürgen. "Der Heimatfilm—der deutsche Western?" *Die Welt,* 29 March 1976 *(Sternstein Manor).*

Sydow, Angelika. "Hans W. Geissendörfer." *Film und Ton,* November 1975, pp. 36–37.

Thieringer, Thomas. "Serien-Konfektionäre und Krämerseelen: *Lobster.*" *Medium,* February 1976, p. 28.

————. "*Sternsteinhof.*" *Medium,* April 1976, pp. 24–25.

Witte, Karsten. "Drohende Gefahr, Angst, Katastrophe." *FR,* 28 April 1978 *(The Glass Cell).*

REINHARD HAUFF

In English

Addiego, Walter V. "German Film of the Politics of Prison." *San Francisco Examiner,* 18 January 1978 *(The Brutalization of Franz Blum).*

Ansen, David. "Brain Damage." *Newsweek,* 12 May 1980 *(Knife in the Head).*

Canby, Vincent, "Screen: German 'Knife in the Head.'" *New York Times,* 23 April 1980.

Curran, Trisha. "Knife in the Head." *Films in Review* 31 (August/ September 1980): 436.

Jacobs, Diane. "Angst, You're Welcome." *Soho News,* 23 April 1980 *(Knife in the Head).*

MacBridge, J. "Die Verrohung des Franz Blum." *Variety,* 26 March 1975.

"Reinhard Hauff and His Films: A Program Presented by Goethe Institut, Munich, Films Department." n.p., n.d., p. 12 (two slightly differing versions of this program brochure exist).

Sarris, Andrew. "Starting from Ground Zero." *Village Voice,* 28 April 1980 *(Knife in the Head).*

Stone, Judy. "Reinhard Hauff: 'Some Call Me a Moralist.'" *San Francisco Examiner,* 15 January 1978.

————. "The Brutalizing of a Man in Prison." *San Francisco Examiner,* 16 January 1978.

Thomas, Kevin. "'Actor' After the First Wrap." *Los Angeles Times,* 6 December 1978 *(The Main Actor).*

In German

Bayer, Eva-Suzanne. "Träume vom sonnigen Südden: Reinhard Hauff inszeniert für den WDR das Fernsehspiel 'Das Haus am Meer.'" *Stuttgarter Zeitung,* 10 July 1972.

Blumenberg, Hans C. "Schere im Kopf: Ein Fall von Ausgewogenheit." *Die Zeit,* 19 January 1979 *(Knife in the Head).*

Buchka, Peter. "Ballade vom leisen Widerstand: Reinhard Hauffs Film 'Zündschnüre' nach dem Roman von Franz-Josef Degenhardt." *SZ,* 6 September 1974 *(Fuses).*

Buschmann, Christel. "Beim Durch-Drehen: Hauff und Wenders an der 'Zonengrenze.'" *FR*, 16 September 1975.

_____. "Gespräch mit Reinhard Hauff." *Film und Ton* 25 (January 1979): 65.

Eder, Klaus. "Ein Gespräch mit Reinhard Hauff über seinen Film 'Zündschnüre' nach F. J. Degenhardts Roman." *Die Tat—antifaschistische Wochenzeitung, Frankfurt/M.*, 7 September 1974 *(Fuses)*.

_____. "Kino—und was dann? Zu Reinhard Hauffs Film 'Der Hauptdarsteller.'" *Deutsche Volkszeitung*, 2 February 1978 *(The Main Actor)*.

Hopf, Florian. "Versuche mit der Wirklichkeit: Gespräche mit den Filmregisseuren Reinhard Hauff und Christian Ziewer." *Die Zeit*, 16 January 1979.

Jansen, Peter W. "Zerstörtes Interieur, neu zu möblieren: 'Messer im Kopf' von Peter Schneider (Buch) und Reinhard Hauff (Regie)." *FR*, 8 December 1978 *(Knife in the Head)*.

Köster, Lothar, and Drechsel, Günter. "Interview mit Reinhard Hauff am 15. 12. 1978." In *Reinhard Hauff und Seine Filme*, edited by Filmclub "e69" Kempten e.V. Kempten: Filmklub "e69," 1979, pp. 39–74 (Program of Hauff retrospective held in Kempten 9–11 March 1979).

Ratschewa, Maria. "Unterhaltung muß weder Cola noch Discothek bedeuten . . ." *Westermanns Monatshefte*, no. 1 (1979).

Timm, Thomas, and Meier-Siem, Christoph. "Reinhard Hauff: Ein Protestant in der Unterwelt." *Kino: Magazin für Film und Kultur*, no. 4 (September 1980), pp. 27–38.

Umbach, Klaus. "Potenter Typ." *Der Spiegel*, 25 March 1974 *(The Brutalization of Franz Blum)*.

Weber, Ingeborg. "Rebell gegen die Obrigkeit: Reinhard Hauffs Fernsehfilm über den Räuber Mathias Kneissl." *Tagesspiegel*, 21 March 1971.

"'Wichtig ist, daß wir gemeinsam kämpfen': Interview mit Reinhard Hauff." *Kino: Magazin für den engagierten Film*, no. 1 (15October 1979), p. 37.

WERNER HERZOG

In English

Andrews, Nigel. "Dracula in Delft." *American Film*, October 1978, pp. 32–38 *(Nosferatu)*.

Ansen, David. "Magnificent Obsessions." *Boston Real Paper*, 16 July 1972 *(Aguirre)*.

_____. "Three Misfits." *Newsweek*, 15 August 1977 *(Stroszek)*.

Bachmann, Gideon. "The Man on the Volcano: A Portrait of Werner Herzog." *Film Quarterly* 31 (Fall 1977): 2–10.

Benelli, Dana. "Mysteries of the Organism: Character Consciousness and Film Form in *Kaspar Hauser* and *Spirit of the Beehive*." *Movietone News*, no. 54 (June 1977), pp. 28–33.

_____. "The Cosmos and Its Discontents." *Movietone News*, no. 56

(November 1977), pp. 8–16 *(Signs of Life* and *Aguirre).*

Benson, Sheila, and Karman, Mal. "Herzog." *Mother Jones,* (November 1976), pp. 40–45.

Canby, Vincent. "Even Dwarfs Started Small." *New York Times,* 17 September 1970.

————. *"Fata Morgana." New York Times,* 8 October 1971.

————. *"Aguirre, the Wrath of God*: Haunting Film by Herzog." *New York Times,* 4 April 1977.

————. "Herzog's Pilgrims Hit the U.S. Road." *New York Times,* 13 July 1977 *(Stroszek).*

Combs, Richard. *"La Soufrière." BFI Monthly Film Bulletin* 46 (January 1974): 203.

————. *"Signs of Life," BFI Monthly Film Bulletin* 41 (January 1974): 9–10.

————. *"Aguirre." BFI Monthly Film Bulletin* 42 (January 1975): 3–4.

————. *"Stroszek." BFI Monthly Film Bulletin* 45 (February 1978): 31.

————. *"Woyzeck." Sight and Sound* 48 (Autumn 1979): 259–60.

Cott, Jonathan. "Signs of Life." *Rolling Stone,* 18 November 1976, pp. 48–56 (interview).

Davidson, David. "Borne out of Darkness: The Documentaries of Werner Herzog." *Film Criticism* 5 (Fall 1980): 10–25.

Dawson, Jan. "Herzog's Magic Mountain." *Sight and Sound* 47 (Winter 1977/78): 57–58 *(La Soufrière, Stroszek).*

————. "In Memoriam: Jan Dawson." *BFI Monthly Film Bulletin* 47 (October 1980): 204 (excerpt from Dawson's unfinished Herzog essay).

Denby, David. "The Germans Are Coming! The Germans Are Coming!" *Horizon* 20 (September 1977): 88–93 (Herzog, Fassbinder).

Dorr, John H. *"Even Dwarves Started Small." Take One* 3 (July/August 1971): 35–36.

Eder, Richard. "A New Visionary in German Films: Werner Herzog." *New York Times Magazine,* 10 July 1977, pp. 24–26ff.

Elley, Derek. *"Aguirre." Films and Filming* 21 (February 1975): 38–39.

————. *"Stroszek." Films and Filming* 24 (April 1978): 34.

Eisler, Ken. *"Aguirre, the Wrath of God." Movietone News,* no. 29 (January/February 1974), pp. 43–44.

————. "Offing the Pig." *Movietone News,* no. 36 (October 1974), pp. 8–11 *(Even Dwarfs Started Small).*

Eisner, Lotte H. "Herzog in Dinkelsbuehl." *Sight and Sound* 43 (Autumn 1974): 212–13 *(Kaspar Hauser).*

Fell, John H. *"Heart of Glass." Film Quarterly* 32 (Spring 1979): 54–55.

Finger, Ellis. "Kaspar Hauser Doubly Portrayed: Peter Handke's *Kaspar* and Werner Herzog's *Every Man for Himself and God Against All." Literature/Film Quarterly* 7 (1979): 235–43.

Forbes, Jill. *"Heart of Glass." Sight and Sound* 46 (Autumn 1977): 255–56.

Gambaccini, Peter. "The New German Film Makers." *Horizon* 23 (June 1980): 88–91 (Herzog, Fassbinder, Wenders).

Gilliatt, Penelope. "Gold." *New Yorker,* 11 April 1977, pp. 127–28 *(Aguirre).*

————. "Hurrah." *New Yorker*, 25 July 1977, pp. 74–77 *(Stroszek)*.

————. "Check." *New Yorker*, 22 May 1978, pp. 115–16 *(La Soufrière)*.

Gleiberman, Owen. "Herzog's Anemic New 'Nosferatu.'" *Michigan Daily*, 4 November 1979.

Gow, Gordon. *"Heart of Glass." Films and Filming* 23 (February 1977): 41–42.

Greenberg, Alan. *Heart of Glass.* Munich: Skellig, 1976.

————. "Notes on Some European Directors." *American Film*, October 1977, pp. 49–53 (Bertolucci, Schroeter, Herzog).

Herzog, Werner. "Why Is There 'Being' At All, Rather Than Nothing?" translated by Stephen Lamb. *Framework*, no. 3 (Spring 1976), pp. 24–27.

————. *Screenplays*, translated by Alan Greenberg and Martje Herzog. New York: Tanam Press, 1980 (translation of *Drehbücher II*).

————. *Of Walking in Ice*, translated by Alan Greenberg and Martje Herzog. New York: Tanam Press, 1980.

Hoberman, J. "Over the Volcano." *Village Voice*, 22 May 1978 (*La Soufrière, How Much Wood Would a Woodchuck Chuck*).

Horak, Jan-Christopher. "Werner Herzog's Ecran Absurde." *Literature/Film Quarterly* 7 (1979): 223–34.

Kael, Pauline. "Metaphysical Tarzan." *New Yorker*, 20 October 1975, pp. 142–49 *(Kaspar Hauser)*.

Kauffmann, Stanley. "Watching the Rhine." *New Republic*, 20 August 1977, pp. 24–25 (Fassbinder, Kluge, Herzog).

Kent, Leticia. "Werner Herzog: 'Film Is Not the Art of Scholars, but of Illiterates.'" *New York Times*, 11 September 1977.

Lloyd, Peter, "Objectivity As Irony: Werner Herzog's *Fata Morgana*." *Monogram*, no. 5 (1974), pp. 8–9.

McCormick, Ruth, and Aufderheide, Pat. "Werner Herzog's *Heart of Glass*—Pro and Contra." *Cineaste* 8 (1978): 32–34.

Milne, Tom. *"Even Dwarfs Started Small." BFI Monthly Film Bulletin* 39 (November 1972): 228.

————. *"Kaspar Hauser." BFI Monthly Film Bulletin* 42 (December 1975): 264–65.

————. *"Heart of Glass." BFI Monthly Film Bulletin* 44 (September 1977): 193.

————. *"Nosferatu: Phantom der Nacht." BFI Monthly Film Bulletin* 46 (July 1979): 151.

————. *"Woyzeck." BFI Monthly Film Bulletin* 46 (November 1979): 235–36.

Morris, George. *"Stroszek." Take One* 5 (November 1977): 8–9.

O'Toole, Lawrence. "I Feel That I'm Close to the Center of Things." *Film Comment* 15 (November/December 1979): 40–50 (interview).

————. "The Great Ecstasy of the Filmmaker Herzog." *Film Comment* 15 (November/December 1979): 34–39.

Overberg, David L. "Every Man for Himself." *Sight and Sound* 44 (Spring 1975): 73–75.

Rayns, Tony. *"Even Dwarfs Started Small." Sight and Sound* 42 (Winter 1972/73): 49–50.

————. *"Fata Morgana." BFI Monthly Film Bulletin* 41 (January 1974): 6.

————. *"Aguirre, the Wrath of God." Sight and Sound* 44 (Winter 1974/ 75): 56–57.

Rogers, Tom. *"Nosferatu the Vampyre." Films in Review* 30 (December 1979): 627.

Rosenbaum, Jonathan. *"Steiner." BFI Monthly Film Bulletin* 44 (January 1977): 7.

Sarris, Andrew. "Werner Herzog Makes a Movie." *Village Voice*, 1 August 1977 *(Stroszek)*.

Siegel, Joel E. *"The Mystery of Kaspar Hauser." Film Heritage* 11 (Winter 1976): 45–46.

Simon, John, "Cinematic Illiterates," *New York*, 20 October 1975, pp. 86–87 *(Kaspar Hauser, Moses and Aaron)*.

Strick, Phillip. *"Nosferatu—The Vampyre." Sight and Sound* 48 (Spring 1979): 127–28.

Thomson, David. "The Many Faces of Klaus Kinski." *American Film*, May 1980, pp. 22–27.

Trojan, Judith. *"How Much Wood Would a Woodchuck Chuck, La Soufrière," Take One* 7 (January 1979): 11–13.

Van Wert, William F. "Hallowing the Ordinary, Embezzling the Everyday: Werner Herzog's Documentary Practice." *Quarterly Review of Film Studies* 5 (Spring 1980): 183–92.

Vogel, Amos. "Herzog in Berlin." *Film Comment* 13 (September/October 1977): 37–38.

Walker, Beverly. "Werner Herzog's *Nosferatu." Sight and Sound* 47 (Autumn 1978): 202–5.

Walsh, Gene, ed. *Images at the Horizon: Workshop with Werner Herzog.* Chicago: Facets Multimedia Center, April 1979 (pamphlet).

Young, Vernon. "Much Madness: Werner Herzog and the Contemporary German Cinema." *Hudson Review* 30 (1977): 409–14.

In German

Herzog, Werner. *Drehbücher I: Lebenszeichen: Auch Zwerge haben klein angefangen: Fata Morgana.* Munich: Skellig, 1977.

————. *Drehbücher II: Aguirre, der Zorn Gottes; Jeder für sich und Gott gegen alle; Land des Schweigens und der Dunkelheit.* Munich: Skellig, 1977.

————. *Vom Gehen im Eis: München-Paris, 23.11 bis 14.12 1974.* Munich: Hanser, 1978.

————. *Stroszek, Nosferatu: Zwei Filmerzählungen (Drehbücher III).* Munich: Hanser, 1979.

Jansen, Peter W., and Schütte, Wolfram, eds. *Herzog/Kluge/Straub, Reihe Film* 9. Munich: Hanser, 1976.

Le Viseur, Raimond, and Schmidmaier, Werner. "Playboy Interview: Werner Herzog." *Playboy* (German edition), January 1977, pp. 29–37.

Pflaum, Hans Günther, ed. *Werner Herzog, Reihe Film 22.* Munich: Hanser, 1979.

ALEXANDER KLUGE

In English

Acuff, Skip. "Excerpts from 'Big Business Bolshevik': The Genesis of Alexander Kluge's *Strong Man Ferdinand.*" *Quarterly Review of Film Studies* 5 (1980): 193–204.

Bean, Robin. "Bubis Kino." *Films and Filming* 13 (February 1967): 49–56.

Canby, Vincent, "Film: 13 Directors Make *Germany in Autumn.*" *New York Times,* 5 April 1979.

Dawson, Jan. *Alexander Kluge and The Occasional Work of a Female Slave.* New York: New York Zoetrope, 1977.

————. "Strong-Man Ferdinand: Directed by Alexander Kluge." *Take One* 6 (1978): 12.

————. "The Sacred Terror: Shadows of Terrorism in the New German Cinema." *Sight and Sound* 48 (1979): 242–45.

————. "A Labyrinth of Subsidies: The Origins of the New German Cinema." *Sight and Sound* 50 (1980/81): 14–20.

Durgnat, Raymond. "Yesterday Girl." *Films and Filming* 13 (May 1967): 27–28.

Eder, Richard. "Strongman Ferdinand." *New York Times,* 10 October 1976.

Falkenberg, Betty. "The New Wave German Style." *Partisan Review* 35 (1968): 599–604.

Franklin, J. C. "Alienation and the Retention of the Self: The Heroines of *Der gute Mensch von Sezuan, Abschied von Gestern,* and *Die verlorene Ehre der Katharina Blum.*" *Mosaic* 12 (1979): 87–98.

Gilliatt, Penelope. "The Current Cinema: Hurrah." *New Yorker,* 25 July 1977, p. 74.

Holloway, Ronald. "Deutschland im Herbst." *Variety,* 29 March 1978.

————. "Die Patriotin." *Variety,* 31 October 1979.

Kauffmann, Stanley. "Watching on the Rhine." *New Republic,* 20 August 1977, pp. 24–25.

Kay, Karyn. "Part-time Work of a Domestic Slave." *Film Quarterly,* 29 (1975): 52–57.

Kluge, Alexander. *Attendance List for a Funeral,* translated by Leila Vennewitz, New York: McGraw-Hill, 1966.

————. *The Battle,* translated by Leila Vennewitz. New York: McGraw Hill, 1967.

————. "A Trained Conscience Will Kiss and Bite at the Same Time," translated by Reinhard Mayer, *Semiotexte* 4 (no. 2, 1982), pp. 112–23.

Kocian, B. "Strong Man Ferdinand." *Variety,* 26 May 1976.

McCormick, Ruth. "Germany in Autumn." *Cineaste* (1979): 53–54.

Moeller, Hans-Bernhard, and Springer, Carl. "Directed Change in the Young German Film: Alexander Kluge and *Artists Under the Big Top: Perplexed.*" *Wide Angle* (1978): 14–21.

Moskowitz, J. "Gelegenheitsarbeit einer Sklavin." *Variety,* 29 May 1974.

————. "In Gefahr und größter Not bringt der Mittelweg den Tod." *Variety,* 27 August 1975.

Pym, John. "Deutschland im Herbst (Germany in Autumn)." *Monthly Film Bulletin* 46 (1979): 5–6.

Rayns, Tony. "Gelegenheitsarbeit einer Sklavin (Occasional Work of a Female Slave)." *Monthly Film Bulletin* 42 (May 1975): 107.

Rosenbaum, Jonathan, and Safran, Yehuda. "Occasional Work of a Female Slave." *Sight and Sound* 44 (1975): 19–20.

Sandford, John. "The New German Cinema." *German Life and Letters* 32 (1979): 206–28.

Sayre, Nora. "Part-Time Work of a Domestic Slave." *New York Times*, 3 October 1974.

Thompson, Howard. "Yesterday Girl." *New York Times*, 22 September 1967.

————. "Artists Under the Big Top: Perplexed." *New York Times*, 27 September 1968.

Wilson, David. "Artistes at the Top of the Big Top: Disorientated." *Sight and Sound* 39 (1969/70): 46–47.

In German

Benjamin, Walter. *Schriften.* 2 vols., edited by Theodor W. Adorno and Gretel Adorno. Frankfurt: Suhrkamp, 1955.

Bitomsky, Hartmut. "Die Patriotin: Entstehungsgeschichte—Inhalt." *Filmkritik* 275 (1979): 503–25.

Brunow, Jochen. "Suchen nach Geschichte: *Die Patriotin* von Alexander Kluge." *tip* 26 (1979): 16–17.

Brustellin, Alfred. "Elefanten und andere zeitgenössische Utopien: Zur Münchner Uraufführung von Alexander Kluges Film *Die Artisten in der Zirkuskuppel: Ratlos.*" *SZ*, 30 October 1968.

Donner, Wolf. "Herrlicher Quatsch: *Die Patriotin* von Alexander Kluge." *Der Spiegel*, 17 December 1977, pp. 144–45.

Dost, Michael; Hopf, Florian; Kluge, Alexander. *Filmwirtschaft in der Bundesrepublik und Europa: Götterdämmerung in Raten.* Munich: Hanser, 1973.

Eder, Klaus. "In Gefahr und größter Not bringt der Mittelweg den Tod." *Medium* 2 (1975): 24–25.

————, and Kluge, Alexander. *Ulmer Dramaturgien: Reibungsverluste.* Munich: Hanser, 1980.

Gregor, Ulrich, et al. *Herzog/Kluge/Straub.* Munich: Hanser, 1976.

Heißenbüttel, Helmut. "Story contra Montage: Zur Form von *Abschied von gestern.*" *Film* 11 (1966): 16–17.

Jansen, Peter W. "Die Artisten in der Zirkuskuppel: Ratlos." *Filmkritik* 12 (1968): 775–77.

Kallweit, Marlies; Sander, Helke; and Kemper, Mädi. "Zu Kluges *Gelegenheitsarbeit einer Sklavin.*" *Frauen und Film* 3 (1974): 12–25.

Kluge, Alexander. *Lebensläufe.* Stuttgart: Henry Goverts, 1962.

————. "Die Utopie Film." *Merkur: Zeitschrift für europäisches Denken,* December 1964, pp. 1134–46.

————. *Abschied von gestern: Protokoll,* compiled by Enno Patalas. Frankfurt: *Filmkritik,* n.d. (1967).

————. *Die Artisten in der Zirkuskuppel. Ratlos; Die Ungläubige. Projekt Z. Sprüche der Leni Peickert.* Munich: Piper, 1968.

_____. *Lernprozesse mit tödlichem Ansgang*. Frankfurt: Suhrkamp, 1973.

_____. *Lebensläufe: Anwesenheitsliste für eine Beerdigung*. Frankfurt: Suhrkamp, 1974.

_____. *Gelegenheitsarbeit einer Sklavin: Zur realistischen Methode*. Frankfurt: Suhrkamp, 1975.

_____. "Gespräche mit Alexander Kluge." *Filmkritik* 20 (1976): 562–93.

_____. *Neue Geschichten: Hefte 1–18, "Unheimlichkeit der Zeit."* Frankfurt: Suhrkamp, 1977.

_____. "Das Theater der Spezialisten: Gespräch mit Martin Schaub." *Cinema* 2 (1978): 15–21.

_____. *Die Patriotin: Texte/Bilder 1–6*. Frankfurt: Zweitausendeins, 1979.

_____, and Reitz, Edgar. "In Gefahr und größter Not bringt der Mittelweg den Tod." *Kursbuch* 41 (1975): 41–84.

Lewandowski, Rainer. *Alexander Kluge*. Munich: C. H. Beck, 1980.

_____. *Die Filme von Alexander Kluge*. Hildesheim & New York: Olms, 1980.

Mitscherlich, Alexander, and Mitscherlich, Margarete. *Die Unfähigkeit zu trauern: Grundlagen kollektiven Verhaltens*. Munich: Piper, 1967.

Negt, Oskar, and Kluge, Alexander. *Öffentlichkeit und Erfahrung: Zur Organisationsanalyse von bürgerlicher und proletarischer Öffentlichkeit*. Frankfurt: Suhrkamp, 1972.

Patalas, Enno. "Abschied von gestern (Anita G.)." *Filmkritik* 11 (1966): 623–25.

Peters, Karsten. "Filme zum Träumen: Gespräch mit Alexandra und Alexander Kluge." *Abendzeitung*, 5 October 1966.

Petz, Thomas. "Klein Glück für den Tüchtigen: Alexander Kluges *Starker Ferdinand* in neuer Fassung." SZ, 6 December 1977.

Schöler, Franz. "Das Publikum soll zufrieden sein: Gespräch mit dem Regisseur Alexander Kluge bei den Dreharbeiten zu *Abschied von gestern*." *Die Welt*, 19 March 1966.

Schütte, Wolfram. "Vergangenheit in der Zukunft: Alexander Kluges Science-fiction-Filme." *FR*, 29 January 1972.

Steinborn, Bion. "Der starke Ferdinand." *filmfaust* 1 (December 1977): 86–105.

_____. "Eine Patriotin der Phantasie." *filmfaust* 15 (1979): 29–36.

Theuring, Gerhard. "Gelegenheitsarbeit einer Sklavin: Gespräch mit Alexander Kluge." *Filmkritik* 6 (1974): 279–83.

PETER LILIENTHAL

In English

Bondy, François. "Munich: The Decline of Cinematic Art." *New York Times*, 22 February 1971.

Canby, Vincent. "Film: 'Calm Prevails.'" *New York Times*, 6 April 1978.

Carroll, Noel. "The Face of Fascism." *Soho News*, 13 April 1978.

Hoberman, J. "Voice Choices: *Calm Prevails over the Country*." *Village Voice*, 10 April 1978.

Holloway, Ronald. "Es herrscht Ruhe im Land (The Country Is Calm)." *Variety*, 30 June 1976.

————. "*Hauptlehrer Hofer* (Schoolmaster Hofer)." *Variety*, 9 February 1977.

————. "A Peter Lilienthal Retro." *Variety*, 30 August 1978.

————. "*Der Aufstand* (The Uprising)." *Variety*, 2 July 1980. Moskowitz, G. "At Berlin Film Fest: David." *Variety*, 7 March 1979.

Rich, B. Ruby. "*David*." *The Reader*, 25 April 1980.

Stone, Judy. "A Parable with the Air of Authenticity." *San Francisco Chronicle*, 5 November 1976.

————. "Exciting New German Directors—Peter Lilienthal and Hark Bohm." *San Francisco Sunday Examiner and Chronicle, Datebook*, 21 October 1979.

————. "'David'—Spirit to Survive." *San Francisco Chronicle*, 25 October 1979.

————. "An Award-Winning Parable." *San Francisco Chronicle*, 28 November 1979.

Ziemann, Ulla, ed. "8 Films by Peter Lilienthal." *Documentation of the 28th International Film Festival in Berlin, 22 February to 5 March 1978*. Berlin: n.p., 1978.

In German

Donner, Wolf. "Lilienthals 'Malatesta.'" *Die Zeit*, 22 May 1970.

————. "Gemeint ist Chile." *Die Zeit*, 16 January 1976.

Erbe, C. "Peter Lilienthal." *Film und Ton* 19 (October 1973): 37–38.

Funk, Barbe. "Die Welt des Peter Lilienthals." *Film* (Velber) 4 (1966), n.p.

Gregor, Ulrich. "Peter Lilienthal." In *Geschichte des Films ab 1960*. Munich: Bertelsmann, 1978, pp. 154–56.

Jung, F. "Es herrscht Ruhe im Land." *Medien und Pädagogik* 20, (1976): 116–17.

Klaist, Christian. "Der lange Atem der Sandinistas." *Tip* (Berlin), 24 October–6 November 1980, pp. 24–29.

Kliess, Werner. "Welche Farbe hat das Grau?: Begegnung mit Peter Lilienthal." *Film* (Velber) 6 (November 1968): 18–22.

Lange, W. "Es herrscht Ruhe im Land." *Film und Fernsehen* 5 (August 1977): 12–13.

Limmer, Wolfgang. "Bevölkerung verhaftet." *Der Spiegel*, 9 February 1976.

Mengershausen, Joachim v. "Lilienthal—die Faszination des Abgelebten." *SZ*, 16/17 April 1966.

Ruf, Wolfgang. "La Victoria." *Medium*, no. 7 (1973), p. 27.

————. "Die Sonne angreifen." *Medium*, no. 3 (1974), pp. 14–17.

————. "Hauptlehrer Hofer." *Medium*, no. 3 (1975), pp. 22–23.

————. "Es herrscht Ruhe im Land." *Medium*, no. 1 (1976), pp. 26–27.

Schober, Siegfried. "Mit Marx und Kitsch." *Der Spiegel*, 24 March 1975.

Schönecker, Leo. "David." *Film-dienst*, 20 March 1979, pp. 6–7.

Schultz-Gerstein, Christian. "Ende der Berührungsangst." *Der Spiegel*, 5 March 1979, p. 238.

Schütte, Wolfram. "Die zerstörte Gemeinschaft der Liebenden." *FR*, 1 March 1979.

Scurla, F. "La Victoria." *Jugend Film Fernsehen* 17 (1973): 160–61.

Skármeta, Antonio. "Verteidigung des 'Aufstands.'" *FR*, 22 November 1980.

Wanzelius, Rainer, and Künsemüller, Sabine, eds. *Dokumentation über den Fernsehregisseur Peter Lilienthal*. Bochum: n.p., 1968.

Witte, Karsten. "Agent der Geschichte sein: Gespräch mit Peter Lilienthal anlässlich seines neuen Films 'Der Aufstand.'" *FR*, 14 June 1980.

EDGAR REITZ

In English

Dawson, Jan. "A Labyrinth of Subsidies: The Origins of the New German Cinema." *Sight and Sound*, Winter 1980/81, pp. 14–20.

Holloway, Ron. "Stunde Null." *Variety*, 27 April 1977.

Stone, Judy. "Zero Hour in Germany, 1945." *San Frnacisco Chronicle*, 18 January 1978.

In German

Bronnen, Barbara, and Brocher, Corinna. "Edgar Reitz." In *Die Filmemacher* (Munich: Bertelsmann, 1973), pp. 101–114.

Dörrie, Doris. "Ein Flieger in Gedanken gefesselt." *SZ*, 6 April 1979 (*The Tailor from Ulm*).

Fischer, Robert, and Hembus, Joe. "Edgar Reitz." In *Der Neue Deutsche Film*, 1960–1980. Munich: Goldmann, 1981, pp. 15–16.

Grafe, Frieda. "Mahlzeiten." *Filmkritik*, March 1967, pp. 143–44.

————, and Patalas, Enno. "Tribüne des Jungen Deutschen Films: 6. Edgar Reitz." *Filmkritik*, March 1967, pp. 128–32.

Kliess, Werner. "Die falsche Liebe zum Schöpferischen: Gespräch mit Edgar Reitz." *Film* (Velbert), November 1969.

Knorr, Günter. "Der Schneider von Ulm und das Kino: Unterhaltung mit Edgar Reitz." *Filmjournal* 5 (August/September 1978): 4–10.

Korn, Karl. "Kommunikation—eine moderne Mythe?" *FAZ*, 17 February 1962.

Reitz, Edgar. "Sie kennen keine Zärtlichkeiten: Zu meinem Film." *Die Zeit*, 7 April 1967.

————; Kluge, Alexander; and Reinke, Wilfried. "Wort und Film." In *Ulmer Dramaturgien: Reibungsverluste*. Munich: Hanser, 1980, pp. 9–27.

Schaaf, Johannes. "Wie sie filmen—wie sie filmen möchten: Gespräch mit Edgar Reitz." *Film* (Velbert), September 1969.

Schütte, Wolfram. "Babylon am Main." *Neue Zürcher Zeitung*, 31 January 1975.

————. "Stunde Null." *FR*, 24 February 1977.

VOLKER SCHLÖNDORFF and MARGARETHE VON TROTTA

Note: Reviews and articles dealing exclusively with von Trotta's films are listed separately. Those treating her collaborations with Schlöndorff are to be found under his name.

In English

Avrech, R. *"The Lost Honor of Katharina Blum."* *Millimeter* 3 (1975): 24–25.

Baker, Rob. "Adaptations: *Coup de Grâce.*" *Soho News*, 16 February 1978.

Binder, David. *"Katharina Blum:* German Parable." *New Republic* 175 (1976): 7–9.

Boyum, Joy Gould. "A Woman's Quest for Independence." *Wall Street Journal*, 24 June 1974 (*A Free Woman*).

Buckley, Tom. *"The Tin Drum* Director to Look at 2 Germanys." *New York Times,* 11 April 1980.

Callenbach, Ernest. *"Young Törless."* *Film Quarterly* 20 (1966–1967): 42–44.

Carroll, Kathleen. "Oppression, Cruelty Rule Classic Film." *Daily News* (New York), 23 July 1968 (*Young Törless*).

Champlin, Charles. *"Tin Drum*—Century of Horror, Hilarity." *Los Angeles Times*, 18 April 1980.

Clurman, Harold . "Film Festival II." *Nation* 221 (1975): 441–43 (*The Lost Honor of Katharina Blum*).

Cocks, Jay. *"Tied Down: A Free Woman."* *Time*, 8 July 1974.

Corliss, Richard. "Keep Off the Grass." *Soho News*, 9 April 1980 (*The Tin Drum*).

Curtiss, Thomas Quinn. *"Tin Drum* Falters as Nazi Fable." *International Herald Tribune*, 10 October 1979.

Dawson, Jan. *"Blechtrommel, Die (The Tin Drum)."* *Monthly Film Bulletin* 47 (1980): 107–8.

Denby, David. "The Boy Who Wouldn't Grow Up." *New York*, 14 April 1980 (*The Tin Drum*).

Elley, D. *"The Lost Honor of Katharina Blum."* *Films and Filming*, no. 23 (1977), p. 30.

Friedman, Lester D. "Cinematic Techniques in *The Lost Honor of Katharina Blum.*" *Literature/Film Quarterly* 7 (1979): 244–52.

Gill, Brendan. "The Current Cinema: The Eye of the Baslisk." *New Yorker*, 21 April 1980 (*The Tin Drum*).

Gilliat, Penelope. "The Current Cinema." *New Yorker*, 1 July 1974 (*A Free Woman*).

Harcourt, Peter. *"The Sudden Wealth of the Poor People of Kombach."* *Film Quarterly* 34 (1980): 60–63.

Harkness, John. "Drumming Up a Storm." *Cinema Canada*, no. 67 (1980), pp. 14–18 (*The Tin Drum*).

Haskell, Molly. *"Katharina Blum* Loses Honor and Finds Sainthood." *Village Voice*, 5 January 1976.

Head, David. "Der Autor muß respektiert werden'—Schlöndorff/von Trotta's *Die Verlorene Ehre der Katharina Blum* and Brecht's Critique of Film Adaptation." *German Life and Letters* 32 (1979): 248–63.

Jacobs, Diane. "Volker Schlöndorff Retrospective." *Soho News,* 21 May 1980.

Kandell, Jonathan. "Schlöndorff Is Still Asking Questions: A German Obsessed with Germany." *International Herald Tribune,* 25 January 1980 (*The Tin Drum*).

Kephart, Edwin. *"The Tin Drum." Films in Review* 31 (1980): 371–72.

McCormick, Ruth. *"Germany in Autumn." Cineaste* 60 (1979): 53–54.

Milne, Tom. *"Fangschuss, Der (Coup de Grâce)." Monthly Film Bulletin* 44 (1977): 67–68.

Morris, George. "Neo-Brechtian Numbness." *Village Voice,* 14 November 1974 (*The Sudden Wealth of the Poor People of Kombach*).

Nogueira, Rui, and Zoloffi, Nicoletta. "Volker Schlöndorff: The Rebel." *Film* 55 (1969): 26–27.

Pachter, Henry. *"The Tin Drum." Cineaste* 10 (1980): 31–32.

Phillips, Klaus. "History Reevaluated: Volker Schlöndorff's *The Sudden Wealth of the Poor People of Kombach." 1978 Film Studies Annual.* West Lafayette, Ind.: Purdue Research Foundation, 1979, pp. 33–39.

Rich, B. Ruby. "War Between the Sexists: *Coup de Grâce." Chicago Reader,* 18 August 1978.

Rosaldo, M. A. *"A Free Woman." American Anthropologist* 79 (1977): 203.

Rosen, Marjorie. "Is *A Free Woman* the Woman We've Been Waiting For?" *New York Times,* 7 July 1974.

⸻. "Margarethe von Trotta on Husbands, Wives, Men, Women and the Delicacy of Creative Collaboration in Filmmaking." *Millimeter,* no. 4 (1976), pp. 36–38.

Sarris, Andrew. "Banging the *Tin Drum* Slowly." *Village Voice,* 21 April 1980.

Sterritt, David. *"The Tin Drum." Christian Science Monitor,* 2 April 1980.

Thomas, Kevin. *"Tin Drum* Marches to a German Beat." *Los Angeles Times,* 4 March 1980.

⸻. "2 Plum Roles Bring Polish Actor to Fore." *Los Angeles Times,* 23 April 1980.

Thompson, Howard. "Feminism Is Defended in *Free Woman: A Free Woman." New York Times,* 18 June 1974.

Thomson, Barry, and Thomson, Greg. "Volker Schlöndorff: An Interview." *Film Criticism* 1 (1976/77): 26–37.

Vinocur, John. "After 20 Years, *The Tin Drum* Marches to the Screen." *New York Times,* 6 April 1980.

Wapshott, Nicholas. "The Winning of Oskar's Oscar." *Times* (London), 10 May 1980.

Wilson, David. *"Michael Kohlhaas—der Rebell (Michael Kohlhaas)." Monthly Film Bulletin* 36 (1969): 259.

⸻. *"Mord und Totschlag (A Degree of Murder)." Monthly Film Bulletin* 36 (1969): 121.

⸻. *"Verlorene Ehre der Katharina Blum, Die (The Lost Honour of Katharina Blum)." Monthly Film Bulletin* 44 (1977): 109.

Zipes, Jack. "The Political Dimension of *The Lost Honor of Katharina Blum." New German Critique,* no. 12 (1977), pp. 75–84.

In German

Baer, Volker. "Zeit im Zwiespalt: Trotta/Schlöndorffs Yourcenar-Verfilmung *Der FangSchuβ.*" *Der Tagesspiegel* (Berlin), 12 November 1976 *(Coup de Grâce).*

Barudio, Günter. "*Die Blechtrommel*: Das hohe Lied auf einen Kaschuben-Caruso." *filmfaust*, no. 14 (1979), pp. 39–40 *(The Tin Drum).*

————. "Interview mit Günter Grass—Berlin, 29.5. 1979." *filmfaust*, no. 14 (1979), pp. 19–27.

Baumgart, Reinhart. "Glanz und Armut einer Politballade: Volker Schlöndorffs *Verlorene Ehre der Katharina Blum* nach Heinrich Böll." *SZ*, 11 October 1975.

Blumenberg, Hans C. "Kollision." *Die Zeit*, 2 May 1975 *(Georgina's Reasons).*

————. "Trotzköpfchen als Terroristin: Nach *Katharina Blum* wieder eine Literaturverfilmung, wieder eine Frauengeschichte." *Die Zeit*, 22 October 1976 *(Coup de Grâce).*

————. "Das war der wilde Osten." *Die Zeit*, 4 May 1979 *(The Tin Drum).*

Bode, Martin, and Nitschke, Uwe, eds. *Volker Schlöndorff*. Munich: Goethe Institut, 1980.

Böll, Heinrich. "Die Verfilmung der *Katharina Blum*: Gespräch mit Viktor Böll am 22.10. 1976." *Heinrich Böll Werke: Interviews.* 1. 1961–1978, edited by Bernd Balzer. Cologne: Kiepenheuer & Witsch, 1978, pp. 666–74.

————. "Die verschobene Antigone." *Heinrich Böll Werke: Hörspiele, Theaterstücke, Drehbücher, Gedichte.* 1. 1952–1978," edited by Bernd Balzer. Cologne: Kiepenheuer & Witsch, 1978, pp. 609–15 (Böll's script for Schlöndorff's contribution to *Germany in Autumn*).

Brocher, Corinna. "Volker Schlöndorff." In *Die Filmemacher: Zur Neuen deutschen Produktion nach Oberhausen 1962*, edited by Barbara Bronnen and Corinna Brocher. Munich: Bertelsmann, 1973, pp. 73–88 (interview with Schlöndorff).

Brustellin, Alf. "Die andere Tradition." *SZ*, 8 February 1971 *(The Sudden Wealth of the Poor People of Kombach).*

————. "Der plötzliche Reichtum der armen Leute von Kombach." *Filmkritik*, no. 3 (1971), p. 159.

Buchka, Peter. "Ein Monstrum wird Gestalt: Volker Schlöndorffs Filmadaption der *Blechtrommel.*" *SZ*, 4 May 1979 *(The Tin Drum).*

Czura, Marian. "*Die Blechtrommel.*" *filmfaust*, no. 14 (1979), pp. 37–39 *(The Tin Drum).*

Deschner, Günther. "Volker Schlöndorffs neuer Film *Der Fangschuβ*: Das Baltikum im groben Raster." *Die Welt*, 4 November 1976 *(Coup de Grâce).*

Donner, Wolf. "Schlöndorffs Film *Die Moral der Ruth Halbfass:* Himbeerwasser mit Schuβ." *Die Zeit*, 21 April 1972.

————. "Frau Schlöndorff emanzipiert sich." *Die Zeit*, 3 November 1972 *(A Free Woman).*

————. "Film. Die Wiederkehr des frechen Oskar." *Der Spiegel*, no. 18 (1979) *(The Tin Drum).*

Fischer, Robert, ed. *"Die Blechtrommel."* In *Kino* 79/80: *Bundesdeutsche Filme auf der Leinwand.* Munich: Monika Nüchtern, 1979, pp. 28–31.

Frise, Maria. "Georginas Abgründe." *FAZ*, 29 April 1975 *(Georgina's Reasons)*.

Greiner, Ulrich. "Wo das Glas zersprang: Nach Danzig, der *Blechtrommel* wegen: Schlöndorffs Dreharbeiten in Polen." *FAZ*, 21 October 1978.

————. "Verspätetes Familienfoto mit Oskar: Volker Schlöndorffs Verfilmung der *Blechtrommel."* *FAZ*, 28 April 1979 *(The Tin Drum)*.

Hopf, Florian. "Ein offenes Gespräch mit Volker Schlöndorff—dem Mann, der bewiesen hat, daß wir als Filmemacher wieder wer sind," *Playboy Interview* 4. Munich: Moewig, 1980, pp. 71–88.

Ignée, Wolfgang. "Abschied von der *Blechtrommel*: Volker Schlöndorff verfilmt Grass' Erzählung." Stuttgarter Zeitung, 4 May 1979 *(The Tin Drum)*.

————. "Infantilismus einer ganzen Epoche." *Der Spiegel*, no. 18 (1979) (interview with Grass and Schlöndorff)

Jeremias, Brigitte. "Eine neure Art von Heimatfilm." *FAZ*, 27 January 1971 *(The Sudden Wealth of the Poor People of Kombach)*.

————. "Das Abenteuerliche an Männerbündnissen: Volker Schlöndorffs neuer Film *Fangschuß."* *FAZ*, 22 October 1976 *(Coup de Grâce)*.

————. "Schneisen geschlagen." *FAZ*, 4 May 1979 *(The Tin Drum)*.

Korn, Karl. "Deutsche Pubertät." *FAZ*, 23 May 1966 *(Young Törless)*.

Loewenstein, Enno von. "Die liebste Heldin Heinrich Bölls." *Die Welt*, 29 May 1978 *(The Lost Honor of Katharina Blum)*.

Lotz, Sebastian. "Trivialität des Luxus: Interview mit Volker Schlöndorff über seinen neuen Film." *Stuttgarter Zeitung*, 24 March 1972 (interview following the release of *The Morals of Ruth Halbfass*).

Luft, Friedrich. "Ein Kraftmeier nimmt Maß." *Die Welt*, 23 April 1970 *(Baal)*.

Nemeczek, Alfred. "Brausepulver in der Nabelgrube." *Stern*, 3 May 1979 *(The Tin Drum)*.

Nettelbeck, Uwe. "Terror im Internal." *Die Zeit*, 19 May 1966 *(Young Törless)*.

————. "Die Beseitigung einer Leiche." *Die Zeit*, 21 April 1967 *(A Degree of Murder)*.

Niehoff, Karena. "Ein Herz aus Glas: Schlöndorffs Grass-Verfilmung *Die Blechtrommel* uraufgeführt," *Der Tagesspiegel* (Berlin), 5 May 1979 *(The Tin Drum)*.

Ohly, Hans. "Begeisterung und Entsetzen." *Filmbeobachter*, no. 9 (1979), p. 4 *(The Tin Drum)*.

Patalas, Enno. *"Michael Kohlhaas—der Rebell."* *Filmkritik*, no. 5 (1969), p. 320.

Rhode, Carla. *"Die Blechtrommel:* In Bilder geronnene Erzähl-situationen." *zitty* (Berlin), no. 11 (1979) *(The Tin Drum)*.

Rühle, Günther. "Die vier schrecklichen Tage der Katharina Blum." *FAZ*, 12 October 1975 *(The Lost Honor of Katharina Blum)*.

Scherer, Marie-Luise. "Ein Kuckucks-Küken in der Kaschubei." *Der Spiegel*, no. 45 (1978) (regarding preproduction on *The Tin Drum*).

Schlöndorff, Volker. "Alain Resnais' neuer Film." *Filmkritik*, no. 5 (1961), pp. 236–38 (report on Resnais's *Last Year at Marienbad*).

————. "*Der plötzliche Reichtum der armen Leute von Kombach.*" Frankfurt: Kommunales Kino, 1970.

————. "*Die Blechtrommel*": *Tagebuch einer Verfilmung*. Darmstadt: Luchterhand, 1979.

————, and Grass, Günter. *Die Blechtrommel als Film*. Frankfurt: Zweitausendeins, 1979.

Schmidt, Eckhart. "Der Filmemacher Volker Schlöndorff: professionell, pragmatisch, ambitioniert." *Medium*, no. 6 (1973), pp. 15–17 (includes interview with Schlöndorff).

————. "Oskar trommelt nur Effekte: Volker Schlöndorffs Verfilmung verjuxt die Qualitäten der Vorlage." *Deutsche Zeitung*, 4 May 1979. *(The Tin Drum)*.

Schmitz, Helmut. "Bilder aus einer deutschen Kindheit: Volker Schlöndorffs Film *Die Blechtrommel* nach dem Roman von Günter Grass." *FR*, 7 May 1979 *(The Tin Drum)*.

Schober, Siegfried. "Film: Die Heilige Johanna der Schlagzeilen." *Der Spiegel*, no. 41 (1975) *(The Lost Honor of Katharina Blum)*.

Schütte, Wolfram. "Volker Schlöndorffs Durchbruch: Zu seinem Film *Die verlorene Ehre der Katharina Blum.*" *Neue Zürcher Zeitung*, 26 September 1975.

————. "*Nicht versöhnt*, fortgesetzt: Schlöndorff/von Trottas *Die verlorene Ehre der Katharina Blum.*" *FR*, 6 November 1975.

Seeßlen-Hurler, Beate. "*Die Blechtrommel.*" *Filmbeobachter*, no. 9 (1979), pp. 3–4.

Seidel, Hans-Dieter. "Politische Macht der Liebe? *Der Fangschuß:* Volker Schlöndorff und Margarethe von Trottas neuer Film." *Stuttgarter Zeitung*, 26 November 1976 *(Coup de Grâce)*.

Steinborn, Bion. "*Deutschland im Herbst* mit: Alf Brustellin, Alexander Kluge, Edgar Reitz, Volker Schlöndorff, Bernd Sinkel—und Theo Hinz (Filmverlag)." *filmfaust*, no. 7 (1978), pp. 3–4 (lengthy interview regarding *Germany in Autumn*).

————. "Interview mit Volker Schlöndorff—München, 31.5.1979. Volker Schlöndorff: Wir sind jetzt die deutsche Filmindustrie." *filmfaust*, no. 14 (1979), pp. 3–17.

Thieringer, Thomas. "Volker Schlöndorff über seine Böll-Verfilmung *Die verlorene Ehre der Katharina Blum*: Grüppchenbild mit Dame." *Kölner Stadt-Anzeiger*, 13 February 1975 (interview with Schlöndorff).

Umbruch, F. "*Der Fangschuß.*" *filmfaust*, no. 1–2 (1976), pp. 52–56 *(Coup de Grâce)*.

Wiedemann, H. "Melville und der Befreiungskampf im Baltikum: Ein Gespräch mit Volker Schlöndorff und Margarethe von Trotta zu *Der Fangschuß.*" *Film und Ton*, no. 22 (1976), pp. 56–59 (Interview with Schlöndorff and von Trotta regarding *Coup de Grâce*).

Other Languages

L'Avant-Scène du Cinéma, no. 181 (1977) (entire issue devoted to *Coup de*

Grâce; includes script, numerous photographs, reviews and a bio-filmography of Schlöndorff and von Trotta).

Cattini, Alberto. *Volker Schlöndorff.* Florence: La Nuova Italia, 1980.

Plard, Henri. "Sur le film *Die Blechtrommel:* de Grass à Schlöndorff." *Etudes Germaniques,* no. 1 (1980), pp. 69–84 (lengthy article on Schlöndorff's film adaptation of Grass's novel).

Schlöndorff, Volker. "L'Etranger." In Luc Moullet, *Fritz Lang.* Paris: Editions Seghers, 1970, pp. 146–47 (Schlöndorff's commentary on Lang's return to post-World War II Germany).

MARGARETHE VON TROTTA

In English

Addiego, Walter V. "Powerful Film of a Replaceable Sister." *San Francisco Examiner,* 25 October 1979 *(Sisters).*

Canby, Vincent. "Screen: *Christa Klages:* Profoundly Political." *New York Times,* 17 May 1979.

Garafola, Lynn. "*The Second Awakening of Christa Klages.*" *Cineaste* 9 (1979): 48–49.

Hoberman, J. "Rosa's Colored Glances." *Village Voice,* 10 December 1979 *(Sisters).*

Johnstone, Diana. "*The Second Awakening of Christa Klages.*" *In These Times,* 30 July–8 August 1979.

Meyer, Marsha. "Interview with Margarethe von Trotta." *Women in German,* no. 14 (1978), pp. 3–5.

Rich, B. Ruby. "*The Second Awakening of Christa Klages.*" *Chicago Reader,* 10 November 1978.

In German

Bär, Willi, and Weber, Hans Jürgen, eds. *Schwestern oder Die Balance des Glücks: Ein Film von Margarethe von Trotta.* Frankfurt am Main: Fischer, 1979 (includes interviews, script, photographs, and diary excerpts).

Blumenberg, Hans C. "Edle Räuberin: Margarethe von Trottas Erstling." *Die Zeit,* 21 April 1978 *(The Second Awakening of Christa Klages).*

Buschmann, Christel. "Gespräch zwischen Margarethe von Trotta und Christel Buschmann." *frauen und film,* no. 8 (1976), pp. 29–33 (interview with von Trotta).

Fischer, Robert, ed. "*Schwestern, oder Die Balance des Glücks.*" *Kino* 80/81: *Bundesdeutsche Filme auf der Leinwand.* Munich: Monika Nüchtern, 1980, pp. 162–65.

Geisel, Beatrix. "Die politische Dimension der privaten Themen: Ein Interview mit Margarethe von Trotta." *Medium,* no. 9 (1979), pp. 34–35.

Hochheiden, Gunar. "Was tun in diesem fremden Land?" *FR,* 29 May 1978 *(The Second Awakening of Christa Klages).*

Knorr, Günter. "Die Prinzipien der Gesellschaft: Margarethe von Trotta über ihren neuen Film." *Filmjournal,* no. 15 (1979), pp. 16–24 (interview following von Trotta's *Sisters).*

Maerker, Christa. "Was ich sagen möchte, kann ich so billig sagen: Gespräch mit Margarethe von Trotta und Helke Sander." In *Jahrbuch Film 78/79: Berichte/Kritiken/Daten*, edited by Hans Günther Pflaum. Munich: Hanser, 1978, pp. 71–84 (interview with von Trotta and Sander).

Möhrmann, Renate. "Margarethe von Trotta." In *Die Frau mit der Kamera: Filmemacherinnen in der Bundesrepublik Deutschland: Situation, Perspektiven, 10 exemplarische Lebensläufe*. Munich: Hanser, 1980, pp. 195–209 (includes interview with von Trotta).

Pflaum, Hans Günther. "Ausbruch aus dem eigenen Gefängnis: Margarethe von Trottas Regie-Debüt." *SZ*, 17 April 1978 *(The Second Awakening of Christa Klages)*.

von Trotta, Margarethe, and Francia, Luisa. *Das zweite Erwachen der Christa Klages*. Frankfurt am Main: Fischer, 1980 (includes interviews, script, photographs, and diary excerpts).

Wittlich, Angelika. "Margarethe von Trotta." In *Frauen Filmbuch*. Munich: Medien-Arbeitskreis der Demokratischen Fraueninitiative, 1978, pp. 172–74 (interview with von Trotta following *The Second Awakening of Christa Klages*).

Ziemann, Ulla. "Interview mit Margarethe von Trotta und Luisa Francia." *Berlin, 8. internationales forum des jungen films* (1978), p. 5 (interview with von Trotta and Francia following *The Second Awakening of Christa Klages*).

MAY SPILS and WERNER ENKE

In German

"Da vorn wird gefummelt: Auszüge aus Drehbüchern junger deutscher Filme." *Der Spiegel*, 25 December 1967 (script excerpt from *Go to It, Baby*).

Feurich, Jörg Peter. "*Nicht fummeln, Liebling.*" *Filmkritik* 3 (1970): 159.

Fischer, Robert, ed. "*Wehe, wenn Schwarzenbeck kommt.*" In *Kino 79/80: Bundesdeutsche Filme auf der Leinwand*. Munich: Monika Nüchtern, 1979, pp. 154–57.

Hau drauf, Kleiner! Press package. Frankfurt: Cinema International Corporation, 1973.

Jansen, Peter W. "*Zur Sache, Schätzchen.*" *Filmkritik* 2 (1968); 129–30.

Limmer, Wolfgang. "Böse Bunken: *Wehe, wenn Schwarzenbeck kommt.*" *Der Spiegel*, no. 4 (1979).

"Männchen im Getreide." *Der Spiegel*, 26 January 1970 *(Nicht fummeln, Liebling!)*.

Manola, Franz, "Was arbeitslose Jugendliche fühlen: *Wehe, wenn Schwarzenbeck kommt . . .*" *Die Presse* (Vienna), 17 February 1979.

Nicht fummeln, Liebling! Press package, Frankfurt: Paramount Pictures, 1969.

Pflaum, Hans Günther, and Prinzler, Hans Helmut, eds. "May Spils." In *Film in der Bundesrepublik Deutschland*. Munich: Carl Hanser, 1979, pp. 268–69.

"Striche in Schwabing." *Der Spiegel,* 15 January 1968 *(Zur Sache, Schätzchen).*
Wehe, wenn Schwarzenbeck kommt . . . Press package, Frankfurt: Cinema International Corporation, 1978.

ULA STÖCKL

In English

Ginsberg, S. "Erika's Passions." *Variety,* 8 November 1978.

In German

"Die Frau von dreißig Jahren: Gespräch mit Ula Stöckl." *Filmkritik* 2 (1969): 93–96.
"Gespräch mit Ula Stöckl." *Frauen und Film* 12 (1977): 2–11.
Ladiges, Peter W. "Neun Leben hat die Katze." *Filmkritik* 12 (1968): 843–45.
Lenssen, Claudia. "When Love Goes Right, Nothing Goes Wrong . . ." *Frauen und Film* 12 (1977): 12–18 *(The Cat Has Nine Lives, A Quite Perfect Couple, Erika's Passions).*
Möhrmann, Renate. *Die Frau mit der Kamera: Filmemacherinnen in der Bundesrepublik Deutschland—Situation, Perspektiven,* 10 *exemplarische Lebensläufe.* Munich/Vienna: Hanser, 1980, pp. 47–64.
"Wir arbeiten ganz anders als der Jungfilm: Gespräch mit Ula Stöckl, Edgar Reitz und Alf Brustellin." *Filmkritik* 10 (1971): 542–47.

JEAN-MARIE STRAUB and DANIÈLE HUILLET

In English

Bachmann, Gideon. "Nicht versöhnt." *Film Quarterly* 19 (Summer 1966): 51–55.
Bennet, E. "The Films of Straub Are Not 'Theoretical.'" *Afterimage* 7 (Summer 1978): 5–11.
Dermody, Susan. "Jean-Marie Straub and Danièle Huillet: The Politics of Film Practice." *Cinema Papers,* no. 10 (September/October 1976), pp. 126–30.
Engel, Andi. "Andi Engel Talks to Jean-Marie Straub, and Danièle Huillet Is There Too." *Enthusiasm,* December 1975, pp. 1–25.
Huillet, Danièle. "Notes on Gregory's Work Journal." *Enthusiasm,* December 1975, pp. 32–55.
Jenkins, Bruce L. "The Counter-Cinemas of Straub/Huillet and Robbe-Grillet." *1976 Film Studies Annual.* West Lafayette, Ind: Purdue Research Foundation, 1976, pp. 144–56.
Lellis, George. "Jean-Marie Straub's *Moses and Aaron.*" *Take One* 4 (December 1975): 37–39.
Magisos, Melanie. "Not Reconciled: The Destruction of Narrative Pleasure." *Wide Angle* 3 (1980): 35–41.
Nowell-Smith, Geoffrey. "After *Othon,* Before *History Lessons*: Geoffrey Nowell-Smith Talks to Jean-Marie Straub and Danièle Huillet." *Enthusiasm,* December 1975, pp. 26–31.

Perez, Gilbert. "Modernist Cinema: The History Lessons of Straub and Huillet." *Artforum* 17 (October 1978): 46–55.

Rickey, Carrie. "Seeing Ideas: Straub and Huillet's *Moses and Aaron*." *Artforum* 16 (November 1977): 66–69.

Rogers, Joel. "Jean-Marie Straub and Danièle Huillet Interviewed: *Moses and Aaron* as an Object of Marxist Reflection." *Jump Cut,* nos. 12/13 (December 1976), pp. 61–64.

Roud, Richard. *Straub.* New York: Viking, 1972.

Straub, Jean-Marie, and Huillet, Danièle. "Scenarios of *History Lessons* and *Introduction to Arnold Schoenberg's Accompaniment to a Cinematograph Scene,*" translated by Misha Donat. *Screen* 17 (Spring 1976): 54–83.

————."*Fortini-Cani*-Script." *Screen* 19 (Summer 1978): 11–40.

Turim, Maureen. "*Ecriture Blanche*: The Ordering of the Filmic Text in *The Chronicle of Anna Magdalena Bach*." In 1976 *Film Studies Annual.* West Lafayette, Ind.: Purdue Research Foundation, 1976, pp. 177–92.

Walsh, Martin R. "Political Formations in the Cinema of Jean-Marie Straub." *Jump Cut,* no. 4 (November/December 1974), pp. 12–18.

————. "Introduction to Arnold Schoenberg's Accompaniment for a Cinematographic Scene: Straub/Huillet: Brecht: Schoenberg." In 1976 *Film Studies Annual.* West Lafayette, Ind.: Purdue Research Foundation, 1976, pp. 193–204.

————. "*Moses and Aaron*: Straub and Huillet's Schoenberg." *Jump Cut,* Nos. 12/13 (December 1976), pp. 57–61.

Woods, Gregory. "A Work Journal of the Straub/Huillet Film *Moses and Aaron.*" *Enthusiasm,* December 1975, pp. 32–55.

In German

Gregor, Ulrich, et al. *Herzog/Kluge/Straub.* Munich: Hanser, 1976.

HANS-JÜRGEN SYBERBERG

In English

Andrews, Nigel. "Hitler as Entertainment." *American Film,* April 1978, pp. 50–53.

Buckley, Tom. "At the Movies." *New York Times,* 23 March 1979 *(Hitler).*

Canby, Vincent. "Screen: 7 1/2-Hour 'Hitler' by Hans-Jürgen Syberberg." *New York Times,* 15 January 1980.

Clarens, Carlos. "Madness and Bad Teeth." *Soho News,* 30 July 1980 *(Ludwig).*

Coleman, J. "The Weight of the Moon." *New Statesman,* 11 February 1977, p. 196 *(Hitler).*

Denby, David. "'Whoever Controls Film Controls History.'" *New York,* 28 January 1980 *(Hitler).*

Dewey, Langdon. "Ludwig: Requiem for a Virgin King." *Film* 48 (April 1977): 8.

Durgnat, Raymond. "Caligari to 'Hitler.'" *Film Comment* 16 (July/August, 1980).

Gessner, Peter. "The Day They Quit Making the Beetle." *Seven Days*, 14 August 1979 *(Hitler)*.

Hamilton, Carol. "Surreal Hitler." *Daily Californian*, 30 March 1980.

Hoberman, J. "The Führer Furor." *Village Voice*, 14 January 1980.

Jaehne, Karen. "Old Nazis in New Films: The German Cinema Today." *Cineaste* 9 (Fall 1979): 32–35 *(Hitler)*.

Kaufman, Stanley. "Dreaming of Hitler." *New Republic*, 2 February 1980.

Kroll, Jack. "The Hitler Within Us." *Newsweek*, 28 January 1980.

Landy, Marcia. "Politics, Aesthetics, and Patriarchy in The Confessions of Winifred Wagner." *New German Critique* 18 (Fall 1979): 151–66.

Mueller, Roswitha. "Hans-Jürgen Syberberg's Hitler: Interview-Montage." *Discourse* 2 (Summer 1980): 60–82.

Pachter, Henry. "Our Hitler, or His." *Cineaste* 10 (Spring 1980): 25–34.

Pym, John. "Winifred Wagner und die Geschichte des Hauses Wahnfried von 1914–1975." *Monthly Film Bulletin* 44 (January 1977): 13.

————. "Syberberg and the Tempter of Democracy." *Sight and Sound* 46 (Autumn 1977): 227.

Rayns, Tony. "Ludwig: Requiem for a Virgin King." *Sight and Sound* 43 (Winter 1973/74): 57.

————. "Ludwig: Requiem für einen jungfräulichen König." *Monthly Film Bulletin* 44 (March 1977): 46–47.

Sontag, Susan. "Eye of the Storm." *New York Review of Books*, 21 February 1980.

Syberberg, Hans-Jürgen. *Hitler: A Film from Germany*, translated by Joachim Neugroschel. New York: Farrar, Straus & Giroux, 1980.

————. "What Can We Do with Hitler?" *Vogue*, May 1980.

Thomas, Kevin. "'Hitler' Explores a Nation's Psyche." *Los Angeles*, 7 April 1979.

Van Gelder, Vincent. "A German Filmmaker Looks at Adolf Hitler." *New York Times*, 13 January 1980.

Wasserman, Steve. "Filmmaker as Pariah." *Village Voice*, 14 January 1980 *(Hitler)*.

Wells, Jeffrey. "Our Hitler." *Films in Review* 31 (March 1980): 176.

Wieseltier, Leon. "German Romanticism Lives: Syberberg's Hitler." *New Republic*, 8 March 1980.

Zimmer, Christian. "Our Hitler." *Telos* 42 (Winter 1979/80): 150–59.

In German

Berg, Robert von. "Deutschland, ein Film von Hitler: Hans-Jürgen Syberberg im Echo der amerikanischen Presse." *SZ*, 28 February 1980.

Blumenberg, Hans C. "Träume in Trümmern." In *Kinozeit: Aufsätze und Kritiken zum modernen Film*. Frankfurt: Fischer, 1980, pp. 139–42.

Brandlmeier, Thomas. "Hitler: Ein Film aus Deutschland." *Medien und Erziehung* No. 1 (1979), 35–41.

Eder, Klaus, ed. *Syberbergs Hitler-Film: Texte von Susan Sontag, Christian Zimmer, Jean-Pierre Oudart u.a.* Munich & Vienna: Hanser, 1980.

Hopf, Florian. "Ein Regisseur greift zur Selbsthilfe: Syberberg und die 'Verlobung in San Domingo.'" *Bonner Rundschau,* 28 November 1970.

Syberberg, Hans-Jürgen. "Zum Drama Friedrich Dürrenmatts: Zwei Modellinterpretationen zur Wesensdeutung des modernen Dramas." Diss. Munich, 1963.

_____. "Nach zehn Jahren: Uber unsere Zustände im heimischen Film." *Filmreport,* no. 19/20 (1975).

_____. *Syberbergs Filmbuch.* Munich: Nymphenburger Verlagsbuchhandlung, 1976.

_____. "Offener Brief an Herrn Augstein, *Spiegel,* Herrn Dr. Sommer, *Die Zeit,* Herrn Dr. Heigert, *Süddeutsche Zeitung,* Herrn Fest, *Frankfurter Allgemeine Zeitung,* und alle anderen, die noch aus Leidenschaft in Deutschland Zeitungen machen." *Filmreport,* no. 11/12 (1977).

_____. *Hitler: Ein Film aus Deutschland.* Reinbek bei Hamburg: Rowohlt, 1978.

_____. "Holocaust: Form ist Moral." *Medium* 9 (April 1979): 15–18.

_____. "Syberbergs Notizen." *Tageszeitung,* 5 September 1980.

_____. "Syberbergs Notizen: La 'Treue.'" *Tageszeitung,* 22 September 1980.

WIM WENDERS

In English

Andrews, Nigel. "Wim Wenders: The Goalkeeper's Fear of the Penalty." *Sight and Sound* 42, (Winter 1972/73): 6–7.

Clarens, Carlos. "King of the Road." *Film Comment* 13 (September/October 1977): 42–46.

Corrigan, Timothy. "The Realist Gesture in the Films of Wim Wenders: Hollywood and the New German Cinema." *Quarterly Review of Film Studies* 5 (Spring 1980): 205–16.

Covino, Michael. "Wim Wenders: A Worldwide Homesickness." *Film Quarterly* 31 (Winter 1977/78): 9–19.

Dawson, Jan. *Wim Wenders.* New York: New York Zoetrope, 1976.

_____. "Filming Highsmith." *Sight and Sound* 47 (Winter 1977/78): 30–36.

Fox, Terry Curtis. "Wim Wenders Crosses the Border." *Village Voice,* 3 October 1977.

Frisch, Shelley. "The Disenchanted Image: From Goethe's *Wilhelm Meister* to Wenders' *Wrong Movement.*" *Literature/Film Quarterly* 7 (Summer 1979): 208–14.

Harcourt, Peter. "Adaptation Through Inversion: Wenders' *Wrong Movement.*" In *Modern European Filmmakers and the Art of Adaptation,* edited by Andrew Horton and Joan Magretta. New York: Ungar, 1981.

Kass, Judith M. "At Home on the Road." *Movietone News*, February 1978, pp. 2–11.

Kauffmann, Stanley. "Wenders." *New Republic*, 29 January 1977.

Keenan, Richard C., and Welsh, James M. "Wim Wenders and Nathaniel Hawthorne." *Literature/Film Quarterly* 6 (Spring 1978): 175–79.

Kinder, Marsha. "The American Friend." *Film Quarterly* 32 (Winter 1978/ 79): 45–49.

Lachman, Edward; Lehman, Peter; and Wood, Robin. "Wim Wenders: An Interview." *Wide Angle* 2 (1978): 72–79.

Monaco, James. "Wim Wenders' *Alice in the Cities*. *Take One* 4 (May/June 1974): 30–31.

Schlunk, Jürgen E. "The Image of America in German Literature and in the New German Cinema: The American Friend." *Literature/Film Quarterly* 7 (Summer 1979): 215–22.

Simon, John. "Of Men and Justice: A Platonic Relationship." *New York*, 25 October 1976, pp. 90–92.

Tarratt, Margaret. "Kings of the Road." *Films and Filming*, May 1969, pp. 31–32.

Thompson, Bill. "A Young German Filmmaker and His Road Movie." 1000 *Eyes*, November 1976, pp. 22–23.

Wenders, Wim, and Müller-Scherz, Fritz. *The Film by Wim Wenders: Kings of the Road (In the Course of Time)*, translated by Christopher Doherty. Munich: Filmverlag der Autoren, 1976.

In German

Blum, Heiko R. "Gespräch mit Wim Wenders." *Filmkritik*, February 1972, pp. 69–77.

Bühler, Wolf Eckhart, and Kleiser, Paul B. "Alice in den Städten." *Filmkritik*, March 1974, pp. 131–35.

Feurich, J. P. "Summer in the City." *Filmkritik*, December 1971, pp. 623–24.

Künzel, Uwe. *Wim Wenders*. Freiburg: Dreisam-Verlag, 1981.

Müller-Scherz, Fritz, and Wiedemann, Horst. "Wim Wenders über 'Im Lauf der Zeit.'" *Film und Ton*, May 1976, pp. 42–54.

Schober, Siegfried. "Mann und Kind." *Der Spiegel*, 4 March 1974.

Theuring, Gerhard. "Filme von Wim Wenders." *Filmkritik*, May 1969, pp. 315–17.

Wenders, Wim. *Texte zu Filmen und Musik*. Berlin: Freunde der deutschen Kinemathek, 1975.